JOURNAL FOR THE STUDY OF THE PSEUDEPIGRAPHA SUPPLEMENT SERIES
33

Editors
James H. Charlesworth
Lester L. Grabbe

Editorial Board
Randall D. Chesnutt, Philip R. Davies, Jan Willem van Henten,
Judith M. Lieu, Steven Mason, James R. Mueller,
Loren T. Stuckenbruck, James C. VanderKam

STUDIES IN SCRIPTURE IN EARLY JUDAISM AND CHRISTIANITY
7

Series Editor
Craig A. Evans

Sheffield Academic Press

This page intentionally left blank

The Interpretation of Scripture in Early Judaism and Christianity

Studies in Language and Tradition

Edited by Craig A. Evans

Journal for the Study of the Pseudepigrapha
Supplement Series 33

Studies in Scripture in Early Judaism and Christianity 7

Copyright © 2000 Sheffield Academic Press

Published by Sheffield Academic Press Ltd
Mansion House
19 Kingfield Road
Sheffield S11 9AS
England

Typeset by Sheffield Academic Press

British Library Cataloguing in Publication Data

A catalogue record for this book is available
from the British Library

ISBN: 978-0-5670-4070-1

CONTENTS

This page intentionally left blank

PREFACE

The present volume is the seventh in the series Studies in Scripture in Early Judaism and Christianity, a series that has grown out of the Society of Biblical Literature program unit Scripture in Early Judaism and Christianity, founded by the editor and long-time colleague James A. Sanders. The program unit is currently chaired by Kenneth E. Pomykala. The series produces occasional volumes that are published as Supplements to the *Journal for the Study of the Old Testament, Journal for the Study of the New Testament* and *Journal for the Study of the Pseudepigrapha*. The first two volumes appeared in 1993: *Paul and the Scriptures of Israel*, edited by C.A. Evans and J.A. Sanders (JSNTSup, 83; SSEJC, 1; Sheffield: JSOT Press) and *The Pseudepigrapha and Early Biblical Interpretation*, edited by J.H. Charlesworth and C.A. Evans (JSPSup, 14; SSEJC, 2; Sheffield: JSOT Press). A third volume appeared in 1994: *The Gospels and the Scriptures of Israel*, edited by C.A. Evans and W.R. Stegner (JSNTSup, 104; SSEJC, 3; Sheffield: Sheffield Academic Press). The fourth and fifth volumes appeared in 1997: *The Things Accomplished among Us: Prophetic Tradition in the Structural Pattern of Luke–Acts*, by R.I. Denova (JSNTSup, 141; SSEJC, 4; Sheffield: Sheffield Academic Press), and *Early Christian Interpretation of the Scriptures of Israel: Investigations and Proposals*, edited by C.A. Evans and J.A. Sanders (JSNTSup, 148; SSEJC, 5; Sheffield: Sheffield Academic Press). The sixth volume appeared in 1998: *The Function of Scripture in Early Jewish and Christian Tradition*, edited by C.A. Evans and J.A. Sanders (JSNTSup, 154; SSEJC, 6; Sheffield: Sheffield Academic Press). As in the case of these previous volumes, *The Interpretation of Scripture in Early Judaism and Christianity: Studies in Language and Tradition* represents a collection of studies concerned with the function of Israel's Scriptures in later sacred writings. The studies in this volume, however, focus on interpretive tradition that grew out of the words and language of Scripture, including key terms and the names of famous (or infamous) biblical personalities. The authors of these studies attempt to understand the hermeneutical principles and exegetical techniques of Jewish and Christian writers of late antiquity, and by doing so throw light on the world of thought out of which Jewish and Christian sacred literature emerged.

Almost all of the papers included in this volume were read at the 1997 and 1998 annual meetings of the Society of Biblical Literature. Papers have been drawn from the Scripture in Early Judaism and Christianity Section and from the Aramaic Section. The paper by Benedict Viviano was read in the 1998 Matthew Seminar, while the paper by Louis Feldman represents a major expansion of smaller portions of work presented in various scholarly settings. Staffan Olofsson's paper was read at the International SBL meeting in Helsinki, while Anthony Saldarini's paper appeared in a *Festschrift* in memory of William Braude. The editor would like to express his thanks to the program unit chairs, the presiders (whose opinions regarding the merits of the papers were solicited), the scholars whose papers appear in this volume and the editorial team at Sheffield Academic Press. Special thanks go to Professor James Charlesworth for agreeing to have this collection of studies appear in the Supplements to the *Journal for the Study of the Pseudepigrapha*. Given that many of the essays interact with the Pseudepigrapha and related writings it is only appropriate that these studies appear in this Supplements series.

Craig A. Evans
February 2000

ABBREVIATIONS

ÄAT	Ägypten und Altes Testament
AB	Anchor Bible
ABD	David Noel Freedman (ed.), *The Anchor Bible Dictionary* (New York: Doubleday, 1992)
AGJU	Arbeiten zur Geschichte des antiken Judentums und des Urchristentums
AKG	Arbeiten zur Kirchengeschichte
ALGHJ	Arbeiten zur Literatur und Geschichte des hellenistischen Judentums
AnBib	Analecta biblica
AnOr	Analecta orientalia
ANTJ	Arbeiten zum Neuen Testament und Judentum
ArBib	Aramaic Bible
AASOR	Annals of the American Schools of Oriental Research
AusBR	*Australian Biblical Review*
AUSS	*Andrews University Seminary Studies*
BAGD	Walter Bauer, William F. Arndt, F. William Gingrich and Frederick W. Danker, *A Greek–English Lexicon of the New Testament and Other Early Christian Literature* (Chicago: University of Chicago Press, 2nd edn, 1958)
BARev	*Biblical Archaeology Review*
BBB	Bonner biblische Beiträge
BBR	*Bulletin for Biblical Research*
BEATAJ	Beiträge zur Erforschung des Alten Testaments und des antiken Judentums
BGBE	Beiträge zur Geschichte der biblischen Exegese
BHS	*Biblia hebraica stuttgartensia*
Bib	*Biblica*
BIOSCS	*Bulletin of the International Organization for Septuagint and Cognate Studies*
BIS	Biblical Interpretation Series
BJS	Brown Judaic Studies
BKAT	Biblischer Kommentar: Altes Testament
BN	*Biblische Notizen*
BO	*Bibliotheca orientalis*
BWANT	Beiträge zur Wissenschaft vom Alten und Neuen Testament
BWAT	Beiträge zur Wissenschaft vom Alten Testament
BZ	*Biblische Zeitschrift*

BZAW	Beihefte zur *ZAW*
BZNW	Beihefte zur *ZNW*
BZRGG	Beihefte zur *ZRGG*
CAD	Ignace I. Gelb *et al.* (eds.), *The Assyrian Dictionary of the Oriental Institute of the University of Chicago* (Chicago: Oriental Institute, 1964–)
CBET	Contributions to Biblical Exegesis
CBL	Collectanca Biblica Latiná
CBQ	*Catholic Biblical Quarterly*
CBQMS	*Catholic Biblical Quarterly*, Monograph Series
CIL	*Corpus inscriptionum latinarum*
CIS	*Corpus inscriptionum semiticarum*
ConBNT	Coniectanea biblica, New Testament
ConBOT	Coniectanea biblica, Old Testament
CPJ	V.A. Tcherikover and A. Fuchs (eds.), *Corpus papyrorum judaicarum* (3 vols.; Cambridge, MA: Harvard University Press, 1957
CRINT	Compendia rerum iudaicarum ad Novum Testamentum
CTA	A. Herdner (ed.), *Corpus des tablettes en cunéiformes alphabétiques découvertes à Ras Shamra–Ugarit de 1929 à 1939* (Paris: Imprimerie nationale Geuthner, 1963)
DDD	K. van der Toorn, B. Becking and P.W. van der Horst (eds.), *Dictionary of Deities and Demons in the Bible*
DJD	Discoveries in the Judaean Desert
DSD	*Dead Sea Discoveries*
ErFor	Erträge der Forschung
EncJud	*Encyclopaedia Judaica*
EstBíb	*Estudios bíblicos*
FAT	Forschungen zum Alten Testament
FN	*Filología neotestamentaria*
FOTL	The Forms of the Old Testament Literature
FRLANT	Forschungen zur Religion und Literatur des Alten und Neuen Testaments
GCS	Griechische christliche Schriftsteller
HALAT	Ludwig Koehler *et al.* (eds.), *Hebräisches und aramäisches Lexikon zum Alten Testament* (5 vols.; Leiden: E.J. Brill, 1967–1995)
HAT	Handbuch zum Alten Testament
HBS	Herders biblischen Studien
HNT	Handbuch zum Neuen Testament
HSCP	Harvard Studies in Classical Philology
HSM	Harvard Semitic Monographs
HTR	*Harvard Theological Review*
HUCA	*Hebrew Union College Annual*
ICC	International Critical Commentary
IEJ	*Israel Exploration Journal*
IOS	*Israel Oriental Studies*
JBL	*Journal of Biblical Literature*

JBR	*Journal of Bible and Religion*
JBTh	*Jahrbuch für biblische Theologie*
JBTh	Jahrbuch für biblische Theologie
JJS	*Journal of Jewish Studies*
JPOS	*Journal of the Palestine Oriental Society*
JQR	*Jewish Quarterly Review*
JRS	*Journal of Roman Studies*
JSHRZ	Jüdische Schriften aus hellenistisch-römischer Zeit
JSJ	*Journal for the Study of Judaism in the Persian, Hellenistic and Roman Period*
JSNT	*Journal for the Study of the New Testament*
JSNTSup	*Journal for the Study of the New Testament*, Supplement Series
JSOT	*Journal for the Study of the Old Testament*
JSOTSup	*Journal for the Study of the Old Testament*, Supplement Series
JSP	*Journal for the Study of the Pseudepigrapha*
JSPSup	*Journal for the Study of the Pseudepigrapha*, Supplement Series
JSQ	*Jewish Studies Quarterly*
Judaica	*Judaica: Beiträge zum Verständnis des jüdischen Schicksals in Vergangenheit und Gegenwart*
KAI	H. Donner and W. Röllig, *Kanaanäische und aramäische Inschriften* (3 vols.; Wiesbaden: Harrassowitz, 1962–64)
KAT	Kommentar zum Alten Testament
KB	Ludwig Koehler and Walter Baumgartner (eds.), *Lexicon in Veteris Testamenti libros* (Leiden: E.J. Brill, 1953)
KTU	M. Dietrich *et al.* (eds.), *The Cuneiform Alphabetic Texts from Ugarit, Ras Ibn Hani and other places* (Münster: Ugarit-Verlag, 2nd edn, 1995)
LAI	Library of Ancient Israel
LSJ	H.G. Liddell, Robert Scott and H. Stuart Jones, *Greek–English Lexicon* (Oxford: Clarendon Press, 9th edn, 1968)
MSU	Mitteilungen des Septuaginta-Unternehmens
NCB	New Century Bible
NIDOTE	Willem A. VanGemeren (ed.), *New International Dictionary of Old Testament Theology and Exegesis* (5 vols.; Grand Rapids: Zondervan, 1997)
NIGTC	The New International Greek Testament Commentary
NovT	*Novum Testamentum*
NovTSup	*Novum Testamentum*, Supplements
NTAbh	Neutestamentliche Abhandlungen
NTS	*New Testament Studies*
OBO	Orbis biblicus et orientalis
OLD	*Oxford Latin Dictionary*
Or	*Orientalia*
OTG	Old Testament Guides
OTL	Old Testament Library
OTP	James Charlesworth (ed.), *Old Testament Pseudepigrapha*
OTS	*Oudtestamentische Studiën*

OTS	Oudtestamentische Studiën
PAT	D.R. Hillers and E. Cussini, *Palmyrene Aramaic Texts* (Baltimore: The Johns Hopkins University Press, 1976)
PEQ	*Palestine Exploration Quarterly*
RB	*Revue biblique*
REJ	*Revue des études juives*
RES	*Répertoire d'epigraphie sémitique*
RevistB	*Revista biblica*
RevQ	*Revue de Qumran*
RGG	*Religion in Geschichte und Gegenwart*
RSR	*Recherches de science religieuse*
RT	*Religious Traditions*
SANT	Studien zum Alten und Neuen Testament
SBAB	Stuttgarter biblische Aufsatzbände
SBL	Society of Biblical Literature
SBLBMI	SBL The Bible and its Modern Interpreters
SBLDS	SBL Dissertation Series
SBLEJL	SBL Early Judaism and its Literature
SBLMS	SBL Monograph Series
SBLSCS	SBL Septuagint and Cognate Studies
SBLSS	SBL Semeia Studies
SBT	Studies in Biblical Theology
SC	Sources chrétiennes
SCL	Sather Classical Literature
SEG	*Supplementum epigraphicum graecum*
SIG	W. Dittenberger (ed.), *Sylloge inscriptionum graecarum* (4 vols.; Leipzig: Hirzel, 3rd edn, 1915–21)
SJLA	Studies in Judaism in Late Antiquity
SJOT	*Scandinavian Journal of the Old Testament*
SPB	Studia Post-Biblical
SR	*Studies in Religion/Sciences religieuses*
SSEJC	Studies in Scripture in Early Judaism and Christianity
ST	*Studia theologica*
STDJ	Studies on the Texts of the Desert of Judah
Str–B	[Hermann L. Strack and] Paul Billerbeck, *Kommentar zum Neuen Testament aus Talmud und Midrasch* (7 vols.; Munich: Beck, 1922–61)
SVMB	E. Schürer, *The History of the Jewish People in the Age of Jesus Christ* (175 B.C.–A.D. 135) (rev. by G. Vermes, F. Millar and M. Black; 4 vols.; Edinburgh: T. & T. Clark, 1973–87)
SVTP	Studia in Veteris Testamenti pseudepigrapha
TAPA	*Transactions of the American Philological Association*
TBü	Theologische Bücherei
TD	*Theology Digest*
TDNT	Gerhard Kittel and Gerhard Friedrich (eds.), *Theological Dictionary of the New Testament* (trans. Geoffrey W. Bromiley; 10 vols.; Grand Rapids: Eerdmans, 1964–)

TDOT	G.J. Botterweck and H. Ringgren (eds.), *Theological Dictionary of the Old Testament*
TEC	Textos y Estudios del Seminaino Filologico 'Cardenal Cisneros' de la Biblia Poliglota Matritense de l'instituto 'Arial montano'
THAT	Ernst Jenni and Claus Westermann (eds.), *Theologisches Handwörterbuch zum Alten Testament* (Munich: Chr. Kaiser, 1971–76)
ThW	Theologische Wissenschaft
ThWAT	G.J. Botterweck and H. Ringgren (eds.), *Theologisches Wörterbuch zum Alten Testament* (Stuttgart: W. Kohlhammer, 1970–)
TP	*Theologie und Philosophie*
TS	*Theological Studies*
TWNT	Gerhard Kittel and Gerhard Friedrich (eds.), *Theologisches Wörterbuch zum Neuen Testament* (11 vols.; Stuttgart, Kohlhammer, 1932–79)
TynBul	*Tyndale Bulletin*
TZ	*Theologische Zeitschrift*
UF	*Ugarit-Forschungen*
VT	*Vetus Testamentum*
VTSup	*Vetus Testamentum*, Supplements
WBC	Word Biblical Commentary
WMANT	Wissenschaftliche Monographien zum Alten und Neuen Testament
WUNT	Wissenschaftliche Untersuchungen zum Neuen Testament
ZAW	*Zeitschrift für die alttestamentliche Wissenschaft*
ZDPV	*Zeitschrift des deutschen Palästina-Vereins*
ZNW	*Zeitschrift für die neutestamentliche Wissenschaft*
ZST	*Zeitschrift für systematische Theologie*
ZTK	*Zeitschrift für Theologie und Kirche*

This page intentionally left blank

LIST OF CONTRIBUTORS

Ellen B. Aitken, Harvard Divinity School

Kenneth R. Atkinson, The University of Northern Iowa

Christian M.M. Brady, Tulane University

John Pairman Brown, The Graduate Theological Union

Stephen B. Chapman, Duke University

Yaron-Zvi Eliav, New York University

Craig A. Evans, Trinity Western University
University of Surrey Roehampton

Louis H. Feldman, Yeshiva University

Bruce N. Fisk, Westmont College

Richard Kalmin, Jewish Theological Seminary

Esther M. Menn, University of Virginia

Hindy Najman, University of Notre Dame

R. Steven Notley, Jerusalem University College

Staffan Olofsson, University of Goethenburg

Josep Ribera-Florit, University of Barcelona

Anthony J. Saldarini, Boston College

Benedict T. Viviano, OP, University of Fribourg

FROM LANGUAGE TO EXEGESIS

Craig A. Evans

Beginning students of biblical interpretation almost always are surprised to learn that New Testament writers and other Jewish and Christian writers of late antiquity often do not follow exegetical rules akin to those taught by modern interpreters. Original text, context and meaning are frequently ignored—or at least so it seems. Instead, key terms, catchwords and turns of phrases appear to provide the interpretive catalyst. The Hosean reminiscence, 'Out of Egypt have I called my son' (Hos. 11.1), becomes for the Matthean evangelist a messianic prophecy fulfilled in Jesus' return to Israel (Mt. 2.13-15). Indeed, Hosea's reference to Egypt itself may underlie the otherwise unattested tradition of the holy family's sojourn in that land. Matthew, furthermore, believes that Jesus' upbringing in Nazareth was surely foretold by prophets who said, in so many words, 'He shall be a Nazarene' (Mt. 2.23; cf. Judg. 13.5; Isa. 11.1). Similarly, one century after the death of Jesus, one Simon bar Kosibah ignited Jewish hopes of freedom from the yoke of Rome. He so captured the biblical and prophetic imagination of his contemporaries that he became known as 'Bar Kokhba', that is, the 'son of the star'. Just as surely as Jesus the *Nazarene* was a fulfillment of prophecies that spoke of either a saving *nazir* (i.e. Judg. 13.5, esp. in some textual traditions) or a branch (*neṣer*) from the stump of Jesse (i.e. Isa. 11.1), so many Jews thought Simon bar Kosibah was the star (*kokhav*, or, in Aramaic, *kokhba*) prophesied in Num. 24.17. Exegesis here revolves around what is perceived to be a key word and a close association.

Of course, in later rabbinic interpretation (i.e. midrash), exegesis based on key words and phrases can become remarkably elaborate. One immediately thinks of meanings unpacked from the scriptural statement that Abram 'went forth from Ur of the Chaldeans' (Gen. 11.31). The Hebrew radicals אור can mean the place 'Ur', but they can also be the noun 'light' or 'fire'. Because elsewhere in Scripture we read that the Chaldeans hurled the Jewish men into the fiery furnace, from which later they 'went forth' unharmed (Dan. 3.26), some ancient interpreters wondered if Abram too had been delivered 'from the *fire* of the Chaldeans' (cf. *Targ. Ps.-J.* Gen. 11.28), or that perhaps his father or brother had died in the fire of the Chaldeans (cf. *Jub.* 12.12-14; *Ps.-Philo* 6.16-18; *Apoc. Abr.* 8.1-6; *Gen. R.* 38.13 [on 11.28]). These imaginative interpretations even help answer the question on what grounds God chose Abram (e.g. he refused to help Nimrod build the Tower of Babel; he rejected his father's idols).

Paul, early Christianity's apostle to the Gentiles, gives evidence of his Jewish training in Scripture in many places in his epistles. His appeal to the singular form of 'seed' (*sperma*/*zera'*) in Gal. 3.16 is a classic example of rabbinic exegesis. In Gen. 12.7 God promised Abraham a 'seed', not 'seeds'. Surely the singularity of the word implies prophecy of a particular coming one, the Messiah. Paul, of course, would readily allow that the promise to Abraham also envisions a multitude of people (the *peshat*, or plain meaning of the text), but the singularity of the word 'seed' also implies a special, singular fulfillment (the *midrash*, or 'searching' for less obvious meaning). Arguments of this nature are plentiful in rabbinic literature.

In Romans 10 Paul makes use of Jewish interpretive tradition and once again innovatively extracts christological significance that clarifies the advent and resurrection of Christ. This time Pauline exegesis shows acquaintance with Aramaic tradition. Alluding to Deut. 30.12-13, Paul asks rhetorically in Rom. 10.6-7: 'Say not in your heart, "Who shall ascend into heaven?" that is, to bring Christ down; or, "Who shall descend into the abyss?" That is, to bring Christ up from the dead.' The allusion to Deuteronomy seems clear enough: 'It is not in heaven above, saying, "Who will ascend for us into heaven and receive it for us, so hearing it we should do it?" Neither is it beyond the sea, that you should say, "Who will go over the sea for us, and bring it to us, that we may hear it and do it?"' Paul's 'descend into the abyss' and his explanation that it is 'Christ' who will come down from heaven and go up from the dead appears to be an innovative adaptation of Jewish interpretation of Deut. 30.12-13, as preserved in the Aramaic paraphrase of Scripture. According to Neofiti, '*The Law* is not in the heavens, that one should say: "*Would that we had one like the prophet Moses,* who would ascend to heaven and fetch it for us and make us hear the command-

ments, that we might do them". Neither is the Law beyond the Great Sea
that one may say: *"Would that we had one like the prophet Jonah,* who
would *descend into the depths* of the Great Sea and bring it up for us
and make us hear the commandments, that we might do them"' (*Targ.
Neof.* Deut. 30.12-13). The words placed in italics represent the significant departures from the Hebrew text. Neofiti agrees at important
points with Paul's paraphrase and interpretation. The targum speaks of
one who would 'descend into the depths' of the sea, which approxi-
mates Paul's 'descend into the abyss', while the targum's appeal to
Moses, who ascended into heaven, and Jonah, who descended into the
sea, represents a similar personalizing of the text. For Paul, of course,
the great Moses and Jonah are but typologies of Christ; he is the one
who has brought the final, saving word. The fact that in the Gospel
tradition itself Jesus is compared with Moses (cf. Jn 3.14; Acts 3.22-23;
7.37) and Jonah (cf. Mt. 12.38-40) would only have encouraged Paul's
exegesis.

The studies that make up the present volume treat more important and
more complicated issues than the ones just mentioned. These studies fall
into three relatively broad categories, though their concerns are remarkably unified and consistent. Gathered in Part One, 'Interpretation in Intertestamental Traditions', are papers concerned with interpretive tradition and styles attested in writings that antedate the writings of the New
Testament. Stephen Chapman wonders if the phrase, 'the Law and the
Words', functioned as an early designation for Scripture. His study
reaches back into the latter period of the Hebrew Bible itself and takes
into consideration the evidence of intertestamental literature, such as
the Dead Sea Scrolls. He finds that indeed a 'core canon' existed as early
as the Persian period and that it is misleading to speak of a 'loosely defined collection' of Scriptures in the late intertestamental period.
Staffan Olofsson probes the textually difficult Ps. 49.15 in the MT and
LXX. He wonders if a double meaning underlies the text, a meaning that
could then account for the variants and uncertain meaning. Kenneth
Atkinson draws our attention to the use of Scripture in the development
of militant Davidic messianism at Qumran. He believes *Psalms of Solomon* 17 potentially sheds important light on the development of messianism in the time of Herod the Great and the ways this messianism
was adapted to fit different circumstances in subsequent generations.
Veteran Josephan scholar Louis Feldman treats us to a lengthy study of
how Josephus comments on contemporary issues through biblical para-

phrase (not unlike much of modern preaching). Of especial interest is how Josephus is able to vilify rivals by drawing close parallels between them and biblical villains. For Josephus, the Bible was a guide for understanding the immediate past and the present. In this sense his hermeneutic was similar in perspective to the hermeneutical systems with more obvious typological and eschatological orientation, such as evidenced in the Dead Sea Scrolls and in parts of the New Testament. Hindy Najman studies the authority conveyed upon Scripture by its description as the 'Torah of Moses'. Ezra's legal innovations, prompted by the need to adapt to new social and political realities, had to be grounded in the authoritative law of Moses. Thus the phrase, 'Torah of Moses', did not primarily function as a reference to a collection of writings, but conferred authority on the updated tradition. Finally, Bruce Fisk probes the hermeneutics that lie behind the use of secondary biblical stories in the development of the narratives in *Pseudo-Philo* and the *Testaments of the Twelve Patriarchs*. He argues that scholars frequently underestimate, even overlook, the fundamentally exegetical nature of efforts in late antiquity to rewrite or retell biblical narratives.

Part Two, 'Interpretation in the New Testament', comprises five studies that probe the use of the Old Testament in Jesus, the Gospels and the epistle of *Barnabas*. John Brown investigates the Aramaic nouns that may underlie the sayings of Jesus. Though this study is primarily lexical and philological in nature, it reveals at various points the influence of biblical language in the vocabulary of Jesus. Steven Notley investigates a difficult text that has bedeviled interpreters for centuries: What does it mean to take the kingdom 'by force' (Mt. 11.12; cf. Lk. 16.16)? Notley believes an exegetical tradition, informed by texts such as Mic. 2.13, lies behind Jesus' words and has important eschatological significance. Benedict Viviano's study considers the influence of Exod. 4.10-17 on Mt. 16.13-20. He detects the presence of a Mosaic/Aaronic typology which clarifies Petrine succession in the Matthean church. Ellen Aitken investigates the Jacob traditions that lie behind the story of the woman at the well in John 4. Aitken believes this woman may have been understood to correspond to Rachel, the mother of the Samaritans. Yaron Z. Eliav probes the epistle of *Barnabas* for evidence of early Christian attitudes towards the Temple Mount. He concludes that *Barn.* 11.2-3 represents an early Christian midrash, based on Jer. 2.12-13 and Isa. 16.1-2, that corresponds in places with Jewish interpretation, but also breaks away at other important points.

Part Three, 'Interpretation in the Rabbis and the Targumim', is made up of four studies. Christian Brady investigates the role of the Attribute of Justice in the targumim, a common figure in the midrashim but relatively rare in the Aramaic paraphrases of Scripture. In the targumim this figure is personified, stands beside God, and—in contrast to the midrashim—rarely functions as an agent of judgment. Anthony Saldarini explores Targum Jonathan's presentation of King Saul as a scribe, in keeping with this targum's tendency to transform prophets into scribes, especially when the prophet is portrayed as a community leader. Ecstatic prophets are also sometimes transformed into scribes 'and the atmosphere of the divine spirit unleashed is tamed by the milieu of worship and study proper to the school and groups of scholars'. Saldarini believes this tendency reflects views of religious leaders in the time of the meturgeman (Aramaic translator/interpretor), perhaps even reaching back to the time of Jesus. Richard Kalmin investigates the fascinating midrashic traditions revolving around Doeg the Edomite, tracing his evolution from biblical villain to rabbinic sage and spokesman for Rome. Josep Ribera-Florit investigates the use of *derash* in the Ezekiel targum. He finds that this interpretive method was not designed to unpack enigmatic or symbolic meaning from the text of Scripture, but was intended simply to clarify the meaning of the text. Accordingly, the meturgeman attempts to offer 'realistic' versions of Ezekiel's allegories. Esther Menn's study of the Song of Songs targum and the dynamics of historical allegory brings our collection of essays to a fitting conclusion. She exposes the targum's portrait of God as a Torah scholar who calls Israel to repent, pray and praise him. The great Song, the penultimate of the ten songs Israel is destined to sing, prepares Israel for the final song that will be sung when God redeems Israel. Until then, Israel is to continue singing Solomon's famous Song.

It is hoped that this latest effort to set forth recent scholarship concerned with biblical intertextuality and the exegetical assumptions and techniques practiced in late antiquity will stimulate further research in this important field. Research of this nature not only sheds light on particular passages of Scripture and elements of sacred tradition, but sharpens our understanding of the canonical process and the forces at work within ancient communities of faith.

This page intentionally left blank

Part I

INTERPRETATION IN INTERTESTAMENTAL TRADITIONS

'THE LAW AND THE WORDS' AS A CANONICAL FORMULA WITHIN THE OLD TESTAMENT[*]

Stephen B. Chapman

1. A Consensus? Titles and Canon Formation

The only word *within* the Old Testament generally considered to be a *terminus technicus*[1] for scripture is תורה.[2] There exists a variety of תורה expressions which by their usage imply to varying degrees the definiteness of their referent: תורה אחת,[3] חקת התורה,[4] (הזאת) התורה,[5]

*   An earlier version of this essay was given as a paper at the 1998 Annual Meeting of the Society of Biblical Literature in Orlando, Florida. I would like to thank the Deutsche Forschungsgemeinschaft for sponsoring my research, Professor B. Janowski for his warm hospitality at the University of Tübingen and my colleagues in the Tübingen Graduiertenkolleg *Die Bibel—ihre Entstehung und ihre Wirkung* for their interest and questions.

1.   See the cautionary remarks on 'technicity' by R.W. Cowley, 'Technical Terms in Biblical Hebrew?', *TynBul* 37 (1986), pp. 21-28. I use the term loosely in the sense of a specified meaning within a particular context, here a reference to scripture—but the historical existence of this kind of linguistic specificity must itself be proved rather than assumed, as Cowley points out.

2.   On the variety of canonical titles outside of the Old Testament, see: Roger Beckwith, *The Old Testament Canon of the New Testament Church and its Background in Early Judaism* (London: SPCK, 1985), esp. pp. 105-109; S.Z. Leiman, *The Canonization of the Hebrew Scriptures: The Talmudic and Midrashic Evidence* (Transactions, 47; Hamden, CT: Archon, 1976). For treatments of the term תורה, see: F. García López and H.-J. Fabry, 'תורה *tôrāh*', *ThWAT* VIII (1995), pp. 597-637. Cf. G. Liedke and C. Petersen, 'תורה *tôrâ* Weisung', *THAT* II (1976), pp. 1032-43.

3.   Exod. 12.49; Lev. 7.7; Num. 15.16 (// משפט אחד // v. 15 חקה אהת), 29. On the significance of this formula, see Rolf Rendtorff, *Die Gesetze in der Priesterschrift: Eine gattungsgeschichtliche Untersuchung* (Göttingen: Vandenhoeck & Ruprecht, 1954), p. 72 n. 38.

4.   Num. 19.2; 31.21. Cf. Num. 27.11 (חקת משפט).

5.   Without זאת: Exod. 24.12 (// המצוה); Deut. 17.11 (// המשפט // הדבר); Jos.

הזה [8](דברי) ספר התורה (הזאת),[7](כל־)דברי התורה (הזאת)[6], כל־התורה (הזאת)
(ספר)תורת אלהים,[11](ספר) תורת משה[10], ספר התורה הזאת[9],ספר התורה
(ספר) תורת יהוה.[13] Certain related expressions appear without תורה, but
with words like ספר, משה or ברית used similarly: הספר הזה,[14]משה
הספר [18](כל־דברי) ספר הברית [16],דת אלה [15],ספר יהוה (הזה)[17],ספר

22.5 (// המצוה); 2 Kgs 17.34 (// המצוה), 37 (// המצוה); Jer. 2.8; Zech. 7.12 (//
הדברים); Mal. 2.8 (// ברית הלוי), 9; Neh. 8.2, 7, 14; 10.35, [34]; 10.37[36]; 12.44;
13.3; 2 Chron. 14.3[4] (// המצוה); 25.4 (// ספר משה); 31.21 (// במצוה). With הזאת:
Deut. 1.5; 17.18; 31.9, 11. Cf. זאת התורה in: Lev. 7.37; 14.54; Num. 19.14; Deut.
4.44. On this formula without the definite article, see below (n. 27). I have not listed
here those forms with pronominal suffixes, although they are also to be considered
definite.

6.   Without הזאת: Josh. 1.7; 2 Kgs 17.13; 21.8; 2 Chron. 33.8 (// החקים //
המשפטים). With הזאת: Num. 5.30; Deut. 4.8.

7.   Without כל and הזאת: Josh. 8.34; 2 Kgs 23.24; Neh. 8.9, 13; 2 Chron. 34.19.
With הזאת only: Deut. 27.26; 31.24. With כל only: Josh. 8.34. With both כל and
הזאת: Deut. 17.19 (// החקים האלה); 27.3, 8; 28.58; 29.28[29]; 31.12; 32.46 (//
כל הדברים).

8.   Without דברי: Josh. 8.34; 2 Kgs 22.8; Neh. 8.3; 2 Chron. 34.15. With דברי:
2 Kgs 22.11.

9.   Deut. 29.20[21]; 30.10; 31.26; Josh. 1.8.

10.   Deut. 28.61. Cf. Deut. 17.18.

11.   Without ספר: Josh. 8.32; 1 Kgs 2.3; 2 Kgs 23.25 (with כל); Mal. 3.22[4.4];
Dan. 9.11, 13; Ezra 3.2; 7.6; 2 Chron. 23.18; 30.16 (// משפטם). Cf. Josh. 1.7; 22.5;
2 Kgs 21.8; Neh. 8.14. With ספר: Josh. 8.31; 23.6; 2 Kgs 14.6; Neh. 8.1. Cf. 2
Chron. 34.14.

12.   Without ספר: Isa. 1.10 (אלהינו); Hos. 4.6 (// הדעת); Ps. 37.31; Neh.
10.29[28] (האלהים), 30[29] (האלהים). With ספר: Josh. 24.26; Neh. 8.8, 18; 9.3
(יהוה אלהיהם); Ps. 37.31. Cf. Ps. 40.8-9[7-8].

13.   Without ספר: Exod. 13.9; 2 Kgs 10.31 (also with אלהי־ישראל); Isa. 5.24
(also with צבאות, // אמרת קדוש־ישראל); 30.9 (// יד־עולם in v. 8); Jer. 8.8; Amos 2.4
(// חקיו); Ps. 1.2; 19.8 (// ידות יהוה in v. 8 // מצות יהוה, // פקודי יהוה in v. 9 //
יראת יהוה, משפטי־יהוה in v. 10); 119.1 (// דתיו in v. 2); Ezra 7.10; 1 Chron. 16.40;
22.12 (also with אלהיך); 2 Chron. 12.1; 31.3, 4; 35.26. With ספר: Neh. 9.3 (also
with אלהיהם); 2 Chron. 17.9; 34.14.

14.   Here תורה is implied. Deut. 28.58; 29.19[20], 26[27]; 2 Kgs 23.3; 2 Chron.
34.31.

15.   Ezra 6.18 (Aram.); Neh. 13.1; 2 Chron. 25.4 (// בתורה); 35.12. See
A. Hurvitz, 'On the Borderline between Biblical Criticism and Hebrew Linguistics:
The Emergence of the Term ספר משה', in M. Cogan, B.L. Eichler and J.H. Tigay
(eds.), *Tehillah le-Moshe: Biblical and Judaic Studies* (Festschrift Moshe
Greenberg; Winona Lake, IN: Eisenbrauns, 1997), pp. 37*-44* (Hebrew)—English
abstract, pp. 316-17. Hurvitz argues that תורת משה, תורת יהוה, ספר התורה ,התורה

דברי,[19] דברי אלהים,[20] (כל־)דברי יהוה,[21] דברי הברית (הזאת).[22] These various expressions cannot always be located securely within discrete sources and traditions, but often seem to function rhetorically as synonyms.[23] Other expressions of authority (e.g. משפט/־ים, עדות מצוה־ות, חק/־ים/־ות)[24] or references to no longer identifiable 'books'[25] have been

---

and ספר תורת משה are all deuteronomistic, and that widespread Second Temple usage indicates ספר משה is not a stylistic variation but a post-deuteronomistic development. The precise referent (the Pentateuch?) is unclear, he maintains. Hurvitz's thesis is plausible; however, given the high degree of stylistic variation with these terms generally, I would advocate caution in drawing any significant implications from this possibility.

16. (Aram.) Only in Ezra 7.14, 25 (pl.), 26. One possible Hebrew equivalent might be ספר אלהים, which is, however, unattested in the entire Old Testament. Cf. (also with תורה) Josh. 24.26; Neh. 8.8, 18.

17. Isa. 34.16. The question is whether this term refers to an earthly 'book' or the tradition of a heavenly 'book of life' (cf. Exod. 32.32-33; Isa. 4.3; Mal. 3.16; Dan. 12.1). For discussion, see: H. Donner, ' "Forscht in der Schrift Jahwes und lest!": Ein Beitrag zum Verständnis der israelitischen Prophetie', *ZThK* 87 (1990), pp. 285-98; W. Herrmann, 'Überlegungen zu den Vorstufen der Kanonbildung', in M. Weippert and S. Timm (eds.), *Meilenstein* (Festschrift Herbert Donner; ÄAT, 30; Wiesbaden: Otto Harrassowitz, 1995), pp. 73-78.

18. Exod. 24.7. With כל־דברי: 2 Kgs 23.2; 2 Chron. 34.30. With הזה: 2 Kgs 23.21.

19. 2 Kgs 22.13, 16 (with כל); Isa. 29.11(K), 18 (without article); Jer. 29.1; 36.32; 2 Chron. 34.21.

20. Jer. 23.36 (with אלהים חיים יהוה צבאות אלהינו); Ezra 9.4 (with אלהי־ישראל); 1 Chron. 25.5 (with האלהים).

21. Without כל: Num. 11.24; Josh. 3.9 (also with אלהיכם); 1 Sam. 15.1 (also with קול); Jer. 36.6, 8 (also with ספר); 37.2; Amos 8.11 (probably דבר here); 2 Chron. 11.4; 29.15. With כל: Exod. 4.28; 24.3 (// כל־המשפטים), 4; 1 Sam. 8.10; Jer. 36.4, 11 (also with מעל הספר); 43.1 (also with אליהם); Ezek. 11.25.

22. Without הזאת: Exod. 34.28 (עשרת הדברים in apposition); Deut. 28.69[29.1]; Jer. 34.18; 2 Chron. 34.31. With הזאת: Deut. 29.8[9]; 2 Kgs 23.3; Jer. 11.2, 3, 6, 8 (with כל).

23. See Norbert Lohfink, *Das Hauptgebot: Eine Untersuchung literarischer Einleitungsfragen zu Deuteronomium 5–11* (AnBib, 20; Rome: Pontifical Biblical Institute Press, 1963), pp. 54-55. Cf. García López and Fabry, 'תורה', p. 608.

24. In addition to the standard lexicon articles covering these and other terms, see: G. Braulik, 'Die Ausdrücke für "Gesetz" im Buch Deuteronomium', *Bib* 51 (1970), pp. 39-66 = *idem, Studien zur Theologie des Deuteronomiums* (SBAB, 2: Altes Testament; Stuttgart: Katholisches Bibelwerk, 1988), pp. 11-38 (I cite from the latter version); Gerhard Liedke, *Gestalt und Bezeichnung alttestamentlicher*

understood as 'pre-scriptural' references to various legal traditions or collections. However, only תורה is thought to have gained the sense of 'Scripture' already within the biblical period.

In order to reach this conclusion, a gradual expansion of the word תורה's semantic range has usually been reconstructed: from referring at first to individual priestly rulings,[26] to collections of such rulings,[27] to the book of Deuteronomy,[28] to the Pentateuch as a whole.[29] More recent linguistic work has emphasized the possibility of non-priestly originating traditions for תורה (e.g. prophecy, wisdom),[30] but still locates the

Rechtssätze: Eine formgeschichtlich-terminologische Studie (WMANT, 39; Neukirchen–Vluyn: Neukirchener Verlag, 1971); Lohfink, *Hauptgebot*, pp. 54-58.

25. See Leiman, *Canonization*, pp. 17-24.

26. E.g. Lev. 26.46; Deut. 33.10; Ezek. 44.24; Hag. 2.10-14; Mal. 2.6-9. The classic exposition is found in J. Begrich, 'Die priesterliche Tora', in J. Hempel, F. Stummer, and P. Volz (eds.), *Werden und Wesen des Alten Testaments* (BZAW, 66; Berlin: Alfred Töpelmann, 1936), pp. 63-88 = *idem*, in W. Zimmerli (ed.), *Gesammelte Studien zum Alten Testament* (TBü 21; Munich: Chr. Kaiser Verlag, 1964), pp. 232-60 (I cite from the latter version).

27. For evidence of such תורת collections within the priestly literature, see: זאת תורה as an introductory formula in Lev. 6.2[9], 7[14], 18[25]; 7.1, 11; 14.2; Num. 6.13, and as concluding formula in Lev. 11.46; 12.7; 13.59; 14.32, 57b; 15.32; Num. 5.29; 6.21a; and also זאת התורה as an introductory formula in Num. 19.14; (Deut. 4.44), and as concluding formula in Lev. 7.37; 14.54. Cf. Ezek. 43.11, 12; 44.5. The inclusios provided by Lev. 14.2, 57b and Num. 6.13, 21 make for especially good examples. Cf. Begrich, 'Tora', p. 257; García López and Fabry, 'תורה', p. 605.

28. B. Lindars, 'Torah in Deuteronomy', in P.R. Ackroyd and B. Lindars (eds.), *Words and Meanings* (Festschrift David Winton Thomas; Cambridge: Cambridge University Press, 1968), pp. 117-36.

29. García López and Fabry, 'תורה', p. 634. Cf. D.N. Freedman, 'The Formation of the Canon of the Old Testament: The Selection and Identification of the Torah as the Supreme Authority of the Postexilic Community', in E.B. Firmage, B.G. Weiss and J.W. Welch (eds.), *Religion and Law: Biblical-Judaic and Islamic Perspectives* (Winona Lake, IN: Eisenbrauns, 1990), pp. 315-31; E. Zenger, 'Der Pentateuch als Tora und als Kanon', in E. Zenger (ed.), *Die Tora als Kanon für Juden und Christen* (HBS, 10; Freiburg: Herder, 1996), pp. 5-34.

30. See: Gunnar Östborn, *Tora in the Old Testament: A Semantic Study* (Lund: Hakan Ohlsson, 1945); Liedke, *Rechtssätze*. The question with regard to prophecy has to do with the origins of the so-called 'prophetic torah'. See T. Lescow, 'Die dreistufige Tora: Beobachtungen zu einer Form', *ZAW* 82 (1970), pp. 362-79. On the problem of 'prophetic torah' in Isaiah, see Joseph Jensen, *The Use of tôrâ by Isaiah: His Debate with the Wisdom Tradition* (CBQMS, 3; Washington: Catholic

critical step in the process of its semantic expansion at the time of the literary frame to the book of Deuteronomy.[31]

Within Deuteronomy all the references to תורה—with three exceptions—appear in the literary frame to the book now found in chs. 1–11 and 27–34.[32] All three exceptions are located in ch. 17, long suspected of exhibiting later redaction.[33] The references to תורה in the framing

Biblical Association, 1973), pp. 18-26, although in my judgment Jensen is too extreme in his conclusion that '…the Old Testament does not use *tôrâ* to designate the prophetic word' (p. 25). See Dan. 9.10! Also, Jud. 13.8 (unless amended); Isa. 28.9, 26 may provide evidence of an early independent prophetic context for תורה. Cf. Lindars, 'Torah', p. 121; García López and Fabry, 'תורה', p. 631. For an alternative proposal on the relation between תורה and prophetic traditions, see E. Myers, 'The Use of *tôrâ* in Haggai 2:11 and the Role of the Prophet in the Restoration Community', in C.L. Meyers and M. O'Connor (eds.), *The Word of the Lord Shall Go Forth* (Festschrift David Noel Freedman; AASOR Special Vol. Ser. 1; Winona Lake, IN: Eisenbrauns, 1983), pp. 69-76.

On the other hand, both Östborn (p. 115) and Liedke (pp. 197-99) suggest that תורה may ultimately have its semantic 'home' within the family, noting that Prov. 1.8; 6.20, (23); (31.26) refer to the תורה of the mother. As Liedke notes, the תורה of a father/teacher is also referred to in Prov. 3.1; 4.2 (cf. the verbal forms in Job 8.10; Prov. 4.4, 11). Cf. Prov. 28.7. There is also mention of a תורת חכם in Prov. 13.14. On the wisdom context of תורה, see further: Jensen, *Use*, pp. 28-44; García López and Fabry, 'תורה', p. 624; Klaus-Dietrich Schunck, 'Der alttestamentliche Tora-Begriff', in his *Alten Testament und heiliges Land: Gesammelte Studien zum Alten Testament und zur biblischen Landeskunde*, I (BEATAJ, 17; Bern: Peter Lang, 1989), pp. 243-55; T. Willi, 'Tôrâ: Israels Lebensprinzip nach dem Zeugnis des späteren Alten Testaments', in *Meilenstein*, pp. 339-48.

31. M. Köckert, 'Das nahe Wort: Zum entscheidenden Wandel des Gesetzesverständnisses im Altes Testament', *TP* 60 (1985), pp. 496-519; *idem*, 'Leben in Gottes Gegenwart: Zum Verständnis des Gesetzes in der priesterschriftlichen Literatur', in I. Baldermann *et al.* (eds.), *'Gesetz' als Thema Biblischer Theologie* (JBTh 4; Neukirchen–Vluyn: Neukirchener Verlag, 1989), pp. 29-61. It should be noted that Begrich ignores any deuteronomistic shift in the meaning of תורה, locating the change in usage from priestly rulings to written law at the time of Ezra instead (Begrich, 'Tora', p. 258).

32. Within the frame, in Deut. 1.5; 4.8, 44; 27.3, 8, 26; 28.58, 61; 29.20[21], 28; 30.10; 31.9, 11, 12, 24, 26; 32.46; 33.4, 10. Within the body of the book, Deut. 17.11, 18, 19. In addition to Lindars, 'Torah', p. 130, see Lohfink, *Hauptgebot*, p. 58, and Braulik, 'Ausdrücke', p. 17.

33. E.g. Wellhausen argued that Deut. 17.14-20 already assumed Deut. 31.9, 26. See Julius Wellhausen, *Die Composition des Hexateuchs und der historischen Bücher des Alten Testaments* (Berlin: W. de Gruyter, 4th edn, 1963), p. 192. Lindars ('Torah', p. 130) argues for 17.18-19 as a later addition; 17.11 he regards

material are interesting not only because they appear to have selected this word from among other legal terms to refer to the Mosaic covenant,[34] but also because they use תורה to refer to the book of Deuteronomy itself as the embodiment of that covenant. Within the literary frame, a deictic pronoun is often used together with תורה to refer to the book of Deuteronomy as such:[35] 'all the words of *this* תורה which are written in *this* book',[36] 'the book of *this* תורה',[37] '*this* book of the תורה'.[38]

The correspondence between these deuteronomistic expressions and the similar expressions found in 2 Kings 22–23 reinforces the theory that the 'lawbook' found in the Temple during Josiah's reign was in fact an earlier version of the book of Deuteronomy.[39] Thus, the basic expressions דברי התורה,[40] ספר התורה הזה,[41] הספר הזה[42] and דברי הברית[43] are shared between both accounts. Similar expressions appear in the books of Ezra–Nehemiah and Chronicles,[44] leading not only to the usual conclusion that after the time of the frame to the book of Deuteronomy the scope of the term תורה expanded to include other pentateuchal materials, but also that the confession of one all-embracing תורה for Israel

---

simply as a noun cognate of the verb, meaning priestly instruction rather than Mosaic תורה. Cf. Braulik, 'Ausdrücke', p. 36 n. 115. Deut. 24.8 provides a deuteronomic example of the verbal form.

34.   Not without precedent, perhaps: the date and interpretation of references to תורה in Hos. 4.6 and 8.1 continue to be debated. In Hos. 8.1, ברית // תורה. Cf. Hos. 8.12.

35.   On the literary significance of 'deictic repetition', see B. Peckham, 'Writing and Editing', in A.B. Beck *et al.* (eds.), *Fortunate the Eyes that See* (Festschrift David Noel Freedman; Grand Rapids: Eerdmans, 1995), pp. 364-83.

36.   Deut. 28.58; cf. 27.3, 8; 29.28[29]; 31.12, 24 (also with עד תמם!); 32.46.

37.   Deut. 28.61.

38.   Deut. 29.20[21]; 30.10; 31.26.

39.   Moshe Weinfeld, *Deuteronomy 1–11: A New Translation with Introduction and Commentary* (AB 5; New York: Doubleday, 1991), pp. 81-84.

40.   Deut. 17.19; 27.3, 8, 26; 28.58; 29.28[29]; 31.12, 24; 32.46 and 2 Kgs 23.24.

41.   Deut. 29.20[21]; 30.10; 31.26 and 2 Kgs 22.8.

42.   Deut. 28.58; 29.19[20], 26[27] and 2 Kgs 23.3; cf. דברי הספר in 2 Kgs 22.13, 16.

43.   Deut. 28.69[29.1]; 29.8[9] and 2 Kgs 23.2, 3; cf. ספר הברית in 2 Kgs 23.2, 21.

44.   See: דברי התורה in Neh. 8.9, 13; 2 Chron. 34.19; ספר התורה in Neh. 8.3; 2 Chron. 34.15; הספר הזה in 2 Chron. 34.31; ספר הברית in 2 Chron. 34.30; דברי הברית in 2 Chron. 34.31; דברי הספר in 2 Chron. 34.21.

was a deuteronomistic innovation which was then retained and expanded by subsequent traditions.[45] On this theory Ezra–Nehemiah[46] and Chronicles[47] do not initiate but *continue* the deuteronomistic language of a single Mosaic 'lawbook'.[48]

Previous scholarly debate has turned on the extent of the literature referred to as תורה within a particular layer of biblical literature and the particular historical period that layer may reflect. That is, does a particular mention of תורה refer to deuteronomic legislation (D), to the

---

45. Lindars, 'Torah', p. 120: 'Thus the use of תורה in this holistic sense throughout 1 and 2 Chronicles, Ezra, Nehemiah and Daniel 9 depends not on the Priestly Code, even though these books have obvious affinities with the priestly literature, and even though it is the Priestly Code, or rather the Pentateuch, to which it refers in them. On the contrary, it is to be traced to the influence of the Deuteronomic literature, and the link is provided by such passages as Zech 7:12 and Mal 3:22'.

46. Although this deuteronomistic language is absent from the book of Ezra *per se*, I consider these two books to have comprised one book already in antiquity (see Josephus, *Apion*, 1.40; Melito of Sardis [Eusebius, *Historia Ecclesiastica* 4.26.14]), following Joseph Blenkinsopp, *Ezra–Nehemiah: A Commentary* (OTL; Philadelphia: Westminster Press, 1988), pp. 38-39. For arguments against an 'original' unity, see: D. Kraemer, 'On the Relationship of the Books of Ezra and Nehemiah', *JSOT* 59 (1993), pp. 73-92; J.C. VanderKam, 'Ezra–Nehemiah or Ezra and Nehemiah', in E. Ulrich *et al.* (eds.), *Priests, Prophets and Scribes: Essays on the Formation and Heritage of Second Temple Judaism* (Festschrift Joseph Blenkinsopp; JSOTSup, 149; Sheffield: JSOT Press, 1992), pp. 55-75.

47. I also think it prudent not to assume the common authorship of Ezra–Nehemiah and the books of Chronicles, although the distinction is not crucial to this essay. For important arguments against common authorship, see: Kenneth G. Hoglund, *Archaemenid Imperial Administration in Syria-Palestine and the Missions of Ezra and Nehemiah* (SBLDS, 125; Atlanta: Scholars Press, 1992), pp. 36-40; S. Japhet, 'The Supposed Common Authorship of Chronicles and Ezra–Nehemiah Investigated Anew', *VT* 18 (1968), pp. 330-71; *idem*, 'The Relationship Between Chronicles and Ezra–Nehemiah', in J.A. Emerton (ed.), *Congress Volume: Leuven 1989* (VTSup, 43; Leiden: E.J. Brill, 1991), pp. 298-313; Simon J. De Vries, *1 and 2 Chronicles* (FOTL, 11; Grand Rapids: Eerdmans, 1989), pp. 1-12; H.G.M. Williamson, *1 and 2 Chronicles* (NCB; Grand Rapids: Eerdmans, 1982), pp. 5-11.

48. Thus: López García and Fabry, 'תורה', pp. 629-30; Rudolf Smend, *Die Entstehung des Alten Testments* (ThW 1; Stuttgart: W. Kohlhammer, 1978), p. 35. Cf. U. Kellermann, 'Anmerkungen zum Verständnis der Tora in den chronistischen Schriften', *BN* 42 (1988), pp. 49-92; D. J. McCarthy, 'Covenant and Law in Chronicles–Nehemiah', *CBQ* 44 (1982), pp. 25-44; T. Willi, 'Thora in den biblischen Chronikbüchern', *Judaica* 36 (1980), pp. 102-105, 148-51.

priestly literature (P), to a combination of both (D+P), or to the Pentateuch in its entirety? Also at issue is whether תורה terminology refers only to the pentateuchal material now extant, or perhaps also to other material that has not survived, in written or even oral form.[49]

This latter question arises because some of the references in Ezra–Nehemiah and Chronicles to the Mosaic 'lawbook' refer to traditions not explicitly included in the received form of the Pentateuch.[50] For example, the duties assigned to priests and levites by authority of the תורת משה in 2 Chron. 30.16 and by the ספר משה in 2 Chron. 35.12 have 'no antecedent legislative basis in the Pentateuch', according to a study by J. Shaver.[51] He sees the same problem of missing warrants in Ezra 10.3, Neh. 8.15 and 10.35[34].[52] On the other hand, references to תורה in Ezra–Nehemiah seem to indicate a combination of deuteronomic and priestly traditions had occurred by at least the time of the final redaction of that book.[53]

Even with some uncertainties, therefore, it appears to be the case that תורה eventually functioned as a *terminus technicus* for Scripture even in the biblical period. Moreover, the apparent lack of other terminology for a broader collection of Scriptures or scriptural collections within the

49. For debate on the contents of Ezra's 'lawbook', see U. Kellermann, 'Erwägungen zum Esragesetz', *ZAW* 80 (1968), pp. 373-85; R. Rendtorff, 'Esra und das "Gesetz"', *ZAW* 96 (1984), pp. 165-84; C. Houtman, 'Ezra and the Law: Observations on the Supposed Relation between Ezra and the Pentateuch', in B. Albrektson *et al.* (eds.), *Remembering All the Way: A Collection of Old Testament Studies Published on the Occasion of the Fortieth Anniversary of the Oudtestamentisch Werkgezelschap in Nederland* (*OTS*, 21; Leiden: E.J. Brill, 1981).

50. For description of the problem, see C. Houtman, *Der Pentateuch: Die Geschichte seiner Erforschung neben einer Auswertung* (CBET, 9; Kampen: Kok Pharos, 1994), pp. 348-50; J. Shaver, *Torah and the Chronicler's History Work: An Inquiry into the Chronicler's References to Law, Festivals and Cultic Institutions in Relationship to Pentateuchal Legislation* (BJS, 196; Atlanta,: Scholars Press, 1989), pp. 87-121.

51. Cf. Ezra 6.18. Shaver, *Torah*, p. 117.

52. Shaver, *Torah*, p. 127.

53. For a summary, see: Shaver, *Torah*, 127; Blenkinsopp, *Ezra*, pp. 152-54. E.g. Neh. 10.32b[31b] appears to combine the law of the seventh fallow year (Exod. 23.10-11; Lev. 25.1-7 = P) with the law of the seventh year of release (Deut. 15.1-18; cf. Exod. 21.2-6 = D). Similarly, the instructions to gather wood for the wood-offering (Neh. 10.35[34]) are not included in the Pentateuch, but Blenkinsopp argues they would be logically necessary. Shaver believes all of the pentateuchal legal traditions are represented in Neh. 10.29[28]-39[38].

biblical text, especially those which would later come to be applied to
the other canonical subcollections (כתובים, נביאים),[54] has played a decisive role in supporting the standard theory of canon formation.

According to the standard canonical theory, as established at the end
of the nineteenth century, the Hebrew canon was formed in three
discrete stages corresponding to the major divisions of the Masoretic
Text.[55] The Pentateuch was thought to have become the first 'Bible' of
Israel in the second half of the fifth century BCE, probably under the
influence of Ezra. The 'Prophets' were said to have been granted canonical status approximately two hundred years later, just before being
mentioned in Dan. 9.2 (c. 165 BCE) and the prologue to the book of Ben
Sira (c. 132 BCE).[56] The 'Writings' were not thought to have become
canonical until two to three hundred years later still.[57]

54.   The term נביאים is found, of course, but not as a title for a literary collection (cf. Ezra 9.11; Neh. 9.26, 30; Lam. 2.9; Dan. 9.10). The closest biblical form to
the later כתובים may be מכתב/בכתב ('writing'?) in 1 Chron. 28.19; 2 Chron. 35.4.
This form is normally used for a letter, e.g. 2 Chron. 2.10[11]. The earliest refer-
ence to כתובים as a canonical subcollection appears to be a statement attributed to
Rabbi Akiba in *M. Yad.* 3.5 (late first/early second century CE?). See Beckwith,
Canon, p. 164 n. 133.
    55.   Above all, see Herbert Edward Ryle, *The Canon of the Old Testament: An
Essay on the Gradual Growth and Formation of the Hebrew Canon of Scripture*
(London: Macmillan, 1892). Cf. Karl Budde, *Der Kanon des Alten Testaments*
(Giessen: J. Ricker, 1900); Frants Buhl, *Kanon und Text des Alten Testaments*
(Leipzig: W. Faber, 1891); Gerrit Wildeboer, *Het ontstaan van den kanon des
Ouden Verbonds* (Gröningen: Wolters, 1889) = idem, *Die Entstehung des alttes-
tamentlichen Kanons* (Gotha: F.A. Perthes, 1891). Recent scholarship has set later
dates for each of the subcollections, but nevertheless retained the three-stage model
as a 'rough guide'. See John Barton, 'The Significance of a Fixed Canon of the
Hebrew Bible', in *Hebrew Bible/Old Testament: The History of its Interpretation.
Volume I: From the Beginnings to the Middle Ages (1300). Part I: Antiquity* (ed.
M. Sæbø; Göttingen: Vandenhoeck & Ruprecht, 1996), pp. 67-83, esp. 68.
    56.   Ryle, *Canon*, pp. 122-23. In their commentary, Skehan and DiLella argue
for a date of 117 BCE for the prologue to Ben Sira. See Patrick W. Skehan with
Alexander A. DiLella, *The Wisdom of Ben Sira* (AB, 39; New York: Doubleday,
1987), p. 135.
    57.   The final 'closing' of the Writings, and thus the entire canon, was thought
to have happened at a rabbinical council in Jamnia toward the end of the first century CE. This is now widely doubted. See: D.E. Aune, 'On the Origins of the "Council" of Javneh Myth', *JBL* 110 (1991), pp. 491-93; Beckwith, *Canon*, pp. 276-77;
J.P. Lewis, 'What Do we Mean by Jabneh?', *JBR* 32 (1964), pp. 125-32; G. Maier,
'Der Abschluß des jüdischen Kanons und das Lehrhaus von Jabne', in G. Maier

What appears to represent the single terminological exception to the exclusive use of תורה as a title for Scripture—the allusion to הספרים in Dan. 9.2,[58] in which Jeremiah's prophecy of 70 weeks is cited explicitly—is argued to prove the rule: only at a later stage of canon formation did prophetic and wisdom traditions acquire a stable literary form, canonical status and thus the *need* to be named. According to the standard reconstruction of canon formation the categorization and naming of the biblical writings could only *begin* once they were literarily complete and possessed a fixed text.

L.M. McDonald has now radicalized this view, asserting: 'The absence of an appropriate term to describe a collection of Scriptures both before and immediately following the time of Jesus suggests that such notions were not the current *lingua franca* in that ancient context'.[59] McDonald argues for this and other reasons that the Old Testament canon was not 'closed' until the end of the fourth century CE.[60]

An important connection exists, then, between the terminology for Scripture that one is able to locate *inside* the Old Testament and how

(ed.), *Der Kanon der Bibel* (Giessen: Brunnen; Wuppertal: Brockhaus, 1990), pp. 1-24; P. Schäfer, 'Die sogenannte Synode von Jamnia', *Judaica* 3 (1975), pp. 54-64; G. Stemberger, 'Jabne und der Kanon', *JBTh* 3 (1988), pp. 163-74; G. Veltri, 'Zur traditionsgeschichtlichen Entwicklung des Bewußtseins von einem Kanon: die Yavneh-Frage', *JSJ* 21 (1990), pp. 210-26.

58. The noun is preceded by ־ב in the text, but is definite in the MT. To judge from later rabbinic usage, הספרים here most likely refers to 'non-pentateuchal Scripture' rather than prophetic Scripture *per se*. See Beckwith, *Canon*, pp. 149-50; Leiman, *Canonization*, p. 57. The term ספר is used to mean 'writing' or 'letter' (see Jer. 29.1, 25; 32.14; 2 Chron. 32.17), but can also indicate a lengthier literary work or literary collection (see Eccl. 12.12; Ezra 6.1[Aram.]; 1 Macc. 12.9).

59. L.M. McDonald, 'The First Testament: Its Origin, Adaptability, and Stability', in C.A. Evans, S. Talmon (eds.), *The Quest for Context and Meaning. Studies in Biblical Intertextuality* (Festschrift James A. Sanders; Biblical Interpretation Series, 28; Leiden: E.J. Brill, 1997), pp. 287-326, here p. 322. The anachronism *lingua franca* seems an especially poor construction to employ when arguing that scholarly reference to a 'canon' in the first century CE represents an anachronism. Cf. *idem*, 'The Integrity of the Biblical Canon in Light of its Historical Development', *BBR* 6 (1996), pp. 95-132; esp. 103-105.

60. McDonald, 'Testament', pp. 317-18. Macdonald sets the 'closure' of the Christian Old Testament at the end of the fourth century, but the 'closure' of the Hebrew canon within Judaism not until the fifth or sixth century CE. Cf. his book-length treatment, *The Formation of the Christian Biblical Canon* (Peabody, MA: Hendrickson, rev. edn, 1995).

one reconstructs the process of canon formation. The fact that the expression 'the law and the prophets' (ὁ νόμος καί οἱ προφῆται) has been thought to appear for the first time within the prologue to the book of Sirach[61] rather than within the Old Testament itself has also been taken as providing evidence for the secondary canonization of prophetic Scripture at the beginning of the second century BCE.[62]

Rarely asked, however, is the question: even if the expression 'the law and the prophets' is not found until later extra-biblical writings,[63] when and how did it arise? In particular, how did the prophetic corpus receive the title 'Prophets'? How did the 'other books' receive the title 'Writings'? If only תורה functions as a *terminus technicus* within the Old Testament for Israel's scriptural inheritance, how is it that נביאים

---

61. Sir. Prol. 1, 3, 7. See R. Beckwith, 'Formation of the Hebrew Bible' in M.J. Mulder (ed.), *Mikra: Text, Translation, Reading and Interpretation of the Hebrew Bible in Ancient Judaism and Christianity* (CRINT, 2.1; Assen: Van Gorcum; Philadelphia: Fortress Press, 1988), pp. 39-86, here pp. 51-52. It should be emphasized, however, that the author of the prologue is familiar with the non-pentateuchal Scripture in Greek translation (Sir. Prol. 6), suggesting an earlier date for such Scripture in Hebrew (cf. Buhl, *Kanon*, p. 12). The specific books, however, are not named. From the time of main body of the book (c. 180 BCE), Sir. 38.34b–39.1 may provide an even earlier allusion to non-pentateuchal Scripture. Moreover, the twelve minor prophets are cited as one book (Sir. 49.10).

Now the earliest explicit mention of נביאים as literature seems to occur in 4QMMT, which refers to 'the book of Moses and the books of the prophets and of David...' (4Q397 [4QMMT[d]] 14–21.10-11). 4QMMT is comprised of six fragments (4Q394-99) dated paleographically from 75 BCE to 50 CE. See E. Qimron and J. Strugnell (eds.), *Qumran Cave 4.V: Miqṣat Ma'ase Ha-Torah* (DJD, 10; Oxford: Clarendon Press, 1994), p. 107. These fragments, however, are apparently copies of an older text. Cf. J. Kampen and M.J. Bernstein, 'Introduction', in *idem* (eds.), *Reading 4QMMT: New Perspectives on Qumran Law and History* (SBLSS, 2; Atlanta: Scholars Press, 1990), pp. 1-7. In the same volume, H. Eshel makes a thoughtful case ('4QMMT and the History of the Hasmonean Period', pp. 53-65, esp. p. 64) for a date of 152 BCE for the text's composition.

62. The prologue to Sirach also mentions 'the other/rest of the books' (καὶ τὰ ἄλλα πάτρια βιβλία // καὶ τὰ λοιπὰ τῶν βιβλίων), a somewhat vague reference which has often been interpreted to mean that the third canonical subcollection of the Writings was still forming and not yet closed. See also 4Q397 (4QMMT[d]) 14–21.10-11; Philo, *Vit. Cont.*, 25; 2 Macc. 2.13; Lk. 24.44.

63. Sirach may or may not be considered extra-biblical. For the issues involved, Beckwith, *Canon*, pp. 366-79; *idem*, 'Formation', pp. 72-73; Skehan and DiLella, *Ben Sira*, pp. 17-20.

and כתובים emerged as distinct categories at all, instead of being completely subsumed under reference to תורה?

2. *A Problem?* Tôrâ *and* Tôrôt

In my judgment a response to these questions must first re-evaluate whether later biblical traditions may be said to use תורה as a title for a canonical Pentateuch.

Moshe Weinfeld has attempted to differentiate between deuteronomistic and priestly uses of the term: 'Unlike JE (Gen. 26.5; Exod. 18.16; cf. Ps. 105.45) and P (Exod. 16.28; Lev. 26.46; cf. Ezek. 44.24) Deuteronomy and the deuteronomic literature never use *tôrôt* but always use *tôrâ* in the singular, in compliance with the notion of a canonized Torah'.[64] Although there do exist differences in the way various traditions use the term תורה, Weinfeld's formulation overlooks a number of similarities and the significance of these similarities for the history of canonization.

For example, it is not at all clear that the plural תורות only appears outside of the deuteronomistic literature. Weinfeld's attribution of Gen. 26.5 to JE proves problematic in light of more recent studies of Genesis. Gen. 26.5 not only contains the plural ותורתי, but places this word at the end of a series of legal terms (or *Rechtssatz*) in which the individual terms (משמרתי מצותי הקותי) appear to function as synonyms. For this reason and others, Gen. 26.5 has been identified as part of a deuteronomistic compositional unit (Gen. 26.3bβ-5)[65] or as a 'semi-deuteron-

---

64. Moshe Weinfeld, *Deuteronomy and the Deuteronomic School* (Oxford: Clarendon Press, 1972), p. 338. I employ the term 'deuteronomic' only in reference to Deuteronomy 12–26 and the traditions these chapters reflect; since the references to תורה as an umbrella term are from a later date, I have used the term 'deuteronomistic' in contrast to Weinfeld, who does not make the same distinction.

65. Erhard Blum, *Die Komposition der Vätergeschichte* (WMANT 57; Neukirchen–Vluyn: Neukirchener Verlag, 1984), pp. 362-64. Blum, however, seems to believe that here (i.e. before Sinai) תורות must be used in the sense of priestly instructions rather than Mosaic תורה. It is not evident to me that the 'anachronism' he finds problematic would have been considered a difficulty by deuteronomistic tradents. The issue at hand is the righteousness of Abraham, which is here measured by the standard of the Sinai legislation so that Abraham can be considered to have been truly righteous. It is precisely this impossibly 'anachronistic' view against which Paul is constrained to argue in Romans 4 (cf. Rom. 4.13).

omistic' redaction of non-priestly Genesis tradition.[66] Similarly Exod. 16.28, which Weinfeld assigns to P, has also been increasingly viewed as a deuteronomistic gloss.[67] Weinfeld also overlooks the *kethib* of Jer. 32.23, a clearly deuteronomistic passage which gives the form וּבתרותך, although later Masoretes read it as singular.[68] ותורתך in Deut. 33.10 should probably also be read as a plural.[69]

A related problem is that Weinfeld's thesis also obscures the significant number of deuteronomistic passages in which תורה (although in the singular) appears within *Rechtssätze* without any clear indication that it functions differently from other terms.[70] Thus, Deut. 17.19 mentions not only כל־דברי התורה הזאת, but also החקים האלה as required reading for the king.[71] Joshua 22.5 cites את־המצוה ואת־התורה.[72] In 2 Kgs 17.34, 37, תורה appears in two expanded *Rechtssätze*, suggesting that its status here is not that of an umbrella term for the entirety of the law—all of which is thought of here as having been written (כתב) by God (v. 37)—although these verses are generally attributed to deuteronomistic redaction.[73] Jer. 44.10, 23 provide further deuteronomistic examples of תורה in combination with other terms.

Despite sometimes seeming to be subordinated to תורה within deuteronomistic tradition,[74] the term מצוה continues to exhibit a high status within deuteronomistic literature, often appearing either parallel to

66.   David M. Carr, *Reading the Fractures of Genesis: Historical and Literary Approaches* (Louisville, KY: Westminster/John Knox Press, 1996), pp. 153-59.

67.   Josef Scharbert, *Exodus* (Die Neue Echter Bibel, 24; Würzburg: Echter Verlag, 1989), p. 68; Liedke and Petersen, 'תורה', p. 1041. Liedke and Petersen call attention to Exod. 13.9 and 16.4 as similar deuteronomistic glosses. Weinfeld identifies (*Deuteronomy*, p. 334, #7) the phrase הלך בתורת יהוה as deuteronomistic, but argues that in Exod. 16.4 תורה 'refers to general instruction and not to the specific "Law"'.

68.   Blum, *Komposition*, p. 362.

69.   See Begrich, 'Tora', p. 233 n. 10, citing Gressman.

70.   On *Rechtssätze* in Deut. 4.45–28.68, see the list in Lohfink, *Hauptgebot*, pp. 295-96; on *Rechtssätze* within the entire Old Testament, see the helpful charts in Liedke, *Rechtssätze*, pp. 13-17.

71.   See also המצוה in Deut. 17.20. According to Lohfink (*Hauptgebot*, p. 58), Deut. 17.19 proves that התורה is not 'reihenscheu' in deuteronomistic usage.

72.   The language of the rest of the verse is clearly deuteronomistic.

73.   R.D. Nelson, *The Double Redaction of the Deuteronomistic History* (JSOTSup, 18; Sheffield: JSOT Press, 1981), pp. 64-65.

74.   E.g. Deut. 30.10; 2 Kgs 17.13.

תורה[75] or in its place.[76] Similarly 'subordinated' in deuteronomistic tradition,[77] חקים-/ות can also share תורה's elevated status[78] or replace it.[79] Thus Weinfeld's thesis fails to account for the inconsistency of 'canonical' terminology within deuteronomistic tradition.

Such inconsistency has led E. Blum to argue instead for 'einen späten, nachdeuteronomistischen Gebrauch des Plurals'[80] and prompted R.D. Nelson to advance the possibility of a later 'demotion' of תורה authority.[81] In my judgment, however, this move does not relieve the burden placed upon the standard theory of canon formation: how and why would a pluralizing tendency emerge in the very period of the תורה's canonization? If singular תורה was selected by the deuteronomists as the *terminus technicus* for canonical scripture, as Weinfeld maintains, how is it that deuteronomistic tradition also preserved expressions which appear to subvert that *terminus*, by acknowledging מצוה or חקים alongside תורה or by alluding to plural תורות?

Although plural forms exist within the deuteronomistic tradition, they are clearly in the minority. However, even if Weinfeld's distinction is granted a certain legitimacy as an approximation, the presence of *any* plural forms within priestly literature and post-deuteronomistic traditions provides ample reason to call the standard theory of canon formation into question.[82]

---

75. Exod. 16.28; 24.12 (dtr? cf. Deut. 9.9-11); Josh. 22.5; 2 Kgs 17.34.

76. Lohfink, *Hauptgebot*, pp. 55-56. Singular in Deut. 5.31; 6.1, 25; 8.1; 11.8, 22; 15.5; 17.20; 19.9; 27.1; 28.1, 9, 13; 30.11. Plural in Deut. 5.29; 8.6; 11.13, 27, 28; 13.5; Judg. 2.17; 3.4; 2 Kgs 17.16 (pl.), 19 (pl.).

77. E.g. Deut. 4.8, 44-45; 30.10; 2 Kgs 17.13, 34. As pointed out by Lohfink (*Hauptgebot*, pp. 56-57) and Braulik ('Ausdrücke', p. 36 n. 118), the framework to the book of Deuteronomy clearly conceives of chs. 5–26 as comprised of the חקם (Deut. 5–11) and משפטים (Deut. 12–26). See Deut. 4.45; 5.1, 31; 11.32; 12.1; 26.16. Cf. Begrich, 'Tora', p. 237 n. 40.

78. Deut. 17.19; 2 Kgs 17.37; Isa. 24.5; Jer. 44 10, 23; Amos 2.4. See García López and Fabry, 'תורה', p. 613.

79. Deut. 4.6; 6.24; 16.12; 2 Kgs 17.8 (חקות הגוים); Jer. 31.35-36; Zech. 1.6(?).

80. Blum, *Komposition*, p. 363.

81. Nelson, *Redaction*, pp. 64-65.

82. Some have attempted to solve this dilemma by positing two *different* understandings of תורה in the post-exilic period—the 'deuteronomistic' view of a single canonical 'book' and the 'priestly' view of a plurality of oral cultic instructions. E g. Liedke and Petersen, 'תורה', p. 1042; García López and Fabry, 'תורה', pp. 629-30; Willi, 'Tôrâ', pp. 343-48. The problem with this argument, as formulated by

If, as has often been suggested, the initial canonization of the Pentateuch alone reflects the priestly elevation of תורה over against prophetic traditions,[83] then the use (or even the retention) of the plural תורות in priestly and post-deuteronomistic texts is quite puzzling.[84] As F. García López has pointed out, the singular form also lacks the definite article in some of the latest texts of the Pentateuch.[85] Moreover, sometimes the word תורה is absent in precisely those places where it would be expected if it had already been selected as a *terminus technicus* for a scriptural canon.[86] Terms such מצוה/-ת and חק/ם-ים/-ות also continue to function in priestly and other late texts without being consistently sub-

Liedke and Petersen, is that *priestly* תורה in the post-exilic period is sometimes described as *singular* rather than plural (2 Chron. 15.3), and *written* rather than oral (1 Chron. 16.40; 2 Chron. 31.3; Ezra 3.2; Neh. 10.35[34]). In my view, their argument does not adequately explain the understanding of תורה presented in the texts. García López attempts a synthesis of 'both' traditions, but as Lindars pointed out, 'the new meaning which resulted from the work of the Deuteronomists can scarcely have been absent from the minds of the [priestly] compilers' ('Torah', p. 135). Lindars himself argued that the priestly literature has simply retained an older usage, but how could they have understood this terminology unchanged in the light of the term's new connotations?

83.   If the Pentateuch alone was canonized in the fifth century BCE, then it must have been elevated *over against* prophetic traditions, some of which would have already existed in written form(s). For a description of the Pentateuch's canonization along these lines, see Joseph Blenkinsopp, *Prophecy and Canon: A Contribution to the Study of Jewish Origins* (University of Notre Dame Center for the Study of Judaism and Christianity in Antiquity, 3; Notre Dame: University of Notre Dame Press, 1977), p. 34; F. Crüsemann, 'Israel in der Perserzeit: Eine Skizze in Auseinandersetzung mit Max Weber', in Wolfgang Schluchter (ed.), *Max Webers Sicht des antiken Christentums. Interpretation und Kritik* (Frankfurt: Suhrkamp, 1985), p. 216. D.N. Freedman argues ('Formation') that this move was also, in effect, anti-Davidic and anti-eschatological.

84.   Exod. 18.20; Lev. 26.46 (also in a *Rechtssatz*); Neh. 9.13 (also in a *Rechtssatz*); Isa. 24.5; Ezek. 43.11; 44.5 (*qere*), 24; Dan. 9.10. It should be noted that the plural form does not appear within the books of Chronicles. See, however, those passages where תורה is singular but functions within a *Rechtssatz* rather than as a single term: e.g. Neh. 9.14; 2 Chron. 19.10; 33.8. Note that Exod. 18.20 and Lev. 26.46 even use the definite article with תורות. Cf. CD 7.15; 2 Macc. 6.28; Josephus, *Ant.* 13.298.

85.   He cites Exod. 12.49; Lev. 7.7; Num. 15.16, 29. See García López and Fabry, 'תורה', p. 617.

86.   E.g. Ezek. 18.8-9; Neh. 1.7; 1 Chron. 29.19; 2 Chron. 7.17, 19; 34.31; 36.15-16.

ordinated to תורה.[87] If the status of תורה as *terminus technicus* for a scriptural canon was decided at the time of the framework to the book of Deuteronomy, it seems strange that this usage would not be reflected within the priestly circles which such a decision supposedly favored.[88]

In my judgment, we should continue to attribute to the deuteronomistic tradition a new application of the word תורה to written scripture.[89] However, in light of the variety of terminology in deuteronomistic, priestly and post-deuteronomistic sources we cannot assume that from the time of the framework to Deuteronomy onward תורה consistently referred to a *single book*[90] or to a *particular text*.[91] If the

---

87. For מצוה and תורה together: Exod. 24.12 (dtr?—the only time מצוה is sg. in the Tetrateuch; otherwise pl.); Prov. 3.1; 6.20, 23; 7.2; Ezra 10.3 (מצות אלהינו); Neh. 9.13 (ומצוות וחקים ותורה), 14 (משפטים ישרים ותורות אמת חקים ומצות טובים); כל־מצות יהוה אדנינו) 10.30[29] // מצותיך // עדותיך // 34 (// מצותיך // משפטיך 29 (// ומשפטי וחקי); 2 Chron. 14.3[4] (המצוה); 19.10 (// מצוה); 31.21. For מצוה without תורה: Lev. 4.13 (כל־מצות יהוה); 27.34 (אלה המצות); Num. 15.31 (// דבר־יהוה), 39 (כל־מצותי), 40 (כל־מצותו־יהוה); Deut. 5.29 (pl.); 8.6 (pl.); 11.13 (pl.), 22 (sg.), 28 (pl.); 13.5[4] (pl. // קל); 19.9 (sg.); 28.13 (מצות יהוה אלהיך // כל־הדברים in v. 14); Eccl. 12.13 (pl.); Ezra 7.11 (מצות־יהוה וחקיו); 9.10 (pl.), 14 (pl.); Neh. 1.9 (pl.); 9.16 (pl.); 2 Chron. 8.13 (מצות משה); 17.4 (pl.); 24.20 (מצות יהוה). For חק and תורה together: Exod. 18.16 (את־חקי האלהים ואת־תורתיו); Num. 15.15 (חקה לכל־חקות) in v. 15, // תורה אחת ומשפט אחד in v. 16); Ezek. 44.5 (ואת־תורתי ואת־חקתו); Ezra 7.10 (// משפט // חק); Neh. 9.14 (see above); 10.30[29] (see above); 1 Chron. 22.12-13 (תורת יהוה אלהיך in v. 12, // את־החקים in v. 13); 2 Chron. 33.8 (כל־התורה והחקים ואת־המשפטים והמשפטים). For חק without תורה: Exod. 29.28 (חק־עולם); Lev. 6.11[18] (חק־עולם), 15[22] (חק־עולם); 10.11 (כל־החקים), 15 (חק עולם); 16.34 (חקת עולם); 18.4 (// משפטי), 5 (// משפטי), 30 (חקות התועבה); 19.37 (// כל־משפטי); 20.8 (חקתי); Num. 18.19 (ברית מלח עולם // חק עולם); 27.11 (חקת משפט); 30.17[16] (אלה החקים); Ps. 2.7 (חק יהוה); 2 Chron. 35.26. Cf. תורה // משפט in Isa. 42.4; 51.4; Hab. 1.4; 2 Chron. 30.16.

88. Cf. Willi's observation ('Tōrâ', p. 340) that Begrich's theory of an *original* priestly תורה, partly identifiable by plural usage, was too heavily based on post-exilic passages: e.g. Hag. 2.10-14; Mal. 2.1-9.

89. See the use of כתב in Deut. 17.18-19; 27.3, 8; 28.58; Josh. 8.34. See also García López and Fabry, 'תורה', p. 609. For a similar judgment, although for other reasons, see Lindars, 'Torah', p. 135. He thinks a 'generalizing' use of the term began before the Deuteronomists and that the use of תורה in Jeremiah is thus parallel rather than redactional.

90. Despite its frequent appearance together with the word ספר, it is clear that the term תורה does not refer to a single scroll of the entire Pentateuch within the biblical period. See E.M. Meyers, 'The Torah Shrine in the Ancient Synagogue',

attribution of 'canonization' requires the existence of a fixed text, then not even the Torah is likely to have been 'canonical' before the early first century CE.[92]

JSQ 4 (1997), pp. 303-38, esp. pp. 309-10. The Pentateuch was customarily copied on five individual scrolls until talmudic times. Cf. M. Haran, 'Book-Size and the Device of Catch-Lines in the Biblical Canon', *JJS* 36 (1985), pp. 1-11. For references in the Mishnah to the Torah as a single book or scroll, see Jacob Neusner, *Rabbinic Judaism: Structure and System* (Philadelphia: Fortress Press, 1995), p. 49.

91.   Houtman, *Pentateuch*, pp. 349-50; 363; 450-55. Cf. J. Trebolle Barrera, *The Jewish Bible and the Christian Bible: An Introduction to the History of the Bible* (trans. W.G.E. Watson; Leiden: E.J. Brill; Grand Rapids: Eerdmans, 1998), pp. 158-59: 'To the extent that during the Persian period there were laws not included in the Pentateuch but considered as the Torah from Sinai in some circles, it is necessary to make a *distinction between Torah and Pentateuch*, for this does not represent the only and complete Torah rooted in the revelation of Sinai...' (his emphasis). Trebolle Barrera argues that the received text of the Pentateuch reflects the results of a later (Hasmonean) compromise. As Brevard S. Childs has pointed out (*The Old Testament as Scripture* [Philadelphia: Fortress Press, 1979], p. 94), canonical status does not result from textual fixity; textual stabilization and fixity are 'derivative of the concept of canon'. Cf. *idem*, 'Biblische Theologie und christlicher Kanon', in I. Baldermann *et al.* (eds.), *Zum Problem des biblischen Kanons* (JBTh 3; Neukirchen–Vluyn: Neukirchener Verlag, 1988), pp. 13-27, here, p. 18: 'Der Text eines Buches wäre nicht festgeschrieben worden, hätte es nicht bereits selbst kanonischen Status erlangt'.

92.   Frank Moore Cross, 'The Stabilization of the Canon of the Hebrew Bible', in *idem*, *From Epic to Canon: History and Literature in Ancient Israel* (Baltimore: The Johns Hopkins University Press, 1998), pp. 219-29. Cross sets the *terminus post quem* for the fixation of the canon at the time of the proto-Theodotionic recension (late first century BCE), since this recensional activity continued into the book of Baruch and a longer version of Daniel, material later not included within the Pharisaic canon (p. 222). Josephus, writing at the end of the first century CE (*Apion*, 1.37-43), sets a reliable a *terminus ante quem* for Cross (pp. 220-222). In between lies the hermeneutical tradition of Hillel, to whom Cross gives the lion's share of the credit for fixing the text and closing the canon (p. 223). Cf. *idem*, 'The Fixation of the Text of the Hebrew Bible', in the same volume, pp. 205-218 esp. pp. 216-17. Note here, however, that already in the late second or early first century BCE the proto-Lucianic recension of the Old Greek version of the books Samuel–Kings had sought to conform them to a pre-Masoretic text-type, evidence that even at this point *a* Hebrew text was considered to possess controlling authority. Note also the counter-argument of Beckwith (*Canon*, pp. 340-41; p. 432 n. 254), that even though *additions* to Jeremiah (i.e. Baruch) and Daniel were reworked in the proto-Theodotionic recension, no *book* of the Apocrypha appears otherwise to have been included.

Before its fixation, however, תורה should not be construed as free-floating oracular activity without a textual basis. Instead, תורה denotes a *cumulative hermeneutical process* in which the attempt was made to retain, clarify and transmit the Mosaic legacy *in words* from one generation to the next.[93] Thus, תורה continued to function in the post-exilic period as the category-designation for a particular revelation[94] of God's character and purpose, traditionally recognized as Mosaic.[95] This revelation included in its scope not only Moses' own words, but also the words of others—oral as well as written—which were correspondingly 'Mosaic'.[96] G.J. Brooke notes: 'It seems as if the whole Moses tradition in a variety of forms carries authority' (i.e., at Qumran).[97] Even though

93. For an explication of this view, with its implications for text criticism and historical reconstruction, see E. Tov, 'The Original Shape of the Biblical Text', in Emerton (ed.), *Congress Volume: Leuven 1989*, pp. 345-59 esp. p. 351. The Temple Scroll from Qumran (11QT) also appears to belong within this same cumulative process of tradition. See G.J. Brooke, 'The Temple Scroll: A Law unto Itself?', in B. Lindars (ed.), *Law and Religion: Essays on the Place of the Law in Israel and Early Christianity* (Cambridge: James Clarke & Co., 1988), pp. 34-43. Brooke argues that 'the' תורה is still 'pre-canonical' as late as the second century BCE. Cf. H.-J. Fabry, 'Der Begriff "Tora" in der Tempelrolle', *Rev Q* 18 (1997), pp. 63-71; J. Maier, 'Zur Frage des biblischen Kanons im Frühjudentum im Licht der Qumranfunde', in Bultmann *et al.* (eds.), *Problem*, pp. 135-46 esp. pp. 141-42.

94. García López and Fabry, 'תורה', p. 618: '...*tôrâ* wird zu einer Chiffre für eine Kategorie authoritativer Offenbarung'.

95. Note that the activity of the priests in Deut. 17.8-11 resembles Moses' activities as portrayed in Exod. 18.15-23; cf. García López and Fabry, 'תורה', p. 606.

96. In my judgment, however, even the distinction between 'Moses' words' and the 'Mosaic words of others' represents an anachronism on our part. The distinction between 'Mosaic' and 'non-Mosaic' was qualitative, not chronological. See L. Jacobs, 'Halakhah', *EncJud* VII, pp. 1156-66 esp. p. 1157.

97. G.J. Brooke, 'Tora in the Qumran Scrolls', in H. Merklein, K. Müller and G. Stemberger (eds.), *Die Bibel in jüdischer und christlicher Tradition* (Festschrift Johann Maier; BBB, 88; Frankfurt: Anton Hain, 1993), pp. 97-120; here, p. 119. Brooke goes too far, however, when he asserts that even by this time no form of the Pentateuch had greater authority than any other. Cf. the views of Emanuel Tov, *Textual Criticism of the Hebrew Bible* (Philadelphia: Fortress Press; Assen: Van Gorcum, 1992), who holds (p. 117) that the significant number of proto-Masoretic texts found at Qumran (40% of the total) 'probably reflects their authoritative status' in the period between the third century BCE and the first century CE. See also his 'Groups of Biblical Texts Found at Qumran', in D. Dimant and L.H. Schiffman (eds.), *Time to Prepare the Way in the Wilderness. Papers on the Qumran Scrolls*

תורה continued to exist in a variety of instantiations (תורות) during the post-exilic period, it could also be considered unitary—not because of its own (literary) fixity, but because of Israel's belief in the unity of God's purpose and will (cf. Sir. 24.23).[98] E. Zenger has summarized the dynamic brilliantly: 'Die Kanonisierung schreibt nicht den Buchstaben fest, sondern die Sinnrichtung der Offenbarung'.[99]

I conclude that use of the term תורה within later biblical traditions does *not* provide the kind of support for the standard reconstruction of canon formation that is generally assumed. Certainly there are other factors involved in reaching a conclusion that the Pentateuch did or did not acquire canonical status before other biblical books or collections, and that its authority was or was not correspondingly elevated above them, but the argument from terminology is surprisingly weak.[100]

On the other hand, even if biblical references to תורה appeal to a hermeneutical tradition rather than exclusively to a given text, this should not be understood in a way that plays Scripture and tradition off against each other.[101] While biblical references to תורה may never be

by the Fellows of the Institute for Advanced Studies of the Hebrew University, Jerusalem, 1989–90 (STDJ, 16; Leiden: E.J. Brill, 1995), pp. 85-102; esp. p. 94, for Tov's argument regarding the antiquity of the proto-Masoretic texts in comparison to those written in the 'Qumran practice'. Cf. Tov's distinction (*Criticism*, pp. 192-95) between 'vulgar' and 'non-vulgar texts'.

98. E.g. 1 Chron. 22.12-13; 2 Chron. 12.1; 14.3; 15.3; 35.26. Of course, this hermeneutical process had a social dimension as well. On the importance of this dimension, see J.N. Lightstone, 'Tora Is *Nomos*—Except when It Is Not: Prolegomena to the Study of the Law in Late Antique Judaism', *SR* 13 (1984), pp. 29-37 esp. p. 32, although his particular reconstruction of the social dynamics I find problematic. Cf. Philip R. Davies, *Scribes and Schools: The Canonization of the Hebrew Scriptures* (LAI; Louisville, KY: Westminster/John Knox Press, 1998), pp. 155-57. Davies has similarly warned against assuming that religious motives were more important than scholarly ones for the fixation of the text. However, his implication that religious and scholarly motives were somehow distinct seems hopelessly anachronistic.

99. Zenger, 'Tora', p. 22.

100. On תורה/תורות within the LXX, see S.H. Blank, 'The LXX Renderings of Old Testament Terms for Law', *HUCA* 7 (1930), pp. 259-83; esp. pp. 278-80. Blank was of the opinion that most of the MT plurals were original; most, but not all, appear as singulars in the LXX. Interesting as well is his sense that νόμος in the LXX functions as a collective term (p. 280).

101. *Contra* Shaver, p. 128: '...at least for the Chronicler, the canonization of the Torah had not yet occurred'. This statement merely begs the question of what is

restricted in scope to the Pentateuch *per se*, or even to written Scripture, they also never appeal to tradition in a way that functions without regard for Scripture or over against it.[102]

3. Tôrâ *as More than the Pentateuch?*

If תורה in the post-exilic period refers to a tradition of Mosaic revelation, which was *in the process of* being committed to written form(s),[103] there remains the question of which 'books' (or portions of what are now books) such references to תורה might include. As we have already noted, there are indications that the books of Ezra–Nehemiah and Chronicles know and refer to both D and P traditions. However, the approximate character of these references and the presence of other unknown תורה traditions in these books makes a precise identification of the literary scope of the referent extremely difficult, if not impossible.[104]

I would now like to take this problem one step further: if it is clear that biblical references to תורה do not consistently specify a single edition or text of the Pentateuch, can such references even be restricted to *pentateuchal* writings or traditions? Is it possible that תורה can also refer to biblical traditions and literature which we might consider 'non-mosaic' or 'non-pentateuchal'? Put more sharply, can we afford the assumption that references to תורה never include non-pentateuchal traditions or writings within their scope?

---

meant by 'canonization'. In my judgment, here Shaver makes the anachronistic assumption that a canonical text must be literarily fixed. For an interesting argument on behalf of an ongoing continuum between orality and textualization 'even in the postexilic period', see Susan Niditch, *Oral World and Written Word* (LAI; Louisville, KY: Westminster/John Knox Press, 1996), esp. pp. 89-98.

102. This is true, I would argue, even in the case of Jer. 8.8-9. See García López and Fabry, 'תורה', p. 615. For a different view, see R.P. Carroll, 'Inscribing the Covenant: Writing and the Written in Jeremiah', in A.G. Auld (ed.), *Understanding Poets and Prophets* (Festschrift George Wishart Anderson; JSOTSup, 152; Sheffield: Sheffield Academic Press, 1993), pp. 61-76.

103. For the continuities and discontinuities that emerge from a synchronic approach, see Phillip R. Callaway, 'The Ancient Meaning of the Law of Moses', in M.P. Graham, W.P. Brown, and J.K. Kuan (eds.), *History and Interpretation* (Festschrift John H. Hayes; JSOTSup, 173; Sheffield: Sheffield Academic Press, 1993), pp. 160-72 esp. p. 171, where he concludes that the 'law of Moses' became 'an authoritative and convenient rubric under which to subsume a plethora of laws'.

104. See Houtman, 'Ezra'. Cf. *idem*, *Pentateuch*, pp. 450-55.

Such usage has long been familiar from post-biblical writings.[105] In the New Testament, 'law' (νόμος)[106] can be used to refer to non-pentateuchal scripture[107] because 'law' is also a designation for the entire Old Testament canon.[108] 'The law' also designates the entire written canon in *4 Ezra* 14.21-22. The *Testament of the Twelve Patriarchs* cites Eccl. 3.5 as 'law'.[109] Philo can cite non-pentateuchal Scripture as 'law'.[110] Mattathias' call for his sons to obey the 'law' in 1 Macc. 2.49-68 (c. 100–90 BCE)[111] includes references to the deuteronomistic history, the book of Daniel and Psalm 37.[112] The prologue to Sirach (132–117 BCE) uses 'law' as an umbrella term[113] at the same time as employing the formula 'the law and the prophets and the other/rest of the books of the fathers'. This overarching usage of 'law' dates at least to the time of the body of the book (Sir. 38.34b–39.1), *circa* 180 BCE.[114]

The question to be asked, therefore, is just how old this usage may be and whether it may also appear within the Old Testament itself. The term תורה in Ps. 40.9[8] offers one possible example. Because sacrificial traditions are criticized in v. 7, it would appear difficult to understand this term as a reference to priestly instruction *or* written pentateuchal traditions. Could not prophetic passages such as Amos 5.21-24 or Hos. 6.6 be included within the scope of this reference? Ps. 1.2

105. For the following examples and others, see: Buhl, *Kanon*, p. 8; Beckwith, *Canon*, pp. 105-109.

106. On νόμος as the standard translational equivalence for תורה within the LXX, see Blank ('Renderings', p. 275). Cf. S. Westerholm, '*Torah, nomos* and Law: A Question of "Meaning"', *SR* 15 (1986), pp. 327-36.

107. Jn 10.34 quotes Ps. 82.6 as γεγραμμένον ἐν τῷ νόμῳ ὑμῶν; 1 Cor. 14.21 quotes Isa. 28.11-12 as ἐν τῷ νόμῳ γέγραπται; Jn 15.25 quotes a selection of Psalms as ἐν τῷ νόμῳ αὐτῶν γεγραμμένος; cf. Paul's mention of the law in Rom. 9.31 with his citation of Isa. 8.14; 28.16 (καθὼς γέγραπται) in Rom. 9.33.

108. See 'the law' in Mt. 12.5; Lk. 10.26; Jn 1.17; 7.19, 49, 51; 8.5, 17. 'Law of Moses' appears in Lk. 2.22-24, 39; Jn 7.23; Acts 15.5; 1 Cor. 9.9; Heb. 10.28. Cf. 'Moses' in Lk. 5.14; Jn 7.22; Acts 15.21; Rom. 10.5, 19.

109. *Test. XII Patr.* 8.7-8.

110. E g. *Vit. Cont.*, 78: ἡ νομοθεσία.

111. For this dating, H. Attridge, 'Jewish Historiography', in R.A. Kraft and G.W.E. Nickelsburg (eds.), *Early Judaism and its Modern Interpreters* (SBL BMI, 2; Atlanta, CA: Scholars Press, 1986), pp. 311-43 here, p. 317.

112. Cf. the contrast between 'books of the law' and the 'book of the covenant' in 1 Macc. 1.56-57; 'holy books' in 1 Macc. 12.9.

113. Sir. Prol. 4, 10.

114. Davies, *Scribes*, p. 109; cf. Houtman, *Pentateuch*, p. 445 n. 58.

provides an even clearer example. Not only is תורה likely to mean more than the Pentateuch because Psalm 1 is a late composition, placed at the beginning of the Psalter to function as its introduction, but also because the source for the Psalm probably comes from prophetic Scripture (Jer. 17.5-8). Moreover, as an introduction Psalm 1 sets out the proper manner of reading the Psalter itself (בתורתו יהגה).[115] Therefore תורה in Ps. 1.2 is best interpreted as referring at least to prophetic Scripture and the Psalms in addition to the Pentateuch, if not to the entire Old Testament 'canon' (cf. the 'global' use of תורה in Pss. 19; 119).[116] Scholarly references to 'torah psalms' and 'torah piety' have tended to mask the broader scriptural scope of these references.

It is further interesting to find reference in the MT of Dan. 9.10 to the plural תורת which God set before the people 'by his servants the prophets'.[117] If the prophets were thought to have transmitted תורות from God, would it not also be possible to refer to their words as תורה?[118] Those responsible for the book were clearly familiar with prophetic Scripture (cf. Dan. 9.2). The use of prophetic traditions within the books of Chronicles makes it evident that the prominence of תורה in these books was also not understood in a way which excluded other 'non-pentateuchal traditions'. Numerous examples could be given, but the best is probably found in 2 Chron. 20.20, where Jehoshaphat cites Isa. 7.9b and exhorts the people of Judah to 'believe [God's] prophets'.[119]

---

115. Cf. Ps. 37.30-31, where reference is made to the way in which פי־צדיק יהגה חכמה ולשונו תדבר משפט תורת אלהיו בלבו. Taken together, the mention of a 'righteous one', 'justice' and 'murmuring wisdom' could suggest not only written Scripture, but prophetic and wisdom traditions as well as legal 'pentateuchal' ones.

116. For further discussion, García López and Fabry, 'תורה', pp. 619-21, esp. p. 619 on Psalm 1: '...daß es sich hier um den Pentateuch handelt oder um einen größeren Teil der alttestamentlichen Schriften'.

117. For discussion of the expansion of this notice in vv. 11-12, see below.

118. For a similar conception, but with מצות instead of תורה, see: 2 Chron. 29.25; Ezra 9.10-11.

119. On 2 Chron. 20.20, see: Michael Fishbane, *Biblical Interpretation in Ancient Israel* (Oxford: Clarendon Press, 1985), pp. 386-88; Rex Mason, *Preaching the Tradition: Homily and Hermeneutics after the Exile* (Cambridge: Cambridge University Press, 1990), pp. 68-71. The use of a citation from the prophet Isaiah in a period in the narrative over a century before he actually lived indicates a view in which prophecies are conceived of as 'eternally' authoritative and true. The exhortation to 'believe' (אמן, hi.) the prophets illustrates their remarkable prestige within Chronicles and is paralleled in the Old Testament only by Moses (e.g. Exod. 14.31;

In my judgment, the pervasive use of prophetic *Scripture* within Chronicles[120] calls into question most sharply the textual scope of references to written תורה within those books. Certain תורה references in Chronicles strongly suggest a broader conception of Scripture than the Pentateuch alone.[121] Thus, 2 Chron. 30.18 refers to Moses with the prophetic appellation איש־האלהים, inviting comparison with 2 Chron. 35.18 where the authority of the prophet Samuel is also mentioned. J. Shaver has noted the possibility that the תורה traditions mentioned in 2 Chron. 31.3 may have been derived from the book of Ezekiel.[122] They are anyway absent from what is now the Pentateuch. Similarly, the prohibition of trading on the Sabbath in Neh. 10.32a[31a] is not to be found in the Pentateuch, but in Amos 8.5.[123] In my judgment it would be anachronistic to assume that halakhic-type judgments could not be based upon non-pentateuchal Scripture in the pre-rabbinic period.[124]

cvc. 4.31; 19.9). See H. Wildberger, '"Glauben": Erwägungen zu האמין', in *Hebräische Wortforschung* (Festschrift Walter Baumgartner; VTSup, 16; Leiden: E.J. Brill, 1967), pp. 372-86, here p. 380: 'Mose ist Jahwes עבד schlechthin, wie die Propheten seine עבדים genannt werden. Nie aber wird sonst irgendein Repräsentant des Jahwevolkes mit ב האמין als "Glaubensgrund" namhaft gemacht'.

120. Cf. the citation of Zech. 4.10 in 2 Chron. 16.9a. On the use of prophetic Scripture within Chronicles, see: Mason, *Tradition*, with numerous examples in his exegetical sections; I.L. Seeligmann, 'Die Auffassung von der Prophetie in der deuteronomistischen und chronistischen Geschichtsschreibung (mit einem Exkurs über das Buch Jeremia)', in *Congress Volume: Göttingen 1977* (VTSup, 29; Leiden: E.J. Brill, 1978), pp. 254-84, esp. p. 273; H.G.M. Williamson, 'History', in D.A. Carson and H.G.M. Williamson (eds.), *It Is Written: Scripture Citing Scripture* (Festschrift Barnabas Lindars; Cambridge: Cambridge University Press, 1988), pp. 25-38, esp. p. 34-35.

121. For תורה usage throughout Chronicles: תורת יהוה in 1 Chron. 16.40 (with כל־הכתוב); 22.12 (with אלהיך); 2 Chron. 12.1; 17.9 (with ספר); 31.3 (with ככתוב), 4; 34.14 (with ספר); 35.26 (with ככתוב); see התורה in 2 Chron. 6.16 (תורתי); 14.3[4] (// המצוה); 15.3 (without art.); 19.10 (without art.); 25.4 (// ספר משה); 31.21 (// המצוה); 33.8 (// החקים והמשפטים); 34.15 (with ספר), 19 (with דברי); and see משה תורת in 2 Chron. 23.18 (with ככתוב); 30.16 (with כמשפט).

122. Shaver, *Torah*, pp. 92, 127. If so, then this would also mitigate the observation of Williamson ('History', p. 35) that כתוב is never used with reference to prophetic writings in contrast to תורה.

123. Shaver, *Torah*, p. 88. He also suggests (pp. 121, 127) the possibility of reliance upon Ezekiel in Neh. 13.15-22.

124. Qimron and Strugnell, *Miqṣat*, p. 133. Cf. Lawrence H. Schiffmann, *Reclaiming the Dead Sea Scrolls: The History of Judaism, the Background of Christianity, the Lost Library of Qumran* (Philadelphia: JPS, 1994) p. 248. Schiffmann

2 Chron. 34.21 refers to 'the word of the Lord' as synonymous with Scripture in its description of the 'lawbook' discovered in Josiah's reign, apparently an expansion from the account in 2 Kings (cf. 2 Kgs 22.13). 2 Chron. 35.26-27 reports that, 'the rest of the acts [דברי] of Josiah, and his good deeds [וחסדיו] according to what is written in the law of the Lord and his acts [ודבריו], first and last [הראשים והאחרנים], behold they are written in the Book of the Kings of Israel and Judah' (RSV).[125] Here the RSV translates דברי as 'acts' to match the non-verbal sense of דברי in v. 26 and the idiom ספר דברי הימים,[126] which has given the books of Chronicles their name.

However, it is also possible to translate this crux as 'the תורה of the Lord and his *words*, the former and the latter'. On this interpretation Josiah's deeds would be seen not only to be in conformity with the Torah, but also with prophetic revelation, perhaps conceived of in two periods.[127] That prophecy is here in view is also suggested by references to the prophet Jeremiah (2 Chron. 35.25; 36.12, 21) and the reference to a *cumulative* prophetic tradition (2 Chron. 24.19; 36.15-16). Because Moses was also understood as a prophet (e.g. 1 Chron. 15.15;

notes that prophetic writings were used to derive halakhic judgments at Qumran, although he terms this practice 'sectarian' (p. 277). Interestingly, he cites prophetic texts as the probable warrants for the prohibitions against trading (Isa. 58.13-14) and carrying (Jer. 17.21-22) on the Sabbath in CD 10.20-21 and 11.7-9, respectively. It is clear that the rabbis later explicitly restricted Halakhah to the Pentateuch (p. 226), although their reasons are not; here Schiffman posits anxiety about messianic interpretation of non-pentateuchal Scripture by Christians.

125. Unless otherwise noted, biblical translations used in this essay are adapted from the Revised Standard Version (RSV).

126. E.g. 1 Kgs 14.19, 29; 15.7, 23, 31; 16.5, 14, 20, 27; etc. In 2 Chron. 35.26, however, הימים is missing. Cf. 1 Kgs 11.41.

127. A conception of two eras of prophecy is clearly attested in the Persian period: Zech. 1.4; 7.7, 12; Ezek. 38.17. On the other hand, הראשנים והאחרנים is a formula referring to the totality of a king's 'acts' (דברי) in 1 Chron. 29.29; 2 Chron. 9.29; 12.15; 20.34; 26.22. Moreover, דברי could have originally referred to Josiah (cf. 2 Chron. 13.22; 27.7; 28.26). In the MT, however, דברי refers to יהוה. Furthermore, in 2 Chron. 26.22 the prophet Isaiah is said to have *written* דברי עזיהו and where the formula PN-דברי appears in Jer. 1.1; Amos 1.1; Neh. 1.1 it is normally translated 'the words of PN'. The possibility that דברים once provided a title for a collection of prophetic Scripture is discussed below. For כתובים הראשנים as a later canonical formula for 'early writings', see Leiman, *Canonization*, p. 57; cf. p. 69 for the rabbinic understanding of Haggai, Zechariah and Malachi as the 'latter' prophets and David, Samuel and Solomon as the 'former' (Soṭ. 48a-b).

2 Chron. 30.16; 35.6), I find there is no reason to assume that even references to the תורה of Moses could not also refer to prophetic traditions.

Other literary material might also be included in references to תורה in Chronicles. In 2 Chron. 23.18 Jehoida is said to have arranged temple officials for the burnt offering in the manner in which 'it is written in the תורה of Moses, with joy and singing, according to David's instruction [על ידי דויד]'.[128] That the Psalms are here in view as Scripture is suggested by Ezra 3.10-11, where the same reference (על־ידי דויד) introduces a citation from the Psalms. A similar arrangement of levitical priests at the Temple is referred to in 2 Chron. 29.25 as 'according to the commandment [במצות] of David and Gad the king's seer and the prophet Nathan, because it was the commandment [המצוה] of the Lord by the hand of his prophets'.[129] Neh. 12.44-45 refers to 'the תורה of the priests and the levites' *and* 'the מצות of David and Solomon' when it mentions the Temple arrangements. Here the overall conception would appear to be not only one in which David and Solomon are understood as prophets, but also one in which the מצות of the prophets (which might very well have included Scripture now found in the Writings) have a place *within* Mosaic תורה.

I conclude that the use of תורה in postexilic biblical literature cannot be assumed to have been restricted to 'pentateuchal' traditions any more than to a particular version or text of the Pentateuch.[130] The use of תורה may thus include within its scope much more of Israel's traditions and

---

128. For a connection between על ידי and prophecy, see 1 Chron. 25.2, 3, 6.

129. In light of the following discussion about דברים as a title for prophetic scripture, I find it is noteworthy that 2 Chron. 29.30 refers to David's commandments as the דברי דויד ואסף החזה (cf. Neh. 12.45-46). The arrangement of priests and Levites for the burnt offering also appears to be understood 'prophetically' in 2 Chron. 30.16, judging by the reference to Moses as איש־האלהים.

130. E.g. 1QS 8.1-4, 12-16; 9.9. See Brooke, 'Tora', p. 119; García López and Fabry, 'תורה', pp. 635-37 on the situation at Qumran, where it is clear that תורה sometimes has a broader frame of reference than the Pentateuch alone. Cf. H.-J. Fabry, 'Schriftverständnis und Schriftauslegung der Qumran-Essener', *Bibel*, pp. 87-96. Fabry argues (pp. 67-72) that תורה means the Pentateuch in CD 5.2; 9.17; 15.9, 12; 16.2, 5 (cf. 20.25, 28). He also notes (p. 67), however, that תורה at Qumran cannot be restricted to the Pentateuch alone and appears to include prophetic revelations and the sect's own legal material (1 QS 9.9-10; cf. CD 20.27-34).

writings than is ordinarily taken for granted.[131] It appears likely that תורה sometimes refers to a re-interpretation or an extension of the biblical traditions as a whole.[132] In my judgment, to assume the pre-eminence of pentateuchal traditions over against non-pentateuchal traditions in this period on the basis of a preponderance of תורה references involves a serious anachronism. The halakhic elevation of the Torah (*qua* Pentateuch) above the rest of the canon is characteristic of *medieval* Judaism.[133]

4. *'Words' as a Category for Prophetic Scripture*

The expression 'the law and the prophets' does not appear within the Old Testament itself in a way that clearly refers to written materials or Scripture. Passages such as Neh. 9.26, 29-30 and Lam. 2.9 pair תורה and נביאים as an authoritative sources of revelation within history, not as texts. In my judgment, however, the related term דברים is not only sometimes used to refer to written prophetic traditions, but in combination with תורה can denote a bipartite collection of written Scripture: 'the law and the words'.[134]

---

131. In my judgment, this conclusion is strengthened by comparison of Chronicles with the book of Tobit, which also mentions the 'law of Moses' (e.g. Tob. 6.12; 7.12-13; cf. 14.9) in connection with regulations and customs not explicitly recorded in the received form of the Pentateuch. At the same time, there can be no question about the authority of prophetic Scripture (e.g. Tob. 2.6; 14.4, 8) within this book from the third or second century BCE. For a dating in the third century BCE, see Carey A. Moore, *Tobit: A New Translation with Introduction and Commentary* (AB, 40A; New York: Doubleday, 1996), p. 42. The prophets are clearly adduced as warrants for contemporary behavior (Tob. 4.12). Cf. J. Gamberoni, 'Das "Gesetz des Mose" im Buch Tobias', in G. Braulik (ed.), *Studien zum Pentateuch* (Festschrift Walter Kornfeld; Freiburg: Herder, 1977), pp. 227-42.

132. On 'inner-biblical exegesis' in these books, see Fishbane, *Interpretation*, pp. 108-34, 134-48, 154-59 and *passim*; Williamson, 'History', pp. 25-31; cf. his *Ezra and Nehemiah* (OTG; Sheffield: JSOT Press, 1987), pp. 94-97.

133. I. Robinson, 'Torah and *halakha* in mediaeval Judaism', *SR* 13 (1984), pp. 47-55, esp. p. 48. Cf. Jacobs, 'Halakhah', pp. 1157-58; Schiffman, *Reclaiming*, p. 226.

134. *Contra* García López and Fabry ('תורה', p. 611), this parallelism is not restricted to the prophetic corpus. For important general treatments of דבר, see: James Barr, *The Semantics of Biblical Language* (London: Oxford University Press, 1961), pp. 129-40, 217-18; G. Gerleman, 'דבר *dābār* Wort', *THAT* I, pp. 433-43; Leonhard Rost, 'Bemerkungen zu dibbär', in his *Studien zum Alten Testament*

Like תורה, דבר appears to be 'at home' in three different semantic contexts: law,[135] prophecy[136] and wisdom.[137] It may be that a basic notion of reported speech underlies all three.[138] Also like תורה, דבר seems to have been selected by the Deuteronomists as an umbrella term, but in this case for prophetic revelation.[139] Not only did the Deuteronomists

(BWANT, 101; Stuttgart: W. Kohlhammer, 1974), pp. 39-60; W.H. Schmidt, 'דבר *dābār* II-V', *ThWAT* II, pp. 101-33.

135. See the use of דבר to mean 'legal complaint' or 'cause of action' in: Exod. 18.16, 22, 26; Deut. 1.17; 16.19; 19.15; Isa. 29.1. The plural can be similarly used: Exod. 18.19; 23.8; Deut. 16.19. Cf. the expression בעל דברים in Exod. 24.14. For other possible examples, see: H.J. Boecker, *Redeformen des Rechtslebens im Alten Testament* (WMANT, 14; Neukirchen–Vluyn: Neukirchener Verlag, 1970), esp. pp. 26-31; Schmidt, 'דבר', p. 115. A particularly prominent legal formula is that of עשרת הדברים for the Ten Commandments: Exod. 34.28; Deut. 4.13; 10.4; cf. (without עשרת) Exod. 20.1; 24.8; 34.1, 27; Deut. 5.22; 9.10.

136. The 'foregrounding' of the דבר יהוה is self-evident in the received text of the prophetic corpus. It is extremely difficult to conceive of biblical prophecy without its characteristic understanding of a revelatory 'word': e.g. Jer. 18.18; Amos 3.8. Still, the use of the particular expression דבר יהוה for the prophetic message is surprisingly infrequent within early prophetic literature, and more likely to appear in narratives (e.g. Amos 7.16) or headings that may well be secondary (e.g. Isa. 1.10; Hos. 4.1; cf. Amos 3.1; 4.1; 5.1). For discussion, Schmidt, 'דבר', pp. 117-22. The formula כה אמר יהוה is much earlier. See J. Lindblom, *Prophecy in Ancient Israel* (Oxford: Basil Blackwell, 1962), pp. 103-104. On this problem further, A.G. Auld, 'Prophets through the Looking Glass: Between the Writings and Moses', *JSOT* 27 (1983), pp. 3-23; *idem*, 'Prophets and Prophecy in Jeremiah and Kings', *ZAW* 96 (1984), pp. 66-82; *idem*, 'Word of God and Words of Man: Prophets and Canon', in Lyle Eslinger and Glen Taylor (eds.), *Ascribe to the Lord* (Festschrift Peter C. Craigie; JSOTSup, 67; Sheffield: JSOT Press, 1988), pp. 237-51; and the response of H.M. Barstad, 'No Prophets? Recent Developments in Biblical Prophetic Research and Ancient Near Eastern Prophecy', *JSOT* 57 (1993), pp. 39-60.

137. Wisdom instruction is referred to as דברי חכמים in Prov. 1.6; 22.17; Eccl. 9.17; 12.11 (cf. Eccl. 10.12) and as the 'words' of the father in Prov. 4.4, 20. Cf. 1 Kgs 10.6. Use of the verb in Deut. 32.44; Judg. 5.12; 1 Kgs 5.12-13[4.32-33] suggests an early context of musical balladry; cf. Ezek. 33.30-33. Cf. Liedke, *Rechtssätze*, pp. 194-95.

138. E.g., 2 Kgs 4.13. See S.A. Meier, *The Messenger in the Ancient Semitic World* (HSM, 45; Atlanta: Scholars Press, 1989); *idem, Speaking of Speaking: Marking Direct Discourse in the Hebrew Bible* (VTSup, 46; Leiden: E.J. Brill, 1992); Cynthia L. Miller, *The Representation of Speech in Biblical Hebrew Narrative: A Linguistic Analysis* (HSM, 55; Atlanta: Scholars Press, 1996).

139. See Schmidt, 'דבר', p. 119.

shape prophetic literature according to a concept of prophecy as דבר,[140] they also compiled a scriptural collection (including the book of Deuteronomy and the books of the Former Prophets)[141] as a witness to the revelatory authority of דבר and תורה together.

The frequent interpretive move in the past was to see the plural דברים within a pre-deuteronomistic legal tradition, the one that had given rise to the expression עשׂרת הדברים for the Ten Commandments.[142] However, more recent scholarship has seen this use of דברים as drawing on the prophetic דבר tradition, rather than reflecting an independent evolution of legal terminology.[143] In fact, what proves especially interesting about דברים within the biblical traditions is that this term comes to be used in increasingly canon-conscious ways, with the decisive turn coming here, too, in the frame to the book of Deuteronomy.

Thus the use of the plural הדברים is characteristic of the deuteronomistic shaping of the book. With the exception of Deut. 12.28 (a later addition[144]) and 22.14, 17 (two early legal references), all of the uses of the absolute plural (without suffixes) occur within the book's literary

140. This is not to say on the one hand that דבר language was previously foreign to prophetic traditions, or that, on the other, the prophetic books were subject to a 'deuteronomistic redaction' *per se*. More likely, in my judgment, is that the deuteronomists used existing prophetic terminology to express the true significance of the prophetic message, as they understood it. This semantic 'framing' was then persuasive to the degree that such language was retained and used even by other circles of tradition. Such a reconstruction parallels precisely what has already been argued for תורה.

141. Martin Noth, *The Deuteronomistic History* (JSOTSup, 15; Sheffield: JSOT Press, 1981). For recent criticism, see Mark A. O'Brien, *The Deuteronomistic History Hypothesis: A Reassessment* (OBO, 92; Freiburg: Universitätsverlag; Göttingen: Vandenhoeck & Ruprecht, 1989).

142. Exod. 34.28; Deut. 4.13; 10.4; cf. (without עשׂרת) Deut. 5.22; 9.10; 10.2. For this view, see Gerleman, 'דבר', p. 440.

143. E.g., Deut. 30.1. As Braulik notes ('Ausdrücke', p. 45), within the entire book of Deuteronomy neither דבר or דברים ever appears 'in einer Reihe mit anderen Gesetzesausdrücken'. See also L. Rost, 'Gesetz und Propheten', in *Studien*, pp. 9-38, esp. p. 13; cf. his 'Bemerkungen', pp. 42-46. Liedke offers (*Rechtssätze*, pp. 194-95) important arguments against דברים as a pre-deuteronomistic legal term. However, he calls the later application of דברים to law in deuteronomistic usage 'theologisch höchst bedeutsam' (p. 195 n. 4).

144. Horst Dietrich Preuss, *Deuteronomium* (ErFor 164; Darmstadt: Wissenschaftliche Buchgesellschaft, 1982), p. 127; cf. his helpful 'Schichtentabelle', pp. 4, 6-61 esp. pp. 51-52.

frame.[145] This plural usage appears to draw upon two traditions: the דבר of the Levitical priests[146] and the דבר of the prophets.[147] As with the term תורה, the use of דבר-/ים can refer in the final form of Deuteronomy to the book itself.[148] Although the precise referent of the term is not always clear, there is no doubt that as a collection of דברים the book is conceived of as written Scripture.[149]

The Deuteronomists also apparently coined a new term to express their synthesis of legal and prophetic traditions: דברי התורה.[150] This expression often appears together with the deuteronomistic phrase 'to observe and to do'.[151] In my judgment, this usage suggests the *prophetic* character of דברי התורה,[152] the insistence on lived obedience rather than formal acquiescence. By combining both terms, however, the editors of the book of Deuteronomy made a concerted effort to express the essential unity of law and prophecy.[153] The same is probably also the case with the use of הדברים (עשׂרת) for the Ten Commandments.[154]

---

145. Deut. 1.1, 18; 4.9, 12, 13; 5.22; 6.6; 9.10; 10.2, 4; 28.14; 30.1; 31.1, 28; 32.45-46; always with the definite article, except for Deut. 4.2. On the usage of דבר-/ים in Deuteronomy, see Braulik, 'Ausdrücke', pp. 45-49; Rost, 'Bemerkungen', pp. 47-50.

146. Deut. 1.17 (sg.), 18 (pl.); 17.11 (sg.); 22.14 (pl.), 17 (pl.); cf. Exod. 29.1 (sg.); Lev. 8.36 (pl.).

147. Deut. 18.18 (pl. with suffix), 19 (pl. with suffix), 20 (sg.), 21 (sg.), 22 (sg.); 32.47 (sg.).

148. With כל, the deictic, or both: Deut. 1.1; 28.14; 30.1; 31.1; 32.45-46.

149. Deut. 4.2; 12.32[13.1]. The singular can also be used in the frame as a collective: e.g. Deut 30.14; 32.47.

150. Deut. 17.19; 27.3, 8, 26; 28.58; 29.28[29]; 31.12, cf. 31.24; 32.46. See the parallel expression דברי הברית הזאת in: Deut. 28.69[29.1]; 29.[8]. See García López and Fabry ('תורה', p. 632) for the view that the expression דברי התורה reflects 'die Synthese der Worte und Befehle JHWHs. Es sind nicht nur "Gesetze", sondern die Gesamtheit des Willen Gottes, dessen Promulgation am Horeb geschieht'.

151. Braulik, 'Ausdrücke', p. 37. Thus: קום-עשׂה in Deut. 27.26; עשׂה in Deut. 28.58; 29.28; and שׁמר-עשׂה in Deut. 31.12; 32.46.

152. *Contra* Braulik ('Ausdrücke', p. 37), who sees this usage as accentuating the 'Gesetzescharakter' of תורה. But cf. Deut. 29.28[29] with Deut. 30.1.

153. E.W. Nicholson, *Deuteronomy and Tradition* (Oxford: Basil Blackwell, 1967), p. 58.

154. This connection would provide additional weight for viewing דברים in legal passages as having been influenced by deuteronomistic tradition. See, e.g., Exod. 20.1; 24.3, 4, 8; 34.1, 27, 28. Cf. G.I. Davies, 'The Composition of the Book of

Thus Deuteronomy features a 'prophetization' of the law at the same time as a 'nomisticization' of prophecy.[155] The abiding message of both Mosaic and prophetic revelation are now joined within a book.

However, if דבר/־ים is used in the frame to Deuteronomy as a means of recalling and confirming the authority of prophetic traditions, why is it the plural form which is used? I think the answer lies within the Deuteronomists' understanding of prophecy as a continually-unheeded warning.

This understanding is especially prominent within the book of Jeremiah. As with תורה, דבר sometimes has a collective sense in the singular as the unified word of God represented in and among its various particular moments of expression.[156] However, two distinctions are sometimes made by employing a change in number. Sometimes a distinction is made between the singular 'word of the Lord' (דבר יהוה) within or in contrast to 'the words' of a particular prophet (PN־דברי) or 'the words of the prophets' (דברי הניאבים).[157] Sometimes the change in number is used to differentiate between a single oracle (דבר) and a series of oracles (דברים).[158]

The latter distinction predominates over the former within the MT of Jeremiah, since the divine דבר can also appear in the plural without any weakening of its authority.[159] In fact, this distinction has been used to order the prophetic material within the book, which is made clear by a number of self-referential expressions.[160] Thus, the expression הדבר הזה

Exodus: Reflections on the Theses of Erhard Blum', in M.V. Fox *et al.* (eds.), *Texts, Temples and Traditions* (Festschrift Menahem Haran; Winona Lake, IN: Eisenbrauns, 1996), pp. 71-85, esp. p. 85 on Exod. 34.28.

155. See Liedke, *Rechtssätze*, pp. 194-95. However, Liedke seems to reject any independent use of דבר within early legal traditions. As will have been clear from my discussion, I think there was such a use, but that the application of דברים to the Ten Commandments was a deuteronomistic innovation.

156. E.g. Jer. 5.13-14 (see LXX); 6.10-11; 18.18; 20.8; 23.17-18 (see LXX), 28-29; 29.10; 32.8; 44.28. See esp. כל־הדבר in 42.5.

157. E.g. Jer. 1.1-2; 27.14, 16, 18.

158. E.g. Jer. 19.2-3; 22.4-5; 26.2, 5; 28.6, 7; 38.1, 4; 46.13; 49.34; 50.1; 51.59.

159. E.g. Jer. 1.9; 5.14; 6.19; 11.10; 13.10; 15.16; 18.2; 19.15; 23.9, 22, 30, 36; 23.20, 21, 36; 25.8; 39.15; 44.29.

160. In addition to the self-referential expressions I discuss here, there are a large number of formulations in which the דבר יהוה is said to have 'come' (היה) to the prophet. These are almost always singular, in keeping with the conception of a particular word at a particular moment (but see Jer. 15.16) and reflect the deuteron-

emphasizes a particular oracle at a particular moment.[161] Plural expressions are then used to express the idea of a series of oracles: כל-הדברים (כל-)הדברים[163]. הדברים האלה[162]. Plural forms are also used as introductory headings and conclusions.[164]

Of greatest interest, however, is a nuance that emerges from this second distinction, that between a particular oral 'word' and a written collection of 'words'. Thus, Jer. 30.1-2 tells of 'the word [הדבר] that came to Jeremiah from the Lord, "Thus says the Lord, the God of Israel: Write in a book all the words [כל-הדברים] that I have spoken to you"'. In Jer. 45.1 we read of 'the word [הדבר] which Jeremiah the prophet spoke [דבר] to Baruch ben Neriah when he wrote these words [האלה הדברים] in a book at the dictation of Jeremiah...'. The cumulative dimension of this distinction is evident in Jer. 36.2: '...this word came to Jeremiah from the Lord: "Take a scroll and write on it all the words [כל-הדברים] that I have spoken to you against Israel and Judah and all the nations, from the day I spoke to you, from the days of Josiah until today."' Throughout this crucial chapter, which describes the textualization of the prophet's oracles,[165] plural forms are always used to refer to what is written. As the oracles take on written form in the book of Jeremiah they are referred to consistently in the plural.

One notes, therefore, that Jeremiah 36 speaks consistently of the plural דברי יהוה instead of singular דבר יהוה. Moreover, Jeremiah's words are called the דברי יהוה when he dictates to Baruch, but the

---

omistic theology of the 'word'. In my judgment, the self-referential expressions listed below go further, indicating the increasing textualization of the 'word'.

161. Jer. 5.14; 7.2, 23; 13.12; 14.17; 22.1, 4; 23.38; 26.1; 27.1; 28.7; 31.23; 36.1; 40.3; cf. 30.14; 38.21.

162. Without כל: Jer. 3.12; 29.1; 22.5; 26.7, 10; 38.24; 45.1. With כל: Jer. 7.27; 11.6; 16.10; 25.30; 26.15; 34.6; 36.16, 17, 18, 24, 27(?, see LXX); 38.27; 43.1; 51.60, 61.

163. Jer. 26.2, 12; 30.2; 36.2, 13, 16, 20.

164. E.g. Jer. 1.1; 29.1; 30.4; 51.64b.

165. On the literary significance of this chapter, see R.P. Carroll, 'Manuscripts Don't Burn—Inscribing the Prophetic Tradition: Reflections on Jeremiah 36', in M. Augustin and K.-D. Schunck (eds.), *'Dort ziehen Schiffe dahin...': Collected Communications to the XIVth Congress of the International Organization for the Study of the Old Testament, Paris 1992* (BEATAJ, 28; Frankfurt: Peter Lang, 1996), pp. 31-42. Based on a one-sided view of writing as 'deformation' (37), Carroll cynically concludes, however, that the chapter represents a 'scribal takeover of the words of Jeremiah' (p. 40).

דברי ירמיהו when Baruch reads aloud what has been written. There is
no hint of a difference in content or authority between the two expressions; instead, the distinction reflects the same process of textualization
which has led to the superscription of the book (Jer. 1.1).

As written prophecy, Jeremiah's oracles lose none of their currency.
Passages such as Jer. 25.13 illustrate the prophetic quality of written
דברים: 'I will bring upon the land all my words [כל-דברי], which I have
uttered [דבר] against it, everything written in this book, which Jeremiah
prophesied against the nations'. In fact, the textualization of the prophetic message is considered a means of its actualization. Thus, in Jer.
51.60 the prophet Jeremiah instructs Seraiah to take a book of his oracles
(כל-הדברים האלה) about Babylon and read them (כל-הדברים האלה)
aloud (קרא) in order to ensure their full force.[166]

In this way the composite literary form of the book of Jeremiah match-
es the deuteronomistic conception of repeated warnings which went un-
heeded.[167] This cumulative conception is expressed by the intersection
of two motifs within the book: '[God's] servants the prophets'[168] and
their persistent דברים.[169] The motif of textualization emerges as a response to the failure of Israel to heed the prophetic message.[170] Written
in a book, the 'words' are considered a powerfully abiding witness to a
message so unified that it can be portrayed as a type.[171]

This typification of prophecy and the conception of written דברים is
continued and broadened in subsequent traditions, developing further
the deuteronomistic notions of prophecy as reading aloud,[172] dicta-

---

166. See Isaac Rabinowitz, *A Witness Forever: Ancient Israel's Perception of
Literature and the Resultant Hebrew Bible* (Bethesda, MD: CDL Press, 1993), esp.
pp. 61-65.

167. E.g., Jer. 7.13, 25-26; 11.7-8; 18.18; 25.3-4; 26.5; 29.19; 32.33; 35.14-15;
44.4-5, 16.

168. The phrase '[God's] servants the prophets' appears in 2 Kgs 9.7; 17.13, 23;
21.10; 24.2; Jer. 7.25; 25.4; 26.5; 29.19 (missing in LXX); 35.15; 44.4; Amos 3.7;
Zech. 1.6; Dan. 9.6, 10; Ezra 9.11. Cf. 1QHab 2.9; 7.5. The language is deuteronomistic.

169. Jer. 7.27; 25.8; 26.5; 29.19; 35.13; 44:4 (sg., but as a 'typical' single
oracle); cf. Dan 9.12.

170. Jer. 25.8-14.

171. See Jer. 25.5-7; 26.4-6; 35.15; 44.4; cf. 2 Kgs 17.13; 21.10-15; Zech. 1.3-6.

172. See C.L. Meyers and E.M. Meyers, *Haggai, Zechariah 1–8* (AB, 25B;
Garden City, NY: Doubleday, 1987), pp. 395-96 on קרא in Zech. 7.7, 13 (cf. 2 Kgs
23.2; Jer. 36.6-8).

tion[173] and writing.[174] Particularly striking is the use of the formula
PN-דברי within Chronicles to indicate prophetic writings.[175]

The culmination of this process can be seen in the use of דבר in the
superscriptions to prophetic books. As with תורה, דבר becomes a category-designation for prophetic revelation, written as well as oral. Thus
use of the formula דבר-יהוה אשר היה אל-PN connects several of the
older books and probably indicates that at one time they formed a
deuteronomistic collection of prophetic scripture.[176] The alternate expression היה דבר-יהוה אל-PN suggests a group of later additions to the
genre.[177] The superscriptions not only suggest a literary genre of prophetic דברים,[178] they also suggest a developing scriptural collection of
Isaiah, Jeremiah, Ezekiel, Hosea, Joel, Amos, Micah, Zephaniah, Haggai and (First) Zechariah in the early postexilic period. Often over-

173. Meyers and Meyers, *Haggai, Zechariah*, pp. 419-20 on מפי הנביאים in
Zech. 8.9; Ezek. 3.17 = 33.7. Cf. מפי in Jer. 36.4, 6, 17, 18, 27, 32; 45.1.

174. E.g. Ezek. 2.9-10; 24.2; 37.16; Hab. 2.2; Ezra 9.10-12(?); Josephus, *Apion*
1.37-43. Cf. Barton, *Oracles of God: Perceptions of Ancient Prophecy in Israel
after the Exile* (London: Darton, Longman & Todd, 1986), pp. 19, 224-25.

175. 1 Chron. 29.29; 2 Chron. 9.29; 12.15; 13.22; 20.34; 26.22; 32.32; 33.18-19;
36.8. See T. Willi, *Die Chronik als Auslegung: Untersuchungen zur literarischen
Gestaltung des historischen Überlieferungen Israels* (FRLANT 106; Göttingen:
Vandenhoeck & Ruprecht, 1972), pp. 229-41. The accompanying expressions indicate that this term is used in a prophetic sense rather than simply meaning 'chronicle': 2 Chron. 9.29 (נבואה // חזה // דברי); 13.22 (מדרש הנביא); 32.32 (חזון); 33.18 (דברי)
החזים, 19 (דברי חוזי). 2 Chron. 26.22 clearly states that Isaiah 'wrote' (כתב) the
דברי עזיהו.

176. The formula in Jer. 1.1 and Amos 1.1 is plural (PN-דברי), although in the
LXX Jeremiah follows the singular pattern. See G. Tucker, 'Prophetic Superscriptions and the Growth of the Canon', in G.W. Coats and B.O. Long (eds.), *Canon
and Authority. Essays in Old Testament Religion and Theology* (Philadelphia:
Fortress Press, 1977), pp. 59-70. Tucker envisions a deuteronomistic prophetic collection of Hosea and Amos, probably also with Micah, Zephaniah, Joel, (First) Isaiah and Jeremiah in mid-sixth century (pp. 62-63, 69). Isa. 1.1 (חזון ישעיהו בן-אמוץ
אשר חזה) does not, however, follow the pattern. Cf. James Nogalski, *Literary
Precursors to the Book of the Twelve* (BZAW, 217; Berlin: W. de Gruyter, 1993),
pp. 278-80. Nogalski suggests a deuteronomistic prophetic corpus consisting of
Hosea, Amos, Micah and Zephaniah.

177. Ezek. 1.3 (with dittography of the היה); Hag. 1.1; Zech. 1.1.

178. For more on prophecy as a literary genre, see Terence Collins, *The Mantle
of Elijah: The Redaction Criticism of the Prophetical Books* (Biblical Seminar, 20;
Sheffield: JSOT Press, 1993).

looked is that most of the remaining books (or later additions to books) employ the term דבר, although other terms are also prominent.[179]

Forms of דברים also feature as headings within the Writings,[180] which could reflect an effort early on to fit these books within the prophetic tradition, or a perhaps a common scribal tradition.[181] If some of the material now found in the Writings was at one time included within a bipartite collection of Scripture, then it would have been natural to conceive of such works as דברים or the figures with which they are associated as prophets. We have already seen how David is treated as a prophet within later tradition.[182] The book of Daniel appears to have been considered a 'prophetic' book at Qumran.[183] It is further of interest to note how Ps. 79.2-3 is cited in 1 Macc. 7.16-17 using the formula, 'according to the word' (κατὰ τὸν λόγον). This manner of citation could reflect an earlier positioning of the Psalter within the prophetic corpus, before a (re-?)distribution into a tripartite collection.[184]

In my judgment, tetrateuchal material also uses various forms of דבר to 'prophetize' Moses and Aaron.[185] The device of reported speech is not only used within priestly legislation as a 'narrative trope',[186] but also stylizes the laws as the divine speech.[187] The figure of Moses in the

179. With the heading משׂא דבר-יהוה: Zech. 9.1 (ב); 12.1 (על); Mal. 1.1 (אל); cf. Isa. 13.1 (משׂא בבל אשר חזה ישׁעיהו בן-אמוץ). The book of Jonah has no superscription, but does begin its narrative with reference to the דבר-יהוה. Only the superscriptions to Obadiah (חזון עבדיה), Nahum (ספר חזון נחום האלקשׁי משׂא נינוה) and Habakkuk (המשׂא אשׁר חזה חבקוק הנביא) do not mention דבר.

180. Ps. 18.1; Job 31.30; Prov. 22.17; 30.1; 31.1; Eccl. 1.1; Neh. 1.1. Of course, this would mitigate interpretation of this phrase as original to wisdom.

181. E.g. Exod. 35.1; 2 Sam. 22.1; 23.1. Cf. Tucker, 'Superscriptions', p. 67.

182. E.g. 1 Chron. 13.8; 2 Chron. 29.25; 11QPsª 27.11; Acts 2.30.

183. E.g. 4Q174 2.3: '...as it is written in the book of Daniel the prophet'.

184. John Barton, *Oracles*, pp. 44-55, 75-82; Beckwith, *Canon*, pp. 38-80; Leiman, *Canonization*, p. 168 n. 287.

185. Rost was of the opinion ('Bemerkungen', p. 59) that the priestly literature had consciously rejected the formula היה דבר יהוה in order to elevate Moses over the prophets, preferring the formula וידבר יהוה אל-משׁה לאמר. The actual usage, however, leads to the opposite conclusion; see Rendtorff, *Gesetze*, p. 69.

186. Miller, *Representation*, pp. 285-90; cf. 384.

187. Rendtorff suggests (*Gesetze*, p. 70) that there has been a later (post-deuteronomistic?) reworking in this direction.

Pentateuch may rightly be viewed as 'an idealization of the prophetic role'.[188]

Thus, also like תורה, in the late period דבר comes to mean the entirety of divine revelation,[189] referring to pentateuchal as well as non-pentateuchal scripture. The term retains, however, a prophetic dimension. In my judgment, the notice in 2 Chron. 36.16 provides three parallel terms which in fact are identical.[190] The people of Israel are charged with 'mocking the messengers of God [מלאכי האלהים], despising his words [דבריו], and scoffing at his prophets [נבאיו]'. Reference here to God's דברים, as expressed through his נביאים, functions as a category-designation for prophetic revelation, much of which existed by this time in written forms. Just as with תורה, the authority of the category did not lie with its literary fixity, however, but with its content. Not only what the prophets themselves had said (*ipsissima verba*) was considered authoritative, or even the precise form of what was written in their individual books, but everything that conformed to the character of their combined insight into the nature and purpose of God.[191]

At Qumran דברים often seems to possess a more legal sense.[192] Still, its usage to mean prophetic scripture is evident in passages like 1QpHab 2.9-10: 'to interpret [פשר] all the words of his servants the prophets'.[193]

---

188. Auld, 'Word', p. 248. Note the use of דברים in Exod. 35.1; Lev. 8.36; Num. 11.24; 14.39; 16.31. The figure of Aaron has also been 'prophetized'; cf. Num. Exod. 4.15, 28, 30; 35.1.

189. Ezra 9.4; 1 Chron. 15.15; 2 Chron. 19.11; 30.12; 34.21; 35.6. Cf. W. Zimmerli, 'Wort Gottes I: Im Alten Testament', RGG VI, pp. 1809-12, esp. p. 1811.

190. Contra W.M. Schniedewind, *The Word of God in Transition: From Prophet to Exegete in the Second Temple Period* (JSOTSup, 197; Sheffield: Sheffield Academic Press, 1995), esp. pp. 83-84.

191. R.E. Clements, 'Patterns in the Prophetic Canon', in Coats and Long (eds.), *Canon and Authority*, pp. 42-55, esp. pp. 48-49.

192. Qimron and Strugnell, *Miqṣat*, p. 139, section 5.3.2.3. However, it is not the case that דברים is used exclusively to mean 'commandments' in 4QMMT, as the editors argue. Their own translation makes that clear (e.g. 4Q396 1-2.i; 4Q398 14-17.ii). Perhaps it would be better to think in terms of a more 'halakhic' sense to the term. This seems to be the sense of 1QS 6.24 (mistakenly cited as 1QS 1.24 in Qimron and Strugnell): ואל(ה) המשפטים ישפטו בם במדרש יחד על פי הדברים. Cf. Exod. 34.27; Deut. 17.10-11.

193. Cf. 1QpHab 7.5; CD-B 19.7: 'the word which is written by the hand of Zechariah the prophet' (quoting Zech. 13.7). The phrase '[God's] servants the prophets', appears in 1QpHab 2.9; 7.5; 4QHos[a] 2.5; 4QpsMos[e] (4Q390) 2.5.

Pesher interpretation in general provides a massive illustration of how prophetic writings were viewed as collections of 'words'. J. Maier, however, has advanced the thesis that the elevation of Torah at Qumran is shown by use of pesher interpretation for Prophets but not Torah.[194] While it is true that pesher interpretation was apparently not used for legal texts,[195] there do exist among the Dead Sea Scrolls three pesher interpretations of the book of Genesis,[196] a fact which suggests the use of pesher style was dependent upon genre, not authority.

Of special interest is the notice in CD 7.10-11: 'when there shall come to pass the word, which is written in the words of Isaiah the prophet, son of Amoz, which says...' (quoting Isa. 7.17). Since the 'words of Isaiah' is clearly not a reference to the superscription of the book, the term illustrates the continued notion of a genre of דברים for written prophetic scripture: the 'word' is written in 'the words'. The written nature of these 'words' is reinforced by the continuation of the passage: '...the books of the prophets whose words Israel despised' (CD 7.17-18).

The *Letter of Aristeas* refers to the Pentateuch as 'oracles' (λόγια).[197] The *Assumption of Moses* terms material from Leviticus and Deuteronomy 'prophecies' (3.11-12). In addition to knowing his received Scriptures as 'law', Philo employs the terms 'word' (λόγος), 'words' (λόγια) and 'oracles' (χρησμοί). In the same way, the entire Old Testament tradition is sometimes viewed under the rubric 'word' within the New Testament.[198] Paul can refer to the entire Old Testament as 'the oracles of God'.[199] The prophetic Scriptures in particular are called 'the words of the prophets which are read every sabbath' (Acts 13.27, τὰς φωνὰς τῶν προφητῶν τὰς κατὰ πᾶν σάββατον) or simply 'the words of the prophets' (Acts 15.15, οἱ λόγοι τῶν προφητῶν).[200] Similar to the cita-

194. Maier, 'Frage', pp. 143-44.

195. H.-J. Fabry, 'Schriftverständnis und Schriftauslegung der Qumran-Essener', in *Bibel*, pp. 87-96, here p. 91.

196. Namely: 4QpGen[a], 4QpGen[b], 4QpGen[c]. Fabry also notes the use of Deut. 33 in 4Q174 and suggests 4Q159 could be a pesher on Deut. 4.29-30 ('Schriftverständnis', p. 89).

197. *Ep. Arist.* 177. For these and other examples, see Beckwith, *Canon*, p. 105 nn. 19-22, 25-27; 'Formation', p. 45.

198. E.g. Acts 13.44.

199. Rom. 3.2, τὰ λόγια τοῦ θεοῦ. Cf. Heb. 5.12.

200. Quoted are Jer. 12.15; Amos 9.11-12 and Isa. 45.21. See also Acts 3.18:

tion of Isaiah in CD 7.10-11 at Qumran, Lk. 3.4a refers to 'the book of the words of Isaiah the prophet' (ὡς γέγραπται ἐν βίβλῳ λόγων Ἡσαΐου τοῦ προφήτου, citing Isa. 40.3-5) not because this is the title of the book, but the standard usage for the entire collection. In the letter of *1 Clement*, 'the words of God' (τὰ λόγια τοῦ θεοῦ) continues to be a frequent designation for prophetic scripture.[201]

5. Tôrâ *and* Dᵉbārîm *as Scripture*

Based on the use of דברים within biblical and extra-biblical books to mean prophetic *writings*, I would like to suggest that the pairing of תורה and דברים is sometimes used in the Old Testament to refer to the entirety of Israel's sacred tradition, eventually functioning as a *terminus technicus* for a *bipartite collection of scripture*.[202] The origins of this pairing can be traced back at least to deuteronomistic usage of the mid-sixth century BCE.[203]

Thus, the final form of Deuteronomy is understood as הדברים of Moses (Deut. 1.1) as well as התורה of Moses the lawgiver (Deut. 1.5).[204] This same pairing is evident in Deut. 4.8-9, where כל התורה הזאת and הדברים combine to express the entirety of the Sinai covenant.[205] The late date of these passages suggests that they belong to the final redac-

'by the mouth of all the prophets' (διὰ στόματος πάντων τῶν προφητῶν); cf. v. 21; 2 Pet. 3.2, 'the words of the holy prophets' (ῥημάτων ὑπὸ τῶν ἁγίων προφητῶν); Rev. 1.3; 22.6-7, 10, 18-19. The book of The Twelve is referred to as 'the book of the prophets' in Acts 7.42 (καθὼς γέγραπται ἐν βίβλῳ τῶν προφητῶν, quoting Amos 5.25-27).

201. See *1 Clem.* 19.1; 53.1. The letter also uses the term 'scripture' (γραφή); for examples, see Beckwith (*Canon*, p. 105 nn. 23-24, 30).

202. 'Synonymous parallelism' was argued for instances of this pairing in the prophetic books by G.P. Fowler (*The Meaning of Torah in the Prophetic Books of the Old Testament* [Ann Arbor: University Microfilms, 1969], p. 73 [on Isa. 1.10; 2.3 (= Mic. 4.2); 30.9-12; Jer. 6.19; Zech. 7.12]; cf. p. 154 [on Zech. 7.12]), but with both terms meaning law, not Scripture.

203. Nicholson, *Preaching*, p. 123.

204. On Deut. 1.1 and 5 as an inclusio, see N. Lohfink, 'Der Bundesschluß im Land Moab: Redaktionsgeschichtliches zu Dt 28, 69–32, 47', *BZ* 6 (1962), pp. 32-56 = *idem*, *Studien zum Deuteronomium und zur deuteronomistischen Literatur*, I (SBAB, 8; Stuttgart: Katholisches Bibelwerk, 1990), pp. 53-82, esp. p. 53 n. 2 (I cite the latter version).

205. On Deut. 4.9-10 as a later gloss, see Preuss, *Deuteronomium*, p. 87; cf. his 'Schichtentabelle', p. 47.

tion of the book. An earlier stage of deuteronomistic tradition is prob-ably responsible for the pairing of תורה and the singular דבר יהוה within the prophetic corpus,[206] although it is possible that this usage may be pre-deuteronomistic and have arisen within prophetic tradition.[207] Other potentially pre-deuteronomistic or early deuteronomistic parallelisms suggest a combination of legal and prophetic revelation: תורה // תעודה,[208] תורה // עד,[209] דבר-ים // (יהוה) פי,[210] תורה // חזון.[211] However, only the deuteronomistic motif of 'the law and the words' is used in a way that consistently suggests written Scripture.

The deuteronomistic view is reflected in 2 Kgs 17.13, where '[God's] servants the prophets' are cited as a cumulative revelatory authority, but their message is not yet given the designation 'words'.[212] What unites this passage with later deuteronomistic tradition is not only the lan-guage of '[God's] servants the prophets',[213] but also the view that the

206. See Isa. 1.10; 2.3 (= Mic. 4.2); Jer. 18.18 (cf. Ezek. 7.26, where חזון appears instead of דבר; passages such as Ezek. 1.3; 11.25 are probably later addi-tions for the purpose of uniting Ezekiel's tradition of prophecy as חזון with the deuteronomistic notion of prophecy as דבר); Hos. 4.1, 6.

207. See Isa. 30.9, 12; Jer. 8.8-9.

208. Isa. 8.16, 20. This parallelism in Isa. 8.16 could well mark the beginning of the canonical 'impulse' given its early date; see García López and Fabry, 'תורה', p. 614. If so, then Israel's canonical process involved prophecy as well as law from the very beginning.

209. Isa. 30.8-9; cf. Deut. 31.24? Ps. 119.44?

210. E.g. 1 Sam. 15.24; 1 Kgs 13.26; 2 Chron. 36.12; cf. Josh. 1.18. Note, how-ever, that Fishbane (*Interpretation*, pp. 477-78, citing Kaminka) has given support to the view that פי יהוה is used as a redactional citation formula in late postexilic prophecy. Obad. 17-18 (citing the fulfilment of Num. 24.17) and Isa. 58.14 (allud-ing to Deut. 32.9, 13) provide examples of this technique.

211. Ezek. 7.26; Prov. 29.18; Lam. 2.9.

212. However, their message is related in the form of a quotation; cf. 2 Kgs 21.10 and 24.2 (which do refer to the message of '[God's] servants the prophets' as the דבר יהוה). Nicholson concludes (*Deuteronomy*, p. 118) that in 2 Kgs 17.13 the prophets are viewed as jointly responsible for the 'promulgation and teaching of the divine law to Israel. What Moses did in Deuteronomy, so also did the prophets during the course of Israel's history'.

213. The deuteronomistic conception of the prophets as 'servants' should be interpreted in light of similar deuteronomistic language about Moses, cf. 2 Kgs 21.8 and 10. For 'servant' language with reference to Moses, see Exod. 14.31; Num. 12.7, 8; 31.49; Deut. 34.5; Josh. 1.1, 7, 13, 15; 8.31, 33; 9.24; 11.12, 15; 12.6; 13.8; 14.7; 18.7; 22.2, 4, 5; 1 Kgs 8.53, 56; 2 Kgs 18.12; 21.8; Mal. 3.22[4.4]; Ps. 105.26; Dan. 9.11; Neh. 1.7, 8; 9.14; 10.30[29]; 1 Chron. 6.34; 2 Chron. 1.3; 24.6,

refusal of Israel to observe the prophetic message *as well as* the law was responsible for their exile from the land.[214]

This is the tradition to which Jer. 6.19 gives expression in lapidary fashion: 'Hear, O earth; behold, I am bringing evil upon this people, the fruit of their devices, because they have not given heed to my words [דברי] and as for my law [תורתי] they have rejected it.' It is not certain whether this passage should be attributed to early jeremianic tradition or to deuteronomistic redaction.[215] Especially if the passage is considered deuteronomistic, however, it is likely that written as well as oral traditions are here in view.

The parallelism of דברים with תורה within the rhetorical context of deuteronomistic tradition and the theme of textualization within the book of Jeremiah strongly suggests that such references are not restricted to oral proclamation. Thus in Jer. 26.4-5 a similar formulation appears: 'If you will not listen to me, to walk in my law [בתורתי] which I have set before you, and to heed urgently the words of my servants the prophets [דברי עבדי הנביאים], though you have not heeded, then...I will

9. Cf. Exod. 4.10; 7.10, 20; 8.5, 25, 27; 10.1; Num. 11.11; 32.25; Mic. 6.4. In deuteronomistic tradition and within the final form of the canon, Moses and the prophets are depicted as populating a single line of revelation (Deut. 18.9-22; 34.10-12; Mal. 3.22-24[4.4-6]) and thus as parallel scriptural authorities. For more on the deuteronomistic depiction of Moses as a 'servant', see C. Barth, 'Mose, Knecht Gottes', in E. Busch, J. Fangmeier and M. Geiger (eds.), *ΠΑΡΡΗΣΙΑ* (Festschrift Karl Barth; Zürich: EVZ-Verlag, 1966), pp. 68-81, esp. pp. 69-70 on Moses, p. 72 on the prophets. Later tradition clearly associates the two in this role; see Dan. 9.10-11.

214. 2 Kgs 17.13; Jer. 16.10-13; 25.8-14; 29.19-20; 35.15; 44.4-6. Cf. the chart of parallels between 2 Kgs 17 and various jeremianic passages in Nicholson, *Preaching*, p. 56.

215. Y. Hoffmann, ' "Isn't the Bride Too Beautiful?" The Case of Jeremiah 6:16-21', *JSOT* 64 (1994), pp. 103-20. Hoffmann argues for a late date based upon similarities with other deuteronomistic texts, although he also notes closes verbal links with other earlier jeremianic poetry. There are problems with Hoffmann's argument, however. He sees Jer. 6.19-20 as dependent upon Isa. 1.10-11, a similarity which could be explained in precisely the opposite direction. Also, by separating Jer. 6.19-20 from 6.16-18, Hoffmann appears to disregard the very clear chiastic structure which unifies the entire passage. Certainly Hoffmann's argument that the unit must be secondary because it would be too 'perfect' an example of early jeremianic poetry has little probative value. I conclude that the unit is probably contemporaneous with early deuteronomism but original to jeremianic tradition, although it may well have been subject to deuteronomistic editing.

make this city a curse for all the nations of the earth.'[216] Confirmation of
the authenticity of this oracle is made in the narrative by a citation of
written prophetic Scripture (Mic. 3.12 in Jer. 26.18). As we have already seen, in the book of Jeremiah prophetic 'words' are increasingly
conceived of as a unified message in a variety of written forms.
Dating from the end of the fifth century BCE, Zech. 7.12 continues
in this deuteronomistic tradition by referring to 'the law and the words
[את-התורה ואת-הדברים] which the Lord of hosts sent by his Spirit
through the former prophets'. Both Zech. 7.9-10 and 8.16-17 give
examples of these דברים as consisting of moral instructions, but in the
form of a prophetic oracle. The first oracle offers the same typification
of pre-exilic prophecy found within the books of 2 Kings and Jeremiah
(cf. Zech. 1.4).[217] Here again, the failure of Israel to heed 'the words
[הדברים] which the Lord proclaimed [קרא] by the former prophets
[הנביאים הראשנים]' (Zech. 7.7) is cited as a reason for the exile (Zech.
7.11-14; cf. 8.14). As Carol and Eric Meyers have suggested in their
commentary, the paired terminology in Zech 7.12 (with the definite
article!) does indeed sugggest an early reference to a bipartite Scripture.[218] As we have seen, however, this expression has its roots within
the concerted effort made by deuteronomistic tradition to pair legal and

216. On Jer. 26.5 as a later gloss, see F.L. Hossfeld and I. Meyer, 'Der Prophet
vor dem Tribunal: neuer Auslegungsversuch von Jeremiah 26', *ZAW* 86 (1974),
p. 47.

217. T. Lescow has suggested ('Sacharja 1–8: Verkündigung und Komposition',
BN 68 [1993], pp. 75-99, here p. 99) that Zech. 1.2-6 is intended to introduce the
postexilic prophets of the book of the Twelve and illustrate how to understand what
has come before (Hosea–Zephaniah): 'als an die Väter ergangene Tora-Prophetie'.
He also sees here a conscious allusion to 2 Kgs 17.13.

218. Meyers and Meyers, *Haggai, Zechariah*, p. 402. The Myers suggest that
this expression is 'a new idiom which may very well have a technical connotation'.
They further theorize that 'words' refers either to 'the working canon of prophecy
that would have existed in Zechariah's day' or to something like the Primary His-
tory as described by D.N. Freedman (cf. his 'The Law and the Prophets', in
Congress Volume. Bonn 1962 [VTSup IX; Leiden: E.J. Brill, 1962], pp. 250-65).
On Zech. 7.12 cf. M.A. Klopfenstein, 'Das Gesetz bei den Propheten', in
W. Dietrich (ed.), *Leben aus dem Wort: Beiträge zum Alten Testament* (Bern: Peter
Lang, 1996), pp. 41-57, esp. pp. 42-43 = M.A. Klopfenstein *et al.* (eds.), *Mitte der
Schrift? Ein jüdisch-christliches Gespräch* (Judaica et Christiana, 11; Frankfurt:
Peter Lang, 1987), pp. 283-97.

prophetic terms.[219] Thus the formula is not a 'new idiom' in Zech.
7.12.[220]

After the deuteronomistic use of the formula, there is a retention and
an expansion of terminology expressing the same basic conception of a
bipartite revelation: ‏// אמרה‎,[222]‏דבר-ים‎ // מצוה-ת‎ ‏דרב-ים‎,[221]‏// משפט-ים‎
‏תורה‎,[223]‏משפט-ים‎,[226]‏אמרה‎ // ברית‎,[225]‏ברית‎ // דבר-ים‎,[224]‏קל (יהוה)‎ // תורה‎
‏// אמרי-פי‎,[227]‏מצוה-ת‎ // אמר-ים‎.[228] Despite wide variation, a persistent
parallelism of terms for legal and prophetic revelation is evident in
various circles of tradition.

The pairing of 'words' and 'law' is also present in Josh. 24.26, in
which Joshua is said to have written 'these words [‏הדברים האלה‎] in the
book of the law of God [‏בספר תורת אלהים‎]'. The 'words' in question
are surely understood as Joshua's covenant with the people from the
preceding verse (24.25), the culmination of Joshua's prophetic address

219. See Lindars, 'Torah', p. 135. He dates this phenomenon to the mid-sixth
century BCE.

220. *Contra* Meyers and Meyers, *Haggai, Zechariah*, p. 402. Zech. 1.6, part of
the same literary framework to the earlier collection of visions now found in Zech.
1.7–6.15, refers to 'my words and my statutes' (‏דברי וחקי‎; cf. Ps. 147.19) which
God commanded his 'servants the prophets'. One explanation for this term would
be to see ‏חקי‎ as substituting for ‏תורתי‎ as a umbrella term for legal tradition. Cf. Ps.
147.19Q (‏חקיו ומשפטיו // דבריו‎); Ezra 7.11 (‏דברי מצות-יהוה וחקיו‎).

221. E.g. Exod. 24.3; 1 Kgs 6.38(?); Ps. 119.43, 160; 147.19 (also with ‏חקיו‎); cf.
Deut. 1.17; 17.8-9, 11; 2 Chron. 19.6.

222. E.g. Num. 15.31; Deut. 4.2; 28.13-14; 30.11, 14 (inclusio); 1 Kgs 6.12;
Prov. 4.4; 13.13; Eccl. 12.13(?). Lohfink analyzes (*Hauptgebot*, pp. 55-56) the
plural ‏מצות‎ as surviving from a pre-deuteronomistic usage and the collective use of
‏דבר‎ singular as a deuteronomistic idiom. There could be an earlier levitical use or a
connection with royal justice (2 Kgs 18.36 = Isa. 36.21).

223. E.g. Isa. 5.24; Ps. 78.1 (‏אמרי-פי‎ //); to ‏תורה‎ are also ‏עדות‎ in v. 5 and ‏ברית‎
‏אלהים‎ in v. 10); Job 22.22; cf. Josh. 24.26-27.

224. E.g. Gen. 26.5; Deut. 28.15; 30.10; Jer. 9.12[13]; 32.23; 44.23 (‏חקות‎ //
‏עדות‎); Dan. 9.10-11, 13-14. Cf. Jer. 11.4; 16.11-12. Hag. 1.12 illustrates that ‏קל יהוה‎
is a prophetic term: here ‏קל יהוה‎ and ‏דברי חגי הנביא‎ are parallel.

225. E.g. Deut. 4.13; Isa. 59.21 (‏רוח‎ //); Jer. 11.10; Ps. 105.8 (= 1 Chron. 16.15);
Neh. 9.8. For a discussion of Isa. 59.21 as a late canon-conscious addition, see
A. Rofé, 'The Piety of the Torah-Disciples at the Winding Up of the Hebrew Bible:
Josh. 1.8; Ps. 1.2; Isa. 59.21', in *Bibel*, pp. 78-85.

226. Deut. 33.9; cf. v. 10 (‏תורה // משפטים‎)

227. E.g. Hos. 6.5; Ps. 78.1; cf. Ps. 19.10b[9b], 15[14]; Job 22.22.

228. E.g. Ps. 119.172; Prov. 2.1; 7.1.

beginning in 24.2 (כה-אמר יהוה אלהי ישראל). Thus, 'new' propheti-cally-mediated אמרי יהוה (24.27) are conceived of as being appended to the book of the law![229] Such a pattern echoes the first chapter, where mention of Joshua's 'words' (דבריך, Josh. 1.18) follows the allusion to the תורה in Josh. 1.7-8. The final form of the book of Joshua appears to have an understanding in which authoritative tradition is constituted by *more* than the 'law of Moses'.

It is certainly the case that in the later books of Ezra–Nehemiah and Chronicles sometimes only a legal warrant is cited, sometimes in a *Rechtssatz*, sometimes alone. However, prophetic allusions and warrants are also prominent, as we have previously noted. In addition, however, the terms תורה and דבר-/ים are conspicuously paired in passages such as 2 Chron. 12.1, 7; 15.3, 8. Moreover, the same kind of inner-biblical exegesis may occur where reference is made to prophecy and prophets that we identified earlier with respect to Moses and the law. Thus, in Neh. 1.8 a 'word' (הדבר) of God to Moses his 'servant' is cited by Ne-hemiah without the textual basis of the citation being at all clear. In the same way, Ezra 9.10-12 attributes to God's servants the prophets a series of commandments (מצות) which do not appear as such in any other passage (cf. 2 Chron. 29.25: המצוה ביד-נביאיו). Here it is the entire prophetic tradition that is being invoked, not a particular pro-phecy. Again understood as a persistent act of 'warning' (2 Chron. 24.19), the entire tradition is viewed as a *cumulative revelation* that eventually achieved a *fullness* of expression (2 Chron. 36.15: 'until there was no remedy').

The two late passages that coordinate traditions of law and prophecy most explicitly are Daniel 9 and Nehemiah 9. In Daniel 9, the prophets —including Moses—are those 'servants of God' (9.6, 10, 11) who have persistently set God's תורות before Israel. Thus, Israel's transgression of the law (Dan. 9.11) is one and the same with her refusal to hear the prophets (9.6, 10). According to the rhetoric of the passage, the gravest of sins is that of disobedience to God's voice (קול), which is described as the rejection of the prophets as well as the laws (9.10, pl.!) they have communicated. Even the תורה of Moses is understood prophetically here (9.11, 13). Not only is the present situation conceived as the ful-filment of 'the curse and the oath written in the law of Moses', but also as the 'confirmation' of God's 'words' (9.12K: ויקם את-דבריו; cf. 9.6).

229. See Niditch, *Word*, p. 88.

Mention of God's 'words' serves not only as a link to the general references to the 'prophets' in the passage, but also to the citation from Jeremiah which precedes it (9.2). God's 'words' are now written Scripture and the failure to obey them is fully the same as a failure to obey God himself (9.12K, '*his* words'!).

In Nehemiah 9, the promise to Abraham is also portrayed as prophecy (lit., 'words') which God brought to fulfilment (9.8, ותקם את-דבריך). Here again the language is of 'laws' (9.13: תורות אמת) *among which* is 'a law by Moses your servant' (9.14). The role of the prophets is that of a persistent 'warning' (9.26: העידו בם; cf. vv. 29-30), the goal of which is to turn the people back towards the law (9.26, 29-30). This role involves no subordination of the prophets, only a recognition of their place within the grand scheme of salvation history unfolded in Ezra's prayer. Here, too, the 'warnings' of the prophets are understood to be the 'warnings' of God himself (9.29: ותעד בהם; cf. v. 30). However, the deuteronomistic conception of prophecy as 'word' is not particularly prominent in this tradition. More conspicuous is the pairing of 'law' and 'prophets' within a salvation-historical framework, which provides a textual basis for the later formula 'the law and the prophets'.

When exactly this formula appeared as such is difficult to pinpoint. The use of 'the law and prophets' in 2 Macc. 15.9 probably indicates that this phrase is pre-Christian.[230] The same is probably also the case with 4 Macc. 18.10.[231] At Qumran there exists a variety of usage, but the precise formula 'the law and the prophets' is somewhat surprisingly not prominent.[232] 'Moses' and 'prophets' are alluded to in 1QS 1.2-3.[233]

---

230. Beckwith, 'Formation', pp. 39-40, 57. Although specific Scripture is not cited in the following narrative, Beckwith points out (*Canon*, p. 143 n. 88, citing Harris) that a 'narrow' understanding of 'law and prophets' is unlikely, given the description of the contents of Nehemiah's library in 2 Macc. 2.13. More likely is that 'law and prophets' is used here as a title for the entire canon, not just the first two subcollections. The dating is difficult because of the unresolved literary history of the book, and can only be narrowed to between 124 BCE and 70 CE. See H. Attridge, 'Historiography', pp. 320-21.

231. For a probable date of 40 CE for 4 Maccabees, see B.L. Mack and R.E. Murphy, 'Wisdom Literature', in *Early Judaism*, pp. 371-410, here, p. 398.

232. See D.M. Carr, 'Canonization in the Context of Community: An Outline of the Formation of the Tanakh and the Christian Bible', in R.D. Weis and D.M. Carr (eds.), *A Gift of God in Due Season: Essays on Scripture and Community* (Festschrift James A. Sanders; JSOTSup, 225; Sheffield: Sheffield Academic Press, 1996), pp. 22-64, here p. 38. However, the manner in which Carr has organized his

4Q504 (4QDibHamᵃ), an early text, refers to 'Moses and your servants the prophets'.²³⁴ CD 5.21–6.1 mentions 'the commandments of God' (מצות אל) given by 'Moses' and 'the holy anointed ones' (בקודש במשיחו). CD 8.15-16 refers to 'the תורה he commanded by the hand of Moses' and 'the prophets', although here, too, 'Moses and the prophets' is not employed as an exact formula.²³⁵ CD 7.15-17 comes close to such a formula, with reference to 'the books [pl.!] of the law' and 'books [ספרי] of the prophets', but it is 4Q397 [4QMMTᵈ] 14–21.10-11 that gives the precise phrase 'the book of Moses [and] the book[s of the pr]ophets and of Davi[d...]'

Philo's usage still includes the old formula of 'law and words' with the phrase 'the law and the inspired words of the prophets and the psalms'.²³⁶ However, by the time of the New Testament writings the title 'the law and the prophets' has established itself as the standard usage. Although a degree of variety is evident, most of the variations are stylistic variations of the formula 'law and prophets'.²³⁷ This New Testament usage confirms an inherited conception of Old Testament Scripture as 'the law (of Moses) and the words (of the prophets)', a title which was shortened or adapted in various ways by different groups and traditions, but despite such variation continued to convey a particular construal of the literature to which it referred.

citations tends to blur the fact that the phrase 'the law and the prophets' is not prominent at Qumran.

233. See also: תורת מושה in 1QS 5.8; 8.22; CD 15.2, 9, 12; 16.2, 5; תורה in 1QS 8.15; ספר התורה in CD 5.2; cf. 'Moses says' in CD-A 8.14 (quoting Deut. 9.5).

234. 4Q504 (4QDibHamᵃ) 3.12-13. See M. Baillet (ed.), *Qumrân Grotte 4.III (4Q482–4Q520)* (DJD, 7; Oxford: Clarendon Press, 1982), pp. 141-42. Baillet dates the text (p. 137) to c. 150 BCE.

235. Cf. Ezra 9.30; 4Q381 [4QapPsᵇ] 69.4-5, with similar rhetoric, but the plural 'laws'.

236. Philo, *Vit. Cont.* 25: νόμοι καὶ λογία θεσπισθέντα διὰ προφητῶν καὶ ὕμνοι.

237. E.g. 'law and prophets' in Mt. 5.17; 7.12; 11.13; 22.40; Lk. 16.16; Jn 1.45; Acts 13.15, 39-40; 24.14; 28.23; Rom. 3.21; 'Moses and the Prophets' in Lk. 16.29, 31; 24.27; Acts 26.22; 'the law' in Mt. 5.18; 12.5; 22.36; Lk. 2.23, 24, 27, 39; 10.26; 16.17; Jn 1.17; 7.19, 49, 51; 8.5, 17; 'the law of Moses' in Lk. 2.22; 24.44 ('and the prophets and the psalms'); Jn 7.23; Acts 13.39; 15.5; 28.23 ('and the prophets'); 1 Cor. 9.9; Heb. 10.28; 'Moses' in Lk. 5.14; Jn 1.45; 7.22; Acts 15.21; Rom. 10.5, 19; 'the prophets' in Acts 3.18; 13.40; 26.27; 'words of the prophets' in Acts 15.15.

6. *'The Law and the Words' as Canon*

As is the case with תורה in later texts, not every use of דברים suggests a reference to prophetic traditions or Scripture.[238] However, when the Deuteronomists wanted to express their exilic understanding of a cumulative prophetic message, they employed the term דברים to do so. Moreover, when they sought to communicate the totality of Israel's authoritative revelation, they used the terms תורה and דברים as its twin categories. In time, these categories of revelation developed into literary genres.

Thus, within the Old Testament and later interpretive traditions דברים can provide a designation for prophetic scripture, sometimes functioning together with תורה as an umbrella expression for the totality of Israel's cumulative revelation. If דברים is never exclusively employed to mean written scripture, the same is also true of תורה! Still, with this terminology Moses and the prophets are acknowledged as the twin, almost interchangeable, emissaries of a bipartite revelation.[239] Just as the prophets are said to have communicated God's תורה/-ות,[240] Moses can be portrayed as having delivered God's דבר/-ים.[241] Moses is remembered as a writer of the Scriptures;[242] so, too, are the prophets.[243] This pairing of traditions is evident at Qumran and in the New Testament, with their repeated references to 'the law and the prophets' and 'Moses and the prophets'.

238. In fact, sometimes הדברים is simply used as a scribal convention. E.g. Gen. 15.1; 22.1, 20; 39.7; 40.1; Josh. 24.29; 1 Kgs 21.1; Job 42.7; Est. 2.1; 3.1; Ezra 7.1; 2 Chron. 32.1. Note, however, a certain closeness to prophetic tradition in Gen. 15.1 (with דבר-יהוה); Job 42.7.

239. H.-J. Kraus, 'Zum Gesetzesverständnis der nachprophetischen Zeit', *Kairos* 11 (1969), pp. 122-33, here p. 124: 'Die תורה ist דבר. Ihre Gebote und Anordnungen sind דברים. Mose hat in prophetischer Vollmacht die 'Worte Jahwes' übermittelt (Deut. 18.15ff.). Prophetische Dynamik waltet darum in der תורה'.

240. 2 Kgs 17.13; Isa. 1.10; 2.3 (= Mic. 4.2); 5.24; 8.16, 20; 30.8; Jer. 6.19; Hos. 4.6; 8.1; Zech. 7.12; Dan. 9.10; Ezra 9.10-12 (מוצא); Neh. 9.26, 29-30. Cf. 2 Macc. 2.2.

241. Exod. 24.3, 4; 34.27, 28; Deut. 1.1; 5.5 (whether sg. or pl.); 18.18; 30.1; 31.1; 32.45-46; 1 Chron. 15.15; 2 Chron. 35.6; cf. Sir. 46.1.

242. Exod. 24.4; 34.27; Deut. 31.9, 24.

243. Isa. 8.1; 30.8; Jer. 29.1; 30.2; 36.1-32; Ezek. 24.2; 37.16; Hab. 2.2; 1 Chron. 29.29; 2 Chron. 9.29; 12.15; 13.22; 20.34; 26.22; 32.32; 33.18-19; 36.8; cf. 2 Macc. 2.4.

With roots deep within deuteronomistic tradition, the significant pairing of תורה and דברים suggests yet another reason why it is quite unlikely that the Pentateuch was ever the sole 'Bible' of Israel.[244] Rather, the Law and the Prophets took shape together as a *complementary* collection of Scriptures,[245] but one in which the particular witness of each tradition was not simply harmonized with the other.[246] Following R.E. Clements, I would argue historically that written (as well as oral) collections of Law and Prophets existed already by the time of the Deuteronomists (mid-sixth century), with *both* collections expanding and being redacted within a *common overarching tradition.*[247] In my view,

244. For other reasons, see my *The Law and the Prophets: A Study in Old Testament Canon Formation* (FAT, 27; Tübingen: Mohr Siebeck, forthcoming).

245. Carr notes ('Canonization', p. 33) this pairing in Zech. 7.12 and Neh. 9.26, but then argues that '...certain other late prophetic texts include no such explicit coordination of authority between the various types of literature'. Moreover, he claims to locate late prophetic opposition to the Torah, but this claim seems driven by his thesis that different Jewish groups acknowledged different 'canons': i.e. that Temple circles preferred a 'Torah-only' canon, whereas 'opposition' groups favored a bipartite scripture (pp. 48-49). Despite his assertion to the contrary (p. 45), there is in fact much evidence for a consensus about the shape of the canon during the Second Temple period, as we have seen. Furthermore, if the canon itself had been in dispute in this period, rather than its *interpretation*, I find it exceedingly strange that there is no explicit example in Second Temple literature of the canon itself as a subject of disagreement.

246. I suggest a common process of tradition, as R.E. Clements proposes in his *Prophecy and Tradition* (Atlanta: John Knox Press, 1975), pp. 41-57. Clements argues that a form of Deuteronomy and the Deuteronomistic History formed Israel's first 'canon' already by the middle of the sixth century BCE, perhaps even including some of the material later found in the Latter Prophets. This would provide, as Clements also outlines, a persuasive explanation for the non-mention of the Latter Prophets within the Deuteronomistic History (pp. 48-49). The books of Isaiah, Jeremiah and Ezekiel were in 'something very close to their present shape by the fourth century BC', according to Clements, *Isaiah 1–39* (NCB; Grand Rapids: Eerdmans, 1980), p. 8.

247. Clements, *Tradition*, p. 55; Freedman, 'Law', p. 251; Houtman, *Pentateuch*, pp. 423-32; 441-46. Cf. M. Hengel, 'The Scriptures and their Interpretation in Second Temple Judaism', in D.R.G. Beattie and M.J. Mulder (eds.), *The Aramaic Bible: Targums in their Historical Context* (JSOTSup. 166; Sheffield: JSOT Press, 1994), pp. 158-75, esp. p. 160. See the expanded version of his essay, appearing as '"Schriftauslegung" und "Schriftwerdung" in der Zeit des Zweiten Tempels', in M. Hengel and H. Löhr (eds.), *Schriftauslegung im antiken Judentum und*

the categorization and naming of these two biblical collections thus *preceded* their final form instead of the reverse, which has been a standard assumption in critical scholarship at least since H.E. Ryle. With the collection of the Writings, however, it does appear that its categorization and naming took place at a later stage in its development. There are good reasons to conclude that many of the books now in the Writings were originally included within the scope of 'the Prophets', or perhaps more generally within 'the Law and the Prophets' as a whole.[248] Certainly the use of the phrase 'the law and the prophets' cannot be understood as excluding the possibility that such material already existed in written form(s) and possessed a high degree of religious authority.[249] Despite this literary flexibility, however, Israel's Scriptures conveyed the sense of a coherent and complete revelation.[250] As 'Law and Prophets' they embodied a unique and non-negotiable communication of God's will. This conception not only survived to find a place in later tradition, but also shaped and formed that tradition.[251] I would argue that the resultant bipartite witness to revelation is best termed a 'canon' —or perhaps a 'core canon'[252]—because in my view the theological

im Christentum (WUNT, 73; Tübingen: Mohr Siebeck, 1994), pp. 1-71 (I cite the former version).

248. For discussion, see: Barton, *Oracles*, pp. 35-55; Beckwith, 'Formation', pp. 55-58; *idem, Canon*, pp. 138-49; Carr, 'Canonization', pp. 40-41. Beckwith sets an early date (164 BCE) for the 'closing' of the canon in part by arguing that the canonical status of the Writings preceded their reorganization into a separate collection. Cf. Houtman, *Pentateuch*, pp. 441-46.

249. E.g. 2 Macc. 15.9; 4 Macc. 18.10-19; cf. 1 Macc. 2.49-68. See Beckwith, *Canon*, pp. 142-43.

250. Contra H. Gese, *Zur biblischen Theologie: Alttestamentliche Vorträge* (Munich: Chr. Kaiser Verlag, 1977) = *Essays on Biblical Theology* (trans. K. Crim; Minneapolis: Augsburg, 1981), p. 11 (I cite the later version). See Mt. 7.12; Acts 3.18-24!

251. Hengel, 'Scriptures', p. 175: 'In this struggle which probably finds no parallel in earlier history, Judaism "created" the holy scriptures, but it would be even more correct to say that God's word created Israel and the holy scriptures Judaism'. Cf. Childs, *Old Testament Introduction*, p. 40; G. Wanke, 'Bibel, I: Die Entstehung des Alten Testaments als Kanon', in *TRE*, VI, pp. 1-8, esp. p. 7. To give a sense of the debate on this point, Davies (*Scribes*, p. 51) calls this view an unsubstantiated 'theological dogma', and (p. 182) 'nonsense'. Here Davies assumes not only that the establishment of the canon was 'a political act', but one of the crudest sort ('i.e. calculated to create consensus, counter deviance and establish authority').

252. For similar terminology, see: James Barr, *Holy Scripture: Canon, Author-*

profile of this conception was more sharply defined than the diffuse and unthematized term 'Scripture(s)' suggests. Such a pronounced theological profile is the distinctive quality of the development of the Old Testament which the word 'canon' has been used to represent,[253] but which is often underestimated or completely overlooked by treatments of canon that deal predominantly with exclusivity or canonical lists.[254]

This 'core canon' was exclusive in a material sense, but not yet in a formal one. It was not that any writings absent from an official list were *therefore* considered to lack authority, but that the authority of the accepted writings was explained by their conformity within the scope established by the overarching category, 'Law and Prophets'. Such 'partial' exclusivity does not mean that the canon was still somehow

ity, Criticism (Philadelphia: Fortress Press, 1983), pp. 57, 61 ('backbone'); John Barton, *Holy Writings, Sacred Text: The Canon in Early Christianity* (Louisville, KY: Westminster/John Knox Press, 1997), p. 23 ('core', 'central books'); Beckwith, 'Formation', p. 45 ('agreed nucleus'); Carr, 'Canonization', p. 64 ('a similar core of books'); J.J. Collins, 'Before the Canon: Scriptures in Second Temple Judaism', in J.L. Mays, D.L. Petersen and K.H. Richards (eds.), *Old Testament Interpretation: Past, Present and Future* (Festschrift Gene M. Tucker; Nashville: Abingdon Press, 1995), pp. 225-41, p. 232 ('core canon'); J.C. VanderKam, 'Authoritative Literature in the Dead Sea Scrolls', *DSD* 5 (1998), pp. 382-402, p. 401 ('core of books'); A. van der Kooij, 'The Canonization of Ancient Books Kept in the Temple of Jerusalem', in A. van der Kooij and K. van der Toorn (eds.), *Canonization and Decanonization* (Leiden: E.J. Brill, 1998) , pp. 17-40, p. 19 ('a defined, though not necessarily definitive, collection of biblical books'); Z. Zevit, 'The Second–Third Century Canonization of the Hebrew Bible and its Influence on Christian Canonizing', in *Canonization*, pp. 133-60, p. 150 ('implicit canon'). What is interesting here is not any agreement about the precise literary scope of Scripture by a particular date, but the widespread use of (inclusive) canonical language for the period prior to the time at which the canon is thought to have become (exclusively) 'closed'. Even before final 'closure', scriptural scrolls were not just individually authoritative; they formed an authoritative *collection*. This collective aspect is a crucial connotation of the term 'canon', which the term 'authoritative scripture' lacks.

253. Childs, *OT as Scripture*, pp. 96-99.

254. E.g., Barton's formulation (*Oracles*, p. 91): 'There was "Scripture", but no canon; books other than the Torah were neither grouped together nor listed in any particular way, except for some specific purpose, apologetic or mnemonic; and almost any book could be referred to as the work of a "prophet"'. Non-pentateuchal 'scripture' is also characterized by Barton as 'one single amorphous pool of material, often called "Prophets"' (57).

'open',[255] but instead that the authority of the books was first established by material rather than formal characteristics. This material conception of 'canon' resulted, as might be expected, in a large collection of undisputed books, together with a small number of disputed books.[256] The formal conception of 'canon' as a fixed text or exclusive list of books does not become evident until the early first century CE.[257]

Thus, the Old Testament canon is no creation of the fourth century CE. Already in the Persian period a 'core canon' had existed as a kind of rule-of-faith, understood and referred to as 'the law (of Moses) and the words (of the Prophets)'. It was the Deuteronomists of the exilic period who formulated this conceptual framework and began the work of assembling scriptural materials *accordingly*. From that point on, Israel's 'canon' was not a 'loosely defined collection of Scriptures',[258] but a diverse collection of authoritative Scriptures which nevertheless communicated a sharply defined theological profile, unity and claim.

255. *Contra* Maier ('Frage', p. 146) and Wanke ('Bibel', p. 1).
256. Beckwith, *Canon*, pp. 274-76.
257. Cross, *Epic*, p. 223.
258. *Contra* McDonald ('Testament', p. 325).

DEATH SHALL BE THEIR SHEPHERD: AN INTERPRETATION
OF PSALM 49.15 IN THE MASORETIC TEXT AND THE SEPTUAGINT

Staffan Olofsson

1

Psalm 49 belongs to the category of the wisdom psalms. In most wisdom psalms the general themes of morality based on the wisdom tradition are developed (e.g. Ps. 1). Psalm 49, on the other hand, is concerned with a single but problematic issue, defined in v. 5 as מָשָׁל 'proverb, wisdom saying' and as a חִידָה 'riddle'[1] or, rather, 'hard or perplexing question'.[2]

> אַטֶּה לְמָשָׁל אָזְנִי אֶפְתַּח בְּכִנּוֹר חִידָתִי
> I will incline my ear to a proverb;
> I will solve my riddle to the music of the harp.

Even the text of some parts of this psalm can be characterized as a riddle, which is far from easy to solve. What is the perplexing question, what is the riddle in this text? It is death, 'death in the context of human power and wealth'.[3]

This psalm reflects a kind of wisdom literature containing works which explore 'the difficult intellectual and theological issues raised in moral wisdom',[4] in contrast to a category in which the moral essence of

---

1. See, e.g., Judg. 14.12, 'Samson said to them, "Let me now put a riddle [חִידָה] to you; if you can explain it to me, within the seven days of the feast, and find it out, then I will give you thirty linen garments and thirty festal garments'. The translations of Bible passages in this article are taken from NRSV if not otherwise stated, and the Bible references are given according to the numbering of MT.

2. See 1 Kgs 10.1, 'When the queen of Sheba heard of the fame of Solomon (fame due to the name of the LORD), she came to test him with hard questions' (בְּחִידוֹת).

3. P.C. Craigie, *Psalms 1–50* (WBC, 19; Waco, TX: Word Books, 1983), p. 358. I am much indebted to Craigie for the overall characterization of the psalm.

4. Craigie, *Psalms 1–50*, p. 358.

the wisdom tradition is expressed in a didactic form, for example, the book of Proverbs.[5] Psalm 49 has some similarity with the critical wisdom; the kind of wisdom literature best represented by themes from the books of Job and Ecclesiastes as well as by other wisdom psalms. The closest parallel is perhaps Job 21.7-15, where the empirical problem of the apparent success and prosperity of the wicked and rich is raised, even though the same problem is also urgent in some other wisdom psalms, for example, Psalm 73.

Psalm 49 seems to be a late psalm, certainly postexilic and perhaps late postexilic. It may very well be one of the latest poems in the book of Psalms.[6] This has some bearing on the interpretation of the verse under consideration. The intellectual milieu seems to be one of critical discussion, perhaps related to certain closed circles of the Temple hierarchy.[7] The Temple theologians seem to be close to the *anawim*, 'the poor',[8] people who regarded themselves as persecuted by rich and influential people, but who had their security in God and expected help from him.[9] Thus, rich people are looked upon with great suspicion and even contempt. There are some parallels to this attitude in the book of Psalms, but even more so in certain books which belong to the intertestamental literature.

The psalm begins with an introduction (vv. 2-5), which is addressed to all, although the specific addressees are probably those who are poor and afflicted. Two main sections of the psalm follow: (a) vv. 6-13, which is concerned with the limitations of wealth; and (b) vv. 14-21, which is related to the destinies of the rich and the poor. Both of them conclude with a refrain (vv. 13, 21). The two refrains are similar, but they are not identical, MT has לִין in v. 13, and בִּין in v. 21.[10] The refrains

---

5.   Craigie, *Psalms 1–50*, p. 358. Thus we are far away from the kind of riddle posed by Samson in the book of Judges. See n. 1.

6.   See, e.g., A.A. Anderson, *The Book of Psalms* (NCB; 2 vols.; London: Oliphants, 1972), p. 373. Others suggest that it belongs to the first part of the fourth century. See, e.g., P. Casetti, *Gibt es ein Leben vor dem Tod? Eine Auslegung von Psalm 49* (OBO, 44; Göttingen: Vandenhoeck & Ruprecht, 1982), p. 285. See also the discussion on pp. 283-85.

7.   See, e.g., Casetti, *Leben*, pp. 281-83.

8.   Kraus, *Psalmen* (BKAT, 15.1-2; 2 vols; Neukirchen–Vluyn: Neukirchener Verlag, 1978), p. 519.

9.   See, e.g., Kraus, *Psalmen*, pp. 108-11.

10.   Most modern translations emend to לִין with a few MSS in v. 21. See, e.g., NRSV, 'Man does not remain through the night, he is like the beasts that perish'

give expression to the essence of wisdom on the problem at hand.[11]

The section 49.14-21 is concerned with 'The folly of confidence in wealth'. The wisdom teacher turns his attention to the way of life of wealthy persons. Their quest for wealth as a safeguard against death is revealed as folly. The most common interpretation of MT is that they have no hope of escaping from death, since death (not Yahweh) will be their shepherd and they will be consumed by Sheol. In contrast to this, the fate of the psalmist is presented; God will in some way ransom his soul from Sheol. So much for the introduction of Psalm 49. I will now turn to methodological presuppositions in interpreting the LXX version, and especially discuss the relation between philological analysis and the so-called theological exegesis.

2

It cannot be excluded that even in the philological analysis of the Hebrew the translator was, without being aware of it, influenced by the religious milieu of his time as well as by his own religious convictions.[12] Particularly when he came across words and expressions which he only vaguely comprehended, his choice of equivalents may have been affected by what he regarded as a reasonable interpretation from a theological point of view. This type of theological influence is more or less inherent in the translation process per se and I do not regard it as manifest theological exegesis, which is reflected in the choice of equivalents, that is, cases where the translation is more influenced by the theology of the translator than by the meaning of the words in their context. It is, of course, a complicated or perhaps impossible task to distinguish

(vv. 13, 21). But the distinction is probably original. See, e.g., Craigie, *Psalms 1–50*, p. 358.

11. See, e.g., Craigie, *Psalms 1–50*, p. 358; Anderson, *Psalms*, p. 374.

12. See the competent methodological discussion by M. Rösel in *Übersetzung als Vollendung der Auslegung: Studien zur Genesis-Septuaginta* (BZAW, 223; Berlin: W. de Gruyter, 1994), pp. 16-24. I write 'the translator' in the singular and this is the accepted view; the LXX Psalms appear to be the work of a single translator, because no significant differences in the vocabulary or style within the Psalter can be seen. See, e.g., A. Soffer, 'The Treatment of Anthropomorphisms and Anthropopathisms in the Septuagint of Psalms', *HUCA* 38 (1957), p. 417. But the proposal of Schaper is in fact also possible. He suggests that it was a joint enterprise. Schaper, *Eschatology*, p. 33.

between conscious theological exegesis and mere theological influence, since it presupposes discernment of the translator's intentions.[13]

A fairly recent monograph of Joachim Schaper, *Eschatology in the Greek Psalter*, deals with some important aspects of the interpretative character of LXX Psalms. Discussions concerning the methods of dealing with and describing the interpretative character of LXX texts are always of great interest. Schaper is certainly right in his statement that an exclusive preoccupation with translation technique does not lead to a full understanding of the Septuagint translation and, furthermore, that the interpretative dimension of the book of Psalms is an interesting area of research. Certainly LXX can be studied as a document in its own right, a document that in some respects reflects, its own cultural and historical milieu.[14] On the other hand, I disagree with him in his criticism of the methods of other LXX scholars. In particular, his criticism of the method of scholars dealing with translation technique, not least the so-called Finnish school, misses the point. His description implies that the underlying proposition of these scholars is that the translator is not 'in any way...influenced by his religious and general cultural environment'.[15] Such statements blur necessary distinctions. Furthermore, when Schaper's own method is applied to specific texts in the Psalter the result is far from convincing.

I will thus try to make clear my own methodological presuppositions. The fact that the translator is influenced by the interpretation prevalent in his lifetime and by his cultural and religious environment does not mean that a modern scholar is entitled to suggest from differences between the meaning of the MT and the Greek translation and the use of certain Greek terms in Jewish interpretations of the Hebrew Bible that the translator engages in theological exegesis. That is especially the case

13. See S. Olofsson, *God Is my Rock: A Study of Translation Technique and Theological Exegesis in the Septuagint* (ConBOT, 31; Stockholm: Almqvist & Wiksell, 1990), pp. 11-12.

14. For a stimulating discussion concerning the method of dealing with the interpretative character of the LXX, a discussion that takes the translation technique as the point of departure, see C. Boyd-Taylor, 'A Place in the Sun: The Interpretative Significance of LXX-Psalm 18:5c', *BIOSCS* 31 (1998), pp. 71-105. I got this interesting article into my hand when my paper was near completion.

15. Schaper, *Eschatology*, p. 21. See also his description on pp. 16, 136. Perhaps the Finnish scholars simply do not address the question because the main object of their translation technical studies is the groundwork for the preparation of a syntax of the Septuagint.

if the passages under discussion are in line with the translation equivalents otherwise used by this translator or other translators in the LXX.[16] Thus if the choice of the Greek future for the Hebrew present tense (a standard counterpart in the LXX Psalms) in one passage implies eschatological expectations, this cannot be demonstrated by the choice of tense, since the same interpretation ought then to be applied to the other passages as well.[17]

In my view, what is really essential and what I have tried to make clear on several occasions is that it is only after an investigation of the translation technique, the competence of the translator, the *Vorlage* of his translation, that one is in a position to discuss theological influences seriously.[18] A similar methodological approach is described in a more eloquent way by Albert Pietersma in his review of Joachim Schaper's monograph, *Eschatology in the Greek Psalter*. He emphasizes that if one picks out standard equations in the LXX it is 'not acceptable methodologically, that one (or several) instances be given special treatment and be elevated to a higher level of interpretation...in distinction from the more mundane text-criticism'.[19]

My methodological proposals do not presuppose that the theological convictions of the LXX translator, whose work we investigate, have not affected his translation in any way. They only suggest that in order to

16. Rösel makes an effort to understand the Greek equivalents from more or less contemporary Greek texts. He is to be commended for his well-informed discussion and his reluctance to suggest that his interpretation is the only one possible. But his work also shows that it is a precarious task to suggest an adequate background for the choice of equivalents. See, e.g., the relevant criticism of Rösel, *Übersetzung*, as regards terminological connections with Timaeus of Plato and the interpretation of Gen. 1–2 with reference to the exegesis by Philo in A. van der Kooij, 'Review of Rösel, *Übersetzung*', BO 54.3-4 (1997), p. 458. See also R. Hanhart, 'The Translation of the Septuagint in Light of Earlier Tradition and Subsequent Influences', G.J. Brooke and B. Lindars (eds.), *Septuagint Scrolls and Cognate Writings: Papers Presented to the International Symposium on the Septuagint and its Relation to the Dead Sea Scrolls and other Writings, Manchester 1990* (SBLSCS, 33; Atlanta: Scholars Press, 1992), pp. 339-79 (351).

17. See, e.g., Rösel, *Übersetzung*, p. 19, who says that 'Standardübersetzungen im Normalfall nicht theologisch auszuwerten sind'; H.C. Knuth, *Zur Auslegungsgeschichte von Psalm 6* (BGBE, 11; Tübingen: J.C.B. Mohr [Paul Siebeck], 1971), p. 386.

18. See the discussion in Olofsson, *Rock*, pp. 5-9. See, e.g., also Rösel, *Übersetzung*, pp. 21-23 and Boyd-Taylor, 'A Place in the Sun', pp. 71-105.

19. A. Pietersma, 'Review of Schaper, *Eschatology*', BO 54.1-2 (1997), p. 187.

make that proposition probable one has first to take a look at more obvious possibilities of interpretation, since theological exegesis is not the primary aim of a translator. I think that this applies to most of the translators of the LXX, but in any case it certainly applies to the translator of the book of Psalms.

The burden of proof is thus on the scholar who suggests that an interpretation of the translator of the Hebrew text at variance with the translation of the same or a similar Hebrew text in a modern translation is based on the theological *Tendenz* of the translator. Thus, 'The exegete of the Greek thus needs to *prove* that the translation says something other than the original'.[20] One can perhaps make some qualifications. The exegete needs to *prove* that the translation says something that differs from the translator's philological understanding of the *Vorlage* in front of him.

The method is thus not negative *a priori* towards any suggestion that theological expectations of the translator influenced his translations, far from it.[21] Theological influences can perhaps be illustrated by the translator of the book of Isaiah, but in a literalist translation like the book of Psalms one must be very cautious not to indulge in speculations that are contrary to the whole attitude of the translator.[22]

Thus, it is not easy to picture a translator who at the same time is extremely careful to follow the very order of the words in his Hebrew *Vorlage*, who employs stereotype lexical equivalents, and at the same time suggest that he is involved in a theological rewriting of the Hebrew Psalter. I admit that it is possible to combine a literal rendering with interpretative additions in the translation, since this can be seen in some of the targums, but in that case the *Tendenz* is very easy to recognize. The translator of the LXX Psalms, however, does not seem to have much in common with the *Targum of Psalms*.[23] The choice of

20. Pietersma, 'Review of Schaper, *Eschatology*', p. 187.

21. See, e.g., the discussion in S. Olofsson, *The LXX Version: A Guide to the Translation Technique of the LXX* (ConBOT, 30; Stockholm: Almqvist & Wiksell, 1990), pp. 1-5.

22. A simple question of Satterthwaite in his otherwise positive review of Schaper's work is right to the point: 'Given the kind of document the LXX Psalms is, then, how accurately can we define its theological outlook and, hence, its place among emergent theologies of the period?' P.E. Satterthwaite, 'Review of Schaper, *Eschatology*', *VT* 49 (1998), p. 286.

23. Apart from that, the *Targum of Psalms* is not really the best comparison text, since it is late.

equivalents in the LXX Psalter and other versions of the Psalms may, on the other hand, sometimes have inspired the targumic tradition.[24]

The reluctance to posit a theological motivation for the ordinary choice of equivalents in LXX is based on the generally accepted criticism of the methods of *TWNT*,[25] where the Greek words often are given meanings which are not rooted in the context of the given word but the meaning of the word in other contexts.[26] There is therefore every reason to show great care and only present an interpretation of the Greek that is in accordance with the exact wording in the context and with the Hebrew *Vorlage*. In any case it is much better to err on this side, that is, to be overcautious, rather than turn directly from the Greek word in LXX to uses of this word in other literary or cultural contexts. Furthermore, the ground work done in translation technique may later on be used for relevant discussions concerning the interpretative character of the LXX.

Admittedly, the Greek text in itself might, for the reader who is not acquainted with the Hebrew, lead to interpretations which were prevalent in his time and in his milieu even though they are not the interpretations of the translator. The interpretation of the ordinary reader is, contrary to that of the translator, not an understanding of a Hebrew text but only of the Greek translation.[27] One ought to base the understanding of the translator's exegesis of the Hebrew text on what he intended and disregard the fact that the Greek text in itself creates a potential for different interpretations.[28]

---

24. See, e.g., J.P. Brown, 'The Septuagint as a Source of Loan-Words in the Targums', *Bib* 70 (1989), pp. 194-216.

25. See especially E. Tov, 'Die Septuaginta in ihrem theologischen und traditionsgeschichtlichen Verhältnis zur hebräischen Bibel', in M. Klopfenstein *et al.*, *Mitte der Schrift? Ein jüdisch-christliches Gespräch. Texte des Berner Symposions vom 6.-12. Januar 1985* (Judaica et Christiana, 11; Bern: Peter Lang, 1987), pp. 237-50. See also R. Hanhart, 'Jüdische Tradition und christliche Interpretation', in A.M. Ritter (ed.), *Kerygma und Logos* (Festschrift C. Andresen; Göttingen: Vandenhoeck & Ruprecht, 1979), pp. 288-97 (288-89); Hanhart, 'Earlier Tradition', pp. 341-45.

26. This is in line with the understanding of Rösel (*Übersetzung*, pp. 22-24). That is why he stresses that the connotations of the Greek words must be investigated with great care and precision (p. 24).

27. See especially E. Tov, 'Three Dimensions of LXX Words', *RB* 83 (1976), pp. 529-30, 532, 536, 541, and the discussion in Olofsson, *LXX Version*, pp. 39-40.

28. I of course admit the difficulties with the term, 'the intention of the trans-

At the same time, the possibility that the theological outlook of the translator guided his interpretation is of course much greater in places where the Hebrew is corrupt or very opaque, even for the modern exegete.[29] When the translator has gone as far as he can with the help of his basic understanding of the Hebrew words he will probably try to make some sense out of the text. In that perspective one must take into account the cultural and religious milieu in which the psalm was composed and the milieu in which the translator lived in order to suggest theological tendencies and implications.

3

Now I will turn to the passage that is the object of my presentation. The most problematic text in the psalm is v. 15. Kraus's description may stand as an exponent for the opinion of most scholars: 'The text in v. 15 is irreparably corrupt. Only the first words can tentatively be reconstructed.'[30] Compare A.A. Anderson: 'The text of this verse is rather corrupt, especially the second half'.[31] With this state of affairs in mind I will not try to suggest a plausible original text nor a wholesale interpretation of the text in MT, but rather make some suggestions concerning possible interpretations of certain words in MT. My main object is,

---

lators', but I prefer in any case to use this term in order to make plain the distinction between the understanding of the Greek in relation to its *Vorlage* and all other interpretations of the Greek text that are possible if it is looked upon as a document in its own right and not a translation. See, e.g., Tov, 'Three Dimensions', pp. 529-532, 540-544 and the discussion in Olofsson, *LXX Version*, pp. 39-40. By the term 'intention' I by no means intend to engage in some sort of psycho-linguistic analysis. What we have, in the best case, is the text of the translator. See Boyd-Taylor, 'A Place in the Sun', p. 91 n. 40. See also. H.C. Knuth, who in his investigation of the interpretation of Ps. 6 always makes a distinction between the interpretation of the readers of the LXX and the intention of the translator. For example, he remarks concerning the rendering of לַמְנַצֵּחַ by εἰς τὸ τέλος that 'Man kann von der Wortbedeutung τέλος aus und ebenso von der Phrase εἰς τὸ τέλος keinerlei Rückschlüsse darauf ziehen, was die Übersetzer mit diesen Wörtern im Sinne hatten oder unbewußt in den Text eintrugen. Das wäre alles Spekulation' (Knuth, *Psalm 6*, p. 388).

29. In this regard I fully agree with Schaper. See, e.g., Schaper, *Eschatology*, pp. 136-37. See also Boyd-Taylor, 'A Place in the Sun', p. 73 n. 4, who suggests that 'it is best to begin by examining localized perturbations in the translator's method'.

30. Kraus, *Psalmen*, p. 517.

31. Anderson, *Psalms*, I, p. 378.

however, to try to comprehend how the LXX translator understood the Hebrew text.

First we shall present the text of v. 15 in MT:

כַּצֹּאן לִשְׁאוֹל שַׁתּוּ מָוֶת יִרְעֵם וַיִּרְדּוּ בָם יְשָׁרִים לַבֹּקֶר
וְצִירָם [K] וְצוּרָם [Q] לְבַלּוֹת שְׁאוֹל מִזְּבֻל לוֹ:

It is very hard to translate without emendations. A tentative translation, including alternative meanings suggested by modern scholars, could be as follows:

Like sheep they are appointed; Death shall shepherd them.[33] The upright shall have dominion over them in the morning, and their form/idol [K] form/rock [Q] shall be consumed in Sheol away from his palatial abode.[33]

My interest in this verse is partly based on the existence of the word צוּר (Q), which *could* be a metaphorical epithet for the God of Israel or a foreign god, even though it is mostly understood as a term for 'figure, form'. This is a complicated passage, since I am uncertain if צוּר is to

32. Concerning 'appointed' see, e.g., P.R. Raabe, *Psalm Structures: A Study of Psalms with Refrains* (JSOTSup, 104; Sheffield: JSOT Press, 1990), p. 74. Craigie suggests instead, with reference to Ugaritic, 'shipped' (*Psalms 1–50*, pp. 356-57). See also A. van Selms, 'Yammu's Dethronement by Baal: An Attempt to Reconstruct Texts UT 129, 137 and 68', *UF* 2 (1970), p. 266, who suggests 'like sheep they are dragged to the nether-world'.

33. Instead of 'shall have dominion over them', Raabe has the translation, 'the upright will trample upon them in the morning'. Raabe, *Psalm Structures*, p. 74. It is based on the use of רדה in Mal. 3.21. Raabe regards שְׁאוֹל as subject of the clause and suggests that מִן refers to the palatial abode of שְׁאוֹל, 'Their form is for consumption by Sheol from its palatial abode' (*Psalm Structures*, p. 76). This is an interesting suggestion, but it presupposes that he is to be understood more or less as a god with a זְבֻל 'palatial abode', and 'no deity Sheol has ever been attested' (H.M. Barstad, 'Sheol', *DDD*, col. 1455). See also the interpretation of J.C. de Moor, 'Studies in the New Alphabetic Texts from Ras Shamra I', *UF* 1 (1969), p. 187 n. 148: 'and their form will be devoured, Sheol will dominate it'. Another suggestion worth mentioning is, 'so that his habitation does not exist any more'. See F.E. König, *Historisch-kritisches Lehrgebäude der hebräischen Sprache* (Leipzig, 1881–97), §406p. The term of Raabe, 'palatial abode', is better than the simple, 'habitation', since it is not an ordinary 'habitation'. Raabe, *Psalm Structures*, p. 76. See G.V. Smith, 'זבל', *NIDOTE*, I, p. 1074. Another rendering is 'lofty abode'. See Craigie, *Psalms 1–50*, p. 356. The meaning 'princely estate' from Ugaritic is suggested in, e.g., J. Barr, *Comparative Philology and the Text of the OT* (Oxford: Clarendon Press, 1968), p. 326. זְבֻל has also been interpreted as a name of a god. See later on in this article.

be regarded as a divine epithet here and, furthermore, because of the text-critical decision involved, that is, the distinction between K and Q.[34]

The rendering of this verse in LXX is as a whole in accord with the choice of equivalents in other parts of LXX Psalms, thus the literalistic approach of the translator as well as his standard equivalents are as a whole followed. The rendering of צוּר by βοήθεια is an exception to this literalistic approach, but, on the other hand, it is in line with the translator's equivalents for metaphorical divine epithets. In this case it is a so-called alternative rendering.[35]

Most modern translations presuppose certain emendations and are thereby able to give the text an adequate meaning. Thus, for example, NRSV: 'Like sheep they are appointed for Sheol; Death shall be their shepherd; straight to the grave they descend, and their form shall waste away; Sheol shall be their home', is probably based on the text וְיֵרְדוּ בְמֵישָׁרִים לַקֶּבֶר instead of MT וַיִּרְדּוּ בָם יְשָׁרִים לַבֹּקֶר. Furthermore, it evidently suggests מִזְּבֻל, 'home, habitation', instead of מִזְּבֻל, and לָמוֹ rather than לֹו. Other modern translations have different renderings.

> Like sheep they are herded into the nether world; death is their shepherd, and the upright rule over them. Quickly their form is consumed; the nether world is their palace (NAB).

> They are penned in Sheol like sheep, Death will lead them to pasture, and those who are honest will rule over them. In the morning no trace of them will be found, Sheol will be their home (NJB).

> Like sheep they head for Sheol; with death as their shepherd, they go straight down to the grave. Their bodies, stripped of all honour, waste away in Sheol (REB).

The translation of LXX is as follows

ὡς πρόβατα ἐν ᾅδῃ ἔθεντο, θάνατος ποιμανεῖ [2110] αὐτούς·
καὶ κατακυριεύσουσιν αὐτῶν οἱ εὐθεῖς τὸ πρωΐ,
καὶ ἡ βοήθεια αὐτῶν παλαιωθήσεται ἐν τῷ ᾅδῃ ἐκ τῆς δόξης αὐτῶν
(Rahlf's text, except ποιμανεῖ from 2110).

> Like sheep they are laid in Hades. Death shall shepherd them. And the upright shall have dominion over them in the morning, and their help shall wax old in Hades, away from their glory.[36]

---

34. See the comment in Schaper, *Eschatology*, p. 61 n. 241.
35. See, e.g., Olofsson, *Rock*, pp. 44-45.
36. See, e.g., Boyd-Taylor, 'A Place in the Sun', p. 85.

The support for the future, ποιμανεῖ, in 2110 as well as the translation of aspect-tense in LXX Psalms, suggest that ποιμανεῖ, rather than ποιμαίνει, is the Old Greek.[37] The picture in the text is not that of rich persons who are regarded as sheep ready for slaughter. It is rather the question of the shepherd, who is usually employed as a metaphor of protection and safety, who is now, as in Ps. 2.9 and Mic. 5.5, used ironically as a metaphor of death; that is, death is described as a shepherd, death which was the very thing that the shepherd should protect his sheep against. It is not Yahweh who is their shepherd (cf. Ps. 23) or their king, but Death.[38] This shepherd does not help them 'to lie down in green pastures' (Ps. 23.2), but he leads them right down to Sheol. Thus irony seems very much to be at play here.

The rendering in LXX here is as a whole in accord with the choice of equivalents in other parts of LXX Psalms. כְּצֹאן is translated by ὡς πρόβατα: thus the collective צֹאן has an equivalent in the plural. The LXX translator recognized that צֹאן is used here as a collective term. צֹאן appears 16 times in the book of Psalms. It is always translated by πρόβατα. שְׁאוֹל is invariably rendered by ᾅδης in LXX Psalms and it is a consistent equivalent in LXX as a whole.[39]

שַׁתּוּ is derived from שָׁתַת by the Masoretes. שָׁתַת is probably understood as a by-form of שִׁית, but with intransitive meaning,[40] 'sit down, encamp',[41] or rather, 'to be set' or 'to be appointed'.[42] The LXX translator renders שַׁתּוּ by ἔθεντο (thus also Aquila), that is, he regards it as a form of שִׁית. This means that either the Masoretic tradition of שָׁתַת and שִׁית as two variants with the same meaning was also known for the

---

37. See the argumentation in A. Pietersma, 'Ra 2110 (P. Bodmer XXIV) and the Text of the Greek Psalter', in D. Fraenkel, U. Quast and J.W. Wevers (eds.), *Studien zur Septuaginta: Robert Hanhart zu Ehren* (MSU, 20; Göttingen: Vandenhoeck & Ruprecht, 1990), p. 275 and the positive evaluation of this proposal by Schaper (*Eschatology*, p. 62 n. 245).

38. See especially the discussion in Casetti, *Leben*, pp. 128-32.

39. See Ps. 6.6; 9.18; 16.10; 18.6; 30.4; 31.18; 49.15 (2×), 16; 55.16; 86.13; 88.4; 89.49; 116.3; 139.8; 141.7. In MT as a whole it occurs 65 times.

40. The possibility of an intransitive force of שִׁית, שָׁתַת seems to be confirmed by Casetti. See Casetti, *Leben*, pp. 118-19 nn. 186-87.

41. See, e.g., F. Baethgen, *Psalmen* (HAT, 2.2; Göttingen: Vandenhoeck & Ruprecht, 3rd edn, 1904), p. 144.

42. See, e.g., Raabe, *Psalm Structures*, p. 74.

translator or that he read שָׁתוּ.[43] The same translation also occurs in Ps.
73.9 (שָׁתוּ, ἔθεντο).[44] θάνατος is a standard equivalent of מָוֶת in LXX
Psalms as well as in the rest of the LXX.

רָעָה is always, except in 80.14, translated with ποιμαίνειν in LXX
Psalms.[45] In 45 out of 47 occurrences, where ποιμαίνειν has a Hebrew
Vorlage it renders רָעָה. The only exceptions are Ps. 2.9 and 48.15.[46]

וַיִּרְדּוּ בָם יְשָׁרִים לַבֹּקֶר is regarded as corrupt by most modern scholars.[47] וַיִּרְדּוּ בָם is adequately translated with καὶ κατακυριεύσουσιν
αὐτῶν. וַיִּרְדּוּ is a form of רָדָה qal, but it is often emended to וְיֵרְדוּ, that
is, it is based on √ירד.[48] This is only a question of pointing. The translator followed in any case the Masoretes and derived the consonantal
text of MT from רָדָה. רָדָה qal (68.28; 72.8; 110.2) is always translated
by κατακυριεύειν in the Psalter. The translator of the Psalter had thus
an adequate understanding of the meaning of the word רָדָה,[49] even
though he wrongly derives רֹדֶם from √רדם rather than from √רדה in
68.28.[50]

יְשָׁרִים is literally rendered by οἱ εὐθεῖς.[51] εὐθύς with cognates
εὐθύς,[52] εὐθής,[53] with cognates εὐθύτης,[54] κατορθοῦν, 119.128 (יָשַׁר

43. See, e.g., D.R. Kittel, *Die Psalmen* (KAT, 13.3; Leipzig & Erlangen:
Deichertsche Verlagsbuchhandlung, 4th edn, 1922), p. 181; C.A. Briggs, *A Critical
and Exegetical Commentary on the Book of Psalms*, I (ICC; Edinburgh: T. & T.
Clark, 1906–1907), p. 413.

44. See, e.g., F. Buhl, *Psalmerne, oversatte og fortolkade af Frants Buhl* (Copen-
hagen: Gyldendalske Boghandels Forlag, 1900), p. 338.

45. Ps. 23.1; 28.9; 37.3; 49.15; 78.71, 72; 80.2.

46. Aquila, in contrast, has νεμήσει and Symmachus νεμήσεται. C. Estin, *Les
Psautiers de Jérôme: A la lumière des traductions juives antérieures* (CBL, 15;
Rome: Brepols, Turnhout, 1984), p. 96.

47. See, e.g., Kraus, *Psalmen*, p. 517; Anderson, *Psalms*, pp. 374, 379.

48. This emendation is mentioned in BHS and followed by, e.g., D.W. Thomas,
The Text of the Revised Psalter (London: SPCK, 1963), p. 18.

49. According to Raabe, רָדָה has instead the meaning 'to tread, to trample',
with reference to Mal. 3.21. See Raabe, *Psalm Structures*, p. 74. But there is in fact
the verb עָסַס employed.

50. The translator of the Psalter thus did not employ the equivalent used in
Genesis, ἄρχειν, 1.16, 28, but a term which renders the synonymous כָּבַשׁ in Gen.
1.28 וְכִבְשֻׁהָ וּרְדוּ, καὶ κατακυριεύσατε αὐτῆς καὶ ἄρχετε.

51. In modern translations or commentaries בָּם יְשָׁרִים is often emended to
בְּמֵישָׁרִים (see, e.g., Thomas, *Revised Psalter*, p. 18) or בַּמִּישָׁרִים (BHS), or בְּשָׁרָם
(BHS).

52. יָשַׁר, 7.11; 11.2; 19.9; 32.11; 33.1; 36.11; 37.14; 49.15; 64.11; 94.15; 97.11;

piel) and κατεύθυνον 5.9 (יָשַׁר hiphil), is the most frequent rendering of √יָשַׁר in LXX as a whole and in the book of Psalms. לַבֹּקֶר has τὸ πρωί as counterpart in LXX. Thus the LXX translator has a literal rendering of MT.[55] This lexical equivalent is in fact always employed in the book of Psalms and the same is true for LXX as a whole.

The LXX text seems so far to be a literal translation of a Hebrew text akin to MT, without a specific interpretation being pin-pointed. It is in fact as difficult to understand as the Hebrew.

It is very difficult, to say the least, to make a reasonable interpretation of וַיִּרְדּוּ בָם יְשָׁרִים לַבֹּקֶר.[56] In order to make some sense out of MT, Ziegler has pointed out that the morning is the 'proper time for divine help in the OT'.[57] Ziegler's thesis was anticipated by H. Gunkel and F. Notscher. The idea that God helps 'in the morning' is 'clothed either in the form of a statement of faith or of a prayer of confidence in the Psalms and in Psalm-like songs of the OT'.[58] Even so, it is not at all a certain interpretation, since the word 'help' only occurs in Ps. 46.6 of the Bible passages under consideration.[59] But the morning can perhaps also be understood as the time for the administration of justice, perhaps implying that the righteous rule over the wicked.[60]

Others suggest that there is a connection between Israel's historical experiences and the help of God 'in the morning', because it cannot be

107.7, 42; 111.1; 112.2, 4; 125.4; 140.14; יָשָׁר, 25.21; מִישׁוֹר, 27.11; 143.10; מֵישָׁרִים, 58.2.

53. יָשַׁר, 25.8; 33.4; 92.16; 119.137.

54. יָשַׁר, 11.7; 37.37; 111.8; יָשָׁר, 119.7; מִישׁוֹר, 26.12; 45.7; 67.5; מֵישָׁרִים, 9.9; 17.2; 75.3; 96.10; 98.9; 99.4.

55. לַבֹּקֶר in Ps. 49.15 is often emended to, e.g., לַקֶּבֶר 'to the grave' (see, e.g., Thomas, *Revised Psalter*, p. 18) or לִרְקֹד, 'to rot' (both *BHS*).

56. See, e.g., Raabe, *Psalm Structures*, pp. 74-76.

57. J. Ziegler, 'Die Hilfe Gottes "am Morgen"' (BBB, 1; Bonn, 1950), p. 282. This concept does not belong in the realm of the philological 'meanings'. See L. Delekat, *Asylie und Schutzorakel am Zionheiligtum: Eine Untersuchung zu den privaten Feindpsalmen* (Leiden: E.J. Brill, 1967), p. 9. It is thus not an attempt to interpret the meaning of בֹּקֶר as such, but to explain how it is used in certain contexts.

58. See C. Barth, 'בֹּקֶר', *TDOT*, II, p. 226, who refers to Ziegler, 'Hilfe', p. 281.

59. See Barth, 'בֹּקֶר', p. 227.

60. See, e.g., Schaper, *Eschatology*, p. 60. It is in fact only Jer. 21.12 and Ps. 101.8 that can be interpreted in this way. But these passages have no reference whatsoever to an eschatological judgment. Cf. Schaper, *Eschatology*, p. 60 with footnotes.

excluded that Ps. 46.6 refers to the liberation of Jerusalem in 701 BCE (2 Kgs 19.35; Isa. 37.36), and the miracle at the Red Sea (Exod. 14.30).[61] But the help in fact occurred during the night (בַּלַּיְלָה הַהוּא), before the dawn, and what happens in the morning (בַּבֹּקֶר) is that the Israelites recognize that the Assyrians 'were all dead bodies' (2 Kgs 19.35 = Isa. 37.36). Furthermore, the other passages which were put forward as an argument in favour of the motif of 'help in the morning' (1 Sam. 11.1-13; 2 Chron. 20.1-30; 2 Kgs 3.9-20) are unsatisfactory, because 1 Sam. 11.9 and 2 Chron. 20.16 do not employ the phrase בַּבֹּקֶר but only מָחָר 'tomorrow'. In both passages the rescue comes in the middle of the day.[62] Only 2 Kgs 3.20 refers to בַּבֹּקֶר 'in the morning'. Furthermore, in Ps. 49.15 it is the upright, who will rule over or trample on the rich and wealthy, not God who will intervene on behalf of the upright.

An interpretation of the passage based on the expectation of eschatological judgment is not probable in this psalm, and would be more or less without parallel in the Old Testament.[63] A more adequate interpretation of MT seems to be that the upright will trample upon the graves of the wicked, with reference to Mal. 3.21.[64] The wicked become corpses and these corpses (in their graves) are trampled upon by the righteous. It is also in line with v. 20 that the wicked 'will go to the generation of his fathers, who will never more see the light'. On the other hand, the use of רְדָה in the Old Testament rather suggests the meaning 'rule, dominate',[65] and the supposed meaning 'tread, trample' occurs only in one disputed passage, Joel 4.13. רְדוּ otherwise only appears in MT as the imperative of ירד (Gen. 42.2; Judg. 7.24; 1 Sam. 6.21; 15.6; Amos 6.2; 2 Chron. 20.16).

The temporal phrase לַבֹּקֶר 'in the morning' may refer to בַּל־יָלִין 'do not remain through the night' in v. 13. Since the wicked, that is, the rich, 'do not remain through the night', the righteous will triumph over them 'in the morning'. This would be more in line with the passages

61. This is suggested by Barth, 'בֹּקֶר', p. 228.

62. The criticism is based on the discussion in Barth, 'בֹּקֶר', p. 228.

63. See, e.g., Schaper, *Eschatology*, p. 60, with references.

64. 'And you shall tread down (עֲסַס) the wicked, for they will be ashes under the soles of your feet, on the day when I act, says the LORD of hosts'.

65. Gen. 1.26, 28; Lev. 25.43, 46, 53; 26.17; Num. 24.19; Judg. 14.9; 1 Kgs 5.4; 5.30; 9.23; Isa. 14.2, 6; Jer. 5.31; Ezek. 29.15; 34.4; Ps. 68.28; 72.8; 110.2; Lam. 1.13; Neh. 9.28; 2 Chron. 8.10.

that refer to 'the morning' as the time of reversal 'from suffering to good fortune and vindication'.[66] Note that MT explicitly says that the fact that 'Man does not remain through the night, he is like the beasts that perish' refers to those who have foolish confidence, that is, the wicked rich, not to the wise, even though they will also die (v. 11), and that it is the wicked rich who 'like sheep are appointed for Sheol' (v. 15).

One of the most crucial words to interpret in this verse is צִיר (K), צוּר (Q). The meaning of צִיר is probably 'idol',[67] but it can also be understood as 'form, figure'.[68] But, as a matter of fact, the only place, apart from here, where צִיר IV in *HALAT* occurs, Isa. 45.16, it refers to an 'idol'. The text reads חָרָשֵׁי צִירִים 'the makers of idols'. It is not used as an ordinary term for 'form, figure' in the Old Testament.[69] Even צוּר can be translated 'form', if it is derived from צוּרָה 'form' (in some lexica = צוּר III), but it can also be interpreted as צוּר, 'rock'.[70]

There are thus two main interpretations of צוּר (Q), צִיר (K). One could argue that the Masoretic text reflects an alternation between צוּר 'rock', as a metaphorical designation for God or a foreign god, and צִיר 'idol'. The *Kethiv* form 'idol' could also be easily explained as an explication

---

66. Raabe, *Psalm Structures*, p. 75. Raabe mentions a different explanation of MT, which he, however, does not find satisfactory. See Raabe, *Psalm Structures*, pp. 75-76.

67. See, e.g., Baethgen, *Psalmen*, p. 144. Since צִיר in the sense of 'idol' only occurs here (K) and in Isa. 45.16, it is not probable that the translator of the LXX knew of a Hebrew צִיר 'idol'. צִירִים in Isa. 45.16 seems to be translated with νῆσοι 'islands' in LXX, i.e., צִירִים is understood as אִיִּים. חָרָשֵׁי צִירִים was an expression that the translator evidently failed to understand, since the translation ἐγκαινίζεσθε πρός με, νῆσοι is *verbatim* the same as the counterpart of אִיִּים אֵלַי הַחֲרִישׁוּ in 45.1. The words from 45.1 are thus repeated literally in 45.16. See I.L. Seeligmann, *The Septuagint Version of Isaiah: A Discussion of its Problems* (Mededelingen en verhandelingen 9 van het Vooraziatisch-Egyptisch Genootschap 'Ex Oriente Lux'; Leiden: E.J. Brill, 1948), p. 117. According to Baethgen, *Psalmen*, p. 144, the equivalents in Aquila, Hieronymus, the *Targum* and Peshitta are based on צִיר 'Bild, Götzenbild' = 'idol'.

68. See especially Raabe, *Psalm Structures*, pp. 76-77.

69. See, e.g., Casetti, *Leben*, p. 142.

70. צוּרה 'form, figure' is also extremely uncertain. It only occurs three times in one and the same verse, Ezek. 43.11. Whether this is the original text is doubtful in all of the cases. See, e.g., *HALAT*, 'צורה', p. 954, and W. Zimmerli, *Ezekiel*, II. *A Commentary on the Book of the Prophet Ezekiel Chapters 25–48* (trans. J.D. Martin; Hermeneia; Philadelphia: Fortress Press, 1983), pp. 410-11, who sticks to MT only on the first occurrence.

of צוּר in this sense. The textual transmission goes from the old (perhaps original) ironic *qere* form צוּר, which is easy to misinterpret as referring to God, to the univocal צִיר 'idol'.[71] It is hard to give a reason for the opposite direction. This understanding is in any case the best background for the equivalents used by Greek translators. The reference of Q צוּר, used as a divine epithet in Casetti, is perhaps to be accepted,[72] but I would rather refer צוּר to 'the god of the rich', rather than to the 'God of Israel', with reference to the ironic use of צוּר for 'foreign gods' in Deut. 32.30-31.[73] 'Their rock' may then be understood as 'their god'. Furthermore, the use of the suffix in third person plural, that is, צוּרָם, is typical for the mocking of idols.[74]

> How could one have routed a thousand, and two put a myriad to flight, unless their Rock [צוּרָם] had sold them, the LORD had given them up? Indeed their rock [צוּרָם] is not as our Rock [צוּרֵנוּ]; our enemies are fools[75] (Deut. 32.30-31).

The interpretation of Casetti must convey וְצוּרָם a kind of parenthesis 'submissive (are they) in the morning—and their Rock? (He is prepared) to wear down Sheol, from the dwelling place that he has?!'[76] Furthermore, it hardly makes sense in the context.[77]

---

71. See also Casetti, *Leben*, p. 145. I admit that צוּרָם and צִירָם could reflect two synonyms for 'form', even though it is not very likely.

72. Casetti, *Leben*, pp. 144-45 nn. 239-41.

73. See Olofsson, *Rock*, pp. 39-40. The foreign God (MT) or gods (LXX) evidently refers to Baal and the local forms of worship related to different epithets of Baal. This is suggested by the use of the imagery of abundance and fertility here. Thus, where צוּר occurs referring to a foreign god it refers to Baal.

74. See especially the use of גִּלּוּל, a derogative word for 'idol', with suffixes in second and third plural in Ezekiel. See H.D. Preuss, 'גִּלּוּלִים', *TDOT*, III, p. 4. It has even been suggested that צוּרָם refers to riches. See F.X. Wutz, *Die Psalmen textkritisch untersucht* (Munich: Kösel & Pustet, 1925), p. 125. See also F.X. Wutz, *Systematische Wege von der Septuaginta zum hebräischen Urtext* (Eichstätter Studien, 1.1; Stuttgart: W. Kohlhammer, 1937), p. 981. He proposed that צוּרָם is identical with צְרָרְם 'ihr Beutel = your purse'. Casetti is negative toward this understanding, at least as an interpretation of MT (Casetti, *Leben*, p. 143). Furthermore, it is admittedly an interpretation which hardly has a counterpart in the Hebrew Bible.

75. NRSV does not follow MT, but reads אֱוִילִים. The meaning of MT is uncertain.

76. 'Gefügig (sind sie) am Morgen—und ihr Fels? (Er soll bereit sein) die Scheol zu zermürben, von der Wohnung aus, die er hat?!' (Casetti, *Leben*, p. 294).

77. The antecedent of the suffix of צוּרָם is obviously the wicked mentioned in v. 14. These arrogant rich are godless persons who only trust in themselves and in

The interpretation of צוּר or צִיר in the sense of 'figure, form' is probably the best understanding of the text of MT, but it is easier if certain emendations are made. This meaning was, however, not within the reach of the early translators, apart from Aquila.

The Greek versions may be based on Q, but with two different interpretations, the translation of Aquila, χαρακτήρ, is probably based on צוּר III 'form',[78] while the counterparts of LXX βοήθεια, Symmachus κρατερός[79] and perhaps Quinta ἡ ἰσχύς[80] is best understood as referring to צוּר in metaphorical sense, as an epithet of God or a foreign god.[81] צוּר is also supported by Origen's transcription of the Hebrew text ουσουραμ (= Q וְצוּרָם), Psalterium Romanum and Psalterium Gallicanum *et auxilium eorum*.[82] Thus the understanding of צוּר as a metaphorical epithet of God or a foreign god is in any case an early interpretation of this passage.

The counterpart in LXX, ἡ βοήθεια αὐτῶν, clearly points to the *qere* form צוּר in the sense 'rock', rather than to צִיר ('idol' or 'form'), since צוּר as an epithet of God is as a rule translated by θεός (13×) or βοηθός in the Psalter (18.3; 19.15; 78.35; 94.22). Furthermore, βοήθεια once

their wealth, not in God as the Rock. On the other hand, the destruction of Sheol by God is a concept that is found in the Hebrew Bible (Isa. 25.8), even though בָּלַע rather than בָּלָה is used here. Thus Raabe's statement that the destruction of Sheol is a concept never found in the Hebrew Bible is doubtful. See Raabe, *Psalm Structures*, p. 77.

78. It is hardly based on צִיר 'idol' as suggested by Baethgen, *Psalmen*, p. 144.

79. צוּר is rendered by κραταιός in 18.32, p. 47 and by κραταίωμα (retranslation from Syriac) in 62.3. See J.R. Busto Saiz, *La traducción de Simaco en el libro de los Salmos* (TEC, 22; Madrid: Varona, 1978), p. 537. See Olofsson, *Rock*, pp. 130-31.

80. Quinta has as a rule στερεός as equivalent of צוּר as a divine epithet in the book of Psalms. Thus it has at least an equivalent with a similar meaning. See, e.g., Olofsson, *Rock*, pp. 130-31.

81. See, e.g., Estin, *Les Psautiers de Jérôme*, p. 97; Casetti, *Leben*, pp. 144-46. For the renderings of צוּר as a divine epithet in LXX and in the Greek versions, see Olofsson, *Rock*, pp. 35-42, 128-33 and the table on p. 155. That Q is the basis for the translation in LXX is also confirmed by Briggs, *Psalms*, I, p. 414; F.W. Mozley, *The Psalter of the Church: The Psalms Compared with the Hebrew, with Various Notes* (Cambridge: Cambridge University Press, 1905), p. 86; Buhl, *Psalmerne*, p. 330; Wutz, *Psalmen*, pp. 123, 125; F.X. Wutz, *Die Transkriptionen von der Septuaginta bis zu Hieronymus* (BWANT, 9, Zweite Folge; Lieferung 1–2; Stuttgart, 1925–1933), p. 185.

82. Casetti, *Leben*, p. 144.

renders צֹר, which was read as צוּר and regarded as a metaphor by the translator, because he did not recognize the meaning 'edge (of a sword)', 89.44. He probably understood it as a divine epithet,[83] since βοήθεια is a fairly common equivalent of metaphorical divine epithets in the book of Psalms as well as in other parts of the LXX.[84] θεός is not used in Ps. 49.15, probably because it would imply a reference to Yahweh, and furthermore θεός renders אֱלֹהִים in v. 16.[85]

An interpretation that is in many respects easier, but linguistically less probable from the point of view of the Greek, moreover less probable with reference to צוּר as an epithet of God or a foreign god in the Hebrew, is that ἡ βοήθεια αὐτῶν should be construed with ἐκ τῆς δόξης αὐτῶν. Thus 'the help that they had from their glory will grow old', that is, slowly disappear in Sheol. In that case ἡ βοήθεια ἐκ τῆς δόξης αὐτῶν παλαιωθήσεται ἐν τῷ ᾅδη would have been the natural counterpart.

בלה forms a common Semitic root. Outside the Hebrew, one can find it as a noun as well as a verb both in Akkadian and in the later stages of Babylonian and Assyrian, in the sense 'to die out (go out of use), to waste away (perish), to be in a condition of non-existence'.[86] In the earliest texts in which בָּלָה is found in MT it is employed as a verb as well as an adjective and it has the meaning 'something that is ordinarily used daily which has become worn out, fragile, by time and use, and can hardly continue to be used even if it is repaired'.[87] The text displays a fairly common theme, the contrast between the power of Yahweh and the transitoriness of his enemies; they wear out (בָּלָה) like a garment (e.g. Isa. 50.9; 51.6; Ps. 102.27; Job 13.28).

---

83. See Olofsson, *Rock*, p. 36 nn. 8-9. In this case Boyd-Taylor has no warrant for his proposal that 'the translator of the Greek Psalter exhibits no tendency to allegorize this particular item'. Boyd-Taylor, 'A Place in the Sun', p. 85 n. 32. He certainly refrained from a literal translation, and he always did it! Thus the suggestion that he translates a different *Vorlage* in this case is out of the question. See also Casetti, *Leben*, pp. 144-45 n. 239.

84. See, e.g., Olofsson, *Rock*, pp. 81-84, 155-56. See also Casetti, *Leben*, pp. 144-45 nn. 239-41.

85. The translator of the Psalter did not use θεός, but *always* choses an alternative rendering when θεός occurs as a rendering of אֱלֹהִים or אֵל in the close context. See Olofsson, *Rock*, p. 44-45.

86. J. Gamberoni, 'בָּלָה', *TDOT*, II, p. 128.

87. Gamberoni, 'בָּלָה', p. 128.

It is the Lord God who helps me; who will declare me guilty? All of them will wear out like a garment [כְּבֶגֶד יִבְלוּ]; the moth will eat them up (Isa. 50.9).

Lift up your eyes to the heavens, and look at the earth beneath; for the heavens will vanish like smoke, the earth will wear out like a garment [כַּבֶּגֶד תִּבְלֶה], and those who live on it will die like gnats; but my salvation will be forever, and my deliverance will never be ended (Isa. 51.6).

They will perish, but you endure; they will all wear out like a garment [כַּבֶּגֶד יִבְלוּ]. You change them like clothing, and they pass away (Ps. 102.27).

One wastes away [יִבְלֶה] like a rotten thing, like a garment [כְּבֶגֶד] that is moth-eaten (Job 13.28).

For a similar picture, but without the term בָּלָה, see Isa. 51.8:

For the moth will eat them up like a garment [כַּבֶּגֶד], and the worm will eat them like wool; but my deliverance will be for ever, and my salvation to all generations.

For a close parallel but with the use of בלע piel in a mythological context, see Isa. 25.7-8:

He will swallow up death [בִּלַּע הַמָּוֶת] for ever. Then the Lord GOD will wipe away the tears from all faces, and the disgrace of his people he will take away from all the earth; for the LORD has spoken.

בָּלָה is used in laments and wisdom texts to describe the most severe distress of the worshipper, 'my body wasted away [בָּלוּ]' (Ps. 32.3), or 'He has made my flesh and my skin waste away [בִּלָּה], and broken my bones' (Lam. 3.4). The most general statement of this kind is probably the latest one: Sir. 14.17, 'All flesh becomes old [יִבְלֶה] like a garment, death alone is eternal law'.

לִבְלוֹת has παλαιωθήσεται as counterpart. The passive of παλαιοῦν, παλαιωθήσεται, used by the LXX translator, refers to 'decay through lapse of time' (LSJ) and is thus an almost exact equivalent to the Hebrew. It sometimes refers to the dead.[88] בָּלָה in piel is mostly understood in an active sense 'to wear something out'.[89] It is an uncommon term; it only occurs here in the Psalms. It is otherwise found in Isa. 65.22; Job 21.13 (K); Lam. 3.4; 1 Chron. 17.9; Ezra 4.4 (K). It is ren-

88. See, e.g., οἱ παλαιούμενοι νεκροὶ (Aristoteles, *Metaphysics*, 390ᵃ22).

89. See Wutz, *Wege*, p. 347, where it is suggested that לִבְלוֹת is to be understood as לְסַלּוֹת 'um aufzuwägen'.

dered by παλαιοῦν in Isa. 65.22; Lam. 3.4 and by ταπεινοῦν in 1 Chron. 17.9. In Job 21.13 LXX is based on the *qere* כָּלָה.

בָּלָה qal occurs 11 times in MT and it is mostly rendered by παλαιοῦν, Deut. 29.4 (the first occurrence); Josh. 9.13; Neh. 9.21; Isa. 50.9; 51.6; Job 13.28; Ps. 32.3; 102.27. The only exceptions are Deut. 29.4 (the second occurrence) and Gen. 18.12, where the relation between MT and LXX is complicated. παλαιοῦν is otherwise used for נָבֵל (Ps. 18.45) and עָתַק (Ps. 6.7). בָּלָה in qal is thus always rendered by παλαιοῦν in the Psalter, 32.3 (בָלוֹ עֲצָמַי, ἐπαλαιώθη τὰ ὀστᾶ μου) and 102.27 (כַּבֶּגֶד יִבְלוּ, ὡς ἱμάτιον παλαιωθήσονται).[90] The translator may thus have read qal here, as do many modern scholars.[91]

According to Tov, the choice of παλαιοῦν for בָּלָה is a reflection of the dependence on the Pentateuch. He refers to Deut. 8.4; 29.4.[92] This is, however, hardly a good example of dependence on the Pentateuch, since בָּלָה qal is in Deut. 8.4 rendered with κατατρίβειν and the same is true for the second occurrence of בָּלָה in Deut. 29.4. בלתי in Gen. 18.12 is understood as בִּלְתִּי and thus translated by οὔπω μέν μοι. Furthermore, the rendering is a good semantic equivalent.

שְׁאוֹל has ἐν τῷ ᾅδῃ as equivalent. Wutz maintains that LXX has בַּשְׁאוֹל as *Vorlage*,[93] but this is far from certain. The preposition בְּ is sometimes made explicit, even in a book as literal as the Psalms.[94] See Ps. 9.12 יֹשֵׁב צִיּוֹן, τῷ κατοικοῦντι ἐν σιων; 24.8 יְהוָה גִּבּוֹר מִלְחָמָה, κύριος δυνατὸς ἐν πολέμῳ; 65.7 יִשְׁכֹּן חֲצֵרֶיךָ, κατασκηνώσει ἐν ταῖς αὐλαῖς

---

90. Thus the suggestion by Wutz that LXX reflects √יבל is unfounded. Wutz, *Transkriptionen*, p. 185. See also p. 204. Wutz suggests a different vocalization in LXX, i.e. יִבְלֶה or יָבוֹל (Wutz, *Psalmen*, pp. 123, 125), or יָבֵל (Wutz, *Transkriptionen*, p. 185).

91. See, e.g., Aquila, κατατρίψαι and Symmachus, παλαιώσει, which reflect the active force of MT.

92. See E. Tov, 'The Impact of the LXX Translation of the Pentateuch on the Translation of the other Books', in P. Casetti, O. Keel and A. Schenker (eds.), *Mélanges Dominique Barthélemy: Etudes Bibliques offertes a l'occasion de son 60-e Anniversaire* (OBO, 38; Göttingen: Vandenhoeck & Ruprecht, 1981), p. 586.

93. Wutz, *Transkriptionen*, p. 185. This is, however, not regarded as the original text by Wutz, who suggests a totally different text based on LXX and the *Targum*. See Wutz, *Transkriptionen*, pp. 185, 515.

94. By handling as he did, Boyd-Taylor suggests that the translator in effect transforms a teleological image in the Hebrew into a spatial one and thereby gives the fate of the foolish rich a more concrete expression ('A Place in the Sun', p. 83). But a spatial interpretation of MT is in fact not seldom made.

σου; 138.3 עֹז תְּרְהִבֵנִי בְנַפְשִׁי, πολυωρήσεις με ἐν ψυχῇ μου ἐν δυνάμει. In fact, both 9.12 and 24.8 can also be regarded as in a constructus relationship. The LXX translator probably misunderstands the Hebrew text, but his interpretation conforms with the thought in the psalm about power and wealth. See, for example, vv. 7-8, 11-12, 16, 17-18. מִזְבֵל לֹו in MT has ἐκ τῆς δόξης αὐτῶν as counterpart.[95] The translator has connected v. 15 with v. 18, where לֹא־יֵרֵד אַחֲרָיו כְּבוֹדֹו is translated literally by οὐδὲ συγκαταβήσεται αὐτῷ ἡ δόξα αὐτοῦ.[96] ἡ δόξα refers to 'the riches', which is clearly the denotation of the parallels in v. 17. All commentators agree that כָּבוֹד in vv. 17-18 in MT refers to the wealth of the rich men,[97] and this is the case in LXX too, but if that is the case why should not δόξα in v. 15 have the same reference? Furthermore, the statement in v. 15, ἐκ τῆς δόξης αὐτῶν, must suggest that they or their god have been separated from the riches, that is, it refers to the different destinies of the riches and the rich. This interpretation is in line with the context.[98] Their wealth is of no use to them in Sheol, since they have to leave it behind. See v. 10, 'When we look at the wise, they die; fool and dolt perish together and leave their wealth [חֵילָם, τὸν πλοῦτον αὐτῶν] to others'. See also Job 21.21 for a similar thought: 'For what do they care for their houses after them, when the number of their months is cut off?' (RSV).

LXX, has, contrary to MT, established a conscious terminological connection between v. 15 and vv. 17-18, since זְבֻל is rendered by ἡ δόξα just as כָּבוֹד. It is probable that δόξα in v. 15 refers directly to the riches, and thus it is synonymous with the reference of ἡ δόξα in vv. 17-18,[99]

95. Some scholars vocalize מַזְבֵל 'habitation', i.e. 'Sheol is for him/her (the form) habitation'. But it is doubtful if such a word exists. See, e.g., Baethgen, *Psalmen*, p. 144; Casetti, *Leben*, p. 149. It is not included in *HALAT* or KB.

96. Thus Mozley, *The Psalter*, p. 86. Wutz suggests a different *Vorlage* מִגְּדֻלְמֹו from גִּדֶל 'greatness', with negative connotation, 'arrogance', as in Isa. 9.8; 10.12. Wutz, *Psalmen*, pp. 123, 125; Wutz, *Transkriptionen*, p. 185. See also Wutz, *Wege*, pp. 347, 981 where he proposed that the *Vorlage* of the rendering in LXX is מְזֻבַּל, from זבל pual, 'wertlos, schlaff sein', with reference to Arab. *dbl*. Neither of these interpretations are very probable.

97. It is in fact even rendered by 'wealth' in NRSV.

98. See Mozley, who suggests that it is a guess from the end of v. 18. Mozley, *The Psalter*, p. 86.

99. This in fact is a common denotation of δόξα in LXX. See Gen. 31.1, 16; 45.13; 1 Kgs 3.13; 1 Chron. 29.28; 2 Chron. 1.11, 12; 17.5; 18.1; 32.27; Est. 5.11; Ps. 45.14; 112.3; Prov. 3.16; 8.18; 11.16; Eccl. 6.2; Hag. 2.7; Isa. 66.12.

where it is clearly stated, 'Do not be afraid when some become rich, when the wealth of their houses increases. For *when they die they will carry nothing away; their wealth will not go down after them*'.

17 μὴ φοβοῦ, ὅταν πλουτήσῃ ἄνθρωπος
   καὶ ὅταν πληθυνθῇ ἡ δόξα [כְּבוֹד] τοῦ οἴκου αὐτοῦ·
18 ὅτι οὐκ ἐν τῷ ἀποθνήσκειν αὐτὸν λήμψεται τὰ πάντα,
   οὐδὲ συγκαταβήσεται αὐτῷ ἡ δόξα [כְּבוֹד] αὐτοῦ.

זְבֻל 'exalted dwelling (of God), the place of the moon, a temple for Yahweh'[100] is loosely rendered also in 2 Chron. 6.2 by ἅγιος and in Hab. 3.11 by τάξις. It also occurs in 1 Kgs 8.13; Isa. 63.15. Only in Isa. 63.15, where the translator is firmly guided by the context, an adequate understanding can be found וּרְאֵה מִזְּבֻל קָדְשֶׁךָ, καὶ ἰδὲ ἐκ τοῦ οἴκου τοῦ ἁγίου σου.

זְבֻל has been interpreted as referring to 'arrogated divinity, the exalted status that the wicked delight to claim for themselves through lavish buildings'.[101] This is not far from the understanding of the word by the LXX translator, but that the translator reflected this meaning by the rendering of זְבֻל by δόξα is partly undermined by the fact that the other LXX translators hardly had an adequate understanding of the term, when not guided by the context. Of course the distinction between riches and arrogant divinity and exalted status based on the wealth of the rich is not great in this context, that is, the attitude prevailing in this psalm. The same is true for the possibility that the rendering in LXX reflects the meanings mentioned in KB: 'princedom' (זְבֻל I) or 'elevated place' (זְבֻל II).[102] The understanding of זְבֻל and perhaps the use of δόξα in LXX precludes such an interpretation. It is perhaps a better suggestion that it is used in an ironical way with the denotation 'temple', as in rabbinical Hebrew (see Dalman).[103]

---

100. W.H. Holladay, *A Concise Hebrew and Aramaic Lexicon of the Old Testament* (Leiden: E.J. Brill, 1971). Note the rendering of זְבֻל in Symmachus, מִזְּבֻל לֹי, ἀπὸ τῆς οἰκήσεως τῆς ἐντίμου αὐτῶν. According to Baethgen, this is not based on a different Hebrew text but it is an interpretation employed to make some sense out of the text. Baethgen, *Psalmen*, p. 145.

101. Gamberoni, 'זְבֻל', p. 31. He refers to Ezek. 28.1-19, esp. 2-9, 12-13, 18; Amos 3.15; 5.11; Mic. 2.2, 4; Isa. 14.13-15; 22.15-19; Jer. 51.53; Ps. 73.9.

102. See also Schaper, *Eschatology*, p. 61.

103. That the meaning 'princely estate' from Ugar is supported by δόξα in LXX is suggested in Barr, *Philology*, p. 326, with reference to a suggestion by G.R.

The most common interpretation of מִן in מִזְּבֻל לֹו is 'away from' and this is probably the interpretation in the LXX too.[104] The reference of לֹו in מִזְּבֻל לֹו is probably צוּר, while the explicit reference of αὐτῶν is rather ἄφρων καὶ ἄνους 'the fool and the stupid' in v. 11, who are implicit in vv. 12-14. Thus it refers to the rich in the LXX. The LXX translator either tried to get some sense out of MT or he was reading לָמֹו.[105] 'The fool and the stupid' are persons who are rich but do not realize that they have no help of their riches in Sheol, that is, their riches cannot help them to be delivered from death. The rich are more or less identical with 'the godless' in this psalm. This interpretation is also in accord with v. 16 in MT and LXX, where there is a marked contrast between the fate of the godless (reading לָמֹו) in v. 15 and the righteous psalmist in v. 16.

The rendering of זְבֻל by δόξα is thus a contextual rendering that depends on the translator's lack of knowledge as to the meaning of the Hebrew word. His interpretation is based on the fact that he understood the reference of זְבֻל as the same as that of חַיִל and עֹשֶׁר in v. 7, חַיִל in v. 11, יְקָר in v. 13, עָשַׁר hiphil in v. 17 and כָּבֹוד in vv. 17, 18, and as an antonym הַכֹּל 'nothing' in v. 18. Even though it is a contextual reading, it is not an adequate interpretation of MT, since זְבֻל otherwise always refers to the habitation of God or gods in the Old Testament (1 Kgs 8.13; Isa. 63.15; Hab. 3.11; 2 Chron. 6.2). In that case the LXX version ought to be interpreted, 'and their help [= god] shall waste away in Hades far away from their glory [= riches]'. 'Their help' in LXX is thus the god of riches, who is consumed in Sheol or by Sheol. The god of riches who was such a help to them when they were alive, but now when they are separated from their riches the god in whom they trusted is of no help in Sheol. The crux with this interpretation is that the help of the rich and foolish men is not otherwise mentioned in the context

---

Driver. In MT זְבֻל refers to the temple in 1 Kgs 8.13 (= 2 Chron. 6.2) and to God's heavenly habitation in Isa. 63.15.

104. See G.V. Smith, who emphasizes that 'the word stands in contrast to Sheol, the place of the wicked' (Smith, 'זבל', p. 1074). According to König מִן ought to be understood 'sodass nicht vorhanden ist'. König, *Historisch-kritisches Lehrgebäude*, §406p. See Lev. 26.43; 2 Kgs 11.6; Isa. 10.18; 23.1; 62.10; Jer. 10.14; 15.19; 51.17; 33.21; Ezek. 12.19; 32.15; 25.9; Hos. 9.11, 12; Hag. 1.10; Zech. 7.14; 9.8Q; Prov. 1.33; Job 21.9; 34.30; 1 Chron. 4.10. Thus it is in that case identical in meaning with the common מֵאֵין, e.g., Isa. 5.9.

105. See Briggs, *Psalms*, I, p. 414.

and that the helper, that is, the god of the rich, is consumed in Sheol has no direct parallel in the Hebrew Old Testament. On the other hand, we have seen that the contrast between the power of Yahweh and the transitoriness of his enemies is described in other places of the Old Testament with the same terminology, for example, Isa. 50.9; 51.6; Ps. 102.27; Job 13.28.

If צוּר, as I have made plausible, is a divine epithet even in MT and refers to a foreign god, that is, a god opposed to Yahweh, the meaning of the Hebrew would be that 'their Rock, that is, the god whom the rich persons relied on, shall be consumed in Sheol, away from his habitation' or 'is for consumption by Sheol'. Some other proposals concerning the meaning or the reference of זְבֻל would make this proposal even more fitting, for example, 'temple', 'elevated place', 'throne', 'lofty abode', 'princedom' (i.e. his high position). This could be seen as a counterpart to the separation between the rich person and their riches, which is firmly achored in the context. Furthermore, it could be an analogy to זְבֻל as referring to the Temple of Yahweh, 1 Kgs 8.13; 2 Chron. 6.2, or to God's heavenly habitation, Isa. 63.15, and conforms to the use of זְבֻל in Hab. 3.11, where it refers to the place of the sun and the moon, in a context where they are regarded as gods opposed to Yahweh.

An alternative interpretation of the Hebrew text could be mentioned in this connection, an interpretation which is in line with the mythological imagery here. The noun זבל stands in Ugaritic texts in apposition before compound terms for various gods and as a genitive epithet of the divine throne. It may also occur as a theophoric element in two personal names, one Phoenician and one Punic. As a stereotyped epithet of the gods and as a designation of their 'majesty', זבל signals the honour of the pantheon.[106] It can on that account be used in a derogative sense by the Old Testament theologians.[107] In MT it once occurs in a mythological context, symbolizing the realms of the gods, that is, the sun and moon, in a context where they are enemies of Yahweh (Hab. 3.11).[108]

The mythological associations may be further strengthened by the fact that זבל occurs in combination with בַּעַל in Ugaritic texts as *zbl b'l 'rṣ*, 'the sovereign Lord of the earth' or rather 'the prince of the under-

106. Gamberoni, 'זְבֻל', p. 30.
107. Gamberoni, 'זְבֻל', p. 30.
108. Gamberoni, 'זְבֻל', p. 31.

world'.[109] It is the king whom no other can stand above, the one who gives substance to all living creatures. When his return to the earth is announced people begin to dream of oil and honey, the symbols of abundance.[110] I do not suggest that the reference is directly to this epithet, even though it makes sense in the context. But since זְבֻל בַּעַל seems to be associated with richness and abundance in the Ugaritic texts, especially in regard to the nature,[111] it cannot be excluded that there is a veiled reference here to this god.[112]

If זְבֻל is understood as a god here the meaning of the name is much disputed. Bordreuil suggests the meaning 'prince' or perhaps 'sovereign' of זְבֻל with reference to the meaning in Ugaritic.[113] The use in the Old Testament, where it refers to the Temple or the heavenly abode, has a counterpart both in Ugarit and in Qumran.[114] Thus בַּעַל זְבֻל may

109. See M. Dietrich and O. Loretz, 'Die Ba'Al-Titel B'ṬṢ Arl Und Aliy Qrdm', *UF* 12 (1980), p. 392. See also W. Herrmann, 'Baal Zebub', *DDD*, col. 295.

110. J.C. de Moor, 'בַּעַל', *TDOT*, II, pp. 187-88.

111. de Moor, 'בַּעַל', p. 188.

112. See especially P. Bordreuil, 'Mizzěbul lô: A propos de Psaume 49:15', in L. Eslinger and G. Taylor (eds.), *Ascribe to the Lord: Biblical and other Studies in Memory of Peter C. Craigie* (JSOTSup, 67; Sheffield: JSOT Press, 1988), pp. 96-98. This interpretation is not dependent on the understanding of Bordreuil that מ in מִזְּבֻל לֹו refers to the interrogative pronoun 'who', i.e., 'who is the sovereign of it [=i.e. Sheol]. He assumes that it was written defective and therefore misunderstood by the Masoretes as מִן. He refers to a parallel in Ps. 12.5 מִי אָדוֹן לָנוּ 'who is our master?' His suggestion may have some support from v. 16, where it is emphasized that God has the power to release from Sheol: אַךְ־אֱלֹהִים יִפְדֶּה נַפְשִׁי מִיַּד־שְׁאוֹל 'But God will ransom my soul from the power of Sheol'.

113. Bordreuil, 'mizzěbul lô', pp. 94-96, 97. See, e.g., W.F. Albright, 'Zabûl Yam and Thâpit Nahar in the Combat between Baal and the Sea', *JPOS* 16 (1936), who suggests 'prince' or 'the elevated one'. The reference is taken from Herrmann, 'Baal Zebub', col. 295. 'Prince' is the most common interpretation. See, e.g., A. Cooper, 'Divine Names and Epithets in the Ugaritic Texts', in S. Rummel (ed.), *Ras Shamra Parallels* (AnOr, 51; Rome: Pontificio Istituto Biblico, 1981), III, pp. 333-469 (355, 364); F.B. Knutson, 'Divine Names and Epithets in the Akkadian Texts', in Rummel (ed.), *Ras Shamra Parallels*, III, pp. 471-500 (499), an interpretation that has been included in *HALAT*. 'His Highness' was proposed by J.C. de Moor, 'Studies in the New Alphabetic Texts from Ras Shamra I', *UF* I (1969), p. 188; and 'ruler', T.L.K. Handy, 'A Solution for many *mlkm*', *UF* 20 (1988), p. 59. But this suggestion seems in fact only to be based on the verb זבל II in KB, with the meaning 'rule', but with a question mark appended. In fact, זבל II is dropped in *HALAT*!

114. 1QM 12.1-2; 1QS 10.3; 1QpHab 3.34.

allude to זְבֻל as the exalted dwelling of Baal, that is, it then refers to the heavenly Baal. This is perhaps more in line with the date of the psalm, since the chief rival of Yahweh in the Hellenistic period was the heavenly Baal *b'lšmyn*.[115]

Even though the rendering δόξα fits the connotations of בַּעַל זְבֻל as a god of prosperity fairly well, we cannot otherwise show that the LXX translators used δόξα in this way. Thus the reference of δόξα in LXX is probably to the riches, but it cannot be excluded that the Hebrew contains a veiled reference to בַּעַל זְבֻל, as a god of prosperity or as the prince of the underworld or as the god of heaven.[116] The meaning of MT would in that case be that 'the form (i.e. the body) of the rich person shall waste away in Sheol away from his god, 'the prince/ruler' (of the underworld) or 'the heavenly one'.

The two interpretations could in fact be combined, since צוּר in Deuteronomy 32 refers to Baal and this could be case here too. It would be an interesting case of irony here if בַּעַל זְבֻל 'Baal the prince' (זְבֻל I) or 'Baal of the elevated place', that is, of heaven (זְבֻל II), the one who ought to have the power to save the rich from Sheol, is himself consumed by Sheol, which in fact is in accordance with the Ugaritic myth, far away from 'his elevated place, his throne', that is, זְבֻל II. זְבֻל then refers directly to the temple or the throne of Baal and at the same time points to the epithet בַּעַל זְבֻל. Thus Baal, contrary to the description in the Ugaritic myth, does not return from the underworld and is not enthroned on Mt Ṣafān.[117] The god only appears as בַּעַל זְבֻב 'Lord of

---

115. See especially T.J. Lewis, 'Beelzebul', *ABD*, I, p. 639. The character and appearance of *b'lšmyn* were subject to change, 'In the beginning he is a sort of high-ranked weathergod... Later on he develops many more solar features' (W. Röllig, 'Baal-Shamen', *DDD*, col. 287). Epithets such as 'Lord of the heavens and the earth' and 'Lord of the world' were given to him.

116. See Baal and his worship were as a rule looked upon with aversion, and Baal was often referred to in pejorative terms in the Old Testament or his name was simply ignored (Mulder, 'בַּעַל', pp. 193, 196-97, 200).

117. See, e.g., de Moor, 'בַּעַל', p. 190. Mot overcomes Baal and Baal has to descend into Mot's underworld domain. Baal is thus reported dead, even though he later on defeats Mot and is enthroned on Mt Ṣafān, an enthronement that probably was celebrated. See, e.g., J.F. Healey, 'Mot', *DDD*, cols. 1124, 1172; de Moor, 'בַּעַל', p. 190. Several OT passages can perhaps be understood with reference to the epithets and mythology of בַּעַל and מוּת. See Healey, 'Mot', cols. 1128-1131; M.J. Mulder, 'בַּעַל', *TDOT*, II, pp. 192-99. I admit that the personification may be 'purely poetical' and that 'any attempt to go beyond the texts and ask whether these

the flies' in the Old Testament (2 Kgs 1.2-3, 6.16), but this seems to be a deliberate distortion of זְבֻל בַּעַל or בַּעַל זְבֻל.[118] This enhances the probability of an ironic use of זְבֻל in this text:

> But [אַךְ] God will ransom my soul from the power [lit. hands] of Sheol,
> for he will receive me [יִקָּחֵנִי] [49.16 MT]

> But [πλήν] God will ransom my soul from the power [lit. hands] of Sheol,
> when he receives me [λαμβάνη με] [48.16 LXX]

אַךְ has various equivalents in LXX Psalms, but πλήν is the most common rendering. Thus it emphasizes the contrast between v. 15 and v. 16. At the same time it may be directed against Baal, who himself is consumed by Sheol or in Sheol. It is God who will ransom from the dead. He is the one who has the power over life, not 'Baal the prince' or 'the heavenly Baal'.

כִּי יִקָּחֵנִי is translated by ὅταν λαμβάνη με. כִּי is thus understood in its temporal meaning here, 'when he receives me'. לָקַח is as a rule translated by λαμβάνειν in LXX as a whole. But the meaning of לָקַח in this context is disputed. Casetti without hesitation understands it as a 'translation (to heaven)'.[119] The equivalent in LXX does not reveal any specific interpretation of לָקַח. If the translator understood it as a 'translation' to heaven he might have employed the *terminus technicus* for this experience, μεθιστάναι, which is used for the translation of Enoch in Gen. 5.24:[120]

---

texts ultimately go back to mythological descriptions is bound to end up as sheer speculations' (Barstad, 'Sheol', col. 1454). But some of the textual emendations and interpretations of this verse by scholars are in fact more speculative. See especially Casetti, *Leben*, pp. 117-52 with footnotes for references.

118. Mulder, 'בַּעַל', p. 194; W.A. Maier II, 'Baal-Zebub', *ABD*, I, p. 554; Dietrich and Loretz, '*B'l Arṣ*', p. 392; Lewis, 'Beelzebul', p. 639. See also W. Forster, 'Βεεζεβούλ', *TDNT*, I, pp. 605-606 and n. 4 and *HALAT*. For further references see Herrmann, 'Baal Zebub', col. 295. בַּעַל זְבֻל is probably a god who is part of the cult of the dead, a cult which was strongly forbidden in the law of Moses. Thus it cannot be excluded that there is a negative reference to the cult of the dead here. Dietrich, Loretz, '*B'l Arṣ*', p. 392 and n. 9.

119. Casetti, *Leben*, pp. 222-230. Thus also, e.g., M. Dahood, *Psalms 1–50* (AB, 16; Garden City, NY: Doubleday, 2nd edn, 1966), p. 301.

120. On the other hand, לָקַח is rendered by λαμβάνειν in 2 Kgs 2.3, 5, where a similar experience is recorded. Whether or not v. 16 in MT is to be understood with reference to Gen. 5.24 is disputed. See, e.g., O. Loretz, 'Ugaritisches und Judisches Weisheit und Tot in Psalm 49', *UF* 17 (1985), p. 207 n. 110. For different inter-

Enoch walked with God; then he was no more [וְאֵינֶנּוּ], because God took him [אֹתוֹ לָקַח כִּי]

Enoch pleased God and he was not found [οὐχ ηὑρίσκετο], because God took him up [μετέθηκεν αὐτὸν ὁ θεός]

See also the reference to this verse in Sir. 44.16 'Enoch pleased the Lord, and was taken up [μετετέθη]; he was an example of repentance to all generations'.

It cannot be excluded that the Hebrew refers to redemption from death in this very late psalm. Cf. A.A. Anderson, who writes in his commentary, 'Therefore it seems that either the Psalmist believed that he would not see Sheol (or death) at all...or he hoped that, having died, he would be raised to life again to enjoy the fellowship with God'.[121] But it is hard to say if it refers to a life with God or a continued life on earth. This is true for the Hebrew as well as the Greek.

The interpretation of the psalm must then be seen in relation to the cultural and religious environment in which it was written and in which the translator lived. The fact that the psalm is one of the latest psalms in the Psalter makes it easier to suggest connections with Jewish intertestamental literature. Furthermore, even though it is hard to be specific, the translation of the book of Psalms is, according to many scholars, to be placed in the middle of the second century BCE; other scholars suggest the first century BCE.[122]

pretations of v. 16, see the same article, p. 208 n. 111 and Kraus, *Psalmen*, pp. 522-23.

121. Anderson, *Psalms*, p. 379. See also Kraus, *Psalmen*, pp. 522-23.

122. Regarding the date of the translation of the book of Psalms, an early date from the second century BCE seems to be favoured in, e.g., G. Dorival, M. Harl and O. Munnich, *La Bible Grecque des Septante* (Paris: Cerf, 1988), p. 111. The second century BCE, without being more specific, is also suggested in O. Munnich, 'La Septante des Psaumes et le groupe *kaige*', *VT* 33 (1983), pp. 75-89 and the second half of the second century BCE in J. Schaper, 'Der Septuaginta-Psalter als Dokument jüdischer Eschatologie', in M. Hengel and A.M. Schwemer (eds.), *Die Septuaginta zwischen Judentum und Christentum* (WUNT, 72; Tübingen: J.C.B. Mohr [Paul Siebeck], 1994), p. 61, and in Schaper, *Eschatology*, p. 45. The reception history also points to a date in the second century BCE. See, e.g., Boyd-Taylor, 'A Place in the Sun', p. 72 and n. 3. A. van der Kooij argues for a date in the first century BCE in his article, 'On the Place of Origin of the Old Greek of Psalms', *VT* 33 (1983), pp. 67-74 (73). But the reasons for a dating in the first century are not convincing.

In some circles of Judaism the rich were looked upon with suspicion; they are more or less regarded as sinners and their wealth created at the expense of the poor and righteous of the people. This is, for example, the case in *1 Enoch* (Ethiopian Enoch). This book is patently difficult to date, but all of the books, except book 2, could in fact be pre-Christian. They may date back to the second century BCE.[123] The righteous love God rather than earthly possessions (108.7), they stand opposed to the rich and powerful, who trust in dishonestly won money and property (4.6, 8; 97.8), who exploit their position with injustice and violence (94.6-11; 96.4-8). In the hereafter, when the position will be reversed (94.10; 96.8), the rich will lament, 'Our souls are sated with the unrighteous mammon, but this does not prevent us from plunging into the flames of hell' (63.10).[124] Cf. *1 Enoch* 94.7-8 'those who acquire gold and silver will quickly be destroyed in the judgement. Woe to you, you rich, for you have trusted in your riches, but from your riches you will depart, for you did not remember the Most High in the days of your riches'.[125] The same attitude is easily seen in the New Testament. Compare Lk. 12.15: 'And he said to them, Take care! Be on your guard against all kinds of greed; for one's life does not consist in the abundance of possessions.'

The idea of the impure, the dishonest and worldly, is sometimes personified and connected with the word מָמוֹן. Thus μαμωνᾶς is personified as a rival lord in Lk. 16.13, 'You cannot serve God and wealth' (μαμ-ωνᾶς). The Hebrew word מָמוֹן only occurs in Sir. 31(34).8 in the Old Testament, including the Apocrypha, where it is rendered by χρυσίον, 'gold': 'Blessed is the rich person who is found blameless, and who does not go after gold [ὀπίσω χρυσίου]'.

Thus one can with confidence say that the basic thrust of this late wisdom psalm is in line with attitudes reflected in Jewish intertestamental literature, including the personification of wealth.

123. See H.F.D. Sparks (ed.), *The Apocryphal Old Testament* (trans. M.A. Knibb; Oxford: Clarendon Press, 1984), pp. 173-77.

124. F. Hauck, 'μαμωνᾶς', *TDNT*, IV, p. 389. Cf. also the translation in Sparks (ed.), *The Apocryphal Old Testament*, p. 246, 'Our souls are sated with possessions gained through iniquity, but they do not prevent our going down into the flames of the torment of Sheol'.

125. Sparks (ed.), *The Apocryphal Old Testament*, pp. 296-97.

4

The text in the Hebrew as well as in LXX is not easy to interpret. My understanding of the Greek text, which is admittedly uncertain, as are all interpretations of this verse, has the advantage that it does make sense of the use of δόξα in vv. 15, 17 and 18, and furthermore, that βοήθεια is in accordance with the translation of צוּר as a divine epithet otherwise in LXX as a whole. In favour of this interpretation, it can also be said that the separation of the riches from the rich and foolish persons is clearly indicated in the close context (e.g. vv. 10, 12-13, 16-17). The translator's interpretation of זְבֻל is easy to understand as a consequence of the lack of knowledge as to the meaning of this Hebrew word. His interpretation of the reference of זְבֻל is based on the context, where חַיִל and עֹשֶׁר in v. 7, חַיִל in v. 12, יְקָר in v. 13, עָשַׁר hiphil in v. 17 and כָּבוֹד in vv. 17, 18 and as an antonym הַכֹּל 'nothing' in v. 18 are all related to the wealth of the rich.

The whole section 49.9-17 is a description of the fate of the rich and the separation of the rich from his riches. See especially v. 10, 'When we look at the wise, they die; fool and dolt perish together and *leave their wealth to others*'; vv. 12-13, 'Mortals *cannot abide in their pomp*, they are like animals that perish. Such is the fate of the foolhardy, the end of those who are pleased with their lot'; vv. 16-17, 'Do not be afraid when some become rich, when the wealth of their houses increases. For *when they die they will carry nothing away; their wealth will not go down after them*' (my italics).

Furthermore, the associations with a god of riches are natural in a context where even death is personified. The god of the riches is not as the Lord living for ever. Rather he is subject to decline in Sheol and the rich are separated from the riches themselves, which do not follow the dead into Sheol. Thus the god of the riches is no 'help' to them them since he wears out in Sheol. The contrast between the everlasting power of Yahweh and the transitoriness of his enemies is sometimes described in the Old Testament as a 'wearing out'. See Isa. 50.9; 51.6, 8; Ps. 102.27; Job 13.28. A weak point in the interpretation is that the riches are otherwise not personified in the Psalm. But this must be seen in relation to the fact that even the death is personified as a shepherd in this verse.

I have also tried to give some suggestions concerning the interpretation of MT. With great hesitation I have proposed that a possible interpretation of MT is that the upright will trample upon the graves of the wicked, but I admit that this is based on the traditional view concerning life and death in the Psalms, that the use of רָדָה in the Old Testament rather suggests the meaning 'rule, dominate'.

If צוּר is a divine epithet that refers to a foreign god, the meaning (not the translation) of the Hebrew would be that their 'rock', that is, the god on whom the rich persons relied, shall be consumed in Sheol (or by Sheol), where he is away from his temple, that is, his elevated position. This is in analogy with the separation between the rich persons and their riches, vv. 10, 12-13, 16-17, and with זְבֻל as the temple of God or his heavenly habitation, and can be compared to Hab. 3.11, where זְבֻל refers to the habitation of the sun and the moon, as gods opposed to Yahweh.

An alternative understanding of the Hebrew text is that the bodies of the rich persons shall be consumed in Sheol (or that Sheol will consume their bodies), separated as they are from their god, בַּעַל זְבֻל. This in line with the mythological imagery of the psalm, the use of זבל in Ugaritic texts and the original meaning of 2 Kgs 1.2-3, 6.16 as referring to בַּעַל זְבֻל.

The two interpretations can in fact be combined. Thus זְבֻל may refer directly the throne of Baal and at the same time point to the epithet בַּעַל זְבֻל, and צוּר can denote בַּעַל זְבֻל 'Baal the prince' (זְבֻל I) or 'Baal of the elevated place', that is, of heaven (זְבֻל II), who cannot save the rich from Sheol, but is himself consumed by Sheol, away from 'his temple' or 'his throne' (זְבֻל II). Baal does not return from the underworld and is not enthroned on his זְבֻל, but God is the one who has the power to deliver from the sphere of Sheol.

ON THE USE OF SCRIPTURE IN THE DEVELOPMENT OF MILITANT DAVIDIC MESSIANISM AT QUMRAN: NEW LIGHT FROM *PSALM OF SOLOMON* 17

Kenneth R. Atkinson

The 1991 release of the remaining unpublished Qumran documents has stimulated a resurgence of interest in the phenomenon of post-biblical Jewish messianism. Two recent books, among the first to benefit from complete access to the entire Qumran corpus, challenge many of our past notions concerning the origins of Davidic messianism. In the first work, *The Scepter and the Star: The Messiahs of the Dead Sea Scrolls and other Ancient Literature*,[1] John Collins proposes that messianism was virtually dormant from the early fifth to the late second century BCE and only emerged as an active ideology in the first century BCE. Collins's thesis is also supported in Kenneth Pomykala's study, *The Davidic Dynasty Tradition in Early Judaism: Its History and Significance for Messianism*,[2] which concludes that Davidic messianism emerged at Qumran during the Herodian period, from 35 BCE–70 CE.[3] These two volumes significantly advance our understanding of pre-Christian messianism, and their insights demand a complete re-examination of other messianic documents in light of the new Qumran texts.

This study will expand upon these two works and focus upon the use of Scripture in the development of militant Davidic messianism in the Qumran texts and *Psalm of Solomon* 17 (*Ps. Sol.* 17). Unfortunately,

---

1. (New York: Doubleday, 1995).
2. (SBLEJL, 7; Atlanta, CA: Scholars Press, 1995).
3. For the opposing thesis, that there is a continuing stream of messianic tradition, in which the Davidic Messiah played a role from the exilic period to the second century BCE, see A. Laato, *A Star Is Rising: The Historical Development of the Old Testament Royal Ideology and the Rise of the Jewish Messianic Expectations* (Atlanta: Scholars Press, 1997), pp. 285-89.

the importance of the militant Davidic Messiah has not been fully examined, since many of the Qumran texts which refer to this enigmatic figure were among the unpublished and previously inaccessible scrolls from Cave 4.[4] The present investigation will examine this new evidence and suggest that the militant Davidic Messiah in the Qumran texts and *Psalm of Solomon* 17 was fashioned from a select corpus of scriptural texts which were used to portray this redeemer as a righteous, yet violent, counterpart to Herod the Great.

1. *Scripture and the Militant Davidic Messiah in Psalm of Solomon 17*

Psalm of Solomon 17 has long been considered the earliest explicit postbiblical document to contain an expectation for a 'Son of David' (υἱὸν Δαυίδ; *Ps. Sol.* 17.21) who is also designated the 'Lord's Messiah' (χριστὸς κύριος; *Ps. of Sol.* 17.32; cf. *Ps. Sol.* 18.7).[5] The psalmist

---

4. For photographs of these texts, see R.H. Eisenman and J.M. Robinson, *A Facsimile Edition of the Dead Sea Scrolls* (2 vols.; Washington, DC: Biblical Archaeology Society, 1991); E. Tov and S.J. Pfann (eds.), *The Dead Sea Scrolls on Microfiche: A Comprehensive Facsimile Edition of the Texts from the Judean Desert* (Leiden: E.J. Brill, 1993).

5. All Greek manuscripts read χριστὸς κύριος while the Syriac version (Ps. Sol. 17.36), translated from the Greek, contains the identical reading ܡܫܝܚܐ ܡܪܝܐ. The Greek likely represents a translation error in which an original genitive κυριου was erroneously rendered as a nominative, as in the LXX of Lam. 4.20 (χριστὸς κύριος), which contains the identical mistranslation. See, M. de Jonge, *De toekomstverwachting in Psalmen Salomo* (Leiden: E.J. Brill, 1965), pp. 38-39; M.A. Knibb, 'Messianism in the Pseudepigrapha in the Light of the Scrolls', *DSD* 2 (1995), pp. 169-70; K.G. Kuhn, *Die Älteste Textgestalt der Psalmen Salomos* (Stuttgart: W. Kohlhammer, 1937), pp. 73-74; J. Viteau, *Les Psaumes de Salomon: Introduction, texte Grec et traduction, avec les principales variantes de la version Syriaque par Francois Martin* (Paris: Letouzey & Ané, 1911), pp. 361-62; J. Schüpphaus, *Die Psalmen Salomon: Ein Zeugnis Jerusalemer Theologie und Frömmigkeit in der Mitte des vorchristlichen Jarhunderts* (ALGHJ, 7; Leiden: E.J. Brill, 1977), p. 71; E. Schürer, 'Messianism', in G. Vermes, F. Millar and M. Black (eds.), *The History of the Jewish People in the Age of Jesus Christ (175 BC–AD 135)* (Edinburgh: T. & T. Clark, 1979), II, p. 504; J. Wellhausen, *Die Pharisäer und die Sadducäer* (Greifswald: L. Bamberg, 1874), p. 132; P. Winter, 'Lukanische Miszellen III. Lc 2.11: [XPICTOC KΥPIOC oder XPICTOΥ?', *ZNW* 49 (1958), pp. 68, 75. For an opposing interpretation, see R. Hann, 'Christos Kyrios in Ps Sol 17.32:

adopts language from a variety of scriptural texts, including 2 Samuel 7, Psalm 89, and Jeremiah 33, to recount God's promise that a Davidic descendant would eternally sit upon the throne (*Ps. Sol.* 17.1-4).[6] The writer then condemns those who have 'despoiled the throne of David' (*Ps. Sol.* 17.5-6) who had also forcibly seized the government and established an unlawful monarchy (*Ps. Sol.* 17.5-6). This rather transparent historical allusion clearly refers to the Hasmonean dynasty, who ruled as kings although they were not of the Davidic line. Because of their sins, God permitted a 'man foreign to our race' (*Ps. Sol.* 17.7) to conqueror Jerusalem and exterminate this unlawful Hasmonean royal family (*Ps. Sol.* 17.7-10).

Although the psalmist initially rejoices at this event (*Ps. Sol.* 17.10), the situation quickly becomes worse as this 'lawless' man (*Ps. Sol.* 17.11), after removing the Hasmoneans from power, proceeds to oppress the city's population and forces the author's community to flee Jerusalem (*Ps. Sol.* 17.11-17). The psalmist reflects upon Jerusalem's present situation and concludes that the entire population, from the leaders to the common people, are immoral (*Ps. Sol.* 17.18-20). With this oppression unbearable, the author feels that there is no hope unless God intervenes in human affairs and sends the lawful ruler, the 'Son of David' (*Ps. Sol.* 17.21), to purge Jerusalem of its Gentile and Jewish sinners (*Ps. Sol.* 17.21-46). This anticipated king is not an ordinary Davidic descendant, for the psalmist unambiguously proclaims that he will be none other then the 'Lord's Messiah' (χριστὸς κύριος; *Ps. Sol.* 17.32).

Psalm of Solomon 17's author portrays this Davidic Messiah as a righteous counterpart to the 'man that is foreign to our race' (*Ps. Sol.* 17.7), who had devastated Jerusalem and persecuted the psalmist's community. This Messiah would be a warrior who would engage in a violent conflict with Jerusalem's enemies and '…smash the arrogance of the sinner as a potter's jar' (*Ps. Sol.* 17.23). Following his successful purge of Jerusalem, this militant Davidic Messiah would inaugurate an

---

"The Lord's Anointed" Reconsidered', *NTS* 31 (1985), pp. 620-27; Laato, *A Star is Rising*, pp. 283-84.

6.   The writer, in vv. 1-4, alludes to many scriptural texts, the most prominent of which include: Jer. 23.5 and 33.15 (monarchy restricted to members of David's house); 2 Sam. 7 and Ps. 89 (God's covenant with David); Ps. 145.13 and Dan. 7.27 (God's everlasting kingdom); Pss. 29.10; 97.1; 74.12; 99.1; Exod. 15.18 (The Lord is king).

era of peace in which the psalmist's community would play a leading role (*Ps. Sol.* 17.26-32) as the Jews scattered throughout the earth would return to Jerusalem (*Ps. Sol.* 17.30-32).[7] Although *Psalm of Solomon* 17's author portrays the Davidic Messiah as a violent warrior, the writer expects that he will rule through compassion and wisdom and judge the people of the earth in righteousness (*Ps. Sol.* 17.33-46).

Psalm of Solomon 17 reflects the tumultuous conditions that accompanied Herod the Great's rise to power in 37 BCE when, with the assistance of the Roman general Sosius, he successfully attacked Jerusalem to seize the throne.[8] Herod, the 'man alien to our race' (*Ps. Sol.* 17.7), once in control of Jerusalem, proceeded to systematically hunt down all the surviving members of the Hasmonean family to prevent them from returning to power. The psalmist alludes to Herod's efforts to eradicate this family with the statement that: 'He has sought out their offspring and let not one of them go free' (*Ps. Sol.* 17.9). Herod's campaign to exterminate the Hasmonean family effectively ended in 30 BCE when he executed Hyrcanus II. *Psalm of Solomon* 17 was therefore composed sometime following 37 BCE, since the author documented Herod and Sosius's 37 BCE siege of Jerusalem, but before 30 BCE, when Herod killed the last of the Hasmoneans.[9]

7. For the scriptural basis for this regathering of the exiles, see Ps. 147.2; Jer. 23.8. This expectation that the exiles would be gathered in the messianic age was a common hope and is reflected in many Jewish works. See, Bar. 4–5; Sir. 36.10-13; 48.10; 2 Macc. 1.27-29. See further, A. Hultgard, 'Figures messianiques d'Orient comme sauveurs universels dans le monde Gréco–Romain', in U. Bianchi and J. Vermaseren (eds.), *La soteriologia dei culti orientali nell' impero romano* (Leiden: E.J. Brill, 1982), pp. 735-76 (734-48).

8. For a Herodian dating of *Ps. Sol.* 17, see K. Atkinson, 'Herod the Great, Sosius, and the Siege of Jerusalem (37 BCE) in Psalm of Solomon 17', *NovT* 38 (1996), pp. 313-22; *idem*, 'Toward a Redating of the Psalms of Solomon: Implications for Understanding the *Sitz im Leben* of an Unknown Jewish Sect', *JSP* 17 (1998), pp. 95-112 (104-107).

9. In 37 BCE, immediately following his siege of Jerusalem, Herod convinced Antony to kill Antigonus, who had declared himself king of Judea with the help of the Parthians. See, Josephus, *Ant.* 14.487-91, 15.8-10. In 36 BCE Herod killed Aristobulus III, the high priest, in his palace pool at Jericho. See, Josephus, *Ant.* 15.50-56. Following the battle of Actium in 31 BCE, Herod faced an uncertain future and feared that the Hasmonean dynasty would return. It was this event that compelled Herod to murder Hyrcanus in 30 BCE. See, Josephus, *Ant.* 15.161-64. Josephus also mentions in passing Herod's siege and destruction of the last Hasmonean strong-

Although the author does not accept the Hasmonean's right to rule, and believes that Herod's murder of the Hasmoneans is God's punishment upon this family for taking the throne with violence (*Ps. Sol.* 17.5-9), the psalmist believes that Herod has gone beyond his commission when he besieged Jerusalem and acted like a Gentile (*Ps. Sol.* 17.14).[10] The psalmist denounces Herod and Sosius respectively as the 'alien and the foreigner' (πάροικος καὶ ἀλλογενής; *Ps. Sol.* 17.28), since they were jointly responsible for the atrocities associated with the siege of Jerusalem. Despite the Roman's culpability, the psalmist chose to focus upon Herod's crimes, since he, as a Jew, had betrayed his country when he invited the Romans to assist him in attacking Jerusalem.[11] The writer's denunciation of Herod as a 'man alien to our race' (*Ps. Sol.* 17.7) was undoubtedly a reference to his Idumean ancestry,

hold at Hyrcania, just before the battle of Actium, which had been held by Antigonus's unnamed sister. See, Josephus, *War* 1.364. Additionally, in 29/27 BCE Herod killed his wife, the Hasmonean princess Mariamme, and shortly thereafter her mother and sons by Herod. See Josephus, *Ant.* 15.229-31; *idem*, *War* 1.441-44. For further details concerning the chronological problems in Josephus's account of Mariamme's execution, and for Herod's non-Jewish background, see N. Kokkinos, *The Herodian Dynasty: Origins, Role in Society and Eclipse* (JSPSup, 30; Sheffield: Sheffield Academic Press, 1998), pp. 211-15.

10. The psalmist's perspective here (Ps. Sol. 17.5-9) is similar to 1QpHab and 1QpNah, which portray the Kittim as having been sent by God to punish the Hasmoneans for their sins.

11. The Qumran text 4QCalendrical Doc C[a-e] provides a similar parallel to the denunciation of Herod in Ps. Sol. 17, for its author castigates the Roman legate M. Aemilius Scaurus for a massacre (4Q324a frag. 2 lns. 4 & 8) that apparently followed Pompey's 63 BCE siege of Jerusalem. Although Pompey was in charge, the author of 4QCalendrical Doc C[a-e] only mentions Scaurus by name, since he was the one who had personally carried out Pompey's orders. Likewise, Ps. Sol. 17's author only castigates Herod, and not Sosius, since he had betrayed his own race in cooperating with the Romans and had personally killed many of Jerusalem's citizens and the Hasmonean royal family. For 4QCalendrical Doc C[a-e], see M. Wise, 'Primo Annales Fuere: An Annalistic Calendar from Qumran', in *idem*, *Thunder in Gemini: And Other Essays on the History, Language and Literature of Second Temple Palestine* (JSPSup, 15; Sheffield: Sheffield Academic Press, 1994), pp. 186-221 (211-18); F.M. García Martínez, 'Calendarios en Qumran (II)', *EstBíb* 54 (1996), pp. 540-43; J. VanderKam, *Calendars in the Dead Sea Scrolls: Measuring Time* (New York: Routledge, 1998), pp. 84-87. See also now the nearly identical mention of a massacre by an individual named Potlais (פותלאיס) that possibly followed Herod the Great's death. M. Broshi, 'Ptolas and the Archelaus Massacre (4Q468g=4Qhistorical text B)', *JJS* 49 (1998), pp. 341-45.

which Josephus records had become an effective propaganda tool for those Hasmonean supporters who attempted to undermine his reign, and was intended to further portray Herod as a Gentile.[12] For the author's community, the consequences of Herod's actions were more devastating than any previous sufferings they had endured since the foundation of the Hasmonean dynasty. According to the psalmist, only the direct intervention of the 'Lord's Messiah' could alter Jerusalem's present situation under Herodian rule (*Ps. Sol.* 17.21-46).

Like the author of Lk. 1.30-35, the psalmist's condemnation of those who 'despoiled the throne of David' (*Ps. Sol.* 17.5-6) implies that Herod must be removed. After describing the horrors of Herod's siege, the psalmist turns to Scripture to fashion a Davidic Messiah who will overthrow Herod and his Roman allies and then reign as king in Jerusalem (*Ps. Sol.* 17.21-46). The psalmist alludes to 1 Sam. 2.10 and Ps. 132.17 to express this expectation for a new Davidic ruler, and writes that:

> Behold, O Lord, and raise [ἀνάστησον] up for them their king, the son of David,
> At the time which you have [fore]seen, O God, to rule over Israel your servant (*Ps. Sol.* 17.21; cf. *Ps. Sol.* 17.4).

Here, the psalmist echoes many passages from the Hebrew Bible in which the motif of 'raising' (קום) the new David appears.[13] The psalmist unambiguously depicts this Messiah as a militant figure and, in vv. 23-24, writes:

> May he smash the sinner's arrogance like a potter's jar,
> With a rod of iron may he break in pieces all their substance;
> May he destroy the lawless nations with the word of his mouth.

Here, the author combines Isa. 11.2-4 and Ps. 2.9 to portray a militant Davidic Messiah who will violently shatter his enemies. The psalmist has also creatively transformed Isaiah 11's verbal weapons, namely the

---

12. For Herod's Idumean ancestry, see Josephus, *War* 1.123, 313; *idem, Ant.* 14.8-9, 403. That 'Amalek' in 4Q252 is also a derogatory reference to Herod's Idumean ancestry is suggested by H. Stegemann, 'Weitere Stücke von 4Qp Psalm 37, von 4Q Patriarchal Blessings und Hinweis auf eine unedierte Handschrift aus Höhle 4Q mit Exzerpten aus dem Deuteronomium', *RevQ* 6 (1967), pp. 214-15. See also Kokkinos, *The Herodian Dynasty*, pp. 94-139.

13. Jer. 23.5; 30.9; Ezek. 34.23. See also, Isa. 11.1; Hos. 3.5; Zech. 3.8. Cf. 1 Sam. 2.10; Ps. 132.17; Lk. 1.69 See also, Laato, *A Star Is Rising*, pp. 322-24; Pomykala, *Davidic Dynasty Tradition*, p. 162.

'rod of his mouth' and the 'breath of his lips' into a literal sword to fashion a militant Davidic Messiah who would destroy his enemies with an iron rod as well as with the word of his mouth.[14] Although this Davidic Messiah is violent warrior, vv. 33-34 state that his power does not rest upon his own might, but upon his trust in God.

2. *Scripture and the Militant Davidic Messiah in the Qumran Texts*

Psalm of Solomon 17's depiction of a militant Davidic Messiah is contemporary with a number of Qumran texts that also use many of the same scriptural texts to fashion a violent Davidic Messiah. Among the Dead Sea Scrolls the following four documents clearly use the Davidic dynasty tradition: 4QDibHam[a] (4Q504), 4QpGen[a] (4Q252), 4QMidr-Eschat[a] (4Q174), 4QpIsa[a] (4Q161) and 4QSefer ha-Milḥamah (4Q285).[15] Because 4Q504's author does not clearly mention a Davidic Messiah, but only echoes Psalm 89 which recalls God's promise of a covenant with David, this text is excluded from the present discussion.[16]

---

14. See, G.L. Davenport, 'The "Anointed of the Lord" in Psalms of Solomon 17', in J.J. Collins and G.W.E. Nickelsburg (eds.), *Ideal Figures in Ancient Judaism: Profiles and Paradigms* (Chico, CA: Scholars Press, 1980), pp. 67-92.

15. For the use of the Davidic dynasty tradition in these texts, see F. García Martínez and J.T. Barrera, *The People of the Dead Sea Scrolls: Their Writings, Beliefs and Practices* (Leiden: E.J. Brill, 1995), pp. 161-70; Collins, *Scepter and the Star*, pp. 20-73; Laato, *A Star Is Rising*, pp. 285-89; Pomykala, *Davidic Dynasty Tradition*, pp. 171-229; E. Puech, 'Messianisme, eschatologie et résurrection dans les manuscrits de la mer morte', *RevQ* 70 (1997), pp. 255-98 (274-76); Schürer, 'Messianism', pp. 550-54; J. VanderKam, 'Messianism in the Scrolls', in E. Ulrich and J. Vanderkam (eds.), *The Community of the Renewed Covenant* (Notre Dame: University of Notre Dame Press, 1994), pp. 215-18. Although other Qumran texts contain a belief in a non-Davidic Messiah, these documents are not relevant to the present investigation, which only examines Davidic Messianism in the Scrolls. For these texts, see Pomykala, *Davidic Dynasty Tradition*, pp. 242-45. See also, Collins, *Scepter and the Star*, pp. 60-61.

16. For 4Q504, dated to c. 150 BCE, see M. Baillet, *Qumran grotte 4.III (4Q482-4Q520)* (DJD, 7; Oxford: Clarendon Press, 1982), VII, pp. 137-68; *idem*, 'Un recueil liturgique de Qumrân, grote 4: "Les paroles des luminaires"', *RB* 68 (1961), pp.195-250. See also, E.G. Chazon, 'Is Divrei Ha-Me'orot a Sectarian Prayer?', in D. Dimant and U. Rappaport (eds.), *The Dead Sea Scrolls: Forty Years of Research* (Leiden: E.J. Brill, 1992), pp. 3-52 (3-17); C.A. Evans, 'David in the Dead Sea Scrolls', in S.E. Porter and C.A. Evans (eds.), *The Scrolls and the Scriptures: Qumran Fifty Years After* (JSPSup, 26; Sheffield: Sheffield Academic Press,

4QapocrDan ar (4Q246), although it does not explicitly refer to a Davidic Messiah, describes a 'Son of God' who is nearly identical to the militant Davidic Messiah of *Psalm of Solomon* 17.[17] These five texts (4Q252; 4Q174; 4Q161; 4Q285; 4Q246) all date to the Herodian period (37 BCE-70 CE), thus making them roughly contemporary with *Psalm of Solomon* 17's composition and the period when the entire corpus of *Psalms of Solomon* were collected and redacted.[18] Although none of

1997), pp. 183-97 (189-90); Pomykala, *Davidic Dynasty Tradition*, pp. 172-80. J.C.R. de Roo, 'David's Deeds in the Dead Sea Scrolls', *DSD* 6 (1999), pp. 44-65.

17. For 4Q246, see E. Puech, '4Qapocryphe de Daniel ar', in G. Brooke, *et al.* (eds.), *Qumran Cave 4.XVII: Parabiblical Texts, Part 3* (DJD, 22; Oxford: Clarendon Press), pp. 165-84. See also, J.J. Collins, 'The "Son of God" Text from Qumran', in M. De Boer (ed.), *From Jesus to John: Essays on Jesus and Christology in Honour of Marinus de Jonge* (Sheffield: JSOT Press, 1993), pp. 65-82; J.D.G. Dunn, '"Son of God" as "Son of Man" in the Dead Sea Scrolls? A Response to John Collins on 4Q246', in Porter and Evans (eds.), *The Scrolls and the Scriptures*, pp. 198-210; J. Fitzmyer, 'The Aramaic "Son of God" Text from Qumran Cave 4', in M. Wise *et al.* (eds.), *Methods of Investigation of the Dead Sea Scrolls and the Khirbet Qumran Site: Present Realities and Future Prospects* (New York: New York Academy of Sciences, 1994), pp. 163-75; *idem*, '4Q246: The "Son of God" Document from Qumran', *Bib* 74 (1993), pp. 153-74; E. Puech, 'Fragment d'une apocalypse en aarméen (4Q246=pseudo-Dan^d) et le "royaume de Dieu"', *RB* 99 (1992), pp. 98-131; *idem*, 'Notes sur le fragment d'apocalypse 4Q246-"le fils de Dieu"', *RB* 101 (1994), pp. 533-56.

18. 4Q252 dates between 30 BCE-70 CE. See G. Brooke, '4Qcommentary on Genesis A', in *idem, et al.* (eds.), *Qumran Cave 4.XVII*, pp. 185-207 (190). See also, Pomykala, *Davidic Dynasty Tradition*, pp. 181, 188; Stegemann, 'Weitere Stücke', p. 215; J.T. Milik, *Ten Years of Discovery in the Wilderness of Judaea* (SBT, 26; London: SCM Press, 1959), p. 96 n. 1. For 4Q174, dated between 30 BCE to the first century CE, see, G.J. Brooke, *Exegesis at Qumran: 4QFlorilegium in its Jewish Context* (JSOTSup, 29; Sheffield: JSOT Press, 1985), pp. 83-84, 217; Milik, *Ten Years of Discovery*, p. 96 n. 1; Pomykala, *Davidic Dynasty Tradition*, p. 192; J. Strugnell, 'Notes en marge du volume V des "Discoveries in the Judean Desert of Jordan"', *RevQ* 26 (1970), pp. 163-276 (177, 220). For the dating of 4Q161, written between 30 BCE-20 CE, see, Milik, *Ten Years of Discovery*, p. 96 n. 1; Pomykala, *Davidic Dynasty Tradition*, p. 198; Strugnell, 'Notes', p. 183. 4Q285 has been dated between 30-1 BCE. See, M. Abegg, 'Messianic Hope and 4Q285: A Reassessment', *JBL* 113 (1994), p. 81; Pomykala, *Davidic Dynasty Tradition*, p. 204; B. Nitzan, 'Benedictions and Instructions for the Eschatological Community (11QBer; 4Q285)', *RevQ* 16 (1993), pp. 77-90; A.S. Van der Woude, 'Ein neuer Segensspruch aus Qumran (11Qber)', in S. Wagner (ed.), *Bibel und Qumran* (Leipzig: Evangelische Hauptbibelgesellschaft zu Berlin, 1968), pp. 253-58. 4Q246 has been dated to approximately 25 BCE. See, E. Puech, *Qumran Cave 4.XVII*, p. 166; *idem*, 'Fragment d'une

these Qumran texts uses the two messianic titles that occur in *Psalm of Solomon* 17, namely the 'son of David' (*Ps. Sol.* 17.21) and the 'Lord's Messiah' (*Ps. Sol.* 17.32), they nevertheless display a comparable expectation for a militant Davidic Messiah and demonstrate that the Davidic Messiah was also referred to by designations other than 'Messiah'.

The first text, 4Q252 5 vi 1-7, bases its hope for a Davidic Messiah upon God's everlasting covenant to David and his descendants. The relevant lines (5.1-4) read:

> [1]A ruler shall [not] depart from the tribe of Judah [Gen. 49.10a]. When Israel has dominion one belonging to David who sits on the throne [2][shall not be] cut off for the staff is the covenant of the kingdom [3][and the thou]sands of Israel are the standards. Until the Messiah of Righteousness comes, the Branch of [4]David,
>
> For to him and to his seed was given the covenant of kingship of his people for everlasting generations.

4Q252 demonstrates that at Qumran Jacob's blessing of Judah in Genesis 49 was viewed as a promise for the restoration of the Davidic monarchy. This text refers to the coming of a figure who is called 'the Messiah of Righteousness' (משׁיח הצדק) and 'the Branch of David' (צמח דויד). These terms allude to the 'righteous Branch' (צמח צדיק) of Jer. 23.5 and 33.15 (cf. Zech. 3.8; 6.12), and confirm that Jeremiah's 'Branch' at Qumran was also called the 'Messiah'.[19] This passage attributes the absence of a Davidic ruler to Israel's present lack of dominion. Because 1QM 1.5 and 17.7-8 assert that Israel would achieve dominion following the annihilation of its enemies, 4Q252's writer presumably envisions a similar violent conflict. 4Q252's author, like *Ps. Sol.* 17.5-6 and Lk. 1.30-35, alludes to such scriptural texts as 2 Samuel 7, Psalm 89, and Jer. 23.5 and 33.15 to undermine the legitimacy of the current

---

apocalypse en araméen', p. 105. For the dating of Qumran scripts, see F.M. Cross, 'The Development of the Jewish Scripts', in G.E. Wright (ed.), *The Bible and the Ancient Near East* (Garden City, NY: Doubleday, 1961), pp. 170-264. For the dating and redaction of the *Psalm of Solomon*, see Atkinson, 'Toward a Redating', pp. 101-112.

19. Collins, *Scepter and the Star*, p. 62. See also, Martínez and Barrera, *People of the Dead Sea Scrolls*, p. 163; Knibb, 'Messianism in the Pseudepigrapha', pp. 167-68; Pomykala, *Davidic Dynasty Tradition*, p. 186; Schürer, 'Messianism', pp. 550-51; Puech, 'Messianisme, eschatologie et résurrection', pp. 276-77; J. VanderKam, 'Messianism and Apocalypticism', in J. Collins (ed.), *The Encyclopedia of Apocalypticism*, I (New York: Continuum, 1997), pp. 193-228 (217-18); *idem*, 'Messianism in the Scrolls', pp. 215-18.

monarch, for these passages restrict kingship to David's house. 4Q252 apparently espouses a militant interpretation of Jeremiah in which the messianic Son of David would use violence to bring about his reign, for Jer. 23.6 states that the 'Branch of David' will deliver Israel and bear the epitaph, 'The Lord is our Vindicator'. If 4Q252 is intended as a messianic challenge to the current monarch, then its Herodian date (c. 30 BCE to 70 CE) suggests that this text's use of Scripture was intended to undermine the legitimacy of one of the Herodian kings.

The term 'Branch of David' also appears in 4Q174 1.10-13, which contains the following interpretation of 2 Sam. 7.11-14 and Amos 9.11:

> [10]And the Lord [decla]res to you that he will build you a house. And I will raise up your seed after you, and I will establish the throne of his kingdom [11][for]ever. I will be to him a father, and he will be to me a son [2 Sam. 7.11b-14a]. This [refers to] the Branch of David who will stand with the Interpreter of the Law, who [12][will arise] in Zi[on in] the end of days, as it is written, 'And I will raise up the booth of David which is fallen' [Amos 9.11a]. He is the Branch of [13]David which was fallen, who will take office to save Israel.

This Qumran text, like 4Q252, uses Jer. 23.5 and 33.15 to identify the seed of David as the 'Branch of David'. Additionally, this text's exegesis of 2 Samuel 7 clearly identifies this 'Branch of David' as the Son of God.[20] This text, like *Psalm of Solomon* 17 and 4Q252, uses Scripture to directly challenge the legitimacy of any non-Davidic ruler. Because 4Q174's author believed that only the 'Branch of David' was the rightful monarch, this text's interpretation of Scripture posed a direct threat to the legitimacy of any non-Davidic king.

4Q174's author alludes to a variety of biblical passages that emphasize this Davidic Messiah's function as a warrior.[21] The writer also quotes Amos 9.11 to stress the active role that this 'Branch of David' will have in restoring Israel.[22] Because the messiah of 4Q252 is to as-

---

20. Collins, *Scepter and the Star*, p. 61. Cf. Laato, *A Star Is Rising*, p. 315.

21. 2 Sam. 7.10-14; Jer. 23.5-6; Amos 9.11; Ps. 2; Dan. 12.10. See further, Puech, 'Messianisme, eschatologie et résurrection', pp. 277-78.

22. Although 4Q174 does not delineate the means by which this Branch of David will save Israel, its verb יׁשע suggests that this Davidic Messiah was expected to deliver Israel from its enemies in a battle. This verb is also used in 1QM 10–11 to describe God's deliverance of the righteous from their enemies in a battle. See, Brooke, *Exegesis at Qumran*, pp. 197-207; Pomykala, *Davidic Dynasty Tradition*, pp. 196-97.

sume the throne in order to save Israel, 4Q174's messiah would also presumably fight God's enemies, including the current illegitimate Herodian monarch.

4Q161 contains an interpretation of Isa. 11.1-5 which speaks of a Davidic Messiah who will participate in a battle against the Kittim.[23] The relevant messianic portion of 4Q161, fragment 8-10 iii 17-24, reads as follows:

> [17][The interpretation of the matter concerns the Branch of] David who will stand in the end [of days...] [18][...ene]mies. And God will sustain him with a [spirit of mi]ght [...] [19][...thr]one of glory, a h[oly] crown, and embroider[ed] garments [20][...] in his hand and over all the n[ation]s he shall rule and Magog [21][...a]ll the peoples will his sword judge, and when it says: 'Neither [22][with the sight of his eyes shall he judge] nor with the hearing of his ears shall he decide' [Isa. 11.3b]. The interpretation is that [23][...] and as they instruct him, so will he judge, and according to their command [24][...] with him. One of the priests of name will go out and in his hand the garments of [...]

This text apparently states that the 'Branch of David' will oppose an eschatological enemy of Israel called 'Magog', derived from Ezekiel 38–39, who, according to 1QM 11.16, is delivered by God into the hands of the Lord's poor ones. 4Q161's author, like the writer of *Psalm of Solomon* 17, has transformed Isaiah 11's verbal weapons, the 'rod of his mouth' and the 'breath of his lips', into a literal sword to intensify the militant nature of the Davidic Messiah. 4Q161 also equates Jeremiah's 'Branch of David' with Isaiah's shoot from the stump of Jesse foretold in Isa. 11.1-5. Because this figure is expected to arise at the end

---

23. Some portions of 4Q161 speak of a war against the Kittim. Fragments 5–6.2-3 recalls 1QM 1.3 and reads 'when they return from the wilderness of the p[eopl]es', and then mentions the 'Prince of the Congregation'. Fragments 8–10.7, and other fragments of 4Q161, mention a 'battle of the Kittim' (למלחמת כתיאים). The Prince of the Congregation in 4Q161 appears to be involved in turning aside the Kittim. See, J.M. Allegro with A.A. Anderson, *Qumran Cave 4.I(4Q158-4Q186)* (DJD, 5; Oxford: Clarendon Press, 1969), pp. 11-15 (to be used in conjunction with Strugnell, 'Notes', pp. 183-86); Collins, *Scepter and the Star*, pp. 57, 70 n. 30; Davenport, 'The Anointed of the Lord', p. 72; Martínez and Barrera, *People of the Dead Sea Scrolls*, p. 164; Pomykala, *Davidic Dynasty Tradition*, pp. 198-99; VanderKam, 'Messianism in the Scrolls', p. 219. For a different reconstruction and numbering than Allegro's *editio princeps*, see M. Horgan, *Pesharim: Qumran Interpretations of Biblical Books*, I (CBQMS, 8; Washington, DC: Catholic Biblical Association, 1979), pp. 15-18.

of days there is little doubt that he is an eschatological Davidic king.[24] Like *Psalm of Solomon* 17, 4Q252 and 4Q174, this text, by its focus upon the 'Branch of David' as king, also uses Scripture to restrict the monarchy to a Davidic descendant. Because 4Q161's militant Davidic Messiah will assume the 'throne of glory', this text also threatens the legitimacy of any non-Davidic monarchy.

Because there is a nearly universal agreement among scholars that the Kittim in the *pesharim* are the Romans, it is possible that this text's mention of the Kittim's assault against Jerusalem refers to Herod's 37 BCE siege of that city.[25] Given 4Q161's Herodian date, is also likely that the Kittim symbolized the Romans and their Herodian allies who would be destroyed by the Davidic Messiah, who would then assume the throne. If so, then the Davidic Messiah of 4Q161, like *Psalm of Solomon* 17, also directly opposes Herod and his Herodian allies.

4Q161 is paralleled by 4Q285 fragment 5 which also contains an interpretation of Isaiah 10 and 11 within a description of a military conflict.[26] This text also interprets Jeremiah's 'Branch of David' as the

---

24. For the expression 'end of days' (אחרית הימים) in the Dead Sea Scrolls, and its relationship to the Messiah's war against the Kittim, see J.J. Collins, 'The Expectation of the End in the Dead Sea Scrolls', in C.A. Evans and P.W. Flint (eds.), *Eschatology, Messianism and the Dead Sea Scrolls* (Grand Rapids: Eerdmans, 1997), pp. 74-90 (79-82).

25. 1QpHab 6.1-8 mentions the Romans sacrificing to their legionary standards. Additionally, 4QpNah contains clear references to the reigns of Alexander Jannaeus, Salome Alexandra and both Hyrcanus II and Aristobulus II. See, Collins, *Scepter and the Star*, pp. 57-58; D. Dimant, 'Pesharim, Qumran', *ABD*, V, pp. 245-47; *idem*, 'Qumran Sectarian Literature', in M.E. Stone (ed.), *Jewish Writings of the Second Temple Period: Apocrypha, Pseudepigrapha, Qumran Sectarian Writings, Philo, Josephus* (CRINT, 2/2; Philadelphia: Fortress Press, 1984), pp. 483-50 (511-12); G. Brooke, 'The Kittim in the Qumran Pesharim', in L. Alexander (ed.), *Images of Empire* (Sheffield: JSOT Press, 1991), pp. 135-59; Horgan, *Pesharim*, pp. 80-81; Y. Yadin, *The Scroll of the War of the Sons of Light Against the Sons of Darkness* (Oxford: Oxford University Press, 1962), pp. 23-26. Additionally, the Old Greek version of Dan. 11.30 substitutes 'Romans' for 'Kittim'. For the historical events of Herod's siege, see Atkinson, 'Herod the Great', pp. 313-22.

26. For the text of 4Q285, see G. Vermes, 'The Oxford Forum for Qumran Research Seminar on the Rule of War from Cave 4 (4Q285)', *JJS* 43 (1992), pp. 85-90; B.Z. Wacholder and M. Abegg, *A Preliminary Edition of the Unpublished Dead Sea Scrolls*, II (Washington DC: Biblical Archaeology Society, 1992), pp. 223-27; R. Eisenman and M. Wise, *The Dead Sea Scrolls Uncovered* (Rockport, MA: Element, 1992), pp. 27-29. For the use of Scripture in this text to describe the Da-

fulfillment of Isaiah's prophecy concerning the shoot from the stump of Jesse and reads:

> ln. 1   Isaiah the prophet: [The thickets of the forest] will be cut [down
> ln. 2   with an axe and Lebanon by a majestic one will f]all. And there
>   will come forth a shoot from the stump of Jesse [Isa. 10.34–11.1].
> ln. 3   [...] the Branch of David; and they will enter into judgment with
> ln. 4   [...] and the Prince of the Congregation, the Bran[ch of David],
>   will kill him[27]
> ln. 5   [...]s and with wounds. And a Priest will command
> ln. 6   [the s]lain of the Kittim [...]

This passage describes the rendering of a guilty verdict where the 'Prince of the Congregation' kills the wicked leader with a sword in fulfillment of Isa. 10.33–11.5. 4Q285 clearly identifies the 'Branch of David' with the 'Prince of the Congregation'. Since Isaiah 11 states that the son of Jesse will strike the earth with 'rod of his mouth' and slaughter the wicked with the 'breath of his lips', 4Q285's Branch of David/ Prince of the Congregation is clearly a militant Davidic Messiah.[28] Here, like 4Q161 and *Psalm of Solomon* 17, Isaiah's verbal weaponry has also been transformed into a literal instrument of execution.[29] Given 4Q285's Herodian date, it is possible that its author used Scripture to fashion a militant Davidic Messiah who was also envisioned as a righteous counterpart to the current Herodian ruler.[30]

vidic Messiah's battle against the Kittim, see VanderKam, 'Messianism and Apocalypticism', p. 218; *idem*, 'Messianism in the Scrolls', pp. 217-18; Puech, 'Eschatologie, messianisme, et résurrection', pp. 274-75.

27. The verb (והמיתו) here is a hiphil third person singular with a suffix. See, Abegg, 'Messianic Hope', pp. 88-89; M. Bockmuehl, 'A "Slain Messiah" in 4Q Serekh Milhamah (4Q285)?', *TynBul* 43 (1992), pp. 155-69; Collins, *Scepter and the Star*, pp. 58-60; Laato, *A Star Is Rising*, pp. 294-95; Martínez and Barrera, *People of the Dead Sea Scrolls*, pp. 166-68; Pomykala, *Davidic Dynasty Tradition*, pp. 207-209; Vermes, 'Oxford Forum', pp. 85-90.

28. See, J.J. Collins, 'Messiahs in Context: Method in the Study of Messianism in the Dead Sea Scrolls', in Wise *et al.* (eds.), *Methods of Investigation*, pp. 213-27 (217, 219-20); Laato, *A Star Is Rising*, pp. 294-95; Martínez and Barrera, *People of the Dead Sea Scrolls*, p. 167; Pomykala, *Davidic Dynasty Tradition*, p. 206; Vermes, 'Oxford Forum', pp. 88-89.

29. For the importance of Isa. 11 in the Scrolls' descriptions of the Davidic Messiah, see J.J. Collins, '"He Shall Not Judge by what his Eyes See": Messianic Authority in the Dead Sea Scrolls', *DSD* 2 (1995), p. 154 (145-64).

30. Because 4Q285 and 1QM mention the Kittim, J.T. Milik believes that 4Q285 belongs to the War Rule. See, J.T. Milik, 'Milkî-sedeq et Milî-resa' dans écrits juifs

Although the messianic nature of the Aramaic document 4Q246, commonly referred to as the 'Son of God' text, is still the subject of contentious debate, this work espouses a form of militant Davidic Messianism similar to *Psalm of Solomon* 17. 4Q246 describes the appearance of someone who '... will also be great upon the earth' (col. 1.7). Column 2 then reads 'Son of God he shall be called, and they will name him Son of the Most High (col. 2.1)', and then describes the brief reign of the enemy that will last until the people of God arise.[31] 4Q246 then details the rule of this 'Son of God', who will fight and prevail over his enemies to inaugurate God's everlasting dominion. This Son of God's power does not emanate from within himself, but 'the great God is himself his might' (col. 2.7).

Although the Qumran texts reflect some exegetical variation, John Collins has demonstrated that there is a remarkable degree of consistency in the manner in which messianic titles were combined. Messiahs, therefore, could be referred to by titles other than 'Messiah'. Consequently, the 'Branch of David' is simply another way of referring to the Davidic Messiah.[32] Therefore, the citation of 2 Sam. 7.14 in 4Q174 provides an explicit basis for equating the 'Branch of David' with the 'Son of God'. Because different epithets and titles were applied to the same figure, the equation of the 'Branch of David' with the 'Son of God', provided by 4Q174, demonstrates that the figure here, in 4Q246, is a

et chrétiens', *JJS* 23 (1972), p. 143 (95-144). See also, Abegg, 'Messianic Hope', pp. 82-83. Although the Cave 4 fragments undermine any attempt to date 1QM to the time of Herod the Great, its multiple recensions suggest that it was revised during the Herodian period to include a Davidic messiah. The War Scroll is also extant in six Cave 4 fragments (4Q491–4Q496) that range in date from the first half of the first century BCE to the beginning of the first century CE. See Baillet, *Qumran grotte 4.III*, pp. 12-73. These texts also show evidence of different recensions. See, P.R. Davies, 'War Rule', *ABD*, VI, p. 875 (875-76); Dimant, 'Qumran Sectarian Literature', p. 515. It is likely that 4Q285 represents a different recension of the War Scroll that greatly expands the Davidic Messiah's role. For this suggestion, see Pomykala, *Davidic Dynasty Tradition*, p. 210.

31. I take the text's use of the third person masculine singular suffix in the following lines to refer to the Son of God, who represents the people of God as their ruler. For this interpretation, see Collins, *Scepter and the Star*, pp. 158-60.

32. J.J. Collins, *Apocalypticism in the Dead Sea Scrolls* (New York: Routledge, 1997), pp. 72, 85; *idem*, 'Messiahs in Context', pp. 213-27 (220-22); *idem*, *Scepter and the Star*, p. 60.

Davidic Messiah.[33] 4Q246 clearly portrays this Davidic Messiah as a warrior, for he is expected to cast down his enemies before assuming the throne for an everlasting reign (col. 2.8-9). The role of the 'Son of God' in 4Q246 is similar to the Messiah of *Psalm of Solomon* 17, for both will successfully fight to overthrow their opponents and establish the kingdom of God.[34] Given the militaristic context of this document, its author also apparently envisioned a Davidic Messiah who would overthrow the unlawful non-Davidic king in battle.

3. *Scripture and the Development of Militant Davidic Messianism*

It is significant that the militant Davidic Messiah in *Psalm of Solomon* 17 and these five Scrolls (4Q252; 4Q174; 4Q161; 4Q285; 4Q246) is consistently fashioned after a select corpus of biblical texts, particularly Isaiah 11.[35] Although there is some exegetical variation in the Scrolls, it is significant that Isa. 11.1-5 is cited with reference to the Messiah in 4Q285, 4Q161, and 1QSb, and no non-messianic interpretation is attested.[36] Additionally, this same biblical passage was used in *Psalm of*

---

33. See, Collins, *Apocalypticism*, pp. 72, 82-85; *idem, Scepter and the Star*, pp. 154-72; *idem*, 'The "Son of God" Text', pp. 65-82; C.A. Evans, 'Jesus and the Dead Sea Scrolls from Qumran Cave 4', in Evans and Flint (eds.), *Eschatology, Messianism*, pp. 92-94 (91-100); Laato, *A Star Is Rising*, pp. 315-16; Puech, 'Fragment d'une apocalypse en araméen', pp. 98-131; *idem*, 'Notes sur le fragment d'apocalypse 4Q246', pp. 533-56. For a non-messianic reading of 4Q246, see Fitzmyer, 'Aramaic "Son of God"', pp. 163-75; *idem*, '4Q246', pp. 153-74.

34. See, Collins, *Apocalypticism*, p. 85; *idem, Scepter and the Star*, p. 167; Laato, *A Star Is Rising*, pp. 314-16.

35. See, Collins, 'Messiahs in Context', pp. 220-22; G. Vermes, *Jesus the Jew* (Philadelphia: Fortress Press, 1973), pp. 130-34. Collins additionally comments on this issue that: 'The Jewish sources of the time consistently portray the Davidic messiah as a militant figure who would crush the enemies of Israel... While some portrayals are less violent than others, the militant character of the Davidic messiah is consistent'. J.J. Collins, 'The Works of the Messiah', *DSD* 1 (1994), p. 108 (98-112). See also, R. Kimelman, 'The Messiah of the Amidah: A Study in Comparative Messianism', *JBL* 116 (1997), p. 316 (313-20). For the evidence of the targumim, see C.A. Evans, 'Mishna and Messiah "in Context": Some Comments on Jacob Neusner's Proposals', *JBL* 112 (1993), pp. 267-89, esp. pp. 276-77.

36. Collins, 'Messiahs in Context', pp. 220-21. Although 1QSb 5.20-29 recounts the blessings of the 'Prince of the Congregation', in a paraphrase of Isa. 11.2-5, this text omits any reference to the shoot from the stump of Jesse in Isa. 11.1. Additionally, 1QSb is a pastiche of biblical images, in which such passages as

Solomon 17 to describe the actions of its Messiah. Because *Psalm of Solomon* 17 was not discovered among the Qumran writings, its expectation for a militant Davidic Messiah was not unique, but was apparently common among various strands of early Judaism.

The common use of Scripture in *Psalm of Solomon* 17 and the Qumran texts examined in the present study suggests that their expectation for a militant Davidic Messiah was widespread.[37] Because the militant Davidic Messiah tradition is found in *Psalm of Solomon* 17 and these five Herodian-period Qumran texts, it is likely that this particular form of messianic expectation emerged in reaction to the Herodian dynasty's assumption to power. Pomykala comments upon this possibility, and the earlier use of messianic imagery in the Scrolls, that:

> This evidence leads to the conclusion that davidic messianism did not arise at Qumran until the herodian period (35 BCE–70 CE). After the concept of a davidic messiah was introduced at Qumran, however, at least one of the earlier royal figures, the Prince of the Congregation, was identified with him—or perhaps more accurately, assimilated to him, a development not surprising given some of the similarities in character and role between the Branch of David and the Prince of the Congregation. Both were militant, both envisioned as rulers, and both subordinated to the priests... Only later, in the herodian era, was the davidic dynasty tradition utilized to fashion the conception of a davidic messiah.[38]

Although the 'Prince of the Congregation' appears in such texts as CD, 1QM and 1QSb, this figure was not understood as a Davidic Messiah. Rather, only in 4Q161 and 4Q285 the 'Prince of the Congregation' is

---

Isa. 11 are used apart from connotations of davidic status, with no clear allusion to a Davidic Messiah. Pomykala comments on 1QSb's use of the title נשיא and imagery from Isa. 11.2-5 that these do not constitute sufficient evidence for construing the Prince of the Congregation in 1QSb as a Davidic Messiah, since both designations were used for non-davidic persons and a clear indication of davidic status is absent —particularly the author's failure to cite Isa. 11.1. Pomykala, *Davidic Dynasty Tradition*, pp. 240-41. For a dissenting opinion, that equates 1QSb's 'Prince of the Congregation' with the 'Branch of David' found in 4Q285 and 4Q161, see Collins, *Scepter and the Star*, pp. 60-61.

37. Collins, in a similar fashion, comments that the similarities between Ps. Sol. 17 and these Scrolls suggests that their common understanding of Isa. 11 was widespread. See, Collins, 'Messiahs in Context', p. 221.

38. Pomykala, *Davidic Dynasty Tradition*, p. 240.

clearly identified with the Branch of David.[39] The Qumran texts examined in this study all share the same date of composition (c. 30 BCE–70 CE) and, based upon a select corpus of scriptural texts, employ the same titles for the militant Davidic Messiah. Although certain terms, such as the 'Prince' are found in earlier scrolls, this study suggests that it is important to take into account the dates of each Qumran document, since the 'Prince of the Congregation' was only interpreted as a Davidic Messiah in the Herodian era and not before.[40]

The appearance of the militant Davidic Messiah tradition in these five Herodian-period Qumran texts and *Psalm of Solomon* 17 suggests that Herod the Great's overthrow of the Hasmonean dynasty was accompanied by a widespread use of Scripture to fashion a violent Davidic Messiah who would challenge the legitimacy of the Herodian kings.[41] Although it is possible that some of these Qumran documents actually reflect the activities of the later Hasmoneans, this does not affect the central thesis of this study, for the common expectation for a militant Davidic Messiah was a late development that roughly coincided with the waning years of Hasmonean rule and the inauguration of the Herodian dynasty.[42]

Although the communities responsible for *Psalm of Solomon* 17 and the Qumran texts are commonly regarded as pacifistic, their common image of a militant Davidic Messiah suggests that they looked forward with apparent eagerness to great bloodshed and the destruction of their enemies. It is therefore significant that the author of the Lucan *Benedictus* (Lk. 1.67-79) also emphasizes the appearance of a Davidic Messiah, who would overturn the illegitimate rule of Herod the Great, and writes: 'he has raised up a horn of salvation for us in the house of his servant

39. Because the 'Prince of the Congregation' was clearly identified with the 'Branch of David' in 4Q285, 4Q161's mention of the 'Prince of the Congregation' within the same context as its reference to the 'Branch of David' (4Q161 8-10 iii 11-24) suggests that 4Q161's author also identified the 'Prince of the Congregation' (4Q161 5–6.3) with the 'Branch of David'. See further, Pomykala, *Davidic Dynasty Tradition*, pp. 198-99, 205-12, 243. See also, Horgan, *Pesharim*, p. 79.

40. Pomykala, *Davidic Dynasty Tradition*, p. 241.

41. For a detailed historical examination of Herodian references in Ps. Sol. 17 and the Dead Sea Scrolls, and Herod's relationship with the Romans as reflected in these documents, see my 'On the Herodian Origin of Militant Davidic Messianism at Qumran: New Light from Psalm of Solomon 17', *JBL* 118 (1999), pp. 435-60.

42. See, Collins, 'He Shall Not Judge', p. 148; Pomykala, *Davidic Dynasty Tradition*, pp. 232-46.

David'.[43] The Christian use of Scripture to create a righteous Davidic Messiah, who was also apparently modelled as a counterpart to the Herodian rulers, provides additional evidence that there were exegetical traditions concerning the Davidic messiah that were known across sectarian lines by the first century BCE and which likely fluctuated with contemporary circumstances.[44] The authors of *Psalm of Solomon* 17 and the Qumran texts examined in this study bear witness to the importance of these traditions which were already available when Herod the Great assumed the throne and which were subsequently adapted to fit the new historical circumstances of Herodian rule.

43. See further, Laato, *A Star Is Rising*, pp. 321-22.
44. See further, Collins, 'Messiahs in Context', p. 222; Vermes, *Jesus the Jew*, p. 130.

JOSEPHUS'S BIBLICAL PARAPHRASE AS A COMMENTARY ON CONTEMPORARY ISSUES

Louis H. Feldman

1. *Introduction*

In view of the fact that Josephus came from such distinguished ancestry (*Life* 1–7), belonging to the first of the 24 courses of priests and being descended on his mother's side from the Hasmonean kings, and in view of his excellent education (*Life* 8) and his early beginning, while only 25 years old (*Life* 13), in public life through participating in an important embassy to the Roman court to secure the release of certain priests, and culminating in his appointment as commander of the revolutionary forces in the crucial area of Galilee at the start of the war against the Romans (*Life* 29, *War* 2.568), we should not be surprised that in writing his historical works Josephus would be inclined to view events, even those that had occurred long before his own time, through his own reaction to them and as, in effect, comments on and lessons for the present.

At the very beginning of his *Antiquities of the Jews* (1.3), Josephus, in setting forth the reasons for his writing the history of the Jewish people, identifies himself with those who, induced by the magnitude of useful events, which currently lie in a state of ignorance, have endeavored to bring forth the history of those events for common advantage. That historiography serves such a purpose would seem to reflect the statement of Josephus' major model, Thucydides (1.22.4),[1] that he seeks to make his history profitable for his readers, since he believes that the events of the past will some day, in all human probability, happen again in the same or in a similar way. Though in the *Antiquities* he is not writing about the war with the Romans, Josephus in his proem (1.4) recalls

---

1.   On the profound influence of Thucydides upon Josephus, see my *Josephus's Interpretation of the Bible* (Berkeley: University of California Press, 1998), pp. 177-78.

to the reader his own participation in that war and his aim in writing the history of that war in order to refute those who had misrepresented it. He asserts (1.5) that in writing the *Antiquities* he is addressing the whole Greek-speaking world, the great majority of whom were presumably non-Jews, in order, it would seem, to set the record straight. Again, at the end of the work (*Ant.* 20.262), he proudly declares that no one else, either Jew or Gentile, would have been equal to the task of issuing so accurate a treatise as the *Antiquities* for the Greek world. That he regarded the *Jewish War* and the *Antiquities* as two parts of a single work would seem to follow from his statement (1.6) that his original intention had been to write a single work covering the history of the Jews from their origin through the war against the Romans. The only reason, according to Josephus (1.7), why he did not do so was that such a volume would have been excessively long.

What encouraged Josephus to write the *Antiquities*, he says (1.8), was that there were certain persons who were curious to know about Jewish history. The fact that the one person whom he cites in particular as urging him to write the history is a non-Jew, Epaphroditus, would seem to indicate that the work, when written, would be especially addressed to such people. In fact, the two works, the *Life of Josephus* and the essay *Against Apion*, which are described as appendices to the *Antiquities*, are dedicated to this same Epaphroditus.

Josephus (1.9) lists two other considerations in writing this history, namely whether the ancestors of the Jews had been willing to communicate such information and whether any of the Greeks had been curious to have it presented to them. Both of these show his concern with his primary audience of non-Jews to whom he particularly addresses the work. If, indeed, he is concerned about relations of Jews with non-Jews there are two aspects that he would be particularly eager to address, namely anti-Semitism and proselytism, both of which were fraught with tension.

As to the former, in the very city where Josephus was resident during the last thirty years of his life, Rome, the Jews had experienced two or even three expulsions—in 139 BCE, in 19 CE and during the reign of Claudius, most probably because of their alleged proselyting activities.[2]

---

2. See my *Jew and Gentile in the Ancient World: Attitudes and Interactions from Alexander to Justinian* (Princeton, NJ: Princeton University Press, 1993), pp. 300-304.

Moreover, he wrote much of the *Antiquities* during the reign of Domitian, under whom (Suetonius, *Domitian* 12) the *fiscus Iudaicus* was collected very strictly (*acerbissime*, 'very harshly', 'very bitterly') through informers, and whose hostile attitude seems to have been prompted by Jewish (and/or Christian) success in winning converts, especially at the court itself in the persons of the emperor's cousin Flavius Clemens, who was executed, and the latter's wife Flavia Domitilla (Suetonius, *Domitian* 15.1; Dio Cassius 67.14.1-2; Eusebius, *Historia Ecclesiastica* 3.19-20), who was exiled. Inasmuch as Josephus himself had been accused of being a traitor to the Jewish people because of his surrender to the Romans, he was naturally inclined, in self-defense, to seek ways to prove to his compatriots that he was zealous in defending them.

We shall here consider certain themes in the first half of the *Antiquities* where Josephus, in his additions to, subtractions from, and modifications of the biblical narrative, is, in effect, commenting upon contemporary issues, particularly the recent war of the Jews with the Romans.

2. *Respect for the Concept of a Just War*

The Romans felt strongly about the concept of a 'just war', that is, that a war is permitted to be waged only when all attempts at a peaceful solution have failed and when the enemy is guilty of having launched an unjust attack (Cicero, *De Officiis* 1.11.34-36; *De Re Publica* 3.23.34-35). Thus, for example, before going to war against the Syrians and to justify that war, Josephus (*Ant.* 8.399) carefully expands on the history of Ahab's claims against Syria. On the other hand, one might well wonder whether Saul's war against the Amalekites and especially Samuel's criticism of him for failing to fulfill the commandment to wipe them out were justified. However, Josephus's extra-biblical explanation that the war was justified as vengeance for what the Amalekites had done to the Israelites after the exodus is more convincing (*Ant.* 6.133), since the Romans had such high regard for their ancestors.

Moreover, Josephus, from his own experience with the Romans during the Jewish revolt of 66–73/74, was well aware of the concept of a 'just war.' Hence, it is significant that whereas the biblical account states merely that Ahab told the servants of Jehoshaphat that Ramoth-gilead, which was in the hands of the king of Syria, really belonged to him (Ahab) (1 Kgs 22.3), Josephus expands this by giving the history of

Ahab's claim, namely that the city had first belonged to his father and that it had been taken away by the father of the Syrian king (*Ant.* 8.399); thereby he justifies to Jehoshaphat the military action which they are jointly about to undertake. Furthermore, the Josephan Ahab is a respecter of peace who refuses to be party to its disruption without prior prophetic authorization (*Ant.* 8.401).[3]

3. *Contempt for the Masses*

Josephus stresses that the race of mankind is by nature morose (δυσα-ρέστου, 'discontented', 'grumbling', 'irritable') and censorious (φιλαι-τίου, 'fond of having reproaches at hand') (*Ant.* 3.23). He comments on the effects of the Egyptian famine in the days of Joseph, that it enslaved not only the bodies of the Egyptians but also their minds (διανοίας, 'thought', 'intelligence', 'understanding') and drove them thereafter to degrading means of subsistence (*Ant.* 2.191). Moreover, Josephus adds a snide remark, directed against the rabble (ὄχλος) of women and children, who, he says, were responsible for vitiating the nobler instincts of the Israelites in the desert (*Ant.* 3.5). He returns to the theme of the fickleness of the mob, after King Saul's victory over Nahash the Ammonite, when he speaks sneeringly of 'all that a crowd, elated by success, is wont to utter against those who were of late disparaging the authors of it' (*Ant.* 6.81).

Josephus betrays his contempt for the ignorant mob in his citation of the comment of Plato, who was probably the most important single intellectual force in the process of Hellenization in the East during the Hellenistic period,[4] that it is hazardous to divulge the truth about G-d to the ignorant mob (ὄχλων) (*Apion* 2.224). Thucydides, whom Josephus admired and imitated so much, points out (2.65.4) the truism that the way of the multitude is fickle, as seen by the fine which the Athenians, in their anger at the terrible losses that had befallen them during the great plague, imposed upon their great leader Pericles, only to reverse themselves shortly thereafter and to choose him again as general. Thucydides (2.49-53) graphically portrays the effects of the plague upon the

---

3. So Christopher T. Begg, 'The Death of King Ahab According to Josephus', *Antonianum* 64 (1989), pp. 230-31.

4. So Moses Hadas, 'Plato in Hellenistic Fusion', *Journal of the History of Ideas* 19 (1958), pp. 3-13; *Hellenistic Culture: Fusion and Diffusion* (New York: Columbia University Press, 1959), pp. 72-82.

Athenians, especially upon their minds, noting that it led to despair and lawlessness (2.51.4, 2.53.4, 2.61.3). Consequently, one of the major qualities of the ideal statesman, as we see in Thucydides' portrait (2.60) of Pericles, is the ability to persuade the masses.

Here Josephus followed in the footsteps of Thucydides (2.65.4) and Plato (*Republic* 8.557-61), and here, too, there are clear overtones in his attitude toward the role of the masses in the war against Rome (*War* 3.475, 7.191). It is a truism, according to Josephus in the Korah pericope, that under the stress of want (ἀπορίας, 'privation') and calamity (συμφορᾶς) people become enraged with each other and with their leader (*Ant.* 4.11). Josephus here has in mind a similar scene in one of his favorite authors, Thucydides (2.65.2-3), where he depicts the attitude of the fickle Athenian mob toward Pericles after the plague had afflicted them. He uses the same word, ἀπορία, to explain the strategy of the Roman general Vespasian in blocking Jerusalem, since, he reckoned, the defenders would be reduced by their privations (ἀπορίαις) to sue for mercy (*War* 3.179). Again, during the siege of Jerusalem, Josephus (*War* 6.195) remarks that even those who were dying were not believed to be in want (ἀπορίας).

Josephus stresses the disorderliness of the mob that supported Korah (*Ant.* 4.22). To Josephus the worst political behavior is that of people trooping to the assembly (ἐκκλησίαν) in disorderly wise (ἀκόσμως), with tumult (θορύβου, 'turmoil', 'confusion', 'unrest', 'disorder') and uproar (ταραχῆς, 'confusion', 'unrest', 'disturbance', 'tumult', 'uproar', 'ferment', 'clamor', 'disorder'), the terms θόρυβος and ταραχή being clearly synonymous and intended to emphasize the tumult (*Ant.* 4.22). It is this turbulence (ταραχή) which Korah arouses and which we find referred to no fewer than four times in this brief passage describing the excitement and disorderly conduct of the people (*Ant.* 4.22, 32, 35, 36). The synonymous term, θόρυβος, and its corresponding verb, θορυβέω ('to be noisy', 'to be in ferment'), and adjective, θορυβώδης ('rebellious', 'restless', 'tumultuous'), appear three times in the passage (*Ant.* 4.22, 37, 36). Indeed, Moses appeals to the people to cease from their sedition (στάσεως) and turbulence (ταραχῆς) (*Ant.* 4.32). The fickle mob, in a scene highly reminiscent of the description in Thucydides of the attitude of the Athenians toward Pericles after the plague, in a tumultuous (θορυβώδη) assembly (*Ant.* 4.36), exhibit their 'innate delight in decrying those in authority' and, in their shallowness, swayed by what anyone said, are in ferment. This recalls the way that the masses of the

Athenians vented their disappointment and anger upon Pericles (Thucydides 2.65). Such disorderliness brings about obliteration of the ordered beauty (κόσμος) of the constitution. Indeed, so deeply ingrained is this disorderliness and this seditous tendency that even after the rebels are swallowed up by the earth the sedition continues (*Ant.* 4.59) and, in fact, to a far greater degree and more grievously than before.

Significantly, the same two terms, θόρυβος and ταραχή, which figure so prominently in Josephus's account of Korah's rebellion, are used by him (*War* 5.101) to describe the disorder and confusion in the Temple when John of Gischala attacked the Zealots there. The word θόρυβος ('clamor') is used by Josephus to describe the behavior of the menacing crowd, who with their confused shouts prevented Josephus from hearing them when they made an attempt upon his life (*War* 2.611). Josephus (*War* 2.598) also uses the word ταραχή to describe the ferment which some robbers, rebuffed by Josephus, created against him in the cities around Tarichaeae, with the result that by daybreak a hundred thousand men in arms had been collected against him. As Vespasian and Titus advanced, says Josephus (*War* 4.131), every city in Judea was agitated by tumult (ταραχή) and civil war. Again, Josephus (*War* 4.151) describes how the Zealots seized the Temple and turned it into a fortress and refuge from any outbreak of popular tumult (ταραχῶν). Furthermore, adds Josephus (*War* 4.407), sedition (στάσις) and disorder (ταραχή) during the siege of Jerusalem gave the scoundrels in the country free rein to plunder.

It is precisely because the masses are so fickle that responsible and inspired leadership is so important, as we see particularly in Josephus' treatment of the period of the judges. In particular, in his account of Samuel, Josephus betrays his contempt for the masses. Thus, in an extra-biblical comment, he remarks that Samuel devoted much zeal and care to instilling the idea of righteousness (δίκαιον) *even* into the multitude (πλῆθος) (*Ant.* 6.34). This same multitude, in insisting, despite Samuel's warnings of what a king will do to them, that Samuel find them a king, is described, in a comment without biblical basis (1 Sam. 8.19), as foolish (ἀνόητον) and obstinate (δύσκολον) (*Ant.* 6.43). Whereas the Bible says simply that the people refused to listen to Samuel (1 Sam. 8.19), Josephus stresses the thoughtlessness of the masses by stating that they pressed him importunately (λιπαρῶς) and insisted that he should elect their king immediately and take no thought of the future (*Ant.* 6.43).

An aphoristic contempt for the mob may likewise be seen in Josephus's remark that all the people swarmed around the body of Amasa and, 'as is the way of the multitude [ὄχλος], pressed forward to wonder at it' (*Ant.* 7.287). Similar negative connotations of the word ὄχλος may be seen in the following statements: 'Of the impious multitude [ὄχλου] Azaelos shall destroy some and Jehu others' (*Ant.* 8.352); 'The entire multitude [ὄχλος] [during the reign of Zadekiah] had license to act as outrageously as it pleased' (*Ant.* 10.103).

Again, it is indicative of Josephus's negative attitude toward Jeroboam that the latter was called to power by the leaders of the multitude (τῶν ὄχλων) immediately after the death of King Solomon (*Ant.* 8.212) and that they were consequently responsible for the secession of the northern kingdom. Josephus himself shows his contempt for the masses when he remarks that the advisers of King Rehoboam of Judah were acquainted with the nature of crowds (ὄχλων), implying that such mobs are fickle and unreliable, and that they urged the king to speak to them in a friendly spirit and in a more popular style than was usual for royalty (*Ant.* 8.215).

Egalitarianism, which the aristocratically-minded Josephus despised, also comes to the fore in the extra-biblical promise, ascribed to Jeroboam, to appoint priests and Levites from among the general population (*Ant.* 8.228). To be sure, in the biblical text, we are told that Jeroboam appointed priests from among all the people (1 Kgs 12.31), but it is much more effective to have this come as a promise from Jeroboam directly to his people. Josephus himself clearly opposed such egalitarianism, which smacks of the remarks made by Korah, who likewise had attacked Moses for bestowing the priesthood upon his brother Aaron (*Ant.* 4.15-19) instead of making the appointment democratically and on the basis of sheer merit (*Ant.* 4.23).

Thucydides, whom Josephus admired and imitated so much, cites (2.65.4) the truism that the way of the multitude is fickle. It is, therefore, indeed, significant that when Ezra is first introduced, Josephus, in an extra-biblical addition, notes that he enjoyed the good opinion (δόξης) of the masses (*Ant.* 11.121). With the huge Persian kingdom, consisting, as it did, of so many nationalities and with the Persians themselves being a distinct minority within it, a person such as Ezra, who had the ear of the Jewish masses, would prove extremely useful to his overlord. However, this quality would not necessarily raise Ezra in the esteem of Josephus's reading audience, since Josephus, particularly in his portrayal of Moses, stresses that the true leader is not swayed by the multitude. It is only a rabble-rousing demagogue such as Korah who caters to the multitude and who is consequently the candidate of the people (*Ant.* 4.15, 4.20), whereas the multitude itself is actually bent on stoning Moses (*Ant.* 4.22). Again, Josephus stresses that the natural state of the multitude is anarchy, noting that, once their great leader Joshua had died, the people continued in a state of anarchy for a full 18 years (*Ant.* 6.84).

That Josephus is thinking in contemporary terms in his snide remarks about the masses may be seen particularly in the *Jewish War*. Thus, in *War* 1.172, we read of King Aristobulus of Judea disencumbering himself of his rabble (ὄχλων) of inefficient followers. Such language is also used with reference to the revolutionaries during the war against Rome, as we see in Titus's address to his troops in which he remarks that the Jews, however dauntless and reckless of life they may be, are undisciplined and deserve to be called a mere rabble (ὄχλος...ἄλλως) rather than an army (*War* 3.475). Likewise, we hear of the mere rabble (ὄχλον ἄλλως) of Jews at Machaerus (*War* 7.191). The use of the word in connection with the mob (ὄχλον) of women and children drafted by that most despised of revolutionaries, John of Gischala, is highly significant (*War* 4.107). Similar disparaging remarks in Josephus's *War* about the mob of revolutionaries are found in 3.542: 'The remainder of the mob [who had congregated at Taricheae]—a crowd of seditious individuals and fugitives to whom their infamous careers in peace-time gave war its attractions'; 6.283: 'the poor women and children of the populace and a mixed multitude had taken refuge [in the Temple]'.

4. Disdain for Demagogues

Josephus shares with Thucydides and Plato a disdain for demagogues. This contempt grew out of experiences which each saw as destroying his state in his own lifetime. One is reminded of the way in which, according to Thucydides (3.36, 6.19), the Athenian masses were swayed by demagogues such as Cleon and Alcibiades, as well as of the technique by which the gullible captain of the ship, representing the masses, in Plato's parable, instead of listening to the true navigator, is won over by the fawning sailors (*Republic* 6.488A-89A).

In particular, Josephus connects the act of a demagogue currying favor of the crowd with rebellion, as seen, for example, in his comment that Absalom, when rebelling against his father David, curried favor (δημαγωγῶν, 'acting as a demagogue') with the multitude; when he thought that the loyalty of the multitude (ὄχλων) had been secured, he proceeded to plot against the state, whereupon a great multitude (ὄχλος) streamed to him (*Ant.* 7.196).[5] Here again Josephus followed in the footsteps of Thucydides (3.36, 6.19) and Plato (*Republic* 6.488-89). Korah, on the other hand, is portrayed as a typical demagogue who, as such, wishes to make it appear by his words (λέγων) that he is concerned with the public welfare (τοῦ κοινοῦ) (*Ant.* 4.20), whereas, in reality (ἔργῳ) he is but scheming to have the dignity of leadership transferred by the people from Moses to himself. In his demagoguery he is highly reminiscent of Cleon and Alcibiades in Thucydides' narrative, as well as of the sophists in Plato's parable of the ship (*Republic* 6.488-89).

Josephus depicts the rise to power of Absalom as having come about through the use of techniques associated with demagogues. In the biblical version we read that Absalom would rise early and would stand outside the royal palace, and, like a modern-day politician, would greet those who had come with their lawsuits, putting out his hand, professing interest, flattering them with the view that they were right in their suit, and lamenting the injustice of the system (2 Sam. 15.2-6). By treating every man thus as his friend and equal he adopted a favorite device of demagogues. No wonder, as the biblical account concludes, Absalom stole the hearts of the men of Israel (2 Sam. 15.6).

Josephus goes further in depicting Absalom as a demagogue. He actually uses the word δημαγωγῶν ('be a demagogue', 'have great influence with the people', 'be a distinguished public speaker') in characterizing Absalom's currying favor with the masses (πλῆθος), particularly appealing to those who lost their legal cases and seeking the loyalty (εὔνοιαν) of the multitude (ὄχλων, the key word in Josephus's denunciation of the masses) (*Ant.* 7.196), which streamed (ἐπισυνέρρευσεν, 'flow together', 'join in mass') to him. This is in contrast to the biblical statement that two hundred men—clearly not a great multitude—from Jerusalem went with him as invited guests (2 Sam. 15.11).

Again, we see a political statement by Josephus against democracy in his version of the way Absalom was chosen as king by his followers. The Bible asserts that the conspiracy grew strong, that the number of his adherents kept increasing, and that a messenger came to David with

5. See my 'Il ritratto di Assalonne in Giuseppe Flavio', *RivistB* 41 (1993), pp. 17-21.

the report that 'the hearts of the men of Israel have gone after Absalom' (2 Sam. 15.12-13). In Josephus we have a description of a democratic political process whereby Absalom was chosen by all his followers as king, and we are told specifically that it was he who had contrived (στρατηγήσας, 'be a field-commander', 'use cunning', 'contrive ways and means') to have this method followed (*Ant.* 7.197).

We can see from Josephus's usage elsewhere of the same verb, δημαγωγέω, how contemptuous he was of demagogues. Thus we hear that the people of Ptolemais had been persuaded to change their plans by a certain Demaenetus, who had their confidence at that time and influenced the people (δημαγωγῶν) (*Ant.* 13.330). In particular, Josephus's great rival, Justus of Tiberias, is described as a clever demagogue (ἱκανὸς δημαγωγεῖν) who, through using a charlatan's tricks of oratory, was more than a match for opponents with saner counsels (*Life* 40).

5. *Realistic Attitude and Even High Regard for the Superpower of the Day*

Despite the Bible's strongly positive view of Hezekiah, Josephus is clearly critical of Hezekiah for not realistically accommodating himself to the superior power of that day, Assyria; and, drawing a parallel, in effect, to the situation of the Jews vis-à-vis the Romans, Josephus is less than enthusiastic about him, even going to the point of asserting that it was cowardice that influenced Hezekiah not to come out himself to meet the Assyrians (*Ant.* 10.5).

Inasmuch as it was Isaiah's prophecy that the Assyrian king Sennacherib would be defeated without a battle that encouraged Hezekiah to defy the Assyrians (2 Kgs 19.20-34; *Ant.* 10.13), Isaiah and Hezekiah would seem to be associated in a refusal to submit to the superpower; and hence one can understand why Josephus would seek to minimize and downgrade both of them. After all, if we compare the message of the Assyrian king Sennacherib to Hezekiah, in which he recalls to Hezekiah what has happened to all the nations that have resisted the Assyrians (Isa. 37.11-13, 18.33-35), we see striking parallels with the speech of the Jewish king Agrippa II in which he lists the various nations that have been overcome by the Romans (*War* 2.358-87).

At first thought one might suggest that Josephus's attitude to Jehoiachin may have been influenced by a desire to present this penultimate king of Judah in a positive light in view of his (Josephus's) hope of the renewal of the monarchy at some future time. But this is unlikely, inasmuch as Josephus himself (*Life*) traced his ancestry back, on his mother's side, to the Hasmoneans, who were the great opponents of the Davidic line, whose kingship they usurped. Moreover, the concept of the renewal of the Davidic line was intimately connected with the expectation of a messiah, who, traditionally, was regarded as a descendant of David; and the idea of a messiah was surely anathema to the Romans, Josephus's patrons, inasmuch as a major achievement of the Messiah was to be the establishment of a truly independent state; and this could, of course, occur only with the end of Roman occupation of Judea.

A more fruitful approach will be to consider the possibility that because Josephus saw a striking parallel between the events leading to the destruction of both the First and Second Temples, and because he himself acted in a fashion similar to that of Jehoiachin in surrendering to the enemy, he felt a greater necessity to defend Jehoiachin's decision. It is surely striking that in his address to his rival John of Gischala and to his fellow Jews, Josephus appeals to the same motives that led Jehoiachin to surrender, namely, to spare his country and to save the Temple from destruction (*Ant.* 10.100). As a sole precedent, he cites (*War* 6.103-104) the instance of Jehoiachin (Jeconiah), whose action he refers to as a noble example, in that he voluntarily endured captivity together with his family rather than see the Temple go up in flames. He then, in a veritable peroration and clearly disregarding the biblical statement that Jehoiachin did evil, remarks that because of this action Jehoiachin is celebrated in sacred story by all Jews and will be remembered forever. It is significant, too, that aside from David and Solomon, Jehoiachin is the only king mentioned by name in the *War*.

In his reworking of the narrative of Gedaliah, the client governor of Judea appointed by Nebuchadnezzar, and with clear implications for the contemporary position of Jews vis-à-vis the Romans, Josephus stresses that it was a matter of military necessity for the Jews to remain subservient to the superpower. Gedaliah's position, vis-à-vis the Babylonians at the time of the destruction of the First Temple, was more or less replicated by Josephus at the time of the destruction of the Second Temple, namely, to accept subservience to the superpower in return for religious autonomy. In this he agreed with the rabbinic leadership, at least as exemplified by Johanan ben Zakkai (*Git.* 56a-b). Josephus's identification with Gedaliah's policy of subservience to the superpower should be understood in the light of his sensitivity to the charge that the

Jews constituted a nation within a nation whose allegiance, wherever they were scattered, was to an independent state in the land of Israel and hence that they would forever be subversive until their return from captivity. In effect, Josephus, unlike the Fourth Philosophy, whose adherents fought the Romans during the Great War of 66–73/74, did not regard nationhood as the *sine qua non* of Judaism; a policy such as that advocated by Gedaliah would, he believed, bring peace and prosperity to the Jews.

6. *Opposition to Messianic and Messianic-like Movements and National Independence*

Inasmuch as the concept of a messiah *ipso facto* meant revolt against Rome in order to establish an independent Jewish state, it is not surprising that Josephus avoids any overt inkling that he favored such a doctrine—hence his relative downgrading of Ruth as the ancestor of David, of David as the ancestor of the Messiah, and of Hezekiah, whose messiahship was apparently recognized by some (*Sanh.* 99a).[6] Thus, in the words of Balaam, the goal of the Jews is not to dominate the world but rather merely to be happy (*Ant.* 4.114). Nor is the goal to have an independent state in Palestine but rather to live eternally (δι' αἰῶνος) in the entire habitable world, that is, the Diaspora. Indeed, one reason, we have suggested, why Josephus identified himself more closely with Elisha than with the latter's mentor Elijah, who was clearly the more popular of the two, is that Elijah was regarded as the patron of the zealots and as the forerunner of the Messiah himself.[7]

After Lot and Abraham part from each other, G-d tells Abraham (Gen. 13.14-17) to lift up his eyes in all directions and then proceeds to promise all this land to him and to his descendants forever. Josephus, aware that the political implications of this promise in his own day were an implicit justification for a Jewish state independent of the Romans, judiciously omits this passage completely.[8]

When Abraham laments that he is childless (Gen. 15.2), G-d, according to the Bible (Gen. 15.7), reassures him that he has brought him

---

6.   See my 'Josephus's Portrait of Hezekiah', *JBL* 111 (1992), p. 598.

7.   See my 'Josephus' Portrait of Elijah', *SJOT* 8 (1994), pp. 62-64.

8.   In contrast, the *Genesis Apocryphon*, which has no such apologetic motives, not only includes G-d's promise but greatly elaborates it.

from Ur in order to give him the land of Canaan to inherit. When Abraham then asks for proof that he will, indeed, inherit the land, G-d (Gen. 15.9) tells him to sacrifice a heifer, she-goat, ram, turtle-dove and pigeon, whereupon G-d makes a covenant with Abraham (Gen. 15.18) assuring him that he has given the land from the Nile to the Euphrates to his descendants. Significantly, in Josephus's version of this episode, G-d (*Ant.* 1.183) assures Abraham that a son will be born to him whose posterity will be as numerous as the stars; and after Abraham sacrifices the animals and birds a divine voice announces (*Ant.* 1.185) that his posterity will overcome their enemies, vanquish the Canaanites in battle, and take possession of their land and cities. Thus, there is no indication that the land is a gift from G-d, but rather that it will be won—and presumably lost—on the field of battle. There is no indication as to the extent of the land, which, if the biblical statement is taken literally, would imply that the Jews not only have a claim to an independent state but also regard it as a matter of divine promise that their state should extend far beyond the borders of Judea.

Thus, there is less emphasis on G-d's promise of Palestine to Abraham, in line with Josephus's view that an independent state is hardly a *sine qua non* for Jews, and certainly not when it requires a revolutionary war against the Romans. On the other hand, Josephus, seeking to build up a picture of Abraham and of his descendants as fighters rather than as mere inheritors, has G-d add (*Ant.* 1.185), in his promise to Abraham (Gen. 15.13-16), as we have noted, that his posterity will defeat the Canaanites in battle. Similarly, the Bible (Gen. 17.1-16) tells how G-d appeared to Abraham, reassured him that he was to become the father of a multitude of nations, and changed his name from Abram to Abraham to signify this. In the Bible (Gen. 17.8) G-d assures him that he will give him all the land of Canaan for an everlasting possession and that the seal of this covenant is to be the circumcision which he is now commanded to perform upon himself and upon every male born in his family. Very significantly, in Josephus's version (*Ant.* 1.191-93) there is no mention of the change of name and its implications, and Canaan is described not as a divine gift but rather as a land to be won by human effort in war—something which his rationalized readers could well understand. The limits cited of the land are more modest, extending only from Sidon to Egypt (*Ant.* 1.191), rather than from the Euphrates to Egypt (so Gen. 15.18), perhaps because Jewish territory never actually reached the Euphrates, and Josephus did not wish to have his divine prediction contradicted by the historical facts.[9] As for the circumcision which is commanded, it is not as a seal of a covenant, with its political implications, but rather a means of preventing assimilation.[10]

Josephus's fullest statement (*Ant.* 1.235-36) of G-d's promise of the supremacy which Abraham's descendants will exercise is found in G-d's assertion to Abraham before the appearance of the ram at the climax of the *'Aqedah*, in other words in a purely religious rather than a political context, at a time when Abraham had shown supreme faith and had proven himself worthy of G-d's blessings; here, too, we find the statement (*Ant.* 1.235) that they will subdue Canaan by force of arms and thus be envied of all people.

Whereas in the Bible (Gen. 21.18) an angel reassures Hagar when she has been banished by Abraham by telling her that G-d will make her child into a great nation, Josephus (*Ant.* 1.219) very carefully has the angel tell her merely and very vaguely that great blessings await her through the preservation of her child. Josephus (*Ant.* 1.221) was aware of the tradition that Ishmael was the ancestor of the Arabs, noting, as he does, that the sons of Ishmael occupied the huge expanse of territory known as Nabatea between the Euphrates and the Red Sea; and hence he realized that the biblical promise to Hagar would indicate that the Arabs would become a great—and obviously independent—nation, something which could happen only if the province of Arabia revolted against the Roman Empire, a situation which Josephus, the loyal Roman citizen, could hardly countenance.

The ending of Josephus's version of the *'Aqedah* is a 'lived happily ever after' finale, so typical of Hellenistic novels.[11] Josephus develops further than does the Bible the divine prediction of the blessings that will be showered upon Abraham and his descendants; presumably, he

---

9.   So Samuel Sandmel, *Philo's Place in Judaism: A Study of Conceptions of Abraham in Jewish Literature* (Cincinnati: Hebrew Union College, 1956), p. 66 n. 278.

10.   In this respect, as in several others, Pseudo-Philo is closer to the biblical narrative and to the rabbis than is Josephus's account, for even though he has vastly abbreviated the whole narrative of Abraham, he twice (*Ps. Philo* 7.4 and 8.3) mentions and gives the terms of the covenant between G-d and Abraham. He likewise, unlike Josephus, mentions the change of name of Abraham and Sarah.

11.   So Abraham Schalit (trans. and ed.), *Josephus: Antiquitates Judaicae* (Jerusalem: Bialik, 1944), 2.40 n. 265.

sought thereby to build up Abraham still more. To be sure, Josephus
(*Ant.* 1.191) does have G-d promise Abraham that his descendants will
'subdue Canaan by their arms'. Yet, Josephus has deleted the biblical
theology of covenanted land, apparently because it would be offensive
to his Roman patrons who had just reconquered that land.[12] He does not
want the land to be the focal point, given its significance for the revolutionary theology of the Fourth Philosophy, which insisted that the
Land of Israel must be free from foreign rule.

Josephus was keenly aware that his paraphrase of the Bible would
have considerable contemporary implications. Thus, Josephus, writing
in Rome under the patronage of the Roman Emperor and in the wake of
the disaster of the Jewish revolt of 66–73/74, places less emphasis on
G-d's promise of Palestine to Abraham;[13] Josephus appears more interested in portraying the marriage alliance arranged by Abraham for Isaac
than in the biblical theme of the fulfillment of G-d's promise that Abraham's descendants will inherit the land of Israel.[14] Again, after Isaac
proves his unquestioning faith at the *'Aqedah*, G-d promises him (*Ant.*
1.234) that after a life of felicity he will bequeath to a virtuous and law-
fully begotten offspring a great dominion (ἡγεμονίαν), whose nature
and extent Josephus keeps deliberately vague.

Isaac's prayer, in his blessing of Jacob (Gen. 27.29), that peoples
should serve (*ya'aveduka*) him and nations bow down to him (the latter
half of which becomes in the Septuagint 'let rulers [ἄρχοντες] bow
down to you'), would clearly not be well received by the peoples, nations and rulers of the world, including, of course, the contemporary Romans. Philo's solution is to interpret the passage allegorically (*Quaest.
in Gen.* 4.216-17): it is the nations of the soul that are to be ruled by
reason, while the princes are those who preside over and are in charge
of heterodox principles. Josephus (*Ant.* 1.273) resolves the problem by
omitting all mention of the subservience of nations and rulers and by
substituting a prayer that Jacob will be a terror to his foes and a treasure
and delight to his friends, reminiscent of Simonides' definition of justice in Plato's *Republic* (1.332D).

12. Betsy H. Amaru, 'Land Theology in Josephus' *Jewish Antiquities*', *JQR* 71
(1980–81), pp. 201-29 (208 and 229).
    13. See Amaru, 'Land Theology in Josephus', pp. 201-29.
    14. James L. Bailey, 'Josephus' Portrayal of the Matriarchs', in Louis H. Feld-
man and Gohei Hata (eds.), *Josephus, Judaism and Christianity* (Detroit: Wayne
State University Press, 1987), p. 162.

As one who had participated in the war against the Romans and had come to the conclusion that resistance to Rome was futile and that Rome was divinely destined to rule the world, Josephus constantly seeks to convince his compatriots to give up the dream of national independence. Whereas in the Bible, the promise of land to Abraham is constantly renewed, Josephus shifts the stress from the covenanted land of Israel, so dear to the revolutionaries, to the biblical personalities themselves and to the role of the Diaspora. Thus, Josephus omits the passage (Gen. 26.3-5) which relates G-d's blessing of Isaac promising the land to Abraham's descendants. It is significant that whereas in the Bible (Gen. 27.27-29), in Isaac's blessing for Jacob (whom he thinks to be Esau), he asks G-d for agricultural abundance and for power to demand respect from other nations (the Hebrew reads: 'Nations shall serve thee and peoples bow down to thee'; see the Septuagint: 'Let nations serve thee, and princes bow down to thee'), in Josephus (*Ant.* 1.272) the national aspect is totally omitted, and instead we have a prayer for Esau's personal happiness and satisfaction.

When Isaac blesses Jacob before sending him off to find a wife, whereas the Bible (Gen. 28.3) has him invoke G-d's blessing to 'make thee fruitful and multiply thee, that thou mayest become a multitude of people', and (Gen. 28.4) to inherit the land which G-d gave to Abraham, Josephus (1.278), aware that the Romans were sensitive about the great expansion of the Jewish population especially through proselytism, omits this. Furthermore, whereas the Bible (Gen. 28.14) declares, in G-d's promise in Jacob's dream, that his seed will be 'as the dust of the earth', and that 'thou shall spread abroad to the west and to the east and to the north and to the south', Josephus (*Ant.* 1.282) predicts that the number of Jacob's direct *descendants* (υἱοῖς) will be vast (as, indeed, was the case at the time when Josephus was writing), but is careful to avoid any suggestion that they will seek to convert others to Judaism. Even the Josephan G-d's promise to Jacob that 'to them [thy children] do I grant dominion [κράτος] over this land' indicates nothing more than that the descendants of Jacob will have power or strength in the land of Canaan, though not necessarily political independence there. There is a further omission of land theology by Josephus (*Ant.* 1.309) when Jacob expresses the desire to depart to his own *home* (πρὸς αὐτόν); in the Bible (Gen. 30.25) Jacob asks Laban to send him away, 'that I may go unto my own place, and to my country [*ule'arẓi*]'. When Jacob replies to Laban's objection to his attempt to

escape from him, he speaks, in a long extra-biblical addition (*Ant.*
1.317; cf. Gen. 31.31-32), not in nationalistic terms but rather in terms
of love of native land (πατρίδος), which, he says, is innate (ἐμφῦσαι) in
all.

A key to Josephus's political position may be seen in the scene (*Ant.*
1.331-34) where Jacob wrestles with the angel. In the Hebrew (Gen.
32.28) the angel tells him that his name will from now on be Israel,
because 'you have striven with G-d and with men and have prevailed'.
In Josephus's version (*Ant.* 1.333) the struggle with men (which might,
presumably, include the Romans) is significantly omitted from the explanation of the name, which, we are told, merely 'denotes the oppo-
nent of an angel of G-d.' The assurance which the angel gives Jacob
(*Ant.* 1.332) is not in terms of a future nation but rather that his race
(γένος) will never be extinguished and that no mortal will surpass him
personally in strength. Hence, Josephus has given us a 'gereinigten'
text, where the name 'Israel assumes an eschatological, rather than a
political, significance'.[15]

It is important to note that whereas in the Hebrew (Gen. 35.11) G-d
at Bethel tells Jacob that 'a nation and a company of nations shall come
from you, and kings shall spring from you'—a passage the political
significance of which, especially in view of the recent revolt of the Jews
against the Romans, might well be offensive to the Romans—Josephus
quietly omits the whole scene. Again, when Jacob descends to Egypt,
whereas in the Bible (Gen. 40.3), G-d declares that He will make a great
nation of him there, the word 'nation' is significantly omitted in Josephus (*Ant.* 2.175), who has G-d announce a long era of dominion (ἡγε-
μονία) and glory for his posterity. The phrase 'long era' implies a time
limitation here, and in any case the language of covenanted land is
absent.[16] Striking, moreover, is Josephus's omission (*Ant.* 2.194) of
Jacob's blessing for Judah (Gen. 49.8-10) predicting his militarism and
sovereignty. Furthermore, inasmuch as the increase in numbers of the
Jews, particularly through proselytism, as we have noted, had caused
great anguish to some Romans, Josephus (*Ant.* 2.194) omits Jacob's
statement to Joseph (Gen. 48.4) that G-d would make him fruitful and
multiply, would make of him a multitude of people, and would give his
descendants the land of Canaan as an 'eternal possession'. Moreover, in

15. Annelise Butterweck, *Jakobs Ringkampf am Jabbok: Gen 32,4 ff. in der
jüdischen Tradition bis zum Frühmittelalter* (Frankfurt: Peter Lang, 1981), pp. 51-56.
16. Amaru, 'Land Theology in Josephus', p. 209.

his account of Jacob's death (*Ant.* 2.194) Josephus has him prophesy how each of his descendants is destined to find a habitation (κατοικεῖν) in Canaan; but there is no mention of an independent state for them. Likewise, he omits (*Ant.* 2.195) Jacob's blessing of Ephraim and Manasseh (Gen. 48.16) that they would grow into a multitude in the midst of the earth. Finally, Josephus (*Ant.* 2.201) also changes the biblical statement (Gen. 47.17) that Israel in Egypt 'was fruitful and multiplied exceedingly' into one that the Egyptians became bitterly disposed towards the Hebrews through envy of their prosperity (εὐδαιμονίας), omitting all mention of their increase in numbers.

A political issue on which Josephus felt strongly was nationalism. In the Bible (Exod. 3.8), G-d tells Moses from the burning bush that He will take the Israelites into a good and broad land, the land of the Canaanites, flowing with milk and honey. A similar statement is found a few verses later (Exod. 3.17). The implication is clear: the Israelites are to displace the Canaanites and establish an independent state in the land. In Josephus's version (*Ant.* 2.269), however, there is significantly no mention of the Canaanites who are to be displaced and no suggestion of an independent state; the Israelites are merely to come to the land and settle there.

Of course, inasmuch as Josephus, especially in his paraphrases of the prophets, is highly selective, he might have simply omitted the prediction by Balaam, as he does with the passage foretelling a messianic kingdom which would destroy all previous kingdoms and which itself would last forever (Dan. 2.44), as well as the later passage in Daniel, which makes it clear that the fifth, world-wide, and everlasting empire would be ruled by a people of 'saints of the Most High', that is the Jews (7.18)—a passage which would, to the obvious embarrassment of Josephus as spokesman for the Romans, imply the ultimate overthrow of Rome. The fact that he does not, on the other hand, omit the interpretation of Nebuchadnezzar's dream or the above prophecy of Balaam is an indication of Josephus's deliberate ambiguity reflective of his attempt to reach both of his audiences, the non-Jews and the Jews, the latter with these allusions to an apparently Messianic kingdom which will make an end of the Roman Empire. Perhaps he felt that to omit them altogether would have been taken by Jewish readers as a clear indication that he had sold out to the Romans. In fact, Klausner goes so far as to argue that Josephus's trip to Rome in 64, despite his statements in the *War* that Rome's ascendancy was part of a divine plan, may have actually increased his support for the cause of the revolutionaries, inasmuch as he must have been impressed by the evidence of Rome's decadence and realized that it was only a matter of time before Rome would fall;[17] hence, the passages in *Ant.* 4.125 and 10.210 may be a clue to his real feelings.

In the passage (Num. 24.17-18) corresponding to *Ant.* 4.125, however, what Balaam predicts is that a star out of Jacob and a scepter out of Israel will conquer Edom and Seir. That this is intended as an eschatological prophecy is clear from Balaam's earlier statement that he will advise Balak what the Israelites would do to the Moabites at the end of days (Num. 24.14). That a messianic prophecy is likewise intended seems to be hinted at in the Septuagint's version of Numbers 24.7: 'There shall come a man out of his [i.e. Israel's] seed, and he shall rule over many nations; and the kingdom of Gog shall be exalted, and his kingdom shall be increased'. In any case, the passage was interpreted messianically shortly after the time of Josephus in reference to Bar Kochba (*y. Ta'an.* 4, 7, 68d) by Rabbi Akiva. Of course, such a messianic understanding was avoided by Josephus because of his subservience to the Romans.

It should not surprise us that Josephus has omitted the passages in Isaiah which were interpreted messianically (9.6-7, 11.2-3). And yet, lest he be regarded as having sold out to the Romans, Josephus does not omit but rather adopts cryptic language in referring to Balaam's prophecy of the overthrow of cities of the highest celebrity (*Ant.* 4.125), just as he does not omit but deliberately avoids explaining the meaning of the stone which, in Nebuchadnezzar's dream, destroyed the kingdom of iron (*Ant.* 10.210), which the rabbinic tradition understood to refer to the triumph of the Messiah (*Tanḥ.* B 2.91-92 and *Tanḥ. Terumah* 7).

Josephus is also careful not to offend non-Jews politically. In particular, he is critical of messianic and messianic-like movements, since the goal of such movements was *ipso facto* a political Jewish state independent of the Romans. In view of Josephus's sensitivity to the charge that the Jews constituted a nation within a nation whose allegiance, wherever they were scattered, was to the Land of Israel and that they would be forever subversive until their return from captivity, it is instructive to note Josephus's paraphrase of the warning issued by the prophet Azariah to King Asa. According to the biblical version, if the

---

17. Joseph Klausner, *History of the Second Temple* (in Hebrew) (5 vols.; Jerusalem: Ahiasaf, 1949), V, pp. 167-68.

Jews forsake G-d he will punish them by forsaking them; 'they will be broken in pieces, nation against nation and city against city' (2 Chron. 15.2-7). Josephus, in his paraphrase, introduces a new element when he declares that as a punishment G-d will scatter the Jews over the face of the earth so that they will lead a life as aliens (ἔπηλυν) and wanderers (ἀλήτην) (*Ant.* 8.296-97). From this we might conclude that the Diaspora is a curse and a punishment, whereas one would have expected Josephus, who spent the second half of his life in the Diaspora under Roman protection, to have glorified this event in Jewish history since he clearly opposed an independent Jewish state. However, we must note that there is no hint here of the traditional Jewish hope that the Jews will some day be gathered together from the exile and return to the land of Israel.

Again, in the Bible, when Jehoshaphat, confronted by the invasion of the Moabites and Ammonites, prays to G-d, he says, 'Didst thou not, O our G-d, drive out the inhabitants of this land before thy people Israel, and give it forever to the descendants of Abraham thy friend?' (2 Chron. 20.7). He then reiterates the notion of an eternal divine gift of the land to the Israelites in his statement that the land has been given to the Israelites by G-d as an inheritance (2 Chron. 20.11). In Josephus's version the central focus is not on the land but on the Temple (*Ant.* 9.9); in other words, Josephus has converted a political gift of G-d into a religious one. To be sure, he does mention the land, but it is not as an inheritance that is meant to be an independent state but rather as a dwelling place (κατοίκησιν, 'dwelling', 'residence').

We may see Josephus's opposition to the re-establishment of an independent Jewish state in the fact that whereas in the Bible King Jehoshaphat reminds G-d that it is h-e who has driven out the non-Jewish inhabitants of Judea and has given it to the Jews as a possession which G-d has given the Jews to inherit (2 Chron. 20.5-12), Josephus's Jehoshaphat speaks not of the land as a possession which the Jews have inherited but rather as a place in which to live (κατοίκησιν) (*Ant.* 9.8-9).

In general, Josephus's Daniel, given the additions to the biblical narrative, comes across as having considerable concern for non-Jews. Thus, according to the Bible, Daniel approached his three companions asking them to pray to G-d concerning the mystery so that he and they might not perish with the rest of the wise men (Dan. 2.17-18). In Josephus's version it is Daniel himself who beseeches G-d (*Ant.* 10.199); furthermore, Josephus adds that he did so throughout the night; and in place of the vague term 'mystery' and in place of a concern primarily with saving their own lives, together with those of the non-Jewish wise men, we are told specifically that he sought enlightenment so as to save the Magi and the Chaldaeans, together with whom they were destined to perish. It is thus significantly the fate of the Magi and the Chaldaeans which is his first thought.

That Josephus was highly sensitive to the charge of dual loyalty may be seen in his paraphrase of the biblical passage in which certain Chaldaeans accuse the Jewish youths Shadrach, Mesach and Abednego, whom Nebuchadnezzar had appointed to high administrative posts, of paying no heed to the king, as witnessed by the fact that they did not serve his gods or worship his image (Dan. 3.8-12)—obviously important symbols in maintaining the unity and allegiance of the many ethnic groups in his kingdom. Josephus, in his paraphrase, is careful to shift the emphasis from the failure of the Jews to serve Nebuchadnezzar's gods and to worship his image—a political demand—to the religious motive of the youths, namely their unwillingness to transgress their fathers' laws (*Ant.* 10.214). The Romans, who placed such a great emphasis upon law and upon respect for ancestral tradition, as we can see from the attention given these factors in their great national poem, Virgil's *Aeneid*, would surely have appreciated such a stance.

Elsewhere, Josephus goes even further in shifting the focus away from the conflict between Jewish religious law and the law of the state. Thus, in the Bible Daniel's envious rivals state, in their exasperation, that they are unable to find any complaint against Daniel unless they discover it to be 'in the matter of the law of his G-d' (Dan. 6.5). Realizing that the word 'law' in and of itself was such an important concept to the Romans and that the biblical allusion to a possible conflict between the law of the state and the law of the Jews implied an irreconcilable conflict between two systems, Josephus in his paraphrase of this passage omits the word 'law' altogether and instead couches the issue solely in religious terms with his remark that when his rivals saw Daniel praying to G-d three times a day they realized that they had found a pretext for destroying him (*Ant.* 10.252). When Josephus does subsequently mention the laws of the Jews, he makes clear that his reference is to their religious laws (*Ant.* 10.275), given the immediately following mention of the Temple and its sacrifices. Daniel's envious rivals, on the other hand, according to Josephus's addition to the biblical text (Dan. 6.13), sought to portray Daniel as attempting, by his disregard of the king's edict, to undermine the state, which they claimed others were seeking to keep and preserve (*Ant.* 10.256).[18]

It is surely striking that Josephus omits all reference to David as the ancestor of the Messiah, despite the fact that such a tradition must have been widespread in his era,[19] because he apparently wished to stress for his Hellenistic Jewish readers his own repugnance of an independent state, this being generally regarded as the goal which a messiah as a political leader would accomplish. To the extent that his Roman patrons would have been aware of the beliefs of Jewish messianism, they would have objected to such a political figure who would seek to re-establish an independent Jewish state, precisely the goal of the revolutionaries against Rome in Josephus's own day whom he attacks so bitterly. While it is true, as de Jonge has remarked, that an investigation of Jewish writings dating from the beginning of the Common Era reveals that the term 'Messiah' is not generally used as a desigation for G-d's representative or intermediary who will effect a new age of peace for Israel and for the world, the fact is that messianic movements do seem to have gained impetus precisely during the first century, aided and abetted by the treatment of the Jews by the Roman procurators.[20]

18. There is a lacuna here in the text, but the import appears to be that those who observed the edict not to pray did so not because of impiety but because they realized how important it was to maintain respect for law and order.

19. See my 'Josephus' Portrait of David', *HUCA* 60 (1989), p. 173.

20. Marinus de Jonge, 'Messiah', *ABD*, IV, p. 787. There were several movements in Judea during the first century, particularly at the time of the revolt against Rome, headed by people who claimed the kingship or were proclaimed king by their followers. In view of the fact that these movements were clearly informed by traditional biblical prototypes, 'the conclusion seems obvious that the groups led by the popularly proclaimed kings were "messianic" movements based upon the prototypical messianic movements of biblical history'. So Richard A. Horsley, 'Messianic Movements in Judaism', *ABD*, IV, p. 793. To be sure, Josephus avoids using the word 'Messiah', except (supposing the passages are authentic) in connection with Jesus (*Ant.* 18.63; 20.200); but the movements led by Judas in Galilee, Simon in Peraea, Athronges in Judea, Menahem the leader of the Sicarii, and Simon bar Giora are highly reminiscent of messianic movements, even if the name 'Messiah' is never used with reference to them by Josephus.

7. *Contempt for the Revolutionaries of his own Day*

Like his beloved model, Thucydides, Josephus believed that history more or less repeated itself, inasmuch as its chief ingredients consisted of people, who have not changed very much through the centuries in the factors that drive them. Hence, he finds many parallels between biblical events and personalities and those of his own day, particularly during the war against the Romans.

We see one instance of this in almost the very beginning of Josephus's paraphrase of Genesis. In an addition to the biblical narrative, he notes in vivid detail the continued deterioration in Cain's descendants, each generation becoming worse than the previous one through inheriting and imitating its vices (*Ant.* 1.66). 'They rushed incontinently [ἀκρατῶς] into battle', he adds, 'and plunged [ὡρμήκεσαν] into brigandage [λῃστείαν]; or if anyone was too timid [ὀκνηρός] for slaughter, he would display other forms of bold recklessness (ἀπόνοιαν θράσους) by insolence (ὑβρίζων) and greed (πλεονεκτῶν)'. All this is Josephus's embellishment of a single biblical phrase: 'And he [Cain] built a city' (Gen. 4.17). Significantly, Josephus (*War* 3.9) uses the same word to describe the incontinent (ἀκρατεῖς) ardor of the Jews after they had defeated Cestius Gallus, the Roman governor of Syria, at the beginning of the war against the Romans. Likewise, in reconstructing the speech of the Jewish King Agrippa II seeking to dissuade the Jews from war with the Romans, he twice, within two paragraphs, uses the same verb to describe the way the Jews have plunged (ὡρμημένους, *War* 2.345; ὡρμημένοις, *War* 2.347; similarly ὁρμήσας, *War* 2.396) into rebellion against the Romans. He uses the same verb, ὥρμησαν (*War* 2.408) to describe the assault of the Jewish insurgents on Masada in 66.[21] In a passage highly reminiscent of Thucydides' reflections (3.81-84) on revolution in Corcyra and other Greek cities, Josephus (*War* 4.134) describes the brigandage (λῃστείαν) which various revolutionary factions carried on throughout the country. He describes the revolutionary Simon's attacks as growing more timid (ὀκνηροτέρας, *War* 4.584), as most of his men lost heart. In his address to his troops the Roman general Titus asserts that the Jews are led on by boldness (θράσος) and

---

21. The same verb occurs no fewer than 59 times in the rest of *War*. See Karl H. Rengstorf (ed.), *A Complete Concordance to Flavius Josephus* (Leiden: E.J. Brill, 1979), III, pp. 236-37.

recklessness (ἀπόνοια, *War* 3.479). As to the insolence of the Jewish
rebels, that is a leitmotif throughout the *War*; thus the high priest Ananus
(*War* 4.190) speaks of the insolence (ὑβρισμένον) of the revolutionaries against G-d. As to the atrocities of the rebels, Josephus (*War*
5.429) vividly portrays the greed (πλεονεκτούντων) in grabbing more
than their share from the whimpering weak during the famine in Jerusalem.

The worst form of government, for Josephus as for Plato (*Republic*
566C–580B), is tyranny. The great attack on Moses (*Ant.* 4.146) by
Zambrias (Zimri) accuses him of acting tyrannically (τυραννικῶς)
under the pretext of following the laws and obeying G-d while actually
depriving the Israelites of freedom of action (αὐτεξούσιον, 'self-de-
termination'). Zambrias (*Ant.* 4.148), speaking frankly and as a free
(ἐλεθέρου) man, makes a very strong case for independence of judgment (*Ant.* 4.149) when he declares that he prefers to get at the truth for
himself with the help of many persons, rather than to live under a
tyranny, placing all his hopes for his whole life upon one man, Moses.
Again, when the Israelites, as they so often do, complain against Moses
and decide to defy his leadership, the worst epithet that they can apply
to him is that he is a tyrant (*Ant.* 4.3). The most effective argument of
the most powerful revolutionary that Moses faced, Korah, is (*Ant.* 4.15-
16) that Moses had defied his own laws in acting undemocratically in
giving the priesthood to his brother Aaron, not through a majority vote
of the people but rather acting in the manner of tyrants (τυράννων
...τρόπῳ). And when the multitude, excited by Korah, are bent on stoning Moses, they shout (*Ant.* 4.22), 'Away with the tyrant, and let the
people be rid of their bondage to one who, in the pretended name of
G-od, imposes his despotic orders [βίαια προστάγματα]'.

As we have noted, the worst form of government for Josephus, as for
Plato in the *Republic*, is tyranny. Thus, whereas the Bible describes the
sons of Eli the high priest as base men who did not know the L-rd
(1 Sam. 2.12) and who dealt contemptuously with the L-rd's offerings
(1 Sam. 2.17), Josephus formulates his denunciation of them in terms of
classical political theory: their manner of life differed no whit from a
tyranny (*Ant.* 5.339). Josephus considerably amplifies the degradation
which, Samuel warns them, the Israelites will suffer at the hands of a
king, remarking that they would be treated as chattels at his will and
pleasure and at the impulse of his other passions (*Ant.* 6.61). He adds an
original reason why kings would be less concerned than is G-d with the

welfare of their subjects, namely that they are not the people's authors and creators, as G-d is, and that, consequently, they would not lovingly strive to preserve them, whereas G-d would cherish their care. Similarly, in his account of the Jewish war against the Romans, Josephus says most emphatically that it was the tyrants of the Jews who drew down upon the holy Temple the unwilling hands of the Romans (*War* 1.10). On no fewer than thirty occasions in the *War* he applies the word 'tyrants' to the leaders of the Jewish rebels against Roman rule.

Thus, significantly, Josephus refers to Menahem, the rebel leader, as an insufferable tyrant (τύραννος, *War* 2.442). Josephus himself is accused by his greatest rival, John of Gischala, of seeking to become a tyrant (*War* 2.626). The high priests Ananus and Jesus refer to the Zealots as tyrants (*War* 4.166, 178, 258); and the revolutionaries in general are thus referred to (*War* 6.202, 286). In particular, John of Gischala is referred to as a tyrant (*War* 4.564, 566; 5.5) (often without even being mentioned by name [*War* 6.98, 129, 143]), as is Simon bar Giora (*War* 4.573; 5.11; 6.227, 7.265), and the two together (*War* 5.439; 6.323, 325, 343, 370, 379, 394, 399, 409, 412, 432).

In particular, Josephus felt a need to tone down the revolutionary ideals of David, especially as these might conjure up the goals of the revolutionary groups in the war against the Romans. Thus, whereas the Bible declares that everyone who was in debt or was discontented gathered around David (1 Sam. 22.2), Josephus, apparently realizing that it was just such people who joined the revolutionaries and who burnt the city archives of Jerusalem to destroy the record of debts (*War* 2.427), omits this statement, mentioning merely that all who were in want (χρεία) or in fear of King Saul joined him (*Ant.* 6.247).

On the one hand, Josephus is careful to avoid denominating Phineas, the slayer of Zimri, a zealot, as the Bible does, indeed, term him (Num. 25.11), since Phineas was, like Josephus, a priest, and since G-d himself gave approval, according to the Bible, to his act in ridding the Israelites of succumbing to sexual temptation. On the other hand, Jeroboam, in his 'ambition for great things' (*Ant.* 8.209) is the prototype of Josephus's rivals, John of Gischala and Justus of Tiberias, of whom a similar phrase is used (*War* 2.587, *Life* 36). Josephus decries Jeroboam's lawlessness (*Ant.* 9.282), the very sin which he ascribes to the Sicarii in rebelling against legitimate authority (*War* 7.262).

The key characteristic of Josephus's remolding of the biblical portrait of Elijah is his elimination of its zealot features. Thus, most notably, whereas in the Bible after his victory in the contest with the priests of Baal Elijah tells the Israelites to seize the prophets of Baal and himself kills them (1 Kgs 18.40), in Josephus it is not Elijah but the Israelites who kill the prophets (*Ant.* 8.343).[22] Again, when Elijah, fleeing from Queen Jezebel, takes refuge in a cave and a voice asks him why he has done so, his biblical answer is that he has been very zealous (*qano' qine'ti*) for the L-rd (1 Kgs 19.10); but Josephus's Elijah makes no mention of his zealotry (*Ant.* 8.350). Similarly, when, according to the biblical version, the still small voice again asks Elijah what he is doing, he replies that he has been very zealous (*qano' qine'ti*) for the L-rd (1 Kgs 19.14). He then, zealot that he is, bitterly proceeds to indict the people of Israel for having forsaken the covenant, thrown down G-d's altars, and slain the prophets. All this is omitted in Josephus's version, where the divine voice simply exhorts the prophet not to be alarmed and assures him that none of his enemies will succeed in getting him within their power (*Ant.* 8.352).

Significantly, Josephus identifies more closely with Elisha than with Elijah, who was the popular prototype of the Zealot and the forerunner of the Messiah, as may be seen from the fact that he omits the prophecy that Elisha will kill those who escape the sword of Jehu (1 Kgs 19.17) and, above all, from the notable fact that he has a eulogy for Elisha but not for Elijah. Indeed, Elisha thus emerges as a gentler prophet.

It is important to note in what context Josephus elsewhere uses the same epithets that he applies to Gedaliah. Thus we find that the epithet φιλάνθρωπος and its adverb φιλανθρώπως are employed four times in connection with Titus (*War* 4.96; 5.335; 6.324; 7.107) and twice of Vespasian (*War* 6.340, 341). Moreover, the corresponding noun, φιλανθρωπία, is used with reference to the friendliness of the Romans to the Jews (*Ant.* 14.267), as seen in the many decrees which the Romans issued on behalf of the Jews, in Augustus's treatment of Herod's sons (*Ant.* 15.343), and in Tiberius's courteous reply to Agrippa (*Ant.* 18.162). The particular import of this term may be discerned in Titus's address to the revolutionaries in calling attention to the humanity displayed by the Romans toward the Jews (*War* 6.333), as well as in Agrippa's speech to them emphasizing the same point (*War* 2.399).

---

22. There is, to be sure, an inconsistency in Josephus on this point in that subsequently when Elijah enters the cave and is asked why he had left the city, he replies that he has done so because he has killed the prophets of Baal and is consequently being pursued by Queen Jezebel.

Indeed, it is almost as if Gedaliah is a 'stand-in' for Josephus, and as if Ishmael, who is responsible for the plot to assassinate Gedaliah, is a 'stand-in' for Josephus's great enemy, John of Gischala; in fact, we find that John of Gischala hypocritically affects Gedaliah's very quality of humanity (ὑποκριτὴς φιλανθρωπίας) (*War* 2.587). Furthermore, we find the terms φιλοφρονούμενος (*War* 3.408) and χρητότης (*Life* 423) used of Vespasian's treatment of Josephus himself.

Likewise, we note that Josephus (*Ant.* 10.160), in his description of Ishmael the son of Nethaniel, who was responsible for the assassination of Gedaliah, refers to him as wicked (πονηρός) and very crafty (δολιώτατος). It is no coincidence that these epithets are used by him on a number of occasions of John of Gischala, Josephus's bitter rival. Thus Josephus remarks that John, aspiring to despotic power, began to disdain the position of mere equality in honors with his peers and gathered around himself a group of the more depraved (πονηροτέρων) (*War* 4.389). Again, speaking of the rivalry between John and another revolutionary, Simon bar Giora, Josephus says, quite cynically, that the one who gave his comrades no share in the proceeds from the miseries of others was ranked a scurvy villain (πονηρός) (*War* 5.441). Indeed, Josephus remarks that the people of Galilee, knowing that John was a perjured villain (πονηρός), pressured Josephus to lead them against him (*Life* 102). In point of fact, however, it was no easy matter to shake off one who had gained such influence through his villainy (πονηρίας, *War* 4.213).

As to Ishmael's trickery, we may note that Josephus's source (Jer. 40.8), when first mentioning Ishmael, says nothing about this quality of his. Josephus, however, as we have noted, describes him as wicked and very crafty (*Ant.* 10.161), almost the exact terms which he uses of John of Gischala, whom he calls the most unscrupulous (πανουργότατος) and most crafty (δολιώτατος) of all who have ever gained notoriety by such infamous (πονηρεύμασιν) means (*War* 2.585). Likewise, he describes John as a man of extreme cunning (δολιώτατος) who carried in his breast an insatiate passion for despotic power and who had long been plotting against the state (*War* 4.208).[23]

---

23. Henry St. J. Thackeray, *Josephus the Man and the Historian* (New York: Jewish Institute of Religion, 1929), pp. 119-20, aptly suggests that this passage recalls Sallust's portrait of Catiline (*De Catilinae Coniuratione* 5), where *subdolus* is the equivalent of δολιώτατος.

Josephus assigns the same quality of villainy to his great literary rival, Justus of Tiberias. Thus, using the well-known rhetorical device of *praeteritio*, Josephus remarks that while veracity is incumbent upon a historian, he is nonetheless at liberty to refrain from harsh scrutiny of the misdeeds (πονηρίας) of individuals such as Justus, not from any partiality for the offenders but because of his own moderation (*Life* 339).

Josephus also paints the other revolutionary groups of his own time with the same brush of villainy. Indeed, he remarks, that period had somehow become so prolific of crime (πονηρίας) of every description among the Jews that no deed of iniquity was left unperpetrated (*War* 7.259). In particular, he notes that the Sicarii oppressed only the more those who in righteous self-defense reproached them with their villainy (πονηρίαν) (*War* 7.258). As for the followers of Simon bar Giora, they considered it an act of petty malice (πονηρίας) to do injury to a foreigner (*War* 7.266).

Likewise, in his description of the plot to assassinate Gedaliah, Josephus clearly has John of Gischala in mind. In the biblical version, when Johanan the son of Kareah warns him of the plot and suggests a preemptive strike against Ishmael, Gedaliah's reply is to forbid such a strike, 'for you are speaking falsely of Ishmael' (Jer. 40.16). Josephus develops the scene considerably. In the first place, he adds a motive for the plot (*Ant.* 10.164), namely Ishmael's ambition to rule over the Israelites, inasmuch as he was of royal descent. In his reply to Johanan, Gedaliah notes that Ishmael had been well treated by him and that he could not therefore believe that a person who had not wanted for anything in the midst of such scarcity should be so base (πονηρόν) and outrageous (ἀνόσιον, 'unholy', 'wicked') toward his benefactor; rather, he says, in his trusting naiveté, it would be a wicked thing in itself for such a person not to seek to save him if he were plotted against. Finally, even if it were true that a plot was being hatched to assassinate him, it would be better to die thus than to put to death a man who had taken refuge with him and had indeed entrusted his very life to him (*Ant.* 10.166-67).

The episode is clearly reminiscent of John of Gischala's plot against Josephus. There, too, envy is said to be the motive (*Life* 85), though we may suspect that an additional, and perhaps primary, motive on Ishmael's part was to overthrow Babylonian rule. Likewise, Josephus has no suspicion of any malign (πονηρόν) intention; indeed, he does not prevent John's coming but even goes so far as to write separate letters to those to whom he had entrusted the administration of Tiberias, directing them to show him proper hospitality (*Life* 86).

8. *Deceit and Hypocrisy of Leaders*

It is significant that Josephus adds further details which denigrate the role of Joab. Whereas the Bible asserts merely that Joab sent messengers after Abner (2 Sam. 3.26), Josephus declares that Joab, unable to persuade David, resorted to a course still bolder (τολμηροτέραν, 'more daring', 'more audacious', 'more unscrupulous') in sending men in pursuit of him (*Ant.* 7.33). Josephus's Joab here practices outright deceit and misrepresentation in that he tells the men whom he sends to pursue Abner to call to him in David's name and to say that he had certain things to discuss with him concerning their affairs which he had forgotten to mention when Abner was with him. Again, whereas the biblical narrative proceeds to state very matter-of-factly that Joab took Abner aside to speak with him gently and then smote him fatally in the groin (2 Sam. 3.27), Josephus incriminates Joab much more by expanding on his deceit, noting that he greeted Joab with the greatest show of goodwill (εὔνους) and friendship (φίλος), led him apart from his attendants as if to speak with him privately, and then took him to a deserted part of the gate where he slew him (*Ant.* 7.34). Josephus quite clearly does not accept Joab's explanation that he slew Abner to avenge his brother Asahel and says outright that Abner was deceived (ἐνεδρευθείς, 'plotted against', 'trapped', 'ambushed') by him (*Ant.* 7.36). His real motive, says Josephus, was that he feared that the command of the army and that his place of honor with the king would be taken from him and given to Abner (*Ant.* 7.36). To emphasize this deceit and to teach his readers a lesson from which they may learn for the future—the very function of his history, as we may see from Thucydides (1.22) and from his own proem (*Ant.* 1.14)—Josephus comments on Joab's act by presenting an editorial reflection, that very often those who undertake disgraceful (ἀτόποις, 'perverse', 'wrong', 'evil', 'improper') acts assume (ὑποκρίνονται, 'feign', 'pretend') the part of truly good people in order to avert suspicion of their design (*Ant.* 7.34).

We may further note Josephus's elaboration of Joab's deceit in promising Uriah that he would come to his assistance with his whole army if the enemy would throw down part of the wall and enter the city where they were stationed, while privately instructing the men who were with Joab to desert him when they saw the enemy charge (*Ant.* 7.137).

Another example of Joab's deceit, as we have noted, is to be seen in Josephus's version of Joab's act in slaying Amasa. In an extra-biblical addition, Josephus remarks that he committed this act against a brave youth because he envied him his office of commander and his being honored by the king with a rank equal to his own (*Ant.* 7.284). Josephus then adds that it was for the same reason that Joab had murdered Abner, except that for that murder he had a pretext, namely vengeance for the slaying of his brother Asahel, whereas he had no such excuse for the murder of Amasa (*Ant.* 7.285).

That Josephus is thinking in contemporary terms may be seen in his use of the same verb (ὑπεκρίνετο; cf. *Ant.* 7.34) in describing the hypocrisy of his great literary rival, Justus of Tiberias, in feigning hesitation on the subject of hostilities with Rome, while actually being eager for revolution (*Life* 36).

9. Greed of Leaders

Josephus takes the opportunity to preach at unusual length to the reader that from Joab's action one may perceive to what lengths of recklessness (τολμῶσιν) people will go for the sake of ambition (πλεονεξίας) and power (ἀρχῆς); and that, in their desire to obtain these, people will resort to innumerable acts of wrongdoing and that in their fear of losing power they perform much worse acts, 'their belief being that it is not so great an evil to fail to obtain a very great degree of authority as to lose it after having become accustomed to the benefits derived therefrom' (*Ant.* 7.37-38). Hence they contrive even more ruthless deeds in their fear of losing what they have (*Ant.* 7.38). The passage clearly recalls Josephus's long editorial comment in connection with King Saul, that when people attain power they lay aside their stage masks (such as, we may suggest, Joab here shows with his deceit) and assume instead audacity (τόλμαν), recklessness and contempt for things human and divine (*Ant.* 6.264).

We may likewise note that the vice of avarice (πλεονεξία) which Josephus ascribes to Joab as a motive in his slaying of Abner (*Ant.* 7.37) is precisely the quality which, together with ambition (φιλοτιμίαν), according to Thucydides (3.82.8), was the cause of all the evils produced by the factious rivalry (φιλονικεῖν) at Corcyra.

It is, again, precisely this quality of greed which Josephus attacks in John of Gischala as his motive in obtaining a monopoly of oil (*War* 2.591-92, *Life* 74–76). It is likewise πλεονεξία which, according to Josephus, instigated the Syrians, at the outset of the war against the Romans, to murder the Judaizers in their midst, since they would then with impunity plunder the property of their victims (*War* 2.464). We may see how strongly Josephus feels about the crime of πλεονεξία in that, when he summarizes the qualities of the various revolutionary groups, it is cruelty and avarice (πλεονεξία) which he ascribes to the Sicarii (*War* 7.256). Indeed, Josephus sermonizes that avarice (φιλοχρη-ματία) defies all punishment and concludes that a dire love of gain (κερδαίνειν) is ingrained in human nature, no other passion being so headstrong as greed (πλεονεξία) (*War* 5.558).

10. *The Disastrous Effects of Envy*

Josephus is clearly thinking of contemporary parallels in his constant stress on the theme of envy and its disastrous consequences. In the case of Joab, it is this theme of jealousy that he especially stresses. Thus, in the Bible Joab tries to convince David that Abner's motive in coming to him was to spy (2 Sam. 3.25), whereas in the *Antiquities* (7.31) it is Josephus himself who analyzes Joab's motive and clearly indicates that it is envy, arising out of the fear that David might deprive him of his command and give Abner honors of the first rank as one who was apt (δεινόν, 'clever') in understanding (συνιδεῖν) in matters of state (πράγ-ματα) and who was quick to seize opportunities and who would help him in securing his kingdom. Josephus then specifically adds that Joab feared that he himself might be set down and deprived of his command.

This stress on Joab's envy is particularly evident in Josephus's account of David's dying charge to his son and successor King Solomon. In the Bible (1 Kgs 2.5) David simply tells his son to avenge Joab's murder of Abner and Amasa. Josephus is explicit in ascribing the two murders to envy (ζηλοτυπίαν) (*Ant.* 7.386).

There can be little doubt that Josephus has recast the figure of Joab so as to parallel that of his archenemy John of Gischala, particularly with regard to the theme of envy. John, according to Josephus, was eager for revolution (νεωτέρων) and ambitious (ἐπιθυμίαν ἔχοντα) of obtaining command in Galilee (*Life* 70). In contrast, Josephus emphasizes that he himself was at this time about thirty years old, 'at a time of life when, even if one restrains his lawless passions, it is hard, especially in a position of high authority, to escape the calumnies [διαβολάς] of envy [φθόνου] (*Life* 80). When John, however, observed how loyal the people of Galilee were to Josephus his envy was aroused (ἐφθόνησε) (*Life* 85). When one scheme after another to destroy Josephus failed, John, believing that there was a direct relationship between Josephus's success and his own ruin, gave way to immoderate envy (εἰς φθόνον ...οὔτι μέτριον) (*Life* 122). Indeed, according to Josephus, his failures to assassinate Josephus merely intensified John's envy (φθόνον) (*War* 2.614). He then tried to induce the inhabitants of the three leading cities of Galilee to abandon Josephus and to transfer their allegiance to him. Thereafter, he attempted to induce the Jewish leaders in Jerusalem to deprive Josephus of his command in Galilee and to appoint John instead. Josephus writes that he was particularly distressed by the base ingratitude of his fellow citizens, whose jealousy (φθόνον) had prompted the order to have him put to death (*Life* 204).

We may note that Josephus uses much the same language in describing John of Gischala's intention toward Josephus as πονηρός ('malign') and in depicting himself, like Abner, as being deceived by him (*Life* 86). The Galilaeans, he says, knew John to be a perjured villain (πονηρός) and consequently pressed Josephus to lead them against him (*Life* 102). He likewise speaks of John's κακουργία ('wickedness', 'evil intent', 'fraud') in profiting from the sale of oil (*Life* 76) and, indeed, castigates him in the most extreme terms as the most unscrupulous (πανουργότατος) and most crafty (δολιώτατος) of all who have ever gained notoriety by such infamous means (*War* 2.585). We may note that Josephus uses similar language in describing the knavish tricks (κακουργήματα) of Justus of Tiberias, Josephus's rival in historiography (*Life* 356). John, we are told, made a merit of deceit (ἀπάτην) (*War* 2.586), precisely the quality in Joab which Josephus stresses in his additions to the biblical text.

The envy (φθόνον) of even a few may bring about civil war (πολέμου ἐμφυλίου), as Josephus remarks (*War* 2.620). In particular, Josephus notes that the leaders in Jerusalem, from motives of envy (φθόνον), secretly supplied John of Gischala with money to enable him to collect mercenaries and to make war on Josephus (*War* 2.627). Envy is likewise, according to Josephus, the motive which drove the revolutionary Zealots, whom he so much despised, to massacre the nobility (εὐγένειαν, 'noble ancestry', 'aristocracy') (*War* 4.357). Indeed, the split in the Zealot party itself was brought about, says Josephus, by the fact that some of the revolutionaries were influenced by envy to scorn John, their former equal (*War* 4.393). Moreover, Josephus ascribes the mutiny of the Idumeans within John's army to envy of his power, as much as to hatred of his cruelty (*War* 4.566).

After the war it is again envy (φθόνον) which was excited by Josephus's privileged position and which exposed him once again to danger (*Life* 423). He adds that numerous accusations were made against him by persons who envied him his good fortune, but that he succeeded in escaping them all through the providence of G-d (*Life* 425).

In Josephus's depiction of the relations between Joab and Abner, Joab plays the role of John of Gischala, and Abner that of Josephus. Thus, whereas in the Bible Joab seeks to turn David against Abner by telling him that Abner had come to deceive him and to spy on his comings and goings (2 Sam. 3.34), Josephus, as we have noted, goes much further in condemning Joab. In the first place, he describes Joab's course as dishonest (κακοῦργον, 'malicious', 'deceitful', 'wrongdoing', 'criminal') and evil (πονηρόν). He then proceeds to add that Joab attempted to calumniate (διαβαλεῖν, 'to make someone disliked', 'to put someone into a bad light', 'to cast suspicion upon', 'to detract from someone's reputation', 'to revile', 'to charge falsely') Abner to King David, 'urging him to be on his guard and not to pay attention to the agreements Abner had made; for he was doing everything, he said, in order to secure sovereignty for Saul's son, and, after coming to David with deceit and guile, he had now gone away with the hope of realizing his wish and carrying out his carefully laid plans' (*Ant.* 7.31-32).

In the sequel Josephus adds further details which denigrate the role of Joab. Whereas the Bible asserts merely that Joab sent messengers after Abner (2 Sam. 3.26), Josephus declares that Joab, unable to persuade David, resorted to a course still bolder (τολμηροτέραν, 'more daring', 'more audacious', 'more unscrupulous') in sending men in pursuit of him (*Ant.* 7.33). Josephus's Joab here practices outright deceit and misrepresentation in that he tells the men whom he sends to pursue Abner to call to him in David's name and to say that he had certain things to discuss with him concerning their affairs which he had forgotten to mention when Abner was with him. Again, whereas the biblical narrative proceeds to state very matter-of-factly that Joab took Abner aside to speak with him gently and then smote him fatally in the groin (2 Sam. 3.27), Josephus incriminates Joab much more by expanding on his deceit, noting that he greeted Joab with the greatest show of goodwill (εὔνους) and friendship (φίλος), led him apart from his attendants as if to speak with him privately, and then took him to a deserted part of the gate where he slew him (*Ant.* 7.34). Josephus quite clearly does not accept Joab's explanation that he slew Abner to avenge his brother Asahel and says outright that Abner was deceived (ἐνεδρευ-θείς, 'plotted against', 'trapped', 'ambushed') by him (*Ant.* 7.36). His real motive, says Josephus, was that he feared that the command of the army and that his place of honor with the king would be taken from him and given to Abner (*Ant.* 7.36). To emphasize this deceit and to teach his readers a lesson from which they may learn for the future—the very function of his history, as we may see from Thucydides (1.22) and from his own proem (*Ant.* 1.14)—Josephus comments on Joab's act by presenting an editorial reflection, that very often those who undertake disgraceful (ἀτόποις, 'perverse', 'wrong', 'evil', 'improper') acts assume (ὑποκρίνονται, 'feign', 'pretend') the part of truly good people in order to avert suspicion of their design (*Ant.* 7.34).

That Josephus is thinking in contemporary terms may be seen in his use of the same verb (ὑπεκρίνετο; cf. *Ant.* 7.34) in describing the hypocrisy of his great literary rival, Justus of Tiberias, in feigning hesitation on the subject of hostilities with Rome, while actually being eager for revolution (*Life* 36). Once again, Josephus takes the opportunity to preach at unusual length to the reader that from Joab's action one may perceive to what lengths of recklessness (τολμῶσιν) men will go for the sake of ambition (πλεονεξίας) and power (ἀρχῆς); and that, in their desire to obtain these, men will resort to innumerable acts of wrongdoing and that in their fear of losing power they perform much worse acts, 'their belief being that it is not so great an evil to fail to obtain a very great degree of authority as to lose it after having become accustomed to the benefits derived therefrom' (*Ant.* 7.37-38). Hence they contrive even more ruthless deeds in their fear of losing what they have (*Ant.* 7.38). The passage clearly recalls Josephus's long editorial comment in connection with King Saul, that when people attain power they lay aside their stage masks (such as, we may suggest, Joab here shows with his deceit) and assume instead audacity (τόλμαν), recklessness, and contempt for things human and divine (*Ant.* 6.264).

We may further note Josephus's elaboration of Joab's deceit in promising Uriah that he would come to his assistance with his whole army if the enemy would throw down part of the wall and enter the city where they were stationed, while privately instructing the men who were with Joab to desert him when they saw the enemy charge (*Ant.* 7.137). Another example of Joab's deceit, as we have noted, is to be seen in Josephus's version of Joab's act in slaying Amasa. In an extra-biblical addition, Josephus remarks that he committed this act against a brave youth because he envied him his office of commander and his being honored by the king with a rank equal to his own (*Ant.* 7.284). Josephus then adds that it was for the same reason that Joab had murdered Abner, except that for that murder he had a pretext, namely vengeance for the slaying of his brother Asahel, whereas he had no such excuse for the murder of Amasa (*Ant.* 7.285).

We may likewise note that the vice of avarice (πλεονεξία) which Josephus ascribes to Joab as a motive in his slaying of Abner (*Ant.* 7.37) is precisely the quality which, together with ambition (φιλοτιμίαν), according to Thucydides (3.82.8), was the cause of all the evils produced by the factious rivalry (φιλονικεῖν) at Corcyra.

The natural temptation on the part of apologists for the Jews, in view of the repeated assertions of their opponents, was to try to seek the reasons for such Jew-hatred. In analyzing the attacks upon Jews in Syria on 66, on the eve of the war against Rome, Josephus lists three motives for it: hatred (μῖσος), fear (δέος) and greed (πλεονεξία) for plunder— apparently a combination of economic jealousy and fear of Jewish power and expansionism (*War* 2.464, 478). That Josephus was acutely aware of the power of jealousy as a human drive may be seen from a number of his additions to the biblical narrative. It is thus envy (φθόνος) and jealousy (βασκανία) at their being named governors of the kingdom that are cited by Josephus as the motives that led to the betrayal of Daniel's companions to King Nebuchadnezzar (*Ant.* 10.212). It is envy of the great honor in which Daniel is held by the king that motivates the Median nobles to plot against him; and this gives Josephus the occasion to present the truism, not found in the biblical narrative (Dan. 6.4), that 'men are jealous when they see others held by kings in greater honor than themselves' (*Ant.* 10.250). Similarly, it is envy (φθόνου) that motivates the satraps to accuse Daniel of transgressing the orders of King Darius (*Ant.* 10.256).

It is, again, precisely this quality of greed which Josephus attacks in John of Gischala as his motive in obtaining a monopoly of oil (*War* 2.591-92, *Life* 74-76). It is likewise πλεονεξία which, according to Josephus, instigated the Syrians, at the outset of the war against the

Romans, to murder the Judaizers in their midst, since they would then
with impunity plunder the property of their victims (*War* 2.464). We
may see how strongly Josephus feels about the crime of πλεονεξία
in that, when he summarizes the qualities of the various revolutionary
groups, it is cruelty and avarice (πλεονεξία) which he ascribes to the
Sicarii (*War* 7.256). Indeed, Josephus sermonizes that avarice (φιλοχρη-
ματία) defies all punishment and concludes that a dire love of gain
(κερδαίνειν) is ingrained in human nature, no other passion being so
headstrong as greed (πλεονεξία) (*War* 5.558).

11. *Abhorrence of Civil Strife*

The underlying theme of the *War* is that the ill-fated revolt originated in
the civil strife (στάσις οἰκεία) engendered by the Jewish 'tyrants' (οἱ
Ἰουδαῖοι τύραννοι). Clearly, Josephus's abhorrence of civil strife grew
out of his own experience in the war against the Romans. The Romans
in Josephus's audience, who themselves had experienced a century of
constantly recurring civil strife from the struggle of the Senate against
the Gracchi, of Sulla against Marius, of Caesar against Pompey, of Brutus against Antony, and of Antony against Octavian, and who had a
great tradition of respect for law going back at least to the Twelve Tables
in the fifth century BCE, would surely have appreciated such an emphasis on the dire consequences of internecine bloodshed.

Almost at the beginning of his *Antiquities* Josephus describes the
exalted picture of Seth's descendants (*Ant.* 1.69), completely missing
from the Bible (Gen. 5.6), as inhabiting the same country without dissension (ἀστασίαστοι). This is reminiscent of Thucydides, who especially bewails civil strife (3.80-83) and of Plato (*Laws* 3.678E9–679A2),
who, in his description of the development of society after the great del-
uge, remarks that primitive men felt affection and good will towards
one another and had no occasion for internecine quarrels about their subsistence. Josephus then indicates how self-defeating civil strife is by
stating that this is the penalty imposed by G-d upon the builders of the
Tower of Babel (*Ant.* 1.117).

Throughout the *War* and the last books of the *Antiquities* the reader
can sense the strong feelings that Josephus has about the civil strife that
had torn the Jewish people apart in his own day. Hence, when Josephus (*Ant.* 1.164), in an extra-biblical addition, states that G-d thwarted

Pharaoh's criminal passion for Sarah by inflicting political disturbance (στάσει) upon him, Josephus is emphasizing the gravity of his offense. For Josephus, Korah's rebellion is not so much theological or philosophical as it is political and military,[24] as we can see from his use of the word στάσις ('sedition') in his mention of it (*Ant.* 4.12), as well as from his reference to the people who were swayed by Korah as an army (*Ant.* 4.21). Indeed, the fact that Josephus, in the brief pericope of Korah (*Ant.* 4.11-56), uses the word στάσις four times (*Ant.* 4.12, 13, 32, 36) and the verb στασιάζω ('to revolt') twice (*Ant.* 4.13, 30) underscores the political aspect of this passage. The analogy which Josephus draws is with large armies, which become ungovernable when they encounter reverses (*Ant.* 4.11). That Josephus is here thinking also of the parallel in Thucydides (3.82-84), where he describes στάσις in Corcyra, seems clear, especially since Josephus specifically states that this was a sedition the extent of which knows no parallel, whether among Greeks or barbarians (*Ant.* 4.12). We recall that in his proem to the *Antiquities* Josephus declares that he intends in his work to embrace not only the entire ancient history of the Jews but also their political constitution (διάταξιν τοῦ πολιτεύματος) (1.5). It is under this rubric of politics and, in particular, of political revolution that he discusses the rebellion of Korah. In connection with the war against the Romans, the term στάσις occurs no fewer than 51 times, the verb στασιάζω for 'to be engaged in civil war' occurs seven times, and the noun στασιαστής for a seditionist occurs 67 times in connection with the insurrection of the Jews and their factional strife.

Moses makes it clear, in his address to the assembly, that, in view of Korah's complaint about the choice of Aaron as high priest, his and Aaron's chief aim was to avoid dissension (στασιάζοντας), and this despite the fact that Aaron held his office by the decision of G-d, as ratified by the good will of the people (*Ant.* 4.30).

---

24. Similarly, in his account of the conflict between Midian and Israel, Josephus emphasizes the political and military point of view, in contrast, for example, to Pseudo-Philo, who, as a moralist, emphasizes (particularly in 18.10) the tragic elements in the narrative. See Willem C. Van Unnik, 'Josephus' Account of the Story of Israel's Sin with Alien Women in the Country of Midian (Num. 25.1 ff.)', in M.S.H.G. Heerma von Voss, Ph.H.J. Houwink ten Cate and N.A. van Uchelen (eds.), *Travels in the World of the Old Testament: Studies Presented to Professor M.A. Beek on the Occasion of his 65th Birthday* (Assen: Van Gorcum, 1974), pp. 244-45.

Drawing upon his experience in the recent war against the Romans, Josephus stresses over and over again that the most terrible political evil is civil strife. In particular, unlike the Bible (Deut. 19.14), which merely presents the commandment not to remove one's neighbor's landmark, Josephus (*Ant.* 4.225) adds a reason, again in political terms: removal of landmarks leads to wars and seditions (στάσεων). In an extrabiblical addition, Moses (*Ant.* 4.294) prays that, after they have conquered the land of Israel, the Israelites not be overcome by civil strife (στάσεως), 'whereby you will be led to actions contrary to those of your fathers and destroy the institutions which they established'. Indeed, one of the qualities of Josephus's ideal ruler, as we can see in his portrait of Moses, is that he seeks to prevent dissension.

Most significantly, Josephus asserts that Gideon did a greater service in assuaging the Ephramites and thus avoiding civil strife (ἐμφυλίου... στάσεως), when they were on the brink of it, than he accomplished through his military successes (*Ant.* 5.231). In this connection, we may note a biblical passage which apparently contradicts a picture of Gideon as a peacemaker and as one who avoided civil strife that Josephus wishes to paint, namely the episode with Succoth and Penuel (Judg. 8.4-17). In this case, according to the Bible, the men of those cities, who were apparently Israelites (as we see from Josh. 13.27), had declined to help Gideon's army with bread when they were hungry, and Gideon eventually took revenge and punished them, even to the point of putting the men of Penuel to death. Such a passage reflects badly both on the hospitality of the Israelites in not feeding the hungry and on the ability of Gideon to mollify his anger and to avoid the slaughter of his countrymen. Hence, very typically, Josephus avoids these problems by simply omitting the entire incident.

One of the qualities of the ideal ruler is to seek to prevent dissension. Hence, when Abishai urges David to put Shimei to death for revolting (2 Sam. 19.23), Josephus, while having David answer in substantially the same vein as the Bible, uses political terminology, declaring that the sons of Zeruiah should not stir up new disorders (ταραχαί) and dissension (στάσις) (*Ant.* 7.265). Furthermore, whereas the Bible terms Sheba a base fellow (2 Sam. 20.1) and the Septuagint calls him a transgressor (παράνομος), Josephus again uses political language and calls him a lover of dissension (στάσει χαίρων) (*Ant.* 7.278), thus, in effect, enduing this biblical scene with a contemporary tinge; that is, there is here an implied attack upon those who, in his opinion, had sown dissension in

Jewish ranks and whom he attacks so bitterly in Books 2 and 7 of the *War* and in Books 18 and 20 of the *Antiquities* in discussing the background of the revolution against the Romans in his own day. Hence, whereas G-d tells David in the biblical version that he will give Solomon peace (1 Chron. 22.9), in Josephus G-d promises David that he will give Solomon the greatest of all blessings—not only peace but also freedom from civil dissension (στάσεις ἐμφύλιοι) (*Ant.* 7.337). Similarly, when David commends Solomon to the people (1 Chron. 28.4), he adds, in Josephus's version, the request that his other sons refrain from civil dissension (μὴ στασιάζειν), now that he had chosen Solomon to succeed him, and enjoins the leaders of the people to show obedience (πειθώ) to Solomon (*Ant.* 7.372-73), a quality which, as we have seen, he himself exemplified (*Ant.* 6.160). Furthermore, in his charge to Solomon, the biblical David tells him to be strong and of good courage (1 Chron. 22.12), whereas Josephus has him exhort the chiefs of the people to assist him, ading that, should they do so, they will enjoy peace and good order (εὐνομία), with which G-d repays pious and just men (*Ant.* 7.341). One will recall that εὐνομία is personified as the daughter of Themis ('Law, Justice', Hesiod, *Theogony* 902) and is the title of a poem by Tyrtaeus (2, cf. Aristotle, *Politics* 5.7.1307A1).

In line with his constantly reiterated theme that civil strife had proven disastrous for the Jews during his own lifetime, Josephus stresses the theme of the consequences of civil strife in connection with Joab in particular. He sets the scene by referring specifically to the long war between the house of Saul and that of David as a civil (ἐμφύλιος, 'of kinsmen', 'internal', 'domestic') war among the Hebrews (2 Sam. 3.1). Thus, whereas the biblical Abner remarks to Joab that continued fighting will lead to bitterness in the end (2 Sam. 2.26), Josephus's Abner is more specific in articulating how wrong civil strife is by stating that it is not right to stir up fellow citizens to strife (ἔριδα) and warfare (*Ant.* 7.17).

In particular, we may note that in the Bible the anonymous old woman asks him, when he besieges the city of Abel Beth-Maacah, whether he is seeking to destroying 'a city and a mother in Israel' and furthermore inquires whether he wishes to swallow up 'the inheritance of the L-rd' (2 Sam. 20.19). Josephus, on the other hand, does not put it in the form of a question but rather in the form of an accusation, stressing the innocence of the people of the city: 'You', she charges him, 'are bent on destroying and sacking a mother-city of the Israelites which has done no wrong' (*Ant.* 7.289). In acting thus, she implies, Joab is going against the will of G-d, who had chosen kings and commanders to drive out the enemies of the Hebrews and to secure peace from them, whereas Joab was doing the work of the enemy in thus attacking fellow-Jews.

It is significant that in the biblical text David, in speaking to his son Solomon, recalls G-d's promise that a son would be born to him who would be a man of peace and that G-d would give him peace from all his enemies round about (1 Chron. 22.9). In Josephus's version, however, G-d's promise is not merely that he would bring peace, which, he adds, is the greatest of all blessings, but also, in terms familiar to the student of Thucydides (2.65, 4.7), Xenophon (*Memorabilia* 4.4.11, 4.6.14) and Lysias (25.26, 30.13), freedom from civil dissension (στάσεων ἐμφυλίων) (*Ant.* 7.337). This very phrase, ἐμφύλιος στάσις, 'internecine civil strife', is found in Solon (4.19), Herodotus (8.3) and Democritus (249). It was Solon's belief (3.28) that the punishment inflicted on a state for transgression of its citizens is precisely this, that it is afflicted by party strife and civil war.

When David calls an assembly of his officers and commends Solomon to them, he asks that just as his own brothers accepted without complaint G-d's choice of him to be king, so, in an extra-biblical statement, his other sons should cheerfully accept the choice of Solomon, since it is G-d's choice, and refrain from civil dissension (στάσιάζειν) (*Ant.* 7.372). Then, in an additional statement that, in effect, is a kind of editorial and that clearly reflects Josephus's own present situation in living under Roman patronage in the aftermath of the debacle of the Jewish war for independence, David remarks that 'it is not such a terrible thing to serve even a foreign master, if G-d so wills, and when it is one's brother to whom this honor has fallen, one should rejoice at having a share in it' (*Ant.* 7.373). One is reminded of Josephus's address to his fellow Jews during the siege of Jerusalem, urging them to surrender to the Romans, inasmuch as 'G-d, who went the round of the nations, bringing to each in turn the rod of empire, now rested over Italy' (*War* 5.367). Indeed, he insists, 'The deity has fled from the holy places and taken his stand on the side of those with whom you are now at war' (*War* 5.412).

The case of Jeroboam becomes, for Josephus, an outstanding example of the disaster brought on by secession and civil strife.[25] Thus, when Jeroboam is first introduced by Josephus to his readers, whereas the Bible states that Jeroboam lifted up his hand against King Solomon (1 Kgs 11.26), Josephus remarks that Jeroboam, 'one of his own countrymen' (ὁμοφύλων, the same word which Josephus had used with reference to the revolutionaries' treatment of their fellow countrymen), rose up against the king (*Ant.* 8.205), thus emphasizing the theme of fraternal strife. It is significant that the rabbis, as we have noted, looked with favor upon this confrontation of Jeroboam with Solomon and justified it by stressing that Jeroboam wanted to ensure free access of pilgrims to the Temple, whereas in Josephus's version he is thus so severely condemned.

Indeed, when the kingdom of Israel comes to an end and Josephus seeks to analyze the underlying cause of its demise, he insists that the beginning of Israel's troubles was the rebellion which it undertook against the legitimate king, Rehoboam, when it chose Jeroboam as king (*Ant.* 9.282). It is almost as if Josephus is analyzing the demise of the Jewish state of his own day, which he likewise ascribes to the rebellion against the legitimate authority, in his case Rome. Thus, very typically, Josephus describes Jeroboam's sedition in language very similar to that which he uses to describe his great enemy, John of Gischala (*Ant.* 8.209, *War* 2.587). In a word, Josephus points his finger at Jeroboam's lawlessness (παρανομίαν) (*Ant.* 9.282), the very quality which he denounces in the revolutionaries,[26] particularly in his bitter attack on the Sicarii as the first to set the example of lawlessness (παρανομίας) and cruelty (ὠμότητος) to their kinsmen (*War* 7.262). It is this lawlessness (παρανομίαν) and iniquity (ἀδικίας) which Josephus, in an editorial comment not found in his biblical source (1 Kgs 15.24), stresses brought about the destruction of the kings of Israel, one after the other, in a short space of time (*Ant.* 8.314). That Jeroboam is, for Josephus, the model of lawlessness may be discerned by comparing the Bible (1 Kgs 16.30), which

25. See my 'Josephus' Portrait of Jeroboam', *AUSS* 31 (1993), pp. 43-46.

26. See *War* 4.134, 144, 155, 339, 351; 5.343, 393, 442; 6.122. Likewise, in the *Antiquities* Josephus make a number of changes in his paraphrase of the biblical text to emphasize the importance of observance of the laws. See, for example, 5.185 (vs. Judg. 3.12); 5.198-200 (vs. Judg. 4.1); 5.255 (vs. Judg. 10.6); 7.130 (vs. no biblical parallel); 8.245 (vs. 1 Kgs 13.33); 8.251-53 (vs. 1 Kgs 14.22).

speaks of the evil which Ahab did but which does not mention Jeroboam, and Josephus's statement that Ahab did not invent anything in his wickedness but merely imitated the misdeeds and outrageous behavior (ὕβριν) which his predecessors showed toward the deity (*Ant.* 8.316); of these predecessors and their misdeeds, Josephus here singles out Jeroboam and his lawlessness (παρανομίαν). To the Romans, who had such a deep and long-standing reverence for law and who were so proud of their legal tradition, such an attack on Jeroboam for his lawlessness would be most effective.

That Josephus viewed Jeroboam as the prototype of the revolutionaries of his own day may be seen in Josephus's extra-biblical remark that Jeroboam attempted to persuade the people to turn away (ἀφίστασθαι) and to start a revolt (κινεῖν) (*Ant.* 8.209).[27] We should also note the striking coincidence that the phrase which he uses to describe Jeroboam's sedition, that he was 'ambitious of great things' (μεγάλων ἐπιθυμητὴς πραγμάτων) (*Ant.* 8.209), is so similar to that which he uses to describe the archrevolutionary, John of Gischala, that he was always ambitious of great things (ἀεὶ...ἐπιθυμήσας μεγάλων) (*War* 2.587). Those who responded to John's invitation are similarly depicted as always ambitious for newer things (νεωτέρων ἐπιθυμοῦντες αἰεὶ πραγμάτων), addicted to change and delighting in sedition (*Life* 87). We find similar language applied to those bold Jews in Jerusalem who were admonished by the procurator Cumanus to put an end to their ambition for newer things, that is, revolution (νεωτέρων ἐπιθυμοῦντας πραγμάτων) (*Ant.* 20.109). Josephus employs similar language in describing his archrival Justus of Tiberias as 'ambitious for newer things' (νεωτέρων...ἐπεθύμει πραγμάτων) (*Life* 36).

It is significant that it is this aspect of fratricidal strife that is stressed when Abijah, the king of Judah, wins a great victory over the forces of Jeroboam and slays no fewer than five hundred thousand of them (2 Chron. 13.17). Josephus adds, as we have noted, that the slaughter surpassed that in any war, 'whether of Greeks or barbarians' (*Ant.* 8.284). This latter phrase is found also in Josephus's comment on the incomparable impiety of the slaying of Jesus the son of Joiada by his brother Johanan, the high priest, when Jesus was plotting to become high priest in Johanan's stead (*Ant.* 11.299).

---

27. Josephus is here basing himself on the Septuagint addition (1 Kgs 12.24b).

The underlying theme of Josephus's *War*, as we have noted, is the emphasis on the civil strife engendered by the Jewish 'tyrants' whom he holds responsible for the ill-fated revolt (*War* 1.10). In particular, Josephus's *Life* is largely an account of the attempts of one of these 'tyrants', John of Gischala, to interfere with Josephus's mission in Galilee.

In fact, when Josephus seeks to analyze the underlying cause of the demise of the kingdom of Israel, he insists that the beginning of the nation's troubles was the rebellion which it undertook against the legitimate king, Rehoboam, when it chose Jeroboam as king (*Ant*. 9.282). It is almost as if Josephus were analyzing the demise of the Jewish state of his own day, which he likewise ascribes to the rebellion against the legitimate authority. It is significant that whereas the Bible (1 Kgs 15.6) states that there was a continuous civil war between Rehoboam and Jeroboam, in direct contradiction to the statement (1 Kgs 12.24) that after mustering his troops to fight against Jeroboam and to force an end to the rebellion, Rehoboam listened to the advice of the prophet and did not attack Jeroboam, Josephus (*Ant*. 8.223) very conspicuously omits the former statement and thus presents Rehoboam as resisting the obvious temptation to seek to put an end to the rebellion by force. Furthermore, whereas in the Bible (1 Kgs 12.24; 2 Chron. 11.4) the decision not to go to war against Jeroboam is that of all the people of Judah and Benjamin, in Josephus (*Ant*. 8.223) the decision is that of Rehoboam alone, who thus clearly obtains the credit for preventing civil war. When, to be sure, in his summary of Rehoboam's reign, Josephus (*Ant*. 8.263) asserts that all his days Rehoboam was an enemy of Jeroboam, in the same sentence he declares that he reigned in great quiet (ἡσυχίᾳ). He thus clearly avoids the biblical statement that Rehoboam was constantly at war with Jeroboam. Significantly, too, whereas in the Bible (1 Kgs 12.24) the prophet Shemaiah (*Ant*. 8.223) quotes G-d as asserting that Rehoboam is not to fight against his kinsfolk, presumably in this particular instance Josephus uses this occasion for an editorial comment that it is not just (δίκαιον) as a general rule to make war on one's fellow citizens (ὁμοφύλους), thus stressing that Rehoboam was convinced by the prophet's statement. It is this failure on the part of the Jews to avoid attacks upon their own kinsfolk that Josephus constantly stresses as the basic reason for their tragedies in the biblical period, as in the civil war with the Benjaminites (*Ant*. 5.150-65), where Josephus (*Ant*. 5.151) stresses the wise advice of the Israelite elders that war ought not to be undertaken hurriedly against one's own kinsfolk (ὁμοφύλους).

To be sure, Josephus (*Ant.* 8.264) acknowledges and condemns Rehoboam for being boastful (ἀλαζών) and foolish (ἀνόητος), the same epithets that he uses in condemning the Jewish revolutionaries (*War* 6.395) against the Romans, who were so haughty (ἀλαζόνας) and proud of their impious crimes and whom Josephus says (*Life* 18) that he warned not to expose their country, their families and themselves to dire perils through acting so rashly (προπετῶς) and so stupidly (ἀνοήτως). It is, says Josephus (*Ant.* 8.264), because of Rehoboam's boastfulness and foolishness in not listening to his father's friends that he consequently lost his royal power.

Nevertheless, though it is true that Josephus (*Ant.* 8.251) mentions Rehoboam's unjust and impious acts, Josephus goes out of his way to explain his lawlessness and evil ways by psychologizing that such an attitude arises from the greatness of people's affairs and the improvement of their position, as if to say that it is only natural that someone under those circumstances would have been misled into unjust and impious acts and would consequently have influenced their subjects accordingly. Significantly, precisely the same phrase (μέγεθος τῶν πραγμάτων, 'greatness of affairs') is used by Josephus (*Ant.* 9.223) to explain the degeneration of King Uzziah, who had started his reign so promisingly. Again, whereas we read that Rehoboam was thus misled (ἐξετράπη) into unjust acts, in the case of Jeroboam (*Ant.* 8.245) no such defense is offered for his wickedness; rather, we find not the passive but the active voice, since we are informed that he outraged (ἐξύβρισεν) G-d.

It is significant that whereas the Bible, in praising Jehoshaphat, declares that he did not follow in the ways of the kingdom of Israel (2 Chron. 17.4), Josephus, in his clear desire to promote the unity of the Jewish people, omits all reference to the ways of Israel and says, rather, that he sought to do something pleasing and acceptable to G-d (*Ant.* 8.394).

It is furthermore in the interest of stressing the importance of the unity of the Jewish people that Josephus avoids the awkward implication of the scriptural passage that after making a marriage alliance with Ahab, the king of Israel, Jehoshaphat waited several years before visiting Ahab (2 Chron. 18.1-2). Josephus has quietly reduced the Bible's years to 'some time' (μετὰ χρόνον τινὰ) (*Ant.* 8.398). Likewise, whereas the Hebrew Bible states that it was by guile that Ahab persuaded (*vayesitehu*) Jehoshaphat (2 Chron. 18.2), Josephus, seeking to smooth relations between the Jewish kingdoms, says that Ahab invited (παρ-εκάλεσε) Jehoshaphat to become his ally in a war against the king of Syria (*Ant*. 8.398). Indeed, Josephus increases considerably the warmth with which Ahab greets Jehoshaphat. According to the biblical account, Ahab killed an abundance of sheep and oxen for him and for the people who were with him (2 Chron. 18.2); Josephus expands on this, remarking that Ahab gave him a friendly welcome (φιλοφρόνως) and splendidly (λαμπρῶς) entertained, with an abundance of grain and wine and meat, the army which accompanied him (*Ant*. 8.398).

Likewise, when Ahab approaches Jehoshaphat to induce him to join in the military action to recover Ramoth-Gilead, the Bible quotes Jehoshaphat as saying, 'I am as you are, my people as your people' (1 Kgs 22.4, 2 Chron. 18.3). Josephus amplifies this, remarking that Jehoshaphat willingly offered his aid, and adds, in order that the reader may not think that Jehoshaphat was inferior in military might to Ahab, that he had a force not smaller than Ahab's (*Ant*. 8.399).

Josephus could not avoid the fact that Jehu the prophet in the biblical account does reproach Jehoshaphat, telling him that because he had helped Ahab G-d was angry with him (2 Chron. 19.2). Josephus, however, softens the reproach by having Jehu remark that G-d was displeased (ἀηδῶς) with this act (*Ant*. 9.1).

Again, the Bible cites the castigation of Jehoshaphat by Eliezer the son of Dodavahu for joining Ahaziah, the king of Israel, in an alliance, and his prophecy that as a result of this alliance G-d would destroy what they had made, namely the fleet of ships which they built in Ezion-Geber (2 Chron. 20.37). Josephus, eager to promote the unity of the Jewish people, omits Eliezer's intervention and instead ascribes the loss of the ships to their great size (*Ant*. 9.17).

This same theme of Jewish unity may be seen in another Josephan addition. The Bible states that the kings of Israel, Judah and Edom joined in an expedition against the Moabites (2 Kgs 3.9). Josephus, clearly seeking to show that the alliance was more than one of convenience, adds that Jehoram, the king of Israel, came first to Jerusalem with his army and received a splendid reception by Jehoshaphat there (*Ant*. 9.31). We then have Jehoram and Jehoshaphat portrayed as true partners in devising their military strategy. In the Bible it is Jehoram who makes the decision as to military strategy after Jehoshaphat asks for advice as to which way they should march (2 Kgs 3.8); in Josephus the decision is a joint decision to advance through the wilderness of Idumea, since the enemy would not expect them to attack from this direction (*Ant.* 9.31). Again, when their army lacks water, Jehoshaphat, in an extra-biblical addition, shows warm, brotherly feeling for Jehoram by comforting him; and his doing so is attributed to his righteousness (*Ant.* 9.33).

Jehu, it would seem, was guilty of lawlessness in rebelling against the king of his nation, Israel; and Josephus was clearly in a quandary as to how to differentiate beween this rebellion and the civil strife which he so strongly condemns. It is significant, therefore, that the biblical account states that Jehu conspired (*vayiteqasher*, 'joined together') against Jehoram (2 Kgs 9.14). In Josephus's version, however, there is no mention of conspiracy; we hear only that Jehu collected his army and prepared to set out against Jehoram (*Ant.* 9.112). Again, whereas, after Ahab's sons had been slain, in accordance with Jehu's orders, Jehu admits to the people that it was he who had conspired (*qoshareti*, the same root as *vayiteqasher*) against King Jehoram (2 Kgs 10.9), Josephus omits the element of conspiracy and has Jehu state merely that he had marched στρατεύσαιτο ('made war', 'undertaken a campaign', 'taken the field') against his master (*Ant.* 9.129).

Josephus, moreover, in a comment that has no parallel in the biblical source (2 Kgs 9.15), stresses the loyalty (εὐνοίας), which he clearly implies was well deserved, of Jehu's followers to him, in that they declared him king because of their friendly feeling toward him (*Ant.* 9.113). As evidence of this good will, in another passage which is unparalleled in the Bible (2 Kgs 9.15-16), Josephus notes that Jehu's soldiers, approving (ἡσθέντες, 'delighting in', 'being pleased with', 'taking pleasure in') what Jehu had said, guarded the roads so that no one might escape to Jezreel, where King Jehoram was recuperating from a wound, and betray him to those who were there (*Ant.* 9.114).

Josephus, however, is careful not to give the impression, as does the Hebrew text (2 Kgs 10.16), that Jehu was a zealot, inasmuch as this might associate him with the Zealots, whom Josephus excoriates as having 'copied every deed of ill, nor was there any previous villainy recorded in history that they failed zealously to emulate' (*War* 7.268-74). We may note that just as Josephus avoids labeling as a zealot Phineas, the slayer of Zimri whom the Bible so denominates (Num. 25.11 vs. *Ant.* 4.150-55), likewise here Josephus carefully avoids applying the term to Jehu (*Ant.* 9.133). Instead, Josephus puts a pious truism into the mouth of Jehu, who tells Jonadab that it is the most desirable and pleasant of sights for a good and upright person to see the wicked punished, in keeping, we may add, with the moral lesson which Josephus preaches in the proem to his *Antiquities*, namely that people are rewarded and punished by G-d in accordance with the degree to which they conform with or violate the laws revealed by G-d (*Ant.* 1.14).

12. *Loyalty to Rulers*

One of the most serious charges against the Jews was that of dual loyalty. Thus Apion not only accused the Jews of sedition and failure to worship the civic deities but also expressed astonishment that they were called Alexandrians (*Apion* 2.38). We may conjecture that this charge of double loyalty was also a factor in a well-documented court case. Cicero's client Flaccus had seized money that the Jews of Asia Minor had sought to ship out of the province to the Temple in Jerusalem. This may well have seemed unpatriotic to the Romans because of the scarcity of money at this time throughout the republic. In 63 BCE, four years before the trial, the Senate had passed a resolution fobidding the export of gold and silver from Italy because of the shortage; and Flaccus had sent the Jewish money to Rome for deposit in the public treasury. Thus Cicero took care to imply that the Jews were unpatriotic (*Pro Flacco* 28.66). 'There is no lack of men', he says, 'as you well know, to stir these fellows up against me and every patriotic citizen'. He thus urged the jury to show their concern for the welfare of the state and to rebuff the Jewish pressure group.

That Jews are, however, loyal to their masters is the theme, for example, of Joseph's extra-biblical addition (*Ant.* 2.68-69) in his statement to the butler that even the lure of his own pleasure would not induce him to dishonor his master Potiphar. Josephus is careful to stress Joseph's loyalty to the Pharaoh even when, presumably because of his tremendous achievement in saving the country from starvation, he might have achieved the rule for himself and, in fact, had been robed in purple by the king (*Ant.* 2.90). Josephus (*Ant.* 2.191-93) likewise uses the example of Joseph's fidelity to the Pharaoh to answer the disloyalty charge, noting that when the famine had abated Joseph repaired to each city and bestowed upon the Egyptians in perpetuity the land which they had previously ceded to the king and which he himself might have held and reserved for his own benefit. Consequently, Josephus concludes, Joseph both increased his own reputation with the Egyptians and their loyalty to their sovereign.

That Joseph is obedient to his sovereign may be inferred from the fact that whereas the Bible says simply that Joseph, as Pharaoh's vizier, came home and greeted his brothers without indicating from what place he was coming (Gen. 43.26), Josephus, eager to stress Joseph's loyalty, fills this lacuna by stating that he came from his attendance (θεραπείας, 'service', 'attention', 'homage', 'allegiance', 'concern') upon the king (*Ant.* 2.121). Josephus felt it particularly important, in view of the recent disastrous revolt of the Jews against the Romans to stress that the proper policy for the Jews was to be loyal to their rulers. Thus, despite his high station, Joseph has no design to supplant Pharaoh; indeed, Josephus significantly omits Judah's remark to Joseph, 'Thou art even as Pharaoh' (Gen. 44.18 vs. *Ant.* 2.140).[28] Josephus is careful to avoid repeating the scriptural statement of Joseph's brothers to Jacob that Joseph was the ruler of all the land of Egypt (Gen. 45.26); instead, in Josephus's version we read that Jacob was told that Joseph was sharing (συνδιέπων, 'administering something with someone') with the king the government of Egypt and had almost the whole charge of it in his hands (*Ant.* 2.168). Thus, when G-d describes Joseph's status in the administration of Egypt, he says that he had made him lord of Egypt and that he differed only slightly (ὡς ὀλίγῳ) from the status of the king (*Ant.* 2.174).

As one who had participated in the war against the Romans and who had come to the conclusion that resistance to Rome was futile and that Rome was divinely destined to rule the world, Josephus constantly seeks to prevail upon his compatriots to give up their dream of national independence. We may see an instance of this concern where Josephus avoids terminology suggestive of an independent state (Num. 23.21) in Balaam's remark that G-d has granted untold blessings to the Israelites and has vouchsafed to them his own providence as their perpetual ally (σύμμαχον) and guide (ἡγεμών) (*Ant.* 4.114). This rendering is clearly not merely an equivalent for the biblical concept of covenant but actually a replacement for it.[29] As Josephus's Balaam puts matters, the Israelites are thus to be happy (εὐδαίμων, *Ant.* 4.114) rather than to

---

28. The rabbinic tradition actually speaks of Joseph as having been appointed 'king in Egypt' (*Sifr. Deut.* 334.3). The Septuagint resolves this delicate problem by reading μετὰ Φαραώ, which the Vulgate renders as 'after Pharaoh'.

29. See Harold W. Attridge, *The Interpretation of Biblical History in the 'Antiquitates Judaicae' of Flavius Josephus* (Missoula, MT: Scholars Press, 1976), pp. 79-80.

dominate the world. It is their fame—rather than, it would seem, their sheer force—that will fill the whole earth, as we see in another of Josephus's extra-biblical additions (*Ant.* 4.115). In particular, we may note that in place of the Bible's picture comparing the Israelites to lions that do not lie down until they have eaten their prey and drunk their blood (Num. 23.24), Josephus avoids such sanguinary particulars and speaks only of the land that the Israelites will occupy (*Ant.* 4.115-16).

Indeed, Josephus clearly shifts the focus from the land of Israel to the Diaspora when he has Balaam declare that whereas now the Israelites are circumscribed by the land of Canaan, the habitable world (τήν οἰκουμένην), that is the Diaspora, lies before them as an everlasting habitation (*Ant.* 4.116).[30]

Josephus's chief aim, in his reworking of the biblical Ezra narrative, is to stress Ezra's loyalty to his ruler and, by implication, to underscore the similar loyalty of Jews to the government of the state in which they reside. It is particularly important, therefore, that when Ezra is first introduced to his readers by Josephus he is termed, in an extra-biblical addition not to be found in 1 Esd. 8.4, 'friendly' (φίλος, *Ant.* 11.121) to King Xerxes. A precedent for Ezra's status here may be seen in Josephus's references to Hezekiah, who was invited by the king of Babylon, Berodach-balaban, to become his ally and 'friend' (*Ant.* 10.30), as well as to Daniel, who was given the extraordinarily high honor of being designated by King Darius of Media as the first of his 'friends' (*Ant.* 10.263), and to Zerubbabel, who had an 'old friendship' with King Darius of Persia and who was on that account 'judged worthy of a place in the king's bodyguard' (*Ant.* 11.32).

In Josephus's reworking of the biblical narrative, Nehemiah emerges, in an extra-biblical detail, as the Persian king's loyal servant who gave stability to the land of Palestine at a time when it was being overrun by marauders who plundered it by day, did mischief to it at night, and carried off many captives from the country and even from Jerusalem itself (*Ant.* 11.161). The biblical text simply states that the inhabitants of Palestine were in great affliction and reproach (Neh. 1.3). Josephus adds that highwaymen had made the roads unsafe, so that they were full

---

30. This is clearly a plea for the viability of Jewish life in the Diaspora, as noted by Schalit, *Josephus: Antiquitates Judaicae*, I, p. lxxxi. We may see a parallel in Josephus's version of G-d's blessings to Jacob (Gen. 28.13-15; *Ant.* 1.280-83): Jacob, G-d says, will have good children who will rule over the land of Israel and will fill all other lands (*Ant.* 1.282).

of corpses (*Ant.* 11.161). Inasmuch as roads were the great pride of both the Persians (cf. Herodotus 8.98) and the Romans, the fact that Nehemiah secured the safety of these roads, according to Josephus's extrabiblical addition, must have made an extremely strong impression upon his readers.

Again, Josephus dramatically illustrates the loyalty of Nehemiah to the Persian king by adding to the biblical passage (Neh. 2.1) that Nehemiah, in his fidelity to the king, hastened, just as he was, and without even bathing, to perform the service of bringing the king his drink (*Ant.* 11.163).

The king's confidence in Nehemiah is also illustrated by the omission of a biblical passage. In Neh. 2.6 the king is represented as asking him how long he will be gone and when he will return, whereupon Nehemiah, of course, answers him by setting a time. Apparently, Josephus regarded such an inquiry as itself a sign of lack of confidence in Nehemiah, and so he simply omits it (*Ant.* 11.166). An indication of Nehemiah's persuasiveness and of the king's confidence in him may likewise be seen in Josephus's addition to the biblical text (Neh. 2.8) that it took the king only one day to fulfill his promise to Nehemiah and to give him a letter to the governor of Syria (*Ant.* 11.167).

Nehemiah, as representative of the Persian king, could hardly afford to show hesitation or fear, and yet the biblical text indicates that whereas he heard in Kislev about the difficulties in Jerusalem (Neh. 1.1), it was not until four months later in Nisan that he went to the king with a request to remedy the situation (Neh. 2.1). Such a delay is obviously not consonant with dynamic leadership, and so Josephus has Nehemiah go immediately to the king after hearing of the troubles of the Jews in Jerusalem (*Ant.* 11.163). Moreover, according to the Bible, when the king asked him why he was sad, he became very much afraid (Neh. 2.2). Josephus, however, obviously found such a detail unseemly in a leader and simply omits it (*Ant.* 11.164).

A major ingredient of Nehemiah's character, as highlighted by Josephus and crucial in his capacity as the right-hand man of the Persian king, is respect for law (*Ant.* 11.183). Indeed, it is significant that in his brief encomium for Nehemiah, consisting of a single sentence, Josephus calls attention to his being just (δίκαιος), that is, observant of the proper way (δίκη) (*Ant.* 11.183). We have noted that the same two adjectives used here of Nehemiah, χρηστός and δίκαιος, are employed also for the prophet Samuel (*Ant.* 6.294) and for the model king Hezekiah (*Ant.* 9.260), as well as for Jehonadab (*Ant.* 9.132), Jehoiada (*Ant.* 9.166) and Jehoiachin (*Ant.* 10.100).

In the Nehemiah pericope, Josephus is concerned to underscore the allegiance of the Jews to the state, as we may see in his omission (*Ant.* 11.170) of the biblical charge, made by Sanballat the Horonite, Tobiah the Ammonite servant and Geshem the Arab, that the Jews were rebelling against the Persian king (Neh. 2.19-20, 6.6). These neighbors likewise tried to reduce to absurdity the action of the Jews in rebuilding the wall; indeed, the biblical text observes that they derided and despised them. Josephus omits such disparaging remarks.

The very beginning of Josephus's account of Nehemiah calls attention to his relationship to the king. Whereas in the biblical account it is not until after 11 verses of the first chapter that Nehemiah is identified as the cupbearer of the king (Neh. 2.1), a position of crucial importance requiring the complete confidence of the monarch, Josephus's very first sentence so describes him (*Ant.* 11.159). Nehemiah, indeed, is so loyal that even without bathing he hastens to bring drink to the king (*Ant.* 11.163).

That Josephus was highly sensitive to the charge of dual loyalty may be seen in his paraphrase of the biblical passage in which certain Chaldaeans accuse the Jewish youths Shadrach, Mesach and Abednego, whom Nebuchadnezzar had appointed to high administrative posts, of paying no heed to the king, as witnessed by the fact that they did not serve his gods or worship his image (Dan. 3.8-12)—obviously important symbols in maintaining the unity and allegiance of the many ethnic groups in his kingdom. Josephus, in his paraphrase, is careful to shift the emphasis from the failure of the Jews to serve Nebuchadnezzar's gods and to worship his image—a political demand—to the religious motive of the youths, namely their unwillingness to transgress their fathers' laws (*Ant.* 10.214). The Romans, who placed such a great emphasis upon law and upon respect for ancestral tradition, as we can see from the attention given these factors in their great national poem, Virgil's *Aeneid*, would surely have appreciated such a stance.

Elsewhere Josephus goes even further in shifting the focus off from the conflict between Jewish religious law and the law of the state. Thus, in the Bible Daniel's envious rivals state, in their exasperation, that they are unable to find any complaint against Daniel unless they discover it to be 'in the matter of the law of his G-d' (Dan. 6.5). Realizing that the word 'law' in and of itself was such an important concept to the Romans and that the biblical allusion to a possible conflict between the law of the state and the law of the Jews implied an irreconcilable conflict between two systems, Josephus in his paraphrase of this passage omits the word 'law' altogether and instead couches the issue solely in religious terms with his remark that when his rivals saw Daniel praying to G-d three times a day they realized that they had found a pretext for destroying him (*Ant.* 10.252). When Josephus does subsequently mention the laws of the Jews, he makes clear that his reference is to their religious laws (*Ant.* 10.275), given the immediately following mention of the Temple and its sacrifices. Daniel's envious rivals, on the other hand, according to Josephus' addition to the biblical text (Dan. 6.13), sought to portray Daniel as attempting, by his disregard of the king's edict, to undermine the state, which they claimed others were seeking to keep and preserve (*Ant.* 10.256).[31]

13. *Tolerance and Respect toward Non-Jews and, Especially, Non-Jewish Leaders*

One of the recurring charges against Jews was that they had an implacable hatred of non-Jews. It is to answer this charge, as made by Apollonius Molon and Lysimachus (*Apion* 2.145) and repeated by Tacitus (*Histories* 5.5.1), that Josephus goes out of his way to stress that Jews show concern and compassion for non-Jews. Hence, to the extent that he was the legitimate ruler of his land, Pharaoh in his role as king was above criticism for Josephus. Indeed, the only ground for criticism of the Pharaoh in the incident with Sarai was that he failed to show self-control; in the Bible (Gen. 12.11-12), significantly, the blame is put on the Egyptians, whose licentiousness Abram fears and who take the lead in praising her to Pharaoh, whereas in Josephus (*Ant.* 1.162) this frenzy for women is transferred to Pharaoh himself; and it is the fear that Pharaoh will slay him because of his wife's beauty that leads Abram to devise his scheme of pretending that she is his sister. Josephus, then, in an extra-biblical passage (*Ant.* 1.163-64), remarks that Pharaoh, not content with reports about Sarai's beauty, was fired with a desire to see her and was actually at the point of laying hands upon her, whereupon G-d inflicted upon Pharaoh the punishment that was most dreadful in

---

31. There is a lacuna here in the text, but the import appears to be that those who observed the edict not to pray did so not because of impiety but because they realized how important it was to maintain respect for law and order.

Josephus's eyes, namely an outbreak of disease and political disturbance (στάσει). But even in this instance, Josephus comes to Pharaoh's
defense, carefully remarking (*Ant.* 1.165) that once he discovered the
truth about Sarai's identity (at that point her name had not yet been
changed to Sarah) Pharaoh apologized to Abram, stressing that he had
wished to contract a legitimate marriage alliance with her rather than to
outrage her in a transport of passion. Significantly, whereas in the Bible
(Gen. 12.16) it is before his discovery of her identity that Pharaoh gives
Abram abundant gifts, in Josephus (*Ant.* 1.165) Pharaoh's character is
enhanced by virtue of the fact that it is after the discovery of Sarai's
identity and when he has nothing to gain thereby that Pharaoh gives
abundant riches to Abram.

Josephus was confronted with a dilemma on the question of how to
treat the figure of Esau. On the one hand, there was a long-standing tradition, commencing with the Bible itself, of denigrating him. Thus the
Bible (Gen. 25.27) quite obviously favors Jacob, the 'plain' (*tam*, Septuagint ἄπλαστος, *Targ. Onq.* and *Targ. Neof. shelim*, 'perfect') man,
dwelling in tents, in contrast to Esau the hunter, the man of the field.
Josephus (*Ant.* 1.258) omits this contrast completely, apparently because he seeks to walk a tightrope between degrading and uplifting
either Jacob or Esau. Contrast the prophet Malachi (1.2-3), who quotes
G-d as saying explicitly, 'Jacob I loved, Esau I hated'.

In his depiction of Esau, Josephus, however, was in a quandary, inasmuch as, if he denigrated him, he would be diminishing respect for
Rome, since Esau had already in Josephus's time become identified
with Rome.[32]

We may note Josephus's adept handling of the dilemma already in
his account of the birth of the twins. In the first place, even before their
birth, Josephus (*Ant.* 1.257) omits all mention of the struggle (Gen.
25.22) between them within the womb of Rebekah (the Hebrew, *vayiter-
ozezu*, indicates that they crushed one another). Whereas the oracle,
according to the Hebrew (Gen. 25.23), declares that the older shall
serve (*ya'avod*) the younger, and whereas the Septuagint likewise reads
'will serve' (δουλεύσει), Josephus (*Ant.* 1.257), in order to avoid suggesting that the descendants of Esau are destined to be slaves to the
Jews, writes that 'he that to appearance was the lesser would excel
[προτερήσειν, come before] the greater'. Here Josephus follows the

---

32. See my 'Josephus' Portrait of Jacob', *JQR* 79 (1988–89), pp. 130-33.

import of the Septuagint, which reads that Jacob will ὑπερέξει ('be above') Esau rather than the Hebrew *ye'emaz* ('be stronger') and thus avoids the embarrassing prophetic implication that Rome will ultimately be militarily weaker than Judea, which it had just defeated in a protracted war (66–73/74).

Moreover, the Bible (Gen. 25.25) declares that Esau came out ruddy (*'ademoni*), 'all over like a hairy garment'; the Septuagint faithfully renders this as indicating that he came out 'red, hairy all over like a skin' (πυρράκης, ὅλος, ὡσεὶ δορά, δασύς); and *Targum Onq.* similarly states that he came out 'red, like a hairy mantle all over'. Josephus (*Ant.* 1.258), on the other hand, speaks of Esau's hairiness but says nothing either about his redness or about the struggle between Jacob and Esau in the womb.

In antiquity there was a general prejudice against ruddy or red-haired persons.[33] That Josephus was aware of the negative connotation of redness may be seen in his rendering (*Ant.* 6.164) of the passage (1 Sam. 16.12) in which David is described as ruddy (*'ademoni*; the same word is used to describe Esau in Gen. 25.25). The Septuagint, here as in the case of Esau, renders the Hebrew word by πυρράκης, that is, 'fiery red'; but Josephus speaks, rather, of David's complexion as 'golden'

---

33. See Theodor H. Gaster, *Myth, Legend and Custom in the Old Testament: A Comparative Study with Chapters from Sir James Frazer's Folklore in the Old Testament* (New York: Harper, 1969), pp. 165-66. In the Middle Ages, Judas Iscariot was represented as having red hair. On hairiness as a mark of savagery, see Ephraim A. Speiser (ed.), *Genesis* (Garden City, NY: Doubleday, 1964), p. 196; and Bruce Vawter, *On Genesis: A New Reading* (London: Chapman, 1977), p. 288. Slaves apparently were conventionally said to have red hair, as we may see from the description of three of them in Roman comedies (Plautus, *Asinaria* 400; *Pseudolus* 1218; Terence, *Phormio* 51); and slaves often bore the name Rufus ('Red'). To be sure, George E. Duckworth, *The Nature of Roman Comedy: A Study in Popular Entertainment* (Princeton: Princeton University Press, 1952), p. 89, asserts that there seems to be no good authority for the claim that slaves always wore red wigs in plays. A clue, however, to the fact that this was normally the case may be seen in Plautus, *Captivi* (648), where Philocrates, though a free young man, is described by his countryman as having 'somewhat reddish hair' (*subrufus*), presumably because he had been disguised as a slave earlier in the play. Philo (*Quaest. in Gen.* 4.160), consistent with his practice of denigrating Esau, remarks that Esau's ruddy body and hairy hide were a sign of his character as a savage man who raged furiously in the manner of a wild beast. The rabbis associate redness with the shedding of blood. See Louis Ginzberg, *The Legends of the Jews* (Philadelphia: Jewish Publication Society, 1928), VI, p. 247 n. 13.

(ξανθός, 'yellow with a tinge of red, fair').[34] Josephus (*Ant.* 1.258), aware of the connections of redness with bloodshed and apparently concerned not to imply that the descendants of Esau, the Romans, were slaves, thus totally omits Esau's redness and remarks merely that he was excessively hairy.

Josephus's handling of Esau's sale of his birthright is likewise calculated to mitigate criticism of him. In the first place, he postpones even mentioning the incident until after the reconciliation between Jacob and Esau, since, we may conjecture, if he had mentioned it in its proper biblical time frame this would have served to build up a cumulative dossier of evidence that Esau was really unworthy of Isaac's blessing, inasmuch as he had such a low opinion of his birthright as to sell it. Josephus therefore postpones mention of the sale until he comes to the death of Isaac, whereupon he explains the division of the inheritance. There is further sympathy generated for Esau, because we are told (*Ant.* 2.2) that he was still a lad (παῖς, 'child') at the moment of the sale, whereas the Hebrew text gives no indication of his age. Whereas the parallel Hebrew text (Gen. 25.29) states that Esau was tired (*'ayef*), Josephus uses a stronger word, indicating that he was fatigued (πόνου, implying 'toil', 'strain', 'exertion') and adds that he was famished (λιμώττων, 'hungry', 'starving'). The Hebrew text might tempt one to despise Esau, who was ready to sell so precious a status as his birthright for some mere boiled pottage (*nazid*); Josephus makes Esau's deed more plausible, since in his account the food in question is a dish of lentils of rich (σφόδρα, 'especially') tawny hue, 'which still further whetted his appetite'. Furthermore, whereas in the Hebrew text (Gen. 25.31) Jacob asks Esau merely to sell him the birthright, Josephus obviously aims to arouse more sympathy for Esau, inasmuch as he explicitly (*Ant.* 2.3) states that Jacob took advantage (χρωσάμενος) of Esau's famished state and forced (ἠνάγκαζε) him to sell it. Josephus mentions Esau's hunger three times in this brief section, whereas the Hebrew text does not refer to it at all. Hence, the sale appears more justifiable as a matter of sheer survival for Esau.

34. The word ξανθός is used by Josephus (*Ant.* 2.2, 3) with reference to the 'tawny' pottage which Jacob gave to Esau in exchange for his rights as a first-born son. Hence, in referring to David as ξανθός, far from associating David with the Messiah who will overthrow the Roman Empire, Josephus may be connecting David with Rome, itself to be identified with Esau or Edom.

What is most striking of all, however, is that Josephus says nothing (2.3) about Esau's despising his birthright (Gen. 25.34);[35] instead, he uses the story to explain the etymology of the name of the region of Idumea, which he derives from Esau's nickname 'Edom' (i.e. Edom), referring to the red color of the pottage which Jacob sold to Esau. If, as we suggest, Esau was already in Josephus's time regarded as the ancestor of the Romans, Josephus is being careful not to offend his Roman patrons by diverging from the biblical text, for example (*Ant.* 2.2), in not having Esau ask to swallow down (*hale'iteni*, Gen. 25.30, implying voracious eating) the pottage but rather in asserting simply that Jacob gave him food (τροφήν). In the Hebrew the second half of Genesis 25.34 presents a staccato succession of five verbal forms calculated to emphasize Esau's lack of manners and judgment; that is he ate, drank, rose up, went his way and finally despised (*vayivez*) his birthright;[36] finally, the Septuagint says that 'he held it cheap' (ἐφαύλισεν, 'held of little value'). All this is missing from Josephus's account, presumably because he is being careful not to denigrate Esau.[37] And yet, true to his careful balancing act, Josephus follows the Septuagint (Gen. 25.31; cf. 25.33) in having Esau ask Jacob to 'give in return' (ἀπόδου, 'give back') the birthright, rather than to sell it to him, the implication being that Jacob really had a right to it in the first place, thus mitigating his guilt.

Finally, in contrast to the extremely negative view of Esau found in the Pseudepigrapha, Philo and the New Testament, Josephus, apparently aware of the equation of Esau and Rome, is careful not to offend his Roman patrons and thus says nothing, for example, about Esau's

---

35. Philo (*Quaest. in Gen.* 4.172) remarks that while the literal meaning of the Jacob's statement, 'Sell me this day thy birthright' (Gen. 25.31), suggests Jacob's greed in wishing to deprive Esau of his rights, the allegorical meaning, which Philo obviously prefers, is that an abundance of possessions brings about sin for a wicked man (i.e. someone like Esau) but is necessary for the righteous man alone. Elsewhere (*Leg. All.* 3.69.192–70.195), Philo justifies Jacob's acquisition of the birthright by noting that Esau had a servile character and that, therefore, the birthright and blessings were inappropriate for him, since he was sunk in boundless ignorance. Pseudo-Philo (*Ps.-Philo* 32.5-6) completely omits the actual barter of the birthright.

36. Speiser (ed.), *Genesis*, p. 195.

37. Philo (*Quaest. in Gen.* 4.228) goes much further than Josephus in defending Jacob's deception of his brother. He cites the parallel of athletes, whose use of deceit and trickery in contests is considered honorable.

despising his birthright (Gen. 25.34). He thus arouses more sympathy for Esau in his presentation of Esau's relationship with his father Isaac, as well as in the scene in which Isaac blesses his sons. Moreover, in the biblical text (Gen. 41.37) we read only that Joseph's advice to Pharaoh to gather food during the fat years for the lean years that will follow seemed good to Pharaoh and to all his servants. On the other hand, we admire Josephus's Pharaoh much more, inasmuch as he expresses his appreciation to Joseph with much greater enthusiasm, not merely stating that Joseph was discreet and wise (Gen. 41.39) but actually marvelling (θαυμάσαντος) at the latter's discernment (φρόνησιν) and wisdom (σοφίαν). This appreciation for Joseph is particularly to be seen in that Josephus spells out the fact (Gen. 41.39 vs. *Ant.* 2.89) that Pharaoh doubly (ἀμφοτέρων) admired Joseph, alike for the interpretation of the dream and for his counsel. Moreover, we admire Josephus's Pharaoh, inasmuch as he expresses his appreciation of Joseph with much greater enthusiasm than does his biblical counterpart (Gen. 41.39 vs. *Ant.* 2.89). Josephus emphasizes that Jews, in turn, are considerate toward non-Jews, so that, in an extra-biblical addition, he proudly notes that Joseph sells grain to all people and not merely to native Egyptians (*Ant.* 2.94, 101). The Pharaoh is likewise more magnanimous toward Joseph's brothers in permitting them to continue in their occupation as shepherds (*Ant.* 2.185 vs. Gen. 46.34).

When Josephus comes to that portion of the Bible detailing the sufferings of the Israelites in Egypt, he is careful (in line with the Bible itself, Exod. 1.8) to avoid the identification, which is found in the rabbinic sources (*Soṭ.* 11a), of this oppressor Pharaoh with the one who had appointed Joseph to high estate, and states that the rule had passed to another dynasty (*Ant.* 2.202), in order to emphasize that not all Pharaohs are identical. The Pharaoh of the exodus emerges more favorably, since, in Josephus's version, the blame is placed not on Pharaoh personally but rather on the Egyptians, who are described as a voluptuous and lazy people (*Ant.* 2.201). Josephus's audience would have had little difficulty accepting this statement of contempt for the Egyptian people, if we may judge from the remarks of a host of Greek and Roman writers, from Florus and Achilles Tatius to the author of the *Bellum Alexandrinum* and Juvenal.[38] As Josephus (*Ant.* 2.201-202) presents it, it is not Pharaoh but the Egyptians who are at fault, their bitter disposition

---

38. See John P.V.D. Balsdon, *Romans and Aliens* (London: Gerald Duckworth, 1979), pp. 68-69, p. 271 nn. 61-74.

toward the Israelites being due to their envy of the latter's prosperity, brought about by the latter's work ethic, which they thought was to their own detriment.

As to Pharaoh's decree that the male babies should be put to death, the Bible (Exod. 1.8-10) clearly puts the finger of blame upon Pharaoh, since we are told that it is he who said to his people that the Israelites were too numerous and too mighty. In Josephus's version (*Ant.* 2.205), on the other hand, the blame is placed upon one of the Pharaoh's sacred scribes who predicts to the king that there would be born to the Israelites one who would surpass all others in virtue and who would win everlasting renown and who would abase the sovereignty of the Egyptians.[39] In view of this remark, the reader is not likely to censure the king who, we are told (*Ant.* 2.206), was alarmed (δείσας, 'was afraid') and who, consequently, as we are reminded, on this sage's advice (rather than on his own initiative), ordered all male children to be drowned in the river. Moreover, we are told, it was the Egyptians (rather than Pharaoh) who were stimulated by the advice of this scribe to exterminate the Israelites.

In addition, Josephus's Pharaoh is portrayed as less cruel than his biblical counterpart, inasmuch as in the Bible (Exod. 1.15) we read that he gave orders to the Hebrew midwives to put the male children to death, whereas Josephus (*Ant.* 2.206) specifically says that the orders were given to Egyptian midwives and explains that Pharaoh proceeded in this way because he realized that women who were his compatriots were not likely to transgress his will. If Pharaoh enforces his decree by declaring (*Ant.* 2.207) that those mothers who ventured stealthily to save their offspring are to be put to death along with their babes, the reader might feel at least some understanding for such a measure in view of the importance of obedience to the law, just as the reader of Sophocles' *Antigone* must identify to some degree with Creon's position, inasmuch as non-obedience to the law, even if one feels the law to be unjust or immoral, is an invitation to something even worse, namely anarchy. Even if this Pharaoh, as we shall see, lacks self-control in his personal behavior and in this respect is subject to censure, he, *qua* ruler, must be obeyed.

The very fact that Josephus devotes 2.16 times as much space to the non-Jewish priest, Jethro, Moses' father-in-law, as does the Hebrew is

39. See my 'Josephus' Portraits of the Pharaohs', *Syllecta Classica* 4 (1993), pp. 49-63.

an indication of the importance that Josephus attached to him.[40] Unlike Philo and the rabbis,[41] who were divided in their views of Jethro, Josephus presents a uniformly favorable picture of him. In the first place, when the reader is introduced to him, he is described as a priest held in high veneration (πολλῆς ἠξιωμένου τιμῆς) by the people of the country (*Ant.* 2.258). Presumably, this is intended to counteract the implication of the biblical text that the shepherds drove away Jethro's daughters (Exod. 2.17), which, we may assume, they would not have done if they had had respect for Jethro himself. In fact, in a startling addition to the biblical text, Jethro even adopts Moses as his son (*Ant.* 2.263). The key point is that Jethro is actually identified here as a barbarian; clearly, Josephus's point is to stress that, far from being prejudiced against barbarians, actually, the greatest leader of the Jews married a barbarian and that he was even adopted by a barbarian. In terms of the striking impact upon a reader, only Alexander the Great's marriage with a Persian princess would be comparable.

One of the most delicate problems for Josephus must have been how to deal with the scene in which Jethro criticizes the way in which Moses had been administering justice (Exod. 18.14). In the Bible, Jethro comes right out with his criticism: 'What is this that you are doing for the people? Why do you sit alone?' Such a criticism must have been disconcerting for Moses, especially since there is no indication in the biblical text that Jethro took Moses aside so as to avoid embarrassing him in the presence of the Israelites. On the other hand, in Josephus's version Jethro shows real sensitivity so as to avoid embarrassing his son-in-law. We are told that when he sees the way Moses administers affairs he holds his peace (ἡσυχίαν ἦγε, 'kept quiet') at the moment (τότε), inasmuch as he is reluctant to hinder any who would avail themselves of the talents of their chief. It is only after the tumult of the crowd has subsided that he then discreetly takes Moses aside and in utter privacy (συμμονωθείς, 'be alone in private with someone') that he instructs him what it is necessary to do (*Ant.* 3.67).

The biblical Balaam narrative was a real challenge for Josephus, inasmuch as Balaam was a non-Jew, and Josephus is constantly aware of the charge that Jews are guilty of hating non-Jews. By shifting the focus from Balaam's personality to the historical, military, and political con-

40. See my *Studies in Josephus' Rewritten Bible* (Leiden: E.J. Brill, 1998), p. 38.

41. See my *Studies in Josephus' Rewritten Bible*, pp. 41-46.

frontation between Israel and her enemies, Josephus gives a relatively unbiased portrait of Balaam (see, for example, *Ant.* 4.105, 106, 112), the pagan prophet who sought to curse Israel, especially when we compare his version with that of Philo, the rabbinic tradition, the New Testament and the book of Numbers itself.[42]

Indeed, we find in Balaam's words in the Bible (Num. 23.9) the statement that the Israelites are a people that shall dwell alone and shall not be reckoned among the nations. Significantly, in his version of this passage, Josephus, clearly aware of the above, avoids presenting the Israelites as sundered off from all other peoples and instead words the statement in terms of the *excellence* of the Israelites as compared with other peoples, and has Balaam assert that G-d has lavished upon the Israelites the means whereby they may become the *happiest* of all peoples (*Ant.* 4.114). No one could object to such a prophecy of the Israelites' happiness; the objection, which Josephus carefully avoids mentioning, would be to their cutting themselves off from other peoples.

Again, Josephus does not hesitate to have Balaam prophesy that the Israelites will occupy the land to which G-d has sent them and that the whole earth will be filled with their fame (*Ant.* 4.115). If Balaam foretells the calamities that will befall kings and cities of the highest celebrity (some of which, he says, have not yet been established) (*Ant.* 4.125), he is careful to keep this prophecy cryptic enough so that Gentile readers will not necessarily recognize this as referring to Rome, just as he has a similarly cryptic prophecy in connection with the interpretation of Nebuchadnezzar's dream in his pericope of Daniel (*Ant.* 10.210).

In the biblical passage (Num. 24.17-18) corresponding to *Ant.* 4.125, however, what Balaam predicts is that a star out of Jacob and a scepter out of Israel will conquer Edom and Seir. That this is intended as an eschatological prophecy is clear from Balaam's earlier statement that he will advise Balak what the Israelites would do to the Moabites at the end of days (Num. 24.14). That a Messianic prophecy is likewise intended seems to be hinted at in the Septuagint's version of Num. 24.7: 'There shall come a man out of his [i.e. Israel's] seed, and he shall rule over many nations; and the kingdom of Gog shall be exalted, and his kingdom shall be increased.' In any case, the passage was interpreted messianically shortly after the time of Josephus in reference to Bar Kochba (*y. Ta'an.* 69d) by Rabbi Akiva. Of course, such a messianic

42. See my 'Josephus' Portrait of Balaam', *Studia Philonica Annual* 5 (1993), pp. 48-93.

understanding was avoided by Josephus because of his subservience to the Romans.

In the same line, Josephus is eager to avoid giving the impression that the Israelites are out to destroy their enemies mercilessly (*Ant.* 4.125), as is suggested by the biblical passage in which Balaam predicts that the G-d of Israel will 'eat up the nations that are His adversaries and break their bones in pieces' (Num. 24.8). In Josephus's much milder version we are informed merely that Balaam foretold what calamities were in store for the opponents of the Israelites, without spelling out precisely what those would be (*Ant.* 4.125).[43]

Another example illustrating Josephus' eagerness not to cast aspersions on non-Jews may be seen in his rehabilitation of Eglon, the king of Moab. Instead of blaming Eglon for subjugating the Israelites he places the onus upon the Israelites themselves for their anarchy and for the failure to obey the laws (*Ant.* 5.185). He likewise omits such disparaging elements as Eglon's obesity (Judg. 3.17) and his defecating (Judg. 3.24)[44]

A number of additions in Josephus's portrayal of Solomon are intended, with a view toward Josephus's contemporary scene, to answer the charge of misanthropy and to demonstrate the excellent relations between Jews and non-Jews. Whereas in the Bible we read only that Hiram, the king of Tyre, sent his servants to Solomon when he heard that he had been anointed king (1 Kgs 5.15), Josephus adds that Hiram was overjoyed and sent him greetings and congratulations on his good fortune (*Ant.* 8.50). Solomon, in turn, expresses his gratitude to Hiram

---

43. Cf. Josephus, *War* 5.367: 'G-d, who went the round of the nations, bringing to each in turn the rod of empire, now rested over Italy.' Marinus de Jonge, 'Josephus und die Zukunftserwartungen seines Volkes', in Otto Betz *et al.* (eds.), *Josephus-Studien: Untersuchungen zu Josephus, dem antiken Judentum und dem Neuen Testament: Otto Michel zum 70. Geburtstag gewidmet* (Göttingen: Vandenhoeck & Ruprecht, 1974), p. 211, deduces from the use of the word 'now' in the above quotation that Josephus regarded the Romans as being powerful at the time that he wrote but not forever. We may reply, however, that the use of the word 'now' is perfectly natural in the context, namely a speech delivered by Josephus to his fellow Jews. He is there making an appeal to realism: Right now (but without reference to the future, which really is irrelevant) the Romans are in firm control of the world; hence revolution makes no sense.'

44. See my 'Josephus' Portrait of Joab', *EstBíb* 51 (1994), pp. 190-93.

for his aid in presenting him with cedar wood for the Temple. Whereas the Bible states simply that, in return, Solomon gave Hiram twenty thousand measures of wheat for food for his household and twenty measures of beaten oil (1 Kgs 5.25), Josephus's Solomon goes much further in expressing his gratitude, in that he not only adds twenty thousand measures of wine to the gifts specified in the Bible, but he also commends (ἐπήνεσε) Hiram's zeal (προθυμίαν) and goodwill (εὔνοιαν) (*Ant.* 8.57). Finally, whereas the Bible states that Hiram and Solomon made a league together (1 Kgs 5.26), Josephus elaborates that the friendship of Hiram and Solomon increased through these things, so that they swore that it should continue forever (*Ant.* 8.58).

That the friendship between Solomon and Hiram was important in refuting the charge of misanthropy may be seen from the fact that Josephus devotes a goodly portion of his apologetic treatise *Against Apion* (1.100-127) to reproducing evidence from the Phoenician archives and from the works of Dios and Menander of Ephesus to illustrate the excellent relations beween the two kings and to confirm the antiquity of the Temple (*Apion* 1.106-108). There is good reason, says Josephus, why the erection of the Temple should be mentioned in the Tyrians' records, since Hiram, king of Tyre, was a friend of Solomon and, indeed, had inherited this friendship from his (Hiram's) father (*Apion* 1.109-10). According to Josephus, it is the non-Jew, Hiram, who inherited the friendship from his father, whereas in the Bible it is Solomon who inherits from his father a friendship with Hiram (2 Sam. 5.11; 1 Kgs 5.1). Josephus, for apologetic reasons, exults in this friendship (*Apion* 1.110). Thus, whereas in the Bible Hiram simply sent cedar trees to David (2 Sam. 5.11), Josephus says that Hiram cut down the finest timber from Mount Libanus (*Apion* 1.110). That this friendship carried with it a great deal of prestige may be deduced from the fact, proudly noted by Josephus, that the Phoenicians were an ancient people and that Hiram lived more than 150 years before the founding of Carthage (*Apion* 2.17-18). In a most unusual digression, Josephus calls special attention to the fact that copies of the correspondence between Hiram and Solomon are to be found not only in the Bible but also in the Tyrian archives (*Ant.* 8.55), and then adds that he has recorded these matters in detail because he wanted his readers to know that he has related nothing more than what is true and that he has not, by inserting into his history various plausible (πιθανοῖς) and seductive (ἐπαγωγοῖς) passages meant to deceive (ἀπάτην) and entertain (τέρψιν), attempted to avoid critical inquiry (ἐξέτασιν) (*Ant.* 8.56). This passage is, of course, reminiscent of Thucydides' implied attack (1.21.1) on Herodotus for composing a work with a view rather to pleasing (προσαγωγότερον) the ear than to telling the truth, and of his insistence that his own history is not intended as 'a prize-essay to be heard for the moment but as a possession for all time' (1.22.4). Josephus then concludes with an *apologia* for his craft as historian: 'Nor should we be indulgently held blameless if we depart from what is proper to a historical narrative; on the contrary, we ask that no hearing be given us unless we are able to establish the truth with demonstrations [ἀποδείξεως] and convincing evidence [τεκμηρίων ἰσχυρῶν]' (*Ant.* 8.56).

The fact that, according to Josephus, many of the riddles and problems which Hiram and Solomon sent each other were still preserved in Tyre in Josephus's own day (*Apion* 1.111) is important not only in building up Solomon's reputation for wisdom but also for stressing the friendship and high respect which a Jewish leader had for a non-Jew. While it is true that Josephus does say that Solomon showed greater proficiency and was the cleverer (σοφώτερος) of the two, it is still quite a compliment for Hiram that he could be compared with Solomon and that Solomon found it interesting and challenging to exchange problems and riddles with him. As further evidence of the historicity of the relations between Solomon and Hiram, Josephus on two occasions cites the words of Menander, who translated the Tyrian records from the Phoenician language into Greek (*Ant.* 8.144-46; *Apion* 1.116-25).

The supreme example of Josephus's concern with answering the charge that the Jews were guilty of hating non-Jews is to be found in Josephus's version of Solomon's prayer at the dedication of the Temple. According to the biblical version, Solomon prayed that when non-Jews come to the Temple G-d should grant all of their requests so that all the peoples of the earth may know his name and fear him (1 Kgs 8.41-43). Josephus says nothing about the peoples' fearing him (*Ant.* 8.116-17), perhaps because he thought that this might give the impression that the Jews were seeking proselytes or G-d-fearers—a very sensitive issue for the Romans at this time because they were afraid that the increasing success of Jews in winning such adherents would mean the end of the old Roman way of life. Instead, Josephus adds a new dimension to the discussion by explaining that Solomon's aim in beseeching G-d thus was to demonstrate that Jews 'are not inhuman [ἀπάνθρωποι] by nature nor unfriendly [ἀλλοτρίως] to those who are not of their own country, but wish that all men should receive aid from Thee and enjoy Thy blessings' (*Ant.* 8.117).[45]

Solomon might well have been accused by a non-Jewish audience of an anti-foreign attitude on the basis of the biblical statement that he removed his wife, Pharaoh's daughter, from Jerusalem to a house in another city, 'for, he said, my wife shall not dwell in the house of David king of Israel because the places are holy whereunto the ark of the L-rd hath come' (2 Chron. 8.11). Josephus defuses such a charge by omitting this passage completely (*Ant.* 8.162).

Again, Solomon, in dedicating the Temple, asks that G-d grant the prayers not only of Jews but also of non-Jews (1 Kgs 8.41-43; *Ant.* 8.116-17). Likewise, whereas the biblical Jonah appears to be indifferent to the Gentiles whom he is to warn, since we find him, at the beginning of the account, fast asleep and even, according to the Septuagint, snoring (Jon. 1.5), Josephus's Jonah is not asleep and, we are told, has absented himself only because he did not wish to imitate what the sailors were doing.

Furthermore, when Mesha, the king of the Moabites, sacrifices his own son to his god, the Bible says nothing about the reaction of Kings Jehoshaphat and Jehoram (2 Kgs 3.27); Josephus, on the other hand, calls attention to their humanity and compassion (*Ant.* 9.43).

Josephus had to avoid criticizing the Assyrians more than necessary, as he did not want to offend non-Jews unduly. Hence, in line with this last concern, he omits the biblical statement that Sennacherib wrote letters to cast contempt on the G-d of Israel (2 Chron. 32.17); and, in particular, he omits the degrading remark of the Rab-shakeh warning that the Jews are doomed to eat their own dung and to drink their own urine (2 Kgs 18.27). Indeed, he considerably abbreviates the threats uttered by the Rab-shakeh (*Ant.* 10.10).

Josephus likewise omits, in an obvious show of tolerance, the statement, in Hezekiah's prayer before G-d, that the kings of Assyria had cast the gods of other nations into the fire (2 Kgs 19.17-18 vs. *Ant.* 10.16). He furthermore omits, as apparently too strong, the prophet Isaiah's blistering promise from G-d that He would put His hook in Assyria's nose and His bit in its mouth (2 Kgs 19.28 vs. *Ant.* 10.16). If

---

45. We may also note that, in connection with the rebuilding of the Temple under Zerubbabel, Josephus stresses, in an extra-biblical detail, that the Temple is open to all, including even the schismatic Samaritans, for worship of G-d (*Ant.* 11.87).

Sennacherib is ultimately defeated, it is not a matter of his returning to his own land because of a mere rumor, as the Bible would have it (2 Kgs 19.7), since that presumably, from Josephus's point of view and from that of much of his audience, would have trivialized the whole incident, but rather because he is a victim, in a manner reminiscent of a Greek tragedy, of over-confidence (θράσους) similar to the overweening pride (ὕβρις) characteristic of the generation of the Tower of Babel and of Haman (*Ant.* 10.13). And yet, just as in the Daniel pericope, Josephus shows respect for Nebuchadnezzar, Belshazzar and Darius, so here he shows regard for Sennacherib, despite the latter's attack upon Jerusalem, as we see from his addition to the biblical statement (2 Kgs 19.37), in which he points out that it was by treachery that Sennacherib was slain by his son (*Ant.* 10.23). Finally, the Bible (2 Kgs 20.12-13; Isa. 39.1-2), relates how the king of Babylon sent envoys to Hezekiah bearing letters and a gift (Septuagint, 'gifts') and inviting him to become his ally, and how Hezekiah welcomed them and showed them his treasure house; Josephus, however, eager to demonstrate the high regard that Jews have for non-Jews and, in particular, the importance of hospitality in Hezekiah's scheme of values, adds that Hezekiah feasted the envoys and sent them back with gifts for the Babylonian king.

In general, Josephus's Daniel, given the additions to the biblical narrative, comes across as having considerable concern for non-Jews. Thus, according to the Bible, Daniel approached his three companions asking them to pray to G-d concerning the mystery so that he and they might not perish with the rest of the wise men (Dan. 2.17-18). In Josephus's version it is Daniel himself who beseeches G-d (*Ant.* 10.199); furthermore, Josephus adds that he did so throughout the night, and in place of the vague term 'mystery' and in place of a concern primarily with saving their own lives, together with those of the non-Jewish wise men, we are told specifically that he sought enlightenment so as to save the Magi and the Chaldaeans, together with whom they were destined to perish. It is thus significantly the fate of the Magi and the Chaldaeans which is his first thought.

Even Nebuchadnezzar, who was responsible for the destruction of the First Temple, emerges more favorably, inasmuch as Josephus omits the cruel decree which Nebuchadnezzar issued, in which he declared that anyone who spoke a word against the Jewish G-d should be torn limb from limb (Dan. 3.29). Moreover, Josephus considerably tones down the gruesome picture of Nebuchadnezzar's behaving like an animal (*Ant.* 10.217).

Likewise, one might well be critical of Darius for signing his name to an edict arbitrarily forbidding any petition directed toward any god or man for thirty days (Dan. 6.7, 9); but Josephus protects Darius's reputation by explaining that Darius had approved of the decree only because he had been misled by his advisers (*Ant.* 10.254).[46] Josephus likewise protects Darius's reputation by having him not merely express the hope, as does the Bible (Dan. 6.16), that Daniel's G-d would save him and that he would suffer no harm from the beasts but also, more positively, by having him bid Daniel to bear his fate with good courage (*Ant.* 10.258). Moreover, the fact that he had cast into the lions' den not only his enemies but also their innocent wives and children (Dan. 6.24) would cast discredit upon Darius, and it is therefore significant that Josephus omits this detail (*Ant.* 10.262).

What is most striking about Josephus's version of Ahasuerus is that there is not even a single hint in it that is negative. Josephus stresses Ahasuerus's respect for law. His apparently capricious treatment of Queen Vashti is explained as due to her insolence after she had been summoned repeatedly by her husband (*Ant.* 11.191-92). And even then, Josephus expands on Ahasuerus's deep love for her and on his remorse (*Ant.* 11.195). As to Ahasuerus's relationship with Esther, though there is good reason to question its nature, Josephus insists that it was lawful (*Ant.* 11.202). He expands on his gentle and tender concern for Esther (*Ant.* 11.236). Indeed, Ahasuerus is glorified as the ideal ruler whose goal is peace and good government for his subjects (*Ant.* 11.216). He is particularly magnanimous toward those who do favors for him (*Ant.* 11.252). If he did send out the edict condemning all the Jews in his realm to be put to death the blame is placed upon his advisers (*Ant.* 11.215, 275-76).[47]

14. *Tolerance toward Non-Jewish Religions*

In an interpretation of Exod. 22.27[28], wherein he follows the Septuagint, Josephus declares that Jews are forbidden to speak ill of the religion of Gentiles out of respect for the very word 'god' (*Ant.* 4.207 and *Apion* 2.237). Thus, Josephus simply omits the passage in which

---

46. See my 'Josephus' Portraits of the Pharaohs', pp. 52-54.
47. See my 'Josephus' Portrait of Ahasuerus', *AusBR* 42 (1994), pp. 17-39.

Gideon, upon instructions from G-d, pulls down the altar of Baal and the Asherah tree that was worshipped beside it (Judg. 6.25-32).

Whereas in the Bible Samuel is represented as speaking to the Israelites assuring them that if they put away their foreign gods and direct their hearts to G-d they will be delivered from the hand of the Philistines (1 Sam. 7.3), Josephus's Samuel says nothing about the worship of the foreign gods (*Ant.* 6.19). Presumably he is concerned lest the non-Jews, comprising most of his audience, be offended by such a reference, and instead speaks to the Israelites of liberty (ἐλευθερία) and of the blessings that it brings.

In the case of Asa, Josephus has systematically removed references to his destruction of pagan cults. Thus, though the account of his reign in 1 Kings (15.12) is extraordinarily brief, yet we have mention of the fact that he put away the male cult prostitutes out of the land and that he removed all the idols that his father had made. In the parallel passage in 2 Chronicles (14.3, 5) we have still further details of Asa's mass destruction of pagan cult objects, namely that he took away the foreign altars and the high places, broke down the pillars, and took out of all the cities of Judah the high places and the incense altars. In Josephus's version we hear nothing specific about Asa's destruction of pagan cult objects; rather, the language is quite deliberately vague, with the emphasis on the positive: 'He put his kingdom in order by cutting away whatever evil growths were found in it and cleansing it from every impurity' (*Ant.* 8.290). For similar reasons, Josephus omits the biblical statement that when Asa heard the warning given him by the prophet Azariah he put away the idols from the land of Judah and Benjamin and from the cities which he had taken in the hill country of Ephraim (2 Chron. 15.8).

Given Josephus's concern not to offend his pagan readers, we should also not be surprised to find that he omits the biblical statement that Asa's people entered into a covenant that they would put to death whoever, whether young or old, man or woman, would not seek the L-rd (2 Chron. 15.12-13). Inasmuch as mystery cults were held in such high regard by many non-Jews, it is not surprising that Josephus altogether omits the statement, as found in the Septuagint translation, that King Asa ended the mystery cults (1 Kgs 15.12).

It is in line with Josephus's tolerant attitude toward the religions of others that we find Josephus omitting the biblical statement that Jehoshaphat removed the pagan high places and the Asherim from the land of Judah (2 Chron. 17.6 vs. *Ant.* 8.394).[48] Indeed, whereas, according to the Bible, the prophet Jehu, after reproaching Jehoshaphat for joining Ahab in a military alliance, remarks that there is nonetheless some good to be found in him in that he had destroyed the pagan objects (2 Chron. 19.3), Josephus very diplomatically omits mention of their destruction, since this would imply disrespect for the religion of others, and instead has Jehu declare in the vaguest terms that the king would be delivered from his enemies, despite having sinned, because of his good character (φύσιν) (*Ant.* 9.1).

This emphasis upon Jehoshaphat's liberal attitude toward pagans may be seen in Josephus's version of the biblical remark that the reason why the neighboring kingdoms did not make war against Jehoshaphat was that the fear of the L-rd fell upon them (2 Chron. 17.10). In Josephus's version their fear is replaced by a positive feeling of love, since we read that the neighboring peoples continued to cherish (στέργοντες, 'love', 'be fond of', 'like', 'feel affection towards', 'esteem', 'think highly of') him (*Ant.* 8.396).

Josephus likewise omits King Jehu's conversion of the temple of Baal into an outhouse (2 Kgs 10.27).

The charge that the Jews were intolerant of other religions is sharply refuted by Josephus in his version of the book of Esther, as elsewhere. Thus, though Josephus generally follows the apocryphal Addition C, containing Esther's prayer to G-d, he omits her bitter attack on the idol-worship of the non-Jews (Addition C 19-22):

> And now they [i.e. the enemies of the Jews] have not been satisfied with the bitterness of our captivity, but they have laid their hands (in the hands of their idols), to remove the ordinance of Thy mouth, and to destroy Thine inheritance, and to stop the mouth of them that praise Thee, and to quench the glory of Thy house and Thy altar, and to open the mouth of the nations to give praise to vain idols, and that a king of flesh should be magnified forever. Surrender not, O L-rd, Thy sceptre unto them that be not gods.

48. Perhaps Josephus was troubled by the fact that the Bible seems to contradict itself on this point, inasmuch as 1 Kgs 22.43 says specifically that during Jehoshaphat's reign the high places were not taken away and that the people continued to sacrifice and burn incense there. Josephus resolves the problem by omitting the statements of both Kings and Chronicles on this point.

15. *Intermarriage and Proselytism*

As we see in his handling of the intermarriages of Esau, Joseph, Moses, Samson and Solomon, among others, Josephus was in a quandary. On the one hand, the Bible explicitly prohibits intermarriage (Deut. 7.3); but, on the other hand, too strenuous an objection to the practice on his part would play into the hands of those who accused the Jews of misanthropy and illiberalism.

Significantly, whereas in the Bible it is only after the death of their father Elimelech that his sons Mahlon and Chilion take wives of the women of Moab (Ruth 1.4), Josephus, on the contrary, indicates that it was Elimelech himself who took Moabite women as wives for his sons (*Ant.* 5.319), presumably to indicate that Jews are not prejudiced against non-Jews, even Moabites, this despite the fact that the Torah declares that no Moabite may enter the 'assembly of the L-rd' (Deut. 23.3), because they had shown hostility to the Israelites during their forty years of wandering in the desert after the exodus. Moreover, again to show that Jews are not hostile to non-Jews, Josephus's picture of the two Moabite daughters-in-law of Naomi arouses even more sympathy than does the biblical version. In the latter, when they are urged to return to their homeland of Moab, they reply very simply, 'Nay, but we will return with thee unto thy people' (Ruth 1.10). In Josephus, by contrast, we are told that the daughters-in-law had not the heart (ἐκαρτέρουν, 'endured') to be parted from Naomi (*Ant.* 5.321). And Josephus would have us give even greater credit to the daughters-in-law in light of his extra-biblical detail that Naomi actually begged (παραιτουμένη) and implored (παρεκάλει) them to remain where they were (*Ant.* 5.321-22).

The subject of proselytism was an extremely delicate one. As the Romans saw a decline in religiosity (see, for example, the preface to Livy's history), they became more and more bitter about those who were trying to draw them away from their ancestral religion and values. The expulsion of the Jews from Rome in 139 BCE (Valerius Maximus 1.3.3) and, apparently, in 19 CE (Josephus, *Ant.* 18.81-84; Tacitus, *Ann.* 2.85; Suetonius, *Tiberius* 36; Dio Cassius 57.18.5a) had been connected with the alleged attempt of the Jews to convert non-Jews to Judaism;[49] and

---

49. See my *Jew and Gentile in the Ancient World* (Princeton: Princeton University Press, 1993), pp. 300-304.

we must note that such drastic action had taken place despite the generally favorable attitude of the Roman government toward the Jews. It is surely significant that in the *Antiquities*, aside from the passage about the conversion of the royal family of Adiabene (*Ant.* 20.17-96) (which was, after all, under Parthian domination and hence of no immediate concern to the Romans), Josephus nowhere propagandizes for proselytism as such. If, in the essay *Against Apion*, he declares (2.261) that the Jews gladly welcome any who wish to share their customs, he is careful to note that Jews do not take the initiative in seeking out proselytes and that, in fact, they take precautions (2.257) to prevent foreigners from mixing with them at random. Josephus himself makes a point of stressing that while he was general in Galilee, when the Galilean Jews tried to compel some non-Jews to be circumcised as a condition for dwelling among them, he refused to allow any compulsion to be used, declaring that everyone should worship G-d in accordance with the dictates of his own conscience (*Life* 113).

In the Bible, when Moses tells Jethro all that the L-rd has done to Pharaoh and the Egyptians, Jethro rejoices for all the good which G-d has done to Israel, he blesses G-d for having delivered them from the Egyptians, he declares that he now knows that the L-rd is greater than all gods because of His saving the Israelites, he offers a sacrifice to G-d, and Aaron comes with all the elders to eat bread with him (Exod. 18.8-12). What is striking in this brief passage is that Jethro is brought into immediate juxtaposition with the mention of G-d no fewer than six times, as we have noted. It is not surprising, consequently, as we have remarked, that, according to rabbinic tradition, especially in view of Jethro's outright statement that the L-rd is greater than all gods, Jethro is represented as having become a proselyte to Judaism (*Exod. R.* 1.32, 27.6; *Mek. Yitro* 1; *Mishnat Rabbi Eliezer*.[50] Consequently, Josephus, in his sensitivity to the proselyting movement, quite carefully omits Jethro's statement about G-d's greatness.

Moreover, the biblical narrative actually states that Jethro offered a burnt offering and sacrifices to G-d (Exod. 18.12), an act that would seem to indicate, as some of the rabbis noted above deduced, that he had come to accept the belief in the Israelite G-d. Josephus, sensitive to the Roman opposition to proselytism by Jews, has quite obviously made a deliberate change in having Moses offer the sacrifice (*Ant.* 3.63).

---

50. Ed. Hyman G. Enelow (New York: Bloch, 1933), p. 304.

Furthermore, in distinct contrast to Jethro's outright taking the lead in his blessing of G-d in the Bible (Exod. 18.10) and his offering of sacrifices to G-d (Exod. 18.12), and in contrast to the clearly subordinate role of Aaron in merely coming with the Israelite elders to eat bread with Jethro (Exod. 18.12), Josephus, in the apparent realization that such a role would, in effect, make Jethro a convert to Judaism, makes Aaron the prime mover in chanting hymns to G-d as the author and dispenser of salvation and liberty to the Israelites (*Ant.* 3.64). Jethro's role is clearly subordinate; Aaron merely gets him to join him (προσλαβόμενος).

Likewise, in view of the Roman sensitivity to the great expansion of the Jewish population, especially through proselytism, we can understand Josephus's difficulty when he came to the passage in Balaam's prophecy (Num. 23.10) with regard to the population explosion of the Israelites: 'Who hath counted the dust of Jacob or numbered the fourth part of Israel?' Josephus diplomatically omits this statement altogether.

We may well ask why Josephus refers to Ruth only once as a Moabitess (*Ant.* 5.319), whereas the biblical text designates her thus on six occasions (1.22; 2.2, 6, 21; 4.5, 10). Moreover, we may ask why Josephus has totally omitted all references to Ruth's conversion to Judaism, so crucial in the biblical account. Hence, whereas in the biblical text, it is Ruth who takes the iniative to indicate her desire to join her mother-in-law and the Israelite people, with her words 'thy people shall be my people, and thy G-d my G-d' (Ruth 1.16), and makes the dramatic statement, indicating the degree of her sincerity, that she wishes to join her mother-in-law even in death itself, in Josephus, on the other hand, we are told simply that Ruth could not be persuaded to remain in Moab (*Ant.* 5.322). She makes no declaration of her intention to join her mother-in-law's religion. We are told merely that Naomi 'took her with her, to be her partner in all that should befall' (*Ant.* 5.322).

As to the almost total omission of the identification of Ruth as a Moabitess, we may note that Josephus, in his summaries of Jewish laws pertaining to marriage (*Ant.* 3.274-75; 4.244-45; *Apion* 2.199-203) omits the prohibition of marrying Amorites and Moabites, presumably because he wished to avoid the charge that Jews are illiberal toward other peoples.

According to the biblical version, when Asa was gathering his army, a number of Jews from the kingdom of Israel who happened to be sojourning in the kingdom of Judah deserted to him when they saw that G-d was with him (2 Chron. 15.9). The Septuagint, in its version of the passage, declares that Asa assembled the tribes of Judah and Benjamin, together with strangers (προσηλύτους) that dwelt with them (2 Chron. 15.9). The word here translated as 'strangers' is 'proselytes', and implies that they were actually converts. Again, Josephus avoids the issue by simply omitting this passage.

The picture of the non-Jewish sailors in the book of Jonah is that of pious men who turn from the worship of their own pagan gods to the worship of the Hebrew G-d (Jon. 1.5). When the lot falls upon Jonah as the guilty one and when he asks to be thrown overboard, the sailors shudder to do so, since they shrink from shedding innocent blood and, indeed, invoke the name of the L-rd twice within a single sentence (Jon. 1.14). In fact, we are told that they feared the L-rd exceedingly and that they offered sacrifices to the L-rd and made vows (Jon. 1.16). One is reminded of the Mishnaic statement of the second-century Rabbi Judah in the name of his older contemporary Abba Gurion of Zadian, that most sailors are saintly (*Qid.* 4.14). The picture is very different in Josephus, where there is no indication whether or not the sailors were Jews or that they prayed to their own individual gods; instead, we are told very simply that the sailors began to pray, without being told to whom they were praying (*Ant.* 9.209).[51]

---

51. While it is true that Josephus's sailors regard it as an impious act to cast Jonah into the sea (*Ant.* 9.212), their morality is based not upon the prohibition of shedding innocent blood but rather upon the ancient Greek sanction concerning hospitality for strangers who have entrusted their lives to their hosts, a feature that a reader acquainted with Homer's *Odyssey*, with its emphasis on proper (the Phaeacians') and improper (Polyphemus the Cyclops') hospitality, would have especially appreciated. The rabbinic tradition stresses the non-Jewish origin of the sailors by noting that representatives of the seventy nations of the world were on board the vessel, each with his individual idols, and that they all resolved to entreat their gods for help, with the understanding that the god from whom help would come would be recognized and worshiped as the one true G-d (*PRE* 10; *Tanḥ. Vayiqra* 8; *Midr. Jon.* 97). See Ginzberg, *The Legends of the Jews*, IV, pp. 247-48. (Cf. *Ant.* 1.161, where, in Josephus's addition to the biblical text, Abraham shows a similar open-mindedness in declaring, upon his descent to Egypt, that if he found the doctrines of the Egyptians superior to his own he would adopt them, but that if his own doctrines appeared superior to theirs he would convert them.) When help came from none of the pagan gods, the captain shows his admiration for Judaism by stating that he had heard that the G-d of the Hebrews was most powerful and that if they would cry to him perhaps he would perform miracles. Indeed, Pseudo-Philo (*Homily on Jonah*), on the basis of the biblical statement that Nineveh was saved, conjec-

The biblical statement that the sailors feared the L-rd greatly is surely reminiscent of the 'G-d-fearers', well known from the eleven passages in Acts (10.2, 22, 35; 13.16, 26, 43, 50; 16.14; 17.4, 17; 18.7) referring to φοβούμενοι τὸν θεόν ('fearers of G-d') and σεβόμενοι τὸν θεόν ('reverencers of G-d') and from the passage in Juvenal (14.96) referring to one who fears (*metuentem*) the Sabbath and who has a son who eventually becomes a full-fledged Jew. It is true that these terms, in and of themselves, do not necessarily refer to 'sympathizers' and may, indeed, designate pious Jews.[52] But the new inscriptions from Aphrodisias make it more likely that these are, indeed, terms referring to 'sympathizers', at least in the third century, the apparent date of the inscriptions.[53]

By the third century there can be no doubt that there was such a class, as is clear from a passage in the Jerusalem Talmud which quotes Rabbi Eleazar, a third-century Palestinian rabbi, as saying that only the Gentiles who had nothing to do with the Jews during their bitter past will not be permitted to convert to Judaism in the time of the Messiah, whereas those 'Heaven-fearers' (*yirei shamayim*) who had shared the tribulations of Israel would be accepted as full proselytes, with the Emperor Antoninus at their head (*y. Meg.* 3.2.74a).[54]

Finally, Josephus, we may suggest, is careful not to compliment the Ninevites, since they were, geographically at any rate, as we have noted, the ancestors of the Parthians, the great national enemy of the Romans.[55]

---

tures that proselytism had already reached a high point where Jonah delivered his homily.

52. See my 'Jewish "Sympathizers" in Classical Literature and Inscriptions', *TAPA* 81 (1950), pp. 200-208.

53. See my 'The Omnipresence of the G-d-Fearers', *BARev* 12.5 (1986), pp. 58-69; and my 'Proselytes and "Sympathizers" in the Light of the New Inscriptions from Aphrodisias', *REJ* 148 (1989), pp. 265-305.

54. See Saul Lieberman, *Greek in Jewish Palestine* (New York: Jewish Theological Seminary, 1942), pp. 78-80.

55. On Josephus's anti-Parthian bias see Carsten Colpe, 'Die Arsakiden bei Josephus', in Betz *et al.* (eds.), *Josephus-Studien*, pp. 97-108. Christopher Begg, 'Josephus and Nahum Revisited', *REJ* 154 (1995), pp. 18-19, similarly suggests that Josephus's decision to include a summary of Nahum's prophecy concerning Assyria was inspired by his desire to impress his Roman patrons, who would have been pleased that a Jewish prophet had predicted the overthrow of the ancestor of their national rival, Parthia. On the other hand, Jewish readers, equating Assyria with

16. *Insistence that Gentiles Do Not Hate Jews*

In his effort to establish better relations between Jews and non-Jews, Josephus emphasizes that Gentile nations are not motivated by hatred of the Jews. Thus, Josephus, in the very proem of his *Antiquities*, pays a tremendous compliment to King Ptolemy Philadelphus for sponsoring the translation known as the Septuagint (*Ant.* 1.10-12). But it is not only Ptolemy Philadelphus whom he compliments; he goes out of his way to remark that it became him to assume that 'there are still today many lovers of learning like the king'. Moreover, Balak and Balaam are motivated not by Jew-hatred but rather by a desire to defeat the Jews militarily (*Ant.* 4.112). In Josephus's view, Balaam's readiness to curse the Israelites is due not to hatred for them but rather to his friendship with Balak (*Ant.* 4.120-21).

Josephus introduces an episode (*Ant.* 2.238-53), completely unparalleled in the Bible, in which Pharaoh chooses Moses as general to halt an invasion of Egypt by the much feared Ethiopians. That Pharaoh should have chosen an Israelite for such a difficult and crucial task is clearly complimentary to Pharaoh and shows that he is clearly not prejudiced against the Israelites. Moreover, lest the reader think that Pharaoh is deliberately choosing Moses in order to bring about his death in battle, Pharaoh, we are told (*Ant.* 2.242), swore to do him no injury and reproached those knavish priests who had urged him to put Moses to death as an enemy.[56]

Josephus is also concerned to attribute hatred of the Jewish people not to whole nations but rather merely to individuals. Thus, whereas in the Bible it is the Amalekites as a nation who beset the Israelites in the desert (Exod. 17.8-16), in Josephus it is the kings of the Amalekites who are blamed for sending messages to the kings of neighboring tribes exhorting them to make war against the Israelites (*Ant.* 3.40).

Rome, would have been pleased with a prediction of the overthrow of the Roman Empire.

56. In this reassurance to Moses, Josephus's Pharaoh is be contrasted with the portrait in Artapanus (*ap.* Eusebius, *Praep. Evang.* 9.27.7), who says that Pharaoh became jealous and sought to kill Moses, finding an opportunity to do so by naming Moses to the extremely dangerous position of commander in the war against the Ethiopians. When the war is over Pharaoh welcomes him back in words but plots against him in deed (*ap.* Eusebius, *Praep. Evang.* 9.27.11-13).

Moreover, it is significant that whereas in the biblical statement G-d forbids the Israelites to attack the Moabites, inasmuch as he had not given the Moabites' land to them but rather to the Moabites themselves as the descendants of Lot (Deut. 2.9), Josephus broadens the statement into a sweeping general principle, namely that the Israelites do not interfere in the affairs of any other country (*Ant.* 4.102).

Again, whereas in the rabbinic tradition (*B. Tanḥ.* 4.134; *Num. R.* 20.4; *Sifre Num.* 157; *Sanh.* 105a) the Moabites and Midianites join forces, despite the fact that they are bitter enemies of one another, because their hatred of the Jews is even greater, Josephus (*Ant.* 4.102) assiduously avoids giving the impression that Gentiles by nature hate Jews and instead depicts the two nations as long-time friends and allies. Their motive in going to war with the Israelites, according to Josephus (*Ant.* 4.103), is thus not hatred; in fact, in an extra-biblical addition, Josephus specifically says that it was not Balak's intention to fight against men fresh with success and who had been found to be only the more emboldened by reverse; rather his aim was to check their aggrandizement. Such a presentation casts the Moabites and the Midianites in a much better light.

Moreover, far from imputing anti-Jewish hatred to Balaam, Josephus (*Ant.* 4.106) presents him as counselling the envoys who had been sent by Balak to renounce the hatred which which they bore to the Israelites. By contrast, the rabbinic view (*Tanḥ. Balak* 6; *B. Tanḥ.* 4.136-37; *Midr. Agg.* 22.13 *Midr. Agg.* B. 2.134) and that of Philo (*Vit. Mos.* 1.48.266) is that Balaam was not at all sincere in his initial refusal to accompany the envoys. In the Bible (Num. 22.13) as well, Balaam does not give advice, as Josephus reports him doing here, on his own but merely reports that it is G-d who has refused to allow him to accompany the envoys.

Moreover, Josephus's favorable picture of Balaam is enhanced by the fact that, unlike the rabbinic tradition, which connects Balaam's desire to gratify the ambassadors with his hatred of the Israelites, Josephus has Balaam explicitly inquire of G-d concerning his intention with regard to the invitation of the envoys. When G-d informs him (Num. 22.12) that he is not to curse the Israelites, in the biblical version (Num. 22.13) Balaam tells the envoys that they must return, inasmuch as G-d refuses to allow him to accompany them. To be sure, in Josephus's version (*Ant.* 4.105) Balaam might seem to be even more anti-Israelite, inasmuch as he makes plain to the envoys his readiness (προθυμίαν) and zeal (σπουδήν) to comply with their request to curse the Israelites, which, however, G-d has forbidden him to do. From this statement we see, nevertheless, that Balaam's motive is not actually hatred for the Israelites but rather loyalty to his sovereign, Balak. Moreover, in stating that G-d has vetoed the envoys' request, Josephus has him piously add to the biblical narrative a statement of his recognition that the G-d who refused him is the G-d who had brought him to his high renown for the sake of truth and its prediction (πρόρρησιν).

Josephus's favorable portrayal of Balaam may also be seen in the scene (*Ant.* 4.112) in which he is said, in an extra-biblical addition, to have received a magnificent reception from Balak. According to the Bible (Num. 22.37), Balak begins by berating Balaam, asking why he had not come to him hitherto and whether the reason was that Balak was not able to honor him sufficiently. Josephus, on the other hand, is here clearly stressing that the relationship between Balak and Balaam is, in the first instance, one motivated by friendship rather than by their hatred of the Israelites. In contrast, we find the rabbis describing the reception which Balak gave to Balaam as very cheap and poor; and Philo (*Vit. Mos.* 1.50.275), who, to be sure, remarks that the interview began with friendly greetings, proceeds immediately to note that these were followed by Balak's censure of Balaam for his slowness and failure to come more readily.

Again, the meeting is presented by Josephus not as an occasion for the parties to express their hatred for the Israelites but rather for them to plan their military defeat. Thus, it is the Israelites' camp (στρατόπεδον, *Ant.* 4.112, clearly a military term) that Balak and Balaam go to inspect, rather than, as the Bible would have it (Num. 22.41), 'a portion of the people.' Similarly, the mountain to which they, in an extra-biblical addition, go in order to inspect the Israelites' camp is located (*Ant.* 4.112) by reference to its distance from the camp. Moreover, it is implied in the biblical text (Num. 22.41) that it was Balak who took the initiative to escort Balaam, whereas in Josephus it is Balaam who apparently asks to be conducted to one of the mountains in order to inspect the disposition—which would certainly include their fighting capacity—of the Israelites' camp.

Again, Haman's hatred for the Jews is presented not as part of an eternal Jewish–Gentile conflict but rather as a personal grudge, since he is an Amalekite (*Ant.* 11.212).

17. *Insistence that Jews Are Not Busybodies*

One of the charges which Josephus seeks to defuse in the *Antiquities*, presumably growing out of their tremendous increase in numbers and in influence, especially in the Ptolemaic and Roman Empires, is that the Jews seek to dominate the entire world. Thus, Josephus goes out of his way to state most emphatically that Balak, in his concern that the Israelites were growing so great, had not learned that they were actually content merely with the conquest of Canaan and that G-d himself had forbidden them to interfere in the affairs of other countries (*Ant.* 4.102).

We can see another of the charges against the Jews reflected, for example, in the order given by Marsus, the governor of Syria, to Agrippa I, to break up the conference of various kings which the latter had convened at Tiberias on the suspicion that Agrippa was trying to foment a conspiracy against the Romans (*Ant.* 19.340-42). Hence, in an extra-biblical detail, Josephus, in introducing the narrative of Balaam, remarks that Balak, the king of the Moabites, had formed an alliance with the Midianites when he saw the Israelites growing so great and became concerned that they would seek to expand at his expense (*Ant.* 4.102). In so doing, he had not learned, says Josephus, that the Hebrews were not for interfering with other countries, G-d having forbidden them to do so. The verb which is here used for 'interfering', πολυπραγμονεῖν, implies being meddlesome, being an inquisitive busybody, and is almost always employed in a pejorative sense.[57]

Moreover, it is significant that whereas in the biblical statement G-d forbids the Israelites to attack the Moabites, inasmuch as He had not given the Moabites' land to them but rather to the Moabites themselves as the descendants of Lot (Deut. 2.9), Josephus broadens the statement into a sweeping general principle, namely that the Israelites do not interfere in the affairs of any other country (*Ant.* 4.102).

18. *Jews Are Not Economically Oppressive*

Not only in the treatise *Against Apion* but also in his *Antiquities*, Josephus constantly seeks to answer anti-Jewish canards. This was particularly necessary in connection with Joseph, inasmuch as the scene of

---

57. Cf., e.g., Herodotus 3.15; Xenophon, *Anabasis* 5.1.15; Aristophanes, *Plutus* 913; Plato, *Republic* 433A.

Joseph's activities was Egypt, which had once been overrun by the Hyksos and which was the hotbed of attacks on the Jews on the part of intellectuals such as Manetho, Chaeremon, Lysimachus and Apion. Thus, in the Bible (Gen. 46.33-34) Joseph instructs his brothers that when asked by Pharaoh about their occupation, they should reply not that they are shepherds (as indeed they were)—since shepherds were an abomination to the Egyptians (Gen. 46.34)—but rather that they are owners of cattle. Josephus (*Ant.* 2.185-86), on the other hand, has Joseph himself tell Pharaoh directly and apologetically that his brothers are *good* shepherds and that they follow this calling so that they may not be separated from each other and may look after their father. His Joseph likewise presents the novel economic factor that they engage in this occupation in order to ingratiate themselves to the Egyptians by not competing with them, since Egyptians are forbidden to occupy themselves with the pasture of livestock. He thus answers the charge of those opponents of the Jews who apparently claimed that Jews constituted an economic threat to the Egyptians' livelihood.[58] He also here offers a defense of the 'cliquishness' of the Hebrews in living together, apart from other peoples, namely that they wished to look after their aged father.

19. *Conclusion*

We may conclude by remarking that Josephus not only, like his much admired model Thucydides, looked upon history as a handbook for statesmen but also viewed it, as had the prophets in the Bible, as a guide to understanding the immediate past and the present and as a guide to the future. And to a considerable degree, he viewed the Bible through the lens of the present, and, in particular, the disastrous war which the Jews had fought against the Romans and in which he himself was directly, and many would say ignominiously, involved.

---

58. I have argued that economics was a major factor in the hatred exhibited by non-Jews toward Jews in Alexandria in the popular attack on the Jews in 38 CE. See my 'Anti-Semitism in the Ancient World', in David Berger (ed.), *History and Hate: The Dimensions of Anti-Semitism* (Philadelphia: Jewish Publication Society, 1988), p. 23.

TORAH OF MOSES: PSEUDONYMOUS ATTRIBUTION IN SECOND TEMPLE WRITINGS[*]

Hindy Najman

At the inception of the Second Temple period, Ezra faced a difficult challenge: how was it possible to claim spiritual authority in the absence of political independence? Ezra claimed to have such authority not by purporting to have received new oral revelation, but, rather, by portraying himself, and his entourage, as reading and rendering accessible those ancient cryptic sacred writings associated with Moses.[1]

* An earlier version of this paper was given to the Scripture in Early Judaism and Christianity Section, SBL 1998, Orlando. I am grateful to Moshe Bernstein, Joseph Blenkinsopp, Paul Franks, Jay Harris, James Kugel and Jon Levenson as well as to the participants in the 1998 Scripture in Early Judaism and Christianity Section for their incisive comments.

1. As early as the fifth century BCE, a corpus of texts must have existed that could be called the Torah of Moses and that was substantially similar to what was later called the Pentateuch, for that corpus must have been the basis for the Greek translation known as the Septuagint. But it is unclear how far the processes of text formation and corpus fixation had gone in the days of Ezra. Sid Z. Leiman suggests that the process of canonization can be traced back to the reforms of Josiah in 621 BCE. See Leiman's comprehensive study, *The Canonization of Hebrew Scripture: The Talmudic and Midrashic Evidence* (Transactions; Hamden, CT: Archon, 1976), pp. 21-24, 143 n. 73. See also the recent discussion of canon by James C. VanderKam, 'Authoritative Literature in the Dead Sea Scrolls', *DSD* 5 (1998), pp. 382-402.

On the fluidity of the biblical text see Eugene Ulrich 'The Bible in the Making: The Scriptures at Qumran', in Eugene Ulrich and James C. VanderKam (eds.), *The Community of the Renewed Covenant* (Notre Dame: University of Notre Dame Press, 1994), pp. 77-94; Frank Moore Cross, 'The Old Testament at Qumrân', in *idem*, *The Ancient Library of Qumran* (Sheffield: Sheffield Academic Press, 1994), pp. 121-42; Frank Moore Cross and Shemaryahu Talmon (eds.), *Qumran and the History of the Biblical Text* (Cambridge, MA: Harvard University Press, 1975); John J. Collins, 'The Emergence of "Canonical" Scripture', in *idem*, *Jewish Wisdom in the*

Nehemiah 8 depicts Ezra's public reading of Mosaic Torah, and the simultaneous public explanation of the Mosaic Torah by the *mebinim*, the authorized interpreters. According to Ezra–Nehemiah, this public reading inaugurates the prototypical scene in which we can see what it meant to authorize a leader in Second Temple times. Authority was inextricably linked to Moses and the ancient tradition of Mosaic Torah.[2] Thus, legal or political innovations had to be justified and grounded in terms of this already authoritative tradition of sacred writing. In fact, as we will see shortly, sometimes such legal innovations were said to be already present in the ancient laws of Moses. In other words, Ezra's legal innovations were pseudonymously attributed to the Torah of Moses.

I will consider two examples of pseudonymous attribution to Moses in the writings of Ezra–Nehemiah. These examples illustrate how it was possible to *inscribe* innovations into a culture that recognized only old and established law as the main source of authority that had survived the exile. But it is notable that the important association between authority and writing was already in place long before the return. Only in light of the gradual emergence of authoritative sacred writing can we understand how Mosaic Torah could have come to replace the prophet and claim the authority once accorded to the priest and the king.

Already in the pre-exilic period, sacred writing played an important role. To mention two examples: in Isaiah 8, the prophet is told to in-

Hellenistic Age (Louisville, KY: Westminster/John Knox Press, 1997), pp. 17-20; Julio Trevolle Barrera, 'The Authoritative Functions of Scriptural Works at Qumran', in Ulrich and VanderKam (eds.), *The Community of the Remewed Covenant*, pp. 95-110.

2.   This can be attributed, in large part, to Persian influence. In the Persian empire, the role of sacred writing and written law was central to Cyrus's revival of Persian culture and tradition. This may have had a significant influence on the Jews who lived under Persian domination in the early Second Temple period. Thus, the Jews may have wanted to assert their own authority by insisting on the authenticity of their ancient legal code in the form of Mosaic Torah. On this point see Elias J. Bickerman, 'The Law of the Jews', in *idem*, *The Jews in the Greek Age* (Cambridge, MA: Harvard University Press, 1988), pp. 29-32; James L. Kugel, 'The World of Ancient Interpreters', in *idem*, *The Bible as It Was* (Cambridge, MA: Harvard University Press, 1997), pp. 1-61; Arnaldo Momigliano, 'Persian Historiography, Greek Historiography and Jewish Historiography', in *idem*, *The Classical Foundations of Modern Historiography* (SCL, 54; Berkeley: University of California Press, 1990), pp. 10ff.

scribe his prophecy onto a tablet; in 2 Kings 23, Josiah institutes a series of religious reforms as a response to the discovered Torah Scroll. As the threat of Assyrian and then Babylonian destruction loomed large over the northern and southern regions of Israel, the exchange between God and prophet came increasingly to be imagined as the transmission of a sacred text.[3]

3. There are a number of references to Mosaic Law as an authoritative source of law in the Hebrew Bible. See, e.g., 2 Chron. 30.16-27; Ezra 3.2-5; Neh. 8.1-8. The 'Torah of Moses', or 'Torah of God', probably corresponds to what will later be referred to as the Pentateuch. Throughout the biblical traditions, the collection referred to as the 'book of Torah', 'the Law of Moses', 'the Law of God' seems to be invoked in similar ways, perhaps even interchangeably. See, e.g., 2 Chron. 25.4; 35.12; Ezra 6.18; Neh. 13.1; Neh. 8.2; 2 Chron. 17.9; 34.14; Neh. 8.1; Josh. 8.31; 2 Kgs 14.6; 1 Kgs 2.3; Mal. 3.22; Dan. 9.13; Ezra 3.2; 7.6; 2 Chron. 23.18. On this point see Sara Japhet, 'Law and "The Law" in Ezra–Nehemiah', in David Asaf (ed.), *The Proceedings of the Ninth World Congress of Jewish Studies* (Jerusalem: Magnes Press, 1985), pp. 99-115 (99-100); Jon D. Levenson, 'Sources of Torah: Psalm 119 and the Modes of Revelation in Second Temple Judaism', in Patrick D. Miller, Jr, Paul D. Hanson and S. Dean McBride (eds.), *Ancient Israelite Religion: Essays in Honor of Frank Moore Cross* (Philadelphia: Fortress Press, 1987), pp. 561-63; James L. Kugel, 'The Rise of Scripture', in James L. Kugel and Rowan A. Greer (eds.), *Early Biblical Interpretation* (Philadelphia: Westminster Press, 1986), pp. 20-22.

According to Jacob Milgrom and Israel Knohl, the Priestly Torah referred to traditions (perhaps separate scrolls of law) as *torah*. Traditions of law are part of the Priestly Torah, which was subsequently edited by the Holiness School and, at a later stage, incorporated into the Pentateuch. For some discussion of these collection of 'laws', see Israel Knohl, *The Sanctuary of Silence: The Priestly Torah and the Holiness School* (Minneapolis: Fortress Press, 1995), p. 6, p. 89 n. 91; Jacob Milgrom, *Leviticus 1-16: A New Translation with Introduction and Commentary* (AB, 3; New York: Doubleday, 1991), p. 2, 688 on Lev. 11.46. For a discussion of the characteristics of ancient Torah Scrolls see Etan Levine, 'The Transcription of the Torah Scroll', *ZAW* 94 (1982), pp. 99-105.

See also, Hag. 2 which uses 'torah' to refer to an interpretation of the law. As we will see later, in my discussion of Ezra 9 and 10 below, it is misleading to think of the torah traditions as exclusively those included in the *written* Pentateuch. From a very early stage in what one might call the prehistory of Scripture, traditions which were not found explicitly in the Pentateuch are said to be part of the Mosaic Torah. This claim is very important for the history of interpretation. Later, Second Temple writers and even rabbinic traditions will claim that interpretive traditions are really 'in the torah', that is, if only one would read the sacred texts correctly, one would understand that the interpretation is really part of, or implicit in, the text.

The trauma of the Babylonian exile only heightened the centrality of sacred writing. Both the permanence and the portability of written Scripture must have held a special appeal for the exiles. In the absence of their land and temple, the exiled Judeans focused on the part of their heritage that could be preserved.

Let me now turn to those sacred texts specifically associated with Moses. Certainly, in both pre-exilic and exilic traditions Moses was an authoritative lawgiver. And the Torah of Moses is already invoked as a normative written legal code prior to the Second Temple period. This Torah is often mentioned at moments of succession. For example, when power is transferred from David to Solomon, the Torah of Moses is used to confer authority upon the successor.[4]

It would be a mistake, however, to conclude that there is nothing new about Ezra's invocation of Mosaic Law. By the time of Ezra–Nehemiah, the authority of the Mosaic Law had achieved a certain independence: it was no longer authorized by the prophet's divinely inspired word to the king. Instead, Mosaic Law was the authoritative link to pre-exilic revelation. Traditions in Ezra–Nehemiah suggest that no law is authoritative unless it is appropriately connected to the Law of Moses —perhaps even pseudonymously attributed to the figure of Moses himself.[5] And that clearly was not the case prior to the exile.

---

4.   See 1 Kgs 2.1-4. In this passage, David instructs Solomon to live and rule according to the Torah of Moses. There is a warning, however, implicit in David's words: if Solomon does not adhere to the Mosaic Torah, the monarchic line will be torn from him. David warns Solomon that his succession is not about familial inheritance; rather, Solomon must continue to earn the right to kingship through adherence to Torah of Moses.

5.   For one of the most illuminating discussions of Mosaic authority, see Sara Japhet's article, 'Law and "The Law" in Ezra–Nehemiah', pp. 99-115. There is some literature that discusses traditions which invoked Mosaic authority. See, e.g., Gary A. Anderson, 'The Status of the Torah before Sinai', *DSD* 1 (1994), pp. 1-29; Joseph Blenkinsopp, *Ezra–Nehemiah: A Commentary* (OTL; Philadelphia: Westminster Press, 1988); Samuel S. Cohon, 'Authority in Judaism', *HUCA* 11 (1936), pp. 593-646; Mary Rose D'Angelo, *Moses in the Letter to the Hebrews* (SBLDS, 42; Missoula, MT: Scholars Press, 1979); Burton Mack, 'Moses on the Mountaintop', in John Peter Kenney (ed.), *The School of Moses: Studies in Philo and Hellenistic Religion* (BJS, 304; Atlanta: Scholars Press, 1995), pp. 16-28; James L. Kugel, 'Early Interpretation: The Common Background of Late Forms of Biblical Exegesis', in Kugel and Greer (eds.), *Early Biblical Interpretation*, pp. 11-106; Robert C. Marshall, 'Moses, Oedipus, Structuralism and History', *RT* 5 (1983), pp. 245-66; Crispin Fletcher-Louis, '4Q374: A Discourse on the Sinai Tradition:

Let us now turn to the scene of Ezra's public reading. Here we see clearly how Second Temple Judaism regarded at least from the perspective of Ezra–Nehemiah, was, from its origins, textualized and invested in the Torah of Moses. According to Ezra–Nehemiah, the central unifying event for the returning exiles was neither revelation mediated by a prophet, nor the coronation of a davidic king. Instead, the central event was a public reading of the Mosaic Law, by a scribe, with *interpreters* at hand to supply explanations. Here is an extract from Neh. 8.1-8:

> All the people gathered together... They asked Ezra the scribe to bring the book of the Torah of Moses... Ezra the priest brought the Torah before the assembly, men, women, and all who could hear with understanding... He read aloud from...dawn until midday facing the men, women, and the interpreters, and...all the people were attentive to the book of Torah...Ezra the scribe opened the book before the eyes of the entire people... When he opened it all of the people stood. Ezra blessed the Lord, the great God and the entire people answered: 'Amen, Amen' while raising their hands, bowing down, and prostrating themselves before the Lord with their faces upon the ground... Those interpreting the Torah...read aloud from the book of the Torah of God, explaining, applying insight, and making the reading comprehensible.

In this passage the people publicly requested, publicly heard, and then publicly accepted the law.[6] They experienced a re-enactment of the Sinai event. This time, however, their mediator was not *Moses* who faithfully recorded what God had dictated to him. Rather it was Ezra, who read what Moses had already written long ago and who claimed no direct revelation from God.

It is clear from the above passage that listening to the public reading of the Torah did not insure adequate comprehension. In addition to a public reading, the people were provided with interpreters, *mebinim*, who must have translated Mosaic Torah into a language the people could understand.[7] Perhaps, like later targumim, their translations also re-

---

The Deification of Moses and Early Christology', *DSD* 3 (1996), pp. 236-52; Rolf Rendtorff, 'Esra und das "Gesetz"', *ZAW* 96 (1984), pp. 165-84.

6.   This reading should be compared to an earlier pre-exilic public reading of the Torah of Moses in Josh. 8.30-35.

7.   See James L. Kugel, 'The Need for Interpretation', in Kugel and Greer (eds.), *Early Biblical Interpretation*, pp. 27-39, esp. p. 28 where Kugel discusses the term *meforash*: 'Even those who had stayed behind in Judea during the exile, though they continued to speak their native idiom, were not exempt from linguistic difficulties. For their spoken idiom was certainly not identical to the often elegant

solved difficulties of comprehension and interpretation, and perhaps they resolved these difficulties in ways that had already become traditional.

The contribution of these interpreters was fateful for the development of Second Temple Judaism. Mosaic Torah could not function as the authoritative center of religious life unless apparent anachronisms and legal or narrative inconsistencies were resolved. Thus, the interpreter would supplant the prophet as mediator of God's word. But, unlike the authority of the prophet, the authority of the interpreter would depend upon the sacred text. And the reconstituted postexilic community would, sooner or later, have to face the difficult question, '*Which* interpretation is authoritative?' or 'Who has the authority to interpret?'

There is a puzzling phenomenon in Ezra–Nehemiah which represents an early stage in the development of interpretive authority. Although the Law of Moses must have already assumed a relatively fixed form,

---

literary language of the Bible; moreover, it apparently became corrupted by neighboring dialects (see Neh. 13.24). For this reason, both the Judean exiles and those who had stayed behind might be in need of that most basic act of interpretation, translation into an idiom more familiar to them. This may be precisely what the "interpreters" mentioned in connection with Ezra's public reading of the Torah (Neh. 8.1-8) were engaged in doing. For it was apparently standard practice within the Persian empire to train scribes to turn, for example, a dictated Persian text into Aramaic (in quite mechanical fashion); the Aramaic could then be spontaneously retroverted into Persian, or translated into another language, by a similarly trained scribe when the text reached its destination. The Persians referred to such a text as *huzvarshn*; the Hebrew *meforash* ("interpreted") in Neh. 8.8 is apparently used here as an equivalent (cf. Ezra 4.18)'. see also, Blenkinsopp, *Ezra–Nehemiah*, p. 288. For further discussion of the importance of interpreters of Mosaic Torah during the time of Ezra, see the recent discussion by Moshe Halbertal, *People of the Book: Canon, Meaning, and Authority* (Cambridge, MA: Harvard University Press, 1997), p. 15.

For analogous developments in Neo-Assyrian traditions, see Peter Machinist and Hayim Tadmor, 'Heavenly Wisdom', in Mark Cohen, Daniel Snell and David Weisberg (eds.), *The Tablet and the Scroll: Near Eastern Studies in Honor of William W. Hallo* (Bethesda: CDL Press, 1993), pp. 146-51, esp. pp. 149-50. In this article, Machinist and Tadmor discuss traditions concerning Nabonidus, who was allegedly unable to understand the ancient tablets of *Enuma Elish* until they were read aloud to him. Once they were read aloud, Nabonidus was able to interpret them. Although there is evidence that Nabonidus was illiterate in cuneiform, he nevertheless acquired a reputation as a wise scribe who could interpret these ancient traditions in public.

allowing it to be read in public, and although that form must have been substantially that of the Pentateuch, some non-Pentateuchal laws are attributed to Mosaic Torah. I will consider two examples which should make us think carefully about how to understand the textualization of Judaism at the inception of the Second Temple period.

First, let us consider the courses of the priesthood. No pre-exilic or exilic tradition mentions the particular groupings of priests and levites mentioned in Ezra–Nehemiah.[8] Nevertheless, in Ezra 6.18, these 'courses' of priests and the 'divisions' of levites are said to have been arranged in accordance with 'the book of Moses'.[9]

> They established priests in their courses and levites in their divisions for the service of the God of Jerusalem in accordance with the writing of the book of Moses.

In 2 Chron. 35.4-5, the *very same* priestly organization is also attributed to a pre-exilic source, though this time it is *David and Solomon*. Sara Japhet notes that Ezra–Nehemiah had a choice: the priestly courses could have been attributed to Moses or to David, either of whom were pre-exilic authorities.[10] Thus, the choice of Moses was deliberate and motivated by theological considerations. It seems to me that Japhet's point raises a further question. If the author who ascribed the priestly courses to the book of Moses did so with precision and in deliberate rejection of the idea that they originated with the davidic monarchy, then we are faced with a problem. What could be meant by the ascription of a law to a book in which the law does not appear? How, for that matter,

---

8.   Japhet, 'Law and "The Law" in Ezra–Nehemiah', pp. 114; H.G.M. Williamson, 'The Origins of the Twenty-Four Priestly Courses', in J.A. Emerton (ed.), *Studies in the Historical Books of the Old Testament* (VTSup, 30; Leiden: E.J. Brill, 1979), pp. 251-68.

9.   The term 'courses' as referring to the courses of priests or Levites occurs only in postexilic texts (1 and 2 Chron., Ezra and Nehemiah). There is one additional usage of 'courses' in Ezek. 44.29, where reference is made to the land apportioned to the Levites, but this seems to be an alternative usage, also found in Josh. 12.7 and 18.10, which refers to the portions of land that were granted to the Israelite tribes.

The term 'divisions' appears only twice in postexilic traditions: Ezra 6.18 and 2 Chron. 35.5, and refers to divisions of the priests (Ezra) or to the clans (2 Chron.). N.b., 2 Chron. 35.5 also refers to the division of the Levites. See also the equivalent term in the Aramaic portions of the MT, e.g. Neh. 11.36; 1 Chron. 23.6; 24.1; 26.1; 2 Chron. 8.14.

10.   Japhet, 'Law and "The Law" in Ezra–Nehemiah', pp. 114-15.

could one hope to get away with such an ascription, if the book in question was public property?

I will return to these questions shortly. First, I want to consider the problem of the returnees who married foreigners during the exile.

Intermarriage was a problem for Ezra. When Ezra was told of extensive intermarriage among the returning exile his response was not unlike that of previous Israelites leaders when they were faced with impending doom: he rent his clothing and prayed to God (Ezra 9.3-7):

> When I heard this matter I tore my tunic and my robe and I tore out some hair from my head and my beard and I sat, horrified... I spread out my hands to the Lord, my God and I said: 'My God, I am too ashamed and humiliated to lift up my face to you, my God, for our sins have multiplied upon our head and our guilt has extended to the heavens. Since the days of our ancestors, we are in a state of great guilt, until this very day. Because of our sins, our kings and our priests were given over into the hands of the kings of the lands, to the sword, to captivity, to plunder and to shame, just like this day.'

Soon after, Ezra issued the following proclamation in Ezra 9.12:

> Now, do not give your daughters to their sons, and do not marry their daughters to your sons. Do not seek their welfare and well-being ever.

What follows in the next chapter of Ezra is indeed noteworthy: one of Ezra's officials, Shecaniah ben Yehiel, referred to Ezra's proclamation as divine law. In Ezra 10.3-4, Shecaniah says:

> Let us make a covenant to our God to send out all of the women and anyone born from them in keeping with the plan of the Lord and those who tremble at the command of our God, let him act in accordance with the Torah.

Many scholars have assumed that, when Shecaniah said that intermarriage should be counteracted 'in accordance with the Torah', he was saying that intermarriage was prohibited by the Torah of *Moses*. As Jon Levenson, Blenkinsopp and Kugel (among others) have argued, there is a strong *Pentateuchal basis* for such a prohibition.[11] The Pentateuchal

---

11. Christine Hayes, 'Intermarriage and Impurity in Ancient Jewish Sources', *HTR* 92 (1999), pp. 3-36; Blenkinsopp, *Ezra–Nehemiah*, pp. 184-85; James L. Kugel, 'Foreigners Are Different', and 'Intermarriage Is Forbidden', in *idem, The Bible as It Was*, pp. 236-38; *idem*, 'The Holiness of Israel and the Land in Second Temple Times', in Michael V. Fox *et al.* (ed.), *Texts, Temples, and Traditions: A Tribute to Menahem Haran* (Winona, IN: Eisenbrauns, 1996); Jon D. Levenson,

source that is repeatedly cited is Deut. 7.3, 'do not make marriages with them; do not give your daughter to his son; and do not take his daughter for your son'. Note that this prohibition is specifically about the local nations and does not reflect a general prohibition against intermarriage. Furthermore, despite very insightful and creative attempts to explain the relationship between earlier Pentateuchal traditions and Ezra's prohibition, in Deuteronomy there is no explicit law to divorce foreign women and to expel their children. Indeed, there is no a general prohibition against intermarriage anywhere in the Pentateuch. How are we to explain the suggestion in Ezra 10 that this law is Torah? Is it new law? Or is it part of the old Mosaic Torah?

Most scholars agree that we should understand this passage from Ezra as an early example of inner-biblical interpretation.[12] Namely, that Ezra interprets texts like Deuteronomy 7, and thereby claims that the resulting law reflects the *correct* reading of what was intended by Moses in the Torah.[13] Indeed the same story could be told about Ezra's priestly

---

'Last Four Verses in Kings', *JBL* 103 (1984), p. 358 n.19. For further discussion of the development of the prohibition of intermarriage in the Second Temple period and in the early rabbinic period, see Shaye J. D. Cohen, 'From the Bible to the Talmud: The Prohibition of Intermarriage', *HAR* 7 (1983), pp. 23-39; *idem*, 'Crossing the Boundary and Becoming a Jew', *HTR* 82 (1989), pp. 13-33; Jacob Milgrom, 'Religious Conversion and the Revolt for the Formation of Israel', *JBL* 101 (1982), pp. 169-76; Sheldon H. Blank, 'The Dissident Laity in Early Judaism', *HUCA* 19 (1945–46), pp. 1-42, esp. pp. 1-5; Cana Werman, '*Jubilees* 30: Building a Paradigm for the Ban on Intermarriage', *HTR* 90 (1997), pp. 1-22.

12. E.g. Yehezkel Kaufmann, *History of Israelite Religion* (Tel Aviv: Bialik, 1937–1956), pp. 291-93 (Hebrew); Kugel, *The Bible as It Was*, pp. 237-38; Levenson, 'Last Four Verses in Kings', p. 358 n. 19; Blenkinsopp, *Ezra–Nehemiah*, pp. 175-76. On p. 189, Blenkinsopp writes: 'The requirement that this be done "according to the law" is puzzling at first sight, since Pentateuchal law nowhere requires an Israelite to divorce his foreign wife. We must conclude that what is implied here is a particular interpretation of law, and specifically a rigorist interpretation of the Deuteronomic law forbidding marriage with the native population... This, then, would be one of several indications in the book of the crucial importance of biblical interpretation as a factor in the struggle to determine the identity and character of the community'. On this point see also Michael Fishbane, *Biblical Interpretation in Ancient Israel* (Oxford: Clarendon Press, 1985), pp. 107-129.

13. See also, Gen. 15.19-20; Exod. 3.8, 17; 33.2; 34.11; Lev. 24.10-23; Num. 27.1-11; Judg. 3.5. For texts which are contemporaneous with Ezra 10 and reflect a similar position, namely that *intermarriage* is tantamount to treachery, see Ezra 10.2, 5, 10; Neh. 1.8; 13.25-27 (9.8 is also relevant, although it does not preserve

courses. Namely, this organization of the priests and levites could be said to be what Moses intended or what David envisioned.[14]

I too agree that Ezra is engaged in inner-biblical interpretation. However, it seems to me that this point has been repeatedly misformulated. It is important to understand the specific nature of inner-biblical interpretation and, in particular, inner-biblical Mosaic attribution. For what is at stake here is one of the main strategies through which Second Temple Judaism sought to authorize itself. Moreover, we need an understanding of Ezra's practice of inner-biblical interpretation that will allow us to make sense of pseudonymous attribution to Moses in Second Temple texts.

If we impose a postcanonical conception of Scripture and interpretation onto the Second Temple period, we will not be able to make sense of this practice. We must understand Second Temple conceptions of Scripture within their own context.

Here is an example of anachronistic imposition. Yehezkel Kaufmann suggested that what we find in Ezra (chs. 9 and 10) is one of the earliest examples of inner-biblical interpretation practiced in a manner similar to what will later be designated as *midrash halakhah*. Although he may be correct in identifying Pentateuchal connections with Ezra's prohibition, it cannot be adequate to say, as Kaufmann does, that what we have here is a 'genuine *midrash halakhah*'. Perhaps one could reconstruct a midrashic derivation of the prohibition against intermarriage, or of the priestly courses and the levitical divisions. Nevertheless, it is essential that no such *derivation* is provided in the Ezra passages themselves. Nor is there any suggestion whatsoever that Ezra or Shecaniah might need to *justify* their attributions to the Law of Moses. The context in which

the same verb used in Ezra 10); 1 Chron. 2.7; 5.27; 9.1; 2 Chron. 12.2; 26.1, 6, 18; 28.19, 22; 29.6, 19; 30.7; 33.19; 36.14.

14. Among other serious difficulties, the returnees were clearly divided on the questions of davidic leadership and the constitution of the priesthood. On the former, see Sara Japhet, 'Sheshbazzar and Zerubbabel—Against the Background of the Historical and Religious Tendencies of Ezra–Nehemiah', *ZAW* 94 (1982), pp. 66-98. In this article, Japhet contrasts Zechariah's and Haggai's celebration of a davidic descendant to Ezra–Nehemiah's silence concerning the davidic connections of these Second Temple leaders. On the problem of the priesthood, see, e.g., Ezra 2.61-62. Some scholars have suggested that this difficulty was due to the tensions between the Samaritan community in Shechem and the newly constituted community in Jerusalem. See, e.g., Williamson, 'The Origins of the Twenty-Four Priestly Courses', pp. 251-68.

these attributions were made must have differed significantly from the context in which *midrash halakhah* was practiced. The midrashists could not avoid the question of justification. They had to appeal to tradition and/or reasoning in order to authorize their dicta. In the age of *midrash halakhah*, the text of the Law of Moses had become a settled and stable object. I mean not merely that the corpus and the specific texts were relatively fixed—for this was already true in the time of Ezra —but rather that there was a clear distinction between *reading* or citing a passage and *interpreting* that passage. There is simply no evidence that the distinction between reading or citing and interpreting was clearly established by the time of Ezra.

Ezra could not offer authoritative interpretation without claiming that his reading was Mosaic in origin. Such literal ascription to Moses was no longer possible in Tannaitic or in later Amoraic traditions which had either to offer a derivation from the biblical text or else to appeal to Oral Torah in order to authorize their interpretations.[15]

The concept of Scripture in Ezra–Nehemiah, is, I suggest, the following. Even if there was a collection of writings known as the Torah of Moses, and even if the term 'Torah of Moses' was often used to refer to this collection, it does not follow that the primary function of the term was to *name* this collection of writings. Instead, it may well be that the primary function of this term was to confer authority. Since a particular collection substantially like the Pentateuch had gradually become the most authoritative collection of sacred writings, it makes sense that this

---

15. See, e.g., *m. Qidd.* 4.14; *t. Qidd.* ch. 5; *Sifrei Debarim, Parshat Wezot Habberakha, Pisqa* 351; *Sifra' Parshat Behuqotai*, ch. 8.13; *ARN* (A) 15; *b. Ber.* 5a; *b. Šab.* 31a. On the Oral Torah see James L. Kugel, 'At Mount Sinai (Exodus 19– 24)', in *idem, The Bible as It Was*, pp. 402-404 for discussion of the following two motifs, 'Moses Was Given More than the Torah' and 'Oral Teachings from Moses'. See also Hanokh Albeck, *Introduction to the Mishnah* (Tel Aviv: Bialik, 1967), pp. 3-39, esp. pp. 3-4 and p. 3 n. 7 (Hebrew); Peter Schäfer, 'Das "Dogma" von der mündlichen Torah im rabbinischen Judentum', in *Studien zur Geschichte und Theologie des rabbinischen Judentums* (Leiden: E.J. Brill, 1978), pp. 153-97; Ephraim E. Urbach, 'The Written Law and the Oral Law', in *The Sages* (Cambridge, MA: Harvard University Press, 1979), pp. 286-314. For some useful discussions of the origin, development and application of this term in rabbinic literature see Gerald J. Blidstein, 'A Note on the Term *Torah She-B'al peh*', *Tarbiz* 42 (1973), pp. 496-98; Robert Brody, 'The Struggle against Heresy', in *idem, The Geonim of Babylonia and the Shaping of Medieval Jewish Culture* (New Haven: Yale University, 1998), pp. 83-99, esp. pp. 83-85.

collection was the most pre-eminent example of the Torah of Moses. Yet, it was also possible to describe as Torah of Moses some law or practice without an explicit Pentateuchal basis, for the sake of authorization.

This account of the concept of Scripture helps us to understand how those texts known as Rewritten Bible and Pseudepigrapha could proliferate in the Second Temple period. If we take the term 'Torah of Moses' to designate authoritative sacred writings and their inherited or innovated authoritative interpretations, then we can view Rewritten Bible as an understandable attempt to authorize certain laws and practices by literally inscribing them back into Mosaic Torah. On the other hand, if we anachronistically impose the later conception that 'Torah of Moses' is the name of an authoritative corpus of texts, then attempts to rewrite the Bible can seem like unscrupulous exercises in literary forgery.[16]

What seems to us to be an interpolation did not seem so to Ezra and his contemporaries.[17] Such procedures may have been the continuation of the work of Ezra and his *mebinim*. Just as there was no distinction

16. On literary forgery, see E.M. Forster, *Anonymity: An Enquiry* (London: Hogarth Press, 1925); Michel Foucault, 'What is an Author?', in James D. Faubion (ed.), *Michel Foucault: Aesthetics, Method and Epistemology*, II (trans. Josué V. Harari, modified by Robert Hurley; New York: The New York Press, 1998), pp. 205-222; David G. Meade, *Pseudonymity and Canon: An Investigation into the Relationship of Authorship and Authority in Jewish and Earliest Christian Tradition* (Tübingen: J.C.B. Mohr [Paul Siebeck], 1986); Bruce M. Metzger, 'Literary Forgeries and Canonical Pseudepigrapha', *JBL* 91 (1972), pp. 3-24; Morton Smith, 'Pseudepigraphy in the Israelite Literary Tradition', in K. von Fritz (ed.), *Pseudepigrapha*, I (Vandoeuvres-Geneve: Fondation Hardt, 1972), pp. 189-215 with discussion pp. 216-27.

17. There are, however, well established Muslim traditions that accuse Ezra of such falsification and pseudonymous attribution. But, the Muslim tradition was by no means monolithic. Some writers defended and even praised Ezra, while others challenged the authenticity of Judaism by claiming that Ezra's Torah was inauthentic. For discussion of the challenges and the history of biblical interpretation of Ezra among Muslim writers, see Hava Lazarus-Yafeh, *Intertwined Worlds: Medieval Islam and Bible Criticism* (Princeton, NJ: Princeton University Press, 1992), pp. 19-74; Camilla Adang, *Muslim Writers on Judaism and the Hebrew Bible: From Ibn Rabban to Ibn Hazm* (Leiden: E.J. Brill, 1996), pp. 192-255. For an example of a recent study which insists on the authenticity and reliability of Ezra's Torah and transmission, see David Weiss Halivni, *Revelation Restored: Divine Writ and Critical Responses* (Boulder, CO: Westview Press, 1997).

between citing and interpreting, so too there was no clear distinction between interpreting and interpolating.

Ezra was in special need of authorization that associated his new laws with ancient written traditions. The exile had created a sense of profound rupture. So, continuity with the pre-exilic past had to be emphasized and re-emphasized. In order to authorize the restored Jerusalem community, the authors of Ezra–Nehemiah identified their history with the history of the authoritative figure, Moses. They associated the Babylonian exile with enslavement in Egypt, Ezra's public reading of the Torah with the revelation at Sinai, and the restoration of the Temple with the promise to inherit the land. Second, Ezra claimed authority, not as a prophet, but rather as a scribe, which was both old and new at once.[18] The authority of the scribe was based on his connection to antiquity: the scribe preserved the ancient traditions in the authoritative medium of writing. Yet, the fact that scribal authority had become paramount was itself rather new and was a manifestation of the traumatic rupture of the exile.

As a scribe, Ezra's authority developed out of his close association with a written tradition of prophecy, a tradition in which Mosaic writings had pre-eminent authority. As Moses claimed to defer to the superior authority of God, whose laws he transmitted, so Ezra claimed to defer to the superior authority of Moses, whose Torah he claimed to restore through interpretation and public pronouncement.

Thus, the authority-conferring strategy of attributing a legal innovation or new interpretation to Moses was established at the inception of the Second Temple period. Later Second Temple and rabbinic traditions can be said to continue this practice of pseudonymous attribution to Moses. For example, the book of *Jubilees* attributes its entire text to

---

18. Scribal authority was inextricably linked to the emergence of the sacred text as authoritative in the Second Temple period. For discussion of the emergence of the scribe in this period, see, e.g., Fishbane, *Biblical Interpretation in Ancient Israel*, pp. 23-262; *idem*, 'From Scribalism to Rabbinism: Perspectives on the Emergence of Classical Judaism', in *idem*, *The Garments of Torah: Essays in Biblical Hermeneutics* (Bloomington: Indiana University Press, 1989), pp. 64-78; Lester L. Grabbe, *Priests, Prophets, Diviners, Sages: A Socio-Historical Study of Religious Specialists in Ancient Israel* (Valley Forge, PA: Trinity Press International, 1995); Joseph Blenkinsopp, *Sage, Priest, Prophet: Religious and Intellectual Leadership in Ancient Israel* (Louisville, KY: Westminster/John Knox Press, 1995); James L. Kugel, 'Early Interpretation: The Common Background of Late Forms of Biblical Exegesis', in *idem*, *Early Biblical Interpretation*, pp. 11-106.

Moses, who, as faithful amanuensis, records every word revealed to him by the divinely instructed angel of the presence. Even after the destruction of the Second Temple, rabbinic traditions continue this practice when they call certain laws 'the law of Moses from Sinai'.[19] The laws of Tephillin[20] and the rules of interpretation are two examples.[21]

Ezra's pseudonymous attribution to 'Torah of Moses' may be profitably compared to later rabbinic attributions of new legal and interpretive innovations to Moses. Because rabbinic conceptions of textuality

---

19. Numerous references to 'the law of Moses from Sinai' appear in rabbinic literature, the earliest occurring in the Mishnah and the Tosephta. See, e.g., *m. Pe'ah* 2.6; *m. 'Ed* 8.7; *m. Yad.* 4.3; *t. Yad.* 2.16; *b. Men.* 32a; *b. Meg.* 24b; *b. Ḥag* 3a.

David Weiss Halivni insists that this term should really be understood as an Amoraic development. See his discussion in *Revelation Restored*, pp. 56-57: 'Except for one possible reference in Peah, the Mishnah never alludes to a historical *Halakha le-Moshe mi-Sinai* as a decisive factor in halakha. The Tannaim did not deny the existence of *Halakha le-Moshe mi-Sinai* or, hypothetically, its power to decide halakha, but they did not avail themselves of it for practical decisions'. Underlying Halivni's comments are the echoes of over a century of fierce debate among Rabbis and scholars of rabbinic literature, a debate that has medieval roots.

20. E.g. *b. Šab* 89b; *b. Men.* 32a; *b. Meg.* 24b. For a critical discussion of the rabbinic sources which claim that laws of Tephillin are part of the 'the law of Moses from Sinai', see Isaac H. Weiss, *Dor Dor Vedorshav*, I (1871–1891; repr., Berlin: Platt & Minkus, 1924), p. 73 n.2.

21. See Rashi's commentary to *b. Pes.* 24a, where he claims that the hermeneutical rules are *halakha le-Moshe mi-Sinai*. On the origin of the hermeneutical rules see, e.g., David Daube, 'Rabbinic Methods of Interpretation and Hellenistic Rhetoric', *HUCA* 22 (1949), pp. 239-64. Daube argues in great detail that Hillel was deeply influenced by the Greco-Roman traditions of Hellenistic philosophy and that the formulation of the hermeneutical rules are shaped by stoic writers such as Cicero. While Saul Lieberman also acknowledges the parallels in Greco-Roman traditions, he does not think that one can demonstrate that the Rabbis actually *borrowed* the hermeneutical rules from the Greeks or the Romans and then incorporated them into rabbinic traditions. See Lieberman's study, 'Rabbinic Interpretation of Scripture', in *idem, Hellenism in Jewish Palestine* (New York: Jewish Theological Seminary, 1962), pp. 47-67. For claims that some of the hermeneutical rules reflect Mesopotamian influences see Stephen J. Lieberman, 'A Mesopotamian Background for the So-Called "*Aggadic* Measures" of Biblical Hermeneutics?', *HUCA* 58 (1987), pp. 157-225. For further discussion, see Michael L. Chernick, *Hermeneutical Studies in Talmudic and Midrashic Literature* (Lod: Haberman Institute, 1984) (Hebrew); Jay M. Harris, *How Do We Know This? Midrash and the Fragmentation of Modern Judaism* (Albany: State University of New York Press, 1995), pp. 1-72, 94-101.

and authorship had changed dramatically since Ezra's day, the very fact of their shared strategy of authorization is remarkable. Nevertheless, I want to emphasize that the concept of Scripture in Ezra–Nehemiah differs radically from the concept of Scripture in rabbinic—or any other post-canonical interpretations. For Ezra–Nehemiah, 'Torah of Moses' was an honorific designation used to mark the authority of laws, practices and interpretations that were were rooted in, or traditionally associated with, the written Pentateuchal traditions.

The specific conception of Scripture in Ezra–Nehemiah must be understood in light of the need to authorize the restoration of the Second Temple community. However, as I have suggested, understanding Ezra's ascription of legal innovation to Moses can also help us to understand practices of pseudepigraphy and rewriting the Bible—practices that continued throughout the Second Temple period and even beyond.

ONE GOOD STORY DESERVES ANOTHER: THE HERMENEUTICS OF
INVOKING SECONDARY BIBLICAL EPISODES IN THE NARRATIVES OF
PSEUDO-PHILO AND THE *TESTAMENTS OF THE TWELVE PATRIARCHS*

Bruce N. Fisk

1. *Preliminary Assumptions and Theses*

This paper seeks to test two theses about the exegetical nature of Rewritten Bible in the *Liber Antiquitatum Biblicarum* of Pseudo-Philo (hereafter *LAB*) and the *Testaments of the Twelve Patriarchs*. But first, a pair of assumptions. Assumption number one is the uncontroversial claim that the ancient tradents understood the many parts of their sacred text to be meaningfully interrelated, such that various passages could and should be read together. This is nicely illustrated in a rabbinic tale about R. Simeon ben Azzai, sparring partner of Rabbi Aqiba. Once, when Ben Azzai sat making midrash, mysterious flames of fire were seen surrounding him. When Aqiba pressed for an explanation, Ben Azzai replied that he was

> linking up the words of the Torah with one another and then with the words of the Prophets, and the Prophets with the Writings, and the words rejoiced as when they were delivered from Sinai, and they were sweet as at their original utterance. And were they not delivered from Sinai in fire, as it says, 'And the mountain burned with fire'? (Deut. 4.11)[1]

Daniel Boyarin notes that Ben Azzai 'did what he did, not by linking texts with their *meanings* but by linking texts with *texts*, that is, by revealing the hermeneutic connection between the Prophets and Writings and the Torah'.[2] For Ben Azzai, the task was simply to string together texts that were, so to speak, yearning to be united and delighting to be

---

1.   *Cant. R.* 1.10 §2. Maurice Simon (trans.), *Midrash Rabbah: Song of Songs* (London: The Soncino Press, 1939), p. 74.
2.   *Intertextuality and the Reading of Midrash* (Bloomington: Indiana University Press, 1990), p. 110 (emphasis added).

fulfilling their divinely intended role. This practice of 'linking texts with texts' is ubiquitous in rabbinic literature,[3] but emerges long before the days of Ben Azzai, characterizing a sizable swathe of ancient biblical interpretation, including some works commonly known as 'Rewritten Bible'.[4]

Assumption number two is somewhat more controversial: scholarly preoccupation with the social, historical and ideological settings of early Jewish biblical interpretation runs the risk of ignoring its fundamentally exegetical nature. This point has been demonstrated convincingly by James Kugel, who contends that, although recent studies of early Jewish literature have paid close attention to social, historical and ideological influences,

> scholars have tended to assume that if an ancient author deviated from the biblical narrative in his retelling of it, that deviation must somehow have been motivated by the reteller's political allegiance or religious agenda or some other matter of ideology, or...an attempt...to retroject the

---

3.   James Kugel, *In Potiphar's House: The Interpretive Life of Biblical Texts* (San Francisco: HarperCollins, 1990), p. 262, remarks: 'one of the most characteristic traits of rabbinic exegesis as a whole is its endless establishing of connections between Pentateuchal verses and other, quite "distant" biblical texts'. See also Saul Lieberman, 'Rabbinic Interpretation of Scripture', in H.A. Fischel (ed.), *Essays in Greco-Roman and Related Literature* (New York: Ktav, 1977), p. 291. On *gezerah shawah*, a rabbinic formalization of this general principle, see H.L. Strack and Günter Stemberger, *Introduction to the Talmud and Midrash* (trans. M. Bockmuehl; Minneapolis: Fortress Press, 1992), pp. 18-19.

4.   Although Kugel, *In Potiphar's House*, p. 261, claims 'that one almost never finds such gratuitous integration of distant texts [as is found in rabbinic texts] in prerabbinic sources', he would not dispute the intertextual nature of biblical and early postbiblical literature. (See, e.g., *idem, The Bible as It Was* [Cambridge, MA: Harvard University Press, 1997], p. 20). On the biblical roots of later intertextual biblical exegesis, see esp. Michael Fishbane, *Biblical Interpretation in Ancient Israel* (Oxford: Clarendon Press, 1985), but also Michael Wadsworth, 'Making and Interpreting Scripture', in *idem, Ways of Reading the Bible* (New Jersey: Barnes and Noble, 1981), pp. 7-22. Important studies on early Jewish and Christian biblical exegesis include G. Vermes, 'Bible and Midrash: Early Old Testament Exegesis', in J. Neusner (ed.), *Post-Biblical Jewish Studies* (SJLA, 8; Leiden: E.J. Brill, 1975), pp. 59-91; A. Shinan and Y. Zakovitch, 'Midrash on Scripture and Midrash within Scripture', in Sara Japhet (ed.), *Scripta Hierosolymitana: Studies in Bible* (Publications of the Hebrew University, 31; Jerusalem: Magnes Press, 1986), pp. 257-77; Richard B. Hays, *Echoes of Scripture in the Letters of Paul* (New Haven: Yale University Press, 1989).

realities of the reteller's own time back to the time of the biblical narrative.[5]

Such ideological agenda do of course influence biblical interpretation, but Kugel rightly warns against neglecting another extremely significant factor, namely the tradent's 'desire *to explain* the biblical text, *to account for its particulars* in one fashion or another'. Again, Kugel explains:

> sometimes that 'true' significance does indeed turn out to correspond to something current in the interpreter's own world, some part of the political or religious or intellectual backdrop. Often, however, it does not: the interpretation is just that, *an attempt to make sense of the text.*[6]

Daniel Boyarin has registered similar concerns about recent approaches to rabbinic midrash:

> We will not read midrash well and richly unless we understand it first and foremost as *reading*, as hermeneutic, as generated by the interaction of rabbinic readers with a heterogeneous and difficult text, which was for them both normative and divine in origin.[7]

---

5. *The Bible as It Was*, p. 25.

6. *The Bible as It Was*, p. 26 (emphasis added). See also Kugel, 'The Story of Dinah in the *Testament of Levi*', *HTR* 85.1 (1992), pp. 1-3; *idem, In Potiphar's House*, pp. 247-51. By no means does Kugel treat 'ideological' and 'exegetical' as mutually exclusive categories: 'the ancient interpreter *always* had an axe to grind' (*The Bible as It Was*, p. 26). On the older distinction between '*pure*' exegesis (concered with phenomena in the text) and '*applied*' exegesis (concerned with contemporary customs and beliefs), see esp. Vermes 'Bible and Midrash'. For 'pure' and 'applied' exegesis in *Jubilees*, see John C. Endres, *Biblical Interpretation in the Book of Jubilees* (CBQMS, 18; Washington: Catholic Biblical Association, 1987), pp. 212-13, 219-22.

7. *Intertextuality*, p. 5 (cf. pp. 3-4, 6, 117-19, *et passim*). For Boyarin, the 'traditional research paradigm' 'does not account for the role that interpretation of Torah plays in the formation of ideological and theological positions' (p. 74). Both Devorah Dimant ('Use and Interpretation of Mikra in Apocrypha and Pseudepigrapha', in M.J. Mulder [ed.], *Mikra: Text, Translation, Reading and Interpretation of the Hebrew Bible in Ancient Judaism and Early Christianity* [CRINT; Minneapolis: Fortress Press, 1990], p. 380) and Steven Weitzman ('Allusion, Artifice, and Exile in the Hymn of Tobit', *JBL* 115 [1996], p. 49) contend that students of early postbiblical literature are only now beginning to think 'systematically' about the techniques and hermeneutical strategies that guided ancient tradents to appropriate biblical elements for their own compositions.

Now for our two theses. The first pertains to the phenomenon, common in Pseudo-Philo, but present also in the *Testaments* and elsewhere,[8] of retelling one story by intruding or evoking elements from another: *The rewritten narratives of* LAB *and the* Testaments *integrate secondary biblical episodes into the primary narrative in order to engage in biblical exegesis.*[9] *Intertextuality* (assumption #1) and biblical *exegesis* (assumption #2) belong together; citations or allusions to other, ostensibly unrelated biblical episodes principally serve the author's (or the tradition's) *exegetical* agenda.[10]

8.   On transpositions and correlations of scripture in *LAB*, see Bruce N. Fisk, 'Scripture Shaping Scripture: The Interpretive Role of Biblical Citations in Pseudo-Philo's Episode of the Golden Calf', *JSP* 17 (1998), pp. 3-23; *idem*, 'Offering Isaac Again and Again: Pseudo-Philo's Use of the Aqedah as Intertext', *CBQ* (forthcoming); Howard Jacobson, *A Commentary on Pseudo-Philo's Liber Antiquitatum Biblicarum, with Latin Text and English Translation* (AGJU 31; Leiden: E.J. Brill, 1996), pp. 224-41; *idem*, 'Biblical Quotation and Editorial Function in Pseudo-Philo's *Liber Antiquitatum Biblicarum*', *JSP* 5 (1989), pp. 47-64; Eckart Reinmuth, *Pseudo-Philo und Lukas* (WUNT, 74; Tübingen: J.C.B. Mohr [Paul Siebeck], 1994); Frederick Murphy, *Pseudo-Philo: Rewriting the Bible* (New York: Oxford, 1993); Louis H. Feldman, 'Josephus' *Jewish Antiquities* and Pseudo-Philo's *Biblical Antiquities*', in *idem*, *Studies in Hellenistic Judaism* (AGJU, 30; Leiden: E.J. Brill, 1996), pp. 57-82; Richard Bauckham, 'The Liber Antiquitatum Biblicarum of Pseudo-Philo and the Gospels as "Midrash"', in R.T. France and D. Wenham (ed.), *Gospel Perspectives*. III. *Studies in Midrash and Historiography* (Sheffield: JSOT Press, 1983), pp. 33-76.

9.   On 'implicit' exegesis as a central feature of rewritten Bible, see esp. Dimant, 'Use and Interpretation', but also Philip S. Alexander, 'Retelling the Old Testament', in D.A. Carson and H.G.M. Williamson (ed.), *It Is Written: Scripture Citing Scripture* (Cambridge: Cambridge University Press, 1988), p. 118; and Craig A. Evans, 'Luke and the Rewritten Bible: Aspects of Lukan Hagiography', in J.H. Charlesworth and C.A. Evans (eds.), *The Pseudepigrapha and Early Biblical Interpretation* (Sheffield: JSOT Press, 1993), pp. 171-74. Although Dimant ('Use and Interpretation', pp. 383-84) reserves 'exegesis' for works that clearly distinguish the biblical presursor from its explication, and prefers 'interpretation' for works (like Rewritten Bible) that blur or erase that distinction, I remain unconvinced of the usefulness of this distinction. It is the narrative genre and biblical style of Rewritten Bible that precludes any clear distinction between text and commentary, such as is found in works of *explicit* biblical exegesis.

10.   Infusions from distant passages may also serve the author's *rhetorical* agenda. When an author quietly smuggles in his own (sometimes radically revisionary) biblical exegesis under the guise of other Scripture, the effect on the reader can be

Our second thesis is really a corollary of the first: When two biblical stories are linked, elements and themes in the principal narrative can subtly shape or even transform the meaning of the secondary episode. In Rewritten Bible, the primary episode can exert exegetical leverage back upon the secondary. It should not be surprising that secondary episodes rarely escape hermeneutical transformation, for the mere act of linking two biblical stories constructs an interpretive framework for reading each of them. Almost inevitably, exegesis moves 'backward' as well as 'forward'.[11]

2. *Biblical Exegesis in Pseudo-Philo's* Liber Antiquitatum Biblicarum

Pseudo-Philo's penchant for explicitly correlating biblical episodes is widely known. Too few, however, have evaluated these sorts of correlations as evidence of early Jewish *biblical exegesis*. Perhaps the following examples illustrate the potential value of adopting such an approach.

a. *Moses' Infancy Foreshadowed Greater Things: Exodus 1–2 and Exodus 14 in* LAB *9.10*

As Pseudo-Philo rehearses the birth of Moses, 'the spirit of God came upon Miriam one night' and she had a dream.[12] In that dream, a man in a linen garment gave her a message for her parents:

powerfully coercive. Cf. David Dawson, *Allegorical Readers and Cultural Revision in Ancient Alexandria* (Berkeley: University of California Press, 1992), pp. 129-30.

11. Boyarin (*Intertextuality*, pp. 32, 41-46, 112-15, 163) makes parallel claims about the *mutually* interpretive nature of intertexts in rabbinic midrash. For a rigorous (though not decisive) critique, see Herbert Basser, 'Boyarin's Intertextuality and the Reading of Midrash,' *JQR* 81 (1991), pp. 429-31. It is precisely this sort of mutality (or bi-directionality) of interpretation that characterises the New Testament Gospels. Craig Evans ('Luke and the Rewritten Bible', pp. 198-99) considers *LAB* a close counterpart to Matthew and Luke, since these Gospels 'clarify and update the Jesus story' (in part) by incorporating and reinterpreting elements from other sources (e.g. Mark, Deuteronomy, Isaiah). The evangelists' sources (or 'secondary' passages) function to *interpret* 'the Jesus story' but they are also *interpreted* by it. E.g. Hosea 11.1 helps to shape Matthew's narrative, but that narrative also demands a radical rereading of the Old Testament text.

12. Jacobson, *Commentary*, p. 419, notes similar, but not identical, rabbinic traditions.

Behold he who will be born from you will be cast forth into the water [*in aquam proicietur*]; likewise through him the water will be dried up [*per eum aqua siccabitur*]. And I will work signs through him and save my people, and he will exercise leadership always (*LAB* 9.10).

Allusions both to Moses' infant 'voyage' on the Nile and to Israel's crossing of the Red Sea are unmistakable. What led Pseudo-Philo to pair up these two Moses-and-water stories? Perhaps our author was impressed that both episodes involve Moses and the Egyptians, a brush with a watery death, and a dramatic reversal of fortunes. In the same way that baby Moses was kept from drowning in the waters of the Nile, an aging Moses would keep his people from a similar fate in the Red Sea. Commentaries typically conclude that Pseudo-Philo forges this sort of link in order to buttress his *theological* agenda. Reinmuth, for example, claims that it illustrates Pseudo-Philo's vision of history as a single, connected story unfolding according to God's plan.[13] This is surely correct as far as it goes,[14] but it fails to consider whether this narrative expansion also functions as biblical *exegesis*.

On closer inspection, we discover that *LAB* contains perhaps as many as four additional narrative links between the two Moses-and-water stories. Such evidence strongly suggests that for Pseudo-Philo the two episodes were profoundly and meaningfully related.

1. *The sheer proximity of the two episodes*: Pseudo-Philo's account completely ignores Moses' flight and calling (Exod. 3–6), and compresses Exodus 7–12 into a single verse (*LAB* 10.1). Thus Exodus 3–12 all but disappear in *LAB* so that the stories of Moses' infant voyage *on*

---

13. Reinmuth, *Pseudo-Philo und Lukas*, p. 126, treats this passage under the rubric 'Korrelationsprinzip', a principle presupposing 'daß Ereignisse durch das Wirken Gottes so korreliert sind, daß sie im Verhältnis der einfachen oder reziproken (bzw. kontrapunktischen) Entsprechung zueinander stehen' (*Pseudo-Philo und Lukas*, p. 118). Additional examples noted by Reinmuth include *LAB* 12.3; 14.2; 19.11; 20.6; 31.5; 59.5; 61.3. For Murphy, *Pseudo-Philo*, p. 59, 'it underlines the structure and interconnectedness of history, which in turn illustrates God's control of events'. Likewise, Bauckham, 'Pseudo-Philo and the Gospels', p. 41: 'The presupposition...must be that there is a consistency about God's acts in the history of his people, so that similar situations and events constantly recur'. See also Jacobson, *Commentary*, p. 241.

14. In this passage, it is God's messenger who compares the Nile and Red Sea episodes. Cf. *LAB* 4.11.

the waters and Moses' adult trek *through* the waters are narrated back
to back.

2. *Miriam's elevated status*: The prophetic role Pseudo-Philo accords
to Miriam, which far surpasses the biblical portrait of Exod. 2.4-8,
almost certainly derives from Exod. 15.20-21, the story of her post-Red
Sea celebrations.[15] Not only is she explicitly called a *prophetess*
(הַנְּבִיאָה) but her oracle describes how God had thrown 'horse and rider
...into the sea'. Readers might easily infer that Miriam had *foreseen* the
Red Sea miracle.

3. *The elders' speech to Amram*: No sooner is baby Moses placed on
the river, than the elders quarrel with Amram:

> Are not these our words that we spoke, 'It is better for us to die without
> having sons than that the fruit of our womb be cast into the waters'?
> (*LAB* 9.14)[16]

These antagonistic remarks foreshadow the opposition Moses faced at
the Red Sea, their language of despair echoing the cry of 'the sons of
Israel' as they watched the advance of the Egyptian army:

> Is this not the very thing we told you in Egypt, 'Let us alone and let us
> serve the Egyptians'? For it would have been better for us to serve the
> Egyptians than to die in the wilderness (Exod 14.12).[17]

4. *The advice of the four tribes at the Sea*: According to *LAB* 10.3,
the twelve tribes were 'split in their opinions according to three strategies'.[18] Four of the tribes favor mass suicide by drowning:

---

15. Noted also by Reinmuth, *Pseudo-Philo und Lukas*, p. 47 n. 73. The influence of Num. 12.6-7 is also likely. In direct reply to Aaron and Miriam who
scornfully ask whether God had not spoken to them also, God replies: 'When there
are prophets among you, I the LORD make myself known to them in visions. Not so
with my servant Moses...' Might this imply that Miriam the prophet had heard
from God in a vision?

16. The elders' initial response to the king's edict to drown all Hebrew baby
boys (*LAB* 9.2) concludes, 'For it is better to die without sons until we know what
God may do'. These deliberations of the elders have no parallel in the biblical account.

17. Jacobson, *Commentary*, p. 425, describes it as 'almost a verbatim quotation'.

18. Though Pseudo-Philo may be the earliest surviving witness to the midrashic
tradition of a tribal debate at the Red Sea (but cf. Philo, *Vit. Mos.* 2.248-52), the
tradition is well represented in later sources, and is commonly thought to be older
than Pseudo-Philo. On the likelihood of a pre-*LAB* origin of this debate tradition,

Come, let us cast ourselves into the sea. For it is better for us to die in the water than to be killed by our enemies (10.3).

If these words are indebted to both Exod. 14.12b and *LAB* 9.14 (the elders' cries at Moses' birth), we have further evidence that Pseudo-Philo saw close ties between the two stories.[19]

We note, furthermore, that Pseudo-Philo's rewritten account eliminates several puzzlers in the biblical narrative.[20] Would a Hebrew mother really abandon her child? Why would she choose such a dangerous place to hide him? Why describe the ark's construction in such detail (2.3)? And whose idea was it to have Miriam keep watch (2.4)? All of these 'problems' disappear in Pseudo-Philo's story-infused account, in which Moses' parents enjoy previews of the near, and the distant, future of their unborn son. Curiously independent behavior is recast as faithful obedience.[21] Their putting Moses 'out to sea' is no desperate act of abandonment or mere rescue attempt, but a divinely ordained prophetic *symbol*—a harbinger of Moses' role in the deliverance of Israel at the

and on the similarities and differences between *LAB* 10.3 and targumic, rabbinic and Samaritan traditions, see esp. Saul M. Olyan, 'The Israelites Debate Their Options at the Sea of Reeds: *LAB* 10.3, its Parallels and Pseudo-Philo's Ideology and Background', *JBL* 110.1 (1991), pp. 75-91, but also C. Perrot and P.-M. Bogaert, *Pseudo-Philon, Les Antiquités Bibliques*, II (SC, 230; Paris: Cerf, 1976), pp. 108-109; Kugel, *The Bible as It Was*, pp. 339-40; W.S. Towner, 'Form Criticism of Rabbinic Literature', *JJS* 24 (1973), pp. 113-16. It is clear from later traditions (e.g. *Targ. Neof.*) that Moses' reply in Exod. 14.13-14 was taken as a compressed series of responses to three or four different popular reactions to the crisis. Nothing in *LAB*, however, *explicitly* links his three 'options' (drowning, surrender, armed resistance) to the words of Moses' reply.

19. Note that by itself Exod. 14.12 actually opposes the sentiment of *LAB* 10.3a. In the former, *serving the Egyptians* is said to be preferable to *dying*; in the latter, surrender is ruled out, and *suicide* is said to be preferable to *death in battle*. This intertextual linkage need not undermine Olyan's proposal ('Israelites Debate', pp. 89-90) that Pseudo-Philo's suicide/death-in-battle antithesis may have been shaped by certain events of the Jewish War.

20. Various ancient tradents attest to the troublesome nature of the narrative. Philo (*Vit. Mos.* 1.9-11) wonders why Moses' parents didn't simply expose him at birth, rather than after three months. Josephus (*Ant.* 2.210-23) has Amram (not Miriam) receive a (much longer) dream-vision predicting Moses' survival and future greatness. *Jubilees* (47.4) assures us that Moses was not truly abandoned; his mother secretly nursed him by night, and Miriam protected him from the birds by day.

21. Presumably the initial disbelief of Miriam's parents (*LAB* 9.10) had been reversed when baby Moses was born circumcised (9.13).

Red Sea. The Nile–Red Sea parallels show that Moses was called by God, from the womb, to be Israel's savior and leader.[22] As for 'reverse' exegesis, Pseudo-Philo's intertextual account of Moses' *birth* quietly supplies a framework for interpreting the later episode of the Red Sea. Significantly, this framework is strikingly similar to several other proposals already in circulation:

> And the LORD brought them out through the midst of the sea as through dry land. And all of the people whom he brought out to pursue after Israel the LORD our God threw into the middle of the sea into the depths of the abyss beneath the children of Israel. *Just as the men of Egypt cast their sons into the river he avenged one million. And one thousand strong and ardent men perished on account of one infant whom they threw into the midst of the river from the sons of your people* (Jub. 48.13-14).[23]

> When they had resolved to kill the infants of your holy ones, *and one child had been abandoned and rescued* [καὶ ἑνὸς ἐκτεθέντος τέκνου καὶ σωθέντος], you in punishment took away a multitude of their children; *and you destroyed them all together by a mighty flood* [καὶ ὁμοθυμαδὸν ἀπώλεσας ἐν ὕδατι σφοδρῷ] (Wis. 18.5).[24]

Pseudo-Philo's story whispers what these other tradents loudly proclaim: the drowning of Israel's infants in the Nile and the drowning of

---

22. Similarly Perrot and Bogaert, *Pseudo-Philon*, p. 106: 'Dans le petit enfant jeté à l'eau, l'auteur voit le signe de la puissance de Moïse sur les eaux'. Philo (*Vit. Mos.* 1.12, 17, 19, 67) appeals directly (without intertexts) to the providence of God. Jacobson, *Commentary*, p. 420, in emphasizing the overlap between *LAB* and parallel accounts, misses this important function of *LAB*'s account.

23. O.S. Wintermute, 'Jubilees', in J.H. Charlesworth (ed.), *OTP*, II (New York: Doubleday, 1985), p. 140. *Jub.* 47.3 emphasizes how many were lost: 'And they continued throwing (them into the river) seven months, until the day when you were born'.

24. Although the focus of Wis. 18.5-25 is on the final plague, the 'mighty flood' language (ἐν ὕδατι σφοδρῷ) of the last clause alludes to the Red Sea, and corresponds to the deliverance of Moses in the second clause. This suggests an A-B-A-B structure:

> When they had resolved to kill the infants of your holy ones,
>   *and one child had been abandoned and rescued,*
> you in punishment took away a multitude of their children;
>   *and you destroyed them all together by a mighty flood.*

These correspondences illustrate a broader principle in Wisdom of Solomon: 'For through the very things by which their enemies were punished, they themselves received benefit in their need' (11.5).

Egypt's troops in the Red Sea stand together as crime and punishment.[25]

b. *Israel's Idolatry Made her Blind: Exodus 32, Exodus 34 and Genesis 42.8 in* LAB *12.1*

In *LAB* 12.1, Pseudo-Philo describes how Moses' face was transfigured during the golden calf episode:

> the light of his face surpassed the splendor of the sun and the moon, and he did not even know this. And when he came down to the sons of Israel, they saw him but did not recognize [*non cognoscebant*] him. But when he spoke then they recognized [*cognoverunt*] him. And this was like what happened in Egypt when Joseph recognized [*cognovit*] his brothers but they did not recognize [*non cognoverunt*] him (*LAB* 12.1).

Exodus 32 says nothing about Moses' transfigured face, about his being unrecognizable to the people, or about their recognizing him only when he spoke.[26] For at least some of these additions, Pseudo-Philo has drawn upon the *second* descent-of-Moses story (Exod. 34.29-32),[27] according to which Moses appeared with such altered appearance (cf. *LAB* 12.1) that 'the people were afraid to come near him' (Exod. 34.30) until he 'called to them' and 'spoke with them' (34.31). Whether Pseudo-Philo inferred that what was true of Moses' second descent would also have been true of his first, or whether he thought Exodus 32 was a more appropriate setting for a luminescent Moses, he has clearly smuggled elements from Exodus 34 back into his account of the golden calf.[28]

---

25. Evidence of direct literary dependence is lacking. Other traditions linking Exodus 1–2 with later events include Josephus, *Ant.* 2.205-206; *PRE* 48. See further Kugel, *The Bible as It Was*, pp. 290-95, and Jacobson, *Commentary*, p. 420.

26. The non-recognition of Moses motif is unique to Pseudo-Philo. Ancient readers might have concluded from Exod. 32.19-20 that Moses' arrival in the camp went unnoticed until he broke the tablets, but is more likely that Pseudo-Philo imported the motif from elsewhere.

27. Cf. Jacobson, *Commentary*, p. 483. Moses' second descent all but disappears from the *LAB* account (13.1).

28. See also Jacobson, *Commentary*; Feldman, 'Prolegomenon', in M.R. James (ed.), *The Biblical Antiquities of Philo* (New York: Ktav, 1971); Perrot and Bogaert, *Pseudo-Philon*; Reinmuth, *Pseudo-Philo und Lukas*; Murphy and C. Dietzfelbinger, *Pseudo-Philo: Antiquitates Biblicae (Liber Antiquitatum Biblicarum)* (JSHRZ, 2; Gütersloh: Gerd Mohn, 1975). Reinmuth, *Pseudo-Philo und Lukas*, pp. 101-102, describes *LAB* 12.1 as a 'midraschartige Interpretation' of Exod. 34. The same transposition occurs in *Deut. R.* 3.12: 'God said to him: "When you arranged [the

But the question remains: how did *fear* of Moses become *non-recognition*? Evidently this non-recognition motif derives from a third biblical narrative: Joseph's reunion with his brothers in Egypt (Gen. 42). When Jacob's ten sons arrived to buy grain, they found themselves face to face with their long lost brother but didn't realize it was Joseph:

> When Joseph saw his brothers, he recognized them [נכר], but he disguised himself [נכר] to them and spoke to them harshly [קשׁות]. And he said to them, 'Where have you come from?' And they said, 'From the land of Canaan, to buy food'. But Joseph had recognized [נכר] his brothers, although they did not recognize [נכר] him (Gen. 42.7-8, NASV).

For Pseudo-Philo, these two encounters are strikingly symmetrical: like Joseph, when Moses was reunited with his kinfolk, they failed to recognize him even though he recognized them.[29] Casual readers may not notice any sleight of hand, but in fact the symmetry only works because Pseudo-Philo has already intruded the *non-recognition* motif into his version of the Moses story.[30] Furthermore, Pseudo-Philo conveniently ignores the fact that *Joseph's* identity remained hidden long after he first *spoke* to his brothers. As Reinmuth points out:

> The factual analogy is thus based again on a word congruence which has come about only by surpassing the biblical text. It is precisely the formulation that Moses could be recognized only after he spoke that does not correspond to the narrative of Gen. 42.7ff.

> Die Sachanalogie basiert folglich wieder auf einer erst in Überbietung des Bibeltextes herbeigeführten Wort-Übereinstimmung. Gerade die Formulierung, daß erst nach dem Reden des Mose dieser erkannt worden

Tables] for Israel I gave you as your reward a shining face, and now you have broken them".'

29. Several other correspondences might have encouraged midrashists to propose explicit intertextual links: both Moses and Joseph grew up in Egypt and became holy men; both were called of God and exalted to positions of leadership over Israel; both faced opposition from within their own families and from the Egyptians; and both were reunited with their kinfolk after a period of prolonged absence. We note further that their stories stand back-to-back in Scripture, and that Joseph's last words (Gen. 50.24-25) are a thinly veiled prediction of the Exodus.

30. The repeated use of *cognoscere* in *LAB*-Latin 12.1 almost certainly points back to forms of נכר. Pseudo-Philo's earlier summation of the Joseph episode (*LAB* 8.10) includes this same theme, though without emphasis: 'And Joseph recognized [*cognovit*] his brothers, but was not known [*non est agnitus*] by them.' As often in Pseudo-Philo, a heavily edited and condensed narrative assumes that readers were familiar with the much fuller biblical precursor. Cf. Jacobson, *Commentary*, p. 395.

sei, entspricht nicht dem als Sachanalogie herbeigezogenen Erzählinhalt Gen. 42.7 ff.[31]

What motivated this story-to-story linkage?[32] Was it the tradent's desire to show Israel's story conforming to a divinely ordained pattern?[33] Was it the need to defend Moses and the law against its detractors, or to underscore the gravity of idolatry?[34] Whether or not theology or social setting has influenced his account, *LAB* has used the *transfiguration* motif from Exodus 34 and the *non-recognition* motif from Genesis 42 to interpret the encounter between Moses and the sinning Israelites. Thanks to Exodus 34, the Moses who confronts Israel's idolatry comes as one 'bathed with invisible light' who virtually embodies the law.[35] And by echoing Genesis 42, Pseudo-Philo implicitly casts the Israelites as the moral equivalent of Joseph's scheming brothers. Like those patriarchs in Egypt, the Israelites in the wilderness failed to recognize Moses precisely because of their profound sinfulness. Reinmuth correctly notes:

> Es ist vorauszusetzen, daß das Nicht-Erkennen des Volkes im Erzähl-zusammenhang ursächlich auf die Anfertigung des Goldenen Kalbes zurückzuführen ist.[36]

31. *Pseudo-Philo und Lukas*, p. 101. My translation. When Joseph does finally disclose himself to his brothers (Gen 45.3, 4, 12), it requires their *seeing* as much as *hearing*: 'Joseph said to his brothers, "I am Joseph. Is my father still alive?" But his brothers could not answer him, so dismayed were they at his presence. Then Joseph said to his brothers, "Come closer to me". And they came closer. He said, "I am your brother, Joseph, whom you sold into Egypt... And now *your eyes...see* that it is *my own mouth* that *speaks* to you".'

32. Jacobson, *Commentary*, p. 483, is puzzled by Pseudo-Philo's strategy here: 'Whether the Joseph episode occurred as an afterthought to *LAB* once he had invented the "lack of recognition" theme here or there is a deeper and more significant connection, I do not know'.

33. See above, n. 13, and Murphy, *Pseudo-Philo*, p. 69.

34. On Pseudo-Philo's idealizing of Moses, see G.W.E. Nickelsburg, 'Good and Bad Leaders in Pseudo-Philo's *Liber Antiquitatum Biblicarum*', in G.W.E. Nickelsburg and J.J. Collins (ed.), *Ideal Figures in Ancient Judaism: Profiles and Paradigms* (SBLSCS, 12; Chico, CA: Scholars Press, 1980), p. 53. On idolatry as 'the root of all evil' in *LAB*, see F. Murphy, 'Retelling the Bible: Idolatry in Pseudo-Philo', *JBL* 107.2 (1998), pp. 275-87.

35. Moses is all but identified with the law in *LAB*. See Reinmuth, *Pseudo-Philo und Lukas*, pp. 101-102.

36. *Pseudo-Philo und Lukas*, p. 102.

It is presupposed that the people did not recognize Moses in the adjoining narrative because of their production of the golden calf.

Pseudo-Philo's Moses narrative may also offer a way of reading the Joseph story as well. Various ancient tradents wondered why Joseph's own brothers could not immediately recognize him.[37] The intertextual linkage in *LAB* subtly implies that Joseph's brothers were just like the Israelites who fashioned the golden calf: blinded by their sinfulness. If so, Pseudo-Philo's interpretive leverage also works in reverse.

c. *Not all Israel Was Guilty: Exodus 32 and Numbers 5.11-31 in* LAB *12.7*
The biblical allusion in *LAB* 12.7 is difficult to confirm.[38] According to *LAB* 12.5-6, when Moses descended from the mountain and saw the calf, he noted that the divine writing had disappeared and then broke the tablets.[39] After an hour of 'labor pains',[40] Moses finally determined what to do:

> And he arose and broke the calf and cast it into the water and made the people drink of it. And if anyone had it in his will and mind that the calf be made, his tongue was cut off; but if he had been forced by fear to consent, his face shone (12.7).

37. Philo (*Jos.* 28) says God must have altered Joseph's appearance or distorted their judgment. Josephus's solution (*Ant.* 2.97) is simpler: his brothers only knew Joseph as a lad, and not as an exalted ruler. The midrash (*Gen. R.* 91.7) explains this verse by having Joseph pretend to practice divination before his brothers. That not all tradents perceived a 'gap' at this point in the story is clear from *Jub.* 42.5; 43.15. See further Kugel, *The Bible as It Was*, pp. 265-69.
38. Cf. Jacobson, 'Biblical Quotation', p. 49.
39. On the disappearing script, cf. *LAB* 19.7: 'when they sinned, what was written on [the tablets] flew away'. On parallel traditions and hints in the biblical precursor, see again Kugel, *The Bible as It Was*, pp. 426-27.
40. A puzzling image. Bauckham, 'Pseudo-Philo and the Gospels', p. 48, sees here the influence of 2 Kgs 19.3 (cf. Isa. 37.3 and Jer. 4.31), but concludes that '[n]o reason for the use of these passages can be suggested, except that they furnished appropriate imagery for a powerful simile'. In fact, the larger context of 2 Kgs 19 is particularly apt, since it describes Israel in national crisis, on the verge of extinction, preserved only by the mercy of God mediated through the prophet Isaiah. For Murphy, *Pseudo-Philo*, p. 72, the labor imagery signals 'the disruption of a process through which he was to bring Israel to birth through the giving of Torah'. See Perrot and Bogaert, *Les Antiquités Bibliques*, II, p. 115, for further Old Testament references to the image of birth pangs.

This description of the destruction of the calf, and the drinking of its dust, uses language reminiscent of Num. 5.11-31, a passage that details the 'law of jealousy' (תּוֹרַת הַקְּנָאֹת; 5.29), which required suspected adulteresses to drink the water of bitterness (הַמָּרִים; 5.18, cf. 5.19, 23, 24) containing dust from the tabernacle floor (וּמִן־הֶעָפָר אֲשֶׁר יִהְיֶה בְּקַרְקַע הַמִּשְׁכָּן יִקַּח הַכֹּהֵן, וְנָתַן אֶל־הַמָּיִם 5.17).

Several striking points of correspondence exist between *LAB* 12 and Numbers 5. In both accounts water is the central element, and each text describes a ritual act, a 'trial by ordeal', in which the defendants are forced to drink this water mixed with dust. In both cases there are physical symptoms signifying the suspects' conviction or vindication.[41] When these parallel elements are assembled to form a narrative sequence, the case for the influence of the Numbers 5 ordeal on Pseudo-Philo becomes persuasive:

Plot Element	Numbers 5	LAB 12
Offense	individual: adultery	corporate: spiritual adultery
Ritual Substance	water and dust	water and powder
Overseer of the Ritual	priest	Moses
Double Effect	infertility/fertility	tongue cut off/face transfigured
Plaintiff	jealous husband	jealous God[42]

On the other hand, some points of the analogy are *not* symmetrical. The dust of Numbers 5 comes from *holy* space[43] whereas the source of the powder in *LAB* 12 (and Exod. 32) is a very *unholy* idol. Likewise, the physical effects of drinking the water do not correspond. The ritual in Numbers rendered the guilty infertile ('her abdomen will swell and her thigh will waste away') but enabled the innocent to 'be free and conceive children' (5.27-28). For Pseudo-Philo, flagrant sinners lost their tongues (literally) while the faces of those who had succumbed to intimidation began to shine.

A third, more substantial difference relates to the purpose of the ritual enactment. The 'trial by ordeal' in Numbers 5 was ostensibly intended to discover whether or not the suspect was guilty; Pseudo-Philo, by

---

41. We might also imagine a remote parallel between the disappearing words on the two tablets (*LAB* 12.5) and the priest's act of washing the words off the scroll into the water (Num. 5.23). On the washing of words into a potion, cf. *m. Soṭ* 2.3-4, 3.3; Josephus, *Ant.* 3.271-72; Philo, *Spec. Leg.* 3.62.

42. Cf. Reinmuth, *Pseudo-Philo und Lukas*, p. 120.

43. Cf. Philo, *Spec. Leg.* 3.59.

contrast, has Moses distinguish between two levels of guilt: willful defiance and fearful compliance. Evidently Pseudo-Philo is concerned for the matter of inner disposition; it is not just the *doing* but also the *intending* that counts before God.[44]

Notwithstanding these asymmetrical elements, there can be little doubt that Pseudo-Philo has rewritten Exodus 32 under the influence of Numbers 5.[45] Indeed, Pseudo-Philo may have seen his revisions precisely as an attempt to make *explicit* the bitter-water imagery *implicit* in Exod. 32.20.[46] For him, Moses' act was not simply one of destruction and national humiliation. It was, rather, a symbolic ritual enacting God's covenant justice in response to Israel's covenant infidelity. By the rabbinic period, a link between the bitter water and the golden calf was widely recognized.[47] *LAB* appears to fall along a hermeneutical

---

44. For a similar distinction, between sins of 'cunning' (*astucia*) and sins of 'ignorance' (*ignorantia*), see Joshua's speech in *LAB* 22 (cf. Josh. 22), wherein he cites the golden calf episode as legal precedent (*LAB* 22.5-6). (See also the eight occurences of *nos voluimus* in *LAB* 25.9, 13.) For Pseudo-Philo, only hearts right before God can hope for divine favor. This 'inner' focus contrasts sharply with the biblical concern for external behavior in both Exod. 32 and Num. 5. See Murphy, *Pseudo-Philo*, pp. 72, 119-120, and cf. *4 Macc.* 8.14, 22-25; CD 5.15.

45. Pseudo-Philo's framework was perhaps also shaped by traditions depicting Israel's sin as spiritual adultery (e.g. Exod. 34.12-17; Deut. 31.16; Judg. 2.17; Hos. 1.2; 2.2, 5 [2.4, 7, MT]; 4.10-19; 5.3; Isa. 50.1; 54.4-8; 57.3-13; 62.4-5; Jer. 2.9–3.10; 5.7-9; Ps. 78.58; Mal. 2.14; and esp. Ezek. 16; 23. Cf. also Num. 25.11; Deut. 32.15-21; 1 Kgs 14.22 in which God becomes jealous (קָנָא) because of Israel's idolatry.

46. See N. Sarna, *The JPS Torah Commentary: Exodus* (Philadelphia: Jewish Publication Society of America, 1989), p. 207. Similarly, Brevard Childs, *The Book of Exodus* (OTL; Louisville, KY: Westminster/John Knox Press, 1974), p. 569; U. Cassuto, *A Commentary on the Book of Exodus* (trans. I. Abrahams; Jerusalem: Magnes Press, 1967), p. 419; H.C. Brichto, *Toward a Grammar of Biblical Poetics* (New York: Oxford University Press, 1992), p. 98. Old Testament support for a link between Exod. 32 and Num. 5 is scant. The Deuteronomic parallel (9.21) makes no mention of the people drinking the water. The link may be implied in Ezek. 16.17, 38. On a possible link between Num. 5 and Ezek. 23, see M. Fishbane, 'Accusations of Adultery: A Study of Law and Scribal Practice in Numbers 5.11-31', *HUCA* 45 (1974), pp. 41-43.

47. *Num. R.* 9.45 (on Num. 5.17) identifies the 'true' sense of the bitter water rite: 'And the priest shall take (V,17): "priest" alludes to Moses; holy water...for the *sanctification* of the name of the Holy One... Hence it is written, *And I took...the calf...and beat it in pieces...and I cast the dust thereof into the brook that descended out of the mount* (Deut. IX, 21). In an earthen vessel (V, 17): Just as an

trajectory midway between the intimations of Scripture and the exclamations of the rabbis.

The hermeneutical effect of the Numbers 5 intertext is threefold. First, by introducing legal arraignment and sentencing into the golden calf narrative, Pseudo-Philo shifts the focus away from the sin itself and onto the means and effect of the punishment.[48] Secondly, *LAB* reduces sharply the scope of the punishment meted out in the canonical precursor. Scripture has all Israelites drink the water, and portrays the Levites slaughtering three thousand (Exod. 32.27-28); Pseudo-Philo's guilty Israelites lost only their tongues. Thirdly, by having some Israelite faces shine, Pseudo-Philo symbolically sanctifies (presumably a majority of) the people, acquits them from charges of apostasy[49] and associates them closely with the glorified Moses himself.[50] Even during Israel's darkest hour, many Israelites stood with Moses, brightly transfigured, on the side of God.[51]

---

earthen vessel does not admit of purification after it has been defiled, so there was no remedy for all those who went astray with the Calf, for they all perished'. H. Freedman and M. Simon (eds.), *Midrash Rabbah: Numbers Volume I* (trans. J.J. Slotki; London: Soncino Press, 1939), p. 319. *Pes. R.* 10.8 treats Ps. 75.8 as commentary on the golden calf story and as warrant for appealing to Num. 5. See also *Targum Pseudo-Jonathon*; Exod. 32.20; *PRE* 45; *b. 'Abod. Zar.* 44A-B; *Pes. K* 9.3; and the comments of Rashi, Rashbam, Ibn Ezra, Ramban *inter alia.* See also Sarna, *Exodus*, pp. 207, 261; Fishbane, 'Accusations of Adultery', p. 40 n. 51; L. Feldman in M.R. James, *The Biblical Antiquites of Pseudo-Philo* (New York: Ktav, rev. edn, 1971), p. xcvii; and L. Smolar and M. Aberbach, 'The Golden Calf Episode in Postbiblical Literature', *HUCA* 39 (1968), pp. 102-103. The rabbis also observed that the Tables of the Law pair up the idolatry and adultery commands (cf. *Pes. R.* 21.18).

48.   Similarly, Reinmuth, *Pseudo-Philo und Lukas*, p. 120.

49.   Similarly, *PRE* 45 cites Exod. 24.11 and 32.26 to show that both the 'nobles' and the Levites 'were not associated in the affair of the calf'.

50.   This association is not possible in Scripture, since Moses' face only shines on his *second* descent from Sinai (Exod. 34.29), *after* the golden calf crisis had already been resolved. As we have seen, Pseudo-Philo has Moses descend to confront Israel's idolatry with his face 'bathed with invisible light' (12.1).

51.   *PRE* 45 associates a different phenomenon with the drinking of the water: 'Everyone who had kissed the calf with all his heart, his upper lip and his bones became golden, and the tribe of Levi slew him'. Jacobson, *Commentary*, p. 496, compares *Targ. Song* 1.5. Biblical warrant for a visible connection between Moses and this 'remnant' may come from Exod. 32.26, which has Moses summon those who were 'on the Lord's side' (מִי לַיהוָה אֵלַי).

3. *Biblical Exegesis in the* Testaments of the Twelve Patriarchs

The heavily embellished narratives, ethical appeals and apocalyptic expectations of the *Testaments of the Twelve Patriarchs* have much to teach us about the nature of Second Temple Judaism. The question here is whether they also provide valuable evidence of early biblical *exegesis*.

a. *Shechem's Punishment Long Overdue: Genesis 34.25-31, Genesis 20 and 26 in* Testament of Levi *6.8*

Ancient readers of the 'rape of Dinah' episode (Gen. 34.1-31) had their hermeneutical work cut out for them. If they were not laboring to vindicate Simeon and Levi from charges of deceit or injustice,[52] they were busy indicting Shechem and his fellow Hivites for defiling an Israelite virgin.[53] Perhaps nowhere is a reinterpretation of the Dinah episode more pivotal than in the *Testament of Levi*.[54]

Like most Hellenistic Jewish compositions, *Testament of Levi* heavily idealizes the patriarchs in the story. Thus, Jacob is no longer angry because his reputation and security had been jeopardized (Gen. 34.30), but because the Shechemites had been killed *after being circumcised* (*T. Levi* 6.6).[55] As for Levi, he first confesses his disobedience (6.7),[56]

---

52. See, e.g., *Jub.* 30.3, 12-13; *Jos. Asen* 22.11–23.17; *Targ. Onq. Gen.* 34.13; *Targ. Neof.* 34.13; *Gen. R.* 80.8.

53. See, e.g., Judg. 9.2-4; *Jub.* 30.3-6, 11-14; *Targ. Neof. Gen.* 34.31; Theodotus, frg. 7 in Eusebius, *Praep. Ev.* 9.22.9. Pseudo-Philo (*LAB* 8.7) summarily condemns the act of Hamor, but omits the deceptive ploy of Simeon and Levi, and the mass circumcision of the Hivites. Josephus's willingness to indict Simeon and Levi (*Ant.* 1.337-341) is the exception (cf. Gen. 34.13, 30; 49.5-7). Like Judith, Philo (*Migr. Abr.* 223-25) and Pseudo-Philo, Josephus makes no mention of circumcision, but neither does he attempt to justify the killing. By emphasizing Jacob's displeasure (1.341; cf. Gen. 34.30) and directly linking this episode and the next, he implies that God commanded Jacob to offer sacrifices and purify his household (Gen. 35.1-4) because of the offense of Jacob's sons.

54. Explicit references to the Dinah story include *T. Levi* 2.2; 5.3-4; 6.3-11; 7.1-3; 12.5. By contrast, there is not a whisper of the Dinah story in the *Testament of Simeon*, the other co-conspirator. On biblical exegesis in *Testament of Levi* 's Dinah episode, see Kugel, 'The Story of Dinah', pp. 1-34 (n. 6 above); H.W. Hollander and M. De Jonge, *The Testaments of the Twelve Patriarchs: A Commentary* (Leiden: E.J. Brill, 1985), pp. 129-83; Dimant, 'Use and Interpretation', pp. 396-400.

55. *T. Levi* 6.7 has Jacob immediately become sick, perhaps explaining why he offered no response to his sons (Gen. 34.30-31). Theodotus (frgs 5, 6; in Eusebius,

but then claims he 'saw that God's sentence [on Shechem] was "Guilty"' (6.8).[57] Levi could claim this supernatural insight because of a dream in which an angelic messenger told Levi to 'perform vengeance on Shechem for the sake of Dinah' (5.3).[58]

So far, so good. The tradent has preserved intact Levi's integrity and motives. But surely ancient readers would also wonder *why* heaven authorized such a massacre, particularly since the biblical account (unlike *Testament of Levi*) is almost sympathetic toward Shechem (Gen. 34.3-4, 8, 11-12, 19), and since another passage, Deut. 22.28-29, levies a fine and a wedding, not a slaughter and a funeral, for the kind of crime Shechem commits.

Significantly, the way out of this dilemma offered by the *Testament of Levi* involves an appeal to secondary Scripture. It is precisely by linking the Dinah episode to several earlier, ostensibly unrelated biblical narratives, that *Testament of Levi* can explain *why* 'the wrath of God ultimately came upon them' (6.11). The sons of Hamor deserved death, we are told,

---

Praep. Ev. 9.22.7-9) similarly emphasizes Jacob's concern over circumcision, but does not mention that the Shechemites followed through on the request.

56. Ἡμάρτομεν γὰρ ὅτι παρὰ γνώμην αὐτοῦ τοῦτο πεποιήκαμεν. For similar language, perhaps implicitly condemning their deed, see Josephus, *Ant.* 1.340: πράξαντες δὲ ταῦτα δίχα τῆς τοῦ πατρὸς γνώμης.

57. The *Testament* further idealizes Levi by casting him as a devout man of prayer (2.4) who experienced heavenly dreams and visions (2.5–5.7; 8.1-19), spoke with angels (5.3-6), and was rewarded with the blessing of the priesthood (2.10; 4.2; 5.2; 8.3-17). Levi is further idealized if, with R.H. Charles, Howard Clark Kee and James Kugel, we follow the text of the thirteenth-century Vatican MS (*Cod. Graec.* 731) and render 6.3: 'Then I advised my father and Reuben that they tell the sons of Hamor that they should *not* be circumcised' (H.C. Kee, 'Testaments of the Twelve Patriarchs' [trans.], in J.H. Charlesworth [ed.], *OTP*, I [New York: Doubleday, 1983]). Although the majority of MSS omit 'not' (cf. Hollander and De Jonge, *The Testaments*, pp. 146-47), Kugel ('The Story of Dinah', pp. 6-12) shows that *Testament of Levi* (and Theodotus) portray Levi as originally opposed to the idea of Shechemite circumcision and its corollary, intermarriage.

58. Hollander and De Jonge, *The Testaments*, p. 148, take Levi's 'I saw' (ἐγὼ εἶδον) in 6.8 (cf. 9.2) as an allusion to this dream vision. Prior to receiving this lengthy dream (2.55.7), Levi had been filled with 'a spirit of understanding from the Lord' (2.3). Kugel, 'The Story of Dinah', pp. 25-28, has shown how divine sanction for the massacre was likely derived from the last clause of Gen. 34.7 (see *Jub.* 30.5-6; Judg. 9.2; *Jos. Asen* 23.14; cf. Theodotus, Josephus, LXX).

because [διότι] they had wanted to do the same thing to Sarah and Rebecca that they did to Dinah, our sister. But the Lord prevented them.

It turns out that the rape of Dinah was 'only the latest incident in a series of crimes' dating back to the abduction of great-grandmother Sarah by Abimelech king of Gerar (Gen. 20).[59]

How is it that our author could compare such distant stories as the abduction and safe return of Sarah, and the near abduction of Rebecca with the rape of Jacob's unmarried daughter? Two factors may be significant.[60]

1. *The overlapping identities of the perpetrators.* Hamor and his son Shechem are called 'Hivites' (Gen. 34.2), but since Jacob feared retaliation from 'the Canaanites and the Perizzites' (Gen. 34.30), we may infer that the three groups are closely related (cf. Deut. 7.1; 20.17). The Abimelech of Genesis 20 and 26, we recall, was a *Canaanite* city-king.

2. *The social status of the victims.* Dinah is consistently presented as the *sister* of Jacob's two sons (34.13, 14, 25, 27, 31). Of particular importance is the final, defiant question posed by Simeon and Levi: 'Should he treat *our sister* [אֲחוֹתֵנוּ] as a harlot?' (v. 31). Correspondingly, it was precisely their status as *sisters* that made Sarah and Rebecca available to the Canaanites of Gerar (Gen. 20.2, 5, 12-13; 26.7, 9).

There can be no doubting that *Testament of Levi* justifies Levi's behavior by invoking secondary episodes. It may also have implicitly elevated Dinah's status, since she now has a place alongside the other famous sister-matriarchs. Furthermore, it should not escape our attention that this linkage also implies a substantial revision of the biblical Abimelech episodes (Gen. 20.4-6; 26.9-11). Whereas the biblical accounts of those stories are somewhat ambivalent, bordering on sympathetic, the version implied by *Testament of Levi* categorically condemns

---

59. Kugel, *The Bible as It Was*, p. 241. A more common charge against the Shechemites was the 'crime' of being a *foreigner*, in keeping with Gen. 34.14-16 (see Jud. 9.2; *Jub.* 30.11-14; Josephus, *Ant.* 1.337-38; cf. Kugel, 'The Story of Dinah', p. 17). Only in Theodotus (frg. 7, in Eusebius, *Praep. Evang.* 9.22.9) do we find a parallel indictment of the Shechemites for a string of transgressions: 'God smote the inhabitants of Shechem, for they did not honor whoever came to them, whether evil or noble. Nor did they determine rights or laws throughout the city. Rather, deadly works were their care'.

60. One wonders if a further basis for associating these passages was the similar phrasing in Gen. 34.7 (וְכֵן לֹא יֵעָשֶׂה) and 20.9 (מַעֲשִׂים אֲשֶׁר לֹא־יֵעָשׂוּ) used to refer to the offense.

the motives and conduct of Israel's Canaanite neighbors. As such, the primary passage has exerted 'reverse' exegetical force on the secondary episodes.

b. *God Rewards Those Who Fast: Genesis 39.6 in Light of Daniel 1.8-16 in* Testament of Joseph *3.4*

The greatly expanded account of Joseph's experience in Potiphar's house in the *Testament of Joseph* arguably includes a quiet appeal to another biblical episode: the story of Daniel and his three friends (Daniel 1.8-16).[61] According to *Testament of Joseph* 3, Joseph was tormented by Potiphar's wife for seven agonizing years, during which he led an austere life of fasting and prayer. Notwithstanding this rigorous asceticism, however, Joseph's physical appearance actually improved over time:

> For those seven years I fasted, and yet seemed to the Egyptians like someone who was living luxuriously, for those who fast for the sake of God [οἱ διὰ τὸν θεὸν νηστεύοντες] receive graciousness of countenance [τοῦ προσώπου τὴν χάριν λαμβάνουσιν] (3.4).

In the divine economy, Joseph assures us, devout acts of fasting are rewarded with enhanced physical grace and beauty.[62] Almost certainly, this reference to 'those who fast' (οἱ...νηστεύοντες) was meant to recall the episode of Dan. 1.8-16, in which four pious Israelite slaves, who traded palace fare for vegetables and water, were singled out for their increased beauty.[63]

Ancient tradents surely recognized that Joseph and Daniel had much in common. Both were renowned for their dreams and interpretations; both maintained their integrity under extreme duress; both rose from slavery to prestigious palace appointments; and both were good looking (Gen. 39.6; Dan. 1.4, 15).[64] Such parallels could easily explain the allusion to Daniel in the *Testament of Joseph*. There may be, however,

---

61. Acknowledged, but not explained by H.C. Kee, 'Testaments', p. 820, and Hollander and DeJonge, *The Testaments*, p. 376.

62. This reward-for-piety model of ethics pervades and unites *Testament of Joseph* (cf. 9.2; 11.1; 18.1-4).

63. Since the narrator is the biblical 'Joseph' himself, he cannot appeal *explicitly* to events of a much later period.

64. Joseph is called יְפֵה־תֹאַר וִיפֵה מַרְאֶה ('handsome in form and appearance'); of Daniel and friends it is said נִרְאָה מַרְאֵיהֶם טוֹב וּבְרִיאֵי בָּשָׂר ('their appearance seemed better and they were fatter of flesh'). Note the shared use of מַרְאֶה.

reason to suspect that the Daniel story served an explicitly exegetical function. Genesis 39.6 contains a curious sequence of clauses:

> So he [Potiphar] left all that he had in Joseph's charge; and with him there, he had no concern for anything but the food that he ate (כִּי אִם־הַלֶּחֶם אֲשֶׁר־הוּא אוֹכֵל).
> Now Joseph was handsome and good-looking (וַיְהִי יוֹסֵף יְפֵה־תֹאַר וִיפֵה מַרְאֶה).

Two questions. First, why does the biblical story single out Potiphar's food-related concerns, almost as though Joseph could not be trusted in that one area? Some ancients thought 'the food he ate' euphemistically referred to sexual relations with his wife.[65] Others, among whom we should probably include *Testament of Joseph*, saw a reference to Egyptian dietary restrictions.[66] On this reading, Joseph was barred from eating with, or preparing food for, Potiphar.

Secondly, why does Scripture shift so abruptly from *Potiphar's food* to *Joseph's beauty*? How might these two possibly be related? For the *Testament of Joseph*, the answer comes from reading Gen. 39.6 through the lens of Daniel 1. His handsome *appearance* was not simply the reason women found him so desirable (Gen. 39.6c-7); it was also his reward for piously adhering to Jewish *food* laws (Gen. 39.6b-c; cf. Dan. 1.8, 16).[67]

---

65. Possibly under the influence of Gen. 39.9 and Prov. 30.20. Cf. *Gen. R.* 86.6; *Targ. Ps.-J.*; Rashi. Cf. N. Sarna, *The JPS Torah Commentary: Genesis* (Philadelphia: Jewish Publication Society of America, 1989), p. 272. Some see a more general reference to Potiphar's private affairs. So Claus Westermann, *Genesis 37–50: A Commentary* (trans. J.J. Scullion; Minneapolis: Augsburg, 1996), pp. 63-64; G. Wenham, *Genesis 16–50* (WBC; Waco, TX: Word Books, 1994), p. 374.

66. N. Sarna, *The JPS Torah Commentary: Genesis*, cites Radak and Ibn Ezra among medieval commentators taking this view. Cf. E.A. Speiser, *Genesis* (AB; Garden City, NY: Doubleday, 1982), p. 303; G. Von Rad, *Genesis* (trans. John Marks; OTL; Philadelphia: Westminster Press, 1961), p. 359. Important for this view is Gen. 43.32, which draws attention to ritual separation at Egyptian meals: 'They served him [Joseph] by himself, and them [Joseph's brothers] by themselves, and the Egyptians who ate with him by themselves, because the Egyptians could not eat with the Hebrews, for that is an abomination to the Egyptians'. Some (e.g. *Jub.* 39.4-5; Josephus, *Ant.* 2.41; Philo, *Jos.* 8) omit all references to Potiphar's food.

67. Food and the benefits of fasting are major motifs in *Testament of Joseph*. See 1.5; 3.3, 5; 4.8; 6.1, 3-4, 7; 9.2; 10.1-2.

Astute readers might also sense that the Daniel story has been clarified as well. Although Dan. 1.15 fails to state explicitly the *cause* behind the improved appearance of Daniel and his friends,[68] the *Testament of Joseph* confirms what all readers of Daniel surely suspect—that it was God's doing, 'for those who fast for the sake of God receive graciousness of countenance'.

4. *Conclusion*

Much more needs to be done to test and strengthen the proposals with which we began.[69] But our findings so far suggest that an important *interpretive strategy* in Rewritten Bible involved linking up near or distant stories with one another. These narrative connections could be explicit and clearly marked, or more subtle and allusive; they may strike us as sensible, creative or quite contrived. But it would be a mistake to deny that they attest to early patterns of reading Scripture that were marked by a high respect for the story, and by an intense concern to fill its gaps and resolve its difficulties—in brief, by a genuinely *exegetical* orientation.

---

68. 'At the end of ten days it was observed that they appeared better and fatter than all the young men who had been eating the royal rations'.

69. Test passages in *LAB* are numerous: *LAB* 9.5-6 links Exod. 2.1-2 and Gen. 38.24-25; *LAB* 12.3 links Exod. 32.1-6 and Gen. 11.6; *LAB* 19.11 links Deut. 34 and Gen. 9.13-15; and *LAB* 40.2 links Judg. 11.36 with Gen. 22. Similarly, *T. Reub.* 3.11 interprets Gen. 35.22 by invoking 2 Sam. 11.2; *T. Reub.* 4.8-10 explains Gen. 35.22 by appealing to Gen. 39, and *T. Reub* .5.6, by recalling Gen. 6.1-4.

Part II

INTERPRETATION IN THE NEW TESTAMENT

THE NOUN-VOCABULARY OF JESUS' ARAMAIC[*]

John Pairman Brown

Of all the New Testament strata, at least the sayings attributed to Jesus must largely rest on an Aramaic base. I make few assumptions about it; I guess that Mark's incidents rest on an oral Aramaic base, and that a Greek document behind Matthew and Luke rested on a written Aramaic one, but I hardly use those guesses. I do not ask which sayings are authentic. I add a few sayings from the mouth of other Galilaeans. To avoid wishful thinking, and in view of uncertainties over Palestinian forms, I do not reconstruct sayings as a whole. Rather I focus on their most marked feature, the noun-vocabulary. I chiefly rely on the Gospel versions in dialects of Aramaic: the Syriac of Edessa, first in two unpointed MSS of the Gospels perhaps of the late second century,[1] and then the complete New Testament, the Peshitto (hereafter Pesh.);[2] later a Palestinian dialect in Syriac script.[3] There is little evidence that the translators had an oral tradition of Jesus' Aramaic; but speaking as they did his mother tongue, and living in communities like his, they are our best evidence for it. Differences in dialect and date are partly correctible from the rabbinic literature, Palmyrene and Nabataean, and new papyrus texts. I assume that the loan words of rabbinic Hebrew were available to Aramaic also.

The Aramaic noun-vocabulary underlying Jesus' sayings, far from being one more witness to primeval Semitic, has been infiltrated by the

---

[*] A condensed form of this paper was read to the Society of Biblical Literature in San Francisco, November 1997.

1. The Curetonian MS (London and Berlin) and the Sinaitic palimpsest (St Catherine's, Sinai); F.C. Burkitt (ed.), *Evangelion da-Mepharreshe* (2 vols.; Cambridge: Cambridge University Press, 1904).

2. *The New Testament in Syriac* (London: British and Foreign Bible Society, 1950).

3. A.S. Lewis and M.D. Gibson, *The Palestinian Syriac Lectionary of the Gospels* (London: Kegan Paul, 1899).

languages of imperial rule in Palestine—Akkadian, Iranian, Greek and Latin.[4] Some loans from Akkadian go back to Ugarit; the sturdiness of the loans in Aramaic is shown by their appearance in the Arabic of the Qur'an![5] Our study will make proposals about the overall role of Aramaic in the Near East; and end by sketching the development in Roman Palestine of a *lingua franca* (in a new sense) whose primary witness is the New Testament.

1. Aramaic as the Language of Jesus

First, I offer a brief vindication that Jesus thought and spoke in Aramaic rather than Greek—nobody thinks he spoke Hebrew.[6] *Transcriptions*: κορβᾶν Mk 7.11 'gift'; ῥαββί Mt. 23.7 'Rabbi'; Σατανά Mk 8.33 'Satan'; ῥακά Mt. 5.22 'stupid'; the words of power, Mk 5.41, 7.34; the word from the Cross, Mk 15.34. All are recognized by the Syriac translators. *Calques*: 'son of X'.[7] Debt as sin: Lk. 13.4, 'Do you think that [the eighteen] were "debtors" [ὀφειλέται] more than all the men in Jerusalem?'[8] *Awkwardnesses*: Jesus' prayer surely had a clear adjective for 'bread'; ἐπιούσιον, Mt. 6.11, shows that the translator failed to understand it. Mk 2.21 replaces lost household terms with abstracts: 'Nobody sews a piece [ἐπίβλημα] of unshrunk cloth on an old garment; if one does, the patch [πλήρωμα] tears away from it'. Lk. 11.41, πλὴν τὰ ἐνόντα δότε ἐλεημοσύνην, is barely Greek.[9]

---

4.   See Sebastian P. Brock, 'Greek Words in the Syriac Gospels (*Vet* and *Pe*)', *Le Muséon* 80 (1967), pp. 389-426; John F. Healey, 'Lexical Loans in Early Syriac: A Comparison with Nabataean Aramaic', *Studi Epigrafici e Linguistici sul Vicino Oriente antico* 12 (1995), pp. 75-84 (a special issue on 'The Lexicography of the Ancient Near Eastern Languages').

5.   Arthur Jeffery, *The Foreign Vocabulary of the Quran* (Baroda: Oriental Institute, 1938).

6.   The only indications of Hebrew in the sayings are puns for which Jesus may well be responsible: זְבֻל 'divine residence' in Βεεζεβούλ; μωρέ Mt. 5.22 'fool' with מוֹרֶד 'rebellious', Deut. 21.18.

7.   'Sons of the bridechamber', Mk 2.19; 'sons of the kingdom', straight or ironically, Mt. 8.12, 13.38; 'son of Gehenna', Mt. 23.15; 'son of peace', Lk. 10.6; 'sons of this age, of light', Lk. 20.34; 'sons of the resurrection', Lk. 20.36.

8.   But 'debt' in the Lord's prayer may originally have been literal or ambivalent.

9.   Matthew Black, *An Aramaic Approach to the Gospels and Acts* (Oxford: Clarendon Press, 2nd edn, 1954) stresses alliteration in his restored Aramaic; and

Sobriquets:[10] Jesus as a second Adam renames the persons and agencies around him—including himself. Many of the new names are sardonic; he takes people ironically at their own evaluation or that of others. Rabbinic parallels are distant, since Jesus transforms whatever he takes up. *Transcribed*: Κηφᾶς Jn 1.42, Gal. 1.18 for Peter, 'thick-headed' or, perhaps ironically, 'unstable'; Βοανηργές Mk 3.17 (corrupt) 'sons of thunder'; Βεεζεβούλ perhaps Jesus' own coinage, 'master of the house', οἰκοδεσπότην Mt. 10.25; Μαμωνᾶ personified 'Property'; Γέεννα 'garbage dump'; Ἀββᾶ Mk 14.36, 'Daddy' (if a children's form).

Translated: (1) 'Hypocrites'. ὑποκριτής is an 'actor': surely in Jesus' lifetime there was a theater in Sepphoris seating 4,500.[11] Mt. 7.5 'Actor [ὑποκριτά, Pesh. באפא בסן], first take the beam out of your eye'; the Syriac is an idiom for 'respecting persons', here denoting the actor who wears a wooden mask or a 'beam' on his eye. (2) 'This generation',[12] ἡ γενεὰ αὕτη names Jesus' contemporary world which rejects all messages. It is the exact opposite of the kingdom of God, for they are identically introduced: Lk. 13.18, 'What is the kingdom of God like, and to what shall I compare it?'; 7.31, 'To what shall I compare the men of this generation, and what are they like?' (3) 'Kingdom of heaven/God'. Jesus' single overarching concept is assembled from scattered usages. To recite the Shema' is to take on 'the yoke of the kingdom of heaven', עול מלכות שמים *m. Ber.* 2.2; *Targum Jonathan* on Zech. 14.9, 'And the kingdom of Y. [מלכותא דיוי] shall be revealed upon all the inhabitants of earth in that time'. (4) 'The Son of Man'. Elsewhere[13] I propose that this is truly Jesus' self-designation, drawn from what others called him, 'This fellow'. Lk. 7.34, opponents say 'Lo, a *fellow* [ἄνθρωπος] who is a glutton and winebibber'; it is their response to his self-description, 'The *Son of Man* [ὁ υἱὸς τοῦ ἀνθρώπου] came eating and drinking'.

mistranslations, of which the most plausible is Mt. 7.6 τὸ ἅγιον for קדשא 'gold ring' (see below).

10. My 'The Son of Man: "This Fellow"', *Bib* 58 (1977), pp. 361-87, pp. 370-71.

11. Zeev Weiss, 'Sepphoris', *New Encyclopaedia of Archaeological Excavations in the Holy Land* (4 vols.; New York: Simon & Schuster, 1993), IV, p. 1324. It was the first part of the city you would reach, walking up from the SE.

12. Joachim Jeremias, *New Testament Theology: The Proclamation of Jesus* (trans. John Bowden; New York: Charles Scribner's Sons, 1971), p. 135, notes the fourteen sayings with this phrase as 'of extreme rebuke'.

13. N. 10 above.

Mk 2.1-12, 'Why does *this one* [οὗτος] speak thus?... The *Son of Man* has authority on earth to forgive sins'.[14] (5) 'Sinners', 'publicans and harlots'. Lk. 7.34, opponents define Jesus' entourage by calling him the 'friend of publicans and sinners'; then at Mt. 21.31, 'The publicans and harlots precede you into the kingdom', he ironically so refers to them himself. So at Mk 2.17, 'I did not come to call righteous but sinners'; Lk. 15.7, beside one repentant sinner there are 99 just needing no repentance.[15]

'Amen I say to you': While Jesus says not to swear at all (Mt. 5.33-37; 23.16-22), he certifies his sayings by a formula which once has the grammar of a Hebrew oath: Mk 8.12 ἀμὴν λέγω ὑμῖν εἰ δοθήσεται τῇ γενεᾷ ταύτῃ σημεῖον 'A sign will *not* be given this generation'. 1 Sam. 19.6, Saul says, 'As Yahweh lives, he shall *not* be put to death', חַי־יְהוָה אִם־יוּמָת; LXX like Mark ζῇ κύριος εἰ ἀποθανεῖται. It borrows the grammar of a curse, 2 Kgs 6.30-31, 'Thus may God do to me and more also, *if* Elisha's head remains on him today'. The 'Amen' sayings, predominantly negative, then are perhaps to be expanded with a suppressed curse, 'As I speak truly to you, [may I be proved a false prophet] *if* a sign is given this generation'.

Counterindications that Jesus' language was Greek: Luke in the prodigal son parable has nine aorist participles introducing a main verb, also two genitive absolutes. But (see p. 255 below) the parable also includes four Greek words which went into Aramaic; Luke may have freely translated an Aramaic original but retained Greek vocabulary he found there in transcription. Sometimes the sayings given Jesus presuppose the LXX just where it differs from the Hebrew. That suggests one of two unpalatable conclusions: that the boy Jesus knew Greek, and the Nazareth rabbi explained that difficult book, the Hebrew Bible, out of the LXX; or that such passages were created in Greek out of whole cloth. A third possibility: the rabbi explained the Hebrew text out of a targumic tradition more Hellenistic than that recorded in *Onqelos* and *Jonathan*.

Mk 12.16, Jesus asks 'Whose is this image [εἰκών]?' and goes on 'Give God the things of God', that is, one's whole self. The connection

---

14. Once rabbinic 'son of man' refers to oneself, בר נש דכוותי 'someone like me': M. Sokoloff, *A Dictionary of Jewish Palestinian Aramaic of the Byzantine Period* (Ramat-Gan: Bar-Ilan, 1990), col. 100b.

15. The narrators at Mk 2.15, Lk. 15.1 naively conclude that Galilee had actual social groups of publicans and sinners.

is Gen. 1.26 LXX where humanity is made 'after our image [εἰκόνα] and likeness'; *Targum Pseudo-Jonathan*[16] for 'likeness' has כד"יוקננא, a distortion of אי'קוני; for at Gen. 5.3 the LXX for 'image' has εἰκόνα and *Pseudo-Jonathan* correctly now אי'קוניא. *Exod. R.* 30.16, 'Parable of a man who insulted the image [אי'קונין] of the king and came before his *bema* [בימה]'.

Fitzmyer[17] lists occasions on which Jesus might have conversed in Greek but thinks it unlikely that he would ever 'teach and preach in Greek'. Selby,[18] from Welsh usage, holds that 'in some situations (home, discipleship groups, synagogue) Jesus spoke in Aramaic, whilst, in the world at large, he spoke Greek'. But even on that assumption, the Greek ascribed to Jesus could only have been formulated in Aramaic; I was always sure that César Chavez in his clear English said only what he had previously thought in Spanish. Black follows the demonstration of Burney[19] 'that the sayings of Jesus are cast in the form of Semitic poetry' and concludes :

> Jesus did not commit anything to writing, but by His use of poetic form and language He ensured that His sayings would not be forgotten. The impression they make in [Black's reconstructed] Aramaic is of carefully premeditated style and studied deliverances; we have to do with prophetic utterances of the style and grandeur of Isaiah.[20]

That is not exactly wrong; but it leaves out the whole prehistory of Jesus' Aramaic. Hebrew was the language of a clannish people, whose poets relied on their predecessors; Aramaic from the beginning was the administrative language of a series of empires, and wherever it went picked up local vocabulary. Above all, Jesus, a man of the streets and

16. E.G. Clarke, *Targum Pseudo-Jonathan of the Pentateuch [Brit Mus MS Add 27031]* (Hoboken: Ktav, 1984).

17. Joseph A. Fitzmyer, 'Did Jesus Speak Greek?', *BARev* (Sept./Oct.) (1992), pp. 58-63.

18. G.R. Selby, *Jesus, Aramaic and Greek* (Doncaster: Brynmill, 1990), p. 104.

19. Black, *Aramaic Approach*, p. 105. C.F. Burney, *The Poetry of our Lord: An Examination of the Formal Elements of Hebrew Poetry in the Discourses of Jesus Christ* (Oxford: Clarendon Press, 1925).

20. Black, *Aramaic Approach*, p. 142. Joseph A. Fitzmyer, *A Wandering Aramean: Collected Aramaic Essays* (SBLMS, 25; Chico, CA: Scholars Press, 1979), pp. 16-17, while noting that we have little specifically Aramaic poetry to compare with the sayings, adds, 'I am not calling in question the existence of the rhythmic sayings attributed to Jesus in the Greek gospels or even their poetic character'.

fields, used words in common use to describe the village culture of Galilee from which he drew his examples.

2. *Akkadian in the Aramaic of the Sayings*

Already in the seventh century BCE, Aramaic, the pen-and-ink business tongue of Babylon, was displacing cuneiform Akkadian as vernacular also; the Jewish community deported there in 597 BCE heard Akkadianized Aramaic around it. (The Babel story nicely fits the linguistic mixture.) It picked up that language and sent it back home: the Jewish military colony at Elephantine in the fifth century was wholly Aramaic-speaking; Neh. 8.8 may mean that Ezra read the law in Hebrew and interpreted it in Aramaic. Kaufman[21] distinguishes between Akkadian loan words in Aramaic and cases where both simply record original Semitic stock. The Akkadian loan words in Jesus' Aramaic reflect the exile: (a) Names of occupations and social groups; (b) urban design; besides (c) miscellaneous terms including trade. In the sayings and in rabbinic, as in real life, Babylonian Judaism is marvelously restored from the dead.

Occupations and Social Groups
Babylon was an old city with a stratified society where each social group was distinct and named. The classification is exported to Palestine and recorded by Talmud and Gospel.

(1) 'Physician'. Everywhere he inspires proverbs. Mk 2.17, 'Those who are well do not need a physician [Pesh. אסיא]'; Lk. 4.23, 'Physician, heal yourself [אסיא אסא נפשך]'. From Akkadian *asû*, itself from Sumerian A.ZU;[22] old Israel had no physician class! Its rapacity was proverbial: *y. Ta'an.* 66d26, 'Honor your physician [איקיר לאסייך] before you need him'; *b. B. Qam.* 85a, 'A physician who heals for nothing is worth nothing', a wholly Akkadian phrase: אסיא דמגן במגן.[23] The

---

21. Stephen A. Kaufman, *The Akkadian Influences on Aramaic* (Assyriological Studies 19; Chicago: University of Chicago Press, 1974).

22. Kaufman, *Influences*, p. 75, *CAD* xi.I.112.

23. Aramaic מגן 'freely': Mt. 10.8, 'Freely have you received, freely give', δωρεὰν ἐλάβετε, δωρεὰν δότε; Pesh. מגן נסבתון מגן הבו. A verb in Ugaritic *mgn* (*KTU* 1.4.I.21), Gen. 14.20 מַגֵּן 'delivered'. In the Palmyrene bilingual *PAT* 0282, מגן = προῖκα. Loan word from Vedic *magham*, 'gift' via Hurrian (Kaufman, *Influences*,

'proverb' of Lk. 4.23 is international, likely Akkadian: Aesop 69,[24] the frog claims to be a physician, but the fox objects, πῶς σὺ ἄλλους σώσεις, σαυτὸν χωλὸν ὄντα μὴ θεραπεύων 'How will you save others [cf. Mk 15.31!] when you can't cure your own lameness?'; *Gen. R.* 23.4, 'Physician, physician, cure your lameness!' חֵונְרְתָךְ אָסִי אַסְיָא אַסְיָא.

(2) 'Poor man', πτωχός common, Pesh. מִסְכְּנָא. Qoh. 9.15, 'A poor wise man', א'שׁ מִסְכֵּן חָכָם.[25] From Akkadian *muškēnu*;[26] in one text the poor (*muš-ke-nu*) address Šamaš daily. Frequent in the Qur'an in lists of the needy, 'kinsfolk, orphans, travelers, the poor', for example, 30.28 *miskīnu*. Thence to Spanish *mezquino* 'poor', attested CE 950;[27] perhaps Moorish beggars pointed at themselves, *miskīn, miskīn*! Via Provençal to Italian at Dante's *Inferno* 27.115 *meschini* 'servitors'; French *mesquin*.

(3) 'Merchant'. Mt. 13.45 'a merchant (ἐμπόρῳ, Pesh. תגרא) seeking goodly pearls' (see below). From Akkadian *tamkaru* and Sumerian DAM.GAR. Same equivalence in the *Hymn of the Pearl* 18[28] תגרי מדנחא = ἀνατολικῶν ἐμπόρων 'merchants of the East'; and in Palmyrene *passim*, for example, *PAT* 1373. *b. B. Meṣ.* 40b זבין וזבן תגרא איקרי 'If one buys and sells [at the same price], can you call such a one a trader?' Mt. 22.5 ἐμπορίαν 'business', Pesh. תאגורתא, Qur'an 34.37 *tijāratu* 'merchandise'.

(4) 'Publican', τελώνης = Pesh. מכסא. Same equivalence in the Palmyrene Tariff (*PAT* 0259 I.7), 'disputes between traders [ἐνπόρων =

---

p. 67). Akk. *magannu* 'gift, as a gift': 'My house is worth one talent of silver, *u ana ma-gannu naši* but he has taken it for nothing' (*CAD* x.I.32).

24. E. Chambry (ed.), *Fables* (Paris: Les Belles Lettres, 2nd edn, 1960).

25. Hence a denominative verb: *b. Soṭ.* 11a, 'Whoever makes building his business will get poor [מהמסכן]'; 2 Cor. 8.9 'though rich he became poor [ἐπτώχευσεν]', Pesh. אתמסכן.

26. *CAD* x.II.275; Kaufman, *Influences*, p. 74, who finds himself 'unable to isolate or comprehend the linguistic forces which caused this specific value term to become the most widespread and long-lived of the Akkadian loanwords'.

27. J. Corominas and J.A. Pascual, *Diccionario crítico etimológico castellano e hispánico*, IV (Madrid: Gredos, 1981), pp. 62-63.

28. Syriac text edited by A.A. Bevan, *The Hymn of the Soul* (Texts and Studies, 3; Cambridge: Cambridge University Press, 1897); transcribed by Heinz Kruse, 'The Return of the Prodigal: Fortunes of a Parable on its Way to the Far East', *Or* 47 (1978), pp. 163-214. Greek translation in a single MS, Maximilianus Bonnet, *Acta Apostolorum Apocrypha* II.2 (repr.; Hildesheim: George Olms, 1959), *Acta Thomae* pp. 108-113, 219-224.

תגרא] and publicans [τελώνας = מכסיא]'. Num. 31.28 מֶכֶס is Akk. *miksu*, and so Aram. מכסא from *mākisu*.[29] An Akkadian letter of 740–705 BCE records a *ma-ki-su* at Sidon.[30] With 'publicans and harlots' (Mt. 21.31) see *b. Šab.* 33b where Romans build streets (שווקים) only for harlots (זונות) and bridges only for taxation (מכס). Like banditry, tax-collecting is felt hereditary: *b. Šebu.* 39a, 'You will find no family with a tax-collector [מוכס] whose members may not all be considered tax-collectors, or containing a bandit [ליסטין = λῃστής] in which they are not all bandits'.

Some Others

(5) 'Student', μαθητής with Pesh. תלמידא, see 1 Chron. 25.8 תַּלְמִיד with Akk. *talmīdu*[31]; only in Akk. does this form designate occupations.

(6) 'Carpenter', τέκτων with Pesh. נגרא; Galilaeans call Jesus both 'carpenter' (Mk 6.3) and 'son of a carpenter' (Mt. 13.55), for the trade is hereditary. Akkadian *naggāru*, Sumerian NAGAR; Elephantine 'head of the carpenters', סנן נגריא[32]; Arabic surname *najjār*. *b. 'Abod. Zar.* 50b (Amos 7.14) of a self-taught rabbi, 'I am not a carpenter nor the son of a carpenter [בר נגרא]'. (7) 'Eunuch', Mt. 19.12 εὐνοῦχοι with Pal. Syr. סריסין. But Bib. Heb. סָרִיס of various court officials. Akk. *ša reši* 'head man'[33]; later the harem-keeper monopolized the name. (8) 'Adversary', Mt. 5.25 ἀντίδικος with Pesh. בעל דין; from Akk. *bel dīni* 'master of judgment'.[34] In the divine court (*Avoth* IV.22) God is judge, witness, adversary (בעל דין).

Features of Urban Design

(1) 'Temple'. Alleged saying Mk 14.58, 'I shall destroy this temple [ναόν, Pesh. היכלא] made with hands'. Bib. Heb. הֵיכָל first 'palace' (1 Kgs 21.1), then 'Temple' (Isa. 6.1). Early loan from Akk. *ekallu*[35] 'palace', Sumerian É.GAL 'big house'; at Ugarit (*KTU* 1.4.V.36) *bhth*

---

29. Kaufman, *Influences*, p. 72.

30. H.W.F. Saggs, 'The Nimrud Letters, 1952—Part II', *Iraq* 17 (1955), pp. 126-60; Letter XII.10-20, p. 128.

31. Kaufman, *Influences*, p. 107.

32. A. Cowley, *Aramaic Papyri of the Fifth Century B.C.* (Oxford: Clarendon Press, 1923), 26.9.

33. Kaufman, *Influences*, p. 100.

34. *CAD* iii, p. 155.

35. Kaufman, *Influences*, p. 27.

and *hklh* '[Ba'al's] house, palace' run parallel. Ahiqar 17 היכלא בבב 'in the gate of the palace' of Esarhaddon. Palmyrene in the new sense (*PAT* 1347), 'temple of Bel', היכלא די בל. *Megillath Ta'anith* 11.[36]
(2) 'Street, square'. Pesh. שׁוק stands for both ἀγορά 'market' and πλατεῖα 'broad street, public square'; the latter also went into Aramaic פלטיא. A proverb at Mt. 20.3, 'standing idle in the market', ἑστῶτας ἐν τῇ ἀγορ ἀργούς, Pesh. דקימין בשוק ובטילין; see *b. Pes.* 55a, 'Go and see how many idle there are in the market'; פוק חזי כמה בטלני איכא בשוקא. שׁוק is an Aramaism in late Bib. Heb., Cant. 3.2 (cf. Prov. 7.8; Qoh. 12.4-5) 'in the streets and squares', בַּשְּׁוּקִים וּבָרְחֹבוֹת, LXX ἐν ταῖς ἀγοραῖς καὶ ἐν ταῖς πλατείαις. At Elephantine.[37] At bilingual Palmyra in an elegant calque, רב שוק = ἀγορανομήσαντα *PAT* 0278 'market-overseer', cf. *Num. R.* 20.18 בעל השוק; ἀγορανόμος became Plautine *agoranomus*. From Akkadian *šūqu*.[38] Hence Arabic *sūq*: Qur'an 25.8, 'What ails this messenger [the Prophet] that he eats food and walks in the markets [*'aswāq*]?' Compare Jesus as 'glutton', Mt. 11.19; Lk. 13.26, 'You taught in our streets [πλατείαις, בשׁוקין]'. Hence in picturesque nineteenth-century Orientalism French *souk* and English *suk*.

Further Urban Design
(3) 'Rooftop'. Greeks transferred δῶμα for 'rooftop', Mt. 10.27, Mk 13.15, where Pesh. אגרא; *Ruth R.* 3.2 איגר פלטין 'the roof of the παλάτιον'[39] from Akk. *igāru* 'wall'; Palestinian builders developed a new style with transferred Akk. name.
(4) 'Bridechamber'. Mk 2.19, 'the sons of the bridechamber' οἱ υἱοὶ τοῦ νυμφῶνος, Pesh. בנוהי דגנונא; just so *b. B. Bat.* 14b בני גננא. Kaufman[40] from Akk. *ganūnu* 'living quarters, bedroom', again reapplied.
(5) 'Furnace'. Mt. 6.30 κλίβανος, Pesh. תנורא; Bib. Heb. תַּנּוּר, probably with Akk. *tinūru* 'oven'.[41] In both the Akk. and Aramaic of the Tell Fekherye bilingual in a curse of scarcity (Lev. 26.28), 'And may one hundred women bake bread in an oven [Aram. תנור]'.[42]

---

36. J.A. Fitzmyer and D.J. Harrington, *A Manual of Palestinian Aramaic Texts* (Biblica et Orientalia, 34; Rome: Biblical Institute Press, 1978), p. 186.
37. Cowley, *Papyri*, 5.14)
38. Kaufman, *Influences*, p. 94.
39. Kaufman, *Influences*, p. 57.
40. Kaufman, *Influences*, p. 51.
41. Kaufman, *Influences*, p. 108.
42. E. Lipiński, *Studies in Aramaic Inscriptions and Onomastics* (Orientalia Lovaniensia Analecta, 57; Leuven: Peeters, 1994), chapter 2.

Other Akkadian Loan Words

(1) 'Demon'. δαιμόνιον must rest on some Aramaic word. The Old Syr. in the sayings has Akk. שׁאדא throughout; the Pesh. sometimes Iranian דיוא, probably under Sasanid influence.[43] Deut. 32.17 שֵׁדִים, LXX δαιμονίοις. In a Pseudo-Daniel from Qumran[44] the Israelites 'sacrificed their children to the demons of error', לשׁידי טעותא. Loan from Akk. *šedu*,[45] 'a spirit representing the vital force' of an individual or temple, both propitious and malevolent (*CAD* xv.256-58). The unclean spirit that leaves a man, and then says 'I will return to my house from which I came' (Mt. 12.43-45), is surely one of the *daimonia*, and paralleled in 'the evil (portended) by an evil *š[edu]* that flits about restlessly in the house of a man' (*CAD* xv.258b).

(2) 'Gold ring'. Mt. 7.6 'Give not the holy [τὸ ἅγιον, Pesh. קודשׁא] to dogs, and cast not your pearls before swine'. The one clear mis-translation in sayings: Akk. *qudāšu* 'earring', unconnected with the root *qdš* 'holy'.[46] The Pesh. by accident restores the Aram. original. Jesus doubles Prov. 11.22 'a gold ring in the nose of a pig', נֶזֶם זָהָב בְּאַף חֲזִיר; at Gen. 24.22 *Targum Onqelos* has קדשׁא דדהבא for Heb. נֶזֶם זָהָב 'gold ring'.

(3) 'Pay'. μισθός literal at Lk. 10.7, mostly symbolic; Mt. 5.12, 'Your pay [Pesh. אגרא as always] is great in heaven'. Kaufman[47] finds the Aram. root simply cognate with Akk. *agaru* 'to hire'; but the noun derived from *igru*. Old Assyrian *ig-ri rābiṣi* 'hire of the policeman' (*CAD* i.45). Literal in Aramaic 'a doctor's fee', אגר אסיא—a wholly Akkadian

---

43. At Mt. 12.24 in a saying of Pharisees, Old Syr. and Pesh. agree in a distinction, 'This fellow only casts out demons [שׁאדא] by Beelzebul prince of the demons [רשׁא דדיוא]'. While most Indo-European forms of Sanskrit *deva* are honorific, the Iranian are pejorative. Thus Zarathushtra (*Yasna* 32.1) of the *daeva*; Xerxes (R.G. Kent, *Old Persian: Grammar, Texts, Lexicon* [AOS, 33; New Haven: American Oriental Society, 1953], p. 151 lines 35-41) at Persepolis overthrew worship of the *daiva*. The flying letter in the *Hymn of the Pearl* 50 is sealed to keep it from 'savage demons', דיוא מרירא, δαίμονας. At *b. Pes.* 110a Iranian *Aešma Daēva* 'Demon of Wrath' is described like Beelzebul, אשׁמדai מלכא דשׁידי 'Asmodaios ['Ασμοδαῖος, Tob. 3.8] king of the *šedim*'.

44. Fitzmyer and Harrington, *Manual*, p. 6 = 4QpsDan.

45. Kaufman, *Influences*, p. 101.

46. Kaufman, *Influences*, p. 86, *CAD* xiii, p. 293.

47. Kaufman, *Influences*, p. 33.

phrase.[48] Symbolic, 'the reward of the righteous',[49] אגרהון דצדיקיה. *'ajr* is common and symbolic in the Qur'an, 12.57, 'And the reward [*'ajrun*] of the Hereafter is better'.

(4) 'Throne'. θρόνος mostly Pesh. כורסיא, but at Mt. 19.28b תרנוס as Rabb. תרנוס which can hardly underly the Greek. Akk. *kussû* seems a very early loan[50] to Ugaritic. The curse 'may your throne be overturned' runs from Ugaritic through Byblos and Bib. Heb. to the New Testament: Dan. 5.20 'he was deposed from the throne of his kingship' חָנְחַת מִן־כָּרְסֵא מַלְכּוּתֵהּ with the Aramaic form in *r*.[51] Aram. with *r* כרסא *KAI* 216.7 (Bar-Rekab, eighth century BCE). The divine claim 'Heaven is my throne' runs from Isa. 66.1 (כִּסְאִי) through the New Testament to Qur'an 2.255 'His throne [*kursiyyuhu*] includes heaven and earth'. A unique continuity!

(5) 'Cock'. Mk 14.30 ἀλέκτορα, Pesh. תרנגלא; *y. Suk.* 55c19 'the cock crowed' קרא תרנגלא. Akk. *tarlugallu*,[52] Sumerian DAR.LUGAL. The domestic fowl came late to the Mediterranean. (6) 'Purple'. Dives (Lk. 16.19) wore 'purple and byssus', Pesh. reversed בוצא וארגונא; Est. 8.15 בּוּץ וְאַגְמָן, Dan. 5.7 אַרְגְּוָנָא. Akk. *argamannu* already in Ugaritic *argmn*, either 'tribute' or 'purple'. Like 'temple' and 'throne' an old Akk. loan in West Semitic.

3. *Iranian in the Aramaic of the Sayings*

Jews in Babylon were under Persian rule from its capture by Cyrus in 539 BCE to the victory of Alexander over Darius III at Arbela in 331 BCE. Babylon fell under Arsacid rule about 138 BCE, and the Parthian Pacorus installed the Hasmonean Antigonus in Jerusalem as king in 40 BCE (Josephus, *War* 1.269). Syriac Edessa was controlled by the Sasanid Sapor I from 240 CE. There is abundant evidence of Iranian administration over Jews from the Elephantine papyri, the Arsames dossier (edited by Driver), and the books of Ezra and Nehemiah. Telegdi

48. Sokoloff, *Dictionary*, pp. 34-35, citing the *Fragment Targ.* on Exod. 21.19.
49. *Targum Neofiti* on Num. 24.23.
50. Kaufman, *Influences*, p. 28.
51. My *Israel and Hellas* (BZAW, 231; Berlin: W. de Gruyter, 1995), pp. 276-77.
52. Kaufman, *Influences*, p. 108.

is a guide to Iranian loan words in Aramaic.[53] I cite such attestation of early Iranian as exists: the Old Persian cuneiform (edited by Kent); the Avesta; and the trilingual of Sapor at Naqš-i-Rustam in Greek, Arsacid Parthian and Sasanid Pehlevi, c. 260 CE.[54] Unlike the Akkadian, a number of these Iranian (or other Oriental) words have gone all the way into Latin: *margarita, angaria, gaza, paradisus* (late); and marginally into Greek, ἀσκάνδης, σαμψηρά.

(1) 'Paradise'. Lk. 23.43, 'Today you will be with me in paradise [παραδείσῳ, Pesh. בפרדיסא]'. Elsewhere I hope to chronicle the history of this word from old Iranian beginnings. The *paradeisoi* were the perquisite of the Great King and satraps; so that Jesus, while suffering the penalty inflicted on rebel satraps, claims their legitimacy. Qur'an 18.107, 'Lo, those who believe and do good works, theirs are the gardens of paradise', *jannātu 'lFirdawsi*. By this Qur'anic text, resting square on the LXX, Islam was preformed for its fateful acceptance in Iran.

(2) 'Limb', μέλος Mt. 5.29, 'It is better that one of your limbs [μελῶν, Pesh. הדמך] be lost than that your whole body [σῶμα] be thrown into Gehenna'. Dan. 2.5 הַדָּמִין תִּתְעַבְדוּן 'You shall be cut up into members'. Avestan *handāman*, 'NW Pehlevi' *handām*,[55] 'member'. The idea of persons as 'members' of a 'body' seems Hellenistic: 1 Cor. 12.12 'As the body [σῶμα]...has many members [μέλη, הדמא]'. But see *Odes of Solomon* 3.2 '[The Lord's] members are with him', והדמוהי לותה אנון.

(3) 'Weapon', ὅπλων Jn 18.3, Pesh. זינא. Lk. 11.22, 'panoply', Pesh. זינה. Cowley, *Papyri*, 31.8 זניהום 'their weapons'. Qumran Job Targum לנקשת זין 'in the clash of arms'.[56] *b. Sanh.* 104a זין אוכל זין 'weapon eating up weapon'.[57] Sapor, *Res Gestae* 58, Deran is 'chief of the armory', Parthian *zynpty*, Pehlevi *zynpt*, ζηνιπιτ. Avestan *Hymn to*

53. S. Telegdi, 'Essai sur la phonétique des emprunts iraniens en araméen talmudique: Glossaire', *Journal Asiatique* 226 (1935), pp. 224-56.

54. Nearly full ed. by A. Maricq, 'Res Gestae Divi Saporis', *Syria* 35 (1958), pp. 259-360; full Iranian texts in M. Back, *Die sassanidischen Staatsinschriften* (Acta Iranica, 18; 3rd ser.; Leiden: E.J. Brill, 1978). Glossary by Philippe Gignoux, *Glossaire des inscriptions Pehlevies et Parthes* (Corpus Inscriptionum Iranicarum, Sup. Series, 1; London: Lund Humphries, 1972).

55. Telegdi, 'Essai', p. 241 no. 59.

56. 11QtgJob 33.6, Fitzmyer and Harrington, *Manual*, p. 40.

57. This picks up the international theme, Prov. 27.17, 'iron sharpens iron'.

Mithra 96,[58] Mithra wields the 'strongest of weapons', *amavastəm ə̄m zaēn ̣am*.

(4) 'Time, season', καιρός, Pesh. זבנא, unlike χρόνος marks a *kind of time*. Mark 1.15 is hopeful, 'The time is fulfilled [πεπλήρωται ὁ καιρός, שלם לה זבנא, Vg *impletum est tempus*]'. Mk 13.33 demands watchfulness, 'You do not know when the time is', πότε ὁ καιρός, Pesh. אמתי הו זבנא, Vg *quando tempus sit*. זבנא with *b* is Syriac and Palmyrene; elsewhere זמנא with *Qoh*. 3.1 has two Heb. words for 'time', 'For everything there is a season, and a time for every matter under the heavens': לַכֹּל זְמָן וְעֵת לְכָל־חֵפֶץ תַּחַת הַשָּׁמָיִם. The LXX reverses expectation, τοῖς πᾶσιν χρόνος, καὶ καιρὸς τῷ παντὶ πράγματι.

Most take זְמָן from Iranian, comparing Pehlevi *zamān*, Persian *zāmān*.[59] Kaufman[60] thinks it rather from Akkadian *simānu* 'set time', but the first consonants are problematic. The double coloration of New Testament καιρός[61] also reflects Latin influence. In classical Greek καιρός is by itself positive. But in Polybius it can be by itself 'a dangerous time': 18.11.8 τόν παρόντα καιρὸν ἐκφυγεῖν 'to avoid the difficult current situation'.[62] Latin *tempus* brought about the shift in Polybius, which continued to later Greek: Cicero (*Cat.* 1.22) urges Catiline 'to yield in face of the dangers of the State', *ut temporibus reipublicae cedas*. With the New Testament ambivalence see Valerius Flaccus 1.306 *tempus adest; age, rumpe moras* 'the time is at hand, put off delay'.[63]

(5) 'Mystery'. Mk 4.11, 'The mystery [μυστήριον] of the kingdom of God', Pesh. ארזא. Dan. 2.19, 'the mystery was revealed', רָזָה גְלִי, Theod. τὸ μυστήριον ἀπεκαλύφθη. *Ahiqar* 175, 'in a hiding place of mysteries', בסתר ארזא. Qumran רזי אל 'secrets of El' in the *Rule* (1QS 3.23), *War Scroll* (1QM 3.9 etc.) as one of the rare non-Semitic words in the Scrolls.[64] *Odes* 8.10 'Keep my mystery, you who are kept by

---

58. Edited by Ilya Gershevitch (Cambridge: Cambridge University Press, 1959), p. 121; see Telegdi, 'Essai', p. 242 no. 66.

59. Telegdi, 'Essai', p. 242 n. 68.

60. *Influences*, p. 92.

61. Conversely καιρός goes into rabbinic קירס, but this cannot underly the New Testament Greek.

62. Michel Dubuisson, *Le latin de Polybe: les implications historiques d'un cas de bilinguisme* (Etudes et Commentaires, 96; Paris: Klincksieck, 1985), pp. 177-78.

63. *OLD* at *tempus* includes 'a favorable or convenient time', but not specifically 'a dangerous time', though it cites several passages with that coloration.

64. Another Iranian word in the Scrolls is נחשיר 'slaughter', 1QM 1.9 etc. See

it': טרו. ארזי הנון דמתנטרין בה. Pehlevi *rāz*, probably Avestan *razah* 'Einsamkeit, Abgelegenheit'.[65] Conversely, μυστήριον went into rabbinic, *Gen. R.* 68.12 'who revealed the secret (מיסטירין) of the Holy One'.

(6) 'Lamp'. For λύχνος Pesh. always has שרגא. The same equivalence in a proverb: Diogenes (Diogenes L. 6.41) 'lit a lamp at midday', searching for an honest man, λύχνον μεθ᾽ ἡμέραν ἅψας; *b. Ḥul.* 60b, 'What is the use of a lamp at midday?': מאי רבותיה דשרגא בטיהרא שרגא is Persian *čirāγ*.[66] Perhaps Persians brought an improved model before the Greeks. Symbolic uses: *Odes* 25.7, 'A lamp you set for me', שרגא סמת לי. At Rev. 21.23 New Jerusalem can dispense with sun and moon, 'its lamp [λύχνος, Syriac שרגא] is the Lamb'; Jn 5.35, John Baptist was the 'burning and shining lamp [λύχνος, שרגא]'. These two New Testament themes are echoed in Arabic. Qur'an 71.16, Allah created the heavens 'and made the moon a light in them, and the sun a lamp [*sirājan*]'; the Prophet besides being a 'bringer of good news' (33.45 *mubašširan*) is a 'lamp that gives light', *sirājan munīran*.

(7) 'Treasure', γάζα Acts 8.27, Pesh. גזה (assimilated to Γάζα the city). Bilingual compound Mk 12.43 γαζοφυλάκιον 'treasury', Pesh. בית גזה. Est. 3.9, 'the treasures of the king', גנזי הַמֶּלֶךְ, LXX γαζοφυλάκιον. Often Oriental treasure, Poly. 11.39(34).12 γάζης of a king of India; but naturalized early (Theophrastus, *Hist. Plant.* 8.11.5). Always exotic in Latin, Vergil, *Aen.* 1.119, *Troia gaza*. Persian *ganǰ* and Parthian *gnz*.[67] Ezra 1.18 הַגּוֹבָר 'treasurer'. In the Parthian of Sapor, *Res Gestae* 66 one Mihrkhwast is treasurer, *gnzbr*, γανζοφύλακος. Hence symbolic, *b. Ḥag.* 12b 'the treasures [גנזי] of life, of peace, of blessing'. Qur'an 18.82, 'under the wall was a treasure [*kanzun*]', with the haggadic theme that seeming unjust acts of God turn out for the best when all is known. The Mandaean sacred corpus is the *Ginza*.

(8) 'Sword'. The Pesh. of μάχαιρα varies. In the proverb Mt. 26.52b, 'All those who take the sword...' it has Aram. סיפא. But at 26.52a, 'Put the sword back in its place', it has Iranian ספסרא; so 26.55, 'Have you come out as against a bandit [λῃστήν, Pal. Syr. לסטיא] with swords [μαχαιρῶν, בספסרא]... to take me?' Sapor, *Res Gestae* 64 has 'Papak

---

Gen. 25.27 Onqelos נחשירכן 'hunter'; Hatra 112.3 Vattioni נחשרפט 'huntmaster' just as Parthian *nhšyrpty* Sapor, *Res Gestae* 59.

65. Telegdi, 'Essai', p. 254 n. 125.
66. Telegdi, 'Essai', p. 255 n. 129.
67. Telegdi, 'Essai', p. 237 n. 42; Gignoux, *Glossaire*, p. 51.

the sword-bearer', Parthian *spsyrdr* = σπαθοφόρου. Monobazus was invested in Iranian fashion with a sword, σαμψηράν, Josephus, *Ant.* 20.32; so papyri and Arrian. *b. B. Bat.* 21b 'he drew his sword', שְׁקל סְפסרא; *Odes* 28.5, 'And the dagger shall not divide me from him, nor the sword': והחרב לא תפלגני מנה אפלא ספסרא. Rom. 13.4, 'He bears not the sword [μάχαιραν, Pesh. ספסרא] in vain' anticipates the later *ius gladii* in language the Syriac hears as Iranian.

(9) 'Legate'. For πρεσβεία 'embassy' in the politicized parables, Lk. 14.32, 19.14 Pesh. has concrete איזגדא 'ambassadors'. An Iranian original in Buddhist Sogdian.[68] Plutarch (*Alex.* 18.5) says that Darius III 'became king instead of courier [ἀστάνδου]'. Targums often have איזגדא for מַלְאָךְ. 2 Cor. 5.20, 'We act as ambassadors [πρεσβεύομεν] on behalf of Christ', where Pesh. again has the plural noun. In the background is an Iranian cosmic legate to humanity: for the Mandaeans[69] speak of 'My good messenger of light [אשגאנדי טאבא דנהירא] who travels to the house of its friends'.[70]

(10) 'Conscription'. At Mt. 5.41, 'Whoever conscripts [ἀγγαρεύσει, Vg *angariauerit*] you one mile…' Pal. Syr. has the noun צאד לך אנגריא 'exercises conscription on you'; the conscription of Simon (Mk 15.21) looks back to the saying. Epictetus (Arrian, *Epict.* 4.1.79), 'Treat your body as if it were a laden donkey…then if there is conscription [ἀγγαρεία] and a soldier lays hold on it, let it go'. The Greek form rests on ἄγγαρος 'Persian messenger', but its new meaning on unrecorded Akkadian or Persian practice. Conscription of ships, animals and men in Greek, Roman law (*angaria*) and rabbinic: *m. B. Meṣ.* 6.3, an ass 'becomes *angareia*', שנעשית אנגריא. *y. Ber.* 2d69, R. Zeira is subject to אנגריא to carry myrtles into the king's palace (but others had to pay a big fee to see the inside).

(11) 'Pearl'. Mt. 13.45, the trader finds a pearl (μαργαρίτην, Pesh. מרגניתא, Pal. Syr. מרגלי). Familiar since Theophrastus, *de lap.* 36, Latin *margarita*. From an unknown Oriental language, but see Middle Persian *marvārīt* and Qur'an 55.58 *marjānu*. *y. Kil.* 32c47, one dying outside

68. H. Happ in *Glotta* 40 (1962), pp. 198-201; W.P. Schmid, in *Glotta* 40, p. 321.

69. E.S. Drower, *The Canonical Prayerbook of the Mandaeans* (Leiden: E.J. Brill, 1959), p. 107 sect. 107 (MS at p. 144); transcription in E.S. Drower and R. Macuch, *A Mandaic Dictionary* (Oxford: Clarendon Press, 1963), p. 40.

70. Conversely πρεσβευτής went into rabbinic: *Exod. R.* 42.3, 'Parable of a province that sent a legate [פרוזבוטיס] to crown a king'.

Israel says, 'I am about to lose my pearl [מרגליתי] in the midst of an unclean land'. Matthew's parable seems parodied at *b. Šab.* 119a: Joseph the Sabbath-keeper has a rich Gentile neighbor; Chaldaeans tell the neighbor that Joseph will consume his property. He goes and sells all his property (cf. Matthew!), buys a pearl, and wraps it in his turban; but the wind over a bridge blows it off, a fish swallows it, and Joseph buys the fish on the eve of Sabbath. The parable or *its* source underlies the beautiful *Hymn of the Pearl*, the crown of Syriac literature.

4. *Greek Loan Words in the Aramaic of the Sayings*

Even before Alexander, the Near East was being Hellenized. About 400 BCE a Greek–Phoenician stele (*KAI* 53) at Athens records the names of Artemidoros son of Heliodoros, Ἀρτεμίδωρος Ἡλιοδώρου = עבדתנת בן עבדשמש. Before Alexander, a king of Sidon had the Greek name Στράτων (Athenaeus 531A). On May 12, 257 BCE Toubias the wealthy Jew of Transjordan wrote Greek letters to Apollonios the minister of Ptolemy II.[71] Under Antiochus IV Epiphanes (175–164 BCE) the High Priest Ἰησοῦς (*Yešua'*) changed his name to Ἰάσων (the hero Jason), and his brother Ὀνίας to Μενέλαος (Josephus, *Ant.* 12.239); the same Jason set up a gymnasium in Jerusalem (2 Macc. 4.9). Almost the first recorded rabbi is Antigonos (אנטיגנוס) of Socho (*Avoth* I.3).

Between Alexander and Islam, hundreds of Greek loan words (some masking Latin ones) entered Aramaic and rabbinical Hebrew, which anticipate Israeli Hebrew in sounding like a European language. Here, paradoxically, we note Greek words of the sayings which likely rest on themselves as loan in the underlying Aramaic. Even when (as mostly) they appear in the Peshitto, how can we tell that the translator is not simply lazy? The best criteria are: when the word is well-attested in rabbinic;[72] and names an element of Greek culture imported into Palestine. The mobility of the Greek thing and name (and the similarity of Italy to

---

71. *CPJ*, I, 4-5. Toubias is sending Aeneas the eunuch with four slave boys seven to ten years old (two circumcised, two not) and a menagerie of wild animals for the king. He is surely a younger relative of that Tobiah the Ammonite who gave Nehemiah so much trouble (Neh. 2.19 etc.).

72. Samuel Krauss, *Griechische und lateinische Lehnwörter im Talmud, Midrasch und Targum; mit Bemerkungen von Immanuel Löw* (2 parts; Berlin, 1899; repr. Hildesheim: George Olms, 1964); Daniel Sperber, *A Dictionary of Greek and Latin Legal Terms in Rabbinic Literature* (Jerusalem: Bar-Ilan, 1984).

Palestine) appears when the same word appears in the Vulgate and Latin generally. But judgment is required, and there is a grey area.

(1) 'Stranger'. Mt. 25.44, 'When did we see you…a stranger [ξένον, Pesh. אכסניא] or naked or sick [ἀσθενῆ] or in prison [ἐν φυλακῇ, Pal. Syr. בפילקי]?' Same equivalence in a Palmyrene bilingual under Hadrian (*PAT* 0305) ξένοις = לאכסניא. *Odes* 17.6, Christ says, 'And I seemed to them a stranger', ואיך אכסניא אסתברת לנהון. Hillel (*Lev. R.* 34.3) told his disciples he was going to prepare dinner for a stranger in his house, which turned out to be himself: והדין נפשא עלובתא לאו אכסניא היא בגו גופא (Aram.) 'Is not the poor soul a guest in the body?' See Hadrian's verses:

> animula uagula blandula
> hospes comesque corporis…

'Little soul, wanderer, charming one, the guest and companion of the body…' (Script. Hist. Aug., *Hadrian* 25). Perhaps behind both lies a lost Stoic formula *ἡ ψυχὴ ξένος ἐν τῷ σώματι 'the soul is a stranger in the body'.

(2) 'Inn'. Lk. 10.34 has an inn, πανδοχεῖον, Pesh. לפותקא, Pal. Syr. better פונדקיא, Arabic New Testament[73] *funduq*, Syrian for classical *khān*. With the Arabic article in Italian *alfóndega* (eleventh century), *fóndaco* in Boccaccio. Arrian, *Epict.* 1.24.14 in New Testament vocabulary 'the bunk in the inn', τὸν κράβατον ἐν τῷ πανδοχείῳ. Inns[74] were felt foreign, M. '*Abod. Zar.* 2.1 'inns of idolaters', פונדקאות של עובדי גלולים. The Samaritan parable is parodied at *Gen. R.* 92.6: an innkeeper (פונדק) gets his guests out at night on a pretext; bandits (לסטיא) rob them and share the spoil with him.

(3) 'Gate'. Mt. 7.13, 'Enter through the narrow gate [πύλης]'.[75] The Greek entered Aramaic through a targum at Gen. 19.1 which for LXX τὴν πύλην Σοδόμων has בפילי דסדום. David asked the Holy One, 'Master of the worlds, tell me which gate is opened to the Hereafter':[76] רבון העלמים הודיעני איזה פלון מפורש לעתיד לבא. *Lev. R.* 18.1 on death:

---

73. American Bible Society (1899).

74. A man may sleep with two women in an inn (בפונדק *m. Qid.* 4.12) so long as his wife is with him (as one of the two or a third?).

75. Mt. 16.18, 'the gates of Hades', πύλαι ἅδου, echoes Isa. 38.10 LXX πύλαις ἅδου, which in turn continues *Iliad* 5.646 πύλας Ἀΐδαο; a beautiful archaic parallel to the Hebrew.

76. *Pes. K.* 27.2.

'Parable of a king who enters a city, and with him his *duces* and eparchs and soldiers [אסטרטיוטין]; although each enters by the same gate [בפילין ואחד], each is taken care of according to his rank'.

(4) 'Storehouse...barn'. Lk. 12.14, 'neither storehouse nor barn [ταμεῖον οὐδὲ ἀποθήκη]' (cf. Josephus, *Ant.* 9.274). Latin *apotheca* common. Both nouns טמיון and אפותיקי are rabbinic, once together.[77]

(5) 'Prison'. See Mt. 25.44 above. Rabb. פילקי common.[78] Where a bandit belongs. Barabbas is a λῃστής (Jn 18.40) and in prison (ἐν τῇ φυλακῇ Lk. 23.19). Josephus, *Ant.* 20.215 describes an amnesty, 'The prison [ἡ. . . φυλακή] was cleaned out of captives, and the countryside was filled with bandits [λῃστῶν]'. *Lev. R.* 30.6, 'After some days that bandit [ליסטא] was captured and put in prison [בפילקי]'. Plautus, *Capt.* 751 *abductus...in phylacam* 'carried off to jail'.

(6) 'Chair'. Mt. 23.2, 'the chair of Moses', Μωυσέως καθέδρας, Vg *super cathedram Mosi*. Solomon's throne (1 Kgs 10.19) is 'like the chair of Moses', קתדרא דמשה.[79] Nikagoras, a descendant of Plutarch, was the 'sophist in the chair', ἐπὶ τῆς καθέδρας σοφιστής at Athens.[80] Juvenal 7.203 *paenituit multos uanae sterilisque cathedrae*, 'Many have regretted an empty and useless teaching chair'. *m. Ket.* 5.5, 'If the wife brought four maids, she may sit [all day long] in the chair [בקתדרא]'. *y. Suk.* 55a75, the chief synagogue at Alexandria had seventy golden cathedrae, קתידראות.

(7) 'Footstool'. Mt. 5.34-35: 'Do not swear at all: not by heaven, for it is the throne [θρόνος] of God; nor by earth, for it is the footstool [ὑποπόδιον] of his feet'. Both words at *m. Kel.* 24.5-7, תרונוס...איפופודין. Jesus cites Isa. 66.1, 'Heaven is my throne, and earth the footstool of my feet', where the LXX has ὑποπόδιον. Did Matthew look up the LXX? Did Jesus quote in Greek? Beit Hillel and Beit Shammai debated

---

77. *y. Ned.* 41c40-43: A man has a case against a rich adversary (בעלדיניה). It comes before Rab, who summons the rich one. 'With such a one should I come to court? All the camels of Arabia could not carry the keys to my treasure-houses [אפותיקי]'. Rab curses him. 'Then a decree [קלווסיס = κέλευσις] came from the government confiscating all he owned to the royal treasury [טמיון]'. But Rab by prayer secures his life.

78. Sperber, *Legal Terms*, pp. 143-44.

79. *Pes. K.* 1.7. Cecil Roth, 'The "Chair of Moses" and its Survivals', *PEQ* 81 (1949), pp. 100-111, finds it in functional or symbolic form in ancient synagogues —including one from China!

80. *SIG* 845, c. 250 CE.

which was made first, heaven or earth.[81] Beit Hillel said earth, citing Gen. 2.4 'In the day that the Lord God made earth and heaven'; and then Isa. 48.13, 'My hand laid the foundation of the earth, and my right hand spread out the heavens', 'It is like a king who built a palace [פלטין]; after he has laid the foundation he builds the upper stories'. Beit Shammai (which we now know was right!) naturally quoted Gen. 1.1, and then Isa. 66.1, 'This is like a king who made a throne; after he made it, he made his footstool [אפיפודין]'. In effect Beit Shammai uses a targumic tradition, perhaps known to Jesus, which unlike Jonathan takes ὑποπόδιον from the LXX.

(8) 'Belt', 'sandal'. Mk 6.8-9, 'No copper in your belt [ζώνην] but wearing sandals [σανδάλια, Old Syr. סדלא],[82] and not taking two tunics [χιτῶνας, Pesh. כותינין]'. The Vg has all three words, *neque in* zona *aes sed calciatos* sandaliis *et ne induerentur duabis* tunicis. The words for 'tunic' go back to antiquity. Rabb. זוני and סנדל common, together at *m. Kel.* 26.3-4. *Num. R.* 4.20, 'girt with a belt around his loins', חגור מתנין בזינו ; Mt. 3.4 of John Baptist, 'with a leather belt [ζώνην δερμ-ατίνην, Pal. Syr. זונא דמשיך[83]] around his loins'. Latin *zona* common, *sandalium* rare. Greeks brought their dress with its names to Palestine. This resembles Cynic instructions, but I find none such with the details of dress.

(9) The Prodigal Son. Its fluent Greek holds four words that entered Syriac and Rabbinic.

(9a) 'Robe'. Lk. 15.22, 'the best robe [στολήν, Pesh. אסטלא, Vg *sto-lam*]'. Syriac uses אסטלא as known elsewhere: Old Syr. Mt. 14.36 for ἱματίου. It entered rabbinic through the targum: *Targ. Onq.* Gen. 45.22 has אסטלון for LXX στολή. Latin *stola*, a man's or woman's long robe. Luxury in rabbinic. *b. Šab.* 128a, a debtor should not wear an איצטלא worth one hundred minas. *m. Giṭ.* 7.5, 'In Sidon a man said to his wife, 'This is your *geṭ* on condition you give me back my robe [איצטליתי]'.

(9b) 'Estate'. Lk. 15.12, 'my share of the estate [οὐσίας, Pal. Syr. אוסיא]'. *Gen. R.* 49.2, 'Parable of a king who gave an estate [אוסיא] to his friend'.

---

81. *b. Ḥag.* 12a; *y. Ḥag.* 77c68-77d2; *Gen. R.* 1.14; *Lev. R.* 36.1.

82. The Pesh. for 'sandals' has טלרא, which must be Latin *talaria*, 'winged sandals'!

83. משיך is Akkadian *mašku* 'hide', *Targ. Onq.* Num. 31.20 משך; Old Persian *maškāuvā* 'on [inflated] skins' (Kent, *Old Persian*, p. 203), Greek μέσκος (Nican-der).

(9c) 'Profligacy'. Lk. 15.13, 'living riotously [ἀσώτως]'. At Eph. 5.18, 'wine wherein is excess, [ἀσωτία]', the Pesh. has an abstract אסוטותא (also at Lk. 21.34).[84] Latin adapted the Greek precisely for a youth squandering his estate! Gellius 10.17.3 *sumptum plurimum asotiamque adulescentis*, 'the excess spending and extravagance of a youth'; Plautus, *Merc. Arg.* 2 'A merchant father sends out his dissolute son to make purchases', *Mercator mercatum asotum filium extrudit pater.*

(9d) 'Symphony'. Lk. 15.25, 'music', συμφωνίας, Old Syr. צפוניא, Vg *symphoniam.* In Aramaic some special instrument, Dan. 3.5 סוּמְפֹּנְיָה, LXX συμφωνίας, Vg *symphoniae. m. Kel.* 11.6 'a *symphonia* [סומפוניא] or flute of cast metal'. Latin since Cicero.

(10) 'Key'. Lk. 11.52, 'the key [κλεῖδα, Pesh. קלידא] of knowledge'; Mt. 16.19, 'the keys [κλεῖδας, Pesh. קלידא] of the kingdom of heaven'. Qur'an 39.63, 'the keys [*maqālīdu*] of heaven and earth'. It was common knowledge[85] that the Holy One had three keys (מפתחות): the key of the raising of the dead (תחית המתים), for (Ezek. 37.12) 'I will *open* [פתח] your graves'; the key of the womb, for (Gen. 29.31) 'he *opened* her womb'; and the key of the rain, for (Deut. 28.12) 'The Lord will *open* to you his good treasure'. But elsewhere one is called in Greek style אקלידא.

Now we understand the Elijah story (*b. Sanh.* 113a)! He rashly predicted drought and prayed; in a weak moment the Holy One gave him the key of rain (אקלידא דמטרא). He locked the rain up but couldn't reopen it. The Holy One saw distress in the world and resorted to subterfuge. He sent Elijah to Sarepta to the widow's sick son, and Elijah begged for the key of the raising of the dead (אקלידא דתחית המתים). The Holy One said: 'Three keys have never been given to angel or seraph;[86] people will say, Two are in the hand of the *talmīd* and one in the hand of the *Rab*? Return that one and take this one'. So he got the key of the rain back, and the storm at Carmel follows. But Elijah still holds the key of the raising of the dead.

(11) 'Necessity'. Mt. 18.7, 'It is necessary [ἀνάγκη, Pesh. אנגקא] that scandals come'. Not lazy transcription, for the Greek also in rabbinic. As 'distress' (Lk. 21.23), *Cant. R.* pref. 'A son of man does not recount his distress [אננקי] except in the hour of his relief'; as 'necessity' *Gen. R.* 12.13, 'When a man of flesh and blood stretches a tent, necessarily

---

84. The adjective ἄσωτος is marginal in rabbinic אסיס, *Gen. R.* 17.2.
85. *Gen. R.* 73.4; *Deut. R.* 7.6.
86. These come from *Deut. R.*

[אננק] in course of time it becomes loose'. Perhaps a takeover of the divinity, Aeschylus *P.V.* 105 'The strength of Anangke is irresistible': τὸ τῆς Ἀνάγκης ἔστ' ἀδήριτον σθένος.

(12) 'Mask, sculptured face'.[87] Lk. 12.56, 'Hypocrites, you can discern the face [πρόσωπον, פרצופא] of earth and sky'; Mt. 6.16 the hypocrites 'disfigure their faces [πρόσωπα, פרצופיהון]'. We saw how a 'hypocrite' is one with a 'false face'—an actor's mask or a 'beam in his eye'. Semitic had no word for 'mask': Aristotle, *Poetics*, 5.2 'the comic mask is ugly', τὸ γελοῖον πρόσωπον αἰσχρόν. *b. 'Abod. Zar.* 12a, 'faces [פרצופות] [in fountains] which spurt out water'; *y. 'Abod. Zar.* 42c68, 'There were all kinds of carved faces [פרצופות] in Jerusalem except human'.

(13) 'Yoke'. Lk. 14.19, 'five yoke of oxen', ζεύγη βοῶν, Pesh. זוגין חורא which would be *ζεύγη ταύρων. 'Yoke' in rabbinic has the Greek idea of marriage, Xenophon, *Oec.* 7.18 τὸ ζεῦγος ὃ καλεῖται θῆλυ καὶ ἄρρεν 'the yoke called female and male'. At Heb. 13.4 Pesh. for γάμος has זווגא and so Rabb. זווג 'marriage'. *m. Pe'ah* 2.6 the five 'pairs' of rabbis are זוגות. In Palestine often 'spouse' fem., thus Gen. 7.9 for 'male and female', *Neofiti* has דכר וזוגה. Qur'an 2.230 *zawjun* is 'husband' and so today.

(14) Jewish concepts. Influence of Hellenistic Judaism in Palestine.

(14a) 'Law'. 'The Law and the Prophets' (ὁ νόμος καὶ οἱ προφῆται) Mt. 7.12 in Pesh. is נמוסא ונביא. In the Palmyrene Tariff (1.6) נמוסא = νόμῳ; a marriage contract from Murabba'at[88] envisages birth 'legitimately', כנמסא. Rabb. נימוס may refer to foreign laws, *Gen. R.* 48.14, 'When you enter a city, act according to its laws [בנימוסה]'. Or in the mouth of foreigners to the law of Israel; *y. Ber.* 9a29 a proconsul says, 'Leave him alone; he is studying the law of his creator [בנימוסא דברייה]'. If Jesus ever spoke the Sermon on the Mount in Greek, he had only νόμος for 'Law', which may have affected his Aramaic.

(14b) 'Covenant'. Mt. 26.28, 'this is my blood of the covenant [διαθήκης, Pesh. דייתקא]'. Classical διαθήκη is 'last will and testament', but at Aristoph, *Aves* 439 'unless they make an agreement with me': ἢν μὴ διάθωνταί γ' οἵδε διαθήκην ἐμοί. Rabbinic דייתיקי is *only* 'will, tes-

---

87. As 'face' simply, Mt. 18.10, 'the face [πρόσωπον, פרצופא] of your Father': it likely entered Aramaic through a targum to Ps. 34.17, transcribing πρόσωπον (Krauss, *Griechische*, p. 495).

88. Fitzmyer and Harrington, *Manual*, no. 42.11, p. 142.

tament': *b. B. Bat.* 135b, 'A [new] will cancels an [old] will', דְּיָתִיקִי
מְבַטְלָת דְּיָתִיקִי. Jer. 31.31 בְּרִית חֲדָשָׁה (LXX 38.31 διαθήκην καινήν)
meant 'new *covenant*', Vg *foedus nouum*. Later, God's covenants were
seen as unilateral acts like the will of a testator, and the old sense of
διαθήκη prevailed. Hence the Vg at the accounts of the Last Supper
and at Heb. 8.8 has *nouum testamentum*. If Jesus at the Last Supper (a
kind of testament) used Aramaic, he might have said דְּיָתִיקִי.

(14c) 'Sanhedrin', συνέδρια are local bodies, Mt. 10.17 (= Mk 13.9),
'they will turn you over to *synedria*', where Pesh. לְבֵית דִינָא. But for the
Jerusalem body, the loan word סַנְהֶדְרִין was universal in rabbinic.

(15) A certain meal. ἄριστον is 'dinner' at Mt. 22.4 (roasts), and so
אֲרִיסְטוֹן *y. Ber.* 7b46 (sixth hour). A heavenly banquet, *Lev. R.* 13.3,
'The Holy One will prepare dinner [אֲרִיסְטוֹן] for his righteous servants'.
Parody of Jesus' parable (where only the 'poor' come [Lk. 14.21],
πτωχούς =מִסְכְּנָא) at *y. Ḥag.* 77d51-53: Bar Maʻyan 'the publican [מוֹכֵס]
did no meritorious deed; [except that] one time he made a dinner for his
bouleutai [חַד זְמַן עֲבַד אֲרִיסְטוֹן לְבוּלוֹטַיָּא]. But they did not come. He
said, "Let the poor [מִסְכֵּינַיָּא] eat so it will not go to waste".

(16) 'Platter, tablet', Lk. 11.39, 'the outside of the...platter [πίνακος,
Old Syr פִּינְכָא]'. Mt. 14.8 etc., 'the head of John on a platter [πίνακι
Pesh. בְּפִינְכָא]'. Classical πίναξ 'plank' was anything flat, like a 'writing tablet', *Iliad* 6.169. At Lk. 1.63 Zachariah calls for a πινακίδιον,
Pesh. פִּנְקִיתָא. *y. Šab.* 6b23 פִּינְכָא דְאוֹרְזָא 'a dish of rice [ὄρυζα]'. *Avoth*
III.17 'the ledger is open', הַפִּנְקָס פָּתוּחַ *y. Roš Haš.* 57a58 has three
account books (פִּינְקְסִיּוֹת): one for the fully righteous, one for the fully
wicked, one for those in between. *Odes* 23.21, '[God's] letter [אִגַּרְתָּא]
became a big *pinax* [פִּנְקִיתָא]'.

Further Items

(17) 'Crowd'. Mk 8.2 ὄχλον, Pal. Syr. אָכְלוֹסָא; *y. Dem.* 24a32 אוּכְלוֹסִין;
a new class of village unemployed. (18) 'Steward'. Jesus praises both
the 'faithful steward [οἰκονόμος]' of Lk. 12.42 and the 'steward of
injustice', οἰκονόμον τῆς ἀδικίας 16.8! *y. B. Meṣ.* 11d16 הָאִיקוֹנוֹמוֹס.
(19) 'Scabbard'. Jn 18.11 θήκην, Old Latin *tecam. m. Kel.* 7 'the sheath
of a sword or knife[89] or dagger',[90] תִּיק הַסַּיָּף וְהַסַּכִּין וְהַפֻּגְיוֹן. (20) 'Sick'.
Mk 14.38, 'But the flesh is weak [ἀσθενής]'. *m. Yom.* 3.5, 'If the High

89. Heyschius συκίνη; Qur'an 12.31 *sikkīnan*.

90. Cicero, *Phil.* 2.30, *Brutus...cruentem pugionem tenens*, 'Brutus, holding the
bloody dagger...'(with which he had killed Caesar).

Priest was old or sick [אי׳סטני׳ס]': euphemism of Greek doctors. (21)
'Daughter-in-law'. Mt. 10.35, 'to divide a daughter-in-law [νύμφην,
Pesh. כלתא] from her mother-in-law'. *Exod. R.* 36.1, 'In Greek they call
a כלא *ninfi* [נינפי]'. It entered rabbinic as 'bride', *Targ. Cant.* 4.8 נינפי
from LXX νύμφη.[91] (22) 'Soldier'. Mt. 8.9 (of the 'centurion') στρατι-
ώτας Pesh. אסטרטיוטא. *Exod. R.* 15.22, 'A king of flesh and blood
enlists stout and strong soldiers [סטרטוטין]'. Also of the heavenly hosts
Num. R. 7.3; Hellenistic/Roman discipline warranted a new name.

5. *Latinisms in the Aramaic of the Sayings*

The first recorded contact between Jews and Romans is the embassy
sent by Judas Maccabaeus to Rome (1 Macc. 8, 161 BCE) and the
following treaty, which agrees well with contemporary Roman treaties
(in Greek) on stone. We have from literary sources *senatus consulta* on
Jewish affairs: 1 Macc. 15.16-21 (140–139 BCE); Josephus, *Ant.*
13.260-64 (132 BCE); 14.145-48 (earlier?). Pompey took Jerusalem in
63 BCE; Syria was under Roman governors since M. Aemilius Scaurus
(65–62 BCE, SVMB, I, p. 244). Augustus divided the realm of Herod
the Great after his death in 4 BCE (SVMB, I, p. 333), an event envisaged at Lk. 19.12-14. Judaea was under governors (originally *praefecti*)
since Coponius (CE 6--9).

Rome governed the eastern half of the empire in Greek, and the names
of Roman institutions went into Greek in two ways: (1) as simple
transcription of the Latin; (2) as Greek equivalents, often created by the
chancery in Rome. Aramaic words for Roman things simply transcribe
the Greek, whether it itself is transcription or equivalent; they show no
new knowledge of Latin.[92] The passion narratives and Acts are full of
Latinisms describing Roman affairs.

---

91. Krauss, *Griechische*, p. 361.

92. The fullest listing of Latin loan words in Greek is Herbert Hofmann, 'Die
lateinischen Wörter im Griechischen bis 600 n. Chr.' (Inaugural-Dissertation; Uni-
versity of Erlangen-Nürnberg, after 1989); I was unable to find a copy in the United
States. The fullest study of Latinisms in New Testament Greek is Corrado Marucci,
'Influssi latini sul greco del nuovo testamento', *FN* 6 (1993), pp. 3-30. BAGD
records New Testament Latinisms in secular Greek. For Latinisms in rabbinic see
Krauss, *Griechische*; in Semitic generally, Maria Gabriella Angeli Bertinelli, 'I
Semiti e Roma: Appunti da una lettura di fonti semitiche', in *Serta historica antiqua*
(Rome: Bretschneider, 1986), pp. 145-81.

Three texts of Luke from the 'Q' tradition have Latin idioms unknown to Aramaic lacking from Matthew. They represent either work of the original translator deleted by Matthew; or of Luke on a less Latinate original. —Lk. 7.4 (Galilaeans speaking), 'He is worthy that you should do this for him', ἄξιός ἐστιν ᾧ παρέξῃ τοῦτο, a unique version of a Latin 'relative clause of characteristic'. The Vulgate has just *dignus est ut hoc illi praestes*; classically it would have been **dignus est cui hoc praestes*, thus Plautus, *As.* 80 *me dignum quoi* [for later *cui*] *concrederet habuit*, 'he held me worthy for him to trust'[93]. —Lk. 14.18-19 ἐρωτῶ σε ἔχε με παρῃτημένον, Vg correctly *rogo te, habe me excusatum*, 'I beg you, have me excused'; so exactly Martial 2.79.2, *excusatum habeas me rogo*[94]. —Lk. 12.58 δὸς ἐργασίαν ἀπηλλάχθαι ἀπ' αὐτοῦ 'work hard to be reconciled with him', Vg *da operam liberari ab illo*.[95] The Greek appears in *P. Oxy.* 742.11 (second century BCE) δὸς ἐργασίαν and in a *senatus consultum* of 81 BCE,[96] δίδωσίν τε ἐργασίαν. The Latin in Terence, *Hec.* 553 *dare operam id scire*, 'to take pains to know it'.[97]

Latin Transliterated (via Greek) in the Sayings

(1) 'Napkin'. Lk. 19.20, 'your mina which I kept in a napkin [ἐν σουδαρίῳ, Vg *sudario*]'; Pesh. בסדרא (Bib. Hebr. סָדִין = σινδών). But for Lazarus's shroud (σουδαρίῳ), Jn 11.44 Pesh. has בסודרא. *b. Ket.* 67b,

---

93. Similarly Ovid, *Met.* 10.681-682, Venus complains that Hippomenes failed to show gratitude for her help in winning Atalanta, *Dignane, cui grates ageret... fui?* 'Was I not worthy for him to give me thanks?'; Vergil, *Aen.* 7.653-4, of Lausus the noble son of the arrogant Mezentius, *dignus...cui pater haut Mezentius esset*, 'worthy of not having Mezentius as father'.

94. More distant is *P. Oxy.* 2.292.5 (c. CE 25) παρακαλῶ σε...ἔχειν αὐτὸν συνεσταμένον 'I urge you to treat him as one recommended'.

95. But the Vulgate misinterprets the second half 'to be freed from his lawsuits'. There is another Latinism in Matthew's version, κοδράντην = *quadrantem* Mt. 5.26; perhaps both stood together in an original version, with Luke deleting the transcribed word and Matthew the idiom.

96. R.K. Sherk, *Roman Documents from the Greek East: Senatus Consulta and Epistulae to the Age of Augustus* (Baltimore: The Johns Hopkins University Press, 1969), no. 18.11, p. 109.

97. And above all in the text of the emergency decree of the Senate, which Cicero (*De bello ciuili* 1.5.3) quotes, *dent operam consules, praetores...ne quid res publica detrimenti caperet*, 'Let the consuls, praetors...take care that the state receive no harm'.

'he wrapped *zuz* in his napkin', היה צייר זוזי בסודריה for the poor. A blushing woman 'hides her face with a napkin', *faciem sudario abscondit*, Petronius 67.13.[98]

(2) 'Assarion'. Mt. 10.29, two sparrows go for an ἀσσαρίου, Vg *duo passeres asse*, Pesh. באסר.[99] Greek ἀσσάριον here first; it is a Latin formation, but **assarium* unattested. The *as* was at first $^1/_{10}$ *denarius* (hence its name), but later $^1/_{16}$ (perhaps $^1/_{24}$ in the Mishna). A fee for exchange (*collybus*) was an *as* per *denarius* or 6 $^2/_3$%.[100] Aramaic אסרא and Greek *as* in the Palmyrene Tariff. The *as* is near-worthless in Latin verse: Catullus (5.3) and Lesbia so reckon old men's gossip, *omnes unius aestimemus assis*.

(3) 'Sextarius'. At Mk 7.4, a vessel ξεστῶν, Pesh. קסטא. Greek from Latin *sextarius* by metathesis; so in Diocletian's Edict. As a measure: Arrian, *Epict.* 1.9.34, a coward is 'a corpse and a pint [ξέστης] of blood'. *Lev. R.* 12.1 קסטין דחמרא 'measures of wine'; *m. Kel.* 15.1 המלכים קיסטות 'vessels of kings'. Measures at Palmyra are Roman (Tariff 69), 'Pure salt is taxed one *assarion* [אסרא] per *modius* [למדיא] of 16 *sextarii* [קסטין]'. Qur'an 17.35, a weight, 'and weigh with a right balance [*qisṭās*]'.

(4) 'Quadrans'. Mt. 5.26, 'the last farthing', ἔσχατον κοδράντην, Vg correctly *quadrantem*. The parallel Lk. 12.59 has an even smaller coin, the λεπτόν, which goes two for a *quadrans* at Mk 12.42, the widow's 'mite' (κοδράντην, Vg *quadrans*, Pal. Syr. קודרנטיס). Plutarch, *Cic.* 29.5, makes the smallest copper the κουαδράντην. Rabbinic

---

98. The napkin as means of life and death. At Acts 19.12 healing is brought by σουδάρια (Pesh. סודרא) ἢ σιμικίνθια, Vg *sudaria uel semicintia*, 'sweat-cloths and aprons'; the latter is a unique loan from *semicinctium* Petronius 94.6. A *sudarium* can bring death by suffocation (Valerius Maximus 9.12.7), and so at *m. Sanh.* 7.2 of execution by strangling.

99. At Lk. 12.6 five sparrows go for two assaria, so that Matthew shows slight inflation. The Maximum-Price Edict of Diocletian (4.37, CE 301) records the devaluation of the denarius, no longer silver: 10 *passeres* go for 16 denarii, while in Luke for 4 assaria = $^1/_4$ denarius (above), so that the denarius is $^1/_{64}$ its Gospel value. *m. Ḥul.* 12.5: mother bird and her young (Deut. 22.6) must not both be taken from the nest to cleanse the leper; it adds that this is a 'light commandment the value of an *issar* [איסר]'.

100. W. Dittenberger, *Orientis Graeci inscriptiones selectae* (2 vols.; Leipzig: Hirtel, 1903–1095), no. 484.13; Pergamum, second century CE, καθ' ἕκαστον δηνάριον εἰσέπρασσον ἀσσάριον ἕν.

קדריונטס;[101] at Lepcis in neo-Punic[102] וכנדרם...דנעריא 'denarii...
quadrantes'. Livy 3.18.11, 'plebeians threw *quadrantes* [all they had]
into the consul's house' to give him a grander funeral, *in consulis
domum plebes quadrantes...iactasse.* In Latin verse 'farthing, minimum
coin'.[103] Vulgar usage at Petronius 43 of a self-made man, *ab asse
creuit et paratus fuit quadrantem de stercore mordicus tollere*, 'He
began with a penny and was always ready to pick a farthing out of a
dung-hill with his teeth'.

(5) 'Legion'. 'Twelve legions of angels', Mt. 26.53, λεγιῶνας ἀγγ-
έλων, Pesh. דמלאכא לגיונין, Vg *legiones angelorum.* So the demoniac
of Gadara, Mk 5.9, 'my name is Legion', Pesh. לגיון שמן 'our name'.
λεγεών Diodorus 26.5;[104] also other versions, στρατόπεδον[105] and
τάγμα.[106] The demoniac has a psyche coopted by the legions of Varus,
4 BCE (Josephus, *Ant.* 17.286-89).[107] לגיונא *PAT* 0308. *Gen. R.* 12.16,
'parable of a legion [לגיונא]' first to proclaim a king [i.e. emperor]'.
Exod. R. 15.13 is wholly Latinate: 'Parable of a *dux* to whom his *legions* have thrown the *purple*': משל לדוכוס שדרכו הלגיונות פורפירא.
As for foreign military units (Livy 24.49.4, *Carthaginiensibus legion-
ibus*), so in the Gospels the hosts of unclean spirits and angels are each
structured as a Roman legion. In rabbinic only the heavenly host:
Lev. R. 16.9, 'The Holy One, blessed be he, calls to his legions [ללגיונות
שלו]'.

101. *y. Qid.* 58d33, where the *denarius* (דינר) is 24 *assaria* (איסר) and the *issar*
is 4 *quadrantes*.

102. G. Levi della Vida and M.G. Amadasi Guzzo, *Iscrizioni puniche della
Tripolitania (1927–1939)* (Monografie di Archeologia Libica, 22; Rome: Bretschneider, 1987), p. 42 n. 17.2.

103. Horace, *Sat.* 2.3.93-94; Martial 5.32; Juvenal 7.8; Phaedrus the fabulist
4.21.23.

104. Plutarch, *Rom.* 13 attributes a legion to Romulus. The spelling λεγεών is
preferable because Latin short i was heard by Greeks as e.

105. Polybius calls legions στρατόπεδα because that is his general term for an
army; then Lk. 21.20, 'When you see Jerusalem surrounded by armies [στρατ-
οπέδων]', need not have the specific sense 'legion'.

106. Dionysius Hal. 20.1.4 calls a legion τάγμα numbered πρῶτον etc. So
Josephus, *Ant.* 15.72 of Queen Alexandra προσφυγεῖν τοῖς σημείοις τοῦ Ῥωμαϊκοῦ
τάγματος 'to flee to the standards of the Roman legion'. This usage may apear at
Odes 35.4 דמריא שלאהוית בתגמה ואנא which Charlesworth translates, 'But I was
tranquil in the Lord's legion'.

107. In Palestinian Aramaic (Sokoloff, *Dictionary*, p. 281) לגיונא can be used for
a single soldier or 'legionary'—a peculiar parallel to the Gadarene.

(6) 'Mile'. Mt. 5.41 'And whoever conscripts you one mile. . . [ἀγγαρεύσει μίλιον ἕν]'. *Mille passuum* became just μίλιον (Polybius 34.11.8) with μεμιλιάσθαι; *m. Yom.* 6.4 מיל. In popular use it becomes a 'milestone': so on a milestone from Cyprus[108] *milia erexit* = τὰ μείλι(α) ἀνέστησεν; rabbinic, 'a road on which were no milestones [מילין]'.[109] In a Phrygian bilingual[110] a villager describes requisitioning oxen: 'We provide service for those coming from Synnada from the fifth mile [ἀπὸ πεμπτοῦ μειλίου]. . . also from Meiros to Kamaxos four milestones [τέσσαρες μειλιάρια] are laid on us'.

(7) 'Peck-measure'. Mt. 5.15 etc., 'They do not light a lamp and put it under *the* peck-measure',[111] οὐδὲ καίουσιν λύχνον καὶ τιθέασιν αὐτὸν ὑπὸ τοῦ μοδίου where the Old Syriac recognizes the Latin: ולא אנש מנהר שרגא וסאם לה תחית מודיא, Vg *neque accendunt lucernam et ponunt eam sub modio*. A dry measure of 16 *sextarii*; a μόδιος for grain at Poly. 21.42.9; Josephus, *Ant.* 9.85 μόδιον Ἰταλικόν as Italian. As a container: wooden, ξύλον, Arrian, *Epict.* 1.17.9; tipped with iron, *modium praeferratum*, Cato, *de agr.* 11.3. Cicero, *de amic.* 67, 'many pecks of salt (*multos modios salis*) must be eaten together' before two become friends. *b. 'Erub.* 83a מודיא דקונרס 'a peck of artichokes [κινάρα]'.

A Latin literary motif has precious metal in a peck-measure; Plautus, *Mil.* 1064, *plus mi auri mille est modiorum Philippi*, 'I have more than a thousand pecks of gold Philips'.[112] Livy (23.12.1) says that the gold rings (*anulos aureos*) from the Roman dead at Cannae poured out by Hannibal at Carthage amounted (according to some) to 3 ½ pecks (*dimidium supra tris modios*), although in his opinion only to a single *modius*. *Est. R.* 2.3 extravagantly has the gift to a rabbi of a 'peck of denarii', **modium denariorum*, חד מודיא דדינרין (likely imagined as gold 'dinars').

(8) '*Denarius*'. The standard coin of the Gospels, δηνάριον, Pesh. דינר, *denarius*. *Denarius* is masculine (Cicero, *Verr.* 2.3.220) for a silver coin worth 10 *as*, whence its name, but a Greek neuter. In the *Periplous*

---

108. *CIL* 3.218.10, CE 198.

109. Krauss, *Griechische*, p. 335 citing *Yal. Deut.* 907.

110. *SEG* 16 (1959), p. 754 = W.H.C. Frend, 'A Third-Century Inscription Relating to *Angareia* in Phrygia', *JRS* 46 (1956), pp. 46-56.

111. The lamp is Iranian; the verb-form is an Aramaic passive. This house has just one peck-measure and one lamp (Mk 4.21).

112. *Modium argenti*, Juvenal 3.220, 'a peck of silver'; Trimalchio's wife Fortunata 'measures her sestertii by the peck', *nummos modio metitur* (Petronius 37.4).

Maris Rubri 8, a collective, 'a small amount of coinage of gold and silver', δηνάριον οὐ πολὺ χρυσοῦν τε καὶ ἀργυροῦν. דינרא a pan-Aramaic loanword.[113] Semitic assumes a 'gold dinar', perhaps the aureus = 25 denarii. In a Palmyrene bilingual (*PAT* 0294) of CE 193 דינרין די דהב עתיקין = χρυσᾶ παλαιὰ δηνάρ[ια] 'gold denars of old [weight]'; *Avoth* 6.9 דינרי זהב; the *dīnār* at Qur'an 3.75 is thought gold. At Mt. 20.2 it is a day's wage, ἐκ δηναρίου τὴν ἡμέραν, Pesh. מן דינרא ביומא ; so *b. B. Bat.* 86b היום בדינר. In Diocletian's *Edict* (7.1) a farm laborer gets 25 denarii per diem plus food (*operario rustico p[asto diu]rni*) and skilled workers 50; close to the inflation of 1.64 we found for sparrows.[114]

(9) Other possibilities. 'Bunk', κράβαττος Mk 2.11 is South Italian vernacular; literary in Latin, Catullus 10.22 'the broken leg of an old cot', *fractum...ueteris pedem grabati*. Doubtful if rabbinic: *b. Qid.* 70a אקרפיטא is something to sit on. Word of popular usage and uncertain origin.[115] 'Census', Mt. 22.19, 'money of the census', τὸ νόμισμα τοῦ κήνσου, Pal. Syr. דינרא דקניסין. Elsewhere in the sayings κῆνσος is popularly 'the poll tax' itself. Uncertain if קנם 'fine, compensation' (*m. Ket.* 3.1)[116] is a Greco-Latin loan word, for the root קנם looks original.

Latin becomes concrete when loaned. The numbers in *denarius*, *sextarius*, *quadrans*, *mille* are lost. *Sextarius*, *modius* become vessels; μίλιον from a measure a milestone; *census* from a tax the coin that pays it. *Sudarium* loses connection with sweat; *legio* names celestial or infernal militias. But literary themes carry over: *as* is a trifling amount, *quadrans* an even smaller one carefully held on to; the *modius* holds fortunes in gold and silver.

---

113. From the Babatha archive, Fitzmyer and Harrington, *Manual*, no. 62.12; in the Palmyrene Tariff; in Punic and at Hatra (*KAI* 257.4).

114. A third figure for the inflation comes from Mk 6.37, where 200 denarii is barely adequate to feed 5,000 persons; then a denarius fed about 25. By Diocletian's time a modius of grain (*Edict* 1.1) cost 100 denarii, and surely more on real markets. If a modius fed 50 persons, to feed one person cost 2 denarii, again a 1.50 inflation.

115. Others such are φαινόλης 'cloak' or φαιλόνης (2 Tim. 4.13), *paenula*, rabbinic פלנים; μάκελλον 'market' (1 Cor. 10.25), *macellum*, rabbinic מקולין.

116. Also Nabataean, *CIS* 2.98.8.

Greek Equivalents for Latin Words in the Sayings

This is not a fixed category. Some Greek words exist only to translate Latin: thus ἀνθύπατος, Poly. 28.5.6 for *pro consule* with rabbinic אנטיפטו. At the other extreme are Greek words which went into rabbinic and name things existing in Latin, but with little or no coloration from the Latin; thus φυλακή, 'prison' with rabbinic פילק׳ and Vg *carcer*, reflecting no known special features of a Roman prison. As in (4), the Greek of the sayings rests on itself as loan word in the assumed original Aramaic—with the difference now that both are colored to some degree by the Latin equivalent.

(1) 'Ensign'. Often σημεῖον is just 'sign' and may rest on itself, סימא. Otherwise Mt. 24.30, 'Then will appear the ensign [σημεῖον, Vg *signum*] of the Son of Man in the sky'. At Josephus, *Ant.* 15.72 σημείοις are legionary standards; Augustus, *Res Gestae* 29, recovered such, *signa militaria* (= σημέας). In 37 CE, Vitellius avoided carrying images (εἰκόνας) attached to standards (σημαίαις) through Jerusalem (*Ant.* 18.121); in 26 CE Pilatus had deliberately brought into the city 'the medallions of Caesar attached to the standards', προτομὰς Καίσαρος αἱ ταῖς σημαίαις προσῆσαν (*Ant.* 18.55). The desecration is recorded as reversed by *Meg. Ta'an.* 9, 'On the third of Kislev the standards were removed from the Outer Court':[117] בתלת בכסלב אתנטילו סימאתא מן דרתא. *Targ. Jon.* at Jer 6.1 following LXX σημεῖον has סימותהון.

Rabbinic also has the Latin loanword סנון. *Exod. R.* 45.3, 'Parable of a king who had a legion [לגיון] that rebelled against him. What did the commander of the troops do? He took the king's standard [סנום] and fled'. A papyrus letter of c. 335 CE tells how Athanasius treated the Meletian bishops: his partisans locked them up at Nikopolis 'until the *praepositus* came into the storage-room of the military standards', μέχρις τοῦ τὸν πραιπόσιτον προερθιν [i.e. προελθεῖν] ἐν τοῖς σίγνοις.[118] Hence σίγνον went into Coptic as 'prison' and thence into Arabic:

117. Fitzmyer and Harrington (eds.), *Manual*, p. 187. Eusebius, *Dem. Ev.* 8.2.123 quotes Philo (inaccurately?) as saying that Pilatus 'set up the imperial [standards] by night in the Temple'; anyway *Meg. Ta'an.* supports this version. Discussion by Carl H. Kraeling, 'The Episode of the Roman Standards in Jerusalem', *HTR* 35 (1942), pp. 263-89.

118. H. Idris Bell, *Jews and Christians in Egypt: The Jewish Troubles in Alexandria and the Athanasian Controversy* (London: British Museum, 1914), n. 1914 line 18; p. 59.

Qur'an 12.100 '[Allah] took me out of the prison', *'ahrajāni min 'assijni.*

(2) 'Governor'. Mt. 10.18, 'You will be brought before governors and kings', ἐπὶ ἡγεμόνας καὶ βασιλεῖς, Pesh. וקדם הגמונא ומלכא, Vg *ad praesides et reges.* ἡγεμών and *praeses* both are general terms.[119] Pilatus is ἡγεμών (Mt. 27.2), and so Felix (Acts 23.24). At Acts 26.30 'the king and the governor arose', the king is Agrippa II and the governor Festus; perhaps the saying anticipates the event. At 1 Pet. 2.13-14, 'Be subject to the king, to governors', the 'king' has become the emperor.[120] In Nabataean הגמונא is the Roman governor of a province; at Rawwafa, 'Antistius Adventus the governor [הגמונא]' sets up a dedication to Marcus Aurelius and Lucius Verus.[121] In the Palmyrene Tariff 74 the היגמונא may be Gaius Licinius Mucianus, *legatus Augusti pro praetore* of Syria in 68–69 CE (cf. *PAT* 0278). Vague in rabbinic: *Exod. R.* 31.17, Esau (Rome) is compared to היגמונים, *duces* and eparchs who plunder cities.

(3) 'Steward'. Mt. 20.8, 'The owner of the vineyard says to his steward [ἐπιτρόπῳ, Vg *uineae procuratori*]'. ἐπίτροπος has four senses in the New Testament, each attested in Aramaic as אפיטרופוס or the like.

(3a) 'Steward' of a private estate, as at Mt. 20.8. Classical since Herodotus. *y. B. Meṣ* 10c29-30, 'A Jew who appointed a Gentile as steward...a Gentile who appointed a Jew as steward': ישראל שמינה גוי אפיטרופא...וגוי שמינה ישראל אפיטרופא. Agrippa I (*Ant.* 18.194) made the freedman Thaumastos *'epitropos* of his estate', τῆς οὐσίας ἐπίτροπον; he may be the *'epitropos* of King Agrippa' (*b. Sukk.* 27a), אפיטרופוס של אגריפס המלך with wives in Tiberias and Sepphoris.

(3b) 'Steward' of a realm. Lk. 8.3, 'Chouza [Χουζᾶ] steward [ἐπιτρόπον, Old Syr. אפטרופא, Vg *procuratoris*] of Herod [Antipas]'. In view of the Nabataean name כוזו (*CIS* 2.227), Chouza may be named for the Edomite god Κωζέ (Josephus, *Ant.* 15.253), and so a fellow Edomite with the Herods and perhaps a relative.[122] The Nabataean king governed

119. Macer (*Digest* 1.18.1), *Praesidis nomen generale est...proconsulis appellatio specialis est,* 'The word *praeses* is general...the name *proconsul* is specific'.

120. Strabo 17.3.25 restricts ἡγεμών to governors of imperial provinces, but this distinction is not elsewhere observed.

121. J.T. Milik, 'Inscriptions grecques et nabatéennes de Rawwafah', *Bulletin of the Institute of Archaeology* (London) 10 (1971), pp. 54-58.

122. Discussion in H.W. Hoehner, *Herod Antipas* (Grand Rapids: Zondervan, 1990), p. 303. Chouza has been interpreted as Antipas's "finance minister" (Hoehner,

Petra by a relative of rank ἐπίτροπον whom he called 'brother' (Strabo 16.4.21).[123] In Seleucid usage: Lysias *'epitropos* of the king [Antiochus IV] and a relative and over his affairs [ἐπὶ τῶν πραγμάτων]', 2 Macc. 11.1, also acts as general. Caesar made Antipater ἐπίτροπος of all Judaea (Josephus, *War* 1.199); Roman or Hellenistic usage?

(3c) 'Guardian' of an orphan. Gal. 4.1-2, 'The heir. . . is under guardians [ἐπιτρόπους]', Pesh. אפטרופא. Classical Greek. *m. Giṭ.* 5.4, 'A guardian who was appointed for orphans by their father':[124] אפטרופוס שמינהו אבי יתומים. The Babatha archive from the Dead Sea speaks of the 'guardian of [Babatha's] orphan son Jesus son of Jesus',[125] ἐπίτροπον Ἰησοῦ Ἰησούτος υἱοῦ αὐτῆς ὀρφανοῦ and so in Aramaic אפטרפא דיתמא 'guardian of the orphan'.[126]

(3d) Roman *'procurator'*. A *procurator* was an equestrian finance official; from Claudius on it was the title of the governor of Judaea, in Greek ἐπίτροπος. Before he had been *praefectus* = ἔπαρχος as Pilate's inscription from Caesarea shows.[127] In the Greek, Seleucid and Roman usages flow together. At Palmyra (*PAT* 0286, 262 CE), Septimius Worod is אפטרפא = ἐπίτροπον Σεβαστοῦ. He claims legitimacy inside rather than outside the empire. A Jerusalem targum[128] has Potiphar make Joseph his אפיטרופוס. *Procurator* also was 'steward' of an estate; hence, for it as an equestrian title, the Roman chancery naturally translated ἐπίτροπος.

(4) 'Bandit'. Mt. 26.55, 'Have you come out as against a bandit [ἐπὶ λῃστήν, Pal. Syr. על לסטיא, Vg *ad latronem*]?'. Lk. 10.30, 'A man fell

---

Herod Antipas, p. 120) and as manager of his estate (J.A. Fitzmyer, *The Gospel According to Luke i-ix* [AB, 28; Garden City, NY: Doubleday, 1981], I, p. 698). Either way he could have been present at the execution of John the Baptist and sent the story by his wife Joanna to Jesus' entourage. Was she there when Jesus called Antipas 'jackal' (Lk. 13.32), to convey the word back to her husband?

123. The Nabataean inscriptions show 'brother of the king' (*RES* 675) and 'brother of the queen' (*CIS* 2.351), probably for persons with the rank of *epitropos*.

124. Cited by Sperber, *Legal Terms*, pp. 56-57, with numerous similar texts.

125. Naphtali Lewis *et al.*, *The Documents from the Bar Kokhba Period in the Cave of the Letters: Greek Papyri* (Judaean Desert Studies, 2; Jerusalem: Israel Exploration Society, 1989); n. 15.4, p. 59.

126. Y. Yadin, 'Expedition D—The Cave of the Letters', *IEJ* 12 (1962), p. 247. The publication of these important texts is being long delayed.

127. Josephus varies his usage and at *War* 2.169 calls Pilatus ἐπίτροπος. Tacitus, *Ann.* 15.44 *per procuratorem Pontium Pilatum* shows the same inaccuracy.

128. Krauss, *Griechische*, p. 104; see Sperber, *Legal Terms*, pp. 56-59.

among bandits [λῃσταῖς, Pesh. לסטיא, Vg *in latrones*]'. λῃστής is pejorative in Josephus for one opposing Rome. We saw that banditry like tax collection is hereditary.[129] Mt. 27.38, 'There were crucified with him two bandits [λῃσταί, Pesh. לסטיא, Vg *latrones*]'.[130] *Est. R.* 1.12,[131] 'Where the bandit steals, there is he crucified': הין דליסטאה מקבח תמן מצטלב. This reflects Roman practice (*Digest* 48.19.28.15):

> Famosos latrones in his locis, ubi grassati sunt, furca figendos compluribus placuit, ut et conspectu deterreantur alii ab isdem facinoribus et solacio sit cognatis et adfinibus interemptorum eodem loco poena reddita, in quo latrones homicidia fecissent.
>
> Most authorities have determined that notorious brigands should be crucified at the site of their activities, so that on the one hand others may be deterred from such crimes by the spectacle, and on the other that it may be a solace to the relatives and kin of those killed that the punishment was carried out in the same place where the bandits committed murders.

The Roman claim to have imposed universal peace gave its disturbers a special outlaw status; λῃστής went into Aramaic to express the new category of *latro*.

The social ambiguity of banditry leads severe moralists to find it in established institutions. Mk 11.17, quoting Jer. 7.11 LXX, makes the Temple a 'cave of bandits', σπήλαιον λῃστῶν, Pesh. מערתא דלסטיא, Vg *speluncam latronum*.[132] Augustine asks (*De Civ. Dei* 4.4), *remota*

---

129. *b. B. Qam.* 57b distinguishes an armed bandit (לסטים מזוײן) from an unarmed bandit (לסטים שאין מזוײן). In a Jewish district most bandits will necessarily be Israelites (*b. Beṣ* 15a). *y. Ket.* 26d44 prefers invaders and bandits to regular forces! It treats *m. Ket.* 2.9, 'If a city was overcome by a besieging troop, all women in it of priestly stock become ineligible [for marriage with a priest on the presumption they have been raped]', and distinguishes. The rule applies when the siege was on the part of the (local) government (where soldiers are at leisure); 'But in the case of a siege by another government, they are to be considered in the category of bandits [where both parties must operate quickly and have no leisure to rape indiscriminately]': אבל כרקום של מלכות אחרת כליסטים הן.

130. There is a large literature on Palestinian banditry and political unrest: Richard A. Horsley with John S. Hanson, *Bandits, Prophets and Messiahs: Popular Movements in the Time of Jesus* (San Francisco: Harper & Row, 1988); John Dominic Crossan, *The Historical Jesus: The Life of a Mediterranean Jewish Peasant* (San Francisco: Harper & Row, 1991), pp. 168-206.

131. Cited by Sperber, *Legal Terms*, p. 108.

132. Perhaps some targumic tradition supported the LXX in Jeremiah by reading ליסטים.

iustitia quid sunt regna nisi magna latrocinia? 'without justice, what
are kingdoms but big banditries?' Among the fictional 'Acts of the
Alexandrian Martyrs', Appian[133] calls the Emperor a 'bandit chief',
λήσταρχος. Ezekias of Galilee captured by Herod the Great was a
'chief bandit', ἀρχιλῃστής (Josephus, *War* 1.204);[134] hence ארכיליסטיס
Deut. R. 4.5.

(5) 'Trumpet'. Mt. 24.31, 'He will send out his angels with a great
trumpet [σάλπιγγος, Pesh. שיפורא, Vg. *tuba*)'. σάλπιγξ went into rabbinic סלפנגס for the armies of Gentiles, and the connotations of *tuba*
underly it. Pharaoh[135] sought to hearten his host 'with all kinds of *buci-
nae*, horns, *shophars* and *salpinges*' במיני בוקינוס וקרנות ושופרות
וסלפינוס.

(6) 'Soldier's pay'. Lk. 3.14 (John the Baptist), 'be content with your
pay (ὀψωνίοις, Pesh. אפסוניתכון, Vg. *stipendiis uestris*)'. Rom. 6.23,
'the pay [ὀψώνιον] of sin is death'. ὀψώνιον 'victuals' translated *stipendium*, the soldier's pay (Poly. 6.39.12, then at two *obols* per diem).[136]
Antiochus IV (1 Macc. 3.28) opened his *gazophylakion* 'and gave his
troops their pay [ὀψώνια] for a year'. The Greek was Latinized as
obsonium: Pliny the Younger, *Ep.* 10.118, *athletae...obsonium petunt
pro eo agone*, 'the athletes are asking their upkeep for that game'.
m. Sanh. 2.4, 'the king must not multiply for himself silver and gold'
(Deut. 17.17) 'except to pay [his soldiers'] wages [אפסניא]'.

6. A Lingua Franca

Of the languages we have treated, Akkadian and Iranian are donors, not
recipients. As the Babylonian and Old Persian texts of Darius's Behis-
tun inscription went into Aramaic (preserved at Elephantine), so those
languages contributed vocabulary to Aramaic; at a later date the two
Iranian texts of Sapor's *Res Gestae* went into Greek. But little vocabulary and no texts went from Greek or Aramaic into them; there is no
ancient Persian translation of the Bible. Thus Greek, Aramaic (with

---

133. *CPJ* II.159b, IV.8.

134. Ezekias the bandit was the father of Judas the Galilaean (*Ant.* 17.271); Acts
5.37 refers to Judas, but at the wrong date.

135. *Mid. Ps.* 18.14 (similarly *Lev. R.* 29.4).

136. It was unheard of in the first century CE that it should be a denarius a day,
Tacitus, *Ann.* 1.26, *ut denarius diurnum stipendium foret.*

other West-Semitic languages) and Latin play special roles in the inter-
play of East Mediterranean cultures.

The Role of Greek

Greek is the sole intermediary between Aramaic and Latin (apart from
rare Punic loans in Latin: *sufes* 'judge', Hebrew שֹׁפֵט). Latin words went
into Aramaic in Greek form only, whether transcription or translation.
In the Hellenistic age, Aramaic as substrate hardly contributed to Greek
(or Latin) other than Latin *sabbata*, 'sabbath'. Earlier, when Greek and
Phoenician were trading equals, West-Semitic words of various origin
found parallels in Greek. In the massive borrowing of Greek terms by
Latin, some of those went over also. Thus of old Greek words with
Semitic parallels and appearing in the sayings of Jesus, these appear
in Latin also (including the Gospel Vulgate): *byssus* 'fine linen', *cadus*
'jar', *camelus* 'camel', *cuminum* 'cummin', *lampas* 'torch', *mina*
'weight', *saccus* 'sack', *taurus* 'bull', *tunica* 'tunic' (deformed from
χιτών), *uinum* 'wine' (but the old Semitic was replaced in Peshitto and
Aramaic by חַמְרָא). They form the oldest stratum of what we may call a
lingua franca—the commonalty of Greek, Aramaic and Latin.

The Role of Aramaic

Aramaic became the business language of successive empires, and anticipated the role of Arabic as moving into dialects of Canaanite. It may
have been the intermediary in the takeover of Akkadian words in Ugarit
and Phoenicia. It was surely the language in which unorthodox Jewish
or Christian groups influenced Islam—so that the symbolism of the
'throne' is continuous from Ugarit to the Hebrew Bible to the New Testament to Mecca. As the language of the Jewish exile in Babylon, it
brought the Akkadian names of social classes and urban features—and
their reality—to Palestine. We saw evidence[137] that one source of Greek
loan words in Aramaic was the use of the Septuagint by the oral tradition which developed into the written targums (and by the makers of
midrash, who put אַפּוֹטְרִין into the Aramaic of Beit Shammai); hence
the LXX in Jesus' quotations need not all be the work of the Evangelists.

We saw that the *parables of Jesus* were enough known in Aramaic to
get *polemical reversal or parody*. At Mt. 13.45-46 it is good luck for

---

137. See further my 'The Septuagint as a Source of the Greek Loan-Words in
the Targum', *Bib* 70 (1989), pp. 194-216.

the trader who 'went and sold all he had' to buy a pearl; bad luck for the Gentile who does so (*b. Šab.* 119a). The reliable innkeeper of the Samaritan parable for one wounded by bandits (Lk. 10.30) is replaced by the rascally innkeeper of *Gen. R.* 92.6 in cahoots with bandits. The householder or king who gives a banquet (Mt. 22.4) to which only the poor come (Lk. 14.21) is replaced by the publican (*y. Ḥag.* 77d51) who does no other meritorious deed. At Lk. 18.2-8 the unjust judge is swayed by the insistence of the widow to be vindicated from her adversary (ἀντίδικος, Pal. Syr. אנטדיקך); at *Pes. K.* 15.9, a woman and her adversary (אנטידיקוס) both bribe the judge, and he is swayed by the bigger bribe of her adversary.

The Role of Latin
At first it was the borrower from Greek. The legendary city of Thebes is described in six Greek loans at Plautus, *Amph.* 1011-1012:

> nam omnis *plateas* perreptaui, *gymnasia* et *myropolia*,
> apud *emporium* atque in *macello*, in *palaestra* atque in foro.

'For I walked through all the streets, gymnasia and perfumeries, at the market and in the meat market, at the wrestling-floor and in the forum'. Three appear in the New Testament and four in Semitic: πλατεῖα with פלטיא; ἐμπόριον Jn 2.16 with Rabb. אמפרין; μάκελλον 1 Cor. 10.25 (Pesh. מקלון); *PAT* 1406 גמנסירכס with γυμνασίαρχος 'gymnasium-supervisor'. Later, Latin becomes an equally generous donor to Greek, both in transcription and translation.

Of the Greek words discussed in Section 4 above, Latin borrowed most of the first declension feminines—*apotheca, asotia, cathedra, stola, symphonia, theca, zona*—all of which also went into Aramaic. The spread of Hellenistic culture to Palestine and Italy happened during the same centuries, and social conditions were enough alike that many of the same items and institutions were taken up by both peoples, along with their names. A survey of the remaining New Testament noun-vocabulary would turn up scores of words of Greek or Latin origin equally at home in all three languages.

Where the three languages are on a par, *trilingual texts* appear. Cleon the salt-official dedicates a bronze altar base at Sardinia in 200–150 BCE (*KAI* 66) in Latin, Greek and Punic; the Punic notes that it weighs '100 pounds', לטרם מאת, the south Italian word behind Latin *libra* and

Greek λίτρα. At Palmyra in 174 CE (*PAT* 1413),[138] Lucius Antonius Callistratus, a tax collector of some sort, gets an honorific inscription in Latin, Greek and Palmyrene from Galen his agent (*actor* = πραγματευτής = פרגמטתא).

The New Testament, itself to become a trilingual text, has in it the text billed (Jn 19.20) as 'in Hebrew, Latin and Greek', Ἑβραϊστί, Ῥωμαϊστί, Ἑλληνιστί where presumably John as elsewhere by 'Hebrew' meant Aramaic. (The Vulgate and Peshitto change the order, *hebraice graece et latine*.) The Peshitto of John correctly has ישוע נצריא, for the town Nazareth is known in Hebrew from the Caesarea list[139] of priestly courses as נצרת. In a Crucifixion by El Greco (1605–1610) at Cleveland the *titulus* is a neat board against agitated clouds. The Greek painter, working in Toledo, follows the Vulgate change of order; he correctly puts the Greek in capitals (with ligatures); and so the Latin, with IVDEOR[um] abbreviated. The Hebrew is corrupt; he is copying a learned translation (source unknown) at several removes. In a near-contemporary work, the Crucifixion by Rubens, the figures are in motion, even the *titulus* is wind-blown. Rubens' Greek is in MS style with capitals and small letters, breathings and accents; the Latin is correct. The Hebrew is again corrupt, now with vowel-points in what pass for the letters. The Greek mannerist conveys the feeling of an ancient trilingual in capitals, while the Flemish realist reproduces printed books of his own age.

Lingua Franca

So far as discourse in Greek, Aramaic or Latin aimed at users of one of the other languages, syntax, topics and vocabulary were restricted for maximum ease of translation. While this assimilation never reached mutual intelligibility, it simplified learning another tongue. The asymmetrical process described created a common vocabulary shared by all three tongues (and more by Greek and Aramaic, and by Greek and Latin).

The original lingua franca was the trading language of the eastern Mediterranean during the Renaissance, a fusion of Italian and Provençal with Arabic elements, like other pidgins comprehensible to each party, but in a limited semantic realm. ('Lingua franca' itself is thought a

---

138. Trilingual epitaphs for the local Hairanes (*PAT* 2801, 52 CE); and the Roman Lucius Spedius Chrysanthus, another publican, מכסא (*PAT* 0591, 58 CE).

139. Jack Finegan, *The Archeology of the New Testament* (Princeton, NJ: Princeton University Press, 1969), p. 29 with photo.

calque on Arabic *lisān al-farang*, 'tongue of the French [i.e. foreigner]'.) Molière reports or parodies it in *Le bourgeois gentilhomme* 4.7 on the mufti's lips:

> Se ti sabir, / Ti respondir; / Se non sabir, / Tazir, tazir.
> Mi star mufti, / Ti qui star, ti? / Non intendir? / Tazir, tazir.
>
> If you know, answer; if you don't know, be quiet, be quiet. I am the mufti, who are you? You don't understand? Be quiet, be quiet.

In modern usage, lingua franca is an existing language used for specific purposes beyond the range of its native speakers. French was long the lingua franca of diplomacy, and we all name military ranks after its scheme: *général, colonel, capitain, lieutenant*. English is the lingua franca of business: the French say *software* while the Académie vainly boosts *logiciel*. Rosén finds Roman Palestine 'one of the few areas of intersection [*Überschneidungsflächen*] of these two linguae francae [Greek and Imperial Aramaic]'.[140] Fitzmyer[141] speaks of Aramaic in the Near East as 'serving as the *lingua franca* during the latter part of the Neo-Assyrian Empire and during the Persian period'; and likewise for Greek during the Hellenistic and Roman periods.

Here I use 'lingua franca' in an intermediate sense to denote the commonalty of two or more languages in the same area, increasingly assimilated without ever creating a full pidgin or creole (a trading pidgin become the language of a whole people). The Near Eastern lingua franca is composed almost wholly of nouns: the mutual intercourse of peoples keeps expanding the universe of things that require discourse—sabbaths, inns, legions—while the actions recorded in verbs remain primordial.

The reality of this lingua franca puts a much enlarged burden on lexicography, whether of the New Testament or an ancient language generally. If the sayings of Jesus in our Gospels are truly a translation, their meaning is not exhausted by prior usage of the translator's vocabulary. If the underlying Aramaic is filled with loan words from other languages, we need to look at them also. You would think at least that the New Testament lexica, when they come to a word transliterated from

---

140. Haiim B. Rosén, 'Die Sprachsituation in römischen Palästina', in *idem, East and West: Selected Writings in Linguistics. I. General and Indo-European Linguistics* (Munich: W. Funk, 1982), pp. 489-513 (499). Strictly speaking, *lingua franca*, being Italian, should not have this Latin plural.

141. *Wandering Aramean*, pp. 29, 32, 35.

Latin, would cite Latin texts; they do not. Καιρός is an egregious example: it surely rests on Aramaic זְמָן, which rests on Iranian; and its possible meaning, 'dangerous time', rests on the influence of Latin *tempus* upon Polybius.

The New Testament as Primary Witness to the Lingua Franca
The New Testament thus is really a trilingual text; and the Versions, in particular Syriac and Latin, not merely illustrate the coloration of its vocabulary, but again and again restore to its original form the actual situation. The Peshitto of Jesus' sayings, though not his original Aramaic, is one step closer than the Greek.

The three versions of the New Testament come closest to mutual intelligibility in dealing with the Roman administration. Thus Mt. 27.26-28: 'Then he released Barabbas to them, and *scourged* Jesus and turned him over to be crucified. Then the *soldiers* of the *governor* took Jesus into the *pretorium* and collected the whole *cohort* against him. And they stripped him and put on him a scarlet *cloak*'. All six Greek words italicized receive their correct equivalents in the Vulgate and the Peshitto. Like the Syriac in Jesus' sayings, the Latin restores the original language of the event. And the Peshitto also restores a possible original of the text; for it can pass as reconstruction of an Aramaic eyewitness account.

The borrowed language naming new cultural elements paradoxically confers *invulnerability* upon the tradition deposited in the successive texts. A weaker society is vulnerable when it tries to hold on to old traditions in old language against the attraction and repression of a stronger occupying power. That happened to the Keltic enclaves in the British isles. But where the weaker society adopts the foreign culture in its foreign language, and then proceeds to express its native thought in those borrowed terms, it cannot be touched; the occupying regime has no power over it. Thus the most characteristic features of Jesus' thought are expressed precisely through examples derived from one of the foreign cultures, and named in its language. Since the objects named by the lingua franca have become a common Mediterranean (and modern) heritage, the message they convey is self-explanatory. And since the situation of Galilee was that of poor people on the land under a double layer of control, native and foreign, the message is self-explanatory wherever the narrative situation repeats itself.

Scholars study the Versions mostly as a witness to the earliest form of the Greek text. Since the Old Latin and Old Syriac go back to the second century of our era, from which we have few papyri, this is a valuable use of them. Here we use them less as a witness to an earlier state of the Greek text than to an earlier *cultural and linguistic state of the New Testament materials*. To the historian, the Latin and Syriac Versions are of no less value than their Greek original in assessing the original meaning of the text. For they represent a restoration of the historical setting by well-informed scholars with a vast fund of concrete knowledge and linguistic understanding now lost to us.

The Pentecost story is usually taken as an interpretation of glossolalia —unintelligible ecstatic speech. Luke is presumed to have in mind the spread of the gospel to many of the peoples he lists (Acts 2.9-11). We may extend his interpretation: Jews speaking Parthian recognized the loans from their language in the texts; Jews speaking Babylonian Aramaic, Greek, the Latin of Rome were to acquire full versions of the texts in their own languages. The new church is surprised and delighted that the barriers of Babel have been overthrown. The limitations on the language of Jesus (and in a somewhat different way on that of Luke and Paul), screening off what was not directly transferable to Greek and Latin, were the condition of its universality.

THE KINGDOM OF HEAVEN FORCEFULLY ADVANCES[*]

R. Steven Notley

Few verses have perplexed New Testament translators and interpreters as has Mt. 11.12 (= Lk. 16.16). Davies and Allison commented recently that our saying is 'without a doubt, one of the New Testament's greatest conundrums'.[1] The inherent complexity of the Greek saying is attested by the divergent editorial activity of Matthew and Luke. The fragmented literary context of the Lukan logion has left the aim of the saying more obscure than its synoptic counterpart.[2] On the other hand, Matthew's geminated ἕως,[3] has resulted in ἕως ἄρτι, to suggest that the

* (I want to thank my friend and mentor, Professor David Flusser, and my student Marc Turnage for their helpful discussions and suggestions and the Jerusalem School of Synoptic Research for funding this study.

1. W.D. Davies and D.C. Allison, *The Gospel According to Saint Matthew* (ICC; 3 vols.; Edinburgh: T. & T. Clark, 1988–97), II, p. 254; C. Spicq, 'βιάζομαι', *Theological Lexicon of the New Testament* (3 vols.; Peabody, MA: Hendrickson, 1994), I, p. 287; E. Trocmé, *Jesus and his Contemporaries* (London: SCM Press, 1973), p. 33; I.H. Marshall, *The Gospel of Luke: A Commentary on the Greek Text* (NIGTC; Grand Rapids: Eerdmans, 1986), p. 630.

2. 'Matthew seems more primitive and Palestinian; Luke fits with a later stage in the propagation of the gospel. So we cannot use one text to explain the other; each has it own particular significance'; Spicq, 'βιάζομαι', p. 287; W. Wink, *John the Baptist in the Gospel Tradition* (Cambridge: Cambridge University Press, 1968), p. 20.

3. Mt. 11.13: πάντες γὰρ οἱ προφῆται καὶ ὁ νόμος **ἕως** Ἰωάννου ἐπρο-φήτευσαν. Matthew introduces the duplicative ἕως in Mt. 5.18, again following the mention of 'the law or the prophets' (Mt. 5.17). On the unusual appearance of ἤ in 5.17 see n. 5 below. In Mt. 5.18, however, the Evangelist employs another favorite temporal phrase, ἕως ἄν (cf. Mt. 2.13; 5.26; 10.11, 23; 12.20; 16.28). The use of ἕως ἄν in 5.18 echoes Mt. 24.34, where he agrees with Lk. 21.32 (ἀμὴν λέγω ὑμῖν ὅτι οὐ μὴ παρέλθῃ ἡ γενεὰ αὕτη **ἕως ἄν** πάντα γένηται) against Mark's sole use of μέχρι (Mk 13.30; cf. Lk. 16.16).

kingdom has come to an end[4]—an opinion inconsistent with Matthew's own presentation of the kingdom of heaven. While Matthew and Luke both offer John's advent as a turning point, scholarship has struggled to understand precisely what his appearance signifies. Did he mark the culmination of the 'law and the prophets' (Luke), or the beginning of the 'kingdom of heaven' (Matthew)?

Luke's logion likewise bears the marks of editing with its reordering of Matthew's οἱ προφῆται καὶ ὁ νόμος to present a patently Matthean phrase (Mt. 7.12; 22.40).[5] Moreover, while the manuscript evidence for a shorter Matthean reading which omits καὶ ὁ νόμος is poorly attested, it deserves some consideration simply on the grounds that the law does not prophesy. On the other hand, the phrase 'the prophets prophesied'[6] is a well-attested Hebraism[7] and reinforces the eschatological nature of what Meier has termed 'the second Baptist-block' (Mt. 11.2-15).[8] The notion that the prophets prophesied concerning the End of Days, even though they themselves did not fully understand their prophecy, is heard in the Dead Sea Scrolls.[9]

> And God told Habbakuk to write down that which would happen to the final generation, but he did not make known to him when *the time* [הקץ] would come to an end (1QpHab. 7.1-2).

The sectarian opinion of the eschatological aim of the biblical prophets is echoed in the rabbinic estimation, 'All of the prophets prophesied solely concerning the Days of the Messiah' (כל הנביאים לא נתנבאו אלא לימות המשיח: *b. Ber.* 34b; *b. Šab.* 63a; *b. Sanh.* 99a).[10] What is important for our study is not merely the recognition of the similarities in lan-

---

4. Matthew alone of the synoptists uses ἕως with ἄρτι (Mt. 11.12; 23.39; 26.29; Jn 2.10; 16.24; 1 Cor. 4.13; 8.7; 15.6; 1 Jn 2.9). See J. Jeremias, *New Testament Theology* (London: SCM Press, 1987), pp. 46-47.

5. The simple ὁ νόμος seems more fitting in Mt. 5.17, but it has been augmented with οἱ προφῆται. Editorial revision may be indicated by the atypical conjunction ἤ in an otherwise Matthean phrase: τὸν νόμον ἢ τοὺς προφήτας. Davies and Allison, *Matthew*, I, p. 484.

6. 1 Pet. 1.10: **προφῆται** οἱ περὶ τῆς εἰς ὑμᾶς χάριτος **προφητεύσαντες**...

7. 1 Sam. 19.20; Jer. 14.15; 2 Chron. 18.11.

8. J.P. Meier, *A Marginal Jew* (2 vols.; New York: Doubleday, 1991–94), II, pp. 130-63.

9. See W.H. Brownlee, *The Midrash Pesher of Habakkuk* (Missoula, MT: Scholars Press, 1979), pp. 110-111.

10. Str-B III, pp. 327-29; D. Flusser, *Judaism and the Origins of Christianity* (Jerusalem: Magnes Press, 1988), p. 255 n. 39.

guage between our saying and the Jewish sources, but the shared opinion in Judaism of late antiquity of the eschatological aim of the biblical prophets. According to this opinion, the prophets spoke ultimately of the hope of redemption, whether that expectation is couched in the Qumran vocabulary of קץ[11] or the rabbinical expression ימות המשיח. This understanding also indicates the eschatological milieu for our saying.

The most comprehensive study of the history of interpretation for Mt. 11.12 is that by Cameron.[12] Beginning with a survey of early patristic interpretation, he has traced the significant approaches to our verse. As he rightly notes, the question at the heart of any discussion is the enigmatic use of the verb βιάζεται and its cognate βιασταί. Should the verb be read passively, 'the kingdom *suffers violence*', or in the middle voice, 'the kingdom *forcefully advances*'? Related to this is the question whether βιασταί designates opponents or members of the kingdom of heaven.

In the following study I hope to demonstrate that the historical sense of our saying has been obscured by three points. First, insufficient attention has been given to the saying's reflection of an ancient complex of eschatological testimonia concerning the Jewish expectation for a prophet in the End of Days. Second, the saying's link to these testimonia has been obscured because of a variance in verbal expression between Greek and Hebrew. Our saying possesses an elliptical allusion to an Old Testament passage which has been overlooked, because it is preserved in a non-Septuagintal Greek rendering of a Hebrew term. Finally, the content of Jesus' testimony concerning John and the βιασταί has not been fully appreciated because New Testament scholarship has underestimated the eschatological aim of John's baptism of repentance.

1. *The Kingdom Suffers Violence*

Evidence has been marshaled from literary Greek usage[13] and from the papyri[14] to support both the passive and the middle readings of βιάζεται. While a passive reading is possible in form, the challenge is to de-

---

11. For the use of קץ to signify the era of God's redemption see 1QS 3.23 (לפי קצי אל עד קצו); CD 19.10 (בקץ הפקדה); see also CD 4.10; 1QS 4.18; 1QpHab. 7.7 (הקץ האחרון); 1Q34[bis] 32.5 (רצונך בקץ).

12. P.S. Cameron, *Violence and the Kingdom: The Interpretation of Matthew 11:12* (ANTJ; Bern: Peter Lang, 1988); see J.M. Thacker, 'The Kingdom of Heaven Is Breaking Forth' (MA thesis submitted to Oral Roberts University, 1990).

13. Spicq, 'βιάζομαι', I, pp. 287-91.

termine its sense in this particular setting. In recent years, the most compelling case for a passive (*in malam partem*) rendering has been that put forward by Moore in his study on βιάζω, ἁρπάζω and their cognates in the writings of Josephus Flavius. He observed that the use of these two verbs in combination by the Jewish historian invariably suggests physical violence as a means of coercion.[15] He thus concluded concerning the Matthean saying,[16]

> Since the saying is primarily concerned with the 'kingdom', and since the chief opponents of Jesus are the Pharisees and this Gospel contains stronger denunciations of them than the others, it is the Pharisees who are chiefly in mind.

Moore proposes that Jesus particularly speaks of the 'violent and Zealotic Pharisees' who 'provided the resistance movement with its theology and its apocalyptic inspiration'.[17] While he acknowledges a division of opinion[18] among the Pharisees regarding armed struggle, pacifistic Pharisaism is all but ignored and the reader is left with the impression that the Pharisees of the Gospels are to be identified with those who had abandoned peaceful means to usher in God's reign. He suggests that 'the denunciation of the Pharisees carried with it *ipso facto* a denunciation of the Zealots'.[19]

The problems with Moore's historical and literary assumptions are legion. Apart from the obvious historical problems of identifying the Pharisees in the New Testament with the Zealots, nothing in the literary context anticipates the notion of force *against* the 'kingdom of heaven'. According to Matthew and Luke—the only Gospels in which the saying appears—Jesus' movement has yet to encounter any violent opposition.

---

14. F. Preisigke, *Wörterbuch der griechischen Papyrusurfunden* (3 vols.; Berlin: G. Preisigke, 1925–31), I, p. 266.

15. E. Moore, 'ΒΙΑΖΩ, ΑΡΠΑΖΩ and Cognates in Josephus', *NTS* 21 (1975), pp. 519-43.

16. Moore, 'Cognates', pp. 540-41.

17. Moore, 'Cognates', p. 541.

18. Acts 5.34-39. Moore suggests ('Cognates', p. 541), that Gamaliel's speech gives us insight into the internal Pharisaic debate. Likewise, he notes that the two opinions are exemplified on the one hand by the '*Psalms of Solomon* (militaristic) and on the other (though more tentatively) by the *Assumption of Moses* (pacifist)'. Nevertheless, as we shall see, these same pseudepigraphical works share an apocalyptic perspective regarding events and characters in the End of Days.

19. Moore, 'Cognates', p. 541; D. Hill, *The Gospel of Matthew* (London: Marshall, Morgan & Scott, 1972), pp. 200-201.

While Mk 3.6 presents plotting by the Pharisees at the very outset of Jesus' ministry, such early violent opposition is unknown either to Matthew[20] or Luke.[21]

Even less evidence exists for Pharisaic (zealotic or otherwise) opposition to John. Matthew's patent style of combining 'the Pharisees and the Sadducees' (Mt. 16.1-12; 22.34) to identify those whom John accused of insincerity (Mt. 3.7) leaves the impression that the Pharisees were unsympathetic to John. Yet the essential content of his call— repentance, baptism and the nearness of the kingdom of heaven—all belong to Pharisaism. His message would have appealed to the Pharisees in the same way that Paul's preaching of the resurrection pitted the Pharisees against the Sadducean priests in the Sanhedrin (Acts 23.6-11).

It is significant that Luke lacks the designation, 'the Pharisees and the Sadducees', in his description of those coming to John (Lk. 3.7-9). Indeed, as all the Synoptic Gospels agree (Mt. 21.23-27 par.), it is the Sadducean Temple establishment which was unsupportive of John's movement. Yet, even after his death they were afraid to express their opinion publicly because of his vast popularity among the Jewish populace.

Schrenk also questioned whether the saying in Matthew could be understood as an opposition logion aimed at unprincipled Zealots.[22]

> The difficulty here is that Matthew is concerned with the prophets, the Law, the Baptist, Jesus and the βασιλεία. It is thus hard to see the point of a special reference to an irrelevant subject when we naturally expect an important insight on the situation depicted.

20. Mt. 12.14: 'But the Pharisees went out and took counsel against him, how to destroy him'.

21. Luke does not mention any violent opposition until the reaction to the parable of the wicked tenants (Lk. 20.9-18), which was aimed at the Sadducean priesthood. Even at that point, Jesus' opponents according to Luke are the Sadducean Temple establishment, and not the Pharisees. 'The *scribes and the chief priests* tried to lay hands on him at that very hour, but they feared the people; for they perceived that he had told this parable against them' (Lk. 20.19). J.A. Fitzmyer noted, 'in all of this characterization of the groups that oppose Jesus during his last days *the Pharisees are conspicuously absent...*': *The Gospel According to Luke* (AB; 2 vols.; New York: Doubleday, 1981–85), II, p. 1270. Indeed, no mention is made in any of the Gospels of the Pharisees' participation in the trial and crucifixion of Jesus. D. Flusser, *Jesus* (Jerusalem: Magnes Press, 1998), p. 73. On Lk. 20.9-18 see B.H. Young, *Jesus and his Jewish Parables* (New York: Paulist Press, 1989), pp. 282-305.

22. G. Schrenk, 'βιάζομαι', *TDNT*, I, p. 611.

Moore's proposal is an abrupt intrusion into the Matthean context, and necessitates the disintegration of our saying from the testimony about John. A reading of violence in Luke is equally problematic.[23] While the fragmented state of Luke's literary context does allow for a sudden change of subject, internally one would have expected ἀλλά rather than καί to distinguish between those who 'proclaim the kingdom of God' and those subjecting it to violence.

Scholarship has failed to provide any coherent connection between the advent of John and violence against the kingdom of heaven—of which the Baptist was not even numbered![24] The only element of violence witnessed in Matthew's historical setting is John's imprisonment by Herod Antipas—an historical setting unknown to Luke. Even if we accept Matthew's context for the saying, the issues which led to this tragic set of events have nothing to do with his proclamation of the nearness of the 'kingdom of heaven'. They, instead, were precipitated by John's unyielding criticism of Herod's attempt to legitimize his adulterous affair with his brother's wife by marrying her.[25] Thus, while the passive voice may be plausible in form, there seems to be little within the literary or historical context which would suggest such a passive (*in malam partem*) reading.

2. *Middle Voice: The Kingdom Forcefully Advances*

While the notion of violence to the kingdom of heaven may be ill-fitted to the context, the rendering of βιαζεταί in the middle voice often fails to contribute much to the cohesion of Jesus' testimony about John. Nevertheless, there does exist a correspondence between the sense of βιάζεται in the middle voice and a Semitic equivalent.[26] What is more

---

23. For the reading of Lk. 16.16 as passive but *in bonam partem*, 'to be pressed, encouraged', see J.B. Cortés and F.M. Gatti, 'On the Meaning of Luke 16:16', *JBL* 106 (1987), pp. 247-59; Fitzmyer, *Luke*, II, p. 1117.

24. Mt. 11.11b: 'He who is least in the kingdom of Heaven is greater than he (John)' (Davies and Allison, *Matthew*, II, p. 252).

25. Josephus, *Ant.* 18.109-110. See the discussion by N. Kokkinos, *The Herodian Dynasty* (Sheffield: Sheffield Academic Press, 1998), pp. 267-70.

26. Spicq ('βιάζομαι', I, p. 288 n. 7) states, 'In several of the papyri, and constantly in literary texts, the verb is used for forced entry into a house, a route, or a city...2 Macc. 14.41; Philo, *Moses* 1.108, 1.215; Epictetus, 4.4.20: "no closed door for me, but for those who want to force it"; Josephus, *War* 2.262: "take Jerusalem by force"; 4.554: "Vespasian entered Hebron by main force"; 5.59: "Titus forced a

significant is that this same Semitic term contributes integrally to Jesus' identification of John the Baptist as the prophet of the End of Days. Suggesting Semitic equivalents for Greek terms is always a precarious task. Daube mentions no fewer than a dozen possible Aramaic and Hebrew equivalents for βιάζεται, with little indication which might actually lie behind the Greek term.[27] Cameron rightly criticizes that Semitic solutions to our saying have traditionally suffered from the same weakness as their Greek counterparts.[28]

> The investigation of the Semitic background to the saying was necessary because there seemed to be no adequate control available from its Greek translations. The question now arises: What controls are there over the investigation of the Semitic background?

As he laments, few controls have been applied to either Greek or Semitic solutions. Yet, it is precisely the fresh linguistic and religious data in the Qumran library which can sometimes contribute to the necessary controls for Semitic solutions. The challenge before us is to determine if the linguistic and religious milieu presented by the Dead Sea Scrolls coincides with the literary context of the saying. Our study will proceed along two lines. First, we want to investigate the expectations among the Qumran sectarians and their Jewish contemporaries concerning the prophet of the End of Days. Particular attention will be given to the similarities between these expectations and the content of Jesus' testimony concerning John. Second, within the body of testimonia concerning these expectations we hope to demonstrate that specialized Hebrew vocabulary exists, which relates to the meaning of βιάζεται and βιάσται in Jesus' statement concerning John in Mt. 11.12.

3. *From the Days of John*

Collins's review[29] of the figures portrayed in the messianic expectations of the Dead Sea Sect touches on the eschatological milieu of our say-

way through to his own"; 5.112: "forced entrance"; Josephus, *Ant.* 17.253: "he had attempted to take their fortresses by force, etc."; Thucydides 7.83.5; Diodorus Siculus 2.19.7; 17.68.2: "the Macedonians forced their way, were obliged to withdraw"; Polybius 5.4.9: "force passage"'.

27. D. Daube, *The New Testament and Rabbinic Judaism* (London: Athlone Press, 1956), pp. 285-300.

28. Cameron, *Violence*, p. 98.

29. J.J. Collins, *The Scepter and the Star: The Messiahs of the Dead Sea Scrolls and other Ancient Literature* (New York: Doubleday, 1995).

ing. Of particular relevance is the hope in Judaism of late antiquity for an eschatological prophet who would appear with the advent of the Messiah(s). This anticipation by the Qumran community for the coming of a Prophet is most clearly expressed in the *Community Rule*.

> They shall depart from none of the counsels of the Law to walk in the stubbornness of their hearts, but shall be ruled by the primitive precepts in which the men of the Community were first instructed until there shall come the Prophet and the Messiahs of Aaron and Israel (1QS 9.11).

Scriptural support for the appearance of the Prophet is given in the *Testimonia* (4Q175) with a citation from Deut. 18.18-19:

> I will *raise up for them a Prophet* like you from among their brethren. I will put my words into his mouth and he shall tell them all I command him. And I will require a reckoning of whoever will not listen to the words which the Prophet shall speak in my Name.

While the Qumran description of the eschatological prophet is shaped primarily by the Deuteronomic tradition, one can not assume that the alternative identification of the prophetic messenger of Malachi was unknown to the community. According to sectarian thought, the Prophet would appear at the End of Days—a period marked by divine judgment (1QS 4.18-21; 1QH 13.16; 14.8)[30] when God would refine (זקק) and purify (טהר) creation. Since these verbs occur in combination only in Mal. 3.3, their use to elucidate the eschatology of the Dead Sea Sect suggests that the community was familiar with the prophetic content of Mal. 3.1-3 in which the messenger (מלאכי) appears.[31] Moreover, the

---

30. References to the Thanksgiving Hymns follow E. Puech's proposed restoration, 'Quelques aspects de la restauration du rouleau des hymnes', *JJS* 39 (1988), pp. 38-55.

31. The sectarians employ language from Mal. 3.2-3 where the Day of the Lord's visitation is compared to 'a refiner's fire' (כי־הוא כאש מצרף) in their description of the End of Days. 'The End of Days is the season of refinement which has come: אחרית הימים היאה עת מצרף הבאה (A. Steudel, 'אחרית הימים' in the Texts from Qumran', *RevQ* 61 [1993–95], p. 228). On the question of whether the time is already arrived, see Steudel's comment, 'עת מצרף הבאה designates a period of history which has already begun. Probably the best example illustrating this is found in the pesharim: 4QpPsa II, 17-19 quotes Ps. 37.14-15 and interprets it as follows: Its interpretation concerns the wicked Ephraim and Manasse who have (oftenly) sought to lay hands on (אשר יבקשו לשלוח יד ב) the priest and the men of his council at the time of refining which has come (בעת מצרף הבאה) upon them. But God has

Aramaic fragment published by Starky in 1964 with the reading,[32] אשלח אליהו קדם clearly represents Mal. 3.23, ...הנה אנכי שלח...אליה...אליה לפני. Nevertheless, the emphasis of the Qumran Community on right teaching seems to have influenced its portrayal of the prophet as a teacher cum prophet-like-Moses.[33]

The identification of the eschatological prophet with the Deutero-nomic tradition was not restricted to the Qumran library. Already in the second century BCE, 1 Macc. 4.42-46 records the expectation of a prophet who would determine legal matters.[34] The Jerusalem priests appointed by Judah the Hasmonean faced a dilemma about what to do with the stones of the altar in the Temple which had been defiled by Antiochus Epiphanes. Eventually, they removed the altar but decided to keep the stones in another place until 'there should come a prophet to tell what to do with them'. The involvement of the prophet in deciding a halakhic question suggests a prophet-like-Moses was envisioned. This suspicion is bolstered by the language used in the mention of the ex-pected prophet during the selection of Simon to be leader and high priest. 'And the Jews and their priests decided that Simon should be their leader and high priest for ever, *until a faithful prophet*[35] should

(always) redeemed them (פ[ד]ם) from out of their hand' (Steudel, 'אחרית הימים', pp. 228-29).

32. J. Starcky, 'Un texte messianique araméen de la grotte 4 de Qumran', *Ecole des langues orientales anciennes de l'Institut Catholique de Paris: Mémorial du cinquantenair 1914–1964* (Travaux de l'Institut Catholique de Paris; Paris: Bloud & Gay, 1964), pp. 51-66; J.A. Fitzmyer, 'The Aramaic "Elect of God" Text from Qumran Cave 4', in *idem, Essays on the Semitic Background of the New Testament* (Grand Rapids: Eerdmans, 1997), pp. 127-60.

33. In 11Q13 the eschatological prophet (משיח הרוח) is presented with the responsibility to instruct the community concerning the ages of eternity: ל[ה]שכילמה בכול קצי העולם (11Q13 2.20). This is also the task of the Instructor (משכיל) of the community (cf. 1QS 3.13-15).

34. R.E. Brown, *The Gospel According to John* (AB; 2 vols.; New York: Dou-bleday, 1966–70), I, p. 49.

35. See 4Q375 1.1.6-7 where the rise of false prophets is contrasted with that of a 'true and faithful prophet': (צדיק הואה נביא [נ]אמן). J. Strugnell suggests that Deuteronomy chs. 13 and 18 lie behind the sectarian description: 'Moses-Pseude-pigrapha at Qumran: 4Q375, 4Q376 and Similar Works', in L.H. Schiffman (ed.), *Archaeology and History in the Dead Sea Scrolls* (JSPSup, 8; Sheffield: JSOT Press, 1990), pp. 226-29; *T. Benj.* 9.2 (μονογενοῦς προφήτου); *T. Levi* 8.15 (προφήτου ὑψηλοῦ). Jesus is called later by the Ebionites 'the true prophet'. See Epiphanius, *Panarion* 30.18.5; Eusebius, *Ecclesiastical History* 1.3.7-13; Flusser, *Judaism*

arise' (1 Macc. 14.41: ἕως τοῦ ἀναστῆναι προφήτην πιστόν). The description recalls the description of Moses as 'faithful' (Num. 12.7) and the ideal prophet: 'No prophet *has risen*...like Moses' (Deut. 34.10: לֹא קָם נָבִיא...כְּמֹשֶׁה; Deut. 18.18: נָבִיא אָקִים...כָּמוֹךָ). A similar style of composite description for Moses[36] that is drawn from disparate biblical passages occurs in a Qumran fragment (1Q34^{bis} 3 2.8)[37] where the lawgiver is called 'a faithful shepherd' (רוֹעֶה נֶאֱמָן = Exod. 3.2; Num. 12.7) and a 'humble man' (אִ[ישׁ עָנִי = Num. 12.3).

The Jewish expectation for a Deuteronomic 'prophet-like-Moses' is witnessed also in the New Testament. At Nain, the people respond to the healing of the widow's son: 'A *great prophet*[38] *has arisen* among

p. 234 n. 7; S. Pines, *Studies in the History of Religion* (Jerusalem: Magnes Press, 1996), pp. 222, 281. Some scholars see a reference in 1 Macc. 14.41 to Simon's successor, John Hyrcanus, who is the only Hasmonean ruler who possessed prophetic gifts. While the 'three crowns' (prophet, priest and king) are denied to Simon, according to Josephus, John Hyrcanus possessed all three. 'Now he was accounted by God worthy of three of the greatest privileges, the *rule* of the nation, the office of the *high-priest*, and the gift of *prophecy*' (*Ant.* 13.299-300; *War* 1.68). The opinion that Hyrcanus possessed prophetic gifts may also be hinted in the Aramaic *Targum of Pseudo-Jonathan* on Deut. 33.11 where the Hasmonean leader is mentioned in association with Elijah: 'Bless O Lord the sacrifices of the House of Levi, those who give the tenth from the tithe, and receive with pleasure the oblation from the hand of Elijah the priest which he offered on Mount Carmel. Break the loins of Ahab, his enemy, and the neck of the false prophets who rose against him. As for the enemies of John the High Priest, may they have no foot to stand on'. P. Kahle, *The Cairo Geniza* (Oxford: Basil Blackwell, 1959), pp. 202-203; R. Meyer, 'Elia und Ahab', in O. Betz, M. Hengel and P. Schmidt (eds.), *Abraham unser Vater, Festschrift für Otto Michel zum 60. Geburtstag* (Leiden: E.J. Brill, 1963), pp. 356-68.

36. The reconstruction in line 2.8 מֹשֶׁה to read 'Moses' was proposed to me by David Flusser in private conversation.

37. D. Barthélemy and J.T. Milik (eds.), *Qumrân Cave I* (DJD, 1; Oxford: Clarendon Press, 1955), p. 154.

38. The same title occurs in the *Oracles of Hystaspes*, 17.1-2: 'When the close of time draws nigh, a great prophet [*magnus propheta*] shall be sent from God to turn men to the knowledge of God, and he shall receive power of doing wonderful things. Whenever men shall not hear him, he will shut up the heaven, and cause it to withhold its rains; he will turn water into blood...' The description of the great prophet is a composition of biblical events. The allusions to Elijah (1 Kgs 8.35: 'shut up the heaven, and cause it to withhold its rains') and Moses (Exod. 7.17: 'he will turn water into blood') are clear. The author may have also intended to allude to the prophet-like-Moses in his statement, 'Whenever men shall not hear him...' See Deut. 18.15b: 'You shall hear him' (cf. Mk 9.7 par.). Flusser has demonstrated

us!' (Lk. 7.16).[39] Elsewhere, scholarship has recognized that the three answers to Jesus' question, 'Who do the crowds say that I am?', are in fact three variations on the same answer—'John the Baptist; but others say Elijah; and others, that one of the old *prophets has arisen*' (Lk. 9.19).[40] Apparently, there were those outside of Jesus' inner circle of followers who thought he was the Prophet of the End of Days. Jesus does speak of his work and death in prophetic terms: 'I must go on my way today and tomorrow and the day following; for it cannot be that a prophet should perish away from Jerusalem' (Lk. 13.33; cf. 4.24). Nonetheless, the Gospels never record that Jesus identified himself as the eschatological prophet. He consistently indicates that that role belongs to the Baptist.

Speculation by some that Jesus was Elijah is derived from the belief in postexilic Judaism that the prophet of the End of Days would be none other than Elijah.[41] The postscript in Mal. 3.22-24 (ET 4.4-6)[42] where this notion is first mentioned is considered by scholars to be an addendum to reiterate the importance of the law given to Moses at Sinai, 'Remember the law of my servant Moses [זכרו תורת משה עבדי]' (3.22a). The mention of Elijah was intended to identify the anonymous messenger of Mal. 3.1, 'Behold, I send my messenger to prepare the

---

that the *Oracles of Hystapses* 'were in reality a Jewish book in Greek language, based upon some Zoroastrian material or book' 'Hystapses and John of Patmos', *Judaism*, pp. 390-453).

39. As we witnessed in 1 Macc. 14.41, the verbs (ἀνίστημι/ἐγείρω = קום) which occur in association with the expected prophet of Deut. 18.15-18 and the description of Moses in Deut. 34.10 have influenced the description of the 'coming' of the eschatological prophet. In the New Testament the pattern is continued (cf. Lk. 7.16; 9.18, 19; 16.31; Acts 3.22; 7.37; Jn 7.52).

40. See Lk. 9.7-9; Fitzmyer, *Luke*, I, pp. 759, 774.

41. Scholarly debate continues how early the tradition develops regarding whether Elijah will precede the Messiah: M. M. Faierstein, 'Why do the Scribes say that Elijah Must Come First', *JBL* 100 (1981), pp. 75-86; D.C. Allison, 'Elijah Must Come First', *JBL* 103 (1984), pp. 256-58; J.A. Fitzmyer, 'More About Elijah Coming First', *JBL* 104 (1985), pp. 295-96; *idem*, 'Aramaic "Elect of God" Text', p. 137; J. Marcus, *The Way of the Lord: Christological Exegesis of the Old Testament in the Gospel of Mark* (Louisville, KY: Westminster Press, 1992), p. 110; C. Milikowsky, 'Elijah and the Messiah', *Jerusalem Studies in Jewish Thought* 2 (1982–83), pp. 491-96 (Hebrew).

42. On the question of the literary relationship of Mal. 3.24-26 with the remainder of the prophecy, see A.E. Hill, *Malachi* (AB; New York: Doubleday, 1998), pp. 363-66.

way before me'. Elijah's return is repeated in the second century BCE Wisdom of Ben Sira 48.10:

> You [Elijah] who are ready at the appointed time, it is written, to calm the wrath of God before it breaks out in fury, to turn the heart of the father to the son and *to restore* [καταστῆσαι] the tribes of Jacob.

Ben Sira is the earliest postbiblical interpretation of Elijah's task upon his return.[43] The meaning of the Hebrew verb in Mal. 3.23 (והשׁיב) is extended in Ben Sira to suggest that Elijah would not only restore family relationships, but that he would regather the tribes of Jacob (i.e. '*to return* fathers to their sons').

Nevertheless, Jesus did not base his opinion regarding John on the regathering role of Elijah presented by Ben Sira. He, instead, identified John's significance with the opinion of the scribes (οἱ γραμματεῖς) that Elijah is to come and to restore things as they were in the past, 'Elijah does come, and *he is to restore* [ἀποκαταστήσει: LXX Mal. 4.6; Acts 1.6; 3.21] all things' (Mt. 17.10-11).[44]

Discussion among Israel's sages concerning Elijah's future task is preserved in a first century logion found in *m. 'Ed.* 8.7:[45]

> R. Joshua said: I have received as a tradition from R. Johanan b. Zakkai, who heard from his teacher, and his teacher from his teacher, as a Halakah given to Moses from Sinai, that Elijah will not come to declare unclean or clean, to remove afar or to bring nigh, but to remove afar those families that were brought nigh by violence and to bring nigh those families that were removed afar by violence [i.e. to bring an end to injustice].

The association of Elijah with legal tasks more closely associated with Moses may stem from the fact that both figures received revelation at Mount Horeb (Exod. 3.1; 1 Kgs 19.8). More likely, however, it results from the juxtaposition in which they appear at the end of Mal. 3.22-23:[46]

---

43. While Ben Sira does not quote explicitly from Mal. 3.24, Wright argues the apocryphal work is dependent upon the biblical passage. B.G. Wright, *No Small Difference: Sirach's Relationship to its Hebrew Parent Text* (Atlanta: Scholars Press, 1989), pp. 209-211.

44. The aim of Jesus' statement is confused in Mk 9.11-13. See Davies and Allison, *Matthew*, II, pp. 714-15.

45. See J. Neusner, *Development of a Legend: Studies on the Traditions concerning Yohanan ben Zakkai* (Leiden: E.J. Brill, 1970), pp. 53, 201.

46. See the collaboration of Moses and Elijah in Rabbinic tradition: *t. Soṭ.* 4.7; *t. 'Ed.* 3.4; *b. Soṭ.* 13a; *y. Sanh.* 10.1, 28a; *Exod. R.* 44.1; *Num. R.* 18.12; *Lam. R.* 1.2,

> Remember the law of my servant *Moses*,
> the statutes and ordinances that I commanded him at Horeb for all
> Israel.
> Behold, I will send you *Elijah* the prophet
> before the great and terrible day of the Lord comes.

What is significant for our study is the opinion of some that Elijah's future task would be to decide legal matters ('to declare unclean or clean')—precisely the role of the expected prophet of 1 Macc. 4.46. At the same time, others held that his role was to regather ('to bring near'). The fluid state of opinion in Jewish thought of the first century concerning bott the eschatological prophet's identity and his task is precisely the religious milieu for the literary creativity witnessed in the New Testament.

Typically, the synoptic tradition draws on the anticipation for Elijah *redivivus* to signify John, 'If you are willing to accept it, he is Elijah who is to come' (Mt. 11.14). Yet, Jesus' statement, 'There has arisen no one born of women greater[47] than John', echoes the Deuteronomic testimony about Moses, ולא־קם עוד נביא בישראל כמשה.[48] Likewise, Mark's statement that Jesus was moved with compassion for the Galilean crowds, because they were 'like sheep without a shepherd' (Mk

---

§ 23. For a detailed comparison of their careers see *Pesiq. R.* 4.13. The coupling of Moses and Elijah can even be witnessed in the Emperor Julian's refutation of the Galileans. 'Moses after fasting forty days received the law, and Elijah, after fasting for the same period, was granted to see God face to face. But what did Jesus receive, after a fast of the same length?' (*The Works of the Emperor Julian, Against the Galileans*, fragment 2 [trans. W.C. Wright; Cambridge, MA: Harvard University Press, 1980], pp. 428-29). M. Stern, *Greek and Latin Authors on Jews and Judaism* (3 vols.; Jerusalem: Israel Academy of Sciences and Humanities, 1980), II, p. 549.

47. Flusser has suggested that μείζων in Mt. 11.11a has geminated from its appearance in the second half of the verse: ὁ δὲ μικρότερος ἐν τῇ βασιλείᾳ τῶν οὐρανῶν μείζων αὐτοῦ ἐστιν. Originally, then, the saying would have read, 'There has arisen no one born among women [like] John…', *Jesus*, p. 261 n. 8.

48. Deut. 34.10 is the only passage in the Hebrew Scriptures which begins, 'There has not arisen…' Such an opening phrase to describe John would suggest to the hearers/readers a connection to Moses. Note the Hebraic influence on ἐν (among) and the replacement of 'in Israel' with 'among those born of woman'. Davies and Allison, *Matthew*, II, p. 251. The verbal allusion to Moses from Deut. 34.10 is reinforced by the phrase, 'born among women', itself a phrase connected to Moses. *Ab. R.N.* 2 Ver. A. See L. Ginzberg, *Legends of the Jews* (7 vols.; Philadelphia: Jewish Publication Society of America, 1910), III, p. 113.

6.34),[49] seems linked by the Evangelist to the recent news of John's execution (Mk 6.17-29), and may imply that the crowds included John's former followers. The Markan phrase is drawn from Num. 27.17, where the subject is the absence of leadership after Moses' death. The historical setting presented by Mark leaves little doubt that he attempted to hint through literary means at the opinion held by some that John was the prophet-like-Moses.

What we witness throughout the Synoptic Gospels are the reflections of the two contemporary streams of Jewish opinion which endeavored to identify the eschatological prophet. The dominical saying in Mt. 11.7-14 is a repetitive creative fusion of these two traditions, which climaxes in the sophisticated blending of Exod. 23.20 and Mal. 3.1 in Mt. 11.10:[50]

> This is he of whom it is written, 'Behold, I send my messenger before thy face, who shall prepare thy way before thee'.

Scholarship has noted that elements from both of these Old Testament verses are present,[51] but few have recognized that the combination itself

---

49. Matthew preserves the phrase at an earlier point in Mt. 9.36. Yet, the significance of its connection to John and his prophetic ministry is consequently lost, because John has not yet been executed according to Matthew's chronology. A similar example of Matthew's reordering of sayings material with resulting obscurity is the timing of Jesus' statement in Lk. 13.35b: 'And I tell you, you will not see me until you say, "Blessed is he who comes in the name of the Lord"'! Originally, the saying is intended to refer to Jesus' pending pilgrimage to Jerusalem at Passover. The citation of Ps. 118.26 refers to the commonplace greeting given to Jewish pilgrims to Jerusalem, particularly at Passover. In Matthew, however, placement of the saying *after* Jesus is already in Jerusalem redirects the saying with an eschatological focus. See S. Safrai, *Die Wallfahrt im Zeitalter des Zweiten Tempels* (Neukirchen–Vluyn: Neukirchener Verlag, 1981), p. 158.

50. These same verses are combined in *Deut. R.* 11.9. J. Mann has suggested that Exod. 23.20 and Mal. 3.1 were read together in the triennial cycle of the synagogue readings already during the days of the Second Temple (*The Bible as Read and Preached in the Old Synagogue* [2 vols.; Cincinnati: Hebrew Union College Press, 1940], II, p. 479).

51. See W.F. Albright and C.S. Mann, *Matthew* (AB; Garden City, NY: Doubleday, 1971), p. 136; R.H. Gundry, *Matthew: A Commentary on his Literary and Theological Art* (Grand Rapids: Eerdmans, 1982), pp. 207-208; Meier, *Marginal Jew*, II, pp. 140-41; J.A.T. Robinson, 'Elijah, John and Jesus: An Essay in Detection', *NTS* 4 (1957–58), pp. 253-81.

is a sophisticated example of *gezerah shavah*.[52] Accordingly, two verses may be joined by virtue of the appearance of the same word(s) in both verses. While in later rabbinic tradition even similar word forms or ideas could justify linking verses, the methodology attributed to Jesus reflects the more primitive style whereby the linkage demanded the appearance of *identical* word forms.

In our present citation the two verses are linked by the fact that only in these two verses in the Hebrew Scriptures do we find the combined appearance of מלאכי[53] and שלח (with also דרך and לפני). This type of associative hermeneutic is Jewish, and not the style of Christian exegetes. Moreover, it indicates a profoundly intimate familiarity with the Hebrew Scriptures, and a knowledge of the sophisticated hermeneutical methods employed in Judaism of the period. What is equally significant for our study is the fact that Exod. 23.20 was read by some interpreters to signify Moses,[54] and as we have seen the messenger of Mal. 3.1 was interpreted to be Elijah. Jesus' uncanny combination of two otherwise unrelated verses in reference to the Baptist presents an ingenious fusion of the two Jewish opinions concerning the identity of the eschatological prophet similar to that witnessed in the *Oracles of Hystapses*.[55] There can be little doubt that we possess a primitive stratum of Christian tradition which originates with the historical Jesus.

Jesus' fusion of the Moses and Elijah traditions is repeated in the preaching of the early church, but with a significant change. In the Synoptic Gospels the two opinions are combined in order to signify the importance of John the Baptist. Yet, Peter's sermon in Solomon's Porticoes quotes directly from Deut. 18.15-18 to illustrate the significance of

---

52. On Hillel's hermeneutical principal of *gezerah shavah* see *ARN* 37 Ver. A; H.L. Strack and G. Stemberger, *Introduction to the Talmud and Midrash* (Minneapolis: Fortress Press, 1992), p. 21.

53. This is the reading of Exod. 23.20 according to the Samaritan Pentateuch, the Greek Septuagint and the Latin Vulgate. A similar witness of Jesus' use of a non-Massoretic textual tradition of the Hebrew Scriptures is seen in Lk. 19.46 and par. where he combines Isa. 56.7 and Jer. 7.11. The verbal link between these verses is the joint appearance of בית. While the term does appear in the Massoretic text of Isa. 56.7, in Jer. 7.11 the term is only attested in the variant textual tradition attested by the Septuagint (ὁ οἶκός μου). See J. Frankovic, 'Remember Shilo!', *Jerusalem Perspective* 46/47 (1994), pp. 25-28.

54. See *Exod. R.* 32.2-3; Tacitus, *Histories* 5.3.1; see M. Stern, *Greek and Latin Authors*, II, p. 25.

55. See n. 38.

Jesus (Acts 3.22; cf. 7.37). Bauernfeind suggested an allusion to Elijah in the preceding verse, 'whom heaven must receive until the *restoration* [ἀποκαταστάσεως] of all which God spoke through the mouth of his holy prophets from old' (Acts 3.21).[56] Elijah is the only figure recorded in the Hebrew Scriptures to be taken up into heaven.[57] The theme of restoration which is so closely identified with the advent of Elijah is also repeated. In the context, it is clear that Jesus' ascension and parousia is defined by Peter in terms of the Jewish traditions concerning Elijah.[58]

In the kerygmatic proclamation of the post-Easter Church, it is Jesus who fills the role of the hoped for eschatological prophet—not John! In fact, nowhere in the opinion of the early church is John given the elevated status that we find recorded in the synoptic tradition. He is merely the one who offered a baptism of repentance,[59] and he is never presented as the prophetic forerunner. The Fourth Gospel even places an explicit denial of prophetic significance upon the lips of John himself, 'And they asked him, "What then? Are you Elijah?" He said, "I am not". "Are you the prophet?" And he answered, "No"' (Jn 1.21).[60]

It may be that continuation of John's movement after his death (Acts 19.1-7) raised concerns in the early church to emphasize the relative

---

56. O. Bauerfeind, 'Tradition und Apokatastassisspruch Apostelgeschichte 3,20f', in Betz, Hengel and Schmidt (eds.), *Abraham unser Vater*, pp. 13-23; *idem*, *Kommentar und Studien aus Apostelgeschichte* (Tübingen: J.C.B. Mohr, 1980), pp. 473-86; F.F. Bruce, *The Acts of the Apostles* (Grand Rapids: Eerdmans, 1990), p. 144; C.K. Barrett, *The Acts of the Apostles* (ICC; 2 vols.; Edinburgh: T. & T. Clark, 1994–2000), I, p. 206.

57. 2 Kgs 2.9-12; Sir. 48.9; 1 Macc. 2.58: 'Elijah because of great zeal for the law was taken up into heaven'. Regarding other figures who were traditionally assumed, see M. Stone's discussion on *4 Ezra* 6.26: 'And they shall see the men who were taken up, who from their birth have not tasted death...' (*Fourth Ezra* [Hermeneia, Minneapolis: Fortress Press, 1990], p. 172). On the relationship between the belief in the assumption of Moses (e.g. *Ant.* 4.326) and the title of the first century CE apocryphal '*Assumption of Moses*', see J. Tromp, *The Assumption of Moses* (SVTP, 10; Leiden: E.J. Brill, 1993), pp. 281-85.

58. According to the second-century chronograph, *Seder Olam* ch. 17, Elijah is hidden (ונגנז) until the coming of the Messiah. At that time he will be appear, only to be hidden again until the days of Gog and Magog. See C.J. Milikowsky, 'Seder Olam: A Rabbinic Chronography' (PhD dissertation for Yale University, 1981), pp. 323-24.

59. Acts 1.5; 10.37; 11.16; 13.24; 18.25; 19.4.

60. See Brown, *John*, I, pp. 47-49.

unimportance of John as compared to Jesus.[61] Thus, in the preaching of Paul in Antioch of Pisidia, John's antedating[62] of Jesus is accompanied with an emphatic denial of John's messianic claim, 'And as John was finishing his course, he said, "What do you suppose that I am? I am not he. No, but after me one is coming, the sandals of whose feet I am not worthy to untie"' (Acts 13.25). Outside of the Gospels and Acts, John finds no mention in any other New Testament writing. Standing in such stark contradiction to the preaching of the early church, there can be little doubt that the elevated presentation of John in the synoptic tradition reflects the historical opinion of those who lived in the days of John's ministry—including that of Jesus.

Dodd argued that the use of Deut. 18.15-18 in Acts 3.22 and 7.37 indicates that there may have existed a pre-canonical substructure of testimonia[63] regarding the eschatological prophet.[64] The discovery of the *Testimonia* (4Q175) at Qumran confirmed his suspicions.[65] The Qumran evidence further indicates that these testimonia were not only pre-canonical but pre-Christian. Dodd's theoretical substructure to the New Testament writings accords with observations by Flusser[66] and Smith[67] regarding the existence of ancient Jewish homilies which belong to the world of the New Testament. These compositions were formed

---

61. Mt. 3.14: 'I need to be baptized by you, and do you come to me?' (cf. Jn 3.30). See Jeremias, *New Testament Theology*, p. 47.

62. Note the Fourth Gospel's emphasis that Jesus preceded the Baptist, 'John bore witness to him, and cried, "This was he of whom I said, He who comes after me ranks before me, for *he was before me*"' (Jn 1.15).

63. According to Origen, Dositheus made claims to the Samaritans that he had fulfilled this prophecy (*Contra Celsum* 1.57). See also *Ps.-Clem. Recogn.* 1.36-40.

64. See C.H. Dodd, *According to the Scriptures: The Substructure of New Testament Theology* (London: Nisbet, 1964), pp. 53-55; H. Conzelmann, *Acts of the Apostles* (Hermeneia; Philadelphia: Fortress Press, 1987), pp. 29-30; F.J. Foakes Jackson and K. Lake, *The Beginnings of Christianity: Part I The Acts of the Apostles*. IV. *Translation and Commentary* (London: MacMillan, 1933), p. 38; Bruce, *Acts*, p. 145.

65. J.A. Fitzmyer, '4Q Testimonia and the New Testament', in *idem, Semitic Background of the New Testament*, pp. 59-89.

66. D. Flusser, '"Today if You Will Listen to His Voice": Creative Exegesis in Hebrews 3–4', in B. Uffenheimer and H. Graf Reventlow (eds.), *Creative Biblical Exegesis: Christian and Jewish Hermeneutics through the Centuries* (JSOTSup, 126; Sheffield: JSOT Press, 1988), pp. 55-62.

67. M. Smith, 'Ascent to the Heavens and Deification in 4QMa', in Schiffman (ed.), *Archaeology and History*, pp. 181-88.

around selected biblical passages which were structured to express particular ideas. In the hands of subsequent authors or religious communities, these homilies were often fractured and reshaped. Nevertheless, a careful analysis of the recurrent units from these homilies can assist us in better understanding the larger complex and the concepts they intended to express.

The recent publication of the *editio princeps*[68] of 11Q13 (11QMelch) revisits the question of the existence and shape of primitive pre-Christian testimonia regarding the Eschatological Prophet and the penetration of their formulation into the substrata of the New Testament. Of particular relevance for our study are the apocalyptic structure, specified tasks and scriptural citations employed by the sectarian author of 11Q13 to describe the prophet of the End of Days and the recurrence of these distinctive details in other Jewish literature.

The advent of the Eschatological Prophet in 11Q13 is placed at the dawning of the redemptive era. The structure of events is shaped by the sectarian division of history into periods.[69] Thus, the column opens with a combined citation of Lev. 25.10 and Deut. 15.2. The significance of the Jubilee year for the author is twofold. According to Lev. 25.10, it is in that year that the people of God 'shall proclaim liberty [דרור] in the land'. The time of redemption is also related to the fact that this year will be a time of '*the Lord's release*' (שמיטה ליהוה = LXX: ἄφεσις κυρίῳ). While the biblical verse speaks of a release from debts, the sectarian spiritual interpretation of שמיטה is defined by the fact that redemption will be inaugurated on 'the Day of Atonement [Lev. 25.9: יום הכפורים] at the end of the tenth Jubilee' (11Q13 2.7). Thus, the tenth Jubilee will begin with an atonement for past iniquities (עוונותיהמה), and culminate in redemption with divine vengeance brought upon Belial and his lot.

Mention of the proclamation of liberty (וקראתם דרור) in Lev. 25.10 allows the author to introduce Isa. 61.1 where liberty is also proclaimed (לקרא לשבוים דרור). This period of redemption is called לשנת רצון (Isa. 61.2; cf. Lk. 4.19). Melchizedek will rise (ומלכי צדק יקום) to render

68. F.G. Martínez, E.J.C. Tigchelaar, A.S. Van Der Woude (eds.), *Qumran Cave 11. II.11Q2-18, 11Q 20-31* (DJD, 13; Oxford: Clarendon Press, 1998), pp. 221-41.

69. On the division of history see J. Licht, 'Time and Eschatology in Qumran', *JJS* 15 (1965), pp. 177-82; D. Dimant, 'The "Pesher on the Periods" (4Q 180) and 4Q 181', *IOS* 9 (1979), pp. 77-102.

divine vengeance (נקם משפטי אל = Isa. 61.3) in a fashion similar to the priestly redeemer of the *Assumption of Moses*:[70]

> Then will be filled the hands[71] of the messenger,[72]
> who is in the highest place appointed.[73]
> Yea, he will at once avenge them of their enemies.
> For the Heavenly One will arise from his kingly throne.[74]
> Yea, he will go forth from his holy habitation
> with indignation and wrath on behalf of his sons (*T. Mos.* 10.2-3).

70. See Tromp, *Assumption of Moses*, pp. 228-34.

71. Exod. 28.41; 29.9, 35; Lev. 16.31. In the *Aramaic Prayer of Levi* the patriarch likewise stretches out his hands as he prays to receive the Holy Spirit, which is further defined in terms of Isa. 11.2. Traditionally this verse was associated with the Davidic Messiah (צמח: Jer. 23.5; Zech. 6.12). See M.E. Stone and J.C. Greenfield, 'The Prayer of Levi', *JBL* 112 (1993), pp. 247-66; *idem*, in G. Brooke, J. Collins *et al.* (eds.), *Qumran Cave 4.XVII. Parabiblical Texts, Part 3* (DJD, 22; Oxford: Clarendon Press, 1996), p. 29.

72. Here the messenger (*nuntius* = מלאך) is a priestly human figure and *not* an angel, which strengthens our suggestion that Melchizedek in 11Q13 was also intended to designate a human redemptive figure. His designated task to execute divine judgment may itself suggest his humanity. As we hear in the *Testament of Abraham* (13.5, 8), 'It is not I [God] who judge you, but by man shall every man be judged... For all men have their origin from the first man [*Adam*]; and so by his son [Heb.: *ben 'adam* = Son of Man/Adam, i.e. Abel] they are first judged'. Yet, the eschatological Messenger (*nuntius*) in the *Assumption of Moses* is not a prophetic forerunner but the Redeemer himself. We have already noted that the early church similarly reshaped the significance of Deut. 18.15-18 to support the messianic claim of Jesus. Both of these examples attest to the fluidity of interpretation of important texts in the hands of different religious communities.

73. Melchizedek is depicted by the sectarian writer enthroned in the heavens: ע[לי]ה] למרום שובה... (11Q13 2.6-7). He cites Ps. 7.8-9 (ET 7.7-8) and by so doing echoes Ps. 110 where we hear mention both of Melchizedek (Ps. 110.4) and the theme of being seated in divine judgment, 'The Lord says to my lord: "Sit at my right hand, till I make your enemies your footstool"' (Ps 110.1). Ascent to the heavenly heights (למרום) is elsewhere depicted of human redemptive figures, sometimes using phraseology similar to Ps. 7.8-9 from Ps. 68.19: עלית למרום. This latter verse is cited in *ARN* concerning Moses and his ascent to receive the Torah. In the same passage Moses is referred to as 'the one born of woman' (see above n. 48). Paul also applies the verse in Eph. 4.8 to the ascension of Christ. See Collins, 'A Throne in the Heavens', *Scepter*, pp. 136-53.

74. Although the Heavenly One seated in the *Assumption of Moses* is God, in *Ezekiel the Tragedian* it is Moses himself who is enthroned. 'On Sinai's peak I [Moses] saw what seemed a throne so great in size it touched the clouds of heaven. Upon it sat a man of noble mien, becrowned, and with a scepter in one hand while

Throughout the column the author utilizes words and phrases from Isa. 61.1-3 that are then combined with other verbally connected Old Testament verses. Ps. 82.1 is cited to take advantage of the term אלהים, which already in biblical Hebrew can mean merely 'judge'.[75] The sectarian citation is not intended to suggest that Melchizedek is a heavenly being,[76] but simply to take advantage of the double appearance of אלהים. According to the collective sectarian thought of Qumran, Mel-

with the other he did beckon me. I made approach and stood before the throne. He handed o'er the scepter and he bade me mount the throne, and gave to me the crown; then he himself withdrew from off the throne' (ll. 68-76) ('Ezekiel the Tradgedian' *OTP*, II, pp. 811-12); P.W. Van der Horst, 'Moses' Throne Vision in Ezekiel the Dramatist', *JJS*, (1983–84), pp. 34-35, pp. 21-29. See the crowning of Enoch in *3 En.* 12.1-5. Josephus also reports the legend that the infant Moses 'seizes Pharaoh's crown and smashes it to the ground' (*Ant.* 2.233-234). *Exod. R.* 1.26 knows a similar tradition. However, Moses takes the crown of Pharaoh and crowns himself, 'as he was destined to do when he became great' (C.R. Holladay, *Fragments from Hellenistic Jewish Authors. II. Poets* [Atlanta: Scholars Press, 1989], pp. 362-65 n. 77).

75. Exod. 21.6; 22.8, 9, 28; 1 Sam. 2.25; Judg. 5.8.

76. The clearest statement of belief that the historical figure, Melchizedek, himself would return in the future is that presented in *2 En.* His priestly father, Nir, is told that the child is to be taken to paradise to escape the coming flood in the generation of Noah, 'For the time is now very near when I shall let loose all the waters over the earth, and all that is on the earth shall perish; and I will give him a place of honour in *another generation*, and *Melchizedek shall be chief priest in that generation*' (*2 En.* 23.34). Collins, following de Jonge and Van der Woude, is the leading proponent of the notion that the figure Melchizedek in 11Q13 is the angel Michael. See M. de Jonge and A.S. Van der Woude, '11Q Melchizedek and the New Testament', *NTS* 12 (1965–66), pp. 305-306; P.J. Kolbelski, *Melchizedek and Melchiresa* (CBQMS, 10; Washington: Catholic Biblical Association, 1981), pp. 71-74; Collins, *Scepter*, pp. 142-43. His argument assumes a similar identification of the 'Son of Man' in Dan. 7.13 to be Michael (*Daniel* [Hermeneia; Minneapolis: Fortress Press, 1993], pp. 304-10). However, there is no evidence that Melchizedek in 11Q13 is intended to signify anyone other than the historical figure introduced in Gen. 14.18-20. We have already noted the parallels between the presentation of Melchizedek here and the priestly (*human*) redeemers of the *Aramaic Prayer of Levi* and the *Assumption of Moses*. Regarding the existence of exalted human figures in the thinking of the Qumran community, see E. Eshel, '4Q471B: A Self Glorification Hymn', *RevQ* 17 (1997), pp. 175-202; M. Smith, 'Two Ascended to Heaven and the Author of 4Q491', in S.J.D. Cohen (ed.), *Studies in the Cult of Yahweh: New Testament, Early Christianity and Magic* (Leiden: E.J. Brill, 1996), pp. 68-78. On Melchizedek's role as the eschatological judge, see Flusser, 'Melchizedek and the Son of Man', in *idem, Judaism*, pp. 186-92.

chizedek will not be the only instrument of divine judgment. Instead, he sits among the עדת אל[77] who are likewise defined in Ps. 82.1 as אלהים. The idea of the Congregation's participation with Melchizedek in rendering judgment is repeated in lines 13-14.

> And Melchizedek will carry out the vengeance of God's judgments [and on that day he will f]r[ee them from the hand of] Belial and from the hands of all the s[pirits of his lot]. And all the Oaks [of Righteousness: אילי הצדק :Isa. 61.3][78] are his help [בעזרו].

It is at this point in the sectarian presentation that the eschatological prophet—the Anointed One of the Spirit (משיח הרוח :1Q13 2.15-20)— is introduced. His prophetic tasks are presented through a phrase by phrase citation of Isa. 52.7. He appears standing upon the mountains which we are told represent the biblical prophets (הנביאים [המה] ההרים). His position is one of superiority. Similar to the eschatological message of *Pss. Sol.* 11.1-2,[79] the messenger announces salvation to Zion. He proclaims, 'Your God is King'. The biblical phrase is creatively interpreted to read, 'Your ELOHIM [= judge] is MELECH [= Melchizedek]'. Column two ends with a return to Lev. 25.9, 'And you shall blow the trumpet [of the Jubilee] in all the land...' Thus, the coming of the prophetic Anointed One of the Spirit precedes the inauguration of the Jubilee and the advent of Melchizedek.

De Jonge and Van der Woude have already recognized the important literary and conceptual connections between 11Q13, the *Psalms of Solomon* and a *pisqa* belonging to the earliest stratum[80] of the homiletical midrash *Pesiqta Rabbati*. They noted the verbal parallels between the role of the משיח הרוח in 11Q13 and Elijah in *Pesiqta Rabbati* 35.[81] Pe-

---

77. The title עדת אל is one of the slogans on the banners designating the Congregation and that is carried into battle (1QM 4.9). See Y. Yadin, *The Scroll of the War of the Sons of Light against the Sons of Darkness* (Oxford: Oxford University Press, 1962), pp. 276-77.

78. Brooke, Collins *et al.* (eds.), *Qumran Cave 4.XVII. Parabiblical Texts*, p. 232.

79. H.E. Ryle and M.R. James, *Psalms of the Pharisees* (Cambridge: Cambridge University Press, 1891), p. 101.

80. A. Goldberg dates this *pisqa* to the third or fourth century CE. *Ich komme und wohne in deiner Mitte: Eine rabbinische Homilie zu Sacharja 2:14 (PesR 35)* (Frankfurt, Selbstverlag der Gesellschaft zur Förderung judaistischer Studien in Frankfurt A.M.e.V, 1977), p. 20. See the discussion of the dating and compilation of *Pesiqta Rabbati* in Strack and Stemberger, *Talmud and Midrash*, pp. 325-29.

81. De Jonge and Van Der Woude, '11Q Melchizedek', p. 307.

siqta Rabbati's identification of the prophetic precursor with Elijah also accords with events depicted after the proclamation of the eschatological messenger in the Jubilee year of *Pss. Sol.* 11.2. There redemption begins with the regathering of the people—an event we have already noted is closely associated with the eschatological work of Elijah.

> Sound in Zion the signal trumpet[82] of the sanctuary;
>> announce in Jerusalem the voice of one bringing good news,[83]
>> for God has been merciful to Israel watching over them.
> Stand on a high place, Jerusalem, and look at your children,
>> from the east and the west assembled together by the Lord.
> From the north they come in the joy of their God;
>> from far distant islands God has assembled them.
> He flattened high mountains into level ground for them;[84]
>> the hills fled at their coming (*Pss. Sol.* 11.1-4).

The theme of regathering/restoration is an essential element in the Jewish hope for redemption[85] and the traditional figure for this task is Elijah. Yet, because of the strict dualistic attitude of the Dead Sea Sect towards those outside of the Congregation, scarce mention is made of the theme of restoration. Indeed, it may be the restorative role of Elijah which also contributed to the Qumran preference to define its hope for an eschatological prophet with Deut. 18.15-18, rather than Mal. 3.1, 23-24. If so, the sectarian perspective of the Qumran community may have motivated its intentional omission of Lev. 25.10b in 11Q13: 'Each of you shall *return* to his family'.

---

82. σάλπιγγι σημασίας: LXX Lev. 25.10 (σημασίας = יובל).

83. Cf. Isa. 52.7.

84. Cf. Isa. 40.4. See *Sib. Or.* 3.777-79; *Ass. Mos.* 10.4. Mk 1.2-3 combines Mal. 3.1 and Isa. 40.3, suggesting that the Evangelist may have been aware of the ancient testimonial complex.

85. The ancient cycle of judgment-dispersion-regathering-redemption is heard already in Gen. 15.13-14, 16. It appears often in postbiblical literature (cf. *Pss. Sol.* 11.1-9; *T. Mos.* 2–4) and is most clearly expressed in the apocryphal work of Tobit: 'Our brethren will be scattered over the earth from the good land, and Jerusalem will be desolate. The house of God in it will be burned down and will be in ruins for a time. But God will again have mercy on them, and bring them back into their land... After this they will return from the places of their captivity, and will rebuild Jerusalem in splendor. And the house of God will be rebuilt there with a glorious building for all generations for ever, just as the prophets said of it' (Tob. 14.4b-5). Cf. C.A. Moore, *Tobit* (AB; New York: Doubleday, 1996), p. 291.

All three eschatological presentations define the advent of the מבשׂר
with Isa. 52.7.[86] The *Psalms of Solomon* and 11Q13 reflect attitudes of
early Jewish apocalyptism and its preoccupation with calendaric concerns.[87] Underlying these attitudes was a rigid predeterminism. Divine
sovereignty had foreordained that events in redemptive history coincide
with the biblical festivals and calendaric cycles.[88] *Pesiqta Rabbati*, on
the other hand, represents a subsequent period when these fervid senti-
ments had subsided. Rather than structuring future redemption within a
rigid periodic framework, the stages of redemption are based upon the
tripartite proclamation of the Messenger (מבשׂר) of Isa. 52.7. Redemption thus unfolds over the course of *three* days.

> Three days before the Messiah comes, Elijah will come and stand upon
> the mountains of Israel, and weep and lament upon them, but then will
> say: Behold, O Land of Israel, how short a time before you cease to be
> a waste land, dry and desolate! Elijah's voice will be heard from the
> world's end to the world's end. And then he will say to the children of
> Israel: Peace has come to the world, as it is said, 'Behold upon the
> mountains the feet of him that brings good tidings, that announces peace'
> [Isa. 52.7]. When the wicked hear this, they will rejoice, every one of
> them, saying one to another, 'Peace has come to us'. On the second day
> Elijah will come and stand upon the mountains of Israel, and say: Good
> has come to the world, as is said, 'The messenger of good tidings' [Isa.
> 52.7]. On the third day he will come and say, Salvation has come to the
> world, as is said, 'That announces salvation' [Isa. 52.7]—that is, salva-
> tion is come to Zion and to her children, but not to the wicked. In that
> hour the Holy One, blessed be he, will show his glory and his kingdom
> to all the inhabitants of the world. He will redeem Israel, and he will ap-
> pear at the head of them, as is said, 'The breach-maker will go up before
> them; they will break through and pass the gate, going out by it. The king
> will pass on before them, the Lord at their head' [Mic. 2.13].

86. The appearance of לבשׂר in Isa. 61.1 allowed the sectarian author to introduce the מבשׂר into his sectarian pesher. De Jonge and Van der Woude, '11Q Melchizedek', p. 306.

87. On the complex relationship between the calendar of Qumran and Jewish
apocalyptic see B.Z. Wacholder, *The Dawn of Qumran* (Cincinatti: Hebrew Union
College Press, 1983), pp. 53-60; S. Talmon, *The World of Qumran from Within*
(Jerusalem: Magnes Press, 1989), pp. 147-85.

88. See the comments concerning the theological underpinnings to the calendaric system in the book of *Jubilees* by G.W.E. Nickelsburg, 'The Bible Rewritten
and Expanded', in Michael Stone (ed.), *Jewish Writings of the Second Temple
Period* (CRINT, 2.1; Assen: Van Gorcum; Philadelphia: Fortress Press, 1984),
p. 100; Dimant, 'Pesher on the Period', p. 93.

The distinctive contribution of *Pesiqta Rabbati* to the testimonial complex is the citation from Mic. 2.13. The medieval Jewish scholar, David Kimche,[89] is certainly correct when he states that the midrash intends to portray three figures in this redemptive drama: Elijah, the King–Messiah and the Lord—which correspond to the three figures of Mic. 2.13 (the Breach-maker, King, Lord).

What is important for our study is recognition of the recurrent units of distinctive vocabulary and scriptural citation which appear in 11Q13, *Psalms of Solomon, Assumption of Moses* and *Pesiqta Rabbati*. They suggest that these unrelated presentations share a common world of understanding concerning the future role of the eschatological prophet, which was based upon ancient Jewish testimonia regarding him.

Scriptural–Thematic Units:	*11Q13*	Assumption of Moses	Psalms of Solomon	Pesiqta Rabbati	*Matthew 11.2-14*
1. Mal. 3.1, 22-24	_90	•	•	•	•
2. Deut. 18.15-18	_91	–	–	–	•
3. Isa. 52.7	•	•	•	•	•
4. Isa. 40.3-4	_92	•	•	•	•
5. Mic. 2.13	–	–	–	•	•
6. Jubilee Redemption	•	–	•	–	_93
7. Priestly Redeemer	•	•	–	–	_94
8. Vengeful Judgment	•	•	•	•	_95

Jesus draws upon contemporary expectations for the prophet of the End of Days to signify John. He fused the hopes for a prophet-like-Moses (Deut. 18.18) and Elijah *redivivus* to indicate his importance. Like the sectarian presentation of the prophetic superiority of the Anointed One

89. 'Our Rabbis of blessed memory and the Midrash, teach 'the breaker' is Elijah and 'their king' is the branch, the son of David'. Cited by E. Pococke, *A Commentary on the Prophecy of Micah* (Oxford: Oxford University Press, 1676), p. 24. Kimche's interpretation is also cited by S.R. Driver, 'Notes on Difficult Texts', *The Expositor*, 3rd series 5 (1887), p. 266.

90. See above n. 31.

91. See 4Q175.

92. The Qumran community cites this verse in its own self-definition: 1QS 8.15.

93. See the discussion below concerning John's βάπτισμα μετανοίας εἰς ἄφεσιν ἁμαρτιῶν (Mk 1.4; Lk. 3.3).

94. Cf. Heb. 6.20: Jesus has gone as a forerunner on our behalf, having become a high priest for ever after the order of Melchizedek; cf. Rom. 8.34.

95. Cf. Lk. 12.49-56.

of the Spirit, Jesus emphasized the superiority of John. 'He is more than a prophet', and 'No one born among women is greater than John'. The recurrent units of the complex in non-sectarian literature suggest that the testimonia witnessed at Qumran were not exclusive to the Dead Sea Sect. Instead, they belong to the intricate warp and woof of Jewish opinion during the Second Commonwealth.[96]

> I do not...think that this theme in Jesus' teaching and practice is to be explained by the influence...of any other texts of the Dead Sea circles. Rather, those documents and the Gospels are different mushrooms of the same ring, connected not directly, but by the ramified root system of popular piety from which they independently arose.

4. *The Kingdom Breaks Forth*

Our review of the eschatological expectations among the Qumran sectarians has brought our attention to pre-Christian testimonia regarding the Eschatological Prophet. This homiletical substructure reflects the background to Jesus' testimony about the Baptist. It may also provide the conceptual rubric and vocabulary stock for Matthew's difficult ἡ βασιλεία τῶν οὐρανῶν βιάζεται. As we have noted, the extensive editorial activity of both Matthew and Luke reflects the inherent obscurity of the Greek phrase.[97] Scholarship has suggested a myriad of possible Semitic equivalents to explain the enigmatic βιάζεται in Mt. 11.12.[98] However, the challenge remains to move beyond what is merely linguistically possible.

At the turn of the century, Resch proposed a linguistic solution which was a distant cousin to a notion suggested at least two centuries earlier.[99] He theorized that the term βιάζεται in Mt. 11.12 represented the Hebrew verb פרץ. It is not necessary here to address all the difficulties posed by Resch's theoretical Hebrew *Urevangelium*. Our interest, in-

96. Smith, 'Ascent to the Heavens', p. 188.

97. M. Black, *An Aramaic Approach to the Gospels and Acts* (Oxford: Clarendon Press, 1979), p. 211 n. 2.

98. Black, *An Aramaic Approach*, p. 211; Daube, *New Testament*, pp. 285-300; B.E. Thiering, 'Are the 'Violent Men' False Teachers?', *NovT* 16 (1979), pp. 293-97.

99. A. Resch, *Aussercanonische Paralleltexte zu den Evangelien: Texte und Untersuchungen zur Geschichte der altchristlichen Literatur* (Leipzig: J.C. Hinrichs, 1897), p. 439; *idem*, *Die Logia Jesu* (Leipzig: J.C. Hinrichs, 1898), p. 123.

stead, is simply his observation—repeated by others in more recent studies[100]—that βιάζεται stands as a linguistic equivalent for פרץ[101] In fact, βιάζω does render פרץ three times in the Septuagint (2 Sam. 13.25, 27; 2 Kgs 5.23).

Moore's observations on the usage of βιάζω in Josephus may also indicate why the Septuagintal translators seldom chose to translate פרץ with βιάζω, and more often to render the Hebrew term with δια-κόπτω.[102] He noted, 'βιάζω then in Josephus, appears to require a direct object, or, even when it is used intransitively, to imply one'.[103] In other words, if in the Hebrew Scriptures פרץ appears without a direct object, the peculiarities of the Greek language would naturally discourage the translators from rendering it with βιάζω. Indeed, on the three occasions cited where פרץ is translated with βιάζω, the Hebrew behind the Septuagint is a transitive verb with a direct object.[104]

The linguistic demarcation in Greek and Hebrew verbal expression necessarily would have limited the number of occasions in the Septuagint in which פרץ could have been represented by βιάζω. However, if the New Testament writers have not followed these nuances in Greek and Hebrew grammar in their elliptical allusions to the Old Testament verses—and which were maintained in the Septuagint translation—then a type of linguistic myopia can result for the modern reader who may miss the intended verbal allusions.

The New Testament authors certainly felt no obligation to doggedly reproduce the vocabulary or idiomatic Greek expression of the Septuagint. A growing number of scholars have recognized the presence of

---

100. Daube, *New Testament*, p. 286; Black, *Aramaic Approach*, p. 211 n. 2; B.H. Young, *Jesus the Jewish Theologian* (Peabody, MA: Hendrickson, 1995), pp. 51-55. See the translation of Mt. 11.12 by Fridolin Stier, *Das Neue Testament* (Munich: Kösel-Verlag, 1989), 'Seit den Tagen Johannes des Täufers bis heute drängt mit Gewalt das Königtum der Himmel heran, und Gewalttäter errauben es'.

101. The linguistic equivalency was also noticed by Black, but he interpreted the Hebrew verb to signify violent divine judgment. Black, *Aramaic Approach*, p. 211 n. 2.

102. Gen. 28.29; 2 Kgs 5.20; 6.8; [4 Kgs] 14.13; 1 Chron. 13.11; 14.11; 15.13; Mic. 2.13.

103. Moore, 'Cognates', p. 520.

104. Each time the object is designated with the preposition ב (e.g. 2 Sam. 13.27: ויפרץ־בו: καὶ ἐβιάσατο αὐτὸν) and the sense of the verb is 'to press, encourage'. To these instances should be added the compound Greek verb παραβιάζω in 1 Sam. 28.23 which renders פרץ likewise with the sense 'to press'.

'non-Septuagintal' Hebraisms in the Gospels,[105] and it has long been recognized that at places literalistic Semitisms in the Gospels have resulted in a rough Greek.[106] It is our contention that this is precisely what has contributed to the obscurity of Mt. 11.12/Lk. 16.16.[107] The Evangelist(s)—or their sources—by employing βιάζεται in our saying intended to allude to an Old Testament passage in which the intransitive פרץ occurred, but which the Septuagint—in proper Greek style—had previously chosen to translate with another Greek term (διακόπτω).

John Calvin (1559)[108] and the English Orientalist, Edward Pococke (1676)[109] seem to be the first Christian scholars, citing the work of medieval Jewish scholar, David Kimche,[110] to suggest that the language of Mt. 11.12 is related to Mic. 2.13.

> He who opens the breach (הפרץ) will go up before them; they will break through (פרצו) and pass the gate, going out by it. Their king will pass on before them, the Lord at their head.

As we have seen in *Pesiqta Rabbati*, Mic. 2.13 belongs to an ancient complex of eschatological testimonia, and its pivotal term פרץ was interpreted by some Jewish commentators to signify the advent of the prophet of the End of Days. The biblical verse is frequently cited else-

---

105. W.G. Most, 'Did St. Luke Imitate the Septuagint', in C.A. Evans and S.E. Porter (eds.), *The Synoptic Gospels: A Sheffield Reader* (BibSem, 31; Sheffield: Sheffield Academic Press, 1995), pp. 215-26.

106. E.C. Maloney, *Semitic Interference in Markan Syntax* (Chico, CA: Scholars Press, 1981).

107. The rough Greek in the source(s) to Matthew's and Luke's saying may have caused Luke to edit and refine his saying to conform with better Greek style: πᾶς εἰς αὐτὴν βιάζεται ('and everyone is breaking forth *into it*').

108. 'A breaker shall go before them, that is, there shall be those who, with a hand, strong and armed will make a way open for them; inasmuch as Christ says that the Kingdom of heaven suffereth violence (Mt.11.12), they then mean that the people will have courageous leaders, whom nothing will stop from breaking through...' (J. Calvin, *Commentaries on the Twelve Minor Prophets* [trans. John Owen; Grand Rapids: Eerdmans, 1950], p. 211).

109. 'But if any think, that by *Haporets*, the breaker, and *Malcam*, their king, should be meant two distinct persons, let him hear, what the Ancient Jews say, for exposition of this place. Haporets, the Breaker, that is Elias, and Malcam, their king, that is the Branch, the son of David; and then observe what our Saviour himself hath taught us, that John the Baptist was Elias which was to come' (Pococke, *Micah*, p. 24).

110. E.I.J. Rosenthal, 'Medieval Jewish Exegesis', *JSS* 19 (1964), pp. 265-79.

where in rabbinic literature in reference to the messianic age. In an exposition on Gen. 18.3-4, Rabbi Hiyya relates that in reward for Abraham's hospitality, his children would receive a reward in the wilderness: the land of Israel and the Messiah. Scriptural support for these promises is drawn from the citation of Mic. 2.13.[111] Later Jewish interpreters also read significance in the appearance of Perez (פֶּרֶץ) at the head of the abbreviated genealogy of David in Ruth 4.18-22. Likewise, the episode of the birth of Perez preceding his twin brother in Gen. 38.29 was understood by *Targum Pseudo-Jonathan*[112] and the midrashim to prefigure the precedence of his progeny, through whom would come King David and the hoped for Messiah. In all of these instances the hope for a redeemer is strengthened by the citation of Mic. 2.13.

In the citation from *Pesiqta Rabbati* we have seen that the advent of the Messiah coincides with the appearance of God's kingdom. Flusser's recent study[113] on the stages of redemption according to John and Jesus has brought fresh attention to Jesus' use of the phrase, 'the kingdom of heaven'. He has demonstrated that a fundamental difference of opinion existed between the eschatological expectations of these two spiritual giants. The former embraced the older bipartite view of history which is also witnessed in the writings of the Qumran library. Accordingly, history will be interrupted in the End of Days by the advent of the Messiah(s), who will render divine judgment in roles similar to that depicted of the Danielic Son of Man. Thus, John asked, 'Are you the One who is coming [i.e. to render judgment]?' We can now understand John's disillusionment with Jesus. He had anticipated imminent judgment, 'The winnowing fork is *already* in his hand' (Mt. 3.12).

Jesus qualified his response to the Baptist with provisions from his own tripartite view of history that was more closely aligned to the opinion of Israel's sages. In their opinion between the period of present history and the End of Days there is to exist an intermediate period

---

111. *Gen. R.* on Gen. 48.10. See *Lev. R.* 32.8; *Qoh. R.* 4.1, 1; *Targ. Onq.* on Exod. 12.42.

112. See E.G. Clark, *Targum Pseudo-Jonathan of the Pentateuch* (Hoboken, NJ: Ktav, 1984), p. 48.

והוה כד אתיב וולדא ית ידיה והא נפק אחוי ואמרת מה תקוף סני
תקיפתא ועלך אית למיתקוף דאנת עתיד למחסן מלכותא וקרת שמיה פרץ.

113. Flusser, 'The Stages of Redemption According to John the Baptist and Jesus', in *idem*, *Jesus*, pp. 258-75.

which was designated 'the days of the Messiah'.[114] Jesus' testimony concerning the Baptist points to John's advent as the transitional point to that new era: 'the law and the prophets were until John' (Lk. 16.16). As we have noted, this idea is also the source of Matthew's saying, 'all the prophets have prophesied until John' (Mt. 11.13). Both forms of the saying in Matthew and Luke point to the ushering in of the messianic age. Yet, Flusser has suggested that, because of Jesus' own messianic self-understanding, he employed another term for this period: 'the kingdom of heaven'.[115]

> He [Jesus] adopted contemporary Jewish interpretations which divided history, and he identified the Days of the Messiah with the period of the kingdom of heaven... It had already begun with John the Baptist, and Jesus was now the Messiah. It is also possible to understand how Jesus modified the structure of the concept of the kingdom of heaven. In the understanding of Jesus, the kingdom of heaven became more dynamic than in rabbinic thinking. Since according to Jesus the kingdom was identical with the messianic period, it was no longer, as in rabbinic thought, an eternal suprahistorical entity. It became a dynamic force which broke through into the world at an identifiable point in history. The kingdom of heaven began to break through with John, and Jesus—the Messiah—was in the center of the movement.

5. *Those Who Forcefully Advance*

The double occurrence of פרץ in Mic. 2.13 corresponds to the double occurrence of the Greek root (βία) in Mt. 11.12. Yet, who are these forceful ones (βιασταί)? Clearly, they are associated with the advent of John which marked the inauguration of the kingdom of heaven. But are they enemies or allies of the kingdom of heaven? A clue may lie in the relationship between the role of John as 'the Breach-maker', the significance attributed by the Baptist's movement to its founder, and the aims of his penitent baptism.

Schwartz's study on the similarities between the Benedictus and 11Q13 focused on the linguistic parallels between the sectarian work and Zacharias's prophecy.[116]

---

114. The tripartite structure of redemptive history may also be witnessed in the apocalyptic *Sib. Or.* 3.652-784.

115. Flusser, *Jesus*, pp. 274-75.

116. D.R. Schwartz, 'On Quirinius, John the Baptist, the Benedictus, Melchizedek, Qumran and Ephesus', *RevQ* 13 (1988), pp. 635-46.

And you, child, will be called the prophet of the Most High; for you will go before the Lord to prepare his ways, to give knowledge of salvation to his people in the forgiveness of their sins, through the tender mercy of our God, when the day shall dawn upon us from on high to give light to those who sit in darkness and in the shadow of death, to guide our feet into the way of peace (Lk. 1.77-79).

The affinities of the Benedictus and the Dead Sea Sect have been recognized by others.[117] However, of particular pertinence to our study are Schwartz's observations regarding the testimony of Zacharias about his son. 'You will go before the Lord to prepare his ways, to give knowledge of salvation to his people in the forgiveness of their sins'. The citation of Mal. 3.1 in the opening clause is unmistakable. So likewise is the allusion to Isa. 52.7, 'to guide our feet into the way of peace'. Both of these verses reflect the testimonial complex which lies behind the testimony heard by Jesus in our present block of sayings. Even more intriguing is Schwartz's recognition that in most of the instances in the Septuagint where the nominal Greek term ἄφεσις appears, it renders Hebrew words associated with the sabbatical or Jubilee year (דרור שׁמט, יובל).[118] The only place in extant Jewish literature where the Jubilee is explicitly linked with the notions of salvation and forgiveness of sins is in 11Q13—a sectarian document which we have already suggested shared conceptual and verbal connections with Jesus' testimony about John.

Nevertheless, Schwartz overlooked the fact that the same language is employed to describe John's call to repentance and ritual immersion. Both Mk 1.4 and Lk. 3.3 describe his baptism as one of repentance *for the forgiveness of sins* (εἰς ἄφεσιν ἁμαρτιῶν),[119] the precise phrase which occurs in the Benedictus. If Schwartz is correct that the phrase is intended to correspond to the sectarian understanding of the Jubilee as the era of redemption, then more may have been intended in John's call to the repentance than has been recognized by scholars. Those who

---

117. D. Flusser, 'The Magnificat, the Benedictus and the War Scroll', in *idem, Judaism*, pp. 126-49.

118. Schwartz, 'On Quirinius', p. 640.

119. While John's baptism is called a 'baptism of repentance' in Acts 13.24 and 19.4, the appended purpose for the baptism—εἰς ἄφεσιν ἁμαρτιῶν—is lacking. It seems that in the early church the phrase is refashioned and the notion identified with Jesus rather than John (Mt. 26.28; Lk. 24.47; Acts 2.38; 5.31; 10.43; 13.38; 26.18; Col. 1.14; Heb. 9.22).

responded to the Baptist's call with repentance and ritual immersion understood their actions to be related to the hoped for initiation of the Jubilee redemption when the iniquities of the nation would be atoned.

Josephus records others in those turbulent times who called the people to the regions of the Jordan river with the hope of divine intervention.

> During the period when Fadus was procurator of Judaea, a certain impostor named Theudas persuaded the majority of the masses to take up their possessions and to follow him to the Jordan river. He stated that he was a prophet and that at his command the river would be parted and would provide them easy passage. With this talk he deceived many (*Ant.* 20.97-98).

The fact that Theudas claimed to be a προφήτης and that his promised miracles parallel those performed by Moses (Exod. 14.21), Joshua—the successor to Moses (Josh. 3.7)—Elijah (2 Kgs 2.8) and Elisha—Elijah's successor (2 Kgs 2.14)—are no coincidence.[120] The whole episode reflects the contemporary belief in a future prophetic figure who would come in the spirit of Moses and Elijah to inaugurate the era of divine redemption.

Our suggestion is reminiscent of another figure who understood that his actions had the capacity to bring forward the kingdom of heaven with divine vengeance. We have already seen that the language and eschatological expectations witnessed in the *Assumption of Moses* are related to 11Q13 and *Pesiqta Rabbati*. Prior to the advent of the priestly redeemer in ch. 10, we are introduced to Taxo, a descendant of Levi who lived in a period of abject suffering. Rather than bending to the will of their oppressors and transgressing the commandments, he encouraged his sons to fast (i.e. repent) and withdraw to a cave in order not to be drawn into sin.

> We shall fast for a three-day period and on the fourth day we shall go into a cave, which is in the open country. There let us die rather than transgress the commandments of the Lord of Lords, the God of our fathers. For if we do this, and do die, our blood will be avenged before

---

120. R.A. Horsley and J.S. Hanson, *Bandits, Prophets and Messiahs* (Minneapolis: Winston, 1985), pp. 164-67; cf. Horsley, 'Popular Prophetic Movements at the Time of Jesus, their Principle Features and Social Origins', *JSNT* 26 (1987), pp. 3-27; P.W. Barnett, 'The Jewish Sign Prophets—AD 40–70 their Intentions and Origins', *NTS* 27 (1981), pp. 679-97.

the Lord. Then his kingdom will appear throughout his whole creation. Then the devil will have an end. Yea, sorrow will be led away with him (*Ass. Mos.* 9.6–10.1).

Licht has rightly stated that this is not a story of suicidal martyrdom.[121] Instead, Taxo encouraged his sons *to live* righteously. The levitical figure, however, understood that righteous action might likely lead to persecution and death. In such an event, the unjust death of the righteous would certainly be avenged by the Lord. In effect their life and (possible) death would bring forward the day of divine favor for the righteous and vengeance against the wicked.

It is intriguing to suggest that Jesus saw in John a character much like Taxo. The Baptist also had remained steadfast and refused to bend.[122] His critique of the adulterous marriage of Antipas to Herodias remained unfailing and led to his death. Yet, equally important was his message to the crowds which came out to him. He called them to follow him in acts of repentance and righteousness. Their renewed commitment was signified by the act of ritual immersion. Jesus' statement, therefore, 'those who break through take hold of'[123] it [i.e. the kingdom of Heaven]' is an affirmation of John's message and of those who responded in faithful obedience.

Jesus' testimony concerning the Baptist belongs to an intricate mosaic of Jewish opinions regarding the prophet of the End of Days. Although some have questioned the historical value of Mt. 11.12, we have seen that the enigmatic vocabulary corresponds to scriptural allusions to the hope for the advent of an eschatological prophet. Our study has also shown that Jesus' deft combination of selected passages is further evidence for the existence of an ancient pre-Christian testimonial complex. There seems little doubt that Jesus was intimately familiar with the Hebrew Scriptures and the contemporary hermeneutical methods by which they were employed. We can now understand more clearly his opinion of John. The prophetic Messenger[124] and those who followed him had

---

121. J. Licht, 'Taxo, or the Apocalyptic Doctrine of Vengeance', *JJS* 12 (1961), pp. 95-103.

122. Mt. 11.7b: 'What did you go out into the wilderness to behold? A reed shaken by the wind?' Flusser suggests that the imagery employed by Jesus in this saying is drawn from Aesop's fable of the reed and the oak (*Jesus*, p. 55 n. 31).

123. J. Marcus, 'Entering into the Kingly Power of God', *JBL* 107 (1988), pp. 663-75.

124. Luke's εὐαγγελίζεται in 16.16 is a linguistic equivalent for מבשׂר, which

indeed played a strategic role in inaugurating the era of God's redemption. Yet, the significance of the movement that Jesus now led was so great[125] that it caused the one whom Jesus esteemed as 'more than a prophet' to pale by comparison.

we have seen elsewhere signifies the task of the Messenger of Isa. 52.7. We have noted that this same Old Testament passage is alluded to in the Benedictus (Lk. 1.77-79) to describe John's future role. The verb reappears in Lk. 3.18 to describe the ministry of John. Luke's unique witness of εὐαγγελίζεται in Jesus' testimony about John may be a vestige from his source(s) which was familiar with the ancient testimonial complex and applied the role of the Messenger to John. See J.E. Taylor, *The Immerser: John the Baptist* (Grand Rapids: Eerdmans, 1997), p. 311.

125. 'John's greatness…becomes a foil for the surpassing greatness of the kingdom' (Davies and Allison, *Matthew*, II, p. 251).

PETER AS JESUS' MOUTH: MATTHEW 16.13-20 IN THE LIGHT OF EXODUS 4.10-17 AND OTHER MODELS

Benedict T. Viviano, OP

1. Mosaic Typology

Much has already been written about Peter's confession of messianic faith in Jesus (Mk 8.27-30; Mt. 16.13-16; Lk. 9.18-21) and Jesus' blessing and commissioning of Peter (Mt. 16.17-19).[1] The following essay only has the limited intention of bringing a hitherto unnoticed Mosaic parallel to the attention of the reader. The search for Mosaic typology in the Gospels is becoming somewhat of a trend in recent studies.[2] Yet the principal recent study on Mosaic typology in Matthew,

---

1. The older literature is listed in R.E. Brown, K.P. Donfried and John Reumann (eds.), *Peter in the New Testament* (Minneapolis: Augsburg; New York: Paulist Press, 1973); from this earlier literature, Oscar Cullmann, *Peter* (Philadelphia: Westminster Press, 1962) is especially to be recommended. Among more recent comprehensive works are Rudolf Pesch, *Simon-Petrus* (Päpste & Papsttum, 15; Stuttgart: Hiessemann, 1980); Gérard Claudel, *La confession de Pierre* (EBib NS, 10; Paris: Gabalda, 1988); Christian Grappe, *Images de Pierre aux deux premiers siècles* (Paris: Presses Universitaires de France, 1995); Roland Minnerath, *De Jérusalem à Rome, Pierre et l'unité de l'église apostolique* (Theologie historique, 101; Paris: Beauchesne, 1995); Pheme Perkins, *Peter* (Studies on Personalities of the New Testament; Columbia, SC: University of South Carolina Press, 1994); C.C. Caragounis, *Peter and the Rock* (BZNW, 58; Berlin: W. de Gruyter, 1990); T.V. Smith, *Petrine Controversies in Early Christianity* (WUNT, 2.15; Tübingen: J.C.B. Mohr, 1985). In addition, the three recent major commentaries on Matthew provide very full bibliographies: Joachim Gnilka, *Das Matthäus-Evangelium* (HTKNT, 1.2; Freiburg: Herder, 1988), pp. 70, 80; Ulrich Luz, *Das Evangelium nach Matthäus* (EKKNT 1.2; Zurich: Benziger; Neukirchen–Vluyn: Neukirchener Verlag, 1990), pp. 450-52; W.D. Davies and Dale C. Allison, *The Gospel According to Saint Matthew*, II (ICC; Edinburgh: T. & T. Clark, 1991), pp. 643-48.

2. D.C. Allison, *The New Moses: A Matthean Typology* (Minneapolis: Fortress

excellent though it be in other respects,[3] does not notice this structural parallel or paradigm.

In Exodus, chapters 3 and 4, God calls, accredits and empowers Moses for his great mission to the Israelites and to Pharaoh, to free his people from Egyptian bondage.[4] Such accreditation is necessary not only because of the reluctance of these two bodies, the Israelites and the Egyptians, but also and especially because of Moses' own hesitation. Moses' 'reluctance, expressed in four objections, must be overcome through signs and dialogue with God (3.1-12, 13-22; 4.1-9, 10-17)'.[5] Moses first objection (3.11), 'Who am I that I should go to Pharaoh...', is answered (3.12) enigmatically, '...you shall worship on this mountain'. Moses' second objection is that the people will not believe that he speaks for God; hence he asks for the name of the mysterious voice (3.13). And God reveals his name (3.14). To Moses' third objection, that people will not believe him, God responds with three signs, demonstrations of the divine power that Moses can count on in the future: the rod which becomes a serpent, then a hand which becomes leprous and is immediately thereafter restored (3.1-9). After enumerating these two signs (4.8; cf. Jn 2.11; 4.54; 21.14 and Boismard, *Moses or Jesus*, cited in n. 2 above), God proposes a third sign as a fallback position: changing Nile water into blood. This sign is not however actually performed at

Press, 1993); M.-E. Boismard, *Moses or Jesus: An Essay in Johannine Christology* (Minneapolis: Fortress Press, 1993); D.P. Moessner, *Lord of the Banquet: The Literary and Theological Significance of the Lucan Travel Narrative* (Minneapolis: Fortress Press, 1989); Joel Marcus, *The Way of the Lord: Christological Exegesis of the Old Testament in the Gospel of Mark* (Louisville, KY: Westminster Press, 1992).

3. Allison, *The New Moses*; my review in *RB* 103 (1996), pp. 137-38.

4. According to the usual source analysis, Exod. 3.1-4a, 5, 7-8, 16-22; 4.1-16 are assigned to the Yahwist, while 3.4b, 6, 9-15; 4.17 are attributed to the Elohist. The part that most concerns us, 4.10-17, is Yahwistic except for the last verse about the rod.

5. R.J. Clifford, 'Exodus', in R.E. Brown (ed.), *New Jerome Biblical Commentary* (Englewood–Cliffs, NJ: Prentice Hall, 1990), p. 12. On Exodus, see also Umberto Cassuto, *A Commentary on the Book of Exodus* (Jerusalem: Magnes Press, 1967), pp. 48-52; Martin Noth, *Exodus* (Philadelphia: Westminster Press, 1974), pp. 78-79; Frank Michaeli, *Exode* (Neuchâtel: Delachaux & Niestlé, 1974), pp. 53-54; Benno Jacob, *Exodus* (Hoboken, NJ; Ktav, 1992), pp. 87-100; Cornelis Houtman, *Exodus* (Kampen: Kok, 1993), pp. 403-419; N.M. Sarna, *Exodus* (Philadelphia: Jewish Publication Society of America, 1991), pp. 21-22; M.M. Kasher, *Encyclopedia of Biblical Interpretation*, VII (New York: American Biblical Encyclopedia Society, 1967), pp. 123-37.

this point. It becomes the first plague in Exod. 7.14-24. The first sign and the third are reproduced by Egyptian magicians in Exod. 7.11, 22; the second recurs in Num. 12.9-16 as a punishment for Miriam.

Now comes the fourth objection, Exod. 4.10-17, the one I see as a parallel to Mt. 16.13-20:

> But Moses said to the Lord, 'O my Lord, I have never been eloquent, neither in the past nor even now that you have spoken to your servant; but I am slow of speech and slow of tongue'. Then the Lord said to him, 'Who gives speech to mortals? Who makes them mute or deaf, seeing or blind? Is it not I, the Lord? Now go, and I will be with your mouth and teach you what you are to speak'. But he said, 'O my Lord, please send someone else'. Then the anger of the Lord was kindled against Moses and he said, 'What of your brother Aaron, the Levite? I know that he can speak fluently; even now he is coming out to meet you, and when he sees you his heart will be glad. You shall speak to him and put the words in his mouth, and will teach you what you shall do. He indeed shall speak for you to the people; he shall serve as a mouth for you, and you shall serve as God for him. Take in your hand this staff, with which you shall perform the signs' (NRSV).

At the fourth objection the Lord finally becomes angry (4.14) and this provokes him to propose a remarkable solution. Aaron will serve as the spokesman for Moses (4.15). More shocking still, Moses will be as God to Aaron (4.16). That, for the biblical author, this bold manner of speaking is not a solitary lapse may be seen in Exod. 7.1 where God says to Moses, 'see, I have made you *like God* to Pharaoh, and your brother Aaron shall be your prophet'.[6]

This is a lively, well-developed passage of dialogue. (Some see a fifth objection in v. 13.) It is almost a playlet. It maintains the reader's inter-

---

6. The philological details of the two verses which speak of Moses as god deserve attention. In 4.16, in the key final phrase w^e'attâ tih^{e}yeh-lô lē'lōhîm there is a lamed prefixed to the word for God, elohim. In 7.1 there is no lamed: n^etattiyāk '^{e}lōhîm l^{e}par^e'ōh. How should we understand this lamed? As a lamed of specification? Or as a sign of a label or inscription, not to be translated? Cf. W.L. Holladay (ed.), *A Concise Hebrew and Aramaic Lexicon of the Old Testament* (Leiden: E.J. Brill, 1993), p. 169. The NRSV translates by adding an 'as' or 'like' before elohim. The sense of this addition is to signal to the reader that this bold expression is only a metaphor and is not to be pressed. The ancient versions went even further in this direction. Cf. my article, 'The Trinity in the Old Testament', *TZ* 54 (1998), pp. 193-209. But we must remember that there is no 'as' or 'like' in the original, especially not in 7.1.

est through shifts and surprises both subtle and substantial. For example, in v. 10 Moses claims not to be a man of words, but the rest of the Pentateuch shows him constantly speaking; in v. 11 God is the cause of evil (deafness, muteness, blindness) as well as good (their opposites); in v. 13 Moses' objection is very subtly worded in the original; in v. 15 God will teach Moses what to *do*, not what to *say*, as one would have expected from the preceding dialogue; in v. 16 the shock is that Moses is called God (*'elōhîm*) in relation to Aaron. It is a somewhat neglected passage. The key words which dominate the passage are *dibber* (speak) and *debārîm* (words) which together occur eight times; *pe'h* (mouth), which occurs seven times, and *'ānōkî* (I) which occurs five times. This last word 'I' suggests a battle of wills between Moses and God.

It is fairly easy to see a *general* connection between the structures of Exodus 3–4 and Mt. 16.13-20. They both contain a scene of divine revelation, followed by the authorization of a purely human (and weak, flawed) figure for a role of leadership. But beyond this, both Exodus and Matthew can be seen as attributing divine or semi-divine status to Moses and Jesus respectively, and as proposing a subordinate but important role to a second figure, in the first case Aaron, in the second Peter. To be sure, the texts are not strictly parallel; otherwise the links would have been noticed earlier. In the one case the revelation consists in the transmitting of God's name (Exod. 3.14), in the second case it consists in Peter's confession of Jesus as the Christ, the Son of the living God (Mt. 16.16). The asymmetry is even more obvious in that the phrase 'you shall serve as God for him' (Exod. 4.16) comes not as a major revelation, much less as a confession, but rather at the end of a series of objections and responses, almost as an afterthought. The phrase could have been omitted without damaging the main sense of the passage; so at least one might think, were it not for Exod. 7.1. Further, there is a parallelism between Aaron and Peter, but there are also differences. This can be seen in the succession narratives in Num. 20.22-29 (cf. 33.38-39) and 27.12-23 (cf. Deut. 31.1-8). In the first of these Aaron is to be succeeded as priest by his son Eleazar. (Actually his office as priest is not mentioned explicitly in 20.22-29; the idea is conveyed by the references to putting on and taking off the vestments. But Aaron is named priest in the second account of his death, Num. 33.38-39). In the second succession narrative Moses is succeeded by Joshua, who 'shall stand before Eleazar the priest, who shall inquire for him by the decision of the Urim before the Lord; at his word they shall go out, and at his word they shall come in, both he and all the Israelites with him, the whole congregation' (Num. 27.21). Joshua does not here receive the name or title of an office, but one is to understand that he will be the leader in battle, and thus exercise military, political and civil authority. In other words, he fulfills the function of a king, although he never bears this title. Whether Eleazar is to be subordinate to Joshua, as I am inclined to think, or Joshua is to be subordinate to Eleazar, as Conrad L'Heureux judges,[7] remains uncertain. Perhaps their exact relationship is left undefined. Joshua seems not to have been admitted to the same degree of intimacy with God as Moses.[8] Like Peter, Joshua undergoes a change of name: 'And Moses changed the name of Hoshea son of Nun to Joshua' (Num. 13.16). (This is due to a scruple of the Priestly tradition about the divine name, but nothing is made of it narratively.) Nevertheless, Joshua's role is important: 'On that day the Lord exalted Joshua in the sight of all Israel; and they stood in awe of him, as they had stood in awe of Moses, all the days of his life' (Josh. 4.14; cf. 1.5; 3.7; 6.27). This idea of a direct succession to Moses is quite different from what one finds in Mt. 16.17-19. There is there no idea of a direct successor of Jesus. Rather is there the idea of Peter exercising the role of a foundation stone (v. 18)[9] and of a lieutenant, a grand vizier, a prime minister, with authority to bind and loose (v. 19). This office of grand vizier or prime minister is developed and illustrated in Isa. 22.15-25,

---

7. Conrad l'Heureux, 'Numbers', in Brown (ed.), *New Jerome Biblical Commentary*, p. 56.

8. Martin Buber, *Moses* (New York: Harper, 1958), p. 198; for a different view, see Jean Daniélou, *From Shadows to Reality: Studies in the Biblical Typology of the Fathers* (Westminster, MD: Newman Press, 1960), 'Book V: The Cycle of Joshua', pp. 229-86.

9. Peter Lampe, 'Das Spiel mit dem Petrus-Namen—Matt. 16.18', *NTS* 25 (1979), pp. 227-45. Despite his immense learning, Lampe's attempt to argue that *petra/kepa'* could not serve to refer to a foundation rock because it meant a (rolling) stone, not a rock, fails to convince for two reasons. (1) Even if the first meaning of *kepa'* was stone, it also, as the Dead Sea Scrolls and the targumim show, meant rock (J.A. Fitzmyer, 'Aramaic Kepha and Peter's Name in the New Testament', in *idem*, *To Advance the Gospel: New Testament Studies* [New York: Crossroad, 1981], pp. 112-24). (2) The image behind Mt. 16.18 is of a temple being constructed, and in Judaism the temple was founded not upon a rock but upon a (foundation) stone, the *'eben šetiiyyâ* (cf. the use of *'eben/lithon* in Isa. 28.16) (so Davies and Allison, *Matthew*, II, p. 626). Caragounis, *Peter*, takes a line similar to Lampe; (3) in Mt. 7.24-25 *petra* means a solid foundation.

with imagery which is echoed in Mt. 16.19. There Shebna, whose titles are steward (*śoken*, LXX: *tamias*) and master of the (royal) household (*'ašer 'al-habbayit*, LXX: v. 23 *archon*) is deposed from his office, and Eliakim son of Hilkiah is set in his place. There it is said, 'I will place on his shoulder the key of the house of David; he shall open, and no one shall shut; he shall shut, and no one shall open...he will become a throne of honor to his ancestral house' (Isa. 22.22-23; for the throne cf. Mt. 19.28, par. Lk. 22.29-30). The point here is that, as Aaron serves as Moses' spokesperson and assistant, so Shebna and later Eliakim serve as stewards or prime ministers to the Davidide king, and Peter as authorized lieutenant (in the etymological sense of place-holder or *locum tenens*) to Jesus. It is a case of Mosaic and Davidide typology, but among the characters of secondary rank. These characters play a real but subsidiary role in biblical models of succession and leadership. It is a delicate matter of balance. Their function is not to be exaggerated nor is it to be denied altogether. In each of these three cases the flaws and failures of each character are frankly stated: for Aaron in Num. 20.24; cf. Num. 12.1-16, not to mention the golden calf in Exodus 32; for Eliakim in Isa. 22.25 (prospectively); for Peter in Mt. 16.22-23; 14.30-31; 26.56, 69-75. Yet in each case, and despite their flaws, their function is accepted as a practical necessity.

To return to the matter of differences between Exod. 4.10-17 and Mt. 16.13-20. Despite some later Jewish views of Moses as unique, foundational and unsucceedable, for example in Philo and Maimonides (based on Num. 12.8 and Deut. 34.10), the picture in the Pentateuch at least shows Moses as (a) flawed (see Deut. 1–3, esp. 1.37-38; 3.23-28) and (b) as having Joshua as his successor. Moses' office is not clearly defined or titled in the Pentateuch; he simply functions as what we would call the leader. (Philo would later, in his *Life of Moses*, speak of a fivefold ministry of Moses as legislator, philosopher, king, priest and prophet, book 2.1-2.) But in at least one strand of the Pentateuch Moses is viewed as a prophet and as a prophet who has successors in his office (Deut. 18.18). The expression of Exod. 4.12, 'I will be with your mouth and teach you what you are to speak', is echoed in Deuteronomy ('and I will put my words in his mouth') and also in Jer. 1.9 and less exactly in Isa. 6.7-8.[10] By contrast, in the New Testament generally Jesus is por-

---

10. New Testament echoes have been seen in Mt. 10.19-20, par. Lk. 12.11-12; Mk 13.11; Lk. 21.14-15, but these passages do not at all suggest that anyone succeeds to Jesus' unique, irreplaceable office.

trayed as flawless, as without sin. The exceptions in Mk 3.5, 21 are almost accidental; there is no hint in Mark that he regarded Jesus' anger as a moral fault, or that he shared the view of Jesus' family that Jesus was out of his mind. The sinlessness of Jesus eventually becomes a principle, as in Heb. 4.15, and his superiority to Moses as son to servant is explicit in Heb. 3.1-6. More important for our purposes, in the New Testament, which accepts that Jesus is the Son of God and risen from the dead, Jesus does not require a human successor, because (a) he reigns as risen Lord present in mysterious ways to his people (e.g. Mt. 28.18-20), (b) he sends his Holy Spirit among them as the main mode of his presence.[11] To be sure, in the resurrection narratives Jesus continues to delegate his work to others who continue his ministry. They do so not as successors but as associates who continue to depend upon his authority. This is quite clear in Mt. 28.18-20: 'All power in heaven and on earth has been given to me. Go, therefore, and make disciples of all nations, baptizing them in the name of the Father, and of the Son, and of the Holy Spirit, teaching them to observe all that I have commanded you. And behold, I am with you always, until the end of the age.'[12]

To sum up the main point, we propose to see a rough Mosaic typology, drawn from Exod. 4.10-17, in Mt. 16.13-20, where a scene of revelation of Jesus' messianic and transcendent identity is followed by an authorization of a secondary, quite human, figure, Peter, to exercise important ministerial powers. Peter stands to Aaron as Jesus to Moses.

The obvious question is whether this passage from Exodus was in Matthew's mind as he composed this scene. That he knew Exodus 4 well is clear from his quotation of Exod. 4.19 in Mt. 2.20. That he had Exod. 4.10-17 in his mind on occasion may be seen in the allusion at Mt. 10.19-20. Still, the question remains, was this passage in his mind at Mt. 16.13-20? To answer such a question, D.C. Allison lists six 'devices' and six guidelines.[13] The six devices used in constructing typologies are: explicit statement, inexplicit borrowing, reminiscent circumstances, key words or phrases, structural imitation, and resonant syl-

---

11. R.F. O'Toole, 'Activity of the Risen Jesus in Luke–Acts', *Bib* 62 (1981), pp. 471-98.

12. T.W. Manson, *The Servant Messiah* (Cambridge: Cambridge University Press, 1961), pp. 89-99; R.E. Brown, *The Churches the Apostles Left Behind* (New York: Paulist Press, 1984), pp. 124-50.

13. Allison, *The New Moses*, pp. 19-23, 140.

labic and/or word patterns. The six guidelines are: chronological prior-
ity of type to antitype; the type must be known to the author of the
antitype; if there is no explicit statement, there ought to be a combination of the other devices; the type should be well known, not obscure
(here Moses and Aaron); multiple use of a type strengthens the case;
unusual imagery and uncommon motifs present in both type and antitype increase the probability of the argument. This is organized common sense, helpful nonetheless. Elements of devices three to six are
arguably present in Mt. 16.13-20 in relation to Exod. 4.10-17.

If we look at the Septuagint of Exod. 4.10-17, which contains some
minor but real differences from and additions to the Hebrew,[14] we must
first of all state frankly that the vocabulary of the two passages is quite
different. The vocabulary of Hebrew text Exod. 4.10-17 is on the whole
simple. One might think it a bit anthropomorphic, though the LXX does
not blush at it (except in v. 16).[15] The vocabulary of Mt. 16.13-20 on
the other hand is a complex weave of terminology from various strands
of the biblical and extra-biblical traditions: the Christ Son of God stems
from Israelite royal language, the keys and the mention of Elijah and
Jeremiah are all prophetic, the makarism in v. 17 is sapiential, the image
of the gates of the underworld is found in both prophetic and wisdom
strands, and binding and loosing come from proto-rabbinic usage. (What
makes our two passages parallel is the partial similarity of content and
structure, not a common vocabulary.) Yet there are a few points to
notice. (1) In Exod. 4.10-11 LXX, Moses says: *ischnophōnos kai brad-
iglossos ego eimi*, 'weak voiced and slow of tongue *am I*'. He uses the

---

14. In v. 10 the LXX does not make explicit the nature of Moses' incompetence.
In v. 11 the MT has 'mute or deaf'; LXX transposes this to 'deaf or hard of hearing'.
In v. 12 MT reads 'I will be *with* your mouth'; LXX: 'I will *open* your mouth'. In
v. 14 LXX adds that Aaron will speak *'for you'*, thus anticipating v. 16. In v. 16 MT
reads: 'you will be to him as God'; LXX: 'you will be [there] for him *for relations
with God [ta tou theou]*'. The LXX thus waters down the boldness of the expression
through interpretation. In v. 17 LXX adds to 'this staff' the phrase 'which has been
changed into a snake'. It thus assimilates this staff to the staff of vv. 2-4. Cf. Alain
Le Boulluec and Pierre Sandevoir, *La Bible d'Alexandrie: L'Exode* (Paris: Cerf,
1989), pp. 98-101.

15. The only unusual terms are the technical terms for the handicaps of speech,
hearing and vision, and the twice-repeated (vv. 12 and 15) root *yrh* III, in the hiphil,
with the meaning 'to instruct'. But this word occurs 45 times in Hebrew Text, well-
distributed among the parts of the Bible, so it is not exactly rare. One could think of
it as belonging to the special vocabulary of wisdom but not in an exclusive sense.

ego eimi of self-predication, establishing an identity.[16] In Matthew it is also a question of determining a personal identity. Jesus twice asks about others' opinion of his identity, for example, 16.15 *tina me legete einai*. The words are the same but the grammatical forms are different, as the interrogative sentence differs from the indicative. (2) The anger of God in Exod. 4.14 parallels the angry words of Jesus in Mt. 16.23 which rebuke Peter. (3) There is a parallel in the conferral of a physical instrument or badge of office, in the case of Moses, the staff. 'Take in your hand this staff, with which you shall perform the signs' (Exod. 4.17). Jesus says to Peter, 'I will give you the keys to the kingdom of heaven' (Mt. 16.19a). The material instrument in each case differs: staff, keys. And the staff is real, whereas the keys are normally understood to be symbolic and metaphorical (by exegetes, but not by artists). But both instruments fit into a context of bestowal of an office. (4) Both passages include a reference to an earthly office-holder who has a kind of control over divine matters. In Exod. 4.16 LXX, God says to Moses, *sy de auto esē ta pros ton theon*, 'but you will be for him (in) the matters toward God'. In Mt. 16.19b, the clauses about binding and loosing on earth and in heaven involve a reverent circumlocution in which heaven stands for the deity. Peter will be involved in *ta tou theou*, divine matters. He thus will serve as a kind of mouth for Jesus as Son of God. This is the main link between the two passages.

These four observations do not guarantee that Exod. 4.10-17 was in the Evangelist's mind as he composed 16.13-20, but they do make it more probable.

If we widen the Matthean context slightly to include 17.1-8, we notice that six days after Peter as a new Aaron has made his confession of Jesus as the transcendent Messiah, comparable to the high priest whose duty it is once a year to pronounce the divine name in the Holy of Holies (*m. Yom.* 6.2; 3.8; *Soṭ.* 7.6; *Tam.* 3.8; cf. Lev. 9.4, 22-24; 16), he is privileged with two other leading disciples to witness the revelation of the transfigured Jesus.

Our four plus one observations do suggest the presence in Mt. 16.13-20 and its context of some of the devices proper to (Mosaic) typology which we listed above. Thus Matthew has borrowed implicitly some motifs of the Moses story in this passage. The circumstance of commis-

---

16. Philip B. Harner, *The 'I Am' of the Fourth Gospel* (Philadelphia: Fortress Press, 1970). This provides Old Testament and New Testament usage and further literature.

sioning Peter to a new series of tasks which together make up an office is reminiscent of God calling and accrediting Moses with Aaron as his prophetic mouthpiece or assistant. We have noted similar phrases and motifs (the question of identity, the anger of God/Jesus, the conferral of a symbol of office—staff, keys), the link of the two offices to divine matters. The conditions set by the six guidelines listed by Allison are all easily met, since Exodus is chronologically prior to Matthew and was certainly known to Matthew. There is a combination of the devices. The type (here Moses and Aaron) was well known to Matthew's readership, and the imagery is sufficiently striking and uncommon as to be memorable.

So much for the Mosaic typology which was such a part of Matthew's cultural world. Now we should look at an extra-biblical but early and rival approach to the question of post-paschal leadership in the churches. The *Gospel of Thomas*, logion 12, contains an interesting parallel to Mt. 16.17-19.

> The disciples said to Jesus: We know that you will go away from us. Who is it who will [then] be great over us? Jesus said to them: In the place to which you have come, you will go to James the Just for whose sake heaven and earth came into being.

This text poses the question clearly: who will be the leader ('great') of the disciples after the Ascension? Jesus' answer here, 'James the Just', astonishing as it may be, reflects the view of the Jewish Christian element within early Christianity, its hope, its wish, its ideal, of a Judaism which accepts Jesus as the eschatological Messiah but wants to remain faithful to the Torah and the way of life (customs) to which it leads. Their hero was the by now long dead James the brother of the Lord, not either of the apostles James. He was a man whom Josephus presents as universally admired for his holiness but who died a martyr at the hands of the priests c. 62 CE (Josephus, *Ant.* 20.9.1; Eusebius, *Hist. Eccles.* 2.23). This group opposed Paul's mission principle according to which Gentile converts could be admitted to the church without the obligation to observe the ethnic markers or ceremonial precepts of Judaism, notably circumcision. They needed to exalt a figure who would symbolize and embody an alternative to Pauline leadership. In their eyes, Peter was too weak, too impetuous and unstable, too easily intimidated by Paul, to fill the bill. The extremists of this group eventually drifted into what the great church would regard as heresy, whether Ebionite or Gnostic or both. This passage from the *Gospel of Thomas* represents their option, even though this James was not an apostle. They were willing to forego apostolic authority, mindful of the brief experiment in caliphate government (government of the church of Jerusalem by blood relatives of Jesus).[17] This seemed to them even better than apostolic authority.[18]

The ecclesial position represented by Matthew, while critical of Paul (Mt. 5.19 in relation to 1 Cor. 15.9) was not willing to exclude the Pauline mission entirely from its ecumenical outreach. Therefore, though it parodied Paul's words in Gal. 1.15-16 and applied them to Peter (Mt. 16.17),[19] it continued to learn from Paul (Mt. 10.8b, possibly) and sought a compromise candidate, a wax nose, that could be influenced by both parties during his lifetime (Gal. 2.11-14),[20] but who had unassailable apostolic credentials (even if Andrew was the first called in John's Gospel), who is almost always placed first in lists of the apostles (Gal. 2.9 is the exception) and who acted as the spokesman of the group of the disciples in all the Synoptic Gospels. He was thus a man acceptable to moderates on all sides and a man who had sealed his confession of faith as a martyr for his Lord (*1 Clem.* 5.4). If you had to choose a symbolic figure for church leadership you could not do better than Peter both on historic and on psychological–moral–typological grounds, since he by his life illustrated the real weaknesses as well as the strengths of church leaders of every era. Thus the parallel from the *Gospel of Thomas* is extremely valuable as a means of understanding the struggles behind and the alternatives to Mt. 16.17-19. Matthew's is not a text that fell from the blue, but, as we now have it in our Greek text, the late first century product or end result of considerable early

---

17. Hans von Campenhausen, 'The Authority of Jesus' Relatives in the Early Church', in Henry Chadwick and H. von Campenhausen, *Jerusalem and Rome* (Philadelphia: Fortress Press, 1966), pp. 1-19; Richard Bauckham, *Jude and the Relatives of Jesus in the Early Church* (Edinburgh: T. & T. Clark, 1990).

18. Martin Hengel, 'Jakobus der Herrenbruder—der erste "Papst"?', in Erich Grässer and Otto Merk (eds.), *Glaube und Eschatologie: Festschrift für W.G. Kümmel zum 80. Geburtstag* (Tübingen: J.C.B. Mohr, 1985), pp. 71-104.

19. In its turn, Mt. 16.17-19 is probably modulated by Jn 20.23 and 21.15-19.

20. Cf. the classic albeit polemical article by Karl Holl on later interpretations of this passage, 'Der Streit zwischen Petrus und Paulus in Antiochien und seine Bedeutung für Luthers innere Entwicklung', in his *Gesammelte Aufsätze zur Kirchengeschichte*, III (Darmstadt: Wissenschaftliche Buchgesellschaft, 1964), pp. 134-46.

Christian experimentation and exploration.[21] This experimentation is precisely in the area of ecclesiological organization and authority, as the Thomas parallel helps us to see; it is not only a matter of the personal faith of each individual disciple (of whom Peter is the type) or of the value of faith in general, but of continuity in church structure and teaching.

Some authors read Galatians 2 as indicating a federation of Peter and Paul with a James group. In this reconstruction, Peter and Paul as *choephoroi* represent a fusion and union of diverse groups. The Jamesians drift off, except for moderates represented in the New Testament by the Gospel according to Matthew and by the letter of James, perhaps also by 2 Peter. It may be that Matthew and others stress Petrine authority *against* the challenge represented by the Jamesian caliphate.[22]

2. *Other Models*

Once we grant that the Evangelist Matthew included 16.17-19 as part of an attempt to provide for church leadership and government after Easter, after the crisis of 66–74, the end of the priestly Temple regime in Judaism, and as the original apostles and eyewitnesses were beginning to die off, we may ask the question: what models of central religious government were available to him and to his sources? What models could have contributed to his editorial shaping of the verses?

Let us draw up a list of some of the possibilities, moving from the least likely to the more probable, before going in greater detail into some of the more probable models. Our work will be exploratory, and it

21. On *Gos. Thom.* 12, see K.T. Schäfer, 'Der Primat Petri und das Thomas-Evangelium', in W. Corsten, A. Frotz and P. Linden (eds.), *Die Kirche und ihre Ämter und Stände* (Festschrift Joseph Kardinal; Frings; Cologne: J.P. Bachem, 1960), pp. 353-63; Smith, *Petrine Controversies*, pp. 107-11; Michael Fieger, *Das Thomasevangelium* (NTAbh, NF 22; Münster: Aschendorff, 1991), pp. 63-66.

This dating does not exclude some roots or traces of the blessing of Peter at the level of the historical Jesus. Davies and Allison, *Matthew*, II, pp. 609-15 and, in their train, Donald Hagner, *Matthew 14–28* (Waco, TX: Word Books, 1995), pp. 461-75, have argued for a setting in the life of the historical Jesus. Nevertheless, we hold that the final form of the text in this Gospel is a product of the Matthean redaction, and, as such, bears the marks of several decades of early Christian searching for a viable model of postapostolic authority.

22. Etienne Nodet and Justin Taylor, *The Origins of Christianity: An Exploration* (Collegeville, MN: Liturgical Press/Glazier Books, 1998), pp. 183-254.

must be kept in mind that we are trying to understand the position of *Peter* for Matthew, not of Jesus as the Christ. The distinction is important, since some of the same models could be or have been used in Christology.

We may begin with the Roman emperor. There is nothing explicit in Matthew to suggest this. Matthew stays as much as possible within the perspective of biblical Israel. Only in the trial narrative does the Roman imperial authority come to the surface in a powerful way. In the prologue the child's conflict is with Herod the Great, not with Augustus. The magi come from the east, not the west. The flight to Egypt *de facto* presupposes the unity of the empire, but this is not discussed. The obvious exception is the controversy over paying taxes to Caesar, 22.15-22, but the contrast is between God and Caesar, not between Jesus and Caesar or Peter and Caesar. The references to kings in 10.18; 11.8, 17.25, as well as in the king parables of 18.23, 22.1-14, all seem to allude to the vassal kings of the local variety with which Galileans were familiar. Nevertheless, we must accept that the Roman empire was the remoter horizon of Matthew's political consciousness, and that the emperor bore the title Pontifex Maximus, the title which signified that he was the head of the state religion. Matthew's borrowing of the terms *parousia* and *hypantesis*,[23] technical terms for the arrival of the emperor for a state visit,[24] and his application of them to the arrival or coming of Jesus in future glory, is a strong indication of his mind, even if the immediate source was 1 Thess. 4.13-18 and/or 1 Cor. 15.23. That is, these terms were already part of the early Christian eschatological vocabulary, even if avoided by the other evangelists (cf., however, Jn 12.13). Yet none of this seems to have directly influenced the words about Peter. All that we can conclude is that the Roman emperor was a model of central religio-political authority current in Matthew's day. (Later, after the end of the empire in the West, the Roman popes did try to fill the imperial gap for a time, in collaboration with Byzantium, but this has no bearing on our understanding of Matthew.)

References to Israelite kings are more frequent, especially to the Herods and to David. Matthew refers to David some fifteen times, more often than any other Evangelists, and the christological title Son of David is singularly important for him, often with a healing connota-

---

23. *Parousia*: Mt. 24.3, 27, 37, 39; *hypantesis*: 8.34; 25.1.
24. Erik Peterson, 'Die Einholung des Kyrios', *ZST* 7 (1929–30), pp. 682-702.

tion,[25] and his successor Solomon is mentioned as well (1.6, 7; 6.29; 12.42),[26] whereas his predecessor Saul is passed over in silence. Herod the Great and his son Archelaus figure in ch. 14.1-9. Matthew's interest in and awareness of such local kings is not in doubt. Perhaps his view of them is partly revealed, not only in 10.18 and 11.8 or in king parables (18.23; 22.27), but also in the episode of the temple tax, proper to his Gospel, where Jesus asks Peter (17.25): 'From whom do the kings take tolls or census tax?' What is regrettably absent from these references to kings is any awareness that they were often aided by grand viziers or prime ministers. For example, the gifted assistant to Herod the Great, Nicolaus of Damascus, is not mentioned. This is unfortunate precisely because the symbolism of the key in 16.19 derives from a prophetic reference to such an assisting figure to a Davidic king.

Since the discovery of the Dead Sea Scrolls in 1947, there has been considerable interest in studying the community structure as described in the sectarian documents found in the caves at Wadi Qumran. (This interest picks up an earlier, pre-Qumran, interest in the possible influence of the Essenes, as described by Josephus and Philo, on early Christianity, manifested by Ernest Renan and others in the nineteenth century.[27]) The roles of the priests, the Teacher of Righteousness, the *mēbaqqēr* and/or the *pāqîd* (supervisor) have all been explored for possible influences on Jesus and/or the early church, especially the development of the office of bishop.[28]

As R.E. Brown says,

25. D.C. Duling, 'The Therapeutic Son of David: An Element in Matthew's Christological Apologetic', *NTS* 24 (1978), pp. 392-410; *idem*, 'Solomon, Exorcism and Son of David', *HTR* 68 (1975), pp. 235-52; J.D. Kingsbury, 'The Title Son of David in Matthew's Gospel', *JBL* 95 (1976), pp. 591-602; Christoph Burger, *Jesus als Davidssohn* (FRLANT, 98; Göttingen: Vandenhoeck & Ruprecht, 1970).

26. Edward Schillebeeckx, *Jesus* (New York: Crossroad, 1979), pp. 456-59.

27. Cf. André Dupont-Sommer, *The Essene Writings from Qumran* (Cleveland: World Publishing Company, 1961), p. 13, refers to Frederick II of Prussia and cites Renan: 'Christianity is an Essenism which has largely succeeded'.

28. J.M. Baumgarten, 'The Duodecimal Courts of Qumran, Revelation and the Sanhedrin', *JBL* 95 (1976), pp. 59-78; B.E. Thiering, '*Mebaqqer* and *Episkopos* in the Light of the Temple Scroll', *JBL* 100 (1981), pp. 59-74; R.E. Brown, 'Apocrypha; Dead Sea Scrolls; Other Jewish Literature', nos. 110-112, in *idem*, (ed.), *New Jerome Biblical Commentary* 67 'Apocrypha; Dead Sea Scrolls; Other Jewish Literature', nos. 110-112.

the Christian bishop is an excellent parallel to the Qumran supervisor. *Episkopos*, 'overseer' or 'supervisor', could be a literal translation of either *pāqîd* or *mēbaqqēr*, and the functions attributed to the bishop are much the same as those of the Qumran supervisor, e.g., shepherd of the flock, steward and manager of community property, and inspector of the doctrine of the faithful (1 Pet. 2.25; Acts 20.28; Tit. 1.7-9; 1 Tim. 3.2-7).[29]

Applying these considerations to Matthew, the Evangelist, inspired by this Qumranite structure, could have seen Peter as such a supervisory figure. But apart from the Teacher of Righteousness, who seems to fulfill a unique and unrepeatable role (and thus corresponds more to the role of Jesus in the Gospels), there is nothing in Qumran about a supervisor of supervisors who would have universal authority even in a conciliar structure (Mt. 18.18). But, while I think that Mt. 16.17-19 describes an ongoing office of church leadership, a judge of final instance, I do not exclude a unique, foundational role to Peter and the other members of the Twelve. Their successors do not share in that foundational role, but are nonetheless endowed with sufficient authority to guide the church through its ongoing crises. This seems to be Matthew's idea in this Petrine passage, as in 18.18. Moreover, in regard to Qumran, there is a distinct sacerdotal aspect to their leadership structure, at least as an ideal. And so one could object that Simon Peter is never said to be of priestly or levitical lineage in the Christian tradition. Any connection with Qumran models would then be ruled out. But, alongside the priests, there seem to be non-sacerdotal office-holders at Qumran. (The texts are not absolutely clear about this.) Yet, like the Pharisees, the people of Qumran seem to have striven to live in a state of priestly purity even if they were not of priestly descent, positively to realize the ideal of Exod. 19.6, negatively in atonement for the defilements caused, in their view, by the Hasmonean high priests in the Jerusalem temple.[30] Thus some Qumran influence on Matthew's view cannot be absolutely

---

29. See Brown, 'Apocrypha', p. 112.

30. Brown, 'Apocrypha', p. 108 and the literature there cited; Adrian Schenker, 'Ein Königreich von Priestern (Ex 19,6)', *IKZ Communio* 25 (1996), pp. 483-90; J.M. Baumgarten, 'The Qumran-Essene Restraints on Marriage', in L.H. Schiffman (ed.), *Archaeology and History in the Dead Sea Scrolls* (JSPSup, 8; Sheffield: JSOT Press, 1990), pp. 13-24 (good bibliography); Anton Steiner, 'Warum lebten die Essener asketisch?', *BZ* 15 (1971), pp. 1-98.

excluded. Indeed, we will return to these semi-sacerdotal models after we consider our next model.

In the wake of W.D. Davies's major study of Matthew, *The Setting of the Sermon on the Mount*,[31] some tried to understand Peter's authority in this text as that of a grand rabbi.[32] For Davies, in the most original part of his work, had proposed that Matthew's 'school' was in polemical dialogue with the early rabbinic academy at Jamnia, founded by Rabbanan Johanan ben Zakkai about 75 CE.[33] (Jamnia lies some 30 km south of Caesarea Maritima on the Mediterranean coast.) As the academy developed, it held annual sessions where the sages gathered and made halackhic decisions (hence the label 'synod'). The academy was governed by a *nasi* or patriarch, whose lieutenant was called the *ab beth din* (literally, the father of the court house).Thus Jamnia at times at least involved academic, legislative, judicial and executive activities. The *nasi*'s authority increased once the Romans recognized its usefulness in dealing with the Jews of the region. Should we suppose that this recognition was granted at the outset, then temporarily withdrawn during the Bar Kochba rebellion (132–135) and its immediate aftermath, and eventually renewed when the situation had quieted down and the rabbis could give assurances of a pacific orientation to the restored leadership, with an exilarch or exarch added as civil leader? The historical data are not clear.

Did this institution of the *nasi* inspire Matthew or his sources? One might be inclined to reject such a suggestion until one remembers that Johanan and his colleagues were trying to find a substitute for the lost religious leadership represented by the high priest in the Temple. Their substitute was not an exact copy of the Temple administration (although they were careful to preserve as much of the traditions of Temple procedure as they could, in the latter part of the Mishnah, in the hope that the Temple would soon be restored) but an administration which intended primarily to codify and to continue (and to purify?) the Pharisaic line of tradition within pre-70 Judaism. In the process they created something new, however traditional their intentions. Matthew's community was also interested in preserving a double strain of continuity in

31. W.D. Davies, *The Setting of the Sermon on the Mount* (Cambridge: Cambridge University Press, 1964).

32. For example, P.E. Ellis, *Matthew: His Mind and his Message* (Collegeville, MN: Liturgical Press, 1974), pp. 125-34.

33. Davies, *Setting*, pp. 256-315.

the face of the terrible disruption and discontinuity which occurred when the temple was burned. Its concerns were (a) to be the heirs and continuers of what they judged to be the true Israel, and (b) to be the true Israel as reformed and gathered for the soon-to-come eschaton by Jesus. This too represented a considerable set of innovations. So, even if the Jamnian arrangements were not a model that Matthew followed in detail, still we can see some parallel intentions and procedures.

The last model for Mt. 16.17-19 which we will consider is the Aaronic high priest of the temple in Jerusalem. For Christians, due to the role of the high priest in the trial of Jesus as recorded in the canonical Gospels, this office has rather negative connotations. For modern religious Jews it is associated with the Sadducean party, an unloved group in rabbinic sources. Yet as a religious office, founded in the Pentateuch, it was important as a role which, so long as it lasted, provided a unity, a central focal point, and a certain continuity for the widely scattered Jews of the diaspora as well as for the Jews of the Judean mother country. Even the Essenes, who abominated the group that held office in the first centuries BCE and CE, were fiercely sacerdotal–levitical in their outlook and lived for the day when they could take over the administration of the Temple themselves. In a more quiet manner the Pharisees sought gradually to influence Temple practices. The zealots took over the Temple in the great battle for the city. The average Jew, unaffiliated with any religious faction, doubtless regarded the Temple and its priesthood as the outer symbols of his faith, and tried to observe the three annual pilgrim festivals there as often as he could.[34] Even the early Jewish Christians seem to have taken it for granted as the center for worship. For Matthew this is hinted at unreflectively by 5.23-24, where the believer is told to leave the altar (of the Temple) to be reconciled with one he has offended before offering his gift (cf. 4.5). Mark's passion narrative symbolism, the rending of the Temple veil (15.38), the cutting off of the high priest's servant's ear (14.47),[35] and the like, suggests that for the early Christians a break had occurred, that they regarded the Temple system as spiritually bankrupt. Now in Christ God was doing something new. A new era of salvation history had

---

34. E.P. Sanders, *Judaism, Practice and Belief 63BCE–66CE* (London: SCM Press, 1992), pp. 125-45.

35. B.T. Viviano, 'The High Priest's Servant's Ear: Mark 14:47', *RB* 96 (1989), pp. 71-80; R.E. Brown, *The Death of the Messiah* (New York: Doubleday, 1994).

dawned. All four canonical Evangelists record the cleansing of the Temple (Mt. 21.12-17 par), implying that it needed to be cleansed. Matthew, in his additional v. 14, 'the blind and the lame approached him in the Temple area, and he cured them', further implies a critique of the restrictions placed on who could enter the temple, in the old regime. Yet this entails a conviction of the desirability of participating in the Temple services. Still, after all the implict polemic against the Temple in the passion narratives, we are astounded at the ease and naturalness with which Acts depicts the early Christians regularly frequenting the Temple to teach and to worship (2.46, 'every day'!; 3.1–4.5; 5.19-26). Paul too is there depicted as performing rites in the Temple (21.15-26). The Marcan and Lucan views are so different as to be virtually contradictory. Doubtless there was idealization by both authors. Everything was not crystal clear at the outset. It took time for the early Christians to recognize the hiatus and the other implications of the death of Jesus. This recognition was only further accelerated by the burning of the Temple.[36]

The cessation of the sacrifices by the Levitical priests on the Temple Mount creates the crisis to which both Jamnia and Matthew respond creatively. For Matthew an additional factor for the creation or envisaging of new institutions was the dying out of the apostolic generation after 70. Something had to be done. Many New Testament authors react to this crisis.[37] At the same time, several of the New Testament authors have recourse to Mosaic typology as one of the means to explain and to interpret the Christ event and to meet new difficulties, along with Danielic apocalyptic and chiefly Isaian prophecy and Davidic typology.[38] What is important for our further argument is to see how, even though the early Christians criticized some parts of their Judaic and even their biblical inheritance, they nevertheless continued to make use of it, in the light of Christ to be sure.

---

36. Klaus Baltzer, 'The Meaning of the Temple in the Lukan Writings', *HTR* 58 (1965), pp. 263-77; Alexander Guttmann, 'The End of the Jewish Sacrificial Cult', *HUCA* 38 (1967), pp. 137-48; E. Schürer and G. Vermes, *A History of the Jewish People in the Age of Jesus Christ*, I (Edinburgh: T. & T. Clark, 1973), pp. 521-24.

37. R.E. Brown, *The Churches the Apostles Left Behind*.

38. C.H. Dodd, *According to the Scriptures: The Substructure of New Testament Theology* (London: Nisbet, 1952).

3. *Exegesis, State of the Question and Ecumenical Implications*

The reader is entitled to know what is my own exegesis of the text of
Mt. 16.17-19. But first my presuppositions regarding Matthew may be
briefly stated. I accept the two-source hypothesis; a date of between 80
and 90 CE for the Greek Gospel; composition somewhere in northern
Palestine or south Syria (Caesarea Maritima?); the Evangelist is a mod-
erate Jewish Christian, in polemical dialogue with the formative Judaism
of Jamnia and with the Pauline inheritance. In the new situation created
by the burning of the Temple, he is convinced that his church is the true
Israel, the legitimate successor or heir to the religion(s) represented in
the Hebrew Bible and the Septuagint. One of his subsidiary concerns
then, briefly inserted into his primary concerns, is ecclesiological, to
provide fully accredited leaders for the church in the new situation.[39]
The old center of unity and religious authority, the high priest in the
Temple, was no more. The rival groups who competed for the succession to the mantle of authority in Israel provided for leadership as best
they could. Matthew provides both an office or ministry invested in a
person, represented by Peter, to ensure unity in the sense of a court of
final appeal (16.17-19), and a conciliar or synodical organ for collective
decision making and discipline (18.15-20, not treated in detail in this
essay).

Let us turn now to a brief exegesis of the three verses.[40] Formally,
v. 17 is a macarism or beatitude. By itself it would suffice as an appropriate response by Jesus to Peter's confession. But Matthew adds vv.
18-19. These could be read on one level as an etiological legend explaining Peter's change of name. Together, vv. 17-19 provide a foundation story about post-Easter authority in the church (note the future
tenses in vv. 18 and 19) and a commission to leadership. Verse 17 says
that 'flesh and blood has not revealed this to you'. This may counter
Paul's claim in Gal. 1.15-16 that, when he was called by God, he did

39. Matthew's primary concern was to tell the story of Jesus so as to show him
as Messiah, Son of God, Lord in word and deed, herald of the kingdom, and even
now, in lowliness and suffering, God with us. This primary concern is manifest in
Matthew's redaction of 16.13-20, where a cluster of christological titles occur, and
especially in v. 20, which carefully returns the reader's attention back to the main
point, Jesus as Messiah.

40. For further details, see Benedict T. Viviano, 'The Gospel According to Matthew', in Brown (ed.), *New Jerome Biblical Commentary*, p. 105.

not confer with 'flesh and blood' (often now translated as 'any human being').[41] In v. 18 the rock is a pun on Peter's name (*Petros, petra*); in Aramaic both would be *kêpā* cf. Isa. 28.14-22; 51.1-2; 1QH 3.13-18; 6.25-27. (For the debate between Peter Lampe, Chrys Caragounis and J.A. Fitzmyer on rock versus rolling stone, see n. 9 above.) The word church is found only here and in 18.17 (*bis*) in the four Gospels. It refers to the assembly of the people of God, here understood in their universality, in 18.17 understood more locally. The 'gates of Hades' or death is a common biblical image for the forces of evil, mortality, finitude; cf. Isa. 38.10; Job 38.17; Ps. 9.14; Wis. 16.13. The keys mentioned in v. 19 are symbols of the grand vizier's or chief steward's office; cf. Isa. 22.22-23; Job 12.14; 1 Enoch 1–16.[42] Matthew here relates the church to the kingdom of heaven/God: the church is an interim arrangement which mediates salvation in the time between the earthly ministry of Jesus and the future coming of the kingdom in its fullness. *Shall be bound*: This periphrastic verb and the parallel 'shall be loosed' are future passives in Greek. The passives here are theological or divine passives; that is, if transposed into active verbs, God becomes the subject. It is then God who shall bind and loose what Peter binds and looses. (The verbs binding and loosing are here substituted for the poetically more appropriate opening and shutting, cf. Isa. 22.22-23 and Rev. 3.7, a substitution made for reasons given below.) This verse gives enormous authority to Peter. In popular imagination he becomes the gatekeeper of heaven. But in fact his ministry is earthly. What is the nature of his authority? Binding and loosing are rabbinic technical terms that can refer to binding the devil in exorcism.[43] They also refer to the juridical acts of excommunication and of definitive decision-making (a form of teaching through legislation or policy setting), which can serve the unity of the church through the settling of divisive disputed questions.[44] The authority to bind and loose is given to the disciples in 18.18, but to Peter alone are accorded the revelation, the role of the

---

41. J. Dupont, 'La révélation du Fils de Dieu en faveur de Pierre (Mt 16,17) et de Paul (Ga 1,16)', *RSR* 52 (1964), pp. 411-20, repr. in his *Etudes sur les Evangiles Synoptiques*, II (Leuven: Leuven University Press, 1985), pp. 929-39.

42. G.W.E. Nickelsburg, 'Enoch, Levi, and Peter: Recipients of Revelation in Upper Galilee', *JBL* 100 (1981), pp. 575-600.

43. R.H. Hiers, '"Binding" and "Loosing": The Matthean Authorizations', *JBL* 104 (1985), pp. 233-50.

44. Cf. J. Jeremias, *s.v.* 'Kleis', *TDNT*, III, pp. 744-53.

rock of foundation (Eph. 2.20), and especially the keys. These verses are a development of the historical reminiscence that Peter was the spokesman for the disciples during the earthly ministry of Jesus. But the present form of the text comes from the final redactor, the Evangelist. As a whole vv. 17-19 represent a blend of Old Testament poetic imagery and institutional legislation. Such a combination is not unusual in rabbinic literature, but here it attains a remarkable density.

One last exegetical point. To be sure, Peter's confession of faith makes him in this respect exemplary for all Christian believers, past and present. This is the truth in the oldest patristic interpretations of the passage, for convenience called the Eastern position. But the three verses as a whole cannot be confined to this sense. They make a promise of great ecclesial authority to an individual, particularly v. 19, especially the mention of the keys and the authority to bind and loose on earth. To this extent, as Davies and Allison remark, 'Peter is not just a representative disciple'.[45] To this extent also, Augustine's interpretation that Christ (not Peter) is the foundation rock of the church is not exegetically adequate (exhaustive), as was recognized even in the Reformation tradition.[46]

As for the contemporary state of the question, it would be good to survey recent Roman Catholic,[47] Eastern Orthodox,[48] as well as Protestant interpretations.[49] For the sake of brevity, we will reduce the discussion to the last group, and in particular to the work of Ulrich Luz, who in recent years has devoted no less than five studies to this passage,[50]

---

45. Davies and Allison, *Matthew*, 2.643.

46. Luz, *Matthaeus*, II, p. 478 and n. 173.

47. I think here particularly of Paul Hoffmann's 'Der Petrus-Primat im Matthäusevangelium', in J. Gnilka (ed.), *Neues Testament und Kirche* (Festschrift R. Schnackenburg; Freiburg: Herder, 1974), pp. 94-114, as well as G. Claudel's work mentioned in n. 1.

48. Cf. John Karavidopoulos, 'Le rôle de Pierre et son importance dans l'église du Nouveau Testament: Problématique exégétique contemporaine', *Nicolaus* 19 (1992), pp. 13-29, summarized in *TD* 44 (1997), pp. 149-54, and the studies gathered in John Meyendorff (ed.), *The Primacy of Peter: Essays in Ecclesiology and the Early Church* (Crestwood, NY: St Vladimir's Seminary Press, 1992), especially the essays by Veselin Kesich and by John Meyendorff.

49. See the studies listed in n. 1.

50. Besides his commentary mentioned in note 1, see Ulrich Luz, 'Das Primatwort Matthäus 16.17-19 aus wirkungsgeschichtlicher Sicht', *NTS* 37 (1991), pp. 415-33; 'The Primacy Text (Mt. 16:18)', *Princeton Seminary Bulletin* 12

surely a record. To diminish the line of exegesis which we have just summarized, Luz (at times) takes quite seriously the results of Lampe's research, as applicable on a pre-Matthean level. He must then accuse Matthew of twisting the meaning of the nickname Peter/*kepa'* from its original meaning (loose stone) to its opposite, solid rock, *eine Umdeutung*. Once one sees that Matthew is using both *Petros* and *petra* loosely here in the sense of *lithos*, these complicated considerations become unnecessary. (We have already discussed this issue in n. 9.)[51]

Luz at times can also be hermeneutically skeptical about the possibility or desirability of attaining or even striving to obtain an 'objective' or 'true' interpretation.[52] Such skepticism can lead to total hermeneutical relativism, anarchy and caprice, as if to say that 'all interpretations are equally valid' or that 'those interpretations which are most unlikely and hence perverse are to be preferred because of their shock value as stimuli and entertainment'. Such nihilistic views would render any non-arbitrary discussion of alternative interpretations impossible. Fortunately, Luz does not go that far. At his best, he argues that any major traditional interpretation, even if exegetically inadequate or poorly grounded, should be cherished for whatever grain of truth it contains. To reject it utterly, in this case Augustine's interpretation of our verses, would spell an impoverishment of the tradition and a loss of part of the Christian heritage.[53] Many a traditionalist and patristic romantic thinks the same. Here the distinction between the literal, historical sense of a text, the one primarily intended by the author, and secondary, often edifying, applications or appropriations of a text, usually in homiletic contexts, comes into play.

This brings us to the real ecumenical problem today. Luz's main argument comes not from exegesis but from the history of interpretation, from the postbiblical reception (or rather non-reception) of the text as it

---

(1991), pp. 41-55; *Matthew in History* (Minneapolis: Fortress Press, 1994), ch. 4, 'Peter: The True Christian or the Pope? (Matthew 16)', pp. 57-74; *The Theology of the Gospel of Matthew* (Cambridge: Cambridge University Press, 1995), pp. 96-100. Of these, the commentary is the most careful, thorough and nuanced. We will refer to it in what follows.

51. Luz, *Matthäus*, II, pp. 457-58.
52. Luz, *Matthew in History*, pp. 5-38.
53. Luz, *Matthäus*, II, p. 480.

is commonly understood by exegetes today, a non-reception particularly in the patristic and medieval periods.[54]

The interpretation in terms of a teaching office embodied in a single person, Peter, with or without successors, is not very common or explicit until Jerome and Leo the Great, and remains uncommon in the commentary literature of the first millennium (as opposed to the canonists' decretals). This need not be an enormous difficulty. There are other cases of texts whose modern interpretation is universally accepted yet whose 'correct' (from the viewpoint of contemporary exegesis) interpretation was lost for almost two millennia (due to the influence of the Septuagint or Vulgate for example). A good example is the interpretation of the little historical credo of Deut. 26.5, 'A wandering Aramean was my ancestor'.[55] The difficulty here is rather a confusion due to a foreshortening of historical perspective, whereby, once one sees that Matthew's three verses envisage an authoritative teaching office embodied in a person, one immediately leaps to a discussion of the bishop of Rome. There is no evidence that Matthew had any thought for Rome. Such a leap is anachronistic. The role of the see of Rome is a product of gradual historical development, as is its association with Mt. 16.17-19 in the sense of Rome representing the concrete embodiment of the office there envisaged. One may accept or reject this concrete embodiment (based in part on the presence of Peter's relics in Rome). That has nothing to do with Matthew.

But it does raise the question: Granted that Matthew was writing roughly twenty years after the deaths of Peter, Paul, the Jameses and John, how did he concretely envisage the office he describes in 16.17-19? In this article we have examined some models with which he would have been familiar, the high priest in the Temple at Jerusalem, the head of the rabbinic academy at Jamnia, and so on. Did Matthew envisage a 'Petrine officer' or pope as director of his school wherever it was located (Caesarea Maritima, Sepphoris, Tiberias, Damascus, Tyre, Sidon, Antioch, or someplace else)? Did he think of himself as such an officer?

---

54. See the important surveys of the history of interpretation in Gnilka, *Matthäus*, II, pp. 71-80; Luz, *Matthäus*, II, pp. 472-83; and the helpful study by Gert Haendler, 'Zur Frage nach dem Petrusamt in der alten Kirche', *ST* 30 (1976), pp. 89-122.

55. See the provocative article by F.P. Dreyfus ' 'L'Araméen voulait tuer mon père': L'actualisation de Dt 26,5 dans la tradition juive et la tradition chrétienne', in J. Doré *et al.* (eds.), *De la Tôrah au Messie, Mélanges Henri Cazelles* (Paris: Desclée de Brouwer, 1981), pp. 147-61.

There is no evidence for any of this. The exegetical school at Caesarea continued to function until the Persian invasion of 614 and then the Islamic conquest of 636–638. But this school did not function as a crucial magisterium after the conversion of Constantinople and Alexandria and Rome. Antioch did reassert its independence after Chalcedon (451). Jerusalem played an important role in the reception of Chalcedon in the East, but otherwise its influence was felt largely in the development of liturgy and catechesis: Cyril and John of Jerusalem, John Damascene (at Mar Saba just outside of Jerusalem), Sophronius.[56] Rome began to play an important role in church life even as Matthew was writing, but it cannot be shown that he was thinking of this as he wrote his Gospel. The connection between Mt. 16.17-19, and the Roman see is a leap which the individual believer may make, but has nothing directly to do with the interpretation of Matthew. It has rather to do with a discernment of the divine guidance of the church through history. The historical link between Mt. 16.17-19 and Rome is through the tradition that Peter died a martyr in Rome. But this tradition, so far as we can tell, did not lead Matthew to reflect upon any connection between the office he describes and any particular city, other than Caesarea Philippi, which never played a role in later church history. In any case, Matthew does not reflect on Rome or the Roman see.

Many patristic homiletic commentators tend to give a vague, edifying interpretation of Mt. 16.17-19, which applies it to *all* their hearers in a *generalizing* fashion. This is perfectly understandable from a pastoral point of view. But in the age of redaction criticism, where the interpreter tries to attend to the *specific* point of view of each author, such generalizing interpretations, if judged to be not the precise, immediate intention of the individual biblical author, are inadequate, except as secondary applications. What Christian would deny that we should try to

---

56. D.J. Chitty, *The Desert a City: An Introduction to the Study of Egyptian and Palestinian Monasticism under the Christian Empire* (Oxford: Oxford University Press, 1966); Christoph von Schönborn, *Sophrone de Jérusalem* (Théologie historique, 20; Paris: Beauchesne, 1972). The story of the exegetical school and bishopric of Caesarea Maritima until its closure due to the Persian invasion in 614 is told by Gideon Foerster, 'The Early History of Caesarea', in C.T. Fritsch (ed.), *The Joint Expedition to Caesarea Maritima*, I (Studies in the History of Caesarea Maritima; Missoula MT: Scholars Press, 1975); Hans Bietenhard, *Caesarea, Origenes und die Juden* (Stuttgart: W. Kohlhammer, 1974); N.R.M. de Lange, *Origen and the Jews* (Cambridge: Cambridge University Press, 1976); L.I. Levine, *Caesarea Under Roman Rule* (SJLA, 7; Leiden: E.J. Brill, 1975).

share Peter's confession of faith? But is this Matthew's main or exclusive point in vv. 17-19? No, it is not. In the same way, many patristic and later interpretations are harmonizing of Matthew here with other New Testament passages: for example, these interpretations want to harmonize the statements of Matthew and Ephesians (2.20) about the church being built on the rock (*petra*)/foundation (*themelios*) of Peter and the apostles, with Paul's statement in 1 Cor. 3.10-11, about the church being built on the foundation which is Jesus Christ. (Such a harmonization is not difficult to attain in this case, since Paul here, if one reads the context, clearly states that he himself is laying a foundation, but usually the argument goes the other way: the apostle cannot be a foundation because only Christ is. This ignores 1 Cor. 3.10.) All this harmonization violates the rules of redaction criticism and the historical-critical method.

We have already mentioned in passing that there is a difference between homiletic commentators and canonists. The canonists, who shared the responsibility for administering churches, which kept getting larger and larger, were interested in clear lines of authority and courts of final instance to which one could appeal to settle a divisive question. Mt. 16.17-19 seemed to provide for such a court of final instance, as Mt. 18.15-18 seemed to provide for courts of intermediate instance and synodical–conciliar bodies. The focus audiences of the two types of author are quite different. The canonists early discovered the ecclesiological potential in the two Matthean passages just mentioned. The preachers strove to find a general meaning applicable to all their listeners.

Moreover we may note here an important point made by Luz: 'In contrast with Mt.16.17, Mt. 16.18 was not really *received* in the early period'.[57] That is, the fathers before Leo the Great were so busy making homiletic and harmonizing applications of Jesus' blessing on Peter's confession of faith in v. 17, applications to *every* believer, that they did not bother to develop a careful, literal interpretation of the ecclesiological content of v. 18. This is doubtless true as a generalization. But in Origen's extensive commentary on the whole passage, which to be sure is extremely homiletical, harmonizing and universalizing, he shows that he knows the difference between the literal sense and the broader, pastoral application. He says, 'For on the one hand in this place [Mt. 16.19] these words seem to be addressed as to Peter only...but on the

---

57. 'Mt 16,18 wurde im Unterschied zu Mt 16,17 in der Frühzeit sozusagen nicht rezipiert' (*Matthäus*, II, p. 473).

other hand in the Gospel of John the Savior having given the Holy
Spirit unto the disciples by breathing upon them said...' And he goes
on to quote Jn 20.22 (Origen, *Commentary on Matthew* 12.11; GCS
Orig. X, 87). This passage may be exceptional, but it does show that
Origen saw the specific reference to Peter in Matthew. He simply preferred to relate it to other, non-Matthean passages whose reference to
the disciples as a group is quite clear.

The most difficult case is St Cyprian. Here is a man who had the serious responsibility of administering a local church (he was bishop of
Carthage and died a martyr in 258 CE), yet he quite firmly rejected any
kind of central authority or primacy as exercised by the bishop of
Rome. Despite this he is honored as a saint by the church of Rome. The
historian taking the long view can either say that Cyprian was right, and
later developments were an error. Or he can say that Cyprian, absorbed
as he was by the need to maintain his authority in his own diocese (he
had rivals aplenty), suffered from tunnel vision. He did not see the
usefulness of support and guidance from outside his diocese, nor did he
see the basis for such support in Mt. 16.17-19. To that extent, the text
and later developments will have proved him wrong. This is the decision the historian is left to make. The exegete can only say that, on the
level of Matthean redaction and intentionality, the second alternative
has a stronger case.

To summarize. Three types of interpretation of the *petra*/rock have
circulated since late antiquity. (1) The Eastern interpretation holds that
the *confession* or the *faith* of Peter is the foundation rock of the church.
(2) The Augustinian interpretation holds that Christ is the foundation
rock of the church (based on 1 Cor. 10.4). (3) The Roman interpretation
holds that Peter as an apostle is the foundation rock of the church.[58] Of
these three interpretations, only the third is exegetically correct as a literal interpretation of Mt. 16.17-19, taken as it stands in Matthew, without trying to harmonize it with 1 Cor. 10.4 or with a homiletic application to all believers. Two problems remain. (1) Does this text refer
only to the historical Peter or also to eventual successors of Peter in a
'Petrine ministry'? (2) Should this text be referred or applied to the succession of bishops in the Roman see, that is, the papacy? As for this
second question, we have just seen that it is not a question of the exegesis of Matthew, since there is no evidence that Matthew had ever

---

58. Luz, *Matthäus*, II, pp. 476-79.

thought about it, much less that he had directly addressed it. It is a question of the interpretation of postbiblical, post-Matthean church history and may be left to patrologists, church historians, ecclesiologists and ecumenists to answer.

As for the first question, whether this text refers only to Peter or also to successors of Peter in this ministry of being a judge of final instance in the church—if we again confine ourselves to the level of Matthean final redaction, and if we accept that the final redactor was responsible for the final form of the text as we have it in Greek Matthew, the answer is most likely that the Evangelist envisaged a succession in this ministry. One reason for this is that at the time of the final redaction of the Gospel (80–90 CE), Peter was already dead. Thus the Matthean text would have had comparatively little relevance at the time of writing if no living embodiment of this ministry were intended. This seems far from Matthew's intention.

Now we see more clearly the trap laid by the historical-critical position on Matthew. If one holds that the present form of the text was formulated between 80 and 90 CE, the idea of succession seems most probable. Therefore, some recent commentators have returned to the view of Cullmann: the present form of the text goes back to the historical Jesus and applies only to Peter.[59] While this is improbable on historical-critical grounds, there is no need to deny it partial validity. On the level of the historical Jesus and the historical Peter, there is no reason to doubt that Peter was a prominent figure among the original disciples of the earthly, pre-paschal Jesus. Moreover, Peter seems to have played an important role in the immediate post-paschal situation. All our sources suggest this. Matthew did not create his text out of thin air. It is also commonly held in Christian tradition that Peter and all the original apostles played a unique, unrepeatable role of foundation. But, if the analogy of Aaron and his successors in the high priesthood holds, then, on the level of Matthean exegesis, it is most probable that Matthew envisaged a succession in the Petrine ministry, relevant to his own day, even though the successors do not share in the unique role of foundation. There was only one Aaron, but there were later high priests. How in practice Matthew envisaged the exercise of this ministry is not perfectly clear, apart from the complementary data provided in Mt.

---

59. Davies and Allison, *Matthew*, II, pp. 615 and 643; D.A. Hagner, *Matthew 14–28* (WBC, 33B; Dallas: Word Books, 1995), pp. 461-75.

18.18 and other ecclesiological texts scattered throughout the Gospel (e.g. 10.40-42; 23.34).[60] Matthew did not write a second volume.

Additional Note

When this essay was presented for discussion at the Matthew Seminar of the Society of Biblical Literature at its annual meeting 23 November 1998, the principal respondent was Professor D.C. Allison, Jr, of Pittsburgh Theological Seminary. He was kind enough to give me a copy of his remarks. I would like here to respond briefly to his critical observations. He must first be thanked for his perfect courtesy, modesty and sense of humor. Allison's criticisms boil down to two or even one:

> Your thesis of the influence of Exod. 4.10-17 on Matthew in composing 16.13-20 is doubtful simply because it is new. And it is new because it is not very obvious. It lacks a key word or phrase to point the reader to the typology. Moreover, if you admit all the other suggested allusions, notably to Davidic Messiah in Isaiah 22, you are faced with a potential overload or over-density of intertextual references.

The basic response to this is that the New Testament texts are rich and many-layered. It is quite common for Matthew to combine a Pentateuchal with a prophetic and even a sapiential allusion to achieve a triple support for an assertion from all three parts of the Hebrew Bible (cf. Jer. 18.18 and Sir., Prologue, for the three parts of the Bible; Qoh. 4.12 for the strength of a threefold cord; Mt. 2.15 for a combination of Pentateuch and prophet, viz. Hos. 11.1 and Num. 23.22; 24.8). It suffices to glance at the marginal references to the Nestlé-Aland editors of the Greek New Testament to see this. And, I stress, those marginal references are far from exhaustive. The rabbis did the same thing in Mishnah *Aboth*. Ps. 12.6, 'The words of the Lord are pure...seven times refined', is interpreted by the midrash on Psalms, *in loco*, to mean that each verse of Scripture has forty-nine senses or interpretations. Why was the Exod. 4.10-17 typology not noticed before? No certain answer can be given to such a question, apart from the already admitted absence of a flashing red light in Matthew which would make the link unmistakable. But we may suggest first that after the schisms, even had

---

60. See Tord Fornberg, 'Peter—the High Priest of the New Covenant', *East Asian Journal of Theology* 4 (1986), pp. 113-21; B.T. Viviano, 'Social World and Community Leadership: The Case of Matthew 23.1–12,34', *JSNT* 39 (1990), pp. 3-21.

they noticed it, it would not have been in the confessional interests of Jewish, Eastern Orthodox or Protestant interpreters to make much of it. As for the church fathers, we have seen that they did not fully 'receive' Mt. 16.18-19 before Leo the Great. When they looked at Exodus 3–4, both they and the medieval theologians tended to be dazzled by the revelation of the divine name in Exod. 3.14. They concentrated their discussion on that. Our passage was comparatively neglected. Once Christianity became predominantly Hellenistic in culture, the details of the Moses story were neglected (in the sense of verse-by-verse commentaries on Exodus–Deuteronomy), with the obvious exceptions of Origen's commentaries, Gregory of Nyssa's *Life of Moses* and Thomas Aquinas's treatment of the Mosaic legislation in his *Summa theologiae* I–II, pp. 98-105 (heavily dependent on Maimonides). Moreover, the Greek and Latin versions of Exod. 4.10-17 weakened the force of the passage, especially of v. 16.[61]

Another argument was brought forward in the discussion at the SBL meeting by Professor Robert Gundry. He suggested that the *petra* of Mt. 16.18 could best be explained as the teaching of Jesus which is compared to a *petra* in Mt. 7.24-25. This is an interesting idea and deserves further consideration. First, we note that the rock there is contrasted with the sand (*ammos*) of v. 26. Thus *petra* here cannot refer to a loose or rolling stone. This further refutes Lampe. Next, Gundry's point possesses the methodological advantage of drawing from the wider context of the same author. This is a sound general principle but cannot be blindly followed, as we see from the further uses of *petra* in Mt. 27.51 and 60. These clearly have nothing to do with the teaching of Jesus. This principle must yield before the usage of the word in the *immediate context*. There we see that the *petra* is connected with the person of Peter by a wordplay, and serves as a foundation for the church. Verse 19 reinforces the reading by three personal addresses to Peter: 'I will give to *you*…whatsoever *you* shall bind…whatsoever *you* shall loose…' This cannot all be explained as the teaching of Jesus in such a way as to bypass the instrumental role of Peter. The primary context here is a provision for institutional continuity of leadership in the church in the post-Easter and postapostolic period (the role of the future perfect

---

61. On patristic exegesis of the Pentateuch, see D.L. Balas and D.J. Bingham, 'Patristic Exegesis of the Books of the Bible', in W.R. Farmer (ed.), *The International Bible Commentary* (Collegeville, MN: Liturgical Press, 1998), pp. 64-115, esp. pp. 65-72.

participles). Once this is seen, the point made by Gundry fits in perfectly: Peter and future Petrine ministers function as the church's leaders only insofar as they remain faithful in deed and word to the primordial rock of Jesus' *logous*. The *petra* of 16.18 must first be understood in its own context, before it can be related to other contexts.

AT THE WELL OF LIVING WATER: JACOB TRADITIONS IN JOHN 4*

Ellen B. Aitken

The narrative techniques of the Gospel of John cast a spotlight on the person of Jesus, calling attention in countless ways to the question of who Jesus is. We see in this text the figure of Jesus refracted, to change the metaphor a little, through many lenses, not least of which are the Scriptures of Israel. It is widely recognized that the Gospel of John constructs its portrayal of Jesus and his works with reference to Scripture, employing stories, to name only a few examples, such as Jacob's ladder (Gen. 28.12; Jn 1.51) or the serpent lifted up in the wilderness (Num. 21.9; Jn 3.14) in order to speak of the access to the divine available through Jesus. Investigation of how Scripture has informed John's Gospel has so focused on the figure of Jesus, however, that seldom have questions been asked about the scriptural construction of those whom we may call the minor characters in the narrative.[1] This skewing of the investigation results in reading the Gospel along the grain, that is, going along with the Gospel's theological emphasis on revealing Jesus to its audience and to the world.[2] Yet it is undeniable that John's Gospel shows Jesus in interaction and dialogue with other characters; thus the matter of how Scripture informs the construction of such interaction and the people with whom Jesus engages is as important to explore as is

---

*   This essay is a revised version of a paper of the same title presented in the Scripture in Early Judaism and Christianity Section of the annual meeting of the Society of Biblical Literature, 21–24 November 1999, Orlando, Florida.

1.   For a discussion of the 'minor characters' in the Gospel of John, see R. Alan Culpepper, *Anatomy of the Fourth Gospel: A Study in Literary Design* (Philadelphia: Fortress Press, 1983), pp. 132-44.

2.   Although I do not attempt an explicitly socio-rhetorical reading of Jn 4.4-46 here, I borrow the notion of reading along versus reading against the grain from Elisabeth Schüssler Fiorenza, *But She Said: Feminist Practices of Biblical Interpretation* (Boston: Beacon, 1992), p. 42.

the portrayal of Jesus in order to understand the rhetorical strategies of this Gospel. In this essay I examine the extended dialogue in Jn 4.4-42 between Jesus and the unnamed woman of Samaria at the well. I ask in particular how Scripture is informing the story and its characters, as well as exploring the possible import this story, understood in the context of its scriptural resonance, may have had within the activities of the Johannine community. For this purpose, it is necessary to attend not only to the narrative content of the story of Jesus and the Samaritan woman, but also to its narrative setting.

The narrative setting of the dialogue in Jn 4.4-42 is clearly marked with reference to scriptural traditions. Jesus, traveling through Samaria on his way from Judea to Galilee, arrives at a town called Sychar, which is identified as 'near the field that Jacob gave to his son Joseph' (Jn 4.5). It is also described as the location of 'Jacob's well', mentioned here initially as though it were well known (Jn 4.6), but then defined further in the statement of the Samaritan woman as the well that 'our father Jacob gave us' and from which Jacob, his sons and his animals drank (Jn 4.12). Thus the narrative setting of the dialogue prepares the audience to understand this story in relation to the traditions about Jacob. It is widely accepted that John here understands the plot of land to be that which Jacob purchases in Shechem from the sons of Hamor in Gen. 33.19, bequeaths to his son Joseph in Gen. 48.22, and where Joseph's bones were reburied upon their translation from Egypt in Josh. 24.32.[3] Josh. 24.32 goes on to remark that this portion of land 'became an inheritance of the descendants of Joseph'. By implication then, the woman of Samaria and the other inhabitants of this town whom she brings to Jesus belong to this portion of land and hence are descendants of Joseph. Read against the story of the acquisition of this land in Genesis 33 and the Jacob cycle of stories, the woman and the other inhabitants are significantly not Shechemites, that is, they are not the problematic descendants of Hamor and Shechem, renowned from Genesis 34 for their rape of Jacob's daughter Dinah.[4]

---

3.   See Birger Olsson, *Structure and Meaning in the Fourth Gospel: A Text-Linguistic Analysis of John 2:1-11 and 4:1-42* (Lund: Gleerup, 1974), pp. 139-40. For a discussion of location of Joseph's burial and Jacob's well, see Hans-Martin Schenke, 'Jakobsbrunnen–Josephsgrab–Sychar: Topographische Untersuchungen und Erwägungen in der Perspektiv von Joh. 4, 5.6', *ZDPV* 84 (1968), pp. 159-89.

4.   George J. Brooke, 'The Temple Scroll and the New Testament', in *idem* (ed.), *Temple Scroll Studies: Papers Presented at the International Symposium on*

The audience of the story is further instructed to understand the dialogue in reference to Jacob traditions by the question that the woman asks Jesus, 'Are you greater than our father Jacob, who gave us this well...?' (Jn 4.12). Not only is it significant for our identification of the heritage of the woman that she here speaks of Jacob as 'our father', that is, the ancestor of this people,[5] but we must also note that this comparison of Jesus with a central figure from Scripture—is he 'greater than Jacob'—finds its place among other such comparisons elsewhere in the Gospel. The verbal similarity is closest to that of Jn 8.53, when the *Ioudaioi* ask Jesus, 'Are you greater than our father Abraham, who died?' But there is also a thematic similarity with the comparison of Jesus with Moses in the episode of the multiplication of loaves in Jn 6.25-40. The comparisons, as Jerome Neyrey and others have argued, belong to a Johannine theme that speaks of Jesus' superiority to the foundational figures of Israel.[6] A further question remains, however, namely, that of the particular significance of this comparison for the purposes of Jn 4.4-42. To understand the rhetorical function of this comparison we must look more closely at how the story of Jacob informs the dialogue.

It is a commonplace in discussions of the scriptural context of John 4 to remark on the presence in this story of the *topos*, or narrative convention, of the meeting of a woman and a man at a well. We may observe this literary *topos* in the stories of Abraham's servant who, in seeking a wife for Isaac, meets Rebekah at the well as she comes to draw water in Genesis 24;[7] Zipporah's encounter with Moses at the

the *Temple Scroll, Manchester, December 1987* (JSPSup, 7; Sheffield: JSOT Press, 1989), p. 190.

5.   John MacDonald (*The Theology of the Samaritans* [London: SCM Press, 1964], pp. 327-33) argues for Samaritan traditions that Jacob's dream (Gen. 28.10-22) took place on Mount Gerizim, thus providing a basis for the cult site there. Jacob thus functioned as a foundational figure in arguments about the legitimacy of worship on Mount Gerizim; see Jerome H. Neyrey, 'Jacob Traditions and the Interpretation of John 4:10-26', *CBQ* 41 (1979), pp. 427-28.

6.   See Neyrey, 'Jacob Traditions', pp. 420-21; Olsson, *Structure and Meaning*, p. 179.

7.   Origen, in his *Commentarii in Johannes* (253.31–254.8), draws a parallel between Genesis 24 and John 4; see the discussion in Jean-Michel Poffet, *La méthode exégétique d'Héracléon et d'Origène—commentateurs de Jn 4: Jésus, la Samaritaine et les Samaritains* (Paradosis, 28; Fribourg: Editions Universitaires, 1985), p. 215.

well in Exod. 2.15-22;[8] and the meeting between Rachel and Jacob at the well in Gen. 29.1-14.[9] Common to this *topos* is the theme of betrothal, in that this meeting at the well leads in each case to a marriage, although in the first case, Genesis 24, we should certainly note that it is not a marriage between Rebekah and Abraham's servant, but rather the servant is the agent of Isaac's betrothal to Rebekah. In John 4, the meeting between the Samaritan woman and Jesus does not lead to betrothal and marriage, although the Samaritan woman's marital status becomes a subject of discussion when she asserts that she has no husband and Jesus replies that she has spoken truly because she has had five husbands and the man whom she now has is not her husband (Jn 4.16-18). Although it is not necessary to my argument here, we may speculate then that this element of the *topos* has become submerged or transformed.[10]

Is the relationship of Jn 4.4-42 to Scripture stronger, however, than that of sharing this *topos* of meeting at the well? Does Jn 4.4-42 stand in closer relation to one of these stories of an encounter and, if so, what does that say about the function of the story? Given the prominence of references to Jacob both in the narrative setting and in the framing of

8.   We may note that Aileen Guilding (*The Fourth Gospel and Jewish Worship: A Study in the Relation of St. John's Gospel to the Ancient Jewish Lectionary System* [Oxford: Clarendon Press, 1960], p. 207), in her argument about the composition of John in relation to the lectionary of the synagogue, employs the sayings about the harvest in Jn 4.35 to locate the story of the Samaritan woman in connection with the reading of either Gen. 24 or Exod. 2 in the triennial lectionary cycle. The difficulties with Guilding's argument have been well rehearsed elsewhere; see, for example, Anthony J. Saldarini, 'Judaism and the New Testament', in Eldon Jay Epp and George W. MacRae (eds.), *The New Testament and its Modern Interpreters* (Philadelphia: Fortress Press; Atlanta: Scholars Press, 1989), p. 43.

9.   Neyrey, 'Jacob Traditions', p. 425; see also the discussion of the 'type scene' of the meeting at the well in Robert Alter, *The Art of Biblical Narrative* (New York: Basic Books, 1981), pp. 51-58; followed by P. Joseph Cahill, 'Narrative Art in John IV', *Religious Studies Bulletin* 2 (1982), pp. 41-47.

10.   Teresa Okure (*The Johannine Approach to Mission: A Contextual Study of John 4:1-42* [WUNT, 2nd ser., 31; Tübingen: J.C.B. Mohr [Paul Siebeck], 1988], pp. 87-90) argues that the scenes of meeting at a well can provide only a very general background to John 4 since the element of marriage has, in her terms, been 'transcended'; she proposes instead that the narrative setting indicates the importance of the well as Jacob's gift to his descendants.

Jesus' identity in this passage, it is appropriate to look first to the meeting between Jacob and Rachel in Gen. 29.1-14. Here I follow and, I trust, extend Jerome Neyrey's interpretation of Jn 4.10-26.[11] Responding to the objection that what Jn 4.12 names as the 'well that our father Jacob gave us' cannot be the same as the well in Gen. 29.2, since that well indeed belongs to Rachel's father Laban, Neyrey looks particularly to the targumic and midrashic traditions about the miraculous well of Jacob from which the water bubbled to the top and overflowed once the stone was removed from the top of the well. The targumim to Gen. 29.10 and 12 associate this miracle specifically with (Laban's) well in Genesis 29.[12] Neyrey also compiles a number of correspondences between themes of the dialogue in Jn 4.10-26 and extrabiblical traditions about Jacob and the well.[13] Although Neyrey's article is persuasive in interpreting John 4 in light of Genesis 29, his work focuses on the figures of Jesus and the well, largely ignoring the impact of Genesis 29 for understanding the unnamed Samaritan woman. His reading of the relation between the texts also relies largely on the way in which the *topos* of the encounter at the well is combined with interpretive traditions concerning Jacob, the well, Mount Gerizim and true worship. Thus, he does not look at the thoroughgoing relationship between the narrative structure of the two stories, an analysis to which I now turn.

First, each story begins with a man journeying and arriving at a well. In Genesis 29 Jacob has been traveling from Bethel, comes to 'the land of the people of the East' and sees a 'well in a field' (Gen. 29.1-2). In John 4, Jesus is traveling from Judea, arrives at 'a city of Samaria, named Sychar', and sits down at the well because he is exhausted (Jn 4.6).

Second, in both stories the time of day when the man arrives is specified. It is 'still high day' in Gen. 29.7; and 'about the sixth hour', that is, noonday in Jn 4.6. These two temporal references may reasonably be considered to refer to approximately the same time of day.

---

11. Neyrey, 'Jacob Traditions', pp. 425-26.

12. *Targ. Yer.* 1; *Targ. Yer.* 2 and *Targ. Neof.* Gen. 29.10, 12; the targumim to Gen. 28.10 also connect the miracle more generally to Jacob's stay in Haran. See the discussion in Neyrey, 'Jacob Traditions', pp. 422-23; Olsson, *Structure and Meaning*, pp. 169-70; Martin McNamara, *Targum and Testament—Aramaic Paraphrases of the Hebrew Bible: A Light on the New Testament* (Grand Rapids: Eerdmans, 1972), pp. 145-46.

13. Neyrey, 'Jacob Traditions', pp. 421-25.

Third, although it is a minor feature, both stories mention the animals who come to drink from the well. In Gen. 29.2, there are three flocks of sheep waiting at the well for the arrival of all the flocks and for the well to be opened; in Jn 4.12, the well is described as the place where Jacob's animals drank.

Fourth, in both stories there are obstacles or difficulties to obtaining the well's water. The shepherds in Genesis 29 object that they cannot water the animals until all the flocks are present and the stone is rolled from the mouth of the well (Gen. 29.8); indeed it is Jacob who rolls away the stone and waters Laban's flocks (Gen. 29.10). This provides the occasion for the targumic speculations on the miraculous spring of water from this well. In Jn 4.11, the Samaritan woman objects to Jesus' promise to give 'living water' by saying that he has nothing with which to draw water. This objection then leads directly to the comparison, 'Are you greater than our father Jacob?' (Jn 4.12), and to Jesus' discourse about the water that he will give, the water that wells up to eternal life (Jn 4.14). Thus, not only is there a difficulty presented in getting the water in each story, in both the resolution of that difficulty comes from the man's (Jacob's or Jesus') action or words.[14]

A fifth and obvious correspondence is that in each story a woman comes to the well and finds the man already there. When Rachel comes to the well in Gen. 29.9, we are already well into the story, whereas in John 4, the woman's appearance occurs soon after Jesus' arrival, but still after the fulsome description of the place.

Sixth, in both stories the man already has knowledge about the woman before she arrives. In Gen. 29.5-6, Jacob has asked the shepherds about Laban and discovered that Rachel is about to come to the well; he, an apparent stranger, is then able to use that knowledge not only to recognize Rachel and to kiss her, but then also to reveal to her his own identity (Gen. 29.11-12). In Jn 4.18, Jesus, a stranger to the Samaritan woman, discloses his apparently supernatural knowledge of her marital history; it is on this basis that she declares that he is a prophet (Jn 4.19) and tells the other inhabitants of the city, 'He told me all I ever did' (Jn 4.29). Thus, this prior knowledge about the woman is also essential to the revelation of the man's identity, whether as Jacob, or as the prophet, and eventually, in Jesus' case as the Messiah (Jn 4.26, 29).

14. Neyrey ('Jacob Traditions', p. 423) suggests that a miracle of Jacob's well is presupposed in Jn 4.14.

Seventh, the woman rapidly goes to tell someone else. Rachel runs to tell her father Laban that Jacob has come (Gen. 29.12). The Samaritan woman goes (fairly quickly, since she leaves her water jar behind) to the city and tells the people there about this stranger whom she has met at the well (Jn 4.28-29).

Eighth, when this third party whom the woman informs then meets the man, a revelatory sentence is uttered. In each case, moreover, the utterance crowns the narrative. Laban says to Jacob, 'Surely you are my bone and my flesh' (Gen. 29.14). The Samaritans who have come out to meet Jesus say to the woman, 'No longer do we believe through your word, for we ourselves have heard and know that this is truly the savior of the world' (Jn 4.42).

Finally, each story ends with a statement about how the man stays with these people for a certain length of time. In Gen. 29.14, Jacob stays with Laban for a month; in John, in response to the Samaritans' request, Jesus stays with them two days (Jn 4.40), a temporal reference that is specifically reiterated at the beginning of the next pericope, 'after the two days, he departed to Galilee' (Jn 4.43).[15]

On the basis of these parallels, I contend that the narrative content and movement of the story of the Samaritan woman in John 4 invokes the story of Rachel's encounter with Jacob at the well in Genesis 29 and, moreover, that the audience was expected to recognize the reworking of Gen. 29.1-14 in Jn 4.4-42 in order to understand the significance of the Johannine story. The audience is drawn to the story of Jacob and Rachel not only by the markers of the narrative setting but also by the events of the encounter in John 4. I would simply note that many of the correspondences I have identified between Genesis 29 and John 4 are first not shared with the other scriptural stories of meetings at wells,[16]

---

15. C.K. Barrett, *The Gospel According to John: An Introduction with Commentary and Notes on the Greek Text* (Philadelphia: Westminster Press, 2nd edn, 1978), p. 43.

16. For example, Rebekah's meeting with Abraham's servant at the well (Gen. 24) takes place at evening, not midday; there are no obstacles to obtaining the water; the servant has no prior knowledge by which he recognizes Rebekah; no revelatory sentence is uttered; and although the servant stays overnight, he explicitly does not stay a longer time, but returns immediately to Abraham, bringing Rebekah. The story of Moses' encounter with Zipporah at the well (Exod. 2.15-21) is spare, relating no dialogue between Moses and Zipporah and her sisters. The principal feature is the obstacle that prevents the women from drawing from the well; after Moses drives the shepherds away from the well, he waters the animals that the women are

and furthermore those features that are missing have to do with the real plot of each story, namely, those concerning difficulty of access to the water and its resolution and those having to do with knowledge and recognition.

What then is the import of the correspondence between the story of Rachel and Jacob and that of the Samaritan woman and Jesus, particularly for the rhetorical function of John 4 in the Johannine community? I turn here from consideration of the plot of the stories to the characters.[17] In each story we have three active characters: the man, the woman and the third party (that is, Laban and the Samaritans who come out from the city). The correspondence between Jacob and Jesus is explicitly drawn out in the text by the question, 'Are you greater than our father Jacob?' (Jn 4.12).[18] I would propose, however, that by invoking the story of Jacob and Rachel, John 4 also constructs the woman of Samaria in terms of Rachel. But to what end?

It is important to recall that in the text, the woman is not given a name but only identified as 'the woman from Samaria' or 'the woman'. When we read this Gospel not as reflecting events in Jesus' life but rather interpret it in terms of the situations in which the Evangelist's community was engaged, then this unnamed woman may, like other key unnamed figures in John's Gospel, notably the beloved disciple, stand for a certain group or situations important to the life of this community.[19] It has been proposed by Elisabeth Schüssler Fiorenza, Wayne

tending. Otherwise, the story lacks a temporal reference, prior knowledge of the woman's identity, and a revelatory utterance. Zipporah and her sisters do return more quickly than usual to their father and tell him whom they met; in addition, the story results in Moses agreeing to stay with the family in Midian and marrying Zipporah. Thus, Genesis 24 lacks the motifs both of difficulty of access to the water and of knowledge and recognition, whereas in Exodus 2 only the motif of knowledge and recognition is missing.

17. For a general discussion of plot and character in the Gospel of John, see Culpepper, *Anatomy of the Fourth Gospel*, pp. 77-148.

18. Olsson (*Structure and Meaning*, p. 179) points out that the contrast in Jn 4.4-42 between what God gave through Jacob and what God gives through Jesus is analogous to the contrast elsewhere (for example, Jn 6.30-34) between God's gift through Moses and God's gift through Jesus.

19. Olsson, *Structure and Meaning*, p. 142. A now classic example of reading the plot and characters of the Gospel of John in terms of the situations in which the Johannine community was engaged is J. Louis Martyn, *History and Theology in the*

Meeks, Oscar Cullmann and others that Jn 4.4-42 indicates the significance of what they call missionary activity in Samaria by the Johannine community and that the dialogue deals with questions particular to the Samaritan context.[20] The woman from Samaria is portrayed as a representative of the Samaritan mission by the insertion of the sayings of Jesus about the harvest and labor, which employ the technical vocabulary of mission (κοπιάω) in Jn 4.31-38, that is, it is inserted precisely between the woman's return to the city to tell about 'the Christ' and the statement about the Samaritans' belief.[21] In other words, the unnamed woman of Samaria stands for the Johannine community's activity of proclaiming Jesus in a Samaritan context, and perhaps also for women's leadership in that activity.[22] Does then the construction of John 4 in terms of Jacob and Rachel and the correspondence between Rachel and

Fourth Gospel (Nashville: Abingdon Press, rev. edn, 1979). See also Raymond E. Brown, *The Community of the Beloved Disciple* (New York: Paulist Press 1979).

20. Elisabeth Schüssler Fiorenza, *In Memory of Her: A Feminist Theological Reconstruction of Christian Origins* (New York: Crossroad, 1983), p. 327; Wayne A. Meeks, *The Prophet-King: Moses Traditions and the Johannine Christology* (NovTSup, 14; Leiden: E.J. Brill, 1967), p; 318; Oscar Cullmann, *The Johannine Circle: Its Place in Judaism: A Study in the Origin of the Gospel of John* (London: SCM Press, 1976), pp. 39-56, esp. 48-49; Hugo Odeberg, *The Fourth Gospel Interpreted in its Relation to Contemporaneous Religious Currents in Palestine and the Hellenistic Oriental World* (Uppsala: Almqvist & Wiksell, 1929), pp. 149-89. For a discussion of the Gospel of John and a Samaritan mission, see Robert Kysar, *The Fourth Evangelist and his Gospel: An Examination of Contemporary Scholarship* (Minneapolis: Augsburg, 1975), pp. 160-63. On questions particular to a Samaritan context, see Neyrey, 'Jacob Traditions', pp. 426-30.

21. Schüssler Fiorenza, *In Memory of Her*, p. 327; Martin Scott, *Sophia and the Johannine Jesus* (JSNTSup, 71; Sheffield: JSOT Press, 1992), pp. 193-95. For a reading of the Samaritan woman as a 'witness' to Jesus, but reflecting an incident in the life of Jesus rather than an aspect of the Johannine community, see Robert Gordon Maccini, *Her Testimony Is True: Women as Witnesses According to John* (JSNTSup, 125; Sheffield: Sheffield Academic Press, 1994), pp. 118-44.

22. Turid Karlsen Seim ('Roles of Women in the Gospel of John', in Lars Hartman and Birger Olsson [eds.], *Aspects on Johannine Literature: Papers Presented at a Conference of Scandinavian New Testament Exegetes at Uppsala, June 16–19, 1986* [ConBNT, 18; Uppsala: Almqvist & Wiksell, 1987], pp. 67-70) interprets the story as indicating the inclusion of women and men in missionary activity, but does not speculate on its relation to the history of the Samaritan church. Culpepper (*Anatomy of the Fourth Gospel*, p. 137) proposes that the Samaritan woman is 'a model of the female disciple and possibly a model of Samaritan believers also'.

the unnamed woman have significance for the possible interest of John's Gospel in the Samaritans?

The woman's question, 'Are you greater than our father Jacob?' accurately draws upon the manner in which all Israelites could name Jacob/ Israel as their eponymous ancestor. Rachel, however, could be claimed only as the ancestor of certain of the twelve tribes: as the mother of Joseph (Gen. 30.22-24) and Benjamin (Gen. 35.16-18), as grandmother of Joseph's sons Ephraim and Manasseh (Gen. 46.20; 48.1-7), Rachel is effectively only the ancestor of the tribes of Ephraim, Manasseh and Benjamin.[23] We have already seen how the narrative setting in Jn 4.4-42, by naming the place as near the plot of land that Jacob gave to his son Joseph, carefully identifies the woman and the other Samaritan inhabitants of the city as the descendants of Joseph. It is, moreover, the tribes of Ephraim, Manasseh and to some extent Benjamin who received what became the territory of the Samaritans; although Judean history may have posited a foreign origin for the Samaritans, it appears that Samaritans understood their own history as a descent from these tribes.[24] I therefore contend that in constructing the unnamed Samaritan woman in terms of Rachel, the Gospel of John here draws upon an understanding of Rachel as the mother most particularly of the Samaritans.

Since within the narrative of John 4 the Samaritan woman proclaims to the Samaritans who Jesus is and brings them to meet Jesus, and since they come to belief initially because of her word, the function of portraying this woman, on the level of the narrative, as Rachel, the mother of the Samaritans, in my view, was to authorize the engagement of the Johannine community with Samaritans. Within this setting, we may speculate on the specific rhetorical aim of the story. Perhaps it authorized such missionary activity—including that by women—from the

23. On the importance of the 'geopolitical Joseph' in Samaritan biblical exegesis, see James Kugel, *In Potiphar's House: The Interpretive Life of Biblical Texts* (San Francisco: HarperCollins, 1990), p. 27 n. 7.

24. MacDonald, *Theology of the Samaritans*, p. 15. It is important to recognize that the characterization of postexilic Samaritans as idolatrous foreigners, whom the Assyrians settled in the territory of Ephraim, Manasseh and Benjamin, stems from an 'outsider' or Judean perspective. Attempts to interpret the Samaritan woman's 'five husbands' (Jn 4.18) as an allegorical cipher for the foreign gods in 2 Kings' portrayal of Samaria, whom Josephus (*Ant.* 9.288) counts as five (see, for example, Barrett, *The Gospel According to John*, p. 235), do not take into consideration the emphasis that John 4 places upon the lineage of Jacob for the Samaritans.

Johannine community among the Samaritans. The story itself, if we accept that it existed in some version prior to the compilation of John's Gospel,[25] could have had its origin within the strategies of proclamation and persuasion used among Samaritans by early followers of Jesus. Its inclusion in John's Gospel may then have functioned to recognize and authorize the presence of Samaritan Christians within the Johannine community. The effectiveness of this story within such a setting of engagement would have been strengthened by recognizing that the primary agent of Samaritan adherence to Johannine Christianity is narrated here through the medium of this distinctive ancestor of the Samaritans, Rachel.

To conclude, in investigating here how Gen. 29.1-14 informs the story of the Samaritan woman, we have attended to the narrative setting of Jn 4.4-42 in conjunction with how the content of the narrative is constructed and how a character other than Jesus is portrayed. This change of perspective has permitted an understanding first of how the figure of the unnamed Samaritan woman corresponds to Rachel, the mother of the Samaritans. It has, moreover, assisted in understanding how this dialogue between the woman of Samaria and Jesus would have particular rhetorical uses within the life of the Johannine community in relation to the interests of Samaritans. The story of the woman of Samaria thus serves as an example of how the Scriptures of Israel contribute to the narrative and rhetorical strategies of the Johannine community, evident in the Fourth Gospel.

---

25. See Rudolf Bultmann, *The Gospel of John: A Commentary* (Philadelphia: Westminster Press, 1971), pp. 179-80; Robert Tomson Fortna, *The Gospel of Signs: A Reconstruction of the Narrative Source Underlying the Fourth Gospel* (Cambridge: Cambridge University Press, 1970), pp. 189-95.

'Interpretive Citation' in the Epistle of Barnabas and the Early Christian Attitude towards the Temple Mount[*]

Yaron Z. Eliav

Midrash is a literary product of the encounter between readers and a text they consider sacred. Gary Porton defines it as follows:

> [A] type of literature, oral or written, which has its starting point in a fixed canonical text, considered the revealed word of God by the midrashist and his audience, and in which the original verse is explicitly cited or clearly alluded to.[1]

The midrash takes many forms and variations. Sometimes it confines itself to a few specific words in the text: interpreting them, playing linguistic games with them and reshaping them; at other times it goes off into general ideas for which the verse serves only as background scenery. Some homiletical interpretations remain close to the original ideas of the text; others depart far from them and imbue the verses with new meaning. The common denominator of all these variations is the great importance that the readers ascribe to the written text, using it as a starting point for their literary activity.

* This paper is based on a chapter from my PhD Dissertation (see below n. 12). Earlier versions of it were presented at the Antiquity Graduate Seminar at the Hebrew University (1997), and at the 'Scripture in Early Judaism and Christianity' session at the SBL conference, Orlando, 1998. I am grateful to the members of both groups for their insightful comments and judicious criticism, from which I have benefited immensely.

1. G.G. Porton, 'Midrash', in D.N. Freedman *et al.* (eds.), *ABD*, IV, pp. 818-22 (819). The following theoretical discussion was inspired by A. Shinan and Y. Za-kovitch, 'Midrash on Scripture and Midrash within Scripture', in S. Japhet (ed.), *Scripta Hierosolymitana: Studies in Bible* (Publications of the Hebrew University, 31; Jerusalem: Magnes Press, 1986), pp. 257-62.

There is no midrash without a sacred 'base text', but can there be a midrash without the explicit expression of the interpreter's ideas? The particular type of midrash discussed here acts minimalistically on the verses, and is therefore hard to locate or define. I call it 'Interpretive Citation', and define it as midrash without homily, that is, a literary practice that makes use of biblical verses, but keeps its ideas hidden and does not present them explicitly. At first glance, it seems to be an innocent citation of verses, but careful inspection reveals that the citation cloaks midrashic activity. This midrashic method is well attested in Second Temple Jewish texts, such as the Qumran literature or the *Liber Antiquitatum Biblicarum*, where some scholars speak of the 'Rewritten Bible'. It is also well known in the texts constituting the New Testament, mainly the letters of Paul.[2] Here I would like to present an example from an early Christian text dating to the end of the first century CE.

2. For a short summary and updated bibliography of research on midrash, see Porton, 'Midrash', pp. 818-22. For a short summary of hermeneutic methods in early Christianity, see R.P.C. Hanson, 'Biblical Exegesis in the Early Church', in P.R. Ackroyd and C.F. Evans (eds.), *The Cambridge History of the Bible*, I (Cambridge: Cambridge University Press, 1970), pp. 412-26; W. Horbury, 'Old Testament Interpretation in the Writings of the Church Fathers', in M.J. Mulder (ed.), *Mikra* (CRINT, 2.1; Assen: Van Gorcum; Philadelphia: Fortress Press, 1989), pp. 727-87; F.M. Young, *Biblical Exegesis and the Formation of Christian Culture* (Cambridge: Cambridge University Press, 1997). For a focus on Barnabas, see A.P. O'Hagen, 'Early Christian Exegesis Exemplified from the Epistle of Barnabas', *AusBR* 11 (1963), pp. 33-40. None of these summaries point to the midrashic method discussed here. Nevertheless, scholars dealing with biblical attestations in the various writings of the Second Temple period (Pseudepigrapha, Qumran, letters of Paul etc.) have mentioned this phenomenon, although using other terms to define it. See, e.g., G. Vermes, *Scripture and Tradition in Judaism: Haggadic Studies* (SPB, 4; Leiden: E.J. Brill, 2nd edn, 1983), pp. 1-10, 67-126; R.B. Hays, *Echoes of Scripture in the Letters of Paul* (New Haven: Yale University Press, 1989), esp. pp. 1-33; C.D. Stanley, *Paul and the Language of Scripture: Citation Technique in the Pauline Epistles and Contemporary Literature* (SNTSMS, 74; Cambridge: Cambridge University Press, 1992) (I owe this last reference to Professor Richard Hays); F.J. Murphy, *Pseudo-Philo: Rewriting the Bible* (New York: Oxford University Press, 1993); G.J. Brooke, 'Shared Intertextual Interpretations in the Dead Sea Scrolls and the New Testament', in E. Chazon and M. Stone (eds.), *Biblical Perspectives: Early Use and Interpretation of the Bible in Light of the Dead Sea Scrolls* (STDJ, 28; Leiden: E.J. Brill, 1998), pp. 35-57. The limited scope of this paper does not facilitate a full range discussion on the thematic definitions of 'quotation' as opposed to 'interpretation/midrash', issues debated broadly among scholars. Comprehensive bibliographical references can be found in the above articles.

The Barnabas Epistle 11.2-3: An Early Christian Midrash[3]

The first part of ch. 11, as noted by the author in its opening passage, deals with the Jews' refusal to accept the privilege of baptism—an atonement for sin—and the judgment that was passed on them as a result.[4] As was customary in many texts in those days, after the topic was presented, the rest of the chapter was constructed as a mosaic of verses quoted from the Scriptures. At first glance it seems as though the author has not intervened in the course of the verses, and that he has allowed the scriptural authors to express their ideas, merely separating the various passages, generally by adding the conjunction καί.

A closer look at the first set of verses, however—that in sections 2–3 of the Barnabas text, which, as many scholars have noticed, constitutes a separate unit[5]—shows that much more than simple citation is involved here. Barnabas, or whoever was before him (see below, n. 18), is very active, albeit surreptitiously, in his presentation of the verses—not only choosing and collecting them from various places in the Scriptures and assembling them together in one text, but also excluding parts of the verses and modifying some of the words. All this leads to an essential change in meaning, perhaps even to a reversal of the scriptural sense. This is the 'Interpretive Citation'.[6] Let us see how this process works.

---

3. All the references in the body of the paper are to Chapter 11 of the Lake Edition (vol. I, pp. 378-80), unless otherwise noted.

4. The author does not give the other side of the coin, and he does not reveal the Jewish way of life without baptism, writing only ἀλλ' ἑαυτοῖς οἰκοδομήσουσιν, without specifying the object of the construction. See J.C. Paget, *The Epistle of Barnabas: Outlook and Background* (WUNT, 2.64; Tübingen: Mohr [Siebeck], 1994), p. 154 and nn. 262-63.

5. E.g. K. Wengst, *Tradition und Theologie des Barnabasbriefes* (AKG, 42; Berlin/New York: W. de Gruyter, 1971), p. 39, which says about the relation between sections 2–3 and the rest of the chapter, 'nicht zusammengehören können'.

6. Cf., e.g., H. Windisch, *Der Barnabasbrief* (HNT, Ergänzungsband: Die Apostolischen Väter, 3; Tübingen: Mohr Siebeck, 1920), pp. 366-67; Wengst, *Tradition*, p. 39; Paget, *Epistle*. These scholars as well as all others I have read on this topic claim that this is a citation of a different version of the scriptural text, whether by Barnabas himself or by some source that he drew upon. It is especially strange that Windisch, who carefully analyzed all the changes that Barnabas introduced into the text under discussion, and the tendentiousness that led him to make these changes, nevertheless calls Barnabas's version, 'Zitate ohne jeden Kommentar'.

The passage made of sections 2–3, which is the important one for our purpose, is composed of two consecutive verses from Jeremiah and two from Isaiah, as follows:

Jeremiah 2.12-13

a: ἔκστηθι οὐρανὲ καὶ ἐπὶ τούτῳ πλεῖον φριξάτω ἡ γῆ;

b: ὅτι δύο καὶ πονηρὰ ἐποίησεν ὁ λαὸς οὗτος ἐμὲ ἐγκατέλιπον πηγὴν ζωῆς καὶ ἑαυτοῖς ὤρυξαν βόθρον θανάτου.

Isaiah 16.1-2

c: μὴ πέτρα ἔρημός ἐστιν τὸ ὄρος τὸ ἅγιόν μου Σινα [Σιων].[7]

d: ἔσεσθε γὰρ ὡς πτεινοῦ νοσσοὶ ἀνιπτάμενοι νοσσιᾶς ἀφῃρημένοι

7.   It is the change that drew the attention of most scholars—'Zion' substituting for 'Sinai' and having no parallel in any version of the Scriptures—which does not seem to me an original version of *Barnabas*. A close analysis of the content of the passage clarifies that the mountain symbolizes Israel's 'death pits'. It therefore must undergo the same process as the people of Israel did. Just as they, due to their mistaken choice, were sentenced to destruction, so too the mountain needs to be transformed from 'bloom to doom'. Indeed Mount Sinai is a desolate mountain, but then it always has been. How, then, could it represent such a transformation? Moreover, if the mountain in question is Mount Sinai, what is the logic of the next scene, cited from Isaiah, and portraying the fledglings taken from their nest? Nevertheless, one who insists may be able to find some explanation; see, for example, the interpretations cited by Paget, *Epistle*, p. 155 n. 265. Most intriguing is the attempt to link Mt Sinai here with the famous saying by Paul which draws a parallel between Jerusalem and Mt Sinai (Gal. 4.25). However, the mere resemblance between these two sources is the common use of the name Sinai; Galatians draws the image of slavery, whereas Barnabas depicts destruction. Undoubtedly, Sinai was occasionally used as a literary motif in Christian texts, but, as argued above, it is not compatible with the context here, and the author has nothing to gain by such a change. It seems to me that the structure of Barnabas's 'homily' and the development of its themes, as presented here, leads to the conclusion that Barnabas was using the two verses from Isaiah to depict a scene of destruction. I thus agree with Haffle (cited by Paget, *Epistle*, p. 155 n. 265), who 150 years ago already claimed that this change was 'Schreibfehler'; this conclusion was reiterated recently by Klaus Wengst when he wrote, 'Die Ersetzung von "Zion" durch "Sinai" ist wohl unbewußtes Versehen'. See K. Wengst, *Schriften des Urchristentums: Didache Barnabasbrief, zweiter Klemensbrief, Schrift an Diognet* (Munich: Kösel, 1984), p. 127 n. 118. Perhaps the conversion of Mt Zion into a Christian symbol in the fourth century, which relocated it on the south-western hill of Jerusalem (where it is shown today), far away from its original site, disqualified 'Zion' from being a symbol for the Jewish destruction. This could have caused its replacement with a phonetically similar name.

Comparing these Barnabas 'verses' with other versions of the Scriptures reveals considerable differences. In the second half of the first
verse from Jeremiah (a), the verb φρίσσω appears in the imperative
(φριξάτω), in contrast to the Septuagint, where it appears in the indicative mood of the first aorist (ἔφριξεν). Moreover, in the Barnabas version the subject of the imperative contains the word 'earth' (γῆ), which
does not appear in the Septuagint at all. These changes formulate a
dramatic imperative opening ("Εκστηθι οὐρανέ...φριξάτω ἡ γῆ), that
reminds the reader of the famous addresses of Isaiah and Micah, 'Hear
O heavens and listen O earth'.[8] In addition, there is the phrase βόθρος
θανάτου at the end of the second verse from Jeremiah (b), which is
much more extreme and blatant than the λάκκοι συντετριμμένοι in the
Septuagint, and is intended to create a contrast with the πηγὴ ζωῆς in
the first half of the verse. The tension that is created between the two
limbs—the 'living spring' in the first limb, which here represents baptism, and the 'death pit' in the second limb—is meant to serve Barnabas's argument about baptism. These cannot be variants from lost versions of the Bible: their distance from the wordings that appear in the
other textual witnesses of the Scriptures, on the one hand, and the way
they are adapted to the line being presented by Barnabas, on the other,
lead me to conclude that this is a new formulation, based on the scriptural text but used it for its own ends.

The two verses from Isaiah at the end of the passage make this conclusion even clearer. Although these verses are obscure in all the versions, including the Masoretic text and the Septuagint, Barnabas's use
of them is transparent and sharp. His aim here is apparently to develop
the motif of death with which he concluded the last verse from Jeremiah. For this purpose he introduces two scenes borrowed from Isaiah,
that present the reality of the death of Israel. In the first verse (c) the
author leaves out the first half of the original verse, thus reversing its
meaning. Not only is it no longer a neutral description of a path, as in
the Masoretic text ('from Sela, by way of the desert, to the mount of
daughter Zion'), but it is not even a clause denoting fear with the character of threat, focused on the future, as in the Septuagint ('Αποστελῶ
...μή...). In Barnabas's text it is a rhetorical question about a present
situation that serves as a concrete description of the Jews' death pits:
'Isn't my holy mountain Zion, [see n. 7] a desolated rock?'[9] This is a

8.   Isa. 1.2. See also Mic. 1.2. All biblical translations are from the NRSV.
9.   As Professor Richard Hays rightly indicated to me, the potential weakness

scene of destruction. Calling Zion here 'my holy mountain' has no support in any version of the biblical text, and it therefore reflects Barnabas's wording (more on that below). The next scene, too, which is based on the second verse in Isaiah (d) and describes fledgling birds taken from their nest, is a famous image of destruction incorporated into the New Testament as well, in Jesus' lamentation on Jerusalem.[10]

It thus becomes clear that the author, by incorporating the verses in this way, creates a coherent unit with internal thematic development and lucid expression of ideas that are distant from those in the scriptural source. The main purpose of the passage is to assert that the Jews' refusal to accept baptism means death (b). A dramatic opening precedes this assertion (a), and two scenes concretely expressing the idea of death follow it (c and d). This is a midrash without exegesis, comprising only the words of the scriptural text, whose ideas can be discerned only by the way the interpreter shapes the verses.

The third part of this passage (c) reveals the status of the Temple Mount in the author's view. First there is the terminology: as previously men-

of my reconstruction of Barnabas's ideas lies in this rhetorical question being set forth with the negative particle μή, which usually denotes a suggestive question expecting the answer 'no'. This rule applies in classical Greek. It also applies in *koine*, and although the usage of μή has amplified considerably, and in many instances displaced οὐ, in regard to independent clauses beginning with μή when the verb is in the indicative mode, the classical meaning has usually retained. See, e.g., H.M. Smyth, *Greek Grammar* (rev. by G.M. Messing; Cambridge, MA: Harvard University Press, 1976), pp. 598-99, §2650; E.A. Sophocles, *Greek Lexicon of the Roman and Byzantine Periods*, II (New York: F. Ungar, 1957), p. 756, *s.v.* 2-3; J.H. Moulton, *A Grammar of New Testament Greek*, III (Edinburgh: T. & T. Clarke, 1963), pp. 281-83. Here, however, we must heed the fact that Barnabas was not using his own wording but rather, apart from his 'midrashic' modifications, was quoting from the Scriptures, where μή originally appeared. The question arises whether ancient authors, in applying the 'Interpretive Citation' method, would also rectify the language, and emend it to the correct form of classical Greek. This issue requires further investigation. In the passage discussed here, it is hard to imagine how such a classical suggestive question ('is my holy mountain a desolated rock?'), for which a negative answer is expected ('no, the mountain is not desolate'), would fit into the layout of ideas presented by Barnabas. I would therefore consider the possibility that since the author found μή in the verse he wanted to use, and since the distinctions between μή and οὐ were already blurred in his world, he left the verse as he found it, in its original wording.

10. Mt. 23.37; Lk. 13.34.

tioned, Barnabas labels the mountain τὸ ὄρος τὸ ἅγιον μού. Robert Kraft's question of why a Christian should call Mount Zion 'the holy mountain'[11] is very difficult to answer, unless this was a customary name for this entity among the Jews in those days.

Elsewhere I have discussed at length that, in contrast to what might be expected of people for whom the Scriptures served as a religious foundation and a source of ideas, the Temple Mount had no special significance for the Jews at the time of the Second Temple.[12] Even though Mt Zion is frequently alluded to in the Bible under a variety of names (e.g. 'the holy mountain', 'the mountain of the house of God'), and was considered a sacred cosmic place during the time of the First Temple, this approach did not prevail in the Second Temple period. The Jews at this later age did indeed recognize the appellation 'Mount Zion' and the ideas that were associated with it in the Scriptures, and they even mentioned them from time to time (especially in early writings such as the letter of Aristeas, the book of Enoch and the book of *Jubilees*), but they did not bestow any real significance in their worldview on the mountain of the Temple.

Numerous writings preserved from that period, both in Palestine and in the Diaspora, reveal that there were two places of great importance in Jewish consciousness during the Second Temple period: Jerusalem and the Temple. These two appear hundreds, or perhaps even thousands, of times in texts of that period, and they influenced many varied layers of Jewish perception. They were religiously important and had a prime place in the liturgy, yet they were also linked to social aspects of Jewish life and played a considerable role in the Jews' national and international politics. In contrast, the Temple Mount is not mentioned at all. The phrase 'the Temple Mount' does not appear in any of the writings that have been preserved from the Second Temple period, except for

11. R.A. Kraft, 'Barnabas' Isaiah Text and the "Testimony Book" Hypothesis', *JBL* 79 (1960), pp. 336-50 (347). His second argument, that Mt Zion is often called 'the holy mountain' in the Scriptures (p. 348, end of n. 87), is misleading. In all the verses he cites there, 'the holy mountain' stands by itself, without any connection to Mt Zion, although such a connection does appear in several verses, e.g., Joel 4.17. Also see the following note.

12. See Y.Z. Eliav, 'A "Mount without a Temple"—The Temple Mount from 70 CE to the Mid-Fifth Century: Reality and Idea' (PhD dissertation; Jerusalem 1998), pp. 17-34 (Heb.); *idem*, 'The Temple Mount in Jewish Liturgy: Re-Examination of the Historical Background', in S. Ward *et al.* (eds.), *Aboda and Ibda* (forthcoming).

one source that happens to quote a verse from the Scriptures which mentions it.[13]

To be sure, a number of sources do suggest that the holiness of the Temple extended to the courtyards around it, although to a lesser degree. The view that can be deduced from these sources (especially the Temple Scroll at Qumran, but also Josephus and Philo) is that the area around the Temple protected the Temple at its center,[14] and therefore a certain degree of 'holy' behavior (e.g. bodily purity, exclusion of various people) was required there as a preparation for entering the Temple. But these areas around the Temple did not have independent status; they were considered an organic part of the whole Temple complex, whose *raison d'être* was to serve the Temple. If the Temple no longer existed, they would cease to have value.

Only towards the end of the Second Temple period, and even more so after the destruction of the Temple in 70 CE, does the Temple Mount begin to function as an element of independent value in the Jewish world. The seeds of this phenomenon can be found in the writings of Josephus Flavius, in the Third Sybil and even in ancient traditions that were incorporated into the New Testament. The climax of this process can be seen in rabbinic literature, where 'the Temple Mount' is a common and habitual phrase with considerable status, sometimes even substituting for the Temple itself.[15]

---

13. I.e. 1 Macc. 4.46, which mentions τὸ ὄρος τοῦ οἴκου. Literary analysis of this source reveals that the imagery and vocabulary rely, among other sources, on the famous description of the destruction in Mic. 3.10-12, and this holds true for the term 'the Temple Mount' as well. The term's absence from other places in the book of Maccabees and from all other writings of the period which frequently deal with Jerusalem and the Temple only emphasizes its detachment and meaninglessness in that one particular instance. For a comprehensive analysis of this source see Eliav, 'A "Mount without a Temple"', pp. 29-33.

14. This was already pointed out by M. Avi-Yonah, *Sepher Yerushalayim* (Jerusalem: Mosad Byalik u-Devir, 1956), p. 393. Cf. L.H. Schiffman, 'Architecture and Law: The Temple and its Courtyards in the Temple Scroll', in J. Neusner *et al.* (eds.), *From Ancient Israel to Modern Judaism*, I (BJS, 159; Atlanta: Scholars Press, 1989), pp. 297-80. I expressed my reservations about Schiffman's view in 'A "Mount without a Temple"', pp. 33-34.

15. Eliav, 'A "Mount without a Temple"', pp. 37-44, 51-58, 173-213; *idem*, 'The λίθος ἐπὶ λίθον Prophecy and the Status of the Temple Mount of Jerusalem in Early Christianity', in A. Oppenheimer and M. Mor (eds.), *The Beginnings of Christianity* (forthcoming).

This evolving perception of the Temple Mount as an independent entity is also revealed in Barnabas's terminology. The fact that he calls the mountain 'the holy mountain' without any substantive reason—since an alternative name, 'Mount Zion', was already present in the scriptural verse—and without any connection to the content of the verse, suggests that this was the customary name of the place in his day. The author used this name merely to clarify to which place he referred. It is as if he were saying, 'Mount Zion, which you call "the holy mountain of God", is now desolate'. This does not refute the likelihood that the phrase 'the holy mountain' was taken from the Scriptures,[16] but the fact that it is used precisely here, in a description of the Temple Mount's desolation, indicates the process by which there is now a new significant place in Jewish consciousness, in addition to the city of Jerusalem and the Temple—namely, the area called τὸ ὄρος τὸ ἅγιον μού.

This cultural process can also be seen in the author's use of the term 'desolation' (ἐρῆμος). The motif of desolation, too, is obviously taken from the Scriptures. Chapter 9 of Daniel, for example, one of the key scriptural chapters for early Christians (whose influence can be discerned already in the Gospels) uses the adjective 'desolate' for Jerusalem as a thread running through its entire length. Many other writers of the Second Temple period use this motif to describe the destruction of Jerusalem, whether referring to the ruins which occurred in the past, the upheaval which they confront in the present, or the fate which they anticipate for the future.[17] The author of *Barnabas* thus makes use of this ancient term and image, but for a new purpose. In contrast to the other writings of the Second Temple period, *Barnabas* does not apply the word 'desolation' to Jerusalem or the Temple, as neither of these places is present in the scene of destruction depicted here. The motif of desolation is used to describe 'the holy mountain' alone. This is a new conception exposed in *Barnabas*.

Yet even more important than the terminology is the theological aspect. As mentioned, the Temple Mount is perceived in this ancient

---

16. E.g. Joel 4.17; Ps. 2.6, 'Zion, my holy mountain', which the Septuagint translates literally.

17. Besides Dan. 9.17-18, 26-27 (five times), see also, e.g., 1 Macc. 3.45; *T. Levi* 15 (in M. de Jonge, *The Testament of the Twelve Patriarchs* [Leiden: E.J. Brill, 1978], p. 43), *T. Dan* 5.13 (*idem, Testament*, p. 109). Additional examples are listed by H.W. Hollander and M. de Jonge, *The Testament of the Twelve Patriarchs: A Commentary* (SVTP, 8; Leiden: E.J. Brill, 1985), p. 170, v. 15.1.

Christian homily as a 'wasteland' (πέτρα ἔρημος), and the author considers it a manifestation of the 'death pit' (βόθρος θανάτου) that the Jews brought upon themselves by rejecting the living waterspring of Christian baptism.[18] This desolation of the Temple Mount also plays a central role in the Jewish worldview of the time, making its best-known appearance in the famous legend of Rabbi Akiva, who laughed when he saw a jackal coming out of the ruins of the Temple Mount. This midrashic legend, which is based on the verse 'Because of Mount Zion, which lies desolate; jackals prowl over it' (*Lam.* 5.18), makes use of precisely the same two motifs that appear in *Barnabas*—'desolation' and 'Mount Zion'—to refer to the Temple Mount.[19]

If my interpretation is correct, we are thus granted one of the most ancient examples of the Christian view concerning the desolation and ruin of the Temple Mount, a view which uses precisely the same motifs as the Jewish description, yet gives them its own meaning. Finally, none of these ideas are expressed explicitly, and they can be ascertained only in the slight changes the author introduces in citing the verses. This is a citation that deviates from the original meaning of the quoted material —a citation that is a midrash.

18. I deliberately avoided the lengthy discussion of Barnabas's sources and of the hypothesis of a 'Book of Testimonies' (*testimonia*) from which he took his citations. This issue, which was the central concern of most students of the text, prevented them, in my opinion, from looking at the text from other angles, such as the one presented here. For a summary of their approach, see Kraft, 'Barabas' Isaiah Text', pp. 336-50; Paget, *Epistle*, esp. pp. 78-98, although actually his entire book is based on it. From the standpoint of the present study it makes no difference if Barnabas interpreted the verses himself or found the interpretation in some other book.

19. *Sifre Deut.* 43. Translated by R. Hammer, *Sifre: A Tannaitic Commentary on the Book of Deuteronomy* (Yale Judaica Series, 24; New Haven: Yale University Press, 1986).

Part III

INTERPRETATION IN THE RABBIS AND THE TARGUMIM

THE ROLE OF מדת דינא IN THE TARGUMIM

Christian M.M. Brady

1. Rabbinic Context

The Attributes of Justice and Mercy are well known from their relatively frequent appearances within the midrashim. It is somewhat surprising, therefore, to realize that these figures are rarely employed within the targumim. Furthermore, in all but one instance, it is only the Attribute of Justice which is found in the targumim. So, how often do they occur in the targumim? Specifically, what role does מדת דינא, the 'Attribute of Justice', play in the targumim? As we attempt to answer these questions we will begin with a *very* brief summary of the origins and role of the Attributes of Justice and Mercy within rabbinic literature in general and then move on to examine the occurrences of these terms specifically within the targumim.[1]

Initially the Attributes of Justice and Mercy represented merely alternate expressions of God's traits as judge and these traits were in turn equated with the names of God. Thus יהוה ('the LORD') was equated with the Attribute of Mercy while אלהים ('God') was equated with the Attribute of Justice. As Sifre to *Deut.* 3.23 states:

> The LORD [3.24]: Whenever Scripture says *the LORD* [יהוה], it refers to his quality of mercy, as in the verse, *The Lord, the Lord, God merciful and gracious* [Exod. 34.6]. Whenever it says *God* [אלהים], it refers to his quality of justice, as in the verses, *The cause of both parties shall come*

1. For a general survey, see Ephraim E. Urbach, *The Sages: Their Concepts and Beliefs* (Cambridge, MA: Harvard University Press, 1995), pp. 448-61; and G.F. Moore, *Judaism in the First Centuries of the Christian Era*, I (Cambridge, MA: Harvard University Press, 1927), pp. 386-400. For discussion of *Memra* and the Attribute of Mercy, see C.T.R. Hayward, 'Memra and the Attribute of Mercy', Chapter 4 of his *Divine Name and Presence: The Memra* (Ottowa: Allenheld Osman, 1981). The summary presented here follows Urbach's outline of the development of the Attribute of Justice within rabbinic literature.

before God [אלהים; Exod. 22.8], and *Thou shalt not revile God* [אלהים; Exod. 22.27].[2]

Very quickly, however, the Attributes became hypostases, independent entities whom God consults in his heavenly court.[3] As the Attribute of Justice took on the role of 'prosecuting attorney' the Attribute of Mercy, in the role of advocate appealing for clemency, became equated with God himself.[4] It is therefore as the agent of God's righteous punishment that we most often find the Attribute of Justice.[5] Thus *Leviticus*

---

2. *Sifre Deut.* 3.24 (§26). This translation is slightly modified from Reuven Hammer's *Sifre: A Tannaitic Commentary on the Book of Deuteronomy* (New Haven: Yale University Press, 1986), p. 49. See also *b. Ber.* 60b; *Exod. R.* to 3.6; *Gen. R.* to 12.15, 33 and 21.7.

Hayward, however, has demonstrated that the targumim are 'unaware' of the rabbinic rule that יהוה is equated with mercy and אלהים is equated with justice. 'Nowhere in the Targumim, so far as we are aware, is this element of justice ever attributed to the title *'elohim*; the Targumim seem completely unaware of any distinction in theological sense between YHWH and *'elohim*' (Hayward, *Divine Name*, p. 45). It is important to remember that Hayward's study focuses upon the *acts* of justice and mercy attributed to YHWH/*'lōhîm* rather than upon the figures of the Attributes of Justice and Mercy.

3. See, e.g., *Gen. R.* to 1.26: 'R. Hanina did not say thus, but [he said that] when he came to create Adam he took counsel with the ministering angels, saying to them, *Let us make man.* "What shall his character be?" asked they. "Righteous men shall spring from him", He answered, as it is written, *For the Lord knoweth the way of the righteous* (Ps. 1.6), which means that the Lord made known the way of the righteous to the ministering angels; *But the way of the wicked shall perish*: He destroyed [hid] it from them. He revealed to them that the righteous would arise from him, but he did not reveal to them that the wicked would spring from him, for had he revealed to them that the wicked would spring from him; the Attribute of Justice would not have permitted him to be created'. See also, e.g., *b. Šab.* 55a, *Meg.* 15b, *Sanh.* 94a and 97b.

All translations of midrashim and talmudic texts are from *Soncino Classics Collection* CD-ROM (Chicago: Davka Corporation, 1996), unless otherwise stated.

4. See Urbach, *The Sages*, pp. 460-61. In *b. Meg.* 15b, for example, during an exposition of Isa. 28.5-8 a dialogue is established directly between the Attribute of Justice and God: 'Said the Attribute of Justice before the Holy One, blessed be he: Why this difference between these [Israel] and the others [the nations]? The Holy One, blessed be he, said to him: Israel busy themselves with the Torah, the other nations do not busy themselves with the Torah—he replied to him, *But these also reel through wine, and stagger through strong drink...they totter in judgment* [Isa. 28.7-8]'.

5. See *Lam. R.* 1.13.

Rabbah speaks of the Attribute of Justice as 'acting against' the generation of the flood, Sodom and Gomorrah, and those who worshipped the golden calf.[6] In a similar vein, *Exodus Rabbah* to 6.2 describes how the Attribute of Justice wanted to smite Moses for his insolence at doubting that God would deliver Israel.[7]

> For this reason did the Attribute of Justice seek to attack Moses, as it says: *And God* [אלהים] *spake unto Moses* [6.2]. But when God reflected that Moses only spoke thus because of Israel's suffering, he retracted and dealt with him according to the Attribute of Mercy, as it says: *And he said unto him: I am the LORD* [יהוה, 6.2].[8]

The midrashim also describe מדת דינא as having been active in Jerusalem's destruction. For example, in commenting on Lam. 1.13, 'He spread a net for my feet [וַיִּרְדֶּנָּה פָּרַשׂ רֶשֶׁת לְרַגְלִי]', 'R. Bebai of Sergunieh said: וַיִּרְדֶּנָּה indicates, "*He saw* that the Attribute of *Justice* overtook her".' וַיִּרְדֶּנָה is thus explained as a compound of 'he saw' (ויראה) and 'justice' (דין).[9]

The book of Lamentations is, in fact, a particularly fruitful text for the introduction of מדת דינא. In the *Targum to Lamentations* we find that מדת דינא occurs three times as a fully personified figure who is given speech.[10] It was this comparatively frequent occurrence of the מדת דינא in *Targ. Lam.* that led to my present investigation. Considering the active role played by the Attribute of Justice in the midrashim it might be reasonable to expect that we would find it occurring with similar frequency in the targumim. Yet, *Targ. Lam.* aside, the Attribute of Justice is rarely found in these texts.

---

6. The intersecting verse is Eccl. 3.16, 'Moreover I saw under the sun that *in the place of justice*, wickedness was there, and in the place of righteousness, wickedness was there as well'. See also *Exod. R.* to 32.11. *Exod. R.* to 6.2 has an extended discussion of how the Attribute of Justice wanted to smite Moses for doubting God's promise to deliver the Israelites from Egypt.

7. Exod. 5.22-23, 'Then Moses turned again to the LORD and said, "O LORD, why have you mistreated this people? Why did you ever send me? Since I first came to Pharaoh to speak in your name, he has mistreated this people, and you have done nothing at all to deliver your people."'

8. The two halves of Exod. 6.2 are interpreted based upon the use first of אלהים and then of יהוה.

9. מדת דינא also occurs earlier in *Lam. R.* to 1.13 and again in *Lam. R.* to 2.4.

10. For another example of the Attribute of Justice speaking out see *b. Meg.* 15b.

2. *Targumic Evidence*

Neither the Attribute of Justice nor the Attribute of Mercy occurs at all in *Targum Onkelos, Targum Neofiti, Targum Jonathan* or *Targum Pseudo-Jonathan*. In fact, outside of *Targ. Lam.*, מדת דינא occurs only once in *Targum Qohelet* and twice in *Targum Esther*, I (3.1 and 6.1). The latter occurrence is in conjunction with the מדת רחמין and is only attested in one MS. As we shall see, it is likely that מדת דינא was not the original reading of *Targ. Esther*. I 6.1, therefore it appears that the Attribute of Justice only occurs five times and the Attribute of Mercy only once in all the targumim![11]

Targum of Lamentations
Of the three instances in *Targ. Lam.*, in each case the Attribute of Justice announces the reasons for Israel's suffering and punishment.[12] The Hebrew text of Lam. 1.1 is quite terse.

> How lonely sits the city
>> that once was full of people!
> How like a widow she has become,
>> she that was great among the nations!
> She that was a princess among the provinces
>> has become a vassal.[13]

אֵיכָה יָשְׁבָה בָדָד הָעִיר רַבָּתִי עָם
הָיְתָה כְּאַלְמָנָה רַבָּתִי בַגּוֹיִם
שָׂרָתִי בַּמְּדִינוֹת הָיְתָה לָמַס:

The targumist, however, has greatly expanded this first verse of Lamentations in order to set the context for the reading of the entire book.[14] *Targ. Lam.* seeks to ensure that the audience realizes that Jerusalem was destroyed due to Israel's sin and not because their God has forsaken them. Thus, we are told that Jeremiah declared Jerusalem's punishment by comparing it with the punishment of Adam and Eve. If their

---

11. The corpus of targumic literature is, of course, vast and there remains the possibility that an instance of the Attributes has missed my notice.

12. They are 1.1, 2.20 and 4.13.

13. All biblical quotations are from the NRSV unless otherwise stated.

14. See my 'Targum Lamentations 1.1-4: A Theological Prologue', in Paul V.M. Flesher (ed.), *Targum Studies*. III. *Ernie Clarke Memorial* (Atlanta: Scholars Press, forthcoming).

punishments are similar then the reasons for such judgment must also be similar. Therefore, 'the Attribute of Justice spoke and said, "Because of the greatness of her rebellious sin which was within her, thus she will dwell alone as a man plagued with leprosy upon his skin who sits alone"' (ענת מדת דינא וכן אמרת על סגיאות חובהא אשתדר ומה דבנוהא

.(בגין תהא יתבא בלחודהא כנבר דמכתש סגירו על בסריה דבלחודוהי יתיב

In this case, the Attribute of Justice is not appealing to God to punish Jerusalem, instead it is announcing the punishment that God *has already* decided to mete out. We may contrast this with many of the midrashim where מדת דינא is described as appealing for God to punish the sinner or as carrying out that punishment. In *Targ. Lam.* 1.1 מדת דינא merely states what God has already decided he would do to punish Jerusalem and why God's decision is just. This punishment parallels that of Adam and Eve. Just as the eating of the forbidden fruit was an act of rebellion punished with banishment, so too Israel's rebellion against God would result in the exile of his people from Jerusalem.

The Attribute of Justice appears again in 2.20. The biblical text is a strong accusation against God, as the author cries out horrified by what has befallen his people.

> Look, O LORD, and consider!
>   To whom have you done this?
> Should women eat their offspring,
>   the children they have borne?
> Should priest and prophet be killed
>   in the sanctuary of the Lord?

> רְאֵה יְהוָה יְהֹוָה וְהַבִּיטָה לְמִי עוֹלַלְתָּ כֹּה
> אִם־תֹּאכַלְנָה נָשִׁים פִּרְיָם עֹלֲלֵי טִפֻּחִים
> אִם־יֵהָרֵג בְּמִקְדַּשׁ אֲדֹנָי כֹּהֵן וְנָבִיא׃

The biblical text of v. 20 contains serious charges against God. The fact that women are driven to eat their children and priests and prophets are killed in the sanctuary are the direct result of God's allowing this calamity to befall his people. The targumist represents the initial argument with a few minor changes.

> See, O Lord, and observe from heaven against whom have you turned.
> Thus is it right for the daughters of Israel to eat the fruit of their wombs
> due to starvation, lovely children wrapped in fine linen?

> חזי יי ותהי מסתכל מן שמיא למן אסתקפתא כדנן אם חזי לבנאתא דישר'
> למיכל בכפנא פירי בטניהון עולימיא רגיגתא דהוו מתלפפין בסדינין דמילתין

The women, we are told, are identified specifically as the 'daughters of Israel' and their 'offspring' (פרים) are described as the 'fruit of their womb' פירי בטניהון. The daughters of Israel resort to cannibalism due to starvation (בכפנא) and their young (and the *hapax legomenon* טפחים) are poignantly described as 'lovely children wrapped in fine linen'.[15] At this point in our targum the Attribute of Justice responds to the charges, asking,

> Is it right to kill priest and prophet in the Temple of the Lord, as when you killed Zechariah son of Iddo, the High Priest and faithful prophet in the Temple of the Lord on the Day of Atonement because he told you not to do evil before the Lord?

> ענת מדת דינא וכן אמרת אם חזי למקטל בבית מקדשא די כהנא
> ונבייא כמה דקטלתון לזכריה בר עדוא כהנא רבא ונביא מהימן בבית
> מקדש' דיי ביומא דכפוריא על דאוכח יתכון דלא תעבדון דביש
> קדם יי:

As in 1.1, the Attribute of Justice is employed by our targumist in order to explain why these atrocities have been allowed to happen to Israel. In this instance,[16] the targumist is recasting the biblical text (20c), transforming its meaning by changing the identity of the speaker. The Attribute of Justice goes on to specify the crimes for which Jerusalem and her people were being punished, 'you killed Zechariah son of Iddo... *because* he told you not to do evil before the LORD'. As is often the case in rabbinic literature in general and in *Targ. Lam.* specifically, the principal of מדה כנגד מדה is applied and Jerusalem's punishment is defined by her crime.

The same is true of the statement made by the Attribute of Justice in 4.13.

---

15. The *hapax legomenon* טפחים and the *hapax legomenon* טפחתי in 2.22 are derived from either an Arabic (B. Albrektson, *Studies in the Text and Theology of the Book of Lamentations with a Critical Edition of the Peshitta Text* [Studia Theologica Ludensia, 21; Lund: C.W.K. Gleerup, 1963], p. 120) or Akkadian root (D. Hillers, *Lamentations* [AB, 7A; Garden City, NY: Doubleday, 2nd edn, 1992], p. 98), both of which refer to child birth/rearing. It is likely that our targumist was unaware of this etymology and so rendered both terms with *לפף, 'to swathe, wrap' (M. Jastrow, *A Dictionary of the Targumim, the Talmud Babli and Yerushalmi, and the Midrashic Literature* [New York: Judaica Press, 1992], p. 715b).

16. In 1.1 the Attribute of Justice's speech is not based on the biblical text.

The Attribute of Justice spoke up and said, 'All this would not have happened but for the sins of her prophets who prophesied to her false prophecies and the iniquity of her priests who offered up burning incense to idols. They themselves caused the blood of the innocent to be shed in her midst'.

עַנַת מִדַּת דִּינָא וְכֵן אָמְרַת לָא הֲוַת כָּל דָּא אֶלָּהֵן מֵחוֹבַת נְבִיָּאהָא דְּמִנַבְּאָן
לַהּ נְבוּאַת שְׁקַר וּמֵעֲוָיַית כָּהֲנָתָא דְּאַסִּיקוּ קְטוֹרֶת בּוּסְמִין לְטַעֲוָתָא וְאִנּוּן גְּרַמוּ
לְאַתָשַׁד דַּם נָוָה זַכָּאִין:

In v. 13, as in 1.1 and 2.20, the targumist uses the Attribute of Justice in order to introduce Jerusalem's sins. In this instance the biblical text itself presents a reason for Jerusalem's punishment, stating directly that 'it was for the sins of her prophets and the iniquities of her priests, who shed the blood of the righteous in the midst of her'. Considering the context, it is not surprising that our targumist proceeds to specify what 'the sins of her prophets' and 'the iniquities of her priests' were. The prophets, we are told, gave false prophecies and the priests offered sacrifices to idols. Quite simply, they did the opposite of what God had called each of them to do. Although it is unlikely that our targumist has a specific incident in mind, the fact that the targum specifies that 'they themselves caused the blood of the innocent to be shed' emphasizes the complete abrogation of their duties by the prophets and priests. It is the responsibility of these men, perhaps more than any others, to protect the lives of the innocent and yet, not only did they allow them to killed, 'they themselves *caused*' them to be killed.

Unlike the descriptions of the Attribute of Justice in the midrashim, *Targ. Lam.* has used the figure as a spokesman rather than an agent of destruction.[17] This enables the targumist to explain why these horrible events have come upon Israel and to demonstrate that they were deserved, since a fundamental element of the Attribute of Justice is that its actions are righteous, even if God may temper the punishment with his mercy.[18]

17. As is already found in the biblical text of Lamentations, it is God himself who goes forth like an enemy against his people. The targumist does not require a mediator other than Nebuchadnezzar (2.4).

18. It is important to note that the Attribute of Mercy does *not* appear in *Targ. Lam.* In fact, a consistent theme of the book of Lamentations which is extended in *Targ. Lam.* is that for Jerusalem there is no comforter and there is no mercy (see 1.2, 9; 2.13, etc.). She is denied all solace in her mourning. God himself has no

Targum of Esther I

מדת דינא occurs twice in *Targ. Esth.* I at 3.1 in all MSS and at 6.1 in one MS variant. The targum to 6.1 begins with the cry of the women from the house of Israel being heard in heaven, and God asks, 'What is this voice of young goats that I hear?'

> Then the attribute of compassion replied, saying as follows [ענת מדת רחמין וכן אמרת]: It is not the voice of young goats that you hear but the voice of women from the house of Israel who are destined to be killed upon the decree of the wicked Haman.[19]

Only one MS, Paris Heb. 110 of the Bibliothèque Nationale,[20] includes the Attribute of Justice and reads ענת מדת דינא רחמין וכן אמרת. The targum goes on to tell how God has mercy upon his people, and such a context is a strong indication that the majority reading, which does not include מדת דינא, is probably correct. *Targ. Esth.* I to 6.1 does, therefore, present us with an example of the מדת רחמין within the targumim, but it is an isolated appearance.

The occurrence of מדת דינא in 3.1 is, however, certain and plays a role similar to that found in *Targ. Lam.*

> After these things, the attribute of justice entered before the Master of the World and thus it said [בתר פתגמיא האיליין עלת מדת דינא קדם רבון כל עלמיא וכן אמרת]: Did not the wicked Haman descend and go up from Susa to Jerusalem to abolish the rebuilding of the Temple; and now King Xerxes has promoted Haman, son of Hammedatha, who is descendant from Agag, son of the wicked Amalek, and has appointed him chief over everything and established his throne over those of all the princes that are with him. Replied the Master of the World and said as follows. I do not wish to destroy him from the world as long as he is not [yet] known in the world, let go of him until he will become great and known among all nations, then will I punish him for all the oppression that he and his ancestors have done to the people of the house of Israel.[21]

The additions found in *Targ. Esth.* I, like the midrashim found in *Est. R.*, ascribe to Haman a role in obstructing the reconstruction of the Temple. In the targum we are given a glimpse into the heavenly court

---

mercy in exacting his punishment. See Lam. 2.17, for example: 'He destroyed and had no mercy'.

19. Bernard Grossfeld, *The Aramaic Bible.* XVIII. *The Two Targums of Esther* (Edinburgh: T. & T. Clark, 1991), p. 69.

20. Grossfeld, *Esther*, p. 2.

21. Grossfeld, *Esther*, p. 51.

where the Attribute of Justice comes before God to ask why he has not already destroyed such a wicked man. God responds that he first wants him to be made great so that all the nations might know of his downfall. It is important to note that God instructs מדת דינא to 'let go of him until he will become great', implying that the Attribute of Justice was preparing to enact judgment upon Haman.

In this passage, we find מדת דינא in a role similar to that of both *Targ. Lam.* and the midrashim. As in *Targ. Lam.*, the Attribute of Justice declares the sins committed by the offender. He reminds God that not only did Haman try to 'abolish the rebuilding of the Temple', but he was also descended from Agag, 'son of the wicked Amalek'. Unlike the role played by מדת דינא in *Targ. Lam.*, but similar to what we find in the rest of the rabbinic corpus, it is implied in this text that the Attribute of Justice *will* be the agent of Haman's destruction.

Targum of Qohelet

Finally, in *Targ. Qoh.* 10.8 we again find the Attribute of Justice providing an explanation for Israel's suffering.

> Solomon said by the spirit of prophecy, 'I have seen the people who were enslaved previously to the people of Israel, growing strong and riding on horses like rulers while the people of Israel and their nobles walk like slaves on the ground'. The Attribute of Justice answered and thus said [ענת מדת דינא וכין אמרת]: 'They caused all this themselves just as a man who digs a pit at the crossroads is liable to fall in it so a people who transgressed the decree of the Memra' of the Lord and breached the fence of the world falls into the hand of the wicked king who bites them like a serpent.'[22]

In v. 6 God enables the Edomites[23] to enslave Israel. This, in turn, leads to Solomon's prophetic vision of a subservient Israel. In response, the Attribute of Justice explains that God has allowed the conquest of his people due to their refusal to obey the *Memra* of the LORD. This usage of מדת דינא is directly parallel to that found in *Targ. Lam.* The Attribute of Justice is not the agent of punishment, rather it explains why God

---

22. *Targ. Qoh.* 10.7-8; Peter S. Knobel, *The Aramaic Bible*. XV. *The Targum of Qohelet* (Collegeville, MN: Liturgical Press, 1991), p. 48.

23. On the difficulties of identifying the Edomites in *Targ. Qoh.* see Knobel, *Qohelet*, p. 12. For a more general discussion, see G. Cohen, 'Esau as Symbol in Early Medieval Thought', in A. Altmann (ed.), *Jewish Medieval and Renaissance Studies* (Cambridge, MA: Harvard University Press, 1967), pp. 19-48.

has allowed tragedy to befall his people and how such action (or God's allowing others to act against his people) is just.

3. *Conclusions*

In sum, it appears that מדת דינא, a figure common in midrashic literature, is a relatively rare occurrence in the targumim. In *Targ. Esth. 1* 3.1 the Attribute of Justice asks God why he has not yet punished the wicked Haman. God directs מדת דינא to 'let go of him' since Haman was to grow powerful before he would be destroyed. This characterization is in keeping with that found in the midrashim, as it brings an accusation against the wicked *seeking* their just punishment. Although the book of Esther is *potentially* about the destruction of the Jews, it is, in fact, a story about God's salvation of his people. Thus the role of the Attribute of Justice is confined to indicting Israel's enemy. However, in the majority of instances where the Attribute of Justice appears in the targumim, it announces the charges against *Israel*. In each case, מדת דינא explains *why* God has allowed Jerusalem/Israel to be defeated, and the answer is always that Israel has sinned.

The nature of the Attribute of Justice in *Targ. Lam.* and *Targ. Qoh.* is predicated by the biblical text. In *Targ. Lam.* it is because the biblical text presents a clear challenge to God's justice as the biblical author asks, 'How could God allow such a catastrophe to befall his chosen people?' The targumist uses מדת דינא to answer this charge. Although *Targ. Qoh.* brings this challenge to the text (perhaps precipitated by external events such as contemporary persecution), the role of the Attribute of Justice is the same as that found in *Targ. Lam.*; it explains that Israel has deserved her fate due to her refusal to obey the Word of the LORD.

Within these targumim, the Attribute of Justice is not the *agent* of destruction. This is contrary to the majority of midrashic passages which feature the Attribute of Justice. In the midrashim it is either seeking to punish transgressors, exacting that punishment, or is being restrained from such action by the Mercy of God (sometimes represented by the מדת רחמין). Furthermore, the Attribute of Justice *rarely* (if ever) speaks in the midrashim. The figure found in the targumim is a fully personified character who is granted speech and converses with God and the audience (Lam. 2.20). By contrast, the midrashic figure is more vague, referred to rather than heard. The figure of מדת דינא in the targumim has a distinct and separate identity from God. It stands beside God and converses with him and, in the majority of occurrences, the Attribute of Justice proclaims the sin of Israel and the justice of God's actions.

'IS SAUL ALSO AMONG THE SCRIBES?'
SCRIBES AND PROPHETS IN *TARGUM JONATHAN*[*]

Anthony J. Saldarini

In a number of passages, *Targum Jonathan* transforms prophets into scribes. The most striking example is found in 1 Samuel 10, where Saul, who has just been anointed king of Israel by Samuel, meets a band of ecstatic prophets, is seized by the Spirit, and joins them in prophesying. This manifestation of the power of God's Spirit in Saul has been predicted by Samuel as a sign which authenticates Saul's choice as king of Israel. The targumist translates the biblical passage as follows:

> [5]And when you enter there to the city, you will meet a band of scribes going down from the house of feasting and before them lyres and timbrels and cymbals and lutes and they will be singing praise. [6]And the spirit of prophecy from before the Lord will reside upon you, and you will sing praise with them, and you will be changed into another man...
> [10]And they came there to the hill, and behold a band of scribes met him, and the spirit of prophecy from before the Lord resided upon him, and he sang praise in their midst. [11]And everyone who knew him yesterday and the day before saw it, and behold, he was singing praise with the scribes. And the people said, each man to his neighbor: 'What is this that has happened to the son of Kish? Is Saul also among the scribes?' [12]And a man from there answered and said: 'And who is their master?' Therefore it became a proverb: 'Is Saul among the scribes?' [13]And he ceased from singing praise and entered the house of feasting.

Though the targumist replaces 'prophets' with 'scribes' here, he is not hostile to prophecy, for he necessarily refers to prophets and prophecy often in his translation of the Former and Latter Prophets. In fact, he

[*] This paper appeared originally in H.J. Blumberg *et al.* (eds.), *'Open Thou mine Eyes...' Essays on Aggadah and Judaica Presented to Rabbi William G. Braude on his Eightieth Birthday and Dedicated to his Memory* (Hoboken: Ktav, 1992), pp. 239-53, and has been reprinted in slightly revised form by the courtesy of Temple Beth-El, Providence, Rhode Island, USA.

sometimes adds the words 'prophet', 'prophesy' and 'prophecy' to his translation of the biblical text. He also distinguishes true from false prophets. Thus, the targumist's reason for substituting 'scribes' for 'prophets' in some passages must be sought in the context of his view of prophecy.

An examination of the targumist's translation of words connected with prophecy will give a context for understanding the transformation of prophets into scribes in certain passages of *Targum Jonathan*. In *Targum Jonathan* the words 'prophet' and 'prophecy' occur more frequently than in the Hebrew text of the Bible. The *Targum* also regularizes the terminology for prophets. 'Man of God', the older name for prophet, 'seer' (*rō'eh*), and 'visionary' (*ḥōzeh*) are usually translated 'prophet'.[1] Noun forms such as *ḥāzôn* (1 Sam. 3.1; 2 Sam. 7.17) and *maḥāzêh* (Gen. 15.1) are translated as 'prophecy',[2] and related verbal forms are translated as 'prophesy'.[3] In addition, the words 'prophet' and 'prophecy' are regularly added to the text of the *Targum*. The 'word of God' becomes the 'word of prophecy from before the Lord', and the 'spirit' or 'spirit of God' becomes the 'spirit of prophecy' (1 Sam. 10.10). In the Latter Prophets prophetic oracles are often given the title 'prophecy', and the individual prophets the title 'prophet'. The targumist tries to protect the title 'prophet' by explicitly naming false prophets as such. When the biblical text has simply 'prophet' for someone who is not speaking God's genuine word, the targumist has the qualification, 'lying (or false) prophet' (*nby šqr*').[4]

The targumist's treatment of prophecy implies that he conceives of prophecy as a direct and true contact with God followed by the accurate communication of his message. Any false communication or communicator masquerading under the title of prophecy or prophet is explicitly labeled as such. All visionary phenomena and divine communications

---

1.   See 1 Kgs 13.1 for several examples. 'Seer' is also translated as 'visionary' (*ḥāzôyā'*) in 1 Sam. 9.9, 11, 18, 19.

2.   In Num. 24.4, 16, Balaam's vision is referred to as a *ḥōzeh* in Hebrew and translated by the cognate Aramaic *ḥze'*, perhaps because Balaam is not an Israelite prophet.

3.   For example, in 1 Kgs 13 the Hebrew *qr'* (the prophet 'cried out') becomes *'tnb'* ('prophesied').

4.   For example, 1 Kgs 13.11, 25, 29; 19.1; 22.10, 12, 13. The prophets of Baal (1 Kgs 18.19, 25; 2 Kgs 10.19) remain the same because the name of Baal automatically marks them as false prophets.

are unified as one phenomenon under one Aramaic root, 'to prophesy'. This practice is in contrast to the usage of the Hebrew, where prophecy is a phenomenon found both within and outside Israel and is common to true and false spokespersons for God. The variety of terms and changes in roles of the prophets in the Hebrew text hint at an evolution and variety in the role of prophet. The *Targum* treats prophecy as a more unified phenomenon which is understood as having revelatory significance for Israel and as being confined to that religious context.

In a limited number of cases the *Targum* changes prophets into scribes (or occasionally teachers) and describes them with language connected to learning, instruction, teaching and Torah.[5] Prophets, who are identifies as part of society's leadership group in the Bible by the formula 'priests and prophets', are transformed into scribes. Before reviewing in detail the evidence in the *Targum Jonathan*, a few generalizations may help to orient us. The targumist accepted historical individuals in Israel's past who revealed God's word to Israel as prophets and named them such. He reserved the term 'prophecy' for direct communication from God. But mention of prophets as community leaders or as groups of ecstatics did not fit either his picture of the past or the reality of his own time. Consequently, prophets were transformed into scribes and their activities made to conform to the scholarly and religious activities of these later Jewish leaders.

1. *The Former Prophets*

In 1 Samuel 10, which was cited in the introduction, as in 1 Sam. 19.20-24, Saul meets a band of ecstatic prophets and joins them in prophesying. These two passages end with the proverb, 'Is Saul also among the prophets?' and are alternative explanations for the origin and meaning of that proverb.[6] Both the proverb itself and the stories about the bands of prophets demonstrate the power of God manifesting itself

---

5. Frequently, the 'sons of the prophets' are called the 'students of the prophets', as in 1 Kgs 20.35; 2 Kgs 2.3, 5, 7, 15; 4.38; 5.22; 6.1; 9.1; see slight variations in 1 Kgs 20.41 and 2 Kgs 9.4.

6. See Carole Fontaine, *Traditional Sayings in the Old Testament: A Contextual Study* (Sheffield: Almond Press, 1982), p. 239; William McKane, *Proverbs* (OTL; Philadelphia: Westminster Press, 1970), pp. 26-27. The proverb is so tied to its present two contexts that its original meaning is not clear. In ch. 10 Saul is treated positively and in ch. 19 negatively.

in a direct, strong and uncontrolled way. In ch. 10 one sign of Saul's choice by God as king is that he is to meet a 'band of prophets coming down from the high place with harp, tambourine, flute, and lyre before them, prophesying. Then the spirit of the Lord will come mightily upon you and you shall prophesy with them and be turned into another man' (1 Sam. 10.5-6). The targumist turns that spirit of God into the 'spirit of prophecy from before the Lord', as usual, and the idolatrous-sounding 'high place' into the more innocuous 'house of feasting', as he did in ch. 9 when Saul and Samuel ate at the high place/house of feasting in the unnamed city where they met. But even though the spirit of *prophecy* comes upon Saul in both the Bible and *Targum*, he does not join a band of prophets prophesying in the *Targum*, but a band of scribes singing praise.[7] The targumist translates v. 6 faithfully: that the spirit of prophecy will come upon Saul and he will be changed into another man. But the change is tamed in the *Targum*, because Saul becomes a teacher at worship rather than an ecstatic prophet. This taming is furthered by the question which answers the inquiry about Saul being among the prophets. In the Bible a resident answers/asks, 'Who is their [the prophets'] father?' In the *Targum* he asks, 'Who is their master [*rab*]?'[8] Though the text does not mention a school, it evokes the atmosphere of the later rabbinic school and suppresses the uncontrolled power of prophetic bands, which were seen as a disruptive force in the targumist's world.

The same taming of the ecstatic prophets takes place also in 1 Sam. 19.18-24, which is a variant of the story in ch. 10. In the biblical story David fled from Saul to Samuel at Ramah, in a location designated as Naioth. When Saul sent messengers three times to capture David and finally went himself, each time they saw Samuel at the head of a band of prophets, prophesying, and the spirit of God came over them, and they prophesied too. This enforced ecstatic behavior protected David from capture. This story is more hostile to Saul than the previous one, because when Saul is seized by the spirit, he strips off his clothes and lies naked day and night. The spirit of God is a violent force which attacks those hostile to David. The story concludes with the proverb, 'Is Saul also among the prophets?'

---

7. The *Targum* recognizes the two passages where *'tnb'w* means 'rave' (1 Sam. 18.10 and 1 Kgs 18.29) and translates them accordingly with *'štty*.

8. See *Targum Jonathan* to 2 Kgs 2.12, where Elisha's address of Elijah as 'My father, my father' is changed to 'My rabbi, my rabbi'. In 2 Kgs 5.13 'my father' becomes 'my master' (*mry*).

The targumist has turned the ecstatic prophets into scribes singing praise, as he did in ch. 10. Instead of being in the unknown location designated as 'Naioth', Samuel and David are in the 'house of study'. The spirit of prophecy from before the Lord causes the band of scribes and Saul's messengers to sing praise.[9] As in the previous story, scribes and school stabilize the wild atmosphere of the biblical story.

In one passage of the Former Prophets, scribes replace prophets as members of the leadership group in Judaism. (This change occurs frequently in *Targum Jeremiah*.) In 2 Kings 23 Josiah the King assembles all the people and reads the newly discovered book of the covenant to them. Specific groups mentioned in 2 Kgs 23.1-2 are the elders of Judah and Jerusalem, the priests and the prophets. The *Targum* changes the prophets to scribes, with special justification here because in the Talmudic Aramaic a scribe is pre-eminently a biblical teacher and interpreter.[10] This change from prophets to scribes in the leadership group will recur in the Latter Prophets.

Occasionally scribes even replace prophets in their visionary role. When Saul sought an answer from the Lord concerning his difficulties, he got none by means of dreams, Urim and prophets (1 Sam. 28.6, 15). Here the prophet functions as advisor in a private manner, a role which does not fit the targumist's idea of prophet. So prophet is changed to scribe because the scribe, learned in the law, can interpret for Saul what the Lord requires. In addition, there may be an implication that traditional sources of divine guidance, the dream and the Urim, are subject to the scribe. 2 Kings 17.13 notes that the Lord warned Israel against idolatry by every prophet and seer (*ḥōzeh*). The targumist changes this pair to scribe and teacher (*malîp*). Both the Hebrew and the *Targum* say that this pair told Israel to keep the commandments and statutes in accordance with all the law of God. In this passage the emphasis on the

---

9.   In the Bible, Saul fell down and lay naked a day and a night. In the *Targum*, he fell down (*bršn*). Jastrow has no certain meaning for the word (see *bršʾn*). Perhaps the meaning is 'He fell under those having power', with *rshln* being the pi. pass. part. m. pl. of *ršy*. Thus the targumist removed the shocking word 'naked' and put Saul under the authority of the scribes who have the spirit.

10.   In 2 Sam. 23.8 the names of David's three mighty men have been replaced by a heavily rewritten passage which describes David on thrones of judgment with all the prophets and elders surrounding him. The prophets and elders seem to be the mighty men of the targumist's Judaism.

law leads the targumist to insert those whom he identifies as the guardians of the law—scribes and teachers.

In the Former Prophets the targumist has substituted scribes for prophets in several passages. Though there are not enough data to prove decisively his motives and outlook, several tendencies are clear. The ecstatic prophets are tamed into a group of pious scribes. Scribes take over leadership roles from the prophets and are especially associated with teaching and interpreting the law.

2. *The Latter Prophets*

Some of the phenomena found in the Former Prophets also occur in the Latter Prophets, especially Isaiah and Jeremiah. Prophecy is mentioned often and prophets are fully accepted, as one would expect. Yet in several revealing instances prophets are changed to scribes and teachers.

a. *Isaiah*

In *Targum of Isaiah* the word 'prophet' occurs far more often than in the Bible because many oracles are introduced with the expression, 'The prophet said', rather than 'I said', and because the prophet is more often given the title 'prophet' than in the Hebrew text.[11] In addition, the 'word' becomes more explicit as the 'word of prophecy'.[12] In passages such as 30.27, where the Bible says that the name of the Lord comes from afar, the *Targum* interprets that to mean that the name of the Lord 'concerning which the prophets prophesied of old' is revealed. Prophecy is the direct and reliable channel for divine revelation which was common in the past. As in the Former Prophets, varied terminology is regularized. 'Vision' (the root *ḥzh*) often becomes 'prophecy' (1.1; 2.1; 13.1; 12.1-2). The 'valley of vision' (22.5) becomes the 'valley against which the prophets prophesied'. In general the role and name of the prophets are made more explicit in the *Targum of Isaiah* than in the biblical text, and various Hebrew terms are assimilated to the term 'prophet'.

---

11. E.g. *Targ. Isa.* 5.1, 9; 6.1; 8.17, etc. 'The prophet' often replaces Isaiah's references to himself as 'I'.

12. E.g. 'word of prophecy' (*pitgām nebû'āh*) replaces *dabar* in 2.1; 6.7; 38.4; 51.16; 59.21. 'Oracle of prophecy' (*maṭal nebû'tā'*) replaces 'burden' (*maśśā'*) in 14.28; 22.1, 25.

In a limited number of passages prophets and visionaries are transformed into scribes; or scribes and teachers are added alongside prophets. In 3.1-12 Isaiah describes the breakdown of leadership in Judea and Jerusalem. The tone of the passage implies that the leaders have failed; consequently God removes them. In 3.2 six categories of leader are named: mighty man, soldier, judge, prophet, diviner and elder. The *Targum* changes prophet to scribe, perhaps reflecting the targumist's later view of who was associated with judges in government. In a judgment against Ephraim (9.7–10.3) Isaiah described God's punishment, which includes cutting off the head and tail. In the Hebrew the tail is the prophet who teaches falsehood (9.14). In the *Targum* the prophet is replaced by the scribe who teaches falsehood, and the scribe is identified as 'the feeble one' (*halāšā'*), rather than as the tail. The targumist again identifies teaching with the scribe rather than with the prophet.[13]

Prophets are also replaced by scribes when they are listed as religious leaders along with the priests. In an oracle against the leaders of Ephraim and Judah (28.1-13) the metaphor of drunkenness expresses their lack of leadership, understanding and justice. Verse 7 says, in part:

> The priest and prophet reel with strong drink,
> they are confused with wine,
> they stagger with strong drink;
> they err in vision,
> they stumble in giving judgment.

The targumist makes some significant changes in this passage which reveal Jewish leadership as he conceives of it.

> Priest and scribe are filled with old wine,
> they are ruined with wine,
> they have gone astray because of old wine;
> her judges have turned aside after pleasant food,
> they have gone astray.

The targumist changes 'prophet' to 'scribe', for he holds the priests and scribes responsible for knowing God's law and for leading an orderly society. Consistent with this view, he also eliminates the statement 'they err in vision', because visions are proper to prophets. He

---

13. Bruce Chilton (*The Glory of Israel: The Theology and Provenience of the Isaiah Targum* [JSOTSup, 23; Sheffield: JSOT Press, 1983], p. 54) says on the basis of 9.14 and 28.7 that 'scribe' replaces 'prophet' when the prophet is false. But the targumist's practice is more complex than that.

changes the last clause, which mentions judgment, to refer to judges, a third part of the leadership group as he understands it. The targumist sees prophets as visionaries, but not as part of society's bureaucratic leadership; thus scribes have replaced prophets where societal leadership is involved.

Prophets scribes, and teachers occur alongside one another in the Ariel oracle in ch. 29. Dreams, drunkenness and blindness are the metaphors used of the sad state of Jerusalem. Finally, in v. 10 the prophet says:

> For the Lord has poured out upon you a spirit of deep sleep
> and has closed your eyes, the prophets,
> and covered your heads, the seers [*hōzîm*].

The targumist changes the sleep imagery into statements about truth and the loss of scribes and teachers.

> For the Lord has cast among you the spirit of error,
> and he has hidden from you the prophets;
> and scribes and teachers [*malpayā'*] who were teaching you
> the instruction of the law he hid.

The seers of the biblical text are replaced by scribes and teachers who instruct in the law. Here the prophets are implicitly associated with the role of teaching truth; their visionary roles as well as the symbols associated with visionary revelation are set aside.

In one Isaianic text the seer is changed into a prophet and the visionary is changed to teacher. An oracle against Judah as a rebellious child in ch. 30 is followed by further description of their rejection of instruction (30.10), for they are people

> who say to the seers [*rō'îm*], 'See not';
> and to the visionaries [*hōzîm*], 'Do not envision what is right;[14]
> speak to us smooth things, envision illusions'.

The *Targum* changes 'seers' and 'visionaries' into 'prophets' and adds 'teachers', so that the people say,

> to the prophets you shall not prophesy
> and to the teachers you shall not teach us Torah.
> Speak pleasant things with us; tell us different things.[15]

---

14. Some versions (e.g. the RSV) translate *ḥzh* as 'prophesy'.

15. *Šōnyāyn* has a connotation of 'different' meaning 'strange' or 'foolish' (cf. M. Jastrow, *A Dictionary of the Targumim, the Talmud Babli and Yerushalmi, and the Midrashic Literature* [2 vols.; New York: Pardes, 1950], II, pp. 1606-607).

The emphasis on teachers and teaching Torah in this passage and the previous ones reflects the Talmudic emphasis on Torah which guided the targumist as he interpreted the Prophets.[16]

b. *Jeremiah and Ezekiel*

The *Targum of Jeremiah*, like the *Targum of Isaiah*, uses the words 'prophet', 'prophecy' and 'prophesy' more than the Hebrew text. The 'word of God' becomes the 'word of prophecy from before the Lord'; prophets are given that label more often, and other words like 'seer' and 'visionary' are suppressed. False prophets, mentioned often in Jeremiah, are explicitly designated as such; oracles are called prophecies.

Jeremiah contains a number of passages which refer to 'priest and prophet' as leaders of the community.[17] The same pair occurred in Isa. 28.7 above. In three other passages 'prophet, priest, and people' is used as a description of the whole community (23.33-34; 26.7; 29.1). The *Targum* changes all these mentions of prophets to scribes, since the targumist conceives of the priest and scribes, rather than prophets, as heads of the community.[18] Most of these passages criticize the priest and

---

16. *Targum of Isaiah* contains several passages of lesser interest where teaching, one of the functions of the scribe, is emphasized. Generally, 'instruction of the Lord' becomes 'instruction of the law of the Lord', and 'hear' becomes 'receive instruction'. *Targ. Isa.* 33.22 contains the declaration, 'The Lord is our leader'. 'Leader' is *mḥqqnw*, from a root that means 'engrave' or 'inscribe'. The leader is one who inscribes decrees. The targumist has followed the root meaning and translated the *mḥqqnw* as 'teacher' (*malpanā'*): 'The Lord is our teacher who gave us the instruction of his law from Sinai'.

In 26.16b the Hebrew is not entirely clear. It reads: 'Anguish, whispering, your chastisement to them'. 'Chastisement' is *mûsār*, which also means 'moral instruction'. The targumist transforms the verse to refer explicitly to the law of God: 'In their troubles they used to teach secretly the instruction [*'ûlpān*] of your law'.

In 50.4-5 teaching and prophesying are made more explicit and expanded. In 27.11 the metaphor concerning women who make fire is changed into women who teach in houses of idols. In 43.27 'your mediators [*m'lişeykā*] who rebelled' are changed into 'teachers' (*malpāk*). Finally, the well-known text, 'you will draw water with joy from the wells of salvation' (12.3) becomes; 'You will receive new instruction [*'ûlpān ḥadāt*] with joy from the chosen of righteousness'.

17. *Targ. Jer.* 6.13; 8.10; 14.18; 23.11; 25.11, 16. One additional passage in the minor prophets, Zech. 2.3, has the transformation of 'priest and prophet' to 'priest and scribe'.

18. In several passages (2.26; 5.31; 8.1; 13.13) the *Targum* retains 'priest and prophet' but the prophets are designated as 'false prophets' (*nbyy šqr'*). See Pinchos

scribes for bad leadership of the community.[19] Scribes are criticized elsewhere in the *Targum of Jeremiah*. Jeremiah 8.8 refers to the false pen of the scribes making the instruction (*tōrāh*) of the Lord into a lie. The *Targum* remains faithful to the sense of this statement while avoiding a grammatical difficulty by translating: 'A scribe made a pen of falsehood to falsify [it]'.

In a couple of other passages, 'prophet' and 'prophecy' are transformed into 'teacher' and 'teaching'. The Bible describes those plotting against Jeremiah's life as reassuring themselves that 'the torah shall not perish from priest and counsel from a wise man and a word from a prophet' (18.18), even if Jeremiah is killed. The *Targum* eliminates prophets from this triad because it conceives of scribes as the teachers par excellence and links them with priests and wise men.[20]

Ezekiel has only one passage where 'prophet' is transformed into 'scribe', and it is similar to Jer. 18.18. In 7.26 Ezekiel says that disaster follows upon disaster and rumor on rumor. The people 'will seek a vision from the prophet, but Torah perishes from a priest and counsel from elders'. The targumist translates:

> And they will seek learning from a scribe
> and Torah will cease from a priest
> and counsel from a wise man.

Churgin, *Targum Jonathan to the Prophets* (Yale Oriental Series, 14; New Haven: Yale University Press, 1927), p. 118, for the separation of true prophets from professional prophets in the *Targum*. The claim of C.T.R. Hayward in 'Some Notes on Scribes and Priests in the Targum of the Prophets', *JJS* 36 (1985), pp. 210-21, and in the introduction to his translation of *The Targum of Jeremiah* (ArBib, 12; Wilmington: Glazier, 1987), pp. 36-38, arguing that the association of scribes with priests reflects the first century before the destruction, is based on insufficient evidence. Scribes were well known in talmudic times as copyists and teachers, and the targumist's concept of prophet gave him ample motive for making the substitution.

19.   Note that the priests with their instruction (*tôrāh*), the prophets and the wise men match both the divisions of the Hebrew Bible and the traditional categories of learned leaders in Israel. In addition, the Hebrew for wise man (*ḥākām*) is also used of the latter rabbis, so that the targumist is covertly including the teachers of his day.

20.   One more complex passage substitutes 'teachers' (*malpin*) for 'prophets' (29.15). Jeremiah is speaking of false prophets in Babylon; the *Targum* transforms the prophets into teachers but then goes on to speak of these false teachers as having prophesied.

The targumist again keeps his triad of learned guardians: scribes, priests and wise men.

As in the previous parts of *Targum of Jonathan*, terms concerned with visions, and so on, are standardized under the word 'prophecy' (7.13; 12.22-24; 13.7). However, the targumist to Ezekiel associates teaching with *prophets* (2.5; 12.27; 13.16; 14.10), contrary to the view of prophets in earlier books of the Latter Prophets.[21] In two other passages (13.8-9; 22.28) in which God is speaking against lying prophets, the Bible describes them as 'those seeing delusion and divining falsehood'. The *Targum* translates this as 'those who prophesy falsehood and teach lies'. In the *Targum of Ezekiel* teaching is closely linked to the prophetic role, in contrast to earlier books of the prophets.

c. *Minor Prophets*

Comment on the minor prophets will be limited to the one passage where 'prophets' is changed to 'scribes' and to a few observations on the use of 'prophet and 'prophecy'. In Zech. 7.3 the priests and prophets are asked for guidance concerning proper religious practice. Like *Targum of Jeremiah*, *Targum of Zechariah* transforms the prophets into scribes because the targumist associates interpretation of the law with the priests and scribes, not with the prophets.

Generally, the word 'prophet' is retained in the *Targum* for the minor prophets and the verb 'prophesy' is used.[22] False prophets are explicitly labeled as such here (*Targ. Hos.* 4.5; 9.7-8), as they were elsewhere in *Targum of Jonathan*. Finally, the office of prophet is occasionally connected with teaching (*Targ. Mic.* 3.5-7, *Targ. Amos* 2.12), as it was in *Targum of Ezekiel*.

3. *Conclusions*

Because the provenience of the *Targums* is so controverted, an evaluation of the meaning of the reasons for the alterations introduced by the targumists is difficult. The texts of the *Targums* as we have them evolved over generations and reflect Talmudic and post-Talmudic times. Some claim that certain *Targums* or parts of the *Targums* can be dated early,

---

21. In Ezek. 2.5 to 'hear/listen to' (*šm'*) the prophet is translated as to 'receive his teaching' (*qbl 'lpn*).

22. See *Targ. Zech.* 13.4; *Targ. Hos.* 6.5; 12.11; *Targ. Hag.* 1.1; *Targ. Hab.* 1.1; *Targ. Amos* 7.

while others insist that both language and content reflect talmudic times at the earliest.[23] In this dispute, those who see the *Targums* as late have the more substantial position. Some traditions in the *Targums* can be shown to be earlier if they occur in earlier, dated sources, but the *Targums* themselves cannot attest to the antiquity of a tradition. The texts which we have looked at can most easily be derived from the talmudic period and tend to support a cautious approach to the *Targums*.

The targumist's view of prophets can be elicited from both his faithful translation of words concerned with prophecy and his transformations of them. His view can be summarized in a few observations:

1. Prophecy is a unified phenomenon which involves receiving and communicating the word of God. Consequently, all terms used for prophets in the Hebrew Bible, such as 'seer' and 'visionary', are regularized as 'prophet', and various words for 'oracle' and 'vision' are regularized as 'prophecy'.

2. Prophecy refers only to Israelite prophets communicating the word of God faithfully. Consequently, false prophets are explicitly named as such, and non-Israelite prophets are designated as such or not called prophets.

3. Prophets are involved with the communication of the word of God. Consequently, when they are portrayed as community leaders or as teachers of God's law, they are transformed into scribes, a group whom the targumist sees as community leaders and interpreters of God's law. This is the general tendency of the *Targum of Jonathan*, but the *Targum of Ezekiel* and the *Targum* to some of the minor prophets do associate prophets with teaching and learning.

---

23. The problem of dating the *Targums* has been vigorously argued by New Testament scholars who wish to date at least some of the targumic traditions to the first century CE. Much of the research and argument for an early date has been summarized by Martin McNamara, *The New Testament and the Palestinian Targum to the Pentateuch* (AnBib, 27; Rome: Pontifical Biblical Institute, 1966; 1978 with additions) and *Targum and Testament* (Grand Rapids: Eerdmans; Shannon: Irish University Press, 1972). The argument against early dating has been vigorously made by Joseph Fitzmyer in reviews of Matthew Black, *An Aramaic Approach to the Gospels and Acts* (Oxford: Clarendon Press, 3rd edn, New York: Oxford University Press, 1967) in *CBQ* 30 (1968), pp. 417-28, and McNamara, *New Testament and Palestinian Targum* in *TS* 29 (1968), pp. 322-26.

4. Ecstatic prophets are transformed into scribes in some passages, and the atmosphere of the divine spirit unleashed is
tamed by the milieu of worship and study proper to the school
and groups of scholars.

The targumist seems to accept and defend prophets in a certain role,
that of directly receiving and transmitting the word of God. He restricts
that role to the Israelite prophets only and assigns leadership and stu-
dious learning to scribes and teachers. In doing so, he reflects both his
own view of the past and his experience of his own time. He does not
simply read in the leaders of his own day, because he includes the
priests, who lost power after the destruction of the Temple in 70 CE,
and he excludes the rabbis, who became the leaders after the destruction. Basic obscurities about the role of scribes and other Jewish leadership groups in the postexilic period make it difficult to assign a date to
the targumist's views, but some reflections are possible.

4. *Comparative Data*

The Gospels of the New Testament, with traditions dating from the mid-
to late first century, refer to the scribes, often in conjunction with other
groups, in teaching and leadership roles. Chief priests, scribes, elders
and Pharisees are the leadership groups mentioned most often. Each
Gospel has its own peculiarities which result from the redaction of earlier traditions and the authors' own perceptions (right or wrong) of who
led Judaism and opposed Jesus.[24] Mark, often followed by Matthew,
refers to scribes alone in some instances. Especially in Matthew, the
scribes are not presented as hostile when they are mentioned alone.[25]
Jesus' opponents are most often characterized as 'high priests and
scribes', 'scribes and Pharisees', and 'priests, scribes, and elders' (with
the groups in varied order). Luke most often uses the last mentioned
triad, with 'scribes and Pharisees' also common. None of these passages
is in itself a reliable indicator of who was in charge and what their role

---

24. Many of the data are collected in Michael J. Cook, *Mark's Treatment of
Jewish Leaders* (NovTSup, 51; Leiden: E.J. Brill, 1978), and Sjei van Tilborg, *The
Jewish Leaders in Matthew* (Leiden: E.J.Brill, 1972).

25. See Raymond E. Brown and John P. Meier, *Antioch and Rome* (New York:
Paulist Press, 1983), p. 56 n. 130, with a reference to R. Hummel, *Auseinander-
setzung zwischen Kirche und Judentum in Mattäusevangelium* (Munich: Kaiser
Verlag, 2nd edn, 1966), p. 17.

was in the early to mid-first century, because the traditions about Jesus' opposition and Jewish leadership have undergone a complex evolution. However, one may fairly conclude that these groups were in existence and had some power and influence. They were looked upon as the traditional leaders of the community. And in this the Gospels and the *Targum* agree, for the targumist looks back even to biblical times and thinks of the community leaders as priests and scribes.

In one interesting passage where Jesus is speaking of Israel's faithlessness and rejection of God's message, he refers to 'prophets, wise men, and scribes' (Mt. 23.34), a triad found in *Targ. Jer.* 18.18 and *Targ. Ezek.* 7.26. Besides referring to the past, Matthew may also be referring covertly to the Christian missionaries, teachers and leaders being rejected by Judaism in his own day (the late first century). The targumist is also making covert reference to the teachers of his own day, for the term wise man (*ḥākām*) is used for the rabbinic teachers, the sages. Note that no one set of terms or unified leadership group emerges from this data. Rather, several groups and roles are reported and understood in various ways. Both the *Targum* and the Gospels agree in viewing the priests and scribes as pre-70 CE leaders of Judaism. They disagree concerning the prophets because the emerging Christian community recognizes prophets in its midst who speak in the name of Jesus.[26]

Talmudic literature is similar to the *Targum* and New Testament, in that it views the scribes as leaders in the Second Temple period and prophets as a group which had died out. References to the *soferim* in rabbinic literature are varied and their meaning unsure. An earlier generation of Jewish scholars saw in the Talmudic data an era of the *soferim* extending from the exile down to Simeon the Just (c. 200 BCE), who is the first of the named teachers in Mishnah *Abot*. *Abot* fills the gap

---

26. See R. Leivestad, 'Das Dogma von der Prophetenlosen Zeit', *NTS* 19 (1972–73), pp. 288-99. Leivestad shows that the institution of Temple prophets had died out by Maccabean times, but prophets were common in other areas of society, especially associated with apocalyptic expectations. However, many literary streams within Judaism show an awareness of the loss of the prophets. The later rabbinic idea of the end of the period of prophecy is a polemic against direct revelation and in favor of revelation from the biblical text and its rabbinic interpretations. For further rabbinic treatment of prophecy, see Robert Goldenberg, 'The Problem of False Prophecy: The Talmudic Interpretations of Jeremiah 28 and 1 Kgs 22', in Eugene Rothman and Robert Polzin (eds.), *The Biblical Mosaic* (Semeia Studies; Philadelphia: Fortress Press; Chico, CA: Scholars Press, 1982), pp. 87-103.

between the exile and Simeon with the 'men of the Great Assembly', and some scholars have identified the scribes and the men of the Great Assembly as one.[27] But the Talmud does not assign any age or period to the *soferim*. It uses that title for a variety of scholars, teachers and copyists in various eras.[28] In the Mishnah the term *soferim* is used for teachers in the periods preceding the Mishnah who serve as sources for laws not found in Scripture,[29] or just teachers of the oral law, date unknown.[30] The scribes are conceived of as learned teachers and authorities from a previous period, a role which fits well with that assigned them in the *Targum of Jonathan*.[31]

The targumist uses the term 'scribe' to cover Jewish teachers in all generations from the Bible to his own time, probably the Talmudic era. He reads scribes into biblical stories because to him they are an important avenue for teaching revelation, and he de-emphasizes the spontaneous and uncontrolled power of prophecy as a part of the community structure. In so translating, the targumist refers to the rabbinic teachers of his own day as the model for societal leadership and communication with God.

27. See Alexander Guttmann, *Rabbinic Judaism in the Making* (Detroit: Wayne State University Press, 1970), pp. 3-9, for the standard view and older sources.

28. See Y. Gilat, 'Soferim', *EncJud*, XV (Jerusalem: Keter, 1971), col. 80. Sometimes distinctions are made between scribes who teach the Bible and others who teach Mishnah (*Lev. R.* 9.2 [on Lev. 7.11-12]).

29. *M. 'Or.* 3.9; *m. Par.* 11.5, 6; *m. Yad.* 3.2; *m. Ṭeb. Y.* 4.6.

30. *M. Kel.* 13.7; *m. Sanh.* 11.3; *m. Yeb.* 2.4; 9.3.

31. In *b. Soṭ.* 15a Rabban Gamaliel is said to address his contemporary scholars as 'scribes', but here again the Talmud sees a figure from the *past* applying the term 'scribe' to learned people.

DOEG THE EDOMITE:
FROM BIBLICAL VILLAIN TO RABBINIC SAGE

Richard Kalmin

This essay attempts to describe and account for unique features of Tannaitic, Palestinian Amoraic and Babylonian Amoraic[1] statements about Doeg the Edomite, one of King Saul's officials (1 Sam. 21.8).[2] Our examination of the rabbinic materials supports earlier findings that Tannaim almost never depict biblical personalities as rabbis, but that Amoraim do so with relative frequency.[3] The significance of this finding will be examined below. In addition, Palestinian Amoraim tend to

1. Tannaitic statements are those attributed to rabbis who lived between the first and early third centuries CE. The overwhelming majority of Tannaim lived in the land of Israel under Roman rule. Palestinian Amoraic statements are those attributed to rabbis who lived in Israel from the early third to the early fifth centuries CE, also under Roman rule. Babylonian Amoraic statement are those attributed to rabbis who lived in Babylonia under Persian rule from the early third to the early sixth centuries CE. The conventional boundary between the Tannaitic and Amoraic periods is the publicaiton of the Mishnah in the early third century CE.

The rabbinic documents cited throughout this essay are: the Mishnah; the Yerushalmi (also known as the Palestinian Talmud); the Bavli (also known as the Babylonian Talmud); *Bereshith Rabbah*; *Vayyira Rabbah*; and *Pesiqta deRab Kahana*. Citations from the Mishnah are introduced by the abbrevation *m.*, from the Yerushalmi by the abbreviation *y.*, and from the Bavli by the abbreviation *b.*

2. For further discussion of Doeg in Jewish and non-Jewish traditions, see Louis Ginzberg, *Legends of the Jews* (Philadelphia: Jewish Publication Society of America, 1909–38), IV, pp. 74-77; and VI, pp. 240-34.

3. For earlier discussion of the phenomenon of the sinful sage in rabbinic literature, see Richard Kalmin, *The Sage in Jewish Society of Late Antiquity* (London: Routledge Press, 1999), pp. 101-109; Jeffrey L. Rubinstein, *Talmudic Stories: Narrative Art, Composition, and Culture* (Baltimore: The Johns Hopkins University Press, 1999), Chapter 3. My thanks to Professor Rubinstein for sharing his manuscript with me in advance of its publication.

regard the sinful sage as an anomaly.[4] They tend to view his existence as a serious problem requiring a drastic solution. Babylonian Amoraim, in contrast, tend not to be troubled by the sinful sage. They tend to accept his existence with equanimity and even exploit his wickedness to solve other problems.

Very likely, I argue, my conclusions in an earlier study that Palestinian rabbis were actively involved in society, dependent upon non-rabbinic Jews for social advancement, power, prestige and material support, help explain their greater concern with the problem of the sinful sage. Palestinian rabbis were wary of the sinful sage because he diminished (or they feared he might diminish) their importance in the eyes of non-rabbinic Jews.[5] What is so special about rabbis if they are sinners, non-rabbis might (or actually did) ask? Or what is so special about Torah, the rabbis' prized possession, if it is compatible with sin? Why should we trust rabbis, give them preferential treatment and monetary support, take them into our homes, and give them our daughters in marriage if they can be corrupt and can corrupt others?

Babylonian rabbis, in contrast, were relatively aloof and were less dependent upon non-rabbis for social advancement and material support. They were therefore less concerned with answering real or anticipated attacks against themselves and their Torah by non-rabbinic Jews. They experienced the sinful sage as less of a problem because they were socially less vulnerable than were their Palestinian counterparts. They had less reason to worry that the wicked sage would harm their reputations and do damage to their social aspirations.

It bears emphasizing that I am, of course, sensitive to the problem of false attribution and pseudepigrapha in rabbinic literature. As countless

---

4. In addition, on *y. Sanh.* 10.2 (29a), one Palestinian Amora, either R. Haninah or R. Yehoshua ben Levi, is evidently troubled by the possibility that a sinful sage might serve as a corrupting influence on those who come in contact with him, his very greatness in Torah blinding them to his wickedness. In this case, the Palestinian Amora allows the sinful sage to survive intact, but cordons him off from the rest of society, so he can do no damage (see below).

5. Part of the concern of the statement on *y. Sanh.* 10.2 (29a), cited in the previous note, is that non-rabbis can trust rabbis, that contact with them will be an enriching rather than a corrupting experience. The sinful sage's punishment is to be separated from the rest of society by a ring of fire, which makes it impossible for him to do any damage.

We shall see below that other sinful sages are also rendered harmless: first, by the removal of their Torah, and next, by the destruction of their bodies.

modern studies have emphasized, one cannot assume that everything attributed to a particular rabbi was actually uttered (or first uttered) by that rabbi.[6] I start with no assumptions regarding the reliability of the attributions to particular rabbis or even to particular time periods or geographical locations. However, leaving open the possibility that the attributions may be accurate, or at least helpful as a general indicator of a statement's chronology or geography, I find that the statements about Doeg exhibit clearly definable chronological and geographical patterns. I find it extremely unlikely that these patterns are the creation of later editors, and find it much more likely that the patterns attest to genuine chronological developments and geographical differences. It is these developments and differences which this essay attempts to document and explain.

A description of the Bible's portrayal of Doeg will add perspective to our discussion of the rabbinic materials. The Bible casts Doeg in an unfavorable light, describing his murder of the priests of Nob because they supported David, who King Saul viewed as a threat to his authority. Doeg informs Saul of the priests' kindness to David, and only Doeg is willing to obey Saul's command to put the priests to death for supporting the king's enemy. The story, on 1 Sam. 22.9-23, is as follows:[7]

> Doeg the Edomite, who was standing among the courtiers of Saul, spoke up: 'I saw [David] the son of Jesse come to Ahimelech son of Ahitub at Nob. [Ahimelech] inquired of the Lord on [David's] behalf and gave him provisions; he also gave him the sword of Goliath the Philistine'.
> Thereupon the king sent for the priest Ahimelech son of Ahitub and for all the priests belonging to his father's house at Nob. They all came to the king, and Saul said, 'Listen to me, son of Ahitub'. 'Yes, my lord', he replied. And Saul said to him, 'Why have you and the son of Jesse conspired againt me? You gave him food and a sword, and inquired of God for him—that he may rise in ambush against me, as is now the case'. Ahimelech replied to the king, 'But who is there among all your courtiers as trusted as David, son-in-law of Your Majesty and obedient to your bidding, and esteemed in your household? This is the first time that I inquired of God for him; I have done no wrong. Let not Your

6.   See, most recently, Günter Stemberger, 'Rabbinic Sources for Historical Study', in Jacob Neusner and Alan J. Avery-Peck (eds.), *Judaism in Late Antiquity. Part 3. I. Where We Stand: Issues and Debates in Ancient Judaism* (Leiden: E.J. Brill, 1999), pp. 169-72.

7.   This translation is taken from *Tanakh: The Holy Scriptures* (Philadelphia: Jewish Publication Society of America, 1988), pp. 454-55.

Majesty find fault with his servant [or] with any of my father's house; for
your servant knew nothing whatever about all this.' But the king said,
'You shall die, Ahimelech, you and all your father's house.' And the
king commanded the guards standing by, 'Turn about and kill the priests
of the Lord, for they are in league with David; they knew he was running
away and they did not inform me.' But the king's servants would not
raise a hand to strike down the priests of the Lord. Thereupon the king
said to Doeg, 'You, Doeg, go and strike down the priests.' And Doeg the
Edomite went and struck down the priests himself; that day, he killed
eighty-five men who wore the linen ephod. He put Nob, the town of the
priests, to the sword: men and women, children and infants, oxen, asses,
and sheep—[all] to the sword.

But one son of Ahimelech son of Ahitub escaped—his name was
Abiathar—and he fled to David. When Abiathar told David that Saul had
killed the priests of the Lord, David said to Abiathar, 'I knew that day,
when Doeg the Edomite was there, that he would tell Saul. I am to blame
for all the deaths in your father's house. Stay with me; do not be afraid;
whoever seeks your life must seek my life also. It will be my care to
guard you.'[8]

Turning first to the earliest rabbis, Tannaitic comments about Doeg
are without exception unfavorable, not too surprising given the Bible's
unsympathetic portrayal. In addition, as noted above, Tannaim never
depict Doeg as a rabbi. The problem of the sinful sage, therefore, is not
an issue for the Tannaim in their comments about Doeg. These facts
take on added significance when we bear in mind that some post-Tannaitic statements depict Doeg favorably and also depict him as a rabbi
(see below).

The following Tannaitic statements are critical of Doeg: *m. Sanh.* 10.2
lists Doeg as one of seven biblical personalities who 'have no share in
the world to come' on account of their wickedness. In addition, a Tannaitic source on *b. Sot.* 9a-b includes Doeg on a list of wicked people:
Cain, Korah, Bilaam, Ahitofel, Gehazi, Absalom, Adonijah, Uziah and
Haman, who 'coveted what was not rightfully theirs'. As punishment,
'What they wanted was not given to them and what they possessed was
taken from them'.[9] A Tannaitic statement on *b. Sanh.* 106b begins with
a quotation of Ps. 55.24: 'Murderous and deceitful people will not live
out half of their lives', followed by the claim that 'Doeg lived only

---

8.   This translation is taken from *The Prophets: Nevi'im* (Philadelphia: Jewish
Publication Society of America, 1978), pp. 147-48.

9.   See also the parallel on *Ber. R.* 20.5 (ed. J. Theodor and H. Albeck; Jerusalem: Wahrmann Books, 1965), pp. 187-88.

thirty-four years and Ahitofel only thirty-three'. Doeg and Ahitofel, in other words, are wicked people who died young as punishment for their sins.[10]

Neither these nor any other Tannaitic sources consider Doeg to be a sage. Tannaitic sources tend not to rabbinize non-rabbinic figures and are thus distinguishable from Amoraic sources, both Palestinian and Babylonian, which sometimes portray non-rabbinic figures as rabbis.

As noted above, Babylonian rabbinic sources depict Doeg as a sinful sage and manifest substantially less anxiety about it than do Palestinian Amoraim. According to Rava[11] on *b. Soṭ.* 21a, for example, Doeg and Ahitofel were sages whose study of Torah did not 'protect them' from punishment for sin.[12] According to Rava, the sinful sage is not an intolerable, anxiety-provoking anomaly.

10. A version of this statement on *b. Sanh.* 69b, it will be recalled, designates only the second half as Tannaitic, and cites the verse as an anonymous editorial introduction to the statement. In addition, the term used in the present context to introduce the Tannaitic statement, 'It is also taught in a Baraita', very likely designates it as having been tampered with by later editors. See Judith Hauptman, *Development of the Talmudic Sugya: Relationship Between Tannaitic and Amoraic Sources* (Lanham, MD: University Press of America, 1988). The statement, therefore, very likely attests to Babylonian attitudes toward Doeg, which as noted above are often negative.

11. The printed text of the Talmud reads 'Rabbah'. The fact that the statement is based on that of Rav Yosef suggests strongly that the fourth-generation Mahozan scholar, Rava, is referred to rather than the third-generation Pumbeditan, Rabbah (Mahoza and Pumbedita are rabbinic centers in Babylonia). See Richard Kalmin, *Sages, Stories, Authors and Editors in Rabbinic Babylonia* (Atlanta: Scholars Press, 1994), pp. 175-92.

12. The Talmudic text does not say explicitly from what Doeg and Ahitofel were not protected, but my argument is unaffected no matter which alternative is preferable. See Rashi, *Tosafot Rosh* and *Dikdukei Soferim ha-Shalem* (ed. Avraham Liss; 2 vols.; Jerusalem: Makhon ha-Talmud ha-Yisraeli ha-Shalem, 1977–1979), I, notes on line 22 and n. 104, there; Yaakov Elman, 'The Suffering of the Righteous in Palestinian and Babylonian Sources', *JQR* 80 (1990), pp. 315-40; *idem*, 'Righteousness as its own Reward: An Inquiry into the Theologies of the Stam', *Proceedings of the American Academy for Jewish Research* 57 (1990–1991), pp. 35-67; Rubinstein, *Talmudic Stories*, Chapter 3. See also *The Babylonian Talmud: Seder Nashim: Sotah* (trans. A. Cohen; Hindhead, Surrey: Soncino, 1961), pp. 106-107. Compare *The Talmud of Babylonia, An American Translation: Tractate Sotah* (trans. Jacob Neusner; Chico, CA: Scholars Press, 1984), p. 136. See also the statement by Rav Yosef to which Rava ostensibly responds.

Elsewhere on *b. Soṭ.* 21a, Rav Yosef expresses approval of R. Menaḥem bar

A statement attributed to Rav on *b. Sanh.* 93b[13] states that the lengthy praise of David uttered by 'one of the youths' according to 1 Sam. 16.18 is actually 'evil speech' by Doeg designed to incite Saul's jealousy against David. Rav, a Babylonian Amora, interprets Doeg's false praise as follows: David is 'skilled in music', meaning that 'he knows how to ask questions'. He is a 'hero', meaning 'he knows how to respond'. He is 'a man of war', meaning 'he knows how to engage in the give and take of the war of Torah'. He is 'a handsome man', meaning he knows how to give attractive reasons for his halakhic opinions; 'discerning in speech', meaning 'he knows how to distinguish one matter from another'. 'God is with him', meaning 'the halakhah is always in accordance with him'. After each word of praise Saul is able to say, 'My son Jonathan is like him'. When Doeg says, 'God is with him', a blessing which Jonathan does not possess, Saul becomes jealous.

According to Rav, therefore, Doeg shares the values of the rabbis and is capable of evaluating David's merits as a Torah scholar, suggesting strongly that Rav views Doeg as a rabbi. Significantly, Rav depicts Doeg negatively, claiming that he engages in evil speech and incites Saul's wrath against David. Once again, a Babylonian Amora is not troubled by the phenomenon of the sinful sage.[14]

A discussion on *b. Sanh.* 106b further supports this characterization of Babylonian rabbis. The discussion begins when R. Ami,[15] a Pales-

---

Yosi's interpretation of Prov. 6.23: 'For the commandment is a lamp, Torah is a light'. According to Menahem bar Yosi, this verse teaches that the performance of commandments protects one temporarily but study of Torah never ceases to protect a person from sin.

13. The statement is quoted by Rav Yehudah.

14. In addition, a Babylonian Amoraic statement on *b. Sanh.* 95a alludes rather delicately to Doeg's murder of the priests of Nob. Rav (quoted by Rav Yehudah) quotes God angrily asking David, 'How long will this transgression be hidden by you? On account of you the priests of Nob were killed; on account of you Doeg the Edomite was troubled; and on account of you Saul and his three sons were killed. Do you want your dynasty to end or do you want to be handed over to the enemy?' The same phraseology is employed in another statement attributed to Rav (quoted by Rav Yehudah) on *b. Sanh.* 104a.

15. See *Dikdukei Soferim* (ed. Rafael Rabbinowicz; Jerusalem: Ma'ayan ha-Hokhmah, 1960), n. *resh*. The parallel on *b. Ḥag.* 15b likewise reads R. Ami. The phrase 'and none of them were resolved' is most likely a later addition to Ami's statement, apparently added by someone bothered by the notion that Doeg could be described as a great scholar.

tinian Amora, describes Doeg as a great scholar since he and Ahitofel asked four hundred questions about 'a tower which flies in the air'. Ami, the Palestinian, depicts Doeg as a great sage and nowhere suggests that he was wicked or deserving of punishment.

The Babylonian rabbis who comment on Ami's statement, however, disagree. 'And is it a great thing to ask questions?' Rava objects, implying that Doeg and Ahitofel were not great scholars. The anonymous Babylonian editors next assert that 'the Holy One, blessed be he, requires the heart', meaning that because Doeg and Ahitofel were wicked, their scholarly expertise did not translate into favor in God's eyes.[16]

Rav Mesharshya, another Babylonian Amora, next claims that Doeg and Ahitofel were not adept at studying Torah. Mar Zutra, however, claims that they were great sages, but as punishment for their wickedness their opinions were not accepted as law. We see, therefore, that some Babylonian rabbis manifest no anxiety whatsoever about the phenomenon of the sinful sage.

Along these same lines, on *b. Soṭ.* 21a Rav Yosef very likely depicts Doeg as a sinful sage when he asserts that Doeg and Ahitofel pursued King David because they misinterpreted Deut. 23.15: 'Let him not find in you any forbidden sexual crime'. According to Doeg and Ahitofel, claims Rav Yosef, 'God has abandoned [David]' (Ps. 71.11) because he transgressed this command. The inability of Doeg and Ahitofel to understand a biblical verse is a serious offense, particularly when it results in the unjustified persecution of God's anointed one, King David.

On *b. Ḥag.* 15b, Rav Yehudah weeps because of the fate of Doeg and Ahitofel, who according to *m. Sanh.* 10.2 have no share in the world to come.[17] If even these great sages suffered such a harsh fate, Yehudah

---

16. In other words, Rava probably said only the first phrase, 'And is it a great thing to ask questions?' which taken by itself challenges the idea that Doeg and Ahitofel were great scholars. The subsequent discussion accepts that they were great scholars but claims that this greatness did not translate into greatness in God's eyes. The two sections, therefore, most likely derive from different sources and were not said by a single individual. I doubt that Rava's statement: 'And is it a great thing to ask questions?' is meant as acceptance of their scholarly greatness, but denial that this translates into divine favor, according to which the entire discussion could derive from Rava. I doubt this because Rava's initial emphasis on the questions of Doeg and Ahitofel most likely contradicts R. Ami's claim that the questions of Doeg and Ahitofel are a mark of scholarly greatness.

17. It is chronologically impossible for Rav Yehudah, in dialogue with Shmuel, to cite a statement by R. Ami. A parallel to the statement is preserved on *b. Sanh.*

wonders, what is to become of us? 'They had filthy minds',[18] answers Shmuel.[19] God punished them for their wickedness despite the merit they earned through study of Torah.

This story is an attempt to overcome rabbinic anxiety aroused by contemplation of the harsh punishment suffered by the great sages, Doeg and Ahitofel. Rav Yehudah worries that the harsh punishment inflicted on great biblical 'rabbis' is also in store for him. Shmuel, the dominant voice in the story, attempts to alleviate Yehudah's anxiety by claiming that the fate of Doeg and Ahitofel should be of no concern to Yehudah because these biblical rabbis were wicked.[20] Shmuel, like other Babylonian rabbis, is not at all exercised about the phenomenon of the sinful sage; it is precisely the wickedness of Doeg and Ahitofel which he invokes to allay Yehudah's fears.

Palestinian Amoraim, in contrast, tend to view the sinful sage as a problem in desperate need of solution. For example, they sometimes depict the sinful sage as a temporary anomaly. They tell colorful stories

106b, and according to the printed edition the statement was made by Rabbi (Yehudah Hanasi), which is most likely incorrect. See *Dikdukei Soferim*, n. *samekh*, there.

R. Ami's statement was very likely transferred from *Sanhedrin* to *Ḥag.* 15b by a later Babylonian editor. If so, then the later editor rather than Rav Yehudah depicts Doeg as a sinful sage, but in either case the attitude toward Doeg is that of a Babylonian rabbi.

18. Or 'impure hearts'.

19. In addition to the statements surveyed below, see also *b. Ber.* 17a-b. The statement is critical of Doeg but its authorship is uncertain. It is also uncertain whether or not the statement views Doeg as a rabbi. The statement groups Doeg with Ahitofel, Gehazi and Jesus (see *Dikdukei Soferim*, n. *lamed*).

See also *b. Yom.* 22b, where R. Mani, a later Palestinian Amora, alludes to Doeg's actions at Nob. According to 1 Sam. 22, Saul instructed Doeg to murder the priests of Nob, who he suspected of collaborating with David. Mani mentions Doeg only incidentally, since his main interest is the character of Saul and the contrast between his excessive 'righteousness' when he fails to carry out God's command to utterly destroy the Amalekites, and his wickedness when he orders the murder of the priests of Nob.

See also the statements on *y. Sanh.* 29b and *b. Sanh.* 104b–105a attributed to 'allegorical interpreters'. These statements are most likely Palestinian, but it is uncertain whether they are Tannaitic or Amoraic. See Daniel Boyarin, 'Dorshei Reshumot Amru', *Beer-Sheva* 3 (1988), pp. 23-35, and the literature cited there.

20. Negative statements about Doeg are also attributed to Babylonian rabbis on *b. Yom.* 38b (Ravina), *Sanh.* 69b (anonymous editors), and *Zeb.* 54b (Rava), but in none of these cases is he clearly depicted as a sage.

in which the wicked sage's sin and Torah-learning coexist in uneasy tension with one another. According to these stories, it does not befit the honor of Torah that it dwell in close proximity to sin, or that it dwell inside a person who is being punished for sin. According to these stories, the problem posed by the coexistence of sin and Torah is not resolved until the two are separated.

According to R. Yizhak on *b. Sanh.* 106b, for example, God challenges Doeg, 'Are you not a hero of Torah? Why do you praise yourself for doing evil? Isn't the love of God available to you all of the time?' Doeg is both a sage and wicked, a combination which the Palestinian Amora, in the name of God, finds baffling. God also wonders, claims Yizhak, what Doeg thinks when he reads passages in the Torah prohibiting murder and evil speech. How can Doeg bear to study these passages, wonders God, when he himself is guilty of these crimes? Doeg is a monster, a reality which the Palestinian Amora reacts to with pained amazement.

R. Ami follows with the first of several Palestinian Amoraic attempts to resolve the issue. Ami's solution is to assert that Doeg's Torah was entirely superficial, 'from the mouth and outwards', meaning that he studied Torah without internalizing it.

R. Yizhak, the same R. Yizhak who twice posed the problem above, claims that the sinful sage is only a temporary anomaly. David asks God for the death of Doeg, claims Yizhak, but God responds that Doeg must expel his Torah before he can die, apparently to avoid disrespect toward or mistreatment of the holy Torah inside the unworthy vessel. David asks God to hasten Doeg's demise by forcibly removing the Torah 'from [Doeg's] belly'. The sinful sage must be destroyed, but his destruction must await the Torah's exit from his body.[21]

Two Palestinian Amoraim follow with strikingly similar solutions. According to R. Ami, 'Doeg did not die until he had forgotten his learning', while according to R. Yohanan, one angel caused Doeg to forget

---

21. R. Yizhak next recounts another dialogue between David and God in which God suggests that Doeg should enter the world to come but David urges God to abandon him forever. God suggests that Doeg's statements should be quoted in the study house but David rejects this idea as well. Finally, God suggests that Doeg's children should be rabbis but David wants him totally 'uprooted', that is, lacking all means of self-perpetuation.

his learning, a second burned him up, and a third scattered his ashes in the synagogues and study houses.[22]

Occasionally, Palestinian Amoraim sidestep the problem of the sinful sage by depicting Doeg as a great rabbi and ignoring biblical and Tannaitic claims that he was wicked. Comparable portrayals are never attributed to Babylonian rabbis. As noted above, for example, on *b. Sanh.* 106b R. Ami, a Palestinian Amora, claims that Doeg and Ahitofel were great sages who asked four hundred questions about 'a tower which flies in the air'.

Elsewhere, R. Yohanan on *b. Yeb.* 76b–77a depicts Doeg engaging in brilliant Talmudic dialectic and defeating his colleagues in argument. According to Yohanan, Doeg challenges David's status as a full-fledged member of the Jewish people since David is descended from Ruth the Moabite and the Torah forbids Moabite converts to Judaism. Abner responds by quoting a mishnah which asserts that the Torah explicitly prohibits Moabite male converts, thereby implying that Moabite women are permitted. Ruth, therefore, was a full-fledged member of the Jewish people and David her descendant is likewise.

Doeg, however, continues to argue against David's status as a full-fledged Israelite. Doeg objects that the mishnah does not distinguish between Egyptian male and female converts, despite the Torah's specification that descendants of an Egyptian male convert must wait three generations before being considered full-fledged Israelites (Deut. 23.8-9). It is unreasonable to distinguish between male and female Moabites, argues Doeg, when the mishnah draws no comparable distinction between male and female Egyptians. Therefore Ruth was not a true convert nor is David, her descendant, a true member of the Israelite people.

Abner responds that the Bible's reason for the prohibition of Moabite converts ('Because they did not advance ahead and meet you with bread and water[23]') is applicable only to men, since 'It is the way of a man to advance ahead but it is not the way of a woman to advance ahead'. The mishnah distinguishes between male and female Moabite converts but not between male and female Egyptians, claims Abner, because the Torah offers no comparable explanation applicable only to male Egyp-

22. See also the following statement, apparently attributed to Rav Ashi, a sixth-generation Babylonian Amora. Because it is included in a series of statements by Palestinian Amoraim, however, it may have been authored by R. Asi, a third-generation Palestinian Amora.

23. Deut. 23.4-5.

tians. Ruth was therefore a true convert and David her descendant is a legitimate member of the Israelite people.

Doeg objects that Deuteronomy's explanation of the prohibition of Moabite converts applies to women as well as to men, since the men should have advanced toward the men and the women toward the women. The Moabite men and women are equally blameworthy, reasons Doeg, and since we forbid Moabite male converts we should also forbid Moabite female converts. Ruth is not a legitimate convert, therefore, and neither is David, her descendant, a member of the Israelite people.

Saul instructs Abner to go to the house of study in search of an answer to Doeg's objection, but none is forthcoming. The rabbis are about to declare David unfit when Amasa arrives and summarily puts a halt to the proceedings.[24]

According to R. Yohanan, therefore, Doeg's facility with rabbinic argumentation outstrips that of his colleagues. True, he uses his dialectical skill against David, but the story nowhere faults him for doing so.[25] The Palestinian Amora's positive portrayal of Doeg the sage is in sharp contrast to the negative portrayals of him by Babylonian Amoraim.

Before turning to Doeg's portrayal in Palestinian compilations, it will be helpful to summarize our findings thus far. Tannaitic statements about Doeg tend to be negative, but there is no evidence that Tannaim consider Doeg to be a sage. Several Babylonian Amoraim, in contrast, depict Doeg as a sinful sage, and the coexistence of sin and Torah does not appear to have bothered them in the slightest. These Babylonian Amoraim likewise have little or no difficulty with the idea that a sage, a living vessel containing Torah, might be punished or destroyed while still in full possession of his Torah. Palestinian Amoraim in the Bavli, however, (1) deny or ignore Doeg's wickedness, (2) assert that he was destroyed only after Torah left his body, (3) view the sinful sage as an

---

24. According to Rava, Amasa wins the day by threatening to kill anyone who refuses to obey the law which he, Amasa, received from the court of Samuel: 'A Moabite male [is prohibited]; a Moabite female is not'.

25. Compare the statement on *b. Soṭ.* 21a attributed to Rav Yosef, a Babylonian Amora. Yosef explicitly says that Doeg and Ahitofel pursued David because they 'misinterpreted' a scriptural verse. R. Yohanan, in the statement presently under consideration, does not assert that Doeg's interpretation was incorrect.

anxiety-producing but temporary phenomenon or (4) claim that Doeg's learning was only superficial, that he had internalized sin but not Torah.

The above characterization of Babylonian Amoraic attitudes toward Doeg is in need of a slight qualification. Rava and Rav Mesharshya, Babylonian Amoraim who express opinions about Doeg on *b. Sanh.* 106b (see above), respond to the problem of the sinful sage by denying that Doeg was a sage. It is no surprise, however, to find post-third-generation Babylonians expressing the Palestinian view, since we find in numerous contexts that later Babylonian Amoraim manifest increased receptivity to or awareness of Palestinian modes of thought and behavior.[26]

Turning now to the depiction of Doeg by Palestinian Amoraim in Palestinian compilations, *y. Sanh.* 10.2 (29a) unambiguously declares, 'Doeg was a great Torah scholar'. The source continues:

> Israel came and asked David, 'Does [the preparation of] the shewbread override the Sabbath?' [David] said to them, 'Its arrangement overrides the Sabbath, but its kneading and shaping do not...' Doeg was there and said, 'Who is this who issues practical decisions in my presence?' They said to him, 'It is David son of Jesse.' Immediately [Doeg] went and advised Saul the King of Israel to kill the priests of Nob.

This story depicts Doeg as a sinful sage, although David's action, the impetus for Doeg's crime, is a serious breach of rabbinic etiquette. The story certainly does not excuse Doeg but it supplies a motive for his outrageous behavior.

R. Yehudah ben Pazi, a Palestinian Amora, next asserts that the Bible's peculiar rendering of Doeg's name as Doyeg (1 Sam. 22.18, 22) expresses Saul's contention that Doeg was 'caught like a fish [*dag*]' and had to murder the priests himself since no one else could bring himself to commit the horrible crime.

'How was [Doeg] distanced?' the discussion continues, and either R. Haninah or R. Yehoshua ben Levi, two early post-Tannaitic Palestinian rabbis, answer that students of Torah[27] attached themselves to

---

26. See Zvi Moshe Dor, *Torat Erez-Yisrael be-Bavel* (Tel Aviv: Devir, 1971); Kalmin, *Sages, Stories, Authors and Editors*, pp. 87-110; idem, *The Sage in Jewish Society*, pp. 30-31 and *passim*.

27. Regarding the meaning of the Hebrew term *talmidim vatikim*, translated here as 'students of Torah', see David Golinkin, 'Le-Perush ha-Munahim "Vatikin", "Vatik", ve-"Talmid Vatik" be-Sefer Ben Sira u-ve-Sifrut ha-Talmudit', *Sidra* 13 (1997), pp. 47-60, esp. p. 57.

Doeg and learned while he forgot. This statement, in other words, reflects the Palestinian Amoraic idea familiar to us from the Bavli, according to which the coexistence of sin and Torah is no more than a temporary anomaly.

According to a second opinion recorded here, 'Fire came out of the holy of holies and burned all around [Doeg]'. The exact significance of this statement is unclear. Evidently, its author is troubled by the possibility that (1) a sinful sage might corrupt those who come in contact with him, his very greatness in Torah blinding them to his wickedness; and/or (2) that he might damage the reputation of scholars in general, his actions mistakenly viewed as typical of all rabbis.[28] In this case, the Palestinian Amora allows the sinful sage to survive, but cordons him off from the rest of society so he can do no damage.[29] According to both interpretations, Doeg the sinful sage is neutralized, a menace which requires extreme measures to ensure that he causes no harm. It is not the coexistence of sin and Torah *per se* which is the problem according to the latter statement, but the negative effect the sinful sage will have on society and/or the reputation of the rabbis.

How might we account for the differences between Palestinian and Babylonian Amoraim? As noted above, our conclusion in an earlier study that Palestinian rabbis tend to be involved with non-rabbis but that Babylonian rabbis tend toward insularity[30] helps explain this distinction. Palestinian Amoraim depend on non-rabbis for material support and social advancement. Their vulnerable position in society causes

---

28. Compare *y. Ḥag.* 77b, where the image of fire enveloping scholars is positive: 'They sat and busied themselves with words of Torah. From the Torah to the Prophets and from the Prophets to the Writings, and fire came down from the heavens and encircled them. Abuya said to them, "My masters! Have you come to burn down my house upon me?" They said to him, "God forbid. But we were sitting and turning words of Torah. From the Torah to the Prophets and from the Prophets to the Writings. And the words rejoiced as when they were given at Sinai, and fire enveloped them as the fire enveloped them at Sinai..."' Nothing in the present context, however, would support a positive interpretation.

29. See also *Pes. K.* 18.1 (ed. Bernard Mandelbaum [New York: Jewish Theological Seminary of America, 1962], p. 293). We also find Palestinian Amoraim criticizing Doeg while not portraying him as a sage. See *Ber. R.* 32.1; 38.1 (ed. Theodor-Albeck, pp. 288-89, 351); *Vay. R.* 26.2 (ed. Mordechai Margaliot [New York: Jewish Theological Seminary, 1993], pp. 589-92); *y. Pe'ah* 16a; and *Pes. K.* 3.16; 4.2 (ed. Mandelbaum, pp. 52, 56-58).

30. Kalmin, *The Sage in Jewish Society*, pp. 1-24 and *passim*.

them to go to great lengths to respond to real or imagined challenges, to actual or anticipated charges by non-rabbinic Jews that Torah expertise is worth little if it is compatible with sin, or that Torah scholars should not be materially and socially advanced because they are as capable as anyone of becoming corrupted and serving as a corrupting influence on others. They therefore tend to (1) depict biblical 'rabbis' in positive terms, (2) safeguard the sanctity of Torah, (3) emphasize the Torah's power to protect against sin and its affects or (4) depict the sinful sage as a temporary anomaly incapable of harming either the rabbis themselves or society in general.

Babylonian rabbis, in contrast, have little reason (1) to neutralize the sinful sage by killing him off or cordoning him off from the rest of society; (2) to pretend the sinful sage doesn't exist, or (3) to go to great lengths to maintain the Torah's sanctity by claiming that its co-existence with sin is a temporary anomaly. Babylonian Amoraim, in other words, go about their business with relatively little concern for what non-rabbis might say or think.

As I argued in my earlier study, it is unlikely that this distinction between Palestine and Babylonia is explicable as a purely rabbinic concern. It is unlikely that Palestinian Amoraim are acutely concerned about the sanctity of Torah only because they believe that rabbis should be exposed to such ideas. Or that Palestinian Amoraim go to great lengths to neutralize or deny the existence of the sinful sage only because of the danger such a figure presents to impressionable young rabbis.

Explaining the phenomenon as an entirely internal rabbinic concern fails to account for the distinction between Palestinian and Babylonian Amoraim on this issue. Why are Palestinian Amoraim anxious to portray the Torah as sacrosanct but Babylonian rabbis less so? Why do Palestinian Amoraim deny or neutralize the sinful sage but Babylonian Amoraim tend not to? If we factor in (1) differing Palestinian and Babylonian Amoraic attitudes toward non-rabbis, and (2) their differing positions in society, however, we understand well the distinctions between Palestinian and Babylonian Amoraim on these issues.

What other conclusions can we draw from study of rabbinic comments about Doeg the Edomite? Two traditions preserved in *Pesiqta deRab Kahana* make the intriguing claim that God has removed the kingship from David as a result of his sins. Doeg and Ahitofel are David's chief accusers, but David responds to them with scriptural arguments showing that God has abandoned him only temporarily.

We find this theme in *Pes. K.* 18.1,[31] where David complains that Doeg and Ahitofel (1) contemptuously refer to him as 'son of Jesse', as if he possessed no name of his own, and (2) claim that God has abandoned him and forever removed from him the kingship of Israel. David proves through scriptural quotations that God's abandonment of him is only temporary, that God has removed David's sin and has seen to it that he will not die.

We find the same theme in *Pes. K.* 2.1,[32] where R. Shmuel bar Imi asserts that Doeg and Ahitofel claim that David's 'capture of the sheep and murder of the shepherd', that is, his sinful treatment of Bathsheba and Uriah, leave David with no hope of salvation from God. David worries that God shares their opinion since he writes in his Torah, 'The adulterer and adulteress shall surely die' (Lev. 20.10). Ultimately, however, God restores David to his former position of glory as king of Israel and promises to protect him because of the merit of his ancestors.

What motivates the *Pesiqta's* claim that David lost the throne when nothing in the Bible supports this claim? What accounts for the curious reference in these sources to God removing from David the kingship of Israel? Very likely, these traditions refer to the rabbis' own era, when Israel was deprived of a Davidic king. The *Pesiqta's* statements very likely postdate 429 CE, when the Christian Roman Empire abolished the office of the patriarch. The patriarch claimed Davidic descent and the rabbis recognized this claim; the end of the patriarchate meant the end of an important symbol of Jewish sovereignty in the land of Israel.[33] The two statements in the *Pesiqta* respond to charges levelled at the rabbis by their contemporaries that the loss of Davidic kingship was permanent.

Very likely, Doeg the Edomite serves as a spokesman for Christian Rome, a role often filled in rabbinic literature by Edom, brother of Jacob and Israel's unfriendly neighbor.[34] Against the Christians, who claim

---

31. Ed. Mandelbaum, p. 293.

32. Ed. Mandelbaum, p. 16.

33. See, for example, Ben-Zion Rosenfeld, 'Mashber ha-Nesiut be-Erez Yisrael be-Meah ha-Revi'it la-Sefirah', *Zion* 53 (1988), p. 250 and the literature cited in n. 45.

34. See Gerson D. Cohen, 'Esau as Symbol in Early Medieval Thought', in Alexander Altmann (ed.), *Jewish Medieval and Renaissance Studies* (Cambridge, MA: Harvard University Press, 1967), pp. 19-48; reprinted in Cohen, *Studies in the*

that Jesus is the Davidic king of the true Israel (Christianity), the rabbis insist that David's loss of the throne is only temporary and the true Davidic dynasty will one day be restored to its former glory.

The fact that this concern for Christianity is discernible only in traditions about Doeg found in *Pesiqta deRab Kahana* perhaps reveals important information about the work's *Sitz im Leben* and the nature of the rabbinic group which produced it. It would be premature to draw firm conclusions about these issues, however, on the basis of only two sources.[35]

Variety of Rabbinic Cultures (Philadelphia: Jewish Publication Society of America, 1991), pp. 243-69.

35. For further evidence that passages from *Pesiqta deRab Kahana* might respond to Christianity, see Lou H. Silberman, 'A Theological Treatise on Forgiveness: Chapter Twenty-three of Pesiqta de Rab Kahana', in J. Petuchowski and Ezra Fleischer (eds.), *Studies in Aggadah, Targum and Jewish Liturgy* (Jerusalem: Magnes Press, 1981), pp. 95-107; *idem*, 'Challenge and Response: Pesiqta Derab Kahana, Chapter 26 as an Oblique Reply to Christian Claims', *HTR* 79 (1986), pp. 247-53.

THE USE OF THE *DERASH* METHOD IN THE *TARGUM OF EZEKIEL*

Josep Ribera-Florit

The *Targum of Ezekiel (Targ. Ezek.)* follows the method used by the other targums to explain its exegesis of the Hebrew Bible. Because the targum applies the *derash* method for clarification and elucidation of the contents of the Masoretic Text (MT), the use of one or other kind of rules depends on the context; the same issue (for example, 'justice') will be interpreted in different ways, depending on whether it refers to divinity, the people of Israel or to the heathen nations. This fact must always be born in mind when we deal with the targumic applications of the different rules of the *derash* method.[1]

1. *The Use of the Rule* אל תקרא

One of the most frequent rules of the *derash* method is the hermeneutic one called אלתקרא ('do not read').[2] In Ezek. 1.20 MT explains the

---

1. On the midrashic method and its application to the targum, see R. Le Déaut, 'A propos d'une définition de Midrash', *Bib* 50 (1969), pp. 395-413; A. Díez Macho, *El Targum* (Barcelona: CSIC, 1972), pp. 12-30. G. Vermes, 'Bible and Midrash: Early Old Testament Exegesis', in P.R. Ackroyd and C.F. Evans (eds.), *The Cambridge History of the Bible*, I (Cambridge: Cambridge University Press, 1970), pp. 199-231; P.S. Alexander, 'The Targum and the Rabbinic Rules for the Delivery of the Targum', in J.A. Emerton (ed.), *Congress Volume Salamanca 1983* (VTSup, 36; Leiden: E.J. Brill, 1985), pp. 14-28.

2. This is one of the rabbinic rules, or *middot,* used above all to denote a change in the Masoretic reading of Scripture in order to give meaning to a phrase, other than the literal one, by changing some of its consonants or vowels to another one of similar sound; it is equivalent to metathesis and paronomasia. See A. Arzi, 'Al Tkrei', in *EncJud*, II (1971), col. 775; R. Le Déaut 'Usage implicite de l'al tiqre dans le Targum de Job de Qumran', in D. Muñoz Léon (ed.), *Salvación en la Palabra: Homenaje al Prof. A. Díez Macho* (Madrid: CSIC, 1986), pp. 419-31; D. Muñoz de León, *Derás: Los caminos y sentidos de la palabra divina en la Escritura* (Madrid: CSIC, 1987, pp. 92-94.

mobility of the creatures in this way: 'Wherever the spirit would go, they went...'; *Targ. Ezek.* changes רוח ('spirit') to רעוא ('wish') ('Wherever *they wished* to go, there they will go, according *to their will*...for the spirit like that of the creatures was in wheels'); with this consonant modification, *Targ. Ezek.* avoids identifying 'spirit' with God, and stresses the freedom of the creatures, which, according to the Merkabah ideology, are probably the angels.[3]

There is one case (6.6) in which MT contains an obvious mistake: 'your altars will be waste and guilty', אשם instead of the root שמם ('desolate'), which we find in Peshitta, Septuagint, Vulgate and *Targ. Ezek.*, and corresponds to the context. In addition, in 8.3 *Targ. Ezek.* reads סלם ('statue, image, idol') in place of סמל ('sign, signal'). Another אל תקרא appears when the Hebrew root ברח 'escape, flee' (מברחיו 'his fugitives', 17.21) is transformed by *Targ. Ezek.* into בחר 'choice', reading מבחריו ('And all the *valiant men* [נבורוהו]...shall be slain...').[4] Also, in 24.14 *Targ. Ezek.* translates, 'I will not spare, I will have no *pity*' (from רחם), while MT has 'I will not comfort' (from נחם).

2. *The Function of the Comparative* -כ

Targ. Ezek. seeks to explain the meaning of prophetic metaphors by means of two devices: either by addition of the comparative particle כ and similar particles, or without it; in the latter case, the original metaphor or symbol of the MT disappears.

In *Targ. Ezek.* we find many examples of the first case. MT 3.25 reads: 'and you son of man, cords will be placed upon you...' *Targ. Ezek.* explains the comparison: 'and you son of Adam, *the decree of my sentence will be* upon you *like a tie of* cords', that is, the divine decree fastens the prophet like a chain. Also, the sentence, 'I will take the stony heart out of their flesh' (11.19 according to MT), receives a targumic explanation of the comparison: 'I will *break the evil* heart, *which is as hard as* stone', the stony heart meaning a wicked heart. In the allegory of the unfaithful wife, her birth is described in these terms: 'On the day you were born your umbilical cord was not cut nor were you

---

3. On the main trends in the Merkabah doctrine, see J. Ribera: 'La ideología de la Mercabá en el judaísmo antiguo y en el targum de Ezequiel', in J.R. Ayaso Martínez and V. Collado Bertomeu (eds.), *IV Simposio bíblico español* (Valencia-Granada: Universidad de Granada, 1993), pp. 307-22.

4. Many Hebrew MSS read also מבחריו; see *BHS, ad locum.*

washed with water to cleanse you...' (16.4); *Targ. Ezek.* makes the comparison as follows: '*And also, when your forefathers went down to Egypt, they were sojourners in a land not their own. The congregation of Israel was enslaved and oppressed. It was like a new born child who is abandoned in the field,* whose umbilical cord was not cut...' In the same chapter, v. 35 MT says, 'Therefore, o harlot, hear the word of the Lord'. But *Targ. Ezek.* mitigates the Hebrew text: 'Therefore, *because her deeds were like* a harlot's, *O congregation of Israel, heed* the word of the Lord'. A clear analogy of the lioness with Israel is found in *Targ. Ezek.* 19.2 (MT affirms: 'What a lioness was your mother, she couched among young lions!'): 'How *the Congregation of Israel has been compared to* a lioness! Among *the kings* she couched...'[5] In 28.18 ('By the multitude of your iniquities...so I brought forth fire from the midst of you') for *Targ. Ezek.* the fire symbolizes strength: 'By the multitude of your sins...*I brought nations who are as strong as* fire'.[6] The targumic identification of the two sisters with two countries is apparent from the context (23.2: 'Son of Adam, *prophesy against two countries who are like* two women who were the daughters of one mother'). In the elegy on Tyre (27.26), 'the east wind' receives this analogy: '...*a king as mighty as* the east wind has crushed you in the midst of the seas'. The evocation of Eden (28.13) with reference to the King of Tyre induces a paradisiac description: '*In abundant prosperity and luxuries you delight yourself, as though you were residing* in Eden'. The sentence, 'I will cover the sun with a cloud' (32.7), related to Egypt suggests to *Targ. Ezek.* this analogy: '*a King shall cover you with his armies like* a cloud...'[7] In the same chapter, v. 8, which reads, 'All the bright lights

---

5.   Generally, the lion is understood by *Targ. Ezek.* as king or ruler, and in the targumim to the Torah the lion refers to the Messiah; see M. Pérez, *Tradiciones mesiánicas en el targum Palestinense* (Valencia: Institución San Jerónimo, 1981), pp. 119-22, but it is not found in *Targum of Jonathan*. See G. Vermes, *Scripture and Tradition in Judaism* (SPB, 4; Leiden: E.J. Brill, 1961), pp. 41-42; nevertheless *Targ. Ezek.* has no objection to changing the interpretation, as in this verse. See J. Ribera, *El Targum de Isaías* (Valencia: Institución San Jerónimo, 1988), p. 30; *idem, Traducción del Targum de Jeremías* (Estella, Navarra: Verbo Divino, 1992), p. 30.

6.   The power of fire according to poetic passages of the Bible can be a positive or destructive force; cf. L.I. Rabinowitz, 'Fire', in *EncJud*, VI, cols. 1302-1305. *Targ. Ezek.* catches the double meaning perfectly, and applies it depending on context.

7.   See *Targ. Jeremiah* 4.13; 46.3, 8; Ezek. 30.18; 31.18. On the image of the

of heaven will I make dark over you, and put darkness upon your land',
Targ. Ezek. adds two similes: 'All *the lanes of your roads, which are
kept in good repair and guarded in the midst of you, behold* they are
like the shining lights in the heavens; I will *ruin* them for you, and
trouble shall cover your land *like* thick darkness...'[8]

3. *Derashic Interpretation of Images Related to the World of Plants*

The phrase, 'be not afraid...though briers and thorns are with you' (2.6),
in the context means rebellion for *Targ. Ezek.* ('be not afraid...*even if
they rebel and argue against you*'). However, the same idea in another
context ('for house of Israel shall be no more a brier to prick or a thorn
to hurt them', 28.24) is interpreted differently: 'for house of Israel shall
be no more a *wicked king or an annoying ruler*'. In the allegory of the
cedar[9] (17.22), MT begins, 'Says the Lord God: I myself will take a
spring from the lofty top of the cedar and will set it out; I will break off
from the topmost of its young twigs a tender one, and I myself will
plant it upon a high and lofty mountain'. The targumic exegesis of this
verse is clearly messianic: 'Thus says the Lord God: I myself will bring
near *a child from the kingdom of house of David which is likened to* the
lofty cedar, *and I establish him from among his children's children; I
will anoint and establish him by my Word* on a high and exalted mountain'.

In ch. 31, we find another allegory of the cedar related, according to
Targ. Ezek., directly to the king of Assur, and indirectly to Pharaoh of
Egypt. We also find a noticeable change between MT and *Targ. Ezek.*
regarding the description of the cedar in 31.3; MT notes that 'its top was
among the thick branches', while *Targ. Ezek.* says '...*sending its roots
by the water courses*'; this would be an allusion to the river Nile. Then
(31.4) its growth is described: 'The waters nourished it, the deep made

cloud as a symbol of guidance, protection and divine revelation, see J. Luzárraga,
Las tradiciones de la nube en la Biblia y en el judaísmo primitivo (AnBib, 54;
Rome: Pontificio Istituto Biblico, 1973).

8. The dualism of light and darkness symbolizes from the beginning (Gen. 1.3-
4) the physical order and disorder, and it connotes morally the good and evil as they
appear in Qumran texts; H. Ringgren, *The Faith of Qumran* (New York: Crossroad,
1995), pp. 68-80.

9. The tree of cedar is mentioned seventy times in the Bible and is described
on account of its beauty, hardiness and longevity; see Y. Feliks, 'Cedar', *EncJud*,
V, col. 268.

it grow tall', which *Targ. Ezek.* describes as, 'With numerous peoples
and powerful auxiliaries he subjugates the kings under his dominion';
in this context, other cedars become kings and cypresses are rulers (31.5,
8); the trees of Eden are the kings from Orient (v. 9); the branches
symbolize the armies and auxiliaries (31.5, 12); and also the beauty and
greatness of the cedar (31.7) are understood by *Targ. Ezek.* as the military power of the king and his victories over the enemies; the top of the
cedar is his might and tyranny, but its falling branches symbolize the
corpses of his armies. On the other hand, for *Targ. Ezek.* the choice and
best of Lebanon represent kings, governors and rich men (31.16).[10]

4. Derashic Interpretation of Images Related to Animal World

Chapter 17 deals with the renovation of Israel, and several allegories
are used there. In 17.23 MT, explaining the image of the cedar, adds,
'under it will dwell all kinds of beasts, in the shade of its branches birds
of every sort will nest'; but *Targ. Ezek.* tries to discover its moral meaning: '…and *become a mighty king*, and *all the righteous shall rely upon
him, and all the humble* shall dwell in the shade *of his kingdom*'. The
metaphor of the lion is developed in ch. 19. It is very usual in rabbinic
exegesis to understand the lion as a symbol of the king or the ruler
(19.2), representing young lions as the sons of kings (although with reference to Egypt it means according to *Targ. Ezek.* '*the mightiest of the
nations*'). In 19.6 MT expounds the attitude of the young lion: 'he
learned to catch prey, he devoured men'; *Targ. Ezek.* renders the text in
a human environment: 'a *king* was he, and he learned to *kill mercilessly*; he *slew people*'. In addition, describing the beginning of the
destruction of Jerusalem with the allegory of the cauldron (MT 24.5),
we read, 'take the most select of the flock, and arrange the bones at the
bottom of it [the cauldron]'; and *Targ. Ezek.* interprets: '*Bring near the
kings of the nations, and also equip the siege troops together with
them*'. In this case, the flock is identified with the kings of Israel, and
the animal bones with troops. This likeness is followed in 24.10: 'Pile
on the wood, kindle the fire, boil the meat thoroughly, add spices, and

---

10. The metaphorical use of Lebanon in *Targ. Ezek.* to mean the king, the rich
or the nations is found in the Bible itself and explains something that is already
implicit in Scripture. The exegesis of Lebanon identified with the temple is a later,
more developed interpretation (*Targ. Jer.* 22.6, 20, 23; Hos. 14.8); see Vermes,
Scripture and Tradition, pp. 26-39.

let the bones be burned'; and also in *Targ. Ezek.*'s interpretation: '*Make numerous the kings, gather the armies, equip the seige-troops, and invite warriors against her, so that her valiant men shall be confounded*'.

In the oracle against Egypt, the scene of the fish and the river Nile (29.4, 'I will make the fish of your streams cling to your scales; and I will pull you up from the midst of your streams, with all the fish of your streams clinging to your scales') suggests to *Targ. Ezek.* the awful fate of the Egyptian kings ('I will put chains in your jaws and *I will slay your mighty rulers together with your valiant men, and I will remove you from your kingdom; your mighty rulers together with your valiant men, shall be slain*'). Following the same image, MT 32.2 speaks of the monster of the seas: 'you burst forth in your rivers, stirring up the water with your feet, and fouling their rivers'. *Targ. Ezek.*'s elucidation is also according to the political and historical reality: 'you broke forth with your armies, and you made the nations tremble by your auxiliaries, and you destroyed their countries'.

It is evident that the allegory of the shepherds and the sheep (ch. 34) alludes to the rulers and the people of Israel.[11] In this context the wild beasts are, of course, the kingdoms of the nations. But several features deserve mention: the fat and the strong sheep become in *Targ. Ezek.*'s ideology transgressors and sinners (v. 16); the stray sheep are those that have been exiled (v. 16); the sheep of the holy sacrifices mean the holy people, the people who are cleansed and come to Jerusalem at the time of Passover Festivals. In the report of Gog's defeat (v. 39), 'rams, lambs, goats, bulls, all of them fatlings of Bashan' turn into 'kings, rulers and governors, all of them mighty men, rich in possessions'.

5. *The Symbolic Meaning of Nature Powers*

Chapter 13 remarks the destruction of Jerusalem in spite of the false prophets' predictions of peace. In 13.13 (MT) we read, 'I will make a stormy wind break out in my wrath', which is historically described by *Targ. Ezek.*: 'I will bring *a King who is as mighty as* a powerful windstorm...' For *Targ. Ezek.* the image of a high mountain is the holy

---

11. Throughout ancient Near Eastern history the image of the shepherd was commonly used to designate gods and kings. Ezekiel uses the evil shepherd theme to illustrate selfish and irresponsible leadership and to rebuke rulership based on domination and crushing oppression. See J.W. Vancil, 'Sheep, Shepherd', *ABD*, V, pp. 1187-90.

mountain where the temple is placed (20.40).[12] In the oracles of indictment against Israel it is stated, 'You are a land that is not cleansed, or rained upon in the day of indignation' (22.24). *Targ. Ezek.* moralizes the sentence: 'You are the land *of Israel*, a land that is not cleansed, and *no good deeds have been performed in her, to protect her* in the day of *curse*'.[13] Chapter 24 describes the crimes of Jerusalem in this way: 'She shed it [that is, the blood] upon a bare rock; no lot has fallen on her' (MT v. 7); which *Targ. Ezek.* details in its manner: '*with premeditation, with arm held high did she shed it* [innocent blood], *she did not shed it by mistake, so that she might be repentant for it*'. Likewise, the sentence (v. 8) 'I have set on the bare rock the blood' means 'I have *uncovered their sins*'. As we have seen in the allegory of the cauldron, fire evokes the armies.

The mention of the river Nile associated with the Pharaoh (29.3) calls to the targumic mind the fact that the land irrigated by the Nile is the property of the king; accordingly, the phrase, 'my Nile is my own, I made it' is replaced by 'mine is *the kingdom*, and it is I *who have conquered*'. Narrating the end of Egypt, the MT refers to the cloud which covered the land, while *Targ. Ezek.* understands this cloud as a symbol of the hostile king who covered Egypt with his armies (30.18). Also in this description, the rivers and waters become countries and nations (31.15) which were laid waste. Nevertheless, in another context (32.14), the rivers symbolize kings. When the return of the glory of the Lord in the new Temple is foreseen, MT compares the sound of his coming to the sound of many waters;. *Targ. Ezek.* gives a different vision: Glory[14] does not come, but is revealed, and the sound of the waters is the voice

---

12. Perhaps among the symbols expressing the sacred centrality of the Temple, the chief one is that of Zion, and the Temple built there is the cosmic mountain. The Temple-building on a mountain and a platform replicates the heavenly mountain of Yahweh and also his earlier manifestation at Sinai; see C. Meyers, 'Temple, Jerusalem', *ABD*, VI, pp. 359-60.

13. Water, in the Jewish interpretation, is a symbol of the Torah (*Targ. Isa.* 12.3); water and rain also symbolize morally the good deeds (*Targ. Isa.* 32.20); see J. Ribera, *El Targum de Isaías*, pp. 31, 103 n. 3, 155 n. 9.

14. The epithet of glory, which appears on many occasions with *shekinah* to stress the spectacular vision of God, in *Targ. Ezek.* 1 is associated with the vision of the Merkabah; see D. Muñoz Léon, *Gloria de la shekina en los targumim del pentateuco* (Madrid: CSIC, 1977); J. Ribera: 'La ideología de la Mercabá', pp. 317-21.

of those blessing the name of the Lord; *Targ. Ezek.* in this case alludes to angelic beings related to the ideology of the Merkabah.

6. *The Moral Sense of the Human Body*

We must distinguish between the interpretation of the members and functions belonging to the human body and those metaphorically ascribed to God.

In the oracle against Tyre, MT affirms that 'the Lord will send blood into her streets' (28.31), but *Targ. Ezek.* chooses 'killing' instead of 'blood'. In another context 'blood' for *Targ. Ezek.* means 'sins' in a broad sense, or specifically 'the sin of killing' (8.13; 24.8).[15] In 16.6-7 the detailed report on the growing of the maiden until the age of puberty leads *Targ. Ezek.* to paraphrase by evoking God's care of his people and consequently their liberation from the servitude of Egypt and their prosperity under the Sinaitic Covenant; in this context the blood of circumcision and the blood of Passover have a redemptive virtue. MT reads, 'And when I passed by you, and saw you weltering in your blood, I said to you: by your blood live!' *Targ. Ezek.* interprets: *'Because the memorial of the covenant with your father is before me that you are oppressed in your captivity, I said to you:* because of the blood *of the circumcision I will take care of you,* And I said to you: Because of the blood *of Passover I will redeem you'*; in this context also the naked and bare maiden represents the abandoned and oppressed people (16.6, 39).[16]

The arm is identified with 'power, kingdom' (30.21) and specifically with 'military power, the armies'.[17] Among the punishments of Jewish captives, MT relates that 'they shall cut off your noses and your ears' (23.25); *Targ. Ezek.* understands this as *'your princes and your nobles shall be exiled'*.

15. In the biblical world blood is identified with life; in this sense, to shed blood means to strike the life. According to rabbinic *halakah*, capital punishment is not a crime when it is an act of justice, but the shedding of innocent blood is a crime (*Targ. Jer.* 2.34; *Targ. Ezek.* 22.2, 3).

16. On the theology of circumcision and its relationship with baptism, see Vermes, *Scripture and Tradition*, pp. 190-92.

17. In the anti-anthropomorphic tendency, the translation of arm and hand as power is frequent, but also in this passage (30.21) *Targ. Ezek.* follows the same interpretation, meaning that in both cases the translation of hand and arm by power is, above all, due to the context.

Describing the atonement for the altar, it is said 'and they shall fill its hands' (43.26). For *Targ. Ezek.*, this is an idiomatic expression equivalent to 'and *offer up its sacrifices*'.

It is well known that the Tg usually avoids the anthropomorphisms and anthropopathisms of the Bible. Accordingly, the human members receive spiritual dimensions. The hand and the arm are symbols of the divine might (גבורא 25.7);[18] eyes mean the divine Word (7.4); the face becomes the *shekinah* (39.23);[19] the soles of the feet signify the abode of the *shekinah* (43.7). Some human acts are also converted in a higher level. To look and to know, to come, to enter, are expressed in the passive: 'it is revealed before me' (23.13; 20.5); 'The glory of the God of Israel/come/was revealed' (43.2). *Targ. Ezek.* catches the exact meaning of the idiomatic phrase את ידי נסתי ('I have raised my hand'), translating 'I have *sworn by my Word*' (36.7).[20] In 37.27 MT says, 'My dwelling place shall be with them', but *Targ. Ezek.* identifies the dwelling place with the divine presence. Another typical expression of Ezekiel (40.1 etc.) is 'the hand of the Lord was upon me', which is interpreted prophetically: '*The spirit of prophecy proceeding from* the Lord *rested* upon me'.[21]

18. The power and might of the Lord, his omnipotence (גבורא), play an important role in all the rabbinic literature. See E. Urbach, *The Sages: Their Concepts and Beliefs*, I (Jerusalem: Magnes Press, 1979), pp. 80-96; L. Smolar and M. Aberbach, *Studies in Targum Jonathan to the Prophets* (New York: Ktav, 1983), p. 98; R. Hayward, *The Targum of Jeremiah* (ArBib, 12; Edinburgh: T. & T. Clark, 1987), p. 67 n. 17.

19. שכינה is one of commonest divine attributes in the rabbinic literature; its principal function is related to the divine presence, the immanence of God in the world, especially in order to benefit his chosen people; see Urbach, *The Sages*, I, pp. 40-65.

20. מימרא, 'Word', normally with pronominal suffix 'my' (מימרי), is perhaps the best known targumic paraphrase for God, and it predominates over all other divine attributes in *Targ. Ezek.* The Lord, according to the doctrine of *Targ. Ezek.*, manifests himself to humanity through his Word, acting as creator, revealer, saviour and judge; see D. Muñoz, *Dios-Palabra: Memrá en los targumim del pentateuco* (Granada: Facultad de Teología, 1974), pp. 605-39; C.T.R. Hayward, *Divine Name and Presence: The Memra* (Ottowa: Allenheld Osmun, 1981); B. Chilton, *The Glory of Israel: The Theology and Provenience of the Isaiah Targum* (JSOTSup, 23; Sheffield: JSOT Press, 1982), pp. 56-69.

21. In this sentence we have a clear example of the words being interpreted by *Targ. Ezek.* according to the context. If in another context hand of God means his

In some passages, the statements of MT are objectively blasphemous; for instance 18.29 and 33.17: 'the way of the Lord is not just'; *Targ. Ezek.* needs to change the meaning: '*the good ways* of the Lord *have not been declared to us*'. Similarly, in 20.25 the Lord says, according to MT, 'I gave them statutes that were not good and ordinances by which they could not have life'; in this case *Targ. Ezek.* avoids the moral problem by changing the subject of the sentence: '*they [Israel] followed their stupid inclination and they obeyed religious decrees which were not proper and laws by which they could not survive*'. It is astonishing that God himself becomes the possession of Israel (44.28); therefore *Targ. Ezek.* suggests the modification of the object: '*the gifts that I give them, these are* their possession'.

We must accept that our concept of anthropopathism does not coincide with that of the targumist, who does not consider the passion of anger and wrath to be unworthy anthropopathism. In *Targ. Ezek.* appear expressions such as 'I am *sending my anger* against you' (5.8), which are not found in MT. However, *Targ. Ezek.* assumes that zeal is a human passion unworthy of God; in these cases zeal is replaced by anger (16.38) or vengeance (36.5).[22]

7. The Use of the Concrete instead of Abstract and Vice Versa

The generic term 'sword', frequently mentioned in MT, is transformed by *Targ. Ezek.* into a complete sentence: '*those who slay by* the sword' (5.2). The sentence 'full of bloody crimes' also receives a personal focus: 'full of *those who are guilty of death*' (7.23).[23] When God decides to do something (דברתי ועשיתי) *Targ. Ezek.* chooses a verb more suitable to circumstances: גזרית במימרי ואקיים ('I the Lord have *decreed it by my Memra* and *executed*' (17.24). We find generic information about 'a man with a written case at his side', which *Targ. Ezek.*

---

power, in relation to the divine action upon the prophet the divine hand means his Spirit.

22. The anti-anthropomorphic tendency of *Targ. Ezek.* when it speaks of divinity does not amount to an absolute rejection; besides, our concepts of anthropomorphism and anthropopathism are not identical with those of the targums; cf. M. Klein, *Anthropomorphisms and Anthropopathisms in the Targumim of the Pentateuch* (Jerusalem: Nakor Publishing, 1982) (in Hebrew); Ribera, *Traducción del Targum de Jeremías*, p. 43 n. 145.

23. S.H. Levey, *The Targum of Ezekiel* (ArBib, 13; Edinburgh: T. & T. Clark, 1987), translates differently: 'those who deserve to be executed' (p. 34).

specifies as 'a man with a scribe's *tablet* at his loins' (9.2). MT refers to the chambers of the singers while *Targ. Ezek.* indicates the chambers of the Levites (40.44). Of course the first month means Nisan for *Targ. Ezek.* (45.21) and 'the year of release' becomes 'the year of *the jubilee*' (46.17).

As regards heathen people, the word 'uncircumcised' is too specific for *Targ. Ezek.* which prefers the use of a generic one: 'sinners' (31.18). MT 30.25 relates that the King of Babylon extends his sword over the land of Egypt, but *Targ. Ezek.* interprets the story more broadly: '*he [the king] executes punishment*'. We find a similar generalization when MT deals with 'washing the burning offering' while *Targ. Ezek.* speaks of '*preparing* the burning offering' (40.38). Likewise, MT mentions the measure called אפה (45.10);[24] this measure is probably ignored by *Targ. Ezek.*, which translates simply, 'measure' (מכלתא).

8. *The Addition of some Qualifiers or Attributives*

The *Targum of the Prophets* systematically adds the qualifier 'prophetic' in the usual sentence דבר יהוה, 'the word of the Lord', in this way: פתג ם יי׳ נבואה מן קדם 'the prophetic message proceeding from the Lord' (2.7; 29.17). We also read 'prophetic vision' instead of 'vision'. When we find prophets whose messages are not in accordance with the divine will, *Targ. Ezek.* calls them explicitly 'false prophets' (13.2, 4, 6, 7).

The statement 'The glory of the Lord rested on the Mount which is at the east of the city (11.23), suggests to *Targ. Ezek.* that it deals with the Mount of Olives.[25] For *Targ. Ezek.* it is not enough that the righteous man should do justice (משפט); he must do true justice (דין דקשוט, 18.5).[26] As we have said *Targ. Ezek.* takes trouble to stress that the shedding of any blood is not necessarily a crime, but the shedding of innocent blood really is a sin (22.2, 3); likewise *Targ. Ezek.* expresses accu-

---

24. According to W.F. Albright, אפה־בת is a dry measure equivalent to 22 litres; see E. Sternberg, 'Weights and Measures', *EncJud*, XVI, col. 380.

25. According to the rabbinic tradition (*Lam. R. Pet.* 25), when the *shekinah* left the Temple, made a journey of ten stops, one of which was the Mount of Olives.

26. This expression is very frequent in the *Targ. Jon.*; see Ribera, *El Targum de Jeremías*, p. 84 n. 1. K. Koch, 'Die drei Gerechtigkeiten; die Umformung einer hebräischen Idee im aramäischen Denken nach Jesajatargum', in Y. Friedrich (ed.), *Rechtfertigung Festschrift für E. Käsemann* (Tübingen: J.C.B. Mohr [Siebeck], 1976), pp. 245-67, explains the right meaning of זכ׳, צדק, קשט in *Targ. Ezek.*

rately that not any behaviour is punishable but only evil ways and rotten deeds deserve divine punishment (פרענות, 24.14). Also, the Lord executes not only justice (משפט) but just punishment (דינין, דינין, 25.11).[27] It is significant that *Targ. Ezek.* adds the qualifying 'holy' to the word 'spirit' related to the observance of the law in *Targ. Ezek.* 36.27, and when the Holy Spirit is a sign of the divine presence (שכנא) in Israel 39.29; on the other hand, when the Spirit inspires the prophet it becomes 'prophetic spirit' (11.24).[28]

9. Completing Incomplete Sentences

In 7.12 MT says, 'the time has come, the day draws near', but *Targ. Ezek.* asks, 'what time, what day?' and answers, 'the time *for the repayment of debts*, the day *of punishments of sins*'.[29] MT gives this generic warning: 'Let him who will listen listen, let him who will refrain refrain', which needs a complement; therefore *Targ. Ezek.* translates, 'let him who will *heed heed the instruction*, let him who will refrain refrain *from sinning*' (3.27). The verb 'to remove', רחק, in the context 'remove yourself from the Lord' (11.15), is understood by *Targ. Ezek.* in the cultic and moral sense: 'remove yourself from *the fear of* the Lord' (דחלתא, worship coming from the fear); in contrast, the verb 'approach, come near' (נגש) in the sentence, 'they shall not approach to me' (44.13), is also interpreted in a cultic way: 'they shall not approach for my *worship* [פלחני]', the service to the Lord.[30] That this complement (פולחן) is not simply explained on account of the anti-anthropomorphic tendency

---

27. See Smolar-Aberbach, *Studies in Targum*, pp. 127-28 n. 124, where many targumic examples about the vindicative justice of God are found.

28. See H. Parezen, 'The ruaḥ ha-Kodesh in Tannaitic Literature', *JQR* 20 (1929–1930), pp. 51-76. P. Schäfer, *Die Vorstellung vom heiligen Geist in der rabbinischen Literatur* (SANT, 28; Munich: Kösel, 1972). Chilton, *The Glory of Israel*, pp. 48-52.

29. יום פרענותא is an allusion to the day of great judgment related to eschatologic times; see J. Ribera, 'La escatología en el targum Jonatán y su relación con el targum palestinense', *II Simposio bíblico español* (Córdoba: Publicaciones del Monte de Piedad, 1987), pp. 487-99.

30. The root פלח means 'to serve' and is used from the classical Aramaic to indicate also 'to serve a God'; *Targ. Ezek.* uses especially the word פולחן to refer to 'worship' and particularly to the Temple service; cf. M. Jastrow, *A Dictionary of the Targumim, The Talmud Babli and Yerushalmi* (2 vols.; London; Putnam, 1895–1903), p. 1141.

is proved by the fact that the same complement is added when dealing with idolatrous worship. For instance, we read in the allegory of the sisters, 'she [Oholah] defiled herself with all the idols', while *Targ. Ezek.* expresses the meaning of the text: 'she defiled herself with all of their idol *worship*' (23.7; 14.4). Likewise we find an incomplete sentence in MT 14.5: 'In order to take hold of the hearts of the house of Israel'; which is completed by *Targ. Ezek.* as follows: 'In order *to bring the House of Israel near, to offer repentance in their hearts*'; then, the moral proximity connotes repentance.[31] Similarly the typical verb שׁוב used frequently in the moral sense to convert (we read in MT 18.32: 'return and live') receives a cultural complement in *Targ. Ezek.*: 'return to my *worship* and you shall survive'. The Hebrew word זמה, whose semantic meaning is large ('plan, evil device, licentiousness'), is always paraphrased in *Targ. Ezek.* as חובי עצת חטא ('the guilty of the sinful counsel', 16.58; 23.27). 'If the man did observe [the law] he would live', states MT 20.13, but the question in the mind of the targumist is what kind of life: the present life or the future life. So he adds, 'in eternal life'.[32] In the oracles of indictment against Jerusalem (ch. 22) according to MT the Lord says (v. 3), 'A city that sheds blood in the midst of her, her time has come...' For *Targ. Ezek.* it refers to the time of her 'disgrace' (תברא). Against this background the Lord says to Oholah, 'you shall drink your sister's cup' (23.32); every time that the symbolic phrase 'to drink a cup' is quoted, *Targ. Ezek.* concludes the expression in this manner: to drink a cup of punishment [פרענות, 'vindicative justice']. Also, the sentence 'to descend to the pit' in the mind of *Targ. Ezek.* is related to hell ('to descend to the place of perdition').[33] We find another usual complement in *Targ. Ezek.* related to something near in

---

31. The religious meaning of 'remove' and 'approach' is found in other places in the biblical and rabbinic literature (*Targ. Isa.* 48.16; cf. 2.13). See Str-B, III, pp. 585-87.

32. In this context there is a clear connection between 'eternal life' and 'resurrection' as postmortem reward. See A. Rodríguez Carmona, *Targum y resurrección* (Granada: Facultad de Teología, 1978), pp. 26-44; G.W.E. Nickelsburg, 'Resurrection', *ABD*, V, pp. 687-88.

33. The syntagma בת אבדנא is a synonym of 'gehena' and is found in many places in *Targ. Jon.* (*Targ. Isa.* 14.15, 19; 38.18; Ezek. 26.30; 31.14, 16, 18, 25, 30; 32.18, 23, 29); see Ribera, *El Targum de Isaías*, p. 53 n. 107; Smolar-Aberbach, *Studies in Targum Jonathan*, pp. 184-87.

time in 30.3: 'For near is the day', which is interpreted 'for the time is just to come proceeding from the Lord', stressing its proximity.[34]

Targ. Ezek. elucidates the finality of an action, as in 35.11, 'I will make myself known among you' (following MT), and *Targ. Ezek.* renders: 'I will reveal myself *by being good to them*'. The commentary of *Targ. Ezek.* on the presence of the Lord in Israel is also of interest; MT reads, 'I am the Lord, the Holy one in Israel' (39.7) and *Targ. Ezek.* completes: 'I *have made my shekinah dwell* in Israel'. Warning priests to act as judges, MT says, 'and they shall judge it according to my judgments' (44.24); and *Targ. Ezek.* concludes: 'according to the judgments *of my will*'.

10. *Adaptations for Ideological Reasons*

One of the significant changes made by *Targ. Ezek.* is motivated by the necessity to emphasize monotheism. For this reason, *Targ. Ezek.* always reads 'as I exist' (קיים) when in the MT we find 'as I live' (חי, 5.11). We also find the mutation of the verb שמע 'to hear, listen' to קבל 'to receive, accept' when the object is the Memra or the prophetic messages (20.8). The use of the words אגורא when dealing with the pagan altar, and מדבחא associated with the altar of the Lord are typical of *Targ. Ezek.* (6.4).[35] Chapter 10 deals with the throne of the divine glory, and in v. 20, speaking of the creatures that the prophet saw 'below the God of Israel' (following MT), *Targ. Ezek.* alludes to the divine chariot translating 'below *the Glory of* the God of Israel'.[36] *Targ. Ezek.* reveals a clear knowledge of the synagogues in the following passage, for which MT has, 'Because I scattered them in the countries, yet have I been a small sanctuary for them in the countries where they have gone'(11.16); *Targ. Ezek.* transforms it in this manner: 'Because I scattered them in the countries, therefore I have *given them synagogues, second only to* my holy Temple, *because they are few in number* in the countries to

---

34. Regarding the semantic meaning of the expression למיתי עתיד see J. Ribera, 'Funciones modificadoras de *'atid* en arameo', *Aula Orientalis* 4 (1986), pp. 153-55.

35. See P. Churgin, *Targum Jonathan to the Prophets* (New Haven: Yale University Press, 1927), pp. 113.

36. Ribera, 'La ideología de la Mercabá', pp. 317-20.

which they *have been exiled*'.[37] Every time that we find in Ezekiel the
syntagma 'new heart, new spirit or heart of flesh', *Targ. Ezek.* interprets
as '*fearful* heart, *fearful* spirit', equivalent to worshipful (36.26).[38] On
account of the phrase 'the heart of stone' (36.26), *Targ. Ezek.* gives this
interpretation: '*I will demolish the wicked heart, which is hard as* stone'.
For *Targ. Ezek.* it is evident that שקוציהם and תועבתיהם are synonymous of טעותבון, that is, 'idols'. Therefore *Targ. Ezek.* places the word
פולחן before these words: 'after *the worship of* their detestable and
abominable things'(11.21). Often, the term 'vision' is changed by *Targ.
Ezek.* into 'prophecy or instruction' (13.16);[39] also, 'parable' becomes
'prophecy'; the verb 'to prophesy' is sometimes rendered by *Targ.
Ezek.* 'to teach' (13.6, 8). Ezek. 14.14 concerns the righteous Noah,
Daniel and Job who save their souls because of their 'justice', according to MT. But *Targ. Ezek.* prefers זכותהון ('because of their *merit*'), for
merit is more comprehensive than justice.[40] In 20.16 MT states, 'The
heart of Israel went after their idols', however *Targ. Ezek.* adds some
features: 'for their heart goes *astray* after their idol *worship*'.[41] All the
prophetic targumin translated the biblical expression 'to break the covenant' into a mitigated form 'to *change [violate]*, the covenant' (17.15).
As in all the targumin, the word 'sin' (חטה) is normally translated 'debt'
חוב; it is a debt related to the obligation of the observance of the divine
law which is broken by the sin.[42] It is significant that the word עול of
MT (18.24, 25, 'he commits iniquity') is modified by *Targ. Ezek.* with

---

37. This passage may throw some light on the origin of the synagogue. See
Levey, *The Targum of Ezekiel*, p. 41 n. 5.

38. On the fear of God in the *Targ. Jon.*, see Smolar-Aberbach, *Studies in Targum Jonathan*, pp. 156-59.

39. However *Targ. Ezek.* (1.2) keeps the word 'vision' when it refers to the
merkabian contemplation of the glory of the Lord.

40. The concept of זכות reflects a very developed doctrine about 'merit' from
the ancient Judaism. See A. Marmorstein, *The Doctrine of Merits in Old Rabbinical
Literature* (London: Oxford University Press, 1920; repr. New York: Ktav, 1968);
R. Le Déaut: 'Aspects de l'intercession dans le Judaïsme ancien', *JSJ* 1 (1970), pp.
42-45.

41. Note the Aramaic rhyme בתר טעותיהון לבהון טעי. See J.W. Wesselius, 'Bib-
lical Poetry through Targumic Eyes: Onkelos' Treatment of Genesis 49:8-12', in
E. Dyk (ed.), *Give Ear to my Words: Psalms and other Poetry in and around the
Hebrew Bible. Essays in honour of Prof. N.A. van Uchelen* (Amsterdam: Societas
Hebraica Amstelodamensis, 1996), pp. 131-45.

42. The same translation is found in the New Testament (Mt. 6.12; Lk. 11.4).

שקר ('he *deals falsely*'), because the lie, the falsehood, is for targumic ideology the origin of all iniquity. When the protagonist is the prophet, *Targ. Ezek.* understands that his mission is not to judge but to admonish the people (20.4).

Speaking of sacrifices, MT uses a metaphor (20.41), 'As pleasing odour I will accept you'; as usual *Targ. Ezek.* gives a realistic meaning to the phrase: '*Your sacrifice as an acceptable offering* shall be *readily accepted*'. Similarly, we read in MT 36.25, 'For I will sprinkle clean water upon you', but *Targ. Ezek.* expresses the moral effect of this ritual and renders: 'For *I will forgive your sins, as though you had been purified by the waters of sprinkling*'; it also mentions another ritual action which serves to forgive the sins, that is, '*by the ashes of the heifer sin-offering*'.[43] It is astonishing to realise that every time it deals with peaceful sacrifices (זבח שלמים) *Targ. Ezek.* uses an indeterminate formula: קודשהון נכסת ('their holy sacrifice', literally, 'the cultic slain of their holy things', 43.27).[44] *Targ. Ezek.* makes an interesting change in 45.22; where MT has, 'On that day the prince shall present for himself [בעדו] and for all the people a bull for sin offering', *Targ. Ezek.* changes בעדו into חלפו, that is, not for himself but as a substitute for himself and substituting for all the people, indicating that the victim represents the offering of the prince himself and all the people: a clearly vicarious offering.

11. *Summary and Conclusions*

The *derash* method used by *Targ. Ezek.* is not a device for offering an enigmatic, symbolic interpretation of the Hebrew text of the Bible, but it aims mainly to simply and clarify the meaning (פשט) of the Bible. Accordingly, the targumist seeks to offer a 'realistic' vision of the abundant allegories which are found in the book of Ezekiel. However, there is no common interpretation; the exegesis of each passage depends on the context. We also notice the ideological and moral tendencies highlighted by *Targ. Ezek.* through the hermeneutic resorts of the *derash* method.

43. It refers to Num. 19.17. This verse may display some relation to Christian baptism. See Levey, *Targum of Ezekiel*, p. 101 n. 14.
44. The use of this expression is found in all the targumim. See W.F. Smelik, *The Targum of Judges* (OTS, 36; Leiden: E.J. Brill, 1995), p. 354.

The principal topics which are the object of the application of this method are: the concept of God, his monotheism and spiritualization with the elimination of anthropomorphisms, divine justice expressed with the word פרענות and the allusions to Merkabah ideology. The image of Israel is assumed as community of Faith with the syntagma כנשת דישראל 'Congregation of Israel'; its land is identified with the land of the living. *Targ. Ezek.* transforms ch. 16 into an account about the fidelity of Yahweh and the infidelity of his people, based on the Sinai covenant; Israel shows her relationship with the Lord through fear and worship (פלחן, דחלא). Idolatry is the worst sin (חוב) committed by Israel, and *Targ. Ezek.* uses the root טעי in a double meaning (תרתי משמע), 'to go astray, idol worship', in order to emphasize it. The expression 'to drink the cup' becomes the symbol of the divine justice ('to drink the cup of punishment').

The mission of the prophet is to transmit the divine word that is the prophetic message (פתגם נבואה מן קדם ייי) and to teach the instruction (אלפן) of the Torah. His task is not to judge the people but to admonish them. The prophet is attributed the qualifier 'false' when his prophecies are at odds with divine will.

The sanctuary of God is identified with 'my hill' (34.26). The glory of the Lord covers the *sancta sanctorum*, the place of atonement according to *Targ. Ezek.* which understands the sanctuary as the throne of the glory. *Targ. Ezek.* stresses the holiness of the priests, avoiding any contact with the people. The mission of the priests is more the observance of the divine Word (מימרא) than the performance of sacrifices.

Targ. Ezek. reveals a clear inclination to give an eschatological focus to future events. Sentences like פרענות קיצא ('final retribution') and עדן תשלומת חובין ('the time of sins retribution') evoke final judgment. The targumic phrase, 'to descend to the pit of perdition', also evokes the place of Gehena.

To fulfil this aim, *Targ. Ezek.* makes use of the resources mentioned, and achieves an elementary and genuine exegesis of the biblical text following the ideological trends of primitive Judaism. *Targ. Ezek.* thus follows the trajectory of the scribes (סופרים), who in the last versions of the Bible added those changes and complements that they thought necessary for a clear understanding and updating of the text which was becoming a holy and canonical one.[45]

---

45. This is the opinion extensively explained by M. Fishbane in his book *Biblical Interpretation in Ancient Israel* (Oxford: Clarendon Press, 1985).

TARGUM OF THE SONG OF SONGS AND THE DYNAMICS
OF HISTORICAL ALLEGORY

Esther M. Menn

The *Targum of the Song of Songs*, an Aramaic paraphrase of the Song of Songs from between the fifth and eighth centuries CE,[1] is an exceptional instance of rabbinic interpretation in that it treats the entire biblical book with a sustained hermeneutical approach highlighting Israel's history with God. This essay explores the dynamics of historical allegory in the *Targum of the Song of Songs*, arguing that in the final analysis the *Targum*'s focus on the narratives of Israel's past and of its projected future[2] is not an end in itself. Rather, the recounting of history

1. See the discussions of date and provenance of the *Targum of the Song of Songs* in Raphael Loewe, 'Apologetic Motifs in the *Targum of the Song of Songs*', in Alexander Altmann (ed.), *Biblical Motifs: Origins and Transformations* (Cambridge, MA: Harvard University Press, 1966), pp. 163-69; E.Z. Melamed, 'Targum of Canticles', *Tarbiz* 40 (1971), pp. 201-15 (214-15) [Hebrew].

The critical edition used in this study is that of Raphael Hai Melamed ('The Targum to Canticles according to Six Yemen Mss. Compared with the "Textus Receptus" [ed. de Lagarde]', *JQR* 10 [1919–20], pp. 377-410; *JQR* 11 [1920–21], pp. 1-20; *JQR* 12 [1921–22], pp. 57-117). For an English translation of the work, see Hermann Gollancz, 'The Targum to "The Song of Songs"', in Bernard Grossfeld (ed.), *The Targum to the Five Megillot* (New York: Hermon Press, 1973), pp. 177-252.

2. History, for the purposes of this paper, is defined primarily as narratives about the past, although narratives about a projected future are also included, since the Targum views even the eschatological culmination of history from the perspective of prophetic hindsight. The discussion of history in the *Targum of the Song of Songs* in this essay remains on this narrative level, and does not treat the issue of what actually happened in the past or may happen in the future. Although narratives concerning the future are not ordinarily considered historical, due to the common understanding of history as stories about the past, the *Targum* assumes that Israel's *telos* is an intrinsic component of this people's history with God. Recent discussions of the significance of the narrative future may be found in Frank Kermode,

serves a number of vital purposes with canonical, practical and performative import for the *Targum*'s intended audience.

The *Targum*'s hermeneutical approach creatively combines translation of the Song of Songs from Hebrew to Aramaic, allegorical interpretation of its poetic imagery and assignment of narrative contexts for its dialogues of love.[3] Together these elements form a complex exposition centered upon Israel's narrative traditions from the exodus to the messianic age. Other rabbinic treatments of the Song of Songs, for example *Song of Songs Rabbah* and *Aggadat Shir ha-Shirim*, consist of eclectic anthologies of comments on different aspects of particular verses or even individual words. Within these anthologies, exegesis of verses of the Song of Songs in terms of historical events such as the exodus from Egypt and the giving of the Law at Sinai is certainly not lacking, and indeed the *Targum* draws heavily from these and other traditional repositories of material. Only in the *Targum*, however, are these traditions correlated, modified, and ordered so that Israel's historical narrative emerges as the overarching structure for understanding the entire book of the Song of Songs from beginning to end.[4] At the very outset, the *Targum*'s introduction of its interpretation with a list of ten songs sung during the history of the world from Adam to the eschatological victory[5] signals the chronological orientation of the work. In-

The Sense of an Ending: Studies in the Theory of Fiction (repr. London: Oxford University Press, 1979) and Paul Ricoeur, *Time and Narrative*, I (Chicago: University of Chicago Press, 1984).

3.   For discussions of this technique of assigning narrative contexts for direct speech in the targums, see A. Samely, *The Interpretation of Speech in the Pentateuch Targums* (Tübingen: J.C.B. Mohr [Paul Siebeck], 1992); R.P. Gordon, 'Dialogue and Disputation in the Targum to the Prophets', *JSS* 39 (1994), pp. 7-17.

4.   Although the majority of interpretive traditions found in the *Targum of the Song of Songs* have parallels elsewhere in rabbinic literature, the *Targum* creates an original work by modifying and conjoining this received material. See Phillip S. Alexander, 'Tradition and Originality in the Targum of the Song of Songs', in D.R.G. Beattie and M.J. McNamara (eds.), *The Aramaic Bible: Targums in their Historical Context* (JSOTSup, 166; Sheffield: JSOT Press, 1994), pp. 318-39. For examples of the *Targum*'s employment of midrashic traditions found also in the Babylonian Talmud, see E.Z. Melamed, 'Targum of Canticles', pp. 208-213.

5.   For the origins and history of development of the rabbinic tradition of the ten songs, see Judah Goldin, 'This Song', in S. Leiberman (ed.), *Salo Wittmayer Baron Jubilee Volume on the Occasion of his Eightieth Birthday*, I (Jerusalem: Central Press, 1974), pp. 539-54; James L. Kugel, 'Is There but One Song?', *Bib* 63 (1982), pp. 329-50.

ternally, the *Targum*'s relentless, if at times meandering, movement through Israelite history asserts that a series of key events provides the occasion for the intimate relationship between God and Israel described in the Song of Songs: the exodus from Egypt, the giving of the law at Sinai, and wilderness wanderings, and the conquest of the land;[6] the establishment of the Temple in Jerusalem;[7] the Babylonian exile, the restoration, and the period of Hasmonean rule;[8] the current dispersion under foreign rule and the vision of ultimate redemption.[9] The *Targum*'s remarkable consistency in executing its allegorical interpretation of the Song of Songs in terms of Israel's historical narratives establish this work at the head of a long trajectory of Jewish and Christian exegetical works that similarly understand the Song of Songs in terms of religious history. In the history of interpretation of the Song of Songs, the *Targum* represents the archetype of historical allegory.[10]

At least in part, the *Targum*'s insistence that the erotic lyrics found in the Song of Songs point to a deeper reality involving Israel's history serves to resolve a crisis of textual meaning. The Song of Songs is a decidedly secular work, lacking references to the name of God or to the basic themes of sacred history such as the Torah and the covenant with Israel, and its inclusion within an emerging corpus of traditional, religious literature that eventually formed the biblical canon therefore creates a dissonance. In the *Targum*, the resolution of this dissonance includes identifying elements of the Song of Songs as metaphors, in order to create an exegetical correspondence between the received text and a system of religious meaning extrinsic to it, centred around Israel's history with God. This type of exegetical linkage of two distinct discourses is of course not distinctive to the *Targum*, but is rather a common characteristic of all allegorical interpretation motivated by cultural shifts of one sort or the other, which render traditional texts offensive, incomprehensible, or simply irrelevant. Another well-known example of this phenomenon, the allegorical interpretation of traditional Greek myths

---

6. *Targ. Song* 1.4–3.6.
7. *Targ. Song* 3.7–5.1.
8. *Targ. Song* 5.2–7.11.
9. *Targ. Song* 7.12–8.14.
10. See Phillip S. Alexander, 'The Song of Songs as Historical Allegory: Notes on the Development of an Exegetical Tradition', in Kevin J. Cathcart and Michael Maher (eds.), *Targumic and Cognate Studies in Honour of Martin McNamara* (JSOTSup, 230; Sheffield: Sheffield Academic Press, 1996).

and legends in terms of philosophical concepts, similarly arose at least in part as a response to the perception that the ancient narratives of the culture were problematic, in that they were violent, immoral and seemingly lacking in pedagogical value. The *Targum of the Song of Songs* therefore exemplifies the common quest of all allegorical interpretation: to articulate authoritative and culturally relevant meanings for classic texts which are understood to 'say one thing and mean another'.[11]

Although the *Targum of the Song of Songs* exhibits basic similarities in method and purpose with other examples of allegorical interpretation, including its earlier classical flowering, it is nevertheless exceptional in one important aspect. The *Targum* moves not from the particular details of myth or history-like legend to more universal philosophical truths as one finds in classical allegorical interpretation, but in the opposite direction, from the common, near-universal experience of human love to the particulars of Israel's unique history with God. For example, when one thinks of allegory in the classical world, the moral interpretations common in Cynic and Stoic circles spring to mind including those which present Heracles' labours and other physical feats as spiritual struggles and victories against vices. Herodorus of Heraklea, for one, explains that the three golden apples that Heracles obtained after killing the dragon with his club represent the three virtues the hero gained through philosophy, specifically the virtues of not getting angry, not loving money and not being fond of pleasure.[12] In this instance, some very particular apples, numbered three and described as golden, which are procured by a well-known figure of legend after defeating a certain dragon with the weapon characteristically associated with him, become transformed into a set of universal virtues available to everyone through the cultivation of wisdom.

In contrast to this allegorical movement from particular to universal, consider a very different treatment of fruit in the *Targum of the Song of Songs*:

11. For discussions of the cultural and rhetorical dynamics of allegorical interpretation, see Deborah L. Madsen, *Rereading Allegory: A Narrative Approach to Genre* (New York: St. Martin's Press, 1994); Jon Whitman, *Allegory: The Dynamics of an Ancient and Medieval Technique* (Cambridge, MA: Harvard University Press, 1987).

12. Herodorus of Heraklea frg. 31F14, cited in Karl G. Galinsky, *The Herakles Theme: The Adaptations of the Hero in Literature from Homer to the Twentieth Century* (Oxford: Basil Blackwell, 1972), p. 56.

'The fig tree spices its green figs, and the vines in blossom exude their fragrance. Arise! Come, my love, my beautiful one, come away!' [*Song* 2.13]. The assembly of Israel, which is compared to the first-fruits of fig trees, opened her mouth and uttered the song at the Reed Sea. Even the children and infants praised the Lord of the Universe with their tongues. Then the Lord of the Universe said to them, 'Arise! Come, assembly of Israel, my beloved, my beautiful one, go out from here to the land which I have promised your ancestors.'[13]

In the biblical verse from the Song of Songs, an unidentified male speaker evokes an idealized, fragrant setting for love by describing the early blossoming of figs and grapes, and then urges his anonymous beloved to join him. The *Targum*, for its part, eliminates the indeterminate, universal appeal of the imagery of desire in this verse by identifying the fruits and the lover as specific characters, and by describing the significance of the imagery of tender spring growth and of the words spoken by the lover within a particular narrative context. The figs become Israel, the vines its children, and their scented greening becomes their praise of the Lord of the Universe in response to his parting of the Sea. Reacting to their praise, the lover, identified as God, summons Israel to continue to the land promised earlier to their ancestors.[14]

These contrasting examples illustrate the very different valuation of universal, generally applicable principles versus particular, historical realities in classical allegorical interpretation and in the *Targum*. The emphasis on history as the fundamental and essential truth lying behind other appearances distinguishes the allegorical interpretation of the *Targum* from many other instances of allegorical interpretation, including the Hellenistic allegorical interpretations of the Torah by earlier Jewish exegetes such as Philo, who understands the biblical stories as 'modes of making ideas visible'.[15]

---

13. *Targ. Song* 2.13; Melamed, 'Targum to Canticles', p. 73.

14. For another interpretation of a garden of fruits in terms of Israel's history, see *Targ. Song* 4.16, which transforms an ideal site for a tryst between anonymous lovers into the Temple which Solomon constructed in Jerusalem as a dwelling place for the divinity among his people Israel.

15. Similarly, an even earlier Jewish writer, Aristobulus (late second century BCE), used allegorical theory to reconcile Greek philosophy with the Torah. He explains that 'Moses, using the figures of visible things, tells us the arrangements of nature and the constitutions of important matters'. For these Hellenistic-Jewish authors, the true referent of the historical narratives in the Torah is universally appli-

The ascendancy of historical narrative in the *Targum*'s allegorical interpretation of the Song of Songs appears to correspond with the common assertion that from ancient times Israel was uniquely concerned with the linear and unrepeatable dimensions of historical reality.[16] Although there may well be some truth in this assertion, closer inspection of the shape and details of Israel's history in the *Targum* suggests that other important issues are at stake as well. Especially revealing is the extremely schematic nature of the *Targum*'s presentation of Israel's history, which lacks sustained attention to a number of important biblical periods, including those of the patriarchs,[17] the judges,[18] the establishment of the monarchy with the reigns of Saul and David,[19] or much of

cable philosophical ideas, whereas for the targumist the true referent of the lyric love poetry in the Song of Songs is Israel's history.

Another instructive contrast may be made between the *Targum* and Origen's interpretation of the Song of Songs, which is the earliest extant Christian interpretation of the work. Although Origen's treatment of the Song of Songs is also allegorical, he considers the biblical book not as centrally concerned with religious history, but rather with a spiritual meaning expressed through the secret metaphors of love. For Origen, this spiritual meaning involves the desire of both the individual soul and the wider church for unity with God's Word. For the relation between Origen's commentary on the Song of Songs and that of rabbis, see Ephraim E. Urbach, 'The Homiletical Interpretations of the Sages and the Expositions of Origen on Canticles and the Jewish–Christian Disputation', in Joseph Heinemann and Dov Noy (eds.), *Studies in Aggadah and Folk-Literature* (Jerusalem: Magnes Press, 1971).

16. See Mircea Eliade, *Cosmos and History: The Myth of the Eternal Return* (New York: Harper and Row, 1959), pp. 95-162.

17. The figures of Abraham, Isaac and Jacob appear frequently throughout the *Targum* (*Targ. Song* 1.9, 13; 2.8, 10, 12, 15, 17; 3.5, 6, 8; 5.14; 6.5, 6, 12; 7.6, 9, 10), primarily as sources of merit and examples of piety, but their narratives are not included in the chronological presentation of Israel's history.

18. While two songs from the period of the Judges (the song of Deborah and Barak and the song of Hannah) are included in the list of ten songs at the beginning of the Targum (*Targ. Song* 1.1), there is no mention of this period in the body of the work.

19. Although the period of Davidic reign is not included in the chronological presentation of Israel's history, his name is mentioned in passing several times in the *Targum*, as the author of a famous song of praise (*Targ. Song* 1.1), as the founder of the Davidic dynasty (*Targ. Song* 8.11), as the co-builder of the Temple with Solomon (*Targ. Song* 1.8), as a moral exemplar whose excellence is matched by more contemporary leaders including the Head of the College (*Targ. Song* 4.4; cf. 7.5), and as the ancestor of the Messiah (*Targ. Song* 4.5).

the history of the monarchy after Solomon until the Babylonian exile.[20] The events that the *Targum* does include form a selective historical epitome, structured not only through the basic linear progression of chronology described in the second paragraph of this essay, but also through the repetition of a number of cycles of sin, repentence and restoration,[21] and through the prominent placement of descriptions of ideal, theocratic periods characterized by God's presence among Israel in the Jerusalem Temple.[22] The *Targum*'s elliptical treatment of Israel's past and projected future may be explained at least in part by the fact that its primary purpose is not to present of a comprehensive account of history through its paraphrastic translation of the Song of Songs. Rather than history for its own sake, the truncated and stylized version of Israel's religious narrative that emerges through the *Targum*'s treatment of the Song of Songs becomes the vehicle through which several other important purposes are accomplished. At least three such purposes may be identified, including the canonical purpose to connect the anomalous book of the Song of Songs with the rest of the corpus of sacred Scripture, the practical purpose to outline a way of life capable of sustaining Israel in what the *Targum* describes as its current exile among the foreign governments of Edom and Ishmael, and the performative purpose to include the reader of the *Targum* in the history of Israel's praise. Each of these different purposes will be described in turn, in order to demonstrate the broad accomplishments of the *Targum*'s suggestive historical allegory.

20. In the main body of the *Targum*, the narrative passes immediately from the idealized period of Solomon's rule to the Babylonian exile, although the division of Israel into the Northern and Southern Kingdoms is briefly described in a digression towards the very end of the *Targum* (*Targ. Song* 8.11-12).

21. The three basic repetitions of this cycle move from the sin of the golden calf at Sinai to the construction of the Tabernacle (*Targ. Song* 1.5–3.4, which contains a threefold repetition of this movement), from the sins leading to the Babylonian exile to the rebuilding of the Temple (*Targ. Song* 5.2–6.3), and from sins leading to the current exile under Esau and Ishmael to the messianic age (*Targ. Song* 7.12–8.14).

22. God's presence in the Jerusalem Temple during the reigns of Solomon (*Targ. Song* 3.7–5.1) and the Hasmonean rulers (*Targ. Song* 6.3–7.6) is especially emphasized, although the Tabernacle from the wilderness period (*Targ. Song* 1.14-16; 3.4) and the messianic Temple to be completed at the culmination of Israel's history (*Targ. Song* 1.8, 17; 8.2, 14) also receive positive, if less extensive, attention.

Perhaps most obviously, the *Targum*'s interpretation of the Song of Songs in terms of Israel's history works to forge links between the Song of Songs and the rest of the biblical canon, particularly the narrative portions of the Torah and the Prophets which emphasize the story of Israel's covenantal relationship with God. The *Targum*'s reading of the biblical book therefore plays a canonical function, in that it draws the Song of Songs into the overarching narrative structure of the Hebrew Bible.[23] Instead of a peripheral book celebrating human love, the Song of Songs becomes an elaboration on the emotional, affective side of some of the core events of Israel's history with God, described in more detail elsewhere in Scripture.

While at times the connections between the *Targum of the Song of Songs* and the other canonical books are left vague and suggestive, at other times they are quite concrete and specific. The *Targum* frequently cites Aramaic translations or paraphrases of scriptural verses from the Torah and the Prophets when it identifies historical settings for particular verses from the Song of Songs.[24] The *Targum*'s treatment of Song 1.9 in terms of the exodus from Egypt amply illustrates this phenomenon:

> 'To a *mare* amongst the chariots of Pharaoh, have I compared you, my love' [Song 1.9]. When Israel went out from Egypt, Pharaoh and his host pursued after them with chariots and horsemen, and the way was barred to them on their four sides... What did the Holy One, blessed be he, do? He revealed himself in the power of his might by the Sea and dried up the water, but the mud he did not dry up. The wicked and the mixed multitude of foreigners who were among them said, 'He is able to dry up the water, but the mud he is not able to dry up!' At that time the anger of the LORD grew strong against them, and he intended to drown them in the waters of the Sea, just as Pharaoh and his *mares*, chariots, and horsemen were drowned, had it not been for Moses the prophet who spread out his hands in prayer before the LORD and turned back the anger of the LORD from them. He and the righteous of that generation opened their mouths, uttered the song, and passed through the midst of the Sea on dry land, on account of the merit of Abraham, Issac and Jacob, the beloved of the LORD.[25]

---

23. The *Targum* also extends the narrative structure found in the Hebrew Bible somewhat further, in that it includes an idealized treatment of the Hasmonean period.

24. For descriptions of the *Targum*'s employment of scriptural passages from outside of the Song of Songs, see Alexander, 'Tradition and Originality', pp. 321-30, and Melamed, 'Targum of Canticles', pp. 201-208.

25. *Targ. Song* 1.9. Melamed, 'Targum to Canticles', p. 63.

The comparison between the mare amongst the chariots of Pharaoh and the beloved in Song 1.9 apparently motivates the *Targum*'s interpretation of this verse in terms of Israel's encounter with Pharaoh and his cavalry during the exodus from Egypt. According to the *Targum*, however, the equestrian comparison offered by the Song of Songs is far from complimentary, since it describes the wicked and the mixed multitude of foreigners accompanying Israel from Egypt, whom God almost drowns because of their scornful comments concerning the miracle performed on their behalf, just as he later drowns Pharaoh and his mares, chariots, and horsemen. To advance this interpretation, the *Targum* first sets the scene by summarizing narrative elements from Exod. 14.8-9:

> The LORD hardened the heart of Pharaoh, king of Egypt, and he pursued after the Israelites, for the Israelites were going out with a high hand. And Egypt pursued after them and overtook them camping by the Sea, all the horses and chariots of Pharaoh, and his horsemen and his host, by Pi-hahiroth, in front of Baal-zephon.

The composite narrative that follows the initial setting of the scene at the Sea contains additional biblical allusions that are too numerous to discuss in this context.[26] One allusive sentence in particular, however, stands out not only because of what it derives from the biblical account, but also because of what it adds to that account. The central contention that God would have drowned the scoffers accompanying Israel as he did the Egyptians draws upon the language of Exod. 14.27b-28a: 'The LORD threw the Egyptians into the midst of the Sea, and the waters returned and covered the chariots and the horsemen, the entire army of Pharaoh that had come after them into the Sea.' To incorporate the motif of the drowning of Pharaoh's chariotry from the Exodus narrative into the comparison with the mare from Pharaoh's chariotry in Song 1.9, however, the *Targum* introduces a reference to the Egyptian king's mares alongside the chariots and horsemen when it paraphrases Exod. 14.28a: 'He intended to drown them in the waters of the Sea, just as

---

26. For the barring of the Israelites' way, see Exod. 14.3; for the mixed multitude, see Exod. 12.38 and Num. 11.4; for the drying of the water, see Exod. 14.21; for Moses' prayer, see Exod. 9.33; for the turning back of God's wrath, see Exod. 32.12; for the singing of the song at the Sea, see Exod. 15.1; and for the crossing of the Sea on dry land, see Exod. 14.22, 29; 15.19; Num. 33.8.

For a more complete discussion of the biblical quotations in this passage, as well as of their relation to various targums of the Torah, see Alexander, 'Tradition and Originality', pp. 326-27.

Pharaoh and his *mares*, chariots and horsemen were drowned.'[27] By inserting the detail of Pharaoh's mares from Song 1.9 into its paraphrase of Exod. 14.27-28a, the *Targum* merges the verses from the Song of Songs and the Pentateuchal narrative into a single, meaningful unit.

The canonical connections forged in this manner by the *Targum* are further strengthened by its own presentation of itself, not as an allegorical interpretation of an earlier work as described at the beginning of this essay, but as an allegorical composition that from its very inception envisioned Israel's history with God through metaphorical imagery.[28] While the *Targum*'s implicit claim to be simply drawing out the deeper significance inherent in a received work may not appear particularly remarkable in the history of allegorical interpretation, the effects of this claim on the perceived relation between the Song of Songs and the rest of the biblical canon are nevertheless distinctive and worthy of analysis. The *Targum* asserts that the genre of the Songs of Songs is not secular love poetry, subjected late in its literary history to a revision of meaning, but rather a type of inspired and holy writing from its very origins. The understanding of Solomon's prophetic authorship of the Song of Songs is introduced in the opening line of the *Targum*, which explains

27. Both Song 1.9 and Exod. 14.28 contain explicit references to 'Pharaoh' (פרעה) and his 'chariotry' (ברבבי, Song 1.9; תדכב, Exod. 14.28), and this common vocabulary facilitates an intertextual reading of these two verses. Since Exod. 14.28 also refers to Pharaoh's 'horsemen' (חפרשׁים), there must have been horses present at the battle, even though they are not explicitly mentioned. The *Targum* fills in this gap with information from Song 1.9, which suggests that there were mares in Pharaoh's chariotry, since the speaker makes a comparison 'to a mare (לסמתי)' in Pharaoh's chariotry'. The appearance of the Aramaic plural 'mares' (וסוסוותיה) in the *Targum*'s paraphrase of Exod. 14.28 may actually reflect a plural reading of the Hebrew word in Song 1.9, which contains an archaic singular feminine ending that resembles a plural feminine ending. Incidentally, the comparison between the mares and the wicked rabble accompanying the Israelites appears to be based on an interpretation of the Hebrew word רעיתי not as 'my love' (Hebrew root רעה), but as 'wicked ones' (Hebrew root רעע).

28. The *Targum*'s understanding of the figurative poetry of the Song of Songs corresponds with a second important definition of allegory in the history of literature, one that coexists with the type described earlier, namely the allegorical composition which is written in metaphorical language for the very purpose of expressing a certain idea or reality through the oblique means of symbolic imagery. For a discussion of allegory that takes into account both allegorical interpretation and allegorical compositional technique, as well as the relation between them, see Whitman, *Allegory*.

the biblical superscription, 'The Song of Songs which is Solomon's', with the expansive paraphrase, 'The songs and praises which Solomon, King of Israel, spoke through the holy spirit (קודשא ברוח) before the LORD, Sovereign of the Universe'.[29] Solomon's appearance as a visionary commentator on Israel's history later in the *Targum* confirms the intentional nature of this conceit.[30]

Certainly the status of the Song of Songs as part of a canon of inspired, sacred Scripture is one important issue underlying the emergence of Solomon's prophetic composition of the work.[31] In addition to this concern, however, the assimilation of the Song of Songs to the prophetic genre makes more plausible the *Targum*'s fundamental claim that the Song of Songs deals with the subject of Israel's history, with memories of the past and visions of the future. The prophetic writings of the Bible are essentially historical in their orientation, in that they postulate a correlation between Israel's faithfulness to their covenantal relationship with God and the cycles of national devastation and restoration experienced as divine anger and favor. If this theme is not immediately apparent in the Hebrew poetry of the Song of Songs itself, the

29. Some manuscripts refer to the author of the composition as 'the Prophet (נבי[י]א) Solomon, King of Israel', thereby strengthening the claim concerning the prophetic nature of the work. See Melamed, 'Targum to Canticles', p. 57, critical apparatus.

30. Solomon appears as a prophetic commentator on various periods of Israel's history from the exodus to the messianic age in *Targ. Song* 1.2, 17; 2.8; 7.2, 7; 8.5, 12, 13. In each of these cases, with the exception of *Targ. Song* 8.12, the *Targum* introduces Solomon into its paraphrase of the Song of Songs even though his name does not appear in the biblical verse under discussion. Solomon appears elsewhere in the *Targum* primarily as the builder of the Temple in Jerusalem (*Targ. Song* 1.8; 3.7, 9, 11; 4.1; 6.4), although once he appears as an exemplary judge (*Targ. Song* 7.5). In general the *Targum* understands the numerous references to Solomon in the Song of Songs literally, as references to the historical king. (Exceptions to this rule appear only in *Targ. Song* 1.5 and the first part of 8.11.) By contrast, in other rabbinic sources, the references to Solomon are generally interpreted allegorically as references to the divinity. See Loewe, 'Apologetic Motifs', pp. 162-63.

31. The alignment of Solomonic authorship with the model of prophetic inspiration follows a trend already evident in the Bible itself, in which various literary genres are assimilated the category of prophecy in order to assert their revelatory status. Most striking, of course, is the presentation of Moses, a figure fundamentally associated with the genre of law, as Israel's greatest prophet (Deut. 34.10-12). See Joseph Blenkinsopp, *Prophecy and Canon: A Contribution to the Study of Jewish Origens* (Notre Dame: University of Notre Dame Press, 1977).

targumist might argue that this is due to the highly symbolic style that characterizes the prophetic genre. The Song of Songs is indeed an effusively figurative work, replete with luxurious metaphors, striking similes and eclectic images drawn from a variety of spheres of life that require the reader to identify a referent described through indirection,[32] and in this way the Song of Songs does resemble the writings attributed to Israel's prophets.

It may even be that the central preoccupation of the Song of Songs, the love relationship between a man and a woman, provided some impetus for the metamorphosis from love poetry to prophecy effected by the *Targum*, since it recalls the prophetic employment of marital imagery to describe the relationship between God and Israel (for example, in Hos. 1–3; Jer. 2.3; 3.1; Ezek. 16; 23; Isa. 50.1-2; 62.4-5).[33] One should be cautious about this hypothesis, however, since closer examination of the *Targum*'s interpretation of the Songs of Songs shows that the potential for developing the symbolism of God as the male lover and Israel as the female lover is not consistently developed in the *Targum* even when there are natural openings, and indeed at times this symbolism is explicitly negated.[34]

32. For a discussion of the figurative language of the Song of Songs, see Robert Alter, 'The Garden of Metaphor: The Song of Songs', in Harold Bloom (ed.), *The Bible: Modern Critical Views* (New York: Chelsea House Publishers, 1987), pp. 177-94.

33. For a discussion of the development of the prophetic marital imagery describing the relationship between God and Israel in the *Targum of the Song of Songs*, see Gerson D. Cohen, 'The Song of Songs and the Jewish Religious Mentality', in idem, *Studies in the Variety of Rabbinic Cultures* (Philadelphia: Jewish Publication Society of America, 1991), pp. 3-17.

34. For example, the kiss in the opening line of poetry in Song 1.2 becomes in the *Targum* a friend's kiss, not a lover's: 'As a man kisses his fellow out of the abundance of his affection, loving us more than the seventy nations'. Similarly, interpreting a passage that speaks of erotic love in terms of a man's enjoyment of his garden ('My beloved has gone down into his garden, to the beds of spices to feed in the gardens and to gather roses', Song 6.2), the *Targum* describes Israel as God's son: 'And in a like manner as a man feeds his beloved son with delicacies, thus did he indulge them, and as a man who gathers roses on the plain, so did he gather them from Babylon'. It is indeed striking how the *Targum* preserves and builds upon the emotive intensity of the Song of Songs in its description of Israel and God's relationship in history while subverting the central theme of the relationship between a man and a woman by substituting other types of love relationships, or by otherwise

In any case, the presentation of the Song of Songs as Solomon's prophetic songs and praises argues that there is no radical divorce between
the poetry's original meaning and the *Targum*'s articulation of its significance through the recounting of Israel's history. Far from acknowledging that it is presenting an allegorical interpretation in order to
negotiate a fundamental disjunction between the primary text and its
cultural significance, the *Targum* claims that it is only spelling out more
explicitly the original meaning of the inspired author—a meaning
which is fundamentally historical in its orientation and therefore entirely in keeping with the central concerns of many of the other canonical writings.

In addition to this canonical purpose of consolidating Israel's traditional texts into a cohesive whole, the *Targum*'s retelling of Israel's
history also accomplishes the practical purpose of describing a way of
life capable of sustaining the Jewish people as they live under the authority of oppressive foreign governments. The selected historical narratives forwarded by the *Targum* become the contexts within which to
extol the normative practices, institutions and leadership structures central to rabbinic Judaism. This concern for the current situation of the
Targum's reader is nowhere more apparent than in the direct request of
the great prophet Moses that God provide information about how the
Jewish people may survive their future captivity:

> 'Tell me, you whom my soul loves, where will you pasture [your flock],
> where will you make [your sheep] rest at noon? For why should I be as
> one who is veiled beside the flocks of your companions?' [Song 1.7].
> When the time arrived for Moses, the prophet, to depart from the world,
> he said before the LORD: 'It is revealed to me that this people will sin
> and be carried into exile. Now tell me, how they will sustain themselves,
> and how they will live among the nations, whose decrees are as
> oppressive as the heat, the blazing heat of the noon sun in the summer
> solstice? For why should they wander among the flocks of the children
> of Esau and Ishmael, who associate their idolatry with your service?'[35]

The woman's question about her beloved's shepherding patterns in the
Song of Songs provides the basis for Moses' question about Israel's
survival among the nations. Strikingly, the *Targum* skips over earlier
instances of biblical oppression, such as the Babylonian exile, to focus

---

deflecting attention from the imagery of sexual love. I treat this subject in further
detail in another essay, intended for future publication.

35. *Targ. Song* 1.7. Melamed, 'Targum to Canticles', pp. 61-62.

on Israel's situation under Roman and perhaps Muslim rule (commonly represented by the figures of Esau and Ishmael).[36] The answer to the prophet's question comes in the interpretation of the next verse:

> 'If you do not know, most beautiful of women, go forth in the footsteps of the flock, and feed your kids beside the shepherds' tent' [Song 1.8]. The Holy One, blessed be he, said to Moses, the prophet: 'If you wish to see my soul have compassion on the assembly of Israel, compared to a beautiful girl, then let her walk in the ways of the righteous, let her arrange her prayers by the mouth of the pastors and leaders of the generation, and let her instruct her children, compared to the kids of the goat, to go to the House of Assembly and the House of Learning. Then, by that merit, they will be sustained in the exile, until the time that I send them the King Messiah, who will lead them gently to their dwelling place, the Temple, which David and Solomon, the shepherds of Israel, will build for them'.[37]

In place of the cryptic answer given by the man to his admirer in the Song of Songs, God delivers a very clear message to his prophet Moses, stipulating that righteous behavior, prayers offered by the community's leaders, and the younger generation's attendance at the House of Assembly and the House of Learning will sustain Israel until the restoration of the Temple in the messianic age. The meritorious actions specified in this passage, namely righteous behavior,[38] prayer[39] and attendance at the House of Assembly[40] and the House of Learning,[41] are promoted elsewhere in the *Targum*, as are other pillars of rabbinic Judaism, in-

---

36. *Targ. Song* 1.7. Edom is commonly identified as Rome and Ishmael as Muslim rule, although there is some dispute among scholars whether in the *Targum* Ishmael refers to the Arabic peoples before or after the spread of Islam. The most convincing evidence for the understanding of Ishmael as Muslim rule in the final recension of the work appears in the description of Israel's willingness to pay silver in order to affirm the unity of the divine name in *Targ. Song* 8.9, which apparently refers to the poll tax (*jizra*) in effect after the spread of Islam. See Loewe, 'Apologetic Motifs', pp. 165-67.

37. *Targ. Song* 1.8. Melamed, 'Targum to Canticles', p. 62.

38. *Targ. Song* 1.3, 6, 8, 10, 15; 2.1, 14; 3.5; 4.1, 3, 4, 7; 5.11, 15; 6.7, 9, 10, 11; 7.11; 8.2, 10.

39. *Targ. Song* 1.8, 13, 14; 2.8, 14, 16; 3.3, 6; 4.3; 5.2, 6; 6.1, 2; 7.7, 12, 13; 8.14.

40. *Targ. Song* 7.13.

41. *Targ. Song* 2.4, 5; 3.4; 7.13; 8.13.

cluding study[42] and teaching[43] of the Torah, and the rendering of righteous judicial decisions.[44] The Head of the College[45] and the Sanhedrin[46] are also idealistically portrayed in the *Targum*, indicating that these institutions retained a symbolic importance in discussions of leadership even after their demise prior to the work's final editing.

The advocacy of rabbinic values within discussions of Israel's history emerges most prominently in passages dealing with the idealized periods centered on the establishment of the Tabernacle, the First and Second Temples, and the messianic Temple of the future. The Temple as a symbol of God's indwelling with Israel is one of the central biblical motifs emphasized in the *Targum*, in keeping with the work's attribution to Solomon, the builder of the First Temple in Jerusalem. Although there would have been no standing Temple in Jerusalem at the time of the *Targum*'s composition, the concept of the Temple nevertheless embodies God's presence among Israel and comes to encompass those aspects of rabbinic life that foster a close relationship between the divinity and the people.[47]

One example of this phenomenon of featuring contemporary practices within descriptions of historical events involving the Temple appears in the *Targum*'s commentary on a biblical verse expressing a lover's amorous praise for the object of his desire:

> Behold, you are beautiful, my love! Behold, you are beautiful! Your eyes are doves behind your veil. Your hair is like a flock of goats that appear from Mount Gilead (Song 4.1).

The *Targum* understands these words as the divine voice's address to Israel following Solomon's offering of sacrifices at the dedication of the Temple in Jerusalem:

---

42. *Targ. Song* 1.10; 2.4, 5, 6; 3.4-5; 4.9, 15; 5.10, 12, 13; 6.11-12; 7.2, 3, 13, 14; 8.1.

43. *Targ. Song* 2.4, 5, 6; 4.1, 4; 5.15; 6.5; 7.14; 8.1, 2, 9, 13.

44. *Targ. Song* 5.12; 7.3, 5; 8.13.

45. *Targ. Song* 4.4; 7.3; 8.13.

46. *Targ. Song* 5.12; 7.5; 8.13.

47. As an aside, Rabbi Aqiba's statement that 'All the Writings are holy, but the Song of Songs is the Holy of Holies' (*m. Yad.* 3.5) resonates suggestively with the Targum's emphasis on the Temple in its various forms as a central locus of God's presence with Israel through history.

> On that day Solomon sacrificed upon the altar a thousand burnt offer-
> ings, and his offering was accepted with favor by the LORD. Then the
> divine voice issued from heaven and said, 'How beautiful is the assem-
> bly of Israel, and how beautiful are those leaders and those wise men of
> Israel in the Sanhedrin, who enlighten the house of Israel, resembling
> young pigeons. Even the rest of the assembly of Israel, the people of the
> land, are as righteous as the sons of Jacob, who gathered stones and
> made a heap in the mountain of Gilead'.[48]

Placed in the narrative context of Solomon's sacrifice at the dedication
of the Temple, one might expect the verse from the Song of Songs to be
transformed from a male lover's praise of his sweetheart's charms to
the divine voice's praise of the Temple's beauty or of the bounty of
Solomon's sacrifice. There is a surprising diversion, however, when the
divine voice praises neither the Temple nor the sacrifices, but instead
Israel's wise leaders, who constantly teach the people, and indeed all
the people themselves, who are as righteous as their forefather Jacob.
The emphasis in this passage is clearly not the dedication of Solomon's
Temple, even though this is the event recalled in the narrative recasting
of the verse from the Song of Songs, but rather the people and their
leadership, who survive the destruction of the Temple to learn and to
teach, and to live righteous and praiseworthy lives.

A second example of this type of interpretation in terms of contemporary religious practice appears in connection with the verse, 'A
garden fountain, a well of living waters, and flowing streams from
Lebanon' (Song 4.15), which in the Song of Songs describes a woman's
life-giving potential. The *Targum* treats this verse in the context of a
continuing description of the Temple built in Solomon's time:

> The waters of Siloah proceed gently with the rest of the waters that flow
> from Lebanon to water the land of Israel, on account of those who occupy
> themselves with the words of the Torah, compared to a well of living
> waters, and by virtue of the oblation of water poured out upon the altar in
> the Temple built in Jerusalem, which is called Lebanon.[49]

This passage identifies the garden fountain of the Song of Songs as the
fructifying waters that, in keeping with an ancient Zion tradition,
stream from the Temple in Jerusalem[50] (here and elsewhere in rabbinic

---

48. *Targ. Song* 4.1. Melamed, 'Targum to Canticles', p. 83.

49. *Targ. Song* 4.15. Melamed, 'Targum to Canticles', p. 59.

50. Ezek. 47.1-2; Joel 4.18; Zech. 14.8; Ps. 46.5; Rev. 22.1-2. These biblical

literature equated with Lebanon). The *Targum*'s discussion of the mythical river issuing from the foundation of the Temple identifies two sources of merit that ensure the waters' flow, namely study of Torah, identified as the well of living waters, and oblations of water in the Temple. The anachronistic placement of Torah study in the time of Solomon's Temple gives this activity a prestige of origins and a prestige of association with the sacrificial cult in the Temple. In a later time, when the Temple no longer stands, there is still a virtuous practice with the power to ensure the fertility of the land.

It should be noted that the importance of Torah study stressed in the previous example emerges as a central theme throughout the *Targum*,[51] where it is frequently worked into passages associated not only with Solomon's Temple, but also with the Tabernacle,[52] the Second Temple,[53] and the messianic Temple of the future.[54] The theme of the Torah is so important in fact, that it dominates the *Targum*'s treatment of the opening line of poetry in the Song of Songs, 'Let him kiss me with the kisses of his mouth, for your love is better than wine' (Song 1.2):

> Solomon the prophet said, 'Blessed be the name of the LORD, who has given us the Torah by the hand of Moses, the great scribe—written upon the two tablets of stone, and [who has given us] the six orders of the Mishnah and the Talmud by oral tradition, and has conversed with us face to face, as a man who kisses his fellow out of the abundance of his affection, [loving us] more than the seventy nations'.[55]

passages parallel descriptions in Ugaritic literature of the temple as cosmic mountain flowing with miraculous waters. See Richard J. Clifford, *The Cosmic Mountain in Canaan and the Old Testament* (HSM, 4; Cambridge, MA: Harvard University Press, 1972), and Jon D. Levenson, *Sinai and Zion: An Entry into the Jewish Bible* (San Fransisco: Harper & Row, 1985), pp. 111-37.

51. Moshe J. Bernstein discusses the thematic centrality of the Torah in another targum, the *Targum of Psalms* ('Torah and its Study in the Targum of Psalms', in Yaakov Elman and Jeffrey S. Gurock [eds.], *Ḥazon Naḥum: Studies in Jewish Law, Thought and History, Presented to D. Norman Lamm on the Occasion of his Seventieth Birthday* [New York: Yeshiva University Press, 1997], pp. 39-67).

52. *Targ. Song* 3.4.

53. *Targ. Song* 6.11-12.

54. *Targ. Song* 8.1-2. Especially striking in this passage is the role of the Messiah, who in addition to teaching Israel to fear God and walk in his way, also accompanies the people to the Temple in Jerusalem to study the Torah as their fellow student.

55. *Targ. Song* 1.2. Melamed, 'Targum to Canticles', p. 59.

This remarkable passage compares God's giving of the written and particularly the oral Torah with the intimacy of a kiss arising out of heartfelt ardor. What is more, it transfers the biblical description of Moses' unique prophetic status, as one with whom God communes face to face, to all of Israel who receive the two Torahs.[56] This transfer suggests that, although prophets play an important role in the *Targum*'s understanding of how Israel communicated with God in the biblical period,[57] the medium of divine revelation has since that time shifted to the study of the Torah. In the *Targum*, Torah study becomes the locus of divine revelation and presence, transcending all the different periods in Israel's history within which it is portrayed. The prominence of this theme of Torah study, as well as other themes connected to rabbinic practices, institutions and leadership structures, within the *Targum*'s schematic presentation of Israel's history reveals that one of this work's broad concerns is to support the values central to a distinctive way of life pleasing to God.

The third and final purpose that the *Targum* accomplishes through its intertwining of narratives concerning Israel's past and projected future with the love poetry of the Song of Songs might be described as performative, since it ultimately involves the inclusion of the work's readers themselves in the history of Israel's praise of the divinity.[58] Through the very act of reciting the *Targum*'s version of Solomon's most beautiful song, successive generations join their voices in the exaltation of the divinity heard from the origins of the human race to its final chapter. Internally, the *Targum* develops the significance of the chronological placement of its contemporary readers within the history of Israel's laud. In the *Targum*, history is the context within which Israel and God delight in each other's company, and the two parties express the pleasure of their association through mutual praise that draws on the expres-

---

56. Deut. 34.10. For a discussion of the range of meanings of the divine kiss in rabbinic and medieval Judaism, see Michael Fishbane, *The Kiss of God: Spiritual and Mystical Death in Judaism* (Seattle: University of Washington Press, 1994), pp. 14-86.

57. Prophets appear throughout the *Targum* as the intermediaries between God and Israel. See *Targ. Song* 2.7; 5.2, 3, 8, 9, 16; 6.1; 7.1, 2, 6; 8.11, 12, 13.

58. For the concept of performative speech, which actually effects some type of change through the use of language, see J.L. Austin, *How to Do Things with Words* (Cambridge, MA: Harvard University Press, 2nd edn, 1962); John R. Searle, *Speech Acts: An Essay in the Philosophy of Language* (Cambridge: Cambridge University Press, 1969).

sions of admiration and desire found in the Song of Songs. God praises Israel most extensively during those periods when he determines that the people are righteous, and when he therefore favors them by dwelling among them in the earthly sanctuaries that they construct for his presence.[59]

The people of Israel for their part praise God at various high points of their history, when they experience redemption or restoration. The motif of Israel's praise in response to divine deliverance is emphasized by the placement of the tradition of ten songs sung by Israel, mentioned earlier, as an introduction the entire work.[60] Beginning with Adam's song when he received pardon from his guilt, and moving through a full three songs attributed to Moses and Israel during the Exodus period (when they crossed the Sea, when they received water in the wilderness and when Moses addressed Israel before departing from the world), the list continues with songs and praises offered by Joshua, Deborah and Barak, Hannah, and David, before describing the ninth and penultimate song— the Song of Songs sung by Solomon, which will ultimately be followed by one last song at the final redemption. Within the body of the *Targum* itself, Israel's praise of God in response to divine deliverance from the Egyptians at the Sea emerges as a significant narrative component of this foundational event, which stands as the opening chapter in this version of Israel's history. According to the *Targum*, Moses and all the righteous of his generation 'opened their mouths and recited the song, and passed through the midst of the Sea on dry land'.[61]

---

59. God praises Israel following the building of the Tabernacle (*Targ. Song* 1.15), Solomon's Temple (*Targ. Song* 3.7-8; 4.1-5, 7-15) and the Second Temple (*Targ. Song* 6.4-7). In addition, the *Targum* depicts Solomon's prophetic presentation of the divinity's more general praise of Israel towards the conclusion of the work, as a kind of summarizing epitome of praise (*Targ. Song* 7.2-8).

60. *Targ. Song* 1.1. See above, p. 424.

61. *Targ. Song* 1.9. See also *Targ. Song* 1.1; 2.13-14. The exodus is also mentioned as an exemplary period in Israel's history, matched by the Hasmonean period, in *Targ. Song* 6.9. The liturgical tradition that arose in the medieval period of reading of the Song of Songs during the Passover season creates a performative echo between every generation's reading of Solomon's most praiseworthy song and Moses' and all Israel's song of praise at the Sea. For a description of this liturgical use of the Song of Songs, as well as citations of references that attest to this liturgical usage, see Ismar Elbogen, *Jewish Liturgy: A Comprehensive History* (trans. Raymond P. Scheindin; Philadelphia: Jewish Publication Society of America, 1993), pp. 115, 150.

Even more important for this discussion of the dynamics of reading the *Targum of the Song of Songs* itself, however, the *Targum* presents the actual contents of Israel's praise of God most extensively, not in the wake of a dramatic deliverance such as the exodus, but within the context of the Babylonian exile. The *Targum* interprets a question posed in the Song of Songs by a love-sick woman's friends concerning the virtues that distinguish her beloved ('What is your beloved more than another beloved?' Song 5.9), as a question posed by Israel's prophets, inquiring which God a repentant Israel now wishes to serve. The woman's extended description of her lover's beauty in Song 5.10-16 becomes Israel's detailed description of the God for whose presence she longs in exile.[62] The passage is too long to cite in its entirety, but the treatment of the opening verse of the description serves well to illustrate Israel's praise of the divinity:

> 'My beloved is radiant and ruddy, distinguished by a banner among ten thousand' [Song 5.10]. Then the assembly of Israel began to speak of the praise of the Lord of the Universe, and said, 'I desire to worship that God who by day is wrapped in a robe white as snow, occupied with the twenty-four books of the words of Torah, and with the words of the Prophets and Writings, and who by night is occupied with the six orders of the Mishnah. The glorious splendor of his face radiates as fire, on account of the magnitude of the wisdom and the judgment through which he daily brings forth new arguments, which he will make known to his people on the great day, while his banner waves over myriads of angels who minister before him'.[63]

Israel's praise of her beloved divinity opens with a portrayal of God as a Torah scholar in a white robe, whose glowing face reveals his zealous

---

For the position of the Song of the Sea as the archetypal biblical song of praise, see Steven Weitzman, *Song and Story in Biblical Narrative: The History of a Literary Convention in Ancient Israel* (Bloomington: Indiana University Press, 1997), p. 75.

Songs of praise at other times in Israel's history are explicitly mentioned in *Targ. Song* 4.11; 5.2, 10, 16.

62. The *Targum*'s interpretation of this extended description, which resembles the Arabic *wasf* still performed at Bedouin wedding ceremonies (see Marvin H. Pope, *Song of Songs: A New Translation with Introduction and Commentary* [AB, 70; Garden City, NY: Doubleday, 1977], pp. 55-56, 67, 142-44), displays a sensitivity to the poetic units of the Song of Songs evident elsewhere in the *Targum* as well.

63. *Targ. Song* 5.10. Melamed, 'Targum to Canticles', p. 94.

intelligence in adducing arguments.[64] This initial description of the divinity as a Torah scholar corresponds with the *Targum*'s emphasis on the importance of Torah study described above, in that it portrays the divinity himself constantly occupied in an exemplary fashion with the written and oral Torah; moreover, much of the continuation of the passage recounting Israel's praise of the divinity also deals with the theme of the Torah's excellence.[65]

For the current discussion, however, it is the setting of Israel's most extended praise of the divinity within the historical context of the Babylonian exile that is of central concern. This setting is at least partially due to the appearance of the woman's exuberant description of her beloved in the Song of Songs immediately after a passage that the *Targum* defines as description of the Babylonian exile.[66] But whatever the original impetus behind this placement of Israel's most extensive praise of the divinity within a period of exile, the *Targum* intentionally develops the significance of this setting by preceding Israel's praise with God's call through the prophets: 'Turn in repentance, open your mouth, pray, and praise me!'[67] Israel's praise in exile thus constitutes part of the people's return to God, and leads directly to their restoration, which is depicted at the conclusion of their words.[68] This placement of Israel's most sustained expression of praise in the context of the exile invites a poignant comparison with the situation of the implied reader of the

---

64. The white robe here recalls the white garment or the prayer shawl worn by scholars of the Torah, although in mystical circles it was understood as the primordial light in which the divinity wrapped himself. See Raphael Loewe, 'The Divine Garment and Shiur Qomah', *HTR* 58 (1965), pp. 153-60, and '*Targum of the Song of Songs*', pp. 184-93, for discussions of the apologetic against Jewish esotericism implicit in the *Targum*'s interpretation of this passage.

65. In the continuation of this passage, the Torah continues to be the divinity's own occupation (*Targ. Song* 5.16), as well as the vocation of the righteous who earn the deity's good will for all of Israel (*Targ. Song* 5.13-16) and an inherently lovely gift to the people (*Targ. Song* 5.11, 16).

66. The *Targum* interprets Song 5.2-3, 5-8 as referring to the Babylonian exile. In the midst of this block of material concerning the Babylonian exile, the *Targum* introduces one passage concerning the earlier Assyrian exile in connection with Song 5.4.

67. *Targ. Song* 5.2. This is the *Targum*'s interpretation of the phrase 'Open to me', in Song 5.2.

68. The return under Cyrus, Ezra, Nehemiah, Zerubbabel and the men of Judah (*Targ. Song* 6.2), directly follows the conclusion of Israel's praise of God (*Targ. Song* 5.16) and the prophets prayer for the people's restoration (*Targ. Song* 6.1).

Targum. Just as all of Israel praised God extensively in the Babylonian exile under the leadership of the prophets, so the reader of the *Targum* similarly praises God in the current exile under Edom and Ishmael, by repeating the most beautiful song of all, the Song of Songs written by Solomon through prophetic inspiration.

According to the tradition about the ten songs sung by Israel mentioned previously, the Song of Songs is the ninth and penultimate song,[69] and only the eschatological song, which the *Targum* identifies as that prophesied in Isa. 30.29,[70] remains to be sung by the children of the present exile when they are redeemed from their captivity. Every generation of readers of the *Targum of the Song of Songs* therefore finds themselves positioned late within the context of Israel's history of praise. Suspended in the time after Solomon's composition of the most praiseworthy song of all, which summarizes all of Israel's significant history and anticipates this history's completion, they look forward to the tenth and final song to be sung at the time of redemption.

---

69. Whereas the version of the tradition of the ten songs in an early source, the *Mekilta deRabbi Ishmael* Bešallaḥ, does not include the Song of Songs, a shorter version of the tradition containing seven songs presented by Origen in his *Commentary* and *First Homily* on the Song of Songs concludes with the Song of Songs. Other rabbinic sources, such as the *Tanḥuma* Bešallaḥ 10, include the Song of Songs as the ninth song, exactly as it appears in the *Targum*. See Kugel, 'Is There but One Song?'

70. Isa. 30.29 is associated with Passover in other rabbinic sources, including *Mek. Bešallaḥ, b. Pes.* 95b, and *Gen. Rab.* 6.2, and the interpretive glosses in the version appearing in the *Targum* emphasize this connection with Passover by specifying that the song to be sung will be characterized by the 'joy' of the 'Passover' deliverance. The *Targum*'s employment of this prophetic verse, with its associations with Passover, suggests that Israel's ultimate praise of God will celebrate a victory comparable to the archetypal event of the exodus, which receives such prominent treatment in the *Targum of the Song of Songs*. The version of Isa. 30.29 in the *Targum* continues to explain that Israel's final song will be characterized by a gladness of heart similar to that experienced formerly by those who went up to the Temple three times a year to worship the LORD with song and musical instruments. The themes of the Temple and of musical praise in the *Targum*'s version of this prophetic verse resonate with these same themes as they appear elsewhere in the work. Both the selection of Isa. 30.29 to represent the eschatological song and the wording of the verse in the *Targum* are idiosyncratic (Alexander, 'Tradition and Originality', pp. 329-30), and serve to connect the final song thematically with other important events in Israel's history of praise.

As the *Targum*'s interpretation of some of the concluding verses of the Song of Songs makes clear, however, Israel is not to hurry the time for the singing of the final song. For example, in connection with the biblical verse, 'I adjure you, daughters of Jerusalem, not to awaken, nor arouse love, until it pleases' (Song 8.4), the *Targum* presents the Messiah himself cautioning restraint and patience, until the time that the Lord of the Universe pleases to redeem Israel. Again, in connection with the final verse of the Song of Songs, 'Flee, my beloved, and be like a roe or a young hart upon the spice mountains' (Song 8.14), the *Targum* portrays the leaders of Israel themselves urging God to flee from the polluted earth, until the time that he is pleased to redeem the people and return them to Jerusalem. But to sustain Israel in the intervening period, the *Targum* has disclosed the deeper, affective dimensions of the historical narrative presented in other parts of the biblical canon, and it has disclosed the means for survival under hostile foreign rule, including practices such as Torah study. During this period, marked by the longing and deferment expressed in certain passages of the Song of Songs, Israel continues to join with Solomon, repeating his most praiseworthy of songs in anticipation.

This brief overview of some of the uses of the historical narratives featured so prominently in the *Targum of the Song of Songs* shows that in this work history functions in a number of important ways, to accomplish canonical, practical and performative purposes. These various uses of the narratives concerning Israel's past and projected future in the *Targum* do not disqualify the common designation of this work as a historical allegory, but they certainly do complicate and enrich the significance of this designation. And that is perhaps as it should be, when speaking of such a complicated and rich composition as the *Targum of the Song of Songs*.

INDEXES

INDEX OF REFERENCES

OLD TESTAMENT

NEW TESTAMENT

TARGUMS

TRACTATES OF THE MISHNAH AND TALMUD

War (cont.)

OTHER ANCIENT REFERENCES

INDEX OF AUTHORS

Dahood, M. 101
d' Angelo, M.R. 205
Daniélou, J. 316
Dante 246
Daube, D. 215, 285, 303, 304
Davenport, G.L. 112, 354
Davies, G.I. 54
Davies, P.R. 44, 46, 72, 119
Davies, W.D. 279, 280, 284, 290, 291,
     311, 312, 316, 323, 327, 332, 338
Dawson, D. 221
Delekat, L. 87
della Vida, G.L. 265
Dietrich, M. 99, 101
Dietzfelbinger, C. 226
Dimant, D. 43, 112, 117, 219, 220, 233,
     296, 301
Dittenberger, W. 264
di Lella, A.A. 34, 36
Dodd, C.H. 295, 329
Donfried, K.P. 312
Donner, H. 28
Dor, Z.M. 401
Doré, J. 334
Dorival, G. 102
Dreyfus, F.P. 334
Driver, G.R. 97
Driver, S.R. 302
Drower, E.S. 254
Dubuisson, M. 252
Duckworth, G.E. 177
Duling, D.C. 325
Dunn, J.D.G. 113
Dupont, J. 331
Dupont-Sommer, A. 325
Dyk, E. 420

Eichler, B.L. 27
Eisenman, R. 117
Eisenman, R.H. 107
Elbogen, I. 441
Eliade, M. 428
Eliav, Y.Z. 22, 359
Ellis, P.E. 327
Elman, Y. 394, 439
Emerton, J.A. 32, 43, 208, 406
Endres, J.C. 219
Enelow, H.G. 193

Epp, E.J. 345
Eshel, E. 298
Eshel, H. 36
Eslinger, L. 52, 99
Estin, C. 86, 91
Evans, C.A. 9, 35, 112, 113, 117, 120,
     220, 221, 305
Evans, C.F. 354, 406

Fabry, H.-J. 26, 28-30, 32, 39-41, 43, 45,
     47, 50, 51, 54, 61, 63
Faierstein, M.M. 289
Fangmeier, J. 64
Farmer, W.R. 340
Faubion, J.D. 213
Feldman, L.H. 10, 21, 138, 220
Feliks, Y. 409
Ferster, G. 335
Fieger, M. 323
Finegan, J. 275
Firmage, E.B. 29
Fischel, H.A. 218
Fishbane, M. 47, 51, 63, 210, 214, 218,
     231, 232, 422, 440
Fisk, B.N. 22, 220
Fitzmyer, J. 113, 120, 244, 248, 249, 251,
     260, 267, 268, 270, 276, 283, 284,
     287, 289, 295, 316, 331, 386
Fleisher, E. 405
Flesher, P.V.M. 367
Fletcher-Louis, C. 205
Flint, P.W. 117, 120
Flusser, D. 280, 283, 287, 288, 291, 295,
     298, 306-308
Fontaine, C. 377
Fornberg, T. 339
Forster, E.M. 213
Forster, W. 101
Fortna, R.T. 352
Foucault, M. 213
Fowler, G.P. 62
Fox, M.V. 55, 209
Fraenkel, D. 85
France, R.T. 220
Frankovic, J. 293
Franks, P. 202
Freedman, D.N. 29, 40, 65, 71
Freedman, H. 232

Notscher, F. 87
Noy, D. 428

O'Brien, M.A. 53
O'Connor, M. 30
O'Hagen, A.P. 354
O'Toole, R.F. 318
Odeberg, H. 350
Okure, T. 345
Olofsson, S. 10, 78-82, 84, 90-92
Olsson, B. 343, 344, 346, 349, 350
Olyan, S.M. 224
Oppenheimer, A. 360
Ostborn, G. 29, 30

Paget, J.C. 355, 356, 362
Parezen, H. 417
Pascual, J.A. 246
Peckham, B. 31
Pérez, M. 408
Perkins, P. 312
Perrot, C. 224-26, 229
Pesch, R. 312
Petersen, C.L. 26, 38-40, 73
Peterson, E. 324
Petuchowski, J. 405
Pfann, S.J. 107
Pietersma, A. 79, 80, 85
Pines, S. 288
Pococke, E. 302, 305
Poffet, J.-M. 344
Polzin, R. 388
Pomykala, K. 106, 111-16, 118, 119, 121, 122
Pope, M.H. 442
Porten, G.G. 353
Porter, S.E. 112, 113, 305
Preisigke, F. 282
Preuss, H.D. 53, 62, 90
Puech, E. 112-15, 118, 120, 286

Qimron, E. 36, 48, 60
Quast, U. 85

Raabe, P.R. 83, 85-87, 89, 91
Rabinowitz, I. 57
Rabinowitz, L.I. 408
Rad, G. von 237

Radak 237
Ramban 232
Rappaport, U. 112
Rashbam 232
Rashi 215, 232, 237, 394
Reinmuth, E. 220, 222, 223, 226-28, 230, 232
Rendtorff, R. 26, 33, 59, 206
Rengstorf, K.H. 146
Resch, A. 303
Reumann, J. 312
Reventlow, H.G. 295
Ribera, J. 407, 408, 412, 415-17, 419
Ribera-Florit, J. 23
Richards, K.H. 73
Ricoeur, P. 424
Ringreen, H. 409
Ritter, A.M. 81
Robinson, I. 51
Robinson, J.A.T. 292
Robinson, J.M. 107
Rofé, A. 66
Röllig, W. 100
Roo, J.C.R. de 113
Rösel, M. 77, 79, 81
Rosén, H.B. 276
Rosenfeld, B.-Z. 404
Rosenthal, E.I.J. 305
Rost, L. 51, 53, 59
Roth, C. 257
Rothman, E. 388
Rubinstein, J.L. 390
Rummel, S. 99
Ryle, H.E. 34, 72, 299

Safrai, S. 292
Saggs, H.W.F. 247
Saldarini, A.J. 10, 23, 345
Samely, A. 424
Sanders, E.P. 328
Sanders, J.A. 9, 68
Sandevoir, P. 319
Sandmel, S. 137
Sarna, N. 231, 232, 237, 313
Satterthwaite, P.E. 80
Schäfer, K.T. 323
Schäfer, P. 35, 212, 417
Schalit, A. 137, 172

JOURNAL FOR THE STUDY OF THE PSEUDEPIGRAPHA
SUPPLEMENT SERIES